C.S. LEWIS'S OXFORD

Simon Horobin

BODLEIAN
LIBRARY
PUBLISHING

In Memoriam Walter Hooper (1931–2020)

First published in 2024 by Bodleian Library Publishing
Broad Street, Oxford OX1 3BG
www.bodleianshop.co.uk

2nd impression 2024

ISBN 978 1 85124 564 2

Publisher: Samuel Fanous
Managing Editor: Susie Foster
Editor: Janet Phillips
Picture Editor: Leanda Shrimpton
Designed and typeset by Lucy Morton of illuminati in 12½ on 15 Perpetua
Printed and bound in China by C&C Offset printing Co., Ltd, on 115 gsm Yulong Pure paper

MIX
Paper | Supporting responsible forestry
FSC® C008047

British Library Catalogue in Publishing Data
A CIP record of this publication is available from the British Library

CONTENTS

ACKNOWLEDGEMENTS

I am grateful to Samuel Fanous for suggesting this project and to the staff of Bodleian Library Publishing for seeing it through to publication. Research for this book was greatly facilitated by the helpfulness of the staff of the Department of Special Collections at the Weston Library and their willingness to keep their archives accessible to scholars throughout the pandemic. I have been fortunate to profit from the guidance of the generous community of archivists and librarians in Oxford and Cambridge: Richard Allen, Charlotte Berry, Robin Darwall-Smith, Amy Ebrey, Amanda Goode, Daryl Green, Clare Hopkins, Amanda Ingram, Oliver Mahony, Martin Maw, Peter Monteith, Gaye Morgan, Kate O'Donnell, Anna Petre, Julian Reid, Michael Riordan, Isabel Robinson, Michael Stansfield and Catherine Sutherland. I am indebted to Marjorie Mead and Laura Schmidt of the Marion Wade Center, Wheaton College, for their welcome and assistance during my visit.

My research has benefited greatly from discussions with many scholars who have kindly shared with me their knowledge of C.S. Lewis and the Inklings. In particular I wish to thank Steven Beebe, Colin Duriez, Julia Golding, Grace Khuri, Andrew Lazo, Gregory Lipiatt, Brian McGreevy, Catherine McIlwaine, Rafael Pascual, Michael Piret, Judith Priestman, Tyson Rallens, Andy Reyes, Jerry Root, Tom Shippey, Charlie Starr, Nick Swarbrick and Bradley Wells.

Cosima Gillhammer, Joel D. Heck and Michael Ward kindly read the entire book in draft and suggested numerous improvements.

This book is dedicated to the memory of Walter Hooper, in recognition of his friendship, kindness and encouragement to me, and of all he has done to promote the study of Lewis's works in Oxford and beyond.

TIMELINE

1898 Clive Staples Lewis born in Belfast.
1905 Family moves to 'Little Lea'.
1908 Death of Lewis's mother, Flora Hamilton Lewis.
1910 Spends a term at Campbell College, Belfast.
1911 Attends Cherbourg House, Malvern.
1913 Attends Malvern College.
1914 Meets Arthur Greeves and begins studying with William T. Kirkpatrick.
1917 Arrives in Oxford as a student at University College.
Joins the Cadet force at Keble College.
1918 Is discharged from the army and returns to Ireland.
1919 Resumes his studies in Oxford.
Publication of *Spirits in Bondage*.
1921 Wins the Chancellor's Essay Prize.
1925 Elected fellow of Magdalen College.
Publication of *Dymer*.
1936 Publication of *The Allegory of Love*.
1938 Publication of *Out of the Silent Planet*.
1940 Publication of *The Problem of Pain*.
1941 Elected vice president of Magdalen College.
1942 First meeting of the Socratic Club.
Publication of *The Screwtape Letters*.
1943 Publication of *Perelandra*.

1945 Publication of *The Great Divorce.*

1950 Publication of *The Lion, the Witch and the Wardrobe.*

1954 Elected to the chair of Medieval and Renaissance Literature, University of Cambridge.
Publication of *English Literature in the Sixteenth Century Excluding Drama.*

1955 Publication of *Surprised by Joy.*

1956 Marries Joy Davidman at Oxford Registry Office.
Publication of *Till We Have Faces.*

1960 Death of Joy Lewis.

1961 Publication of *A Grief Observed.*

1963 Death of C.S. Lewis.

OXFORD

It is well that there are palaces of peace
And discipline and dreaming and desire,
Lest we forget our heritage and cease
The Spirit's work – to hunger and aspire:

Lest we forget that we were born divine,
Now tangled in red battle's animal net,
Murder the work and lust the anodyne,
Pains of the beast 'gainst bestial solace set.

But this shall never be: to us remains
One city that has nothing of the beast,
That was not built for gross, material gains,
Sharp, wolfish power or empire's glutted feast.

We are not wholly brute. To us remains
A clean, sweet city lulled by ancient streams,
A place of vision and of loosening chains,
A refuge of the elect, a tower of dreams.

She was not builded out of common stone
But out of all men's yearning and all prayer
That she might live, eternally our own,
The Spirit's stronghold – barred against despair.

C.S. Lewis

FIG. 1 The 'Dreaming Spires' of Oxford, looking west from Magdalen College Tower, 1908.

PREFACE

ARRIVAL

C.S. Lewis first set foot in Oxford in December 1916, travelling from his home in Belfast to sit the university entrance examination. This was not the most auspicious of encounters since, having arrived at the railway station, Lewis set off in the wrong direction. The further he walked, the more disappointed and confused he became. Nevertheless, he pressed on, assuming that the fabled dreaming spires were just around the next corner. It was only when he found himself in the countryside that he realized he had in fact been walking away from the city, through the unprepossessing suburb of Botley; on turning round he was greeted with a spectacular view of the Oxford skyline.

Recounting this episode in his spiritual autobiography, *Surprised by Joy*, Lewis views this adventure as an allegory of his life. This is a striking idea, since, according to an allegorical interpretation, in which his turning round prefigures his later religious conversion, the city of Oxford comes to stand in for the ethereal city of heaven. Having experienced this vision, Lewis trudged back to the railway station and took a cab to his lodgings at the corner of Mansfield Road and Holywell Street, where he spent his first night in the city which would become his home for the remainder of his adult life.

Clive Staples Lewis, known to his friends as 'Jack', was born in Belfast on 29 November 1898 to Albert Lewis, a solicitor, and Flora

Hamilton, the daughter of a clergyman. In 1905 the family moved from the semi-detached villa in which Lewis was born to Leeborough House, or 'Little Lea', a more spacious, detached family residence in Strandtown, East Belfast. It was here that Lewis was able to indulge his love of reading, helping himself to volume after volume from the vast shelves of works that cluttered the rooms and corridors of the new house.

Flora Lewis died of cancer in 1908, an event which shattered the young Lewis, removing the great source of tranquillity and security in his life. The loss of his mother was shortly followed by his being sent to join his older brother Warren, known as Warnie, born in 1895, at Wynyard School, a boarding establishment in Hertfordshire. Lewis was deeply unhappy at Wynyard, under a headmaster whose brutality led to the school being closed in 1910. While his father reconsidered his plan for his younger son's education, Lewis joined Campbell College in Belfast, although he was withdrawn after a term on health grounds.

In January 1911 Lewis accompanied Warnie to Malvern, Worcestershire, where he joined Cherbourg House, a preparatory school, while his brother attended the senior school, Malvern College. Lewis moved to 'The Coll' in 1913, having been awarded a Classical scholarship. But, unlike Warnie, who enjoyed his time at Malvern College, Lewis was miserable at the school, with its institutionalized system of 'fagging' – by which junior boys were required to do menial tasks for their seniors – and pleaded with his father to remove him.

Lewis failed to find like-minded individuals at his boarding schools; however, during a school holiday in 1914, he visited Arthur Greeves, a boy of his own age who was laid up in bed in the house across the street. Lewis was astonished to find Arthur had a copy of H.A. Guerber's *Myths of the Norsemen* (1908) beside his bed; Lewis was deeply interested in Norse mythology and the two quickly developed a strong and long-lasting friendship.

Recognizing the difficulties his son had experienced at school, Albert Lewis turned instead to a private tutor and former headmaster of Lurgan College, the school he himself had attended, William T.

Kirkpatrick, who agreed to take Lewis as a pupil. In 1914 Lewis moved to the village of Great Bookham, Surrey, following in his brother's footsteps, since Warnie spent four months with Kirkpatrick preparing for his army entrance exam. Under Kirkpatrick's supervision, Lewis undertook a rigorous programme of study of the classical languages, spending his leisure time reading widely in English literature and exploring the local countryside. From Kirkpatrick Lewis acquired the skills of dialectic, as the elderly rationalist relentlessly required his charge to engage in disputation over the most innocent of topics. For most teenagers this approach would have been overwhelming; for Lewis it was 'red beef and strong beer'.[1] After two blissful years under Kirkpatrick's tutelage, it was decided that Lewis was ready for the next stage of his education: an application to the University of Oxford.

Lewis was immediately captivated by Oxford. Writing to his father he exclaimed: 'The place has surpassed my wildest dreams. I never saw anything so beautiful, especially on these frosty moonlight nights.'[2] The scholarship examination was taken in the hall at Oriel College, which was so cold that the students resorted to writing in gloves. Lewis and his fellow candidates attempted papers in Latin prose, Greek and Latin unseen translations, a General Paper and an English essay, the topic of which was Dr Johnson's claim that 'People confound liberty of thinking with liberty of talking'. Lewis returned home in dejection, certain that he had failed. However, just before Christmas, he received a letter informing him that, although he had not been selected by New College, to which he had applied, he had been offered a place by University College, along with an exhibition, a scholarship which would contribute to his living costs.

ONE
UNIVERSITY COLLEGE

Every student at Oxford University must also become a member of a college, where they are accommodated, take their meals and receive individual instruction from their tutors, known as 'tutorials'. Lewis was a member of University College, or 'Univ', as the college is affectionately known. His first encounter with the college was a visit he made in January 1917, when he called upon the master in his lodgings. At that time, the master of the college was Reginald Walter Macan, a classical scholar, editor of the works of Herodotus and author of a history of Persia. Despite referring to him as 'the ogre', Lewis came away very positively disposed towards Macan, describing him as 'a clean shaven, white haired, jolly old man'.[1] Lewis was particularly favourably impressed by the large collection of books piled up on the shelves of his study, which included Malory's *Le Morte d'Arthur* in the Temple Classics edition – Lewis was in those days an avid collector of fine editions and considered this copy of Malory's work to be highly desirable. Having been invited to stay to have lunch with the master and his wife, Lewis concluded: 'I am very pleased with my ogre after all.'[2]

His account of subsequent interactions with the Mugger (as he was popularly known) in the termly business of collections is considerably

FIG. 2 University College Freshmen, Trinity term, 1917. C.S. Lewis is in the back row on the right.

less warm. College collections are end-of-term reports which are delivered by tutors in the presence of the master, so called because they were once accompanied by the payment of student fees, or 'battels'. Lewis described it as the 'worst relict of barbarism which yet hangs about the University', but it is a tradition that survives to this day in various forms. For Lewis and his contemporaries, it involved walking the length of the hall to the high table, where the master sat, accompanied by senior college officers, whom Lewis labelled his 'auxiliar fiends'. The master then pronounced upon the student's performance and future prospects. Lewis reported that, in his case, each term's report was identical: 'Well Mr Lewis, I – ah – I – have nothing but – ah – satisfaction to express as regards – ah – ah –. We expect great things of you.' Unexpectedly, at the end of Hilary (Easter) term 1921, the master did not repeat this homily, leaving Lewis to conclude: 'Apparently he has now given up expecting great things of me.'[3]

The result of his initial meeting with the master was the establishment of a plan that Lewis would sit Responsions in March, with the aim of embarking upon his student career at Oxford (referred to in Oxford jargon as 'coming up') at the beginning of Trinity (summer) term, 1917. Responsions was the first of three assessment points in a student's university career; having been accepted by a college, students were still required to pass examinations in Latin, Greek and Mathematics before being admitted to the university. This was a means of ensuring consistency in admissions standards in the days before standardized assessments were introduced for school-leavers.

Having been founded in 1249, Univ vies with Balliol and Merton for the claim to be the oldest college in the university. Today Univ is a bustling educational institution; when Lewis arrived during the First World War there were just a handful of students in residence (see FIG. 2). Because the hall was being used as a hospital for nursing wounded soldiers, Lewis and his fellow students ate dinner in one of the small lecture theatres; other meals were brought to their rooms by a college servant, known as a 'scout'. As Lewis noted in a letter to his friend

Arthur Greeves back in Belfast, Oxford of the war years was 'only a shadow of the real Oxford'; yet even so he declared himself to have never been happier in his life.[4]

On arrival, Lewis was shown to his rooms by the porter, and was pleasantly surprised by their size, comfortable furnishings and generous profusion of rugs. Unfortunately, he had been directed to the wrong rooms; his were considerably more modest and spartan. Lewis's rooms (known in Oxford as a 'set') were number 5 on staircase XII of Radcliffe Quad, the college's second largest quadrangle, built in 1716–19 with funding from Dr John Radcliffe, a former undergraduate and wealthy doctor.

A statue of Dr Radcliffe stands over the archway, allowing him to survey the quad that bears his name, as well as the activities of the students. Despite being built in the eighteenth century, Radcliffe's quad was constructed in a self-consciously archaic style, reflecting the patron's preference for the architecture of the previous century rather than the 'modern' neoclassical architecture reflected in the contemporary Queen's College, situated on the opposite side of the High Street. Staircases X–XII are on the eastern side of the quad and were originally planned to form the master's lodgings. But when the new lodgings were built in 1879–80, they were converted into student rooms.

Having arrived in the Trinity term of 1917, an unusual point in the academic year, which typically began in October (Michaelmas term), Lewis did little formal academic work; instead he spent most of his time receiving instruction from the Officers' Training Corps. Lewis's weekday routine consisted mostly of parades in the University Parks, interspersed with some academic work and moments of leisure, during which he read, bathed in the river, played cards and rode his bike.

Although his academic studies did not begin in earnest, he received tuition in algebra from John Edward Campbell, a tutor at Hertford College, in preparation for sitting the mathematics component of Responsions (also known as 'Smalls' or 'Little Go'). However, despite his mother Flora having obtained a degree in Mathematics from Queen's

University Belfast, Lewis had no aptitude for the subject and never passed the exam; he was spared the ignominy of having to resit it on his return to Oxford after the war by a decree excusing ex-servicemen from having to pass Responsions.

KEBLE COLLEGE

In June 1917 Lewis joined E Company, No. 4 Officer Cadet Battalion (FIG. 3), stationed at Keble College, where he shared a room with Edward Francis Courtenay Moore, known to his friends as Paddy. Although they were only acquainted for a short period, this friendship was to have huge consequences for Lewis's future. Lewis spent time with Paddy and his mother, Mrs Jane King Moore, who had separated from her husband and taken rooms in Wellington Square, now the site of the university's central administrative offices, with her daughter Maureen. Before they left for the Western Front, the two men apparently made an agreement that each would look after the other's surviving parent should one of them be killed in action. Paddy was reported missing in March 1918 and his death was confirmed later that year. Lewis followed through on his promise; after the war, Mrs Moore came to live in Oxford, beginning a long and complex relationship, which is explored in more detail in Chapter 3.

Lewis was dismayed at having to swap his own 'snug quarters' at Univ for a 'carpetless little cell with two beds (minus sheets or pillows) at Keble'.[5] Nevertheless, he adopted a stoical attitude towards his new lifestyle, admitting that hard work, such as digging trenches and marching in the hot sun, might be good for him, even though it left little time for dreaming or reading.[6] Despite this change in fortunes, Lewis was delighted at having been able to remain in Oxford for his training, since it allowed him to return to Univ at weekends. Here he could enjoy the relative comfort and consolations of the college and its library, which was the only place where you could feel warm during

FIG. 3 Lewis and E Company, No. 4 Officer Cadet Battalion, Keble College, 1917.

the winter. But, while being especially conducive to private study, the library did present considerable distractions: 'The temptation to spend all your time rambling over the interesting modern books & the great old worm-eaten folios has to be sternly resisted!'[7] During this period Lewis returned to one of his favourite authors, Homer, though was shocked to discover how strange the Greek appeared to him, prompting an anxiety that he might forget it all during the war. He also found time to dabble in writing poetry, hoping to put together a collection and submit it to a publisher before leaving for France: 'After that, if the fates decide to kill me at the front, I shall enjoy a 9 days immortality while friends who know nothing about poetry imagine that I must have been a genius – what usually happens in such cases.'[8]

In early July, however, access to this oasis of calm was closed off by the dean, the college officer responsible for discipline, who felt that the college was being used as a hotel. This caused Lewis great remorse: 'I am more homesick for this College than ever I was for Little Lea. I love every stone in it.'[9] In September of the same year, he received a temporary commission as a second lieutenant in the 3rd Somerset Light Infantry, and by November he was serving in the trenches on the French–Belgian border.

FRANCE

Having sailed to Le Havre on 17 November, Lewis arrived at the front line twelve days later, his nineteenth birthday. He spent the winter of 1917 in the trenches at Monchy-Le-Preux. Records of the battalion's activities show that, when not actively engaged in fighting, much of his time was occupied with attempting to improve the conditions in the trenches, working tirelessly against the cold and wet. The remainder was spent training, carrying out manoeuvres, practising marching with box respirators, fighting with bayonets, playing rugby, football, boxing and tug-of-war matches with other battalions, and attending Divisional 'Follies' in the evening. Given his lifelong distaste for organized sport, it is hard to imagine Lewis enjoyed many of these activities. What

FIG. 4 Laurence B. Johnson in uniform. He was killed in 1918 by the same shell that injured Lewis.

free time Lewis did have he spent writing letters and reading lengthy prose works, such as George Eliot's *Middlemarch* and Boswell's *Life of Johnson*. In February 1918 he contracted trench fever and spent a month convalescing at No. 10 British Red Cross Hospital at Le Tréport. There he read a collection of essays by G.K. Chesterton, which was to have a profound effect upon his spiritual development.

On 19 March the battalion was moved to Fampoux to prepare for a major assault; on 14 April the Somerset Light Infantry carried out an assault on Riez du Vinage, near Arras. The following day the Germans responded by bombing the village. Lewis was injured and taken to No. 6 British Red Cross Hospital near Étaples; also injured by the same shell was Second Lieutenant Laurence B. Johnson (see FIG. 4).

Lewis and Johnson had become close friends. Lewis wrote warmly of their relationship to Arthur Greeves, praising Johnson's wide reading (especially in modern literature, of which Lewis himself was particularly ignorant), his morality, musical appreciation and philosophical depth. Like Lewis, Johnson had been awarded a scholarship to study at Oxford, at The Queen's College, and Lewis noted with enthusiasm how much he looked forward to renewing their friendship after the war. But Johnson never had the opportunity to take up his place at Oxford, as the shell that had wounded Lewis killed Johnson. His death is a stark reminder of how many brilliant young men like Lewis, with promising Oxford careers ahead of them, never returned to the university.

To recover from his injury Lewis was initially sent to Endsleigh Park Hotel in London and subsequently to Ashton Court in Bristol, a sixteenth-century mansion that had been converted into a recovery hospital. Writing to his father shortly after the move, Lewis lamented the loss of most of his friends from his battalion, especially Johnson: 'I had had him so often in my thoughts, had so often hit on some new point in one of our arguments, and made a note of things in my reading to tell him when we met again, that I can hardly believe he is dead.'[10] Lewis wrote affectionately of Johnson in *Surprised by Joy*, praising him as a dialectician, a lover of poetry and a man of conscience. Lewis admitted to his father that he could 'sit down and cry over the whole business'; instead, he spent his days ensconced in a disused writing room at one end of the house reading Robert Burton's *The Anatomy of Melancholy* (1621). Alongside a passage in which Burton wonders what the Greek philosopher Democritus would have made of 'so many bloody battles, so many thousands slain at once, such streams of blood able to turn mills', Lewis inscribed the word 'WAR' in capitals and drew a heavy line underneath.

Lewis asked his father to send him a copy of *The Anatomy* in February of that year, when he was in hospital at Le Tréport. Burton's seminal study of melancholy – the early modern term for depression and other types of mental illness – was a lifelong favourite of Lewis's; he returned to it during the Second World War, finishing it on 28 June 1945. In *Surprised by Joy*, he cites Burton's thousand-page treatise as an example of the 'gossipy and formless' book that is especially suited to reading at the dinner table, although Lewis evidently took its practical advice and consolations more seriously than that remark might imply.

In November of the previous year, Lewis reminded Arthur Greeves of Burton's advice to the melancholy to 'be not idle, be not solitary', a phrase which he underlined in his copy of the work.[11] Lewis now put the advice into practice, producing a fair copy of his collected poems in the hope of publication. Lewis had deposited the manuscript copy of his early poems with Arthur Greeves for safekeeping before he left for France; this collection, with several additional poems composed during the war, formed the basis of *Spirits in Bondage*, issued under the pseudonym Clive Hamilton, his mother's maiden name, in 1919.

RETURN TO OXFORD

Among the poems that were composed during Lewis's time in France is the short lyric extolling the beauty and values embodied by the city of Oxford quoted in full at the beginning of this book; a reminder that, despite being currently 'tangled in red battle's animal net', humans were 'born divine':

> We are not wholly brute. To us remains
> A clean, sweet city lulled by ancient streams,
> A place of vision and of loosening chains,
> A refuge of the elect, a tower of dreams.[12]

Lewis evidently clung on to that briefly glimpsed vision of Oxford, 'The Spirit's stronghold – barred against despair', while in the trenches; it was to this sweet city and tower of dreams that he returned in January 1919, ready to resume his studies in earnest.

Oxford of the post-war period is perhaps best known from the Arcadian setting of Evelyn Waugh's novel *Brideshead Revisited* (1945). But Waugh's Oxford was that of the 1920s; the men returning from the trenches in 1919 were a much more sombre and serious crowd. In his memoir *Good-Bye to All That*, Robert Graves recalls his first encounter with Oxford as a student at St John's: 'We found the University remarkably quiet. The returned soldiers did not feel tempted to rag about, break windows, get drunk, or have tussles with the police and races with the Proctors' "bulldogs", as in the old days.' Graves quotes G.N. Clarke, a history tutor at Oriel, who was shocked to find his students unusually diligent and dutiful: 'They seem positively to thirst for knowledge and scribble away in their note-books like lunatics.'[13]

Lewis's subject was Literae Humaniores, literally 'more humane letters', known as Lit. Hum. in Oxford and as Classics in most other universities. His tutor was Arthur Blackburne Poynton (1867–1944), fellow and Praelector in Greek, who went on to be master of Univ from 1935 to 1937. The Lit. Hum. degree encompasses the languages, literature, history and philosophy of the ancient world. It is divided into two parts: Honour Moderations, or 'Mods', an examination taken after five terms, and Final Honour School, or 'Greats', taken at the end of the four-year degree. Lewis achieved First-class honours in both sets of exams – what is known as a 'double First'.

Having achieved these grades, Lewis considered applying for a prestigious fellowship at All Souls College, which offers seven-year positions with no teaching duties. He discussed the idea with his friend Eric Beckett, lunching with him in the buttery at All Souls, drinking clear red beer bottled in the nineteenth century, with 'a man called Lawrence (formerly of Jesus College)'. T.E. Lawrence, recently returned from the Middle East, was an undergraduate at Jesus College, where he read History, and a fellow of All Souls from 1919 to 1926, when he rewrote his account of his military exploits, *Seven Pillars of Wisdom* (1926). Lewis found Lawrence 'interesting and agreeable', although, according to Beckett, he cut rather an aloof figure at All Souls, refusing to accept his stipend, not dining in hall and hanging around the common room sporting ordinary clothes and contributing little to the general conversation. Although Lewis was woefully ignorant of international affairs, the two men had similar literary interests, since Lawrence had a particular affection for Malory's *Le Morte d'Arthur*; Lewis, however, later disapproved of the pseudo-archaic style of Lawrence's translation of Homer's *Odyssey* (1932). But, while Beckett considered Lewis to have a strong chance of obtaining an All Souls fellowship, the requirement to reside in the college meant that

Lewis decided not to apply, since it would mean not being able to provide lodging for Mrs Moore and her daughter.[14]

Instead, Lewis enquired about the prospect of employment as a university teacher, but his philosophy tutor, Edgar Carritt, informed him that there were no vacancies, and advised him to take a further degree to make himself more employable. In response to Carritt's advice, Lewis stayed on to undertake the Final Honours School in English Language and Literature.

Before beginning his English studies in the autumn of 1922, an alternative opportunity presented itself in the form of a research fellowship advertised by Magdalen College. Lewis decided to submit an application, which involved the submission of an extended essay, testimonials and an interview with the president, Herbert Warren, whom Lewis found to be a 'stout man with a short grey beard, thick lips, and an affable manner'.[15]

The candidates for the position were then submitted to a gruelling series of three-hour examinations. The first was an English paper requiring an essay on 'The use and abuse of satire', which Lewis admitted he would be sorry to see survive as a specimen of his work. This was followed by unseen translations from Hesiod, Dionysius of Halicarnassus and Ausonius, the first of which Lewis found quite challenging. Another paper required composition in Latin prose; during this exam, one student boldly lit a cigarette, after which all the others followed suit.

The Philosophy paper saw Lewis write an essay on the importance of Time to Ethics, with which he was fairly pleased, although he was less satisfied with his answer on Kant, and considered that he had written a lot of 'poor pudding' about Pragmatism. There followed papers on Ancient History, French Translation, and Political Philosophy and Philosophical Unseens, featuring extracts from Plato, Aristotle and Tertullian, the last of which he had to leave unfinished. Surprisingly, given his expertise in the Latin and Greek languages, Lewis elected not to sit the papers in Greek prose and Greek and Latin verse, considering that his performance in these subjects would not help his application.

A total of eleven candidates sat the fellowship examinations, including two fellow Univ students, E.R. Dodds, later Regius Professor of Greek at Oxford, and A.C. Ewing, who went on to become a celebrated Cambridge philosopher. When he read the announcement in *The Times* newspaper that the Magdalen fellowship had been awarded to H.H. Price, a scholar of New College, Lewis discovered that 'this has affected my spirits very little'.[16] By this point, Lewis had clearly accepted that the position would not be offered to him and had begun to prepare for a new direction in his academic career.

ENGLISH LANGUAGE AND LITERATURE

In the early 1920s the English school was in its infancy; its formal inception dates back to a statute of 1894, but it was not until after the First World War that it witnessed a significant expansion in its student body. In 1913, Final Honours exams in English were sat by twelve men and twenty-five women; in 1923 that number had grown to fifty men and fifty-two women.[17] The discipline still struggled to attract the prestige of other schools; Lewis was initially rather disparaging towards his fellow students, complaining about 'a certain amateurishness in the talk and look of the people'.[18]

An English degree today involves the appreciation of works from all literary periods; when Lewis was an undergraduate the course was heavily focused on texts written before 1500. Texts from this period were composed in Old and Middle English, forms of the language that differ considerably from modern English; studying such works was considered to be equivalent to reading ones composed in Latin and Greek. Lewis, however, viewed Old English, or Anglo-Saxon, to be a relatively straightforward proposition compared to learning to read classical texts. He dismissed Old English words like *cwic* (modern English 'quick'), as 'parodied English badly spelled', and confidently predicted that reading selected passages could be achieved by anyone within a month.

The first piece of translation from Old English that he undertook was the account of Ohthere, a Norwegian sea captain, from the classic student textbook *An Anglo-Saxon Reader in Prose and Verse*, edited by Henry Sweet, first published in 1876. But Lewis's initial foray into Old English translation was not quite the plain sailing he anticipated. He records beginning the work after supper on Saturday 14 October. This is followed by the telling sentence: 'Late to bed.' Later in his diary Lewis recorded a story of how Sweet's tyrannical father had found him a job in a bank to try to prevent him from becoming a philologist, to which Lewis added the sardonic remark: 'wd. God he had succeeded'.[19] Plate 4 shows a page from the notes he made while working on his translation, including an illustration explaining the etymology of Old English *steorbord* 'starboard' (the side on which the rudder was attached) and *bæcbord* (the side of the ship to which the steersman had his back).

Analysis of these texts was focused neither on their historical context nor on their literary qualities, but rather on their status as evidence for the historical study of the language. Lewis's antipathy to this subject can be traced back to his undergraduate tutorials with Miss E.E. Wardale of St Hugh's College, whom he described without affection as an 'elderly, pallid woman, rendered monstrous by a lower lip hanging loose enough to expose an irregular gum'. Lewis had little enthusiasm for philology, the historical study of language, complaining about the time spent trying to reproduce the various 'clucking, growling and grunted noises which are apparently an essential to the pure accent of Alfred [the Great]'.[20]

Lewis also attended lectures delivered by the Merton Professor of English Language, H.C. Wyld, author of a number of seminal philological studies. Lewis took an immediate and intense dislike to Wyld, partly because he considered the content of the lectures to be elementary and self-evident. But he also objected to Wyld's manner: his snobbery and tendency to harangue his audience for coming in late, not concentrating, and not knowing the answers to the questions he fired at them. It was this hectoring style that prompted Lewis to refer to Wyld as 'the cad' throughout his diary.

Lewis's disdain for Wyld prompted him to compose a series of poems castigating him, and his obsession with analysing sounds at the expense of the texts themselves. These poems were written in Lewis's own copy of Wyld's textbook *A Short History of English* (1921), perhaps during one of the lectures. In the following poem, an acrostic spells out 'Henry Cecil Wyld he'. Regrettably, we will never know why Lewis took objection to Wyld's garden marrows.

He opens and closes his glottis at pleasure,
Explosives and stops he is able to measure,
No grunt and no gurgle escapes his attention,
Religiously marking each slackness and tension,
You find him in air-bursts beguiling his leisure.

Can any one blame him if, doomed to mistaking
Each word in its meaning, he studies the making?
Condemned to be blind to the picture, the frame
Instead let him chip at. But why in God's name,
Lead us from Parnassus to join your muck-raking?

Why, pray, should a squire of the Muse and Apollo
Yield thus with a living steam-organ to follow?
Leave us to the spirit and keep your phonetics,
Don't come to the table to talk dietetics.
His Berkshire garden grows, I'm told
Enormous marrows tinged with gold.

But this exercise in poetic parody did not satisfy the young Lewis; on the remaining blank pages he penned a series of additional satirical verses lampooning Wyld: one in English, alongside others in Latin, Greek, French and even Old English.

Lewis's time wasn't entirely taken up with philology and translation from Old English. His other tutor was the literary scholar F.P. Wilson, an expert on Elizabethan drama and general editor of the Oxford History of English Literature series, for which Lewis was to go on to write the volume *English Literature in the Sixteenth Century Excluding*

Drama, published in 1954. Wilson himself authored the companion volume, *The English Drama, 1485–1585*.

Lewis wrote warmly of his tutorials with Wilson, which were spent discussing Middle English poetry. Wilson introduced Lewis to Chaucer's long poem *Troilus and Criseyde*, to which he responded with considerable enthusiasm: 'It is simply amazing. Except *Macbeth* and one or two of the old ballads I don't know that any poetry has affected me more.'[21] Lewis borrowed a copy of W.M. Rossetti's collation of Chaucer's poem with its source, Boccaccio's *Il Filostrato*, thereby beginning a project that would culminate in his groundbreaking essay 'What Chaucer Really Did to *Il Filostrato*' (1932).[22] Even at this early stage in his scholarly career, Lewis had developed firm opinions and was quite willing to disagree with established scholars. He notes in his diary a tutorial discussion in which Wilson quoted a view that Chaucer's Pandarus was merely a transition between Boccaccio and Shakespeare, with no character of his own, to which he responds: 'What nonsense!'[23]

THE MARTLETS

An important feature of Lewis's time at Univ was his involvement in the college society known as the Martlets. Founded in 1892, the Martlets was a literary gathering at which scholars and younger fellows presented papers on specific authors or genres.[24] Lewis was appointed secretary in January 1919, and in October he was elected president. On being appointed to the former position, he observed with his customary self-deprecation: 'I have been elected Secretary – the reason being of course that my proposer, Edwards, was afraid of getting the job himself. And so if I am forgotten of all else, at least a specimen of my handwriting will be preserved to posterity.'[25] It is interesting to note that, even at this early stage in his literary career, Lewis had an eye on his legacy as a writer.

Lewis's first paper to the Martlets was on William Morris; because he was secretary it was read by R.M.S. Pasley, allowing Lewis to keep a record of the ensuing discussion. According to the rather cursory account, Lewis claimed that, as a teller of tales, Morris 'yielded to none except Homer', while his prose works recall the 'melody and charm of Malory'. But the minutes suggest that Lewis's high admiration for Morris was not shared by his audience: 'The general sense of the Society was that rather too high a position had been claimed for William Morris.' Undeterred by this somewhat underwhelming response, Lewis returned to the subject in a paper to the Martlets in November 1937; the record of this event concludes by describing it as 'a very interesting and extraordinarily well-written paper', although it remains unclear whether Lewis had succeeded in converting his audience to his view.[26]

In November 1919, having recently been appointed president of the Martlets, Lewis presented a paper on narrative poetry which, according to the minutes, 'took up, from the first, a fighting attitude': 'In an age of lyrical activity he was come to defend the epic against the prejudice of contemporaries.' This martial attitude to debate, with which he defended the epic against modern poetry, was to become a defining feature of Lewis the scholar, teacher and Christian apologist. His topic – the defence of the long narrative poem – was one that he continued to champion throughout his life. According to the secretary's report, Lewis took issue with the modern unwillingness to invest the effort required for appreciating the epic form, and went on to extol the poetic 'fulness' of narrative poetry, drawing his examples from *Paradise Lost* and *The Faerie Queene* – works that were to be a major focus of his later scholarship. The secretary's account judged the paper to be 'as able a vindication of the narrative form as could well be constructed'. Lewis would have no doubt drawn considerable satisfaction from this judgement, since he himself had been at work on a lengthy narrative poem since 1916 – eventually published in 1926 as *Dymer*.

Subsequent lectures delivered at meetings of the Martlets include what the secretary described as 'a brilliant paper on the poetry of Edmund Spenser', one on James Stephens and another on James Boswell. It was at gatherings of the Martlets that Lewis gave a first

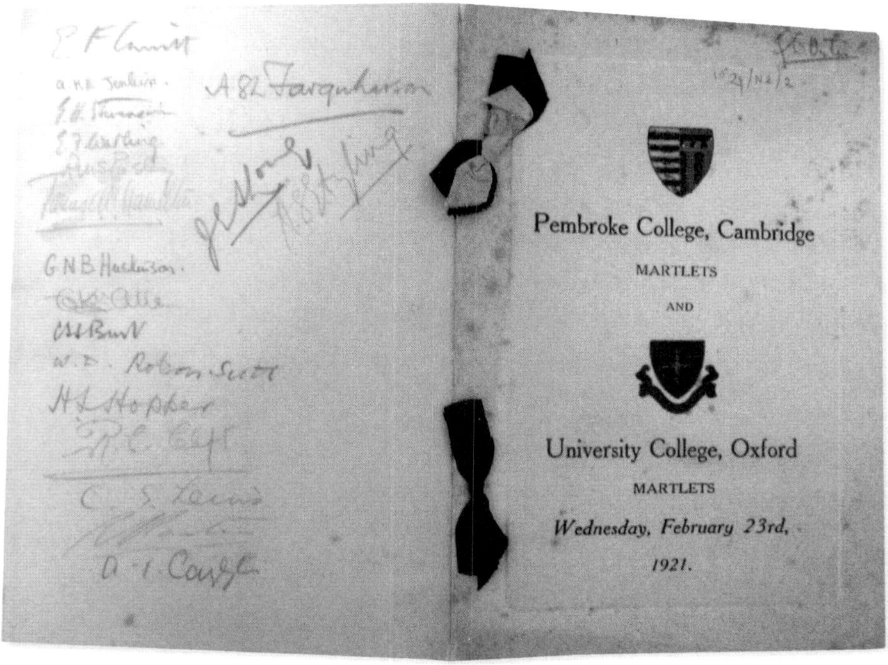

FIG. 5 Signed programme of a joint meeting of the Martlets with Pembroke College, Cambridge, 1921.

airing to some of his most famous essays: 'The Personal Heresy in Poetics' and 'The Kappa Element in Romance', which was subsequently published as 'On Stories'. The Martlets also arranged joint meetings with the Martlets Society of Pembroke College Cambridge; the programme for a combined event held in 1921 was signed by all those who attended, including Lewis (see FIG. 5). The Martlets Society is still active today, although in its modern incarnation it is a forum for graduate students of all disciplines to discuss their research.

At the beginning of 1923 Lewis began to attend another literary discussion group, this one hosted by George Gordon, the Merton Professor of English Literature, comprising students who had been specially selected for the honour by their tutors.[27] The group met weekly, either in an upstairs room of the Examination Schools on the High Street or in Gordon's home. It was at the meeting on 2

February that Lewis first encountered Nevill Coghill, who became a close friend and colleague in the Oxford English Faculty. Lewis took an instant liking to Coghill, describing him as 'an enthusiastic sensible man, without nonsense, and a gentleman'.[28] At the following meeting Lewis read a paper on Edmund Spenser; in keeping with the tradition established by Gordon, the minutes of the event were written in verse. Coghill, adopting the style of the opening of Chaucer's *Canterbury Tales*, began the minutes with a description of the various members of the 'goodlye companye' and then recorded how Professor Gordon, acting as the host Harry Bailley, called upon Lewis to tell his tale of Daun Spenser:

Then to *Sir Lewis* turned the Professour
(That was our tales juge and governour) *judge*
And cried unto hym 'Now by Pigges bones,
'Thou shallt a noble tale for the nones, *occasion*
'Somewhat to quite Daun Darlow and the Cogge. *repay*
'Rede us of Spenser, by Seint James dogge.
'Lordynges, attend, and hear our philosopher *lords*
That hath both wit and beauty in his coffer!'
Anon turned Lewis to a blue boke
He swalwed thrice; hys dewy fingers shooke *swallowed*
And he bigan with right a myrie cheere
His tale anoon; and spake in this mannere.[29]

At the fourth meeting of the term, Lewis acted as secretary and produced his own attempt at Chaucerian pastiche in response to Coghill's effort. Lewis's introductory verses note that the intended speaker, Gilbert Burns, had pulled out because of illness, and that Robert Macdonald read a paper in his absence:

But whan that Coghille had his tale ytold *told*
Our Professour gan round about behold
And lough and seyde 'Unbokeled is the male! *laughed; bag*
Let see now who shal tell another tale;
And namely Sir Burns as thou art able
Telleth anon som matere profitable.' *tell*

This seely man, this Burns, lift up his head, *worthy*
He was al wan to see and nothing red, *pale*
And 'Sir,' he seyd, 'By my devotioun
I shal yow nothing tell at this seasoun
For I have swyche a stounde of hevinesse, *such; pang; sluggishness*
It is the influenza as I guesse.
Another man shal tell. Hit am not I.'
Ther was a Scottis clerke set thereby,
And he was wunder blak and wunder pale,
His vois was high upon the upper scale,
And he was cleped hende Macdonald. *called; noble*

Lewis's private account of the paper in his diary is somewhat less flattering, calling it a 'very bad paper on the adapters of Shakespeare', delivered in a 'monstrous high pitched voice with a Scotch accent'.[30] As well as introducing him to Coghill, these meetings provided Lewis with the model of a sympathetic and inspirational tutor: one who guided the discussion effortlessly, steering the students away from blind alleys and reinforcing the most valuable observations with a few well-chosen words.[31]

In addition to helping to foster his skills as a lecturer, tutor and debater, these early years at Univ were important for nurturing Lewis as an essay writer. In April 1921 he submitted an entry for the prestigious Chancellor's Essay Prize on the subject of optimism. The process was not entirely without hitches. Lewis hired a secretary to type up his manuscript, resulting in a text full of the 'miswriting' that Chaucer feared his poem *Troilus and Criseyde* would be subjected to at the hands of later scribes. Paragraphs had been run together, question marks appeared in the wrong places, 'word' was rendered 'now', and 'hedonism' as 'medonism'. Despite the topic of his essay, Lewis was deeply pessimistic about his chances of winning the prize: 'You see I am afraid I have rather fallen between two stools: it has to aim at being both literary and philosophical, and, in the effort to accomplish the double object, I have made it too literary for the philosophers and too metaphysical for the dons of English Literature.' Lewis noted that the essay would be judged by a panel whose tastes and tempers were unknown and unpredictable: 'it must be difficult to be quite fair to an essay which expresses some view that you have been denouncing to a submissive Senior Common Room for the last half century, however good it may be.'[32]

To his great delight, Lewis was soon to learn that his essay had been awarded the prize. He was rather shocked to be invited to read aloud a section of his prize-winning essay at the university's Encaenia, an annual ceremony at which honorary degrees are conferred. The ceremony is conducted in the Sheldonian Theatre, a seventeenth-century building on Broad Street, built to a design by Christopher Wren, and is attended by the university's great and good. Lewis was generally impressed by the pomp and ceremony, and encouraged to discover that he could follow the Latin in which the ceremony was conducted, though he did not enjoy the experience of having to perform in full subfusc: dark suit and white bow tie, along with cap and gown. He was less impressed by his fellow prizemen, which the programme (see FIG. 6) reveals included James Laver, who went on to be a respected author, art critic and curator at the Victoria and Albert Museum, and George Catlin, a political scientist who was knighted for his services to Anglo-American relations, describing them as a 'collection of scrubby, beetle-like, bespectacled oddities'.[33]

During these years Lewis made considerable use of Oxford's many libraries, especially that of the Oxford Union. Although it is best known today for its political debates and high-profile visiting speakers, Lewis spent his time in the writing room and library, 'where I have already passed many happy hours and hope to pass many more'.[34] A beautiful Victorian building in its own right, the Oxford Union Society Library must have especially appealed to the young Lewis, since its walls are decorated with a series of murals painted by members of the Pre-Raphaelite Brotherhood, William Morris and Dante Gabriel Rossetti, depicting scenes from the Arthurian legends, first collected together by Thomas Malory in his *Morte d'Arthur*, and retold by

¶ THE PROFESSOR OF POETRY *will deliver the* CREWEIAN ORATION '*in commemoration of Benefactors to the University, according to the intention of the Right Honourable Nathaniel Lord Crewe, Bishop of Durham*'.

¶ THE PRIZE COMPOSITIONS *will be recited by the* PRIZEMEN *as follows*:—

THE GAISFORD PRIZE FOR GREEK VERSE.
Vergil, Georgic IV, 425–527 (*Iam rapidus . . . ripae*).
ASHER HYMAN, Scholar of Wadham College.

THE STANHOPE HISTORICAL ESSAY.
The Influence of George III on the development of the Constitution.
ALFRED MERVYN DAVIES, Scholar of Jesus College.

THE CHANCELLOR'S PRIZE FOR LATIN VERSE.
Olympic Games, Ancient and Modern.
ROBERT GRAHAM COCKRANE LEVENS, Scholar of Balliol College.

THE GLADSTONE MEMORIAL PRIZE.
The Constitution and Membership of the ideal Upper Chamber.
GEORGE EDWARD GORDON CATLIN, B.A., New College.

THE CHANCELLOR'S PRIZE FOR AN ENGLISH ESSAY.
Optimism.
CLIVE STAPLES LEWIS, Scholar of University College.

SIR ROGER NEWDIGATE'S PRIZE FOR ENGLISH VERSE.
Cervantes.
JAMES LAVER, New College.

¶ THE VICE-CHANCELLOR *will dissolve the* CONVOCATION, *and the Procession will leave the Theatre.*

TOCCATO FROM SYMPHONY NO. 5 . . . . . *Widor.*

FIG. 6 Oxford University Encaenia programme, 1921.

Tennyson in his cycle of twelve poems titled *Idylls of the King*, published between 1859 and 1885 (see PLATE 3).

Lewis's diary makes many references to trips to the Oxford Union to consult books; unlike the Bodleian, it is a lending library and so Lewis was able to take the volumes home for consultation. In October 1922 Lewis borrowed George Saintsbury's *A History of English Literature* but did not find himself in sympathy with its author.[35] The copy consulted by Lewis is still held by the Union Library, bearing a number of pencil annotations that appear to derive from Lewis's detailed perusal of the volume. Alongside Saintsbury's contention that '*The Faerie Queene* is the only long poem that a lover of poetry can sincerely wish longer', that famous lover of the long narrative poem has scrawled the objection 'No!'

Another of Lewis's favourite Oxford locations was Duke Humfrey's Library, the oldest part of the Bodleian, which dates back to its foundation in the fifteenth century. Lewis described the scene in a letter: 'I sit in "Duke Humphrey's Library", the oldest part, a Fifteenth-Century building with a very beautiful painted wooden ceiling above me and a little mullioned window at my left hand through which I look down on the garden of Exeter.' Off the main aisle is a series of desks hidden away in little cubby holes, which Lewis – with his particular fondness for pubs – described as 'little boxes, in the public house sense of the word'. Lewis appreciated the library's more permissive approach to conversation, which requested readers to 'talk little and tread lightly', rather than insisting upon complete silence. As well as allowing him to appreciate 'the hum of the hive', Lewis took great pleasure in having some friend step into his box and say 'Hello, are you here?' Along with the lack of upholstering and ashtrays, the only other drawback that Lewis identified was that the combination of beauty, antiquity and overheating worked together to 'weave a spell very much more suited to dreaming than to working' (PLATE 23).

Although he spent much of his spare time reading, Lewis enjoyed boating on the river or taking to the waters at the male bathing area known as Parson's Pleasure, where he rejoiced in the opportunity to swim 'without the tiresome convention of bathing things' (an equivalent area for ladies wearing bathing costumes was known as 'Dame's Delight').[36] Parson's Pleasure is located in the University Parks, adjacent to the path that leads to Mesopotamia: so called because it is the meeting point of the rivers Cherwell and Thames – known locally as the 'Isis'. Lewis eulogized it in his diary: 'The bathing place is a lovely backwater surrounded by those level ... daisied & buttercuped fields & overhung by those short fluffy trees – named – I don't know.'[37] A visit from Warnie in 1922 involved some sightseeing at Merton College as well as games of table tennis and croquet.[38]

Despite the disappointment of the Magdalen fellowship, Lewis had determined upon an academic career; indeed, his former tutor, W.T. Kirkpatrick, had already made clear to Lewis's father his unsuitability for any other profession: 'You may make a writer or a scholar of him, but you'll not make anything else.'[39] He had briefly contemplated the Civil Service as a career, but gave the idea up because of a lack of vacancies and a sense that it was an alien territory to which he did not belong.[40] But there were no academic jobs in Oxford either, and Lewis baulked at the prospect of taking up work as a jobbing tutor, which he viewed as the 'prelude to being a mere grinder' (someone who helps students cram for examinations).[41]

Carritt suggested he apply for a position as a junior dean at Wadham College, who were seeking a student taking Greats willing to retrain as a Tutor in Law.[42] A junior dean is responsible for maintaining discipline among the undergraduate body; Lewis gave up on this idea when he realized the impossibility of him breaking up a party of drunk students in a way that was likely to command obedience. Another suggestion proposed by his tutor was to apply for positions at other universities while waiting for a fellowship to fall vacant at Univ; if he should end up with both, he could hold tutorials at weekends, as Carritt himself had done when a lecturer at Edinburgh. However, Lewis's unusual domestic arrangements and responsibilities made it impossible for him to consider jobs further afield. He was interviewed for a post at

Reading University, close enough for him to commute from Oxford, but was not offered the position.

To postpone the need for gainful employment, Lewis entertained the idea of undertaking a period of postgraduate research: either towards a B.Litt. degree, on the subject of translation in the eighth century, or towards the higher degree of D.Phil., for which he planned to focus on the works of the seventeenth-century Cambridge Platonist Henry More. In the meantime he supplemented his meagre income by marking English essays submitted for the Higher Certificate, a kind of entrance examination for Oxford and Cambridge universities. Although he found the work interesting, he was struck by the abundance of errors and particularly unimpressed by the 'almost illiterate Upper VIth of Lancing' – an exclusive private school in West Sussex whose alumni include the novelist Evelyn Waugh.[43]

In 1923 Lewis applied for a research fellowship at Exeter College, submitting a proposal to write a metaphysical critique of modern psychology, and others at St John's and Trinity colleges. It is interesting to reflect that, if one of these applications had been successful, Lewis might have gone on to a career as a professional philosopher. For the Trinity fellowship Lewis got to the final, and crucial, stage of Oxford appointments of this era: the dinner. Although Lewis was not particularly impressed by Trinity's president, Rev. Herbert Blakiston, whom he described as 'quite a nice old man, but shy and a poor talker', he was very taken with the Trinity dons, viewing it as 'one of the best evenings imaginable'. The senior tutor, 'a disreputable old man in Holy Orders and in liquor', was especially entertaining, leading Lewis to conclude that 'if Trinity don't give me a Fellowship, at least they gave me a very good time'.[44]

As part of the selection process, the president solicited views from senior philosophers in the university. One of these was H.W.B. Joseph of New College, who had marked Lewis's final exams and conducted the oral examination, known as the 'viva', the previous summer. At the viva, Joseph challenged Lewis on the content of his written papers, in particular his view that Plato was wrong on just about everything. In assessing Lewis's suitability for the Trinity post, Joseph recalls being struck by a definite impression of philosophical ability, but also by a 'streak of wilfulness and rebellion to customary doctrine in his mind'.[45] In comparing Lewis with his own preferred candidate, H.H. Price, whom he knew well since Price had been a student at New College, he concluded that, while Lewis was the inferior scholar at this point in his career, he may be the stronger thinker, showing an individuality in his examination papers that offset the greater knowledge commanded by Price. But, despite this caveat, the fellowship was offered to H.H. Price, the very person who had beaten Lewis to the temporary Magdalen fellowship the previous year, and whom Lewis had already identified as a 'dangerous man'. Price went on to have an impressive career as a philosopher, holding the Wykeham Professorship of Logic at New College from 1935 to 1959.

Despite these setbacks, Lewis's first period of paid employment was teaching philosophy; during the academic year 1924–5 he was invited to fill in for his former philosophy tutor, E.F. Carritt, who had taken up a visiting position at the University of Michigan.[46] Lewis was tasked with giving fourteen hour-long lectures on the subject of 'The Moral Good – Its Place among the Values', a prospect he found rather daunting: 'I rather fancy I could really tell the world everything I think about everything in five hours.'[47] Despite this, Lewis did manage to assemble a series of fourteen lectures; these covered topics such as Plato's *Philebus* and *Republic*, Utilitarian Ethics and Kantian Ethics, with follow-up lectures offering critiques, and then another entitled 'Fundamental Error of Both These Theories'.

Despite his winning a considerable reputation as a lecturer in later life, this was not an auspicious beginning to Lewis's career. Thanks to a timetable clash with a lecture being delivered by the senior philosopher Harold Arthur Pritchard, combined with a misprint in the lecture list that gave the location as Pembroke College rather than Univ, Lewis's first lecture was attended by just four students.[48] This modest audience subsequently dwindled to two, at which point Lewis moved the event to his rooms and adopted a more informal approach, encouraging the students to interrupt as they so wished. One of the students, an elderly parson, took up this offer so enthusiastically that Lewis was hardly able to get a word in edgeways.

Reflecting on the experience in a letter to his father, Lewis concludes that he will no longer pursue a career in philosophy, considering himself temperamentally unsuited to a life of solitude and 'perpetual questioning of all that plain men take for granted, a chewing the cud for fifty years over inevitable ignorance and a constant frontier watch on the little tidy lighted conventional world of science and daily life'.[49]

Although the 1920s witnessed an expansion in Arts subjects at Oxford, the creation of the school of PPE (Philosophy, Politics and Economics) in 1920 prompted Univ to use a benefaction to create a new fellowship in Economics and Politics. As a consequence, there was no chance of a fellowship in English becoming available; the college's first tutorial fellow in English, Peter Bayley, was not appointed until the late 1940s.[50] With no prospects of employment at Univ, Lewis successfully applied for a Tutorial Fellowship in English Language and Literature at Magdalen College, taking up the post in 1925.

Despite spending the next thirty years at Magdalen, Lewis maintained a close connection with his undergraduate college; students reading English were sent to him for their tutorials into the 1940s, with some receiving tuition in Old English from C.L. Wrenn. Perhaps Wrenn was employed by Univ in response to a concern expressed by Lewis in his termly reports that students were letting themselves down with 'poor Anglo-Saxon', as in the case of J.T. Holland, whom Lewis felt took a cavalier approach to the language and appeared 'genuinely hurt at being asked to find the Nominative and the Verb before translating a sentence'.

Wrenn was later appointed to a chair at King's College London. Writing to a former Univ pupil, Gerald Brodribb, Lewis recounted how, having been evacuated to Bristol, Wrenn drove around the city during the Blitz, bellowing at the locals to keep calm using a megaphone.[51] Brodribb became a schoolteacher, amateur archaeologist and cricket historian. He dedicated his first book to his former tutor;

although Lewis no doubt appreciated the gesture, it's hard to imagine he had much interest in *The English Game: A Cricket Anthology* (1948).

Lewis was especially drawn to students who were prepared to work hard, even when they were not especially gifted. One such pupil, P.A. Wallers, was praised by Lewis as 'the most worthy pupil I have ever had'. 'Starting with no knowledge and scant talents, he has turned himself into a new man by sheer commonsense, teachableness and industry.'[52] In Michaelmas term 1930 Lewis labelled him a 'third class man' and suggested he would never rise beyond this level;[53] however, by Trinity term 1931 Lewis reported his great hopes of a second-class degree. Of his classmate, he noted simply and somewhat less enthusiastically: 'Seems awake and prepared to work.'[54]

Lewis ceased teaching for Univ in 1946, when his friend Hugo Dyson took over. But Lewis continued to have great affection for his alma mater. In 1959 the college elected him to an honorary fellowship; writing to the master, Arthur Lehman Goodhart, to acknowledge the appointment, Lewis described himself as 'quite overwhelmed' by the honour.[55]

TWO

MAGDALEN COLLEGE

Having tried unsuccessfully for various academic positions, Lewis's hopes were not high when he submitted his application for a fellowship in English Language and Literature at Magdalen College in April 1925. The disappointment of his failed attempt for a research fellowship was still keenly felt. However, in the letter informing him that he had been unsuccessful, the president had praised his essay on 'The Hegemony of Moral Value', and implied that, while Lewis had not done himself justice on this occasion, the gates of Magdalen had not permanently closed on him.[1]

What little optimism Lewis nursed regarding this opportunity must have been considerably undermined by his belief that his former tutor, F.P. Wilson, had also applied. Having established the untruth of this rumour, Lewis approached both Wilson and George Gordon for references, but was dealt a further blow on discovering that, since they thought he had decided to pursue a career in philosophy, both had agreed to back Nevill Coghill. But when Coghill was appointed to a fellowship at his own college, Exeter, both Wilson and Gordon transferred their support to Lewis. As part of the appointment process Lewis was invited to dine at high table at Magdalen, causing him some sartorial anxiety. What was the dress code for such an event? Lewis

FIG. 7 Lewis in 1925, from the Magdalen College Senior Common Room photograph album.

was advised to wear white tie and tails; on arriving in the hall, he was dismayed to find his fellow diners sporting black ties and dinner jackets.

After a nervous period waiting for a response, Lewis received an invitation to meet with the president at his lodgings: an imposing building that stands at the heart of St John's Quad, adjacent to the cloisters and the chapel.[2] Lewis spent an anxious thirty minutes loitering outside, listening to the choir boys practising, while preparing to be quizzed on Anglo-Saxon verbs or the 39 Articles. The meeting turned out to be a mere formality, in which he was asked whether he would be willing to tutor Philosophy as well as English. 'I would have agreed to coach a troupe of performing bagbirds in the quadrangle: but I looked very wise and thought over all his points and I hope let no subservience appear.'[3] The process of appointment was a good deal more formal than that by which the second tutorial fellow in English was appointed. J.A.W. Bennett recalled being offered the position by one of the fellows while crossing Magdalen bridge: 'Ah Bennett, we're thinking of making you a Fellow – any objections?'[4]

Lewis was admitted to the Magdalen fellowship in a ceremony that has remained unchanged to the present day. He knelt before the president, who addressed him in Latin; when the time came for Lewis to reply, he realized that he had not been told what to say. He hazarded the formula *Do fidem*, meaning 'I swear', used when receiving a degree in an Oxford graduation ceremony, which turned out to be the correct response.[5] The president and each of the fellows then shook Lewis's hand and wished him joy. Lewis noted of this ceremony: 'You can hardly imagine how odd it sounded by the twenty fifth repetition.' With the Magdalen fellowship today made up of around seventy fellows, the ritual can last considerably longer and sound even stranger.

Although it may have lost some of its meaning by the twenty-fifth repetition, the wording of this salutation seems oddly prophetic, given

FIG. 8 President and fellows of Magdalen College seated in the college cloisters, 1928. Lewis is in the second row, right of centre.

the place that joy went on to occupy in Lewis's biography. The year before his installation, Lewis wrote a poem titled 'Joy' which attempts to capture a feeling of rapture and freedom that is temporary and cannot be recalled, published under the pseudonym Clive Hamilton. The pursuit of joy, and the sense of inconsolable longing that it instilled in him, was so central to Lewis's journey to faith that he titled his spiritual autobiography *Surprised by Joy*, the opening line of a sonnet by William Wordsworth. We will return to the importance of joy in Lewis's life in Chapter 5.

NEW BUILDING

On taking up his fellowship, Lewis was allocated a set of three rooms, up a set of twisting wooden stairs, on the first floor of staircase 3 of the New Building, an impressive Palladian edifice constructed in the 1730s (see PLATE 2). With a sitting room overlooking the Grove, home to the college's herd of fallow deer, Lewis was struck by the sense that, despite its city location, he was living in the countryside. He wrote to his father, proclaiming his external surroundings to be 'beautiful beyond expectation and beyond hope'.[6]

In addition to his rooms, Lewis received a dining allowance, a salary of £500 per year and a pension, meaning that his money worries were finally over. He was, however, rather surprised to learn that the rooms came unfurnished: 'the extent of College's bounty being some linoleum in the smaller sitting room and a washstand in the bedroom'. Lewis bought most of the necessary furnishings second-hand, but it still cost him more than £90. Despite this substantial price tag, Lewis assured his father that he had not been extravagant: 'The rooms certainly do not look as if they had been furnished by a plutocrat.'[7] There was no lavatory; former students recall Lewis interrupting a tutorial to relieve himself in a chamber pot in the bedroom.

That life in the New Building in the 1920s was quite spartan is apparent from some of the details recorded in his letters. The rooms were certainly cold; Lewis regularly woke to find his bedside water had frozen over during the winter months. During a particularly cold snap in early 1940, Lewis went to bed wearing two pullovers and a pair of trousers over his pyjamas. In post-war Oxford, when coal and electricity were in short supply, Lewis would hold tutorials wearing his dressing gown, with a heavy woollen cardigan underneath. At night he was regularly visited by mice; in a letter to an eleven-year-old New Yorker who sent him a picture she had drawn of Reepicheep the mouse, Lewis described how, when he sits up late working, they poke their heads out from behind the curtains as if to say '"Hi! Time for *you* to go to bed. We want to come out and play."'[8]

Alastair Fowler, a student of Lewis's who went on to be a professor of English Literature at Edinburgh University, penned a vivid description of Lewis's rooms in an account of his first visit. He went to seek Lewis's agreement to supervise his doctoral research; this was a daunting prospect, since Lewis was known for his hostility towards research degrees.

Lewis famously divided up the English Faculty into the literate, the illiterate and the B.Litterate: the B.Litt. being a postgraduate research degree. When asked to examine a thesis submitted in 1930 for the B.Litt. on 'The Life and Work of Henry Howard, Earl of Surrey', Lewis produced a brief but damning report: 'We find that Mr. Casady's thesis adds nothing to what is already known of this subject; and that his general knowledge of English literature and history even within the XVIth century is inadequate.'[9] When a revised version was presented for re-examination the following year, Lewis grudgingly passed it: 'Although we found Mr. Casady's general knowledge of English Literature so very inadequate as almost to disqualify him for the degree, the biographical part of his thesis appeared to us to be adequate.'[10]

While Lewis scrutinized a recommendation from Hugo Dyson, Fowler had time to take in his surroundings, which consisted of mountains of shelved literature, a floral-patterned chesterfield and a reproduction of Botticelli's *Mars and Venus*, a painting which Lewis references in a discussion of the proper way of appreciating a work of art in *An Experiment in Criticism*: 'Look. Listen. Receive. Get yourself out of the way.'[11] Lewis's fondness for enlivening an otherwise austere suite of rooms – famously labelled 'arid' by John Betjeman in *Summoned by Bells* – with allegorical paintings of the Italian Renaissance is also noted by Peter Bayley, who recalls his surprise at Lewis's copy of Tintoretto's erotic *The Origin of the Milky Way*, and by Derek Brewer, who remembers Bronzino's *An Allegory of Venus and Cupid* hanging above the mantelpiece.[12]

A photoshoot for *Vogue* magazine shows Lewis, sporting the dressing gown he wore over his clothes to keep out the cold, sitting in front of a fireplace above which hangs a copy of a second work by Tintoretto: *Mercury and the Three Graces.*[13] In Figure 9 Lewis stands in front of bookshelves in the corner of his sitting room, upon which battered copies of Greek, Latin, Anglo-Saxon and English dictionaries stand. On the right-hand wall is a copy of Michelangelo's *The Creation of Adam*, part of the fresco that adorns the roof of the Sistine Chapel.

TUTORING

During his early years at Magdalen, Lewis gave numerous tutorials: hour-long meetings which focus on discussion of an individual student's essay. These were held in the smaller sitting room on the New Building's south side, with views overlooking the neatly mowed lawns, the cloisters and the Great Tower. In Lewis's day the pupil would read the essay aloud, with the tutor interrupting in order to challenge, correct or extend the discussion of a particular point. Rather than being a disquisition on a subject by the more learned tutor, a successful tutorial comprises a debate between tutor and pupil, in which different viewpoints and perspectives are proposed and considered. Even arguments that appear to the tutor misguided and wrong-headed can provoke stimulating discussion in such a forum, especially if the student is prepared to defend them with close reference to the primary

FIG. 9 Lewis in his sitting room on the first floor of the New Building, Magdalen College, 1947. The shelf behind him holds well-used dictionaries.

texts. Lewis considered all ideas on their own merit: his interest was in the point itself, rather than in the person making it.

This method of instruction could be rather daunting for the student, faced with reading an essay on Shakespeare's tragedies, Donne's love poetry or Swift's *Gulliver's Travels* to such a widely read and learned critic. To make matters worse, Lewis's head would usually be wreathed in smoke, so that it became impossible to discern his reaction from any telltale facial expressions.[14] Sir Guenter Treitel (1928–2019), a lawyer who became a fellow of Magdalen College in 1954, was interviewed by Lewis as a 17-year-old scholarship applicant. He recalled having a conversation about Chaucer's *Canterbury Tales* with a cloud of pipe smoke, out of which he could just make the top of his interviewer's bald head.[15]

During the reading of the essay, Lewis would typically make regular interruptions, requesting clarification or further expounding of a particular point. Once the student had finished the recitation, the business of critiquing began in earnest, encompassing both content and style. Rather than attempting to correct a particular viewpoint, or to impose his own, Lewis's aim was to enable students to gain a deeper understanding of the text and to express their own ideas more clearly. That these interactions also stimulated Lewis's thinking is apparent from references in his critical writings. The essay 'On Stories' refers to a discussion with an American pupil about the works of James Fenimore Cooper, which revealed such different attitudes to suspense and atmosphere that Lewis recalls feeling as if he was talking to a visitor from another planet. Elsewhere, he expresses his surprise at hearing an undergraduate's paper on Jane Austen from which, had he not read the books for himself, he would never have guessed that her novels contain the remotest hint of comedy.[16]

Of particular interest are his diary descriptions of failed attempts to teach Anglo-Saxon, the earliest recorded form of the English language, to a reluctant John Betjeman. In one memorable tutorial the future Poet Laureate turned up in a pair of 'eccentric bedroom slippers', expressing the hope that Lewis would not object. Lewis, who cared so little for his own appearance that he was content to wear odd socks – even odd shoes on one occasion – and had little sympathy for Betjeman's preferred apparel of silk dressing gown and shantung ties, responded rather tartly that, while he would mind them very much, he had no objection to his wearing them – 'a view which, I believe, surprised him'.[17] On another occasion Betjeman rang Lewis to excuse himself from a tutorial as he was suspected of having measles. Lewis adds wryly: 'Probably a lie, but what can one do?'[18]

Typical entries in Lewis's diary record a string of aimless and lightweight essays, or tutorials for which Betjeman had done no preparation. Even when he did produce a creditable essay it became clear from the discussion that it could not be his own work, prompting a despairing Lewis to remark: 'I wish I cd. get rid of this idle prig.' If this attitude strikes us as unduly harsh, Lewis's judgements on his other pupils show that he was not singling out Betjeman for criticism. His tutorial partner, D.W. Valentin, is dismissed as a 'useless lump', while De Peyer and L.E. Clark are described as 'a desperately stupid pair'.[19]

Betjeman's academic career had begun promisingly enough, with an alpha in his first sitting of college exams, formally known as the 'Terminal Review of Regularity and Diligence'. But, in Michaelmas Term 1926, Lewis drew the Tutorial Board's attention to Betjeman's unsatisfactory work ethic; a minute of its meeting of 17 November instructs that 'Mr Betjeman be informed that the Board is not satisfied with his industry'. This warning did not have the desired effect. In Michaelmas Term 1927 he obtained a gamma in his college exams; in Hilary term 1928 Betjeman received the only delta awarded to the entire study body, as well as failing the compulsory Divinity exam, or 'Divvers', for the second time. Betjeman was rusticated – that is, suspended – for Trinity term 1928, in order to allow him to concentrate on cramming for the Holy Scripture examination.

Despite their many clashes in tutorials, Lewis and Betjeman's relationship does not appear to have been entirely antagonistic. Lewis was invited to Betjeman's rooms on St Aldates for tea, where he found himself 'pitchforked into a galaxy of super-undergraduates'. Although he had little time for the assembled group, which included the poet Louis MacNeice, whom Lewis described as 'silent and astonishingly ugly', Lewis was taken with Betjeman's book collection.[20] A letter written to his father shortly afterwards suggests the real focus of his interest: 'Did I tell you that I was asked to tea by a pupil not long ago and noticed a copy of *Dymer* in his bookcase? This is fame.'[21] Since Lewis's *Dymer* was published under the pseudonym Clive Hamilton, it is possible that Betjeman was unaware that the poem was the work of his tutor.

But the real damage was done when Lewis refused to support Betjeman's application to be readmitted for an Honours degree, following his rustication. Lewis made it clear he was unwilling to play both 'butt and fairy godfather' in Betjeman's comedy, and advised him to throw himself at the mercy of the Tutorial Board in order to be permitted to undertake a Pass degree.[22]

Betjeman's biographers suggest that he never forgave Lewis for this coldness. It is certainly true that Betjeman passed up few opportunities to make sarcastic remarks at Lewis's expense in print. In *Ghastly Good Taste* (1933) Betjeman acknowledged his debt to his former tutor, 'whose jolly personality and encouragement to the author in his youth have remained an unfading memory for the author's declining years'.[23] In the preface to his collection of poems *Continual Dew* (1937) he thanked 'Mr C.S. Lewis for the fact on page 256'; there are just 45 pages in the volume.

However, an unpublished letter from Lewis to Betjeman dated 10 November 1936 replies to a request from his former pupil to bury the hatchet.[24] Lewis responded positively, making light of the 'few bolts' that Betjeman had shot at him in his prefaces, claiming that their verbal sparring was nothing more than the 'ordinary amoenities of a literary life'. Lewis goes on to concede that he was a very young tutor when Betjeman was his student and that he may have 'much more than I suppose for which to ask a pardon'. He concludes with a friendly benediction: 'Peace be to you and your house' and an invitation to drop in and see him if it is ever convenient.

But, despite this rapprochement, Betjeman's rancour continued to bubble under the surface. In 1939 he penned a lengthy letter to Lewis in which he attempted to explain his resentment at Lewis's treatment of him as a student, critiqued Lewis's approach to modern poetry and offered a self-justification of his aesthetic interests. Betjeman acknowledged feeling 'unpardonably rude' in expressing such sentiments; it was perhaps for this reason that the missive appears never to have been sent. Perhaps simply writing the letter was sufficient catharsis for someone who, some ten years after dropping out without a degree, admitted that he still woke up angry in the night, thinking of the 'mess I made at Oxford'.[25]

One might have expected two aspiring poets with literary interests to have found common ground, but Betjeman's passion for the more obscure writers of the Victorian period was not suited to the Oxford English course, with its focus on medieval literature and philology. Betjeman's friend and fellow-student Henry Yorke, later a prolific novelist under the pseudonym Henry Green, similarly struggled with the historical focus of the English course. In his memoir, *Pack My Bag* (1940), Yorke observed that, as an English student, he was required to learn Anglo-Saxon: 'This I found I could not do.'[26] According to Warnie, Yorke once responded to some fierce criticism of an essay by Lewis with the rejoinder: 'Whenever I read to you I feel I am casting pearls before (pause) an unappreciative audience.'[27] But, for Edward Sniders, who spent a year at Magdalen before flying Mosquitos with RAF Squadron 139, memories of being taught by Lewis, and the 'stark beauty of Anglo-Saxon', offered comfort during a period of solitary confinement in the notorious Stalag Luft III prisoner-of-war camp, following an unsuccessful escape attempt.[28]

Another Magdalen student who served with the RAF during the Second World War was Richard Gwilym Morgan, who was appointed to a demyship (a college scholarship, derived from *demi-socii* 'half fellows') in 1940, but was killed in action in February 1944 when his Spitfire was shot down, just three weeks after his wedding.[29] As a History student, Morgan would have been taught political theory by

Lewis, and it was Lewis who authorized his access to a work kept in the Bodleian's restricted collection: books given the shelfmark ϕ, the Greek letter phi, which were deemed too sexually explicit to be on open access. Students wishing to read such materials were required to submit a letter of authorization from a college tutor; Figure 10 shows Lewis's letter of support for Morgan's request to consult *Vénus la populaire, ou Apologie des maisons de joye*, a translation of the English *A Modest Defence of Publick Stews* (i.e. brothels), attributed to Bernard de Mandeville.

Lewis could take discussions of literature personally and become offended when students failed to appreciate his favourite authors. He was once heard to shout down the staircase at a departing pupil: 'If you think that way about Keats you needn't come here again!'[30] He is reported to have settled a dispute over the merits of Matthew Arnold's poem *Sohrab and Rustum* with swords. According to his colleague J.A.W. Bennett, who was present, the skirmish resulted in Lewis drawing blood.

However, the experience of being educated by Lewis was not all about withstanding criticism or engaging in swordplay. According to Peter Bayley, who was taught by Lewis in the 1940s before going on to a career as an Oxford English tutor, a good essay could prompt Lewis to place two bottles of beer on the hearth to warm, before sharing them with the grateful student. John Harwood, son of Lewis's friend Cecil, who read English at Magdalen in the early 1950s, was struck by Lewis's determination to find any merit, or glimpse of a worthwhile idea, in the 'pretty pedestrian' essays he submitted to his scrutiny.[31]

On one evening Lewis records staying up late with a student reading Anglo-Saxon poetry: 'Ker shares to the full my enthusiasm for the saga world & we had a pleasant evening – with the wind still roaring outside.'[32] N.R. Ker became a leading palaeographer, a scholar who studies ancient scripts, and author of foundational works on medieval manuscripts and libraries. In 1945 he was appointed Reader in Palaeography in the University of Oxford and was elected to a fellowship at Magdalen.

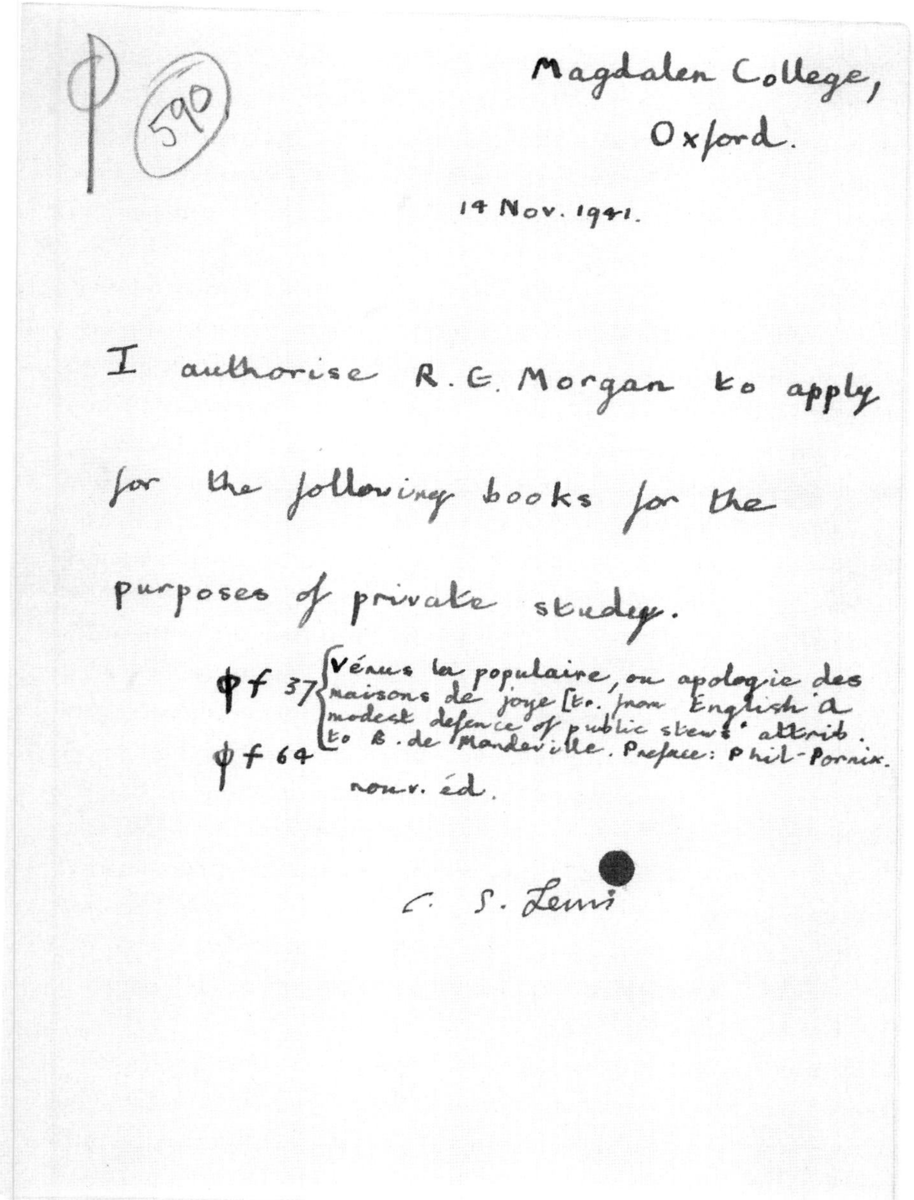

Φ 590

Magdalen College,
Oxford.

14 Nov. 1941.

I authorise R.G. Morgan to apply for the following books for the purposes of private study.

Φf 37 {Vénus la populaire, ou apologie des maisons de joye [tr. from English 'A modest defence of public stews' attrib. to B. de Mandeville. Preface: Phil-Pornix.
Φf 64 nouv. éd.

C. S. Lewis

FIG. 10 Letter from Lewis in 1941 authorizing his student R.G. Morgan to request a book about brothels in the Bodleian Library's Phi Collection, a restricted access collection of sexually explicit works.

Another former student, Derek Brewer, penned an engaging memoir of his years as an undergraduate under Lewis's tutelage. Despite being described as 'lacking pep' by Lewis in an end-of-term collection report, Brewer went on to become one of the leading Chaucer scholars of his generation; in 1964 he was appointed Fellow and Tutor in English at Emmanuel College, Cambridge; from 1977 to 1990 he served as the college's master.

Before coming up to read English in 1941, Brewer wrote to Lewis requesting guidance for his preparatory study. Lewis's response gives an idea of the wide range of reading he expected of an English student embarking on his course. Lewis advised Brewer that, while Greek was largely irrelevant, he should aim to keep up his Latin, focusing particularly on the *Aeneid*, Ovid's *Metamorphoses*, Boethius's *De Consolatione Philosophiae* and Cicero's *De Republica*, adding that 'if you can't scan hexameters, learn how to'. No details are given as to how he should come by this knowledge. Brewer is also advised to acquire a sound biblical background, as this is assumed by most of the early literary writers he will be studying; since the Vulgate is 'very easy Lat.', reading the Bible in St Jerome's Latin translation is a good way of refreshing one's Latin while becoming familiar with the biblical stories. Finally, we come to the recommended reading in English literature, which comprises Chaucer, Shakespeare, Milton, Malory, Spenser, Donne, Dryden, Pope, Swift, Johnson and Wordsworth. Once he has dispatched those writers, Brewer is free to pursue his own tastes. 'The great thing is to be always reading but not to get bored – treat it not like work, more as a vice! Your book bill ought to be your biggest extravagance.'[33]

It was not just students who went on to become professional medievalists themselves that thrived under Lewis's supervision. The writer and theatre critic Kenneth Tynan spoke with great warmth and enthusiasm of his time studying under Lewis. Describing Lewis as 'terribly sound and sunny', Tynan reported having 'rediscovered Milton hand in hand with C.S. Lewis', with God as his co-pilot. In a deathbed interview printed in the *Guardian* in 2001, Tynan recalled how Lewis had talked him out of committing suicide when his fiancée deserted him the day before their wedding; Lewis reminded Tynan that, as a boy, he had narrowly avoided being blown up by a landmine and so should be thankful for every moment of his life. For Tynan, Lewis was both the greatest English literary critic of the twentieth century and a father figure whom he worshipped.[34]

We get an insight into Lewis as a tutor from the comments dotted around the essays written by Kenneth Taylor, who read English at Magdalen from 1944 to 1947, which are now part of the college archives. Along with a scattering of blunt and somewhat acerbic remarks, such as 'wd. like more than two answers' to an unfinished exam paper (see PLATE 10), Lewis's annotations reveal him as a tutor engaging deeply with the style, choice of words and arguments. In an essay on Milton, Lewis supplies a number of counter-examples to Taylor's claim that an epic should follow chronological order, but notes that this is the 'only serious omission in an otherwise good answer', awarding it a beta.

Student recollections of Lewis the tutor often comment on his incredible recall of a vast library of primary texts. Quote a line from *Paradise Lost* and Lewis could give you the following one. When asked why he did not admire the novelist Henry James, Lewis criticized the absurdity of the tea party conversation in chapter 1 of *The Portrait of a Lady*, proceeding to quote the entire passage from memory. His astonishing ability to turn straight to a line or passage within an author's œuvre was thanks to a memory that seemed to have been trained in the Renaissance *ars memorativa*, supported by his extensive annotation of primary texts with detailed thematic indexes. Lewis explained that, to properly enjoy a book, he had to annotate it heavily with a fine-nibbed pen, adding an index of all the highlighted passages at the end; as a result, the book 'acquires the charm of a toy without losing that of a book'.[35] Plate 9 shows a sample page from Lewis's copy of the Arden Shakespeare edition of *Love's Labour's Lost* with his characteristic index.

George Sayer, who read English at Magdalen in the 1930s and went on to be an English master at Malvern College, recalls how often criticism of his tutorial essays focused on Lewis's insistence upon the accurate use of words. Questions such as: 'What exactly do you mean by "sentimental"?' or 'How are you using the word "romantic"?' challenged students to clarify their terms with precision. Failure to do so could lead to the ultimate put-down: 'Wouldn't it be rather better, Sayer, if you're not sure of the meaning of that word, not to use it at all?'[36] A concern with precision in one's terms is apparent in Lewis's underlining of 'attitude' in Plate 10 and the accompanying comment: 'is this quite the right word?' Lewis's rigorous tutorial style clearly ventriloquized his former teacher, W.T. Kirkpatrick, whose opening encounter with Lewis challenged his claim to be surprised by the wildness of the Surrey countryside. When called upon to define exactly what he meant by 'wildness', Lewis found himself unable to do so. 'Do you not see, then ... that your remark was meaningless?', came the stern rebuke from the Great Knock.[37]

Despite being a student at St John's College, from 1943 to 1946, the poet and novelist John Wain was sent to Lewis for his tutorials, during which the two men engaged in a 'breathless game', as Wain learned the skills of the quick-fire debater, equipped with illustration and metaphor, from the master. Looking back on those encounters having read Lewis's autobiographical account of his own training at the hands of W.T. Kirkpatrick, Wain noted that, with a simple substitution of names, it exactly captured his experience of being taught by Lewis.[38]

Wain jotted down brief summaries of these tutorials at the ends of his essays, allowing us glimpses into the nature of Lewis's feedback and the ensuing discussions.[39] Following an essay on Sir Thomas Browne, Lewis reprimanded Wain for being too credulous in accepting a 'history book concept' of the seventeenth century. Instead of using the writers to correct this theory, Wain was guilty of straining them to fit the theory. Lewis also took issue with Wain's use of 'personal revelation' to signal the laying bare of one's own soul; in the seventeenth century it referred to the spirit of God revealed to man.

Similarly, Wain's essay misunderstood Browne's concept of 'paradox', which meant going against accepted doctrine, rather than a seemingly contradictory statement.

An essay on seventeenth-century satire finished with Lewis praising Wain's observations on Samuel Butler, while advising him to replace a quotation that is reproduced by every 'second class female candidate' with a more recondite alternative. This was followed by a long argument about whether *Alice in Wonderland* was 'starkly sadistic'. Wain argued in support of this description, with reference to the original illustrations. This prompted Lewis to produce a copy of the work and the two men proceeded to thumb through it, 'arguing furiously'.

Wain was one of a number of students from other colleges that Lewis tutored, despite his heavy teaching load at Magdalen. In Trinity term 1926 he taught a class of seven female students at Lady Margaret Hall, covering topics such as Plato's *Dialogues*, David Hume's theory of causation and Samuel Alexander's distinction between enjoyment and contemplation, which Lewis himself regarded as 'an indispensable tool of thought'.[40] The first meeting got off to a slow start, since most of the students appeared not to have read the *Dialogues*; the class dynamic also proved quite challenging, with students forming alliances and snubbing others in an effort to assert themselves.

It is reassuring to note that improbable student excuses for tardiness are not a modern phenomenon; Miss Carter blamed her late arrival on having to hunt for her pet tortoise.[41] Despite these unpromising beginnings, the class made good progress. Lewis recorded that Miss Scoones's paper of 5 May was 'really astonishingly good for an amateur' and that it was followed by an excellent discussion. Lewis took the success or failure of his classes very personally. Following a disappointing meeting the next month, he notes: 'The hour was a failure and I am rather ashamed of getting a pound for it.'[42]

In 1932 Lewis taught Mary Shelley, who was reading English at St Hugh's College, at the request of her former tutor, Hugo Dyson, then a lecturer at Reading University. In her final examinations she obtained a fourth-class degree; Lewis wrote to her in an effort to reassure her that this result did not mean she had a fourth-class mind. He explained that the language papers had proved to be her downfall: she obtained an NS (*non satis*, or 'unsatisfactory') and a δ (D, the lowest grade available) in these subjects. He expressed some surprise at her poor performance in the literature papers, where her highest mark was a β+ (B+), blaming himself for not having required her to produce more essays.

That there was some truth in this explanation is suggested by the term's report card, in which Lewis noted that he required fewer essays from Miss Shelley in recognition of her overcrowded schedule.[43] A somewhat terse observation by the senior English tutor below suggests that Lewis ought to have been more diligent in his supervision, and that several tutorials had been cancelled due to illness (Lewis was laid up with flu for several weeks). Mary Shelley's daughter Sarah, to whom Lewis became godfather in 1942, attributed her mother's poor results to a relationship break-up shortly before Finals, combined with a lack of self-confidence.[44]

Lewis and Mary Shelley (later Neylan) remained lifelong friends and corresponded over matters of faith, marriage and parenting – the last invoking the scorn of Mrs Moore, who wondered why anyone would seek Lewis's advice on how to bring up a baby.[45] Lewis introduced Mary to the three-volume *Unspoken Sermons* of George MacDonald, and, in recognition of her enthusiasm for the work of his mentor, dedicated his selection of extracts, *George MacDonald: An Anthology* (1947), to her.

LECTURING

As with most Oxford positions, Lewis's appointment carried both tutorial duties and a requirement to give lectures to the wider student body. In an effort to cut down on the preparation time, Lewis chose a subject with which he was very familiar for his first series of lectures: 'Eighteenth-Century Precursors of the Romantic Movement'. But he soon discovered that F.P. Wilson was planning to lecture on precisely the same texts, requiring Lewis to spend his Christmas vacation earnestly studying the prose works of this period, with which he was much less familiar, in order not to find himself competing for an audience with his former tutor.[46]

Lewis gave his first lecture in January 1926. Having cautiously booked the smallest room in college, he was delighted to discover a large crowd had assembled, requiring him to lead them in a search for a larger venue. This necessitated crossing the High Street in a disorderly mass, suspending the traffic in the process. Despite being exhilarated by the experience, Lewis knew that the success of the lecture would be judged on the following week's turnout: 'I have been weighed, with results as yet unknown – and next week I may have an audience of five or none. Still it is something to be given a chance.'[47]

Alastair Fowler, who attended Lewis's lectures on Spenser and subsequently edited them for publication, described his lecturing style as one of 'avuncular informality'.[48] While each lecture was a carefully crafted rhetorical performance, in which the fuse of a joke or 'coup d'amphitheatre' was lit some minutes before the explosion, it was characterized by improvisations and a conversational style that suggested Lewis thinking through an idea for the first time. Far from engaging in ceremony, Lewis would begin orating as he entered the lecture theatre, and continue to do so until he left the room. The novelist A.S. Byatt was so inspired by Lewis's criticism, especially *The Allegory of Love* (1936), that she approached him at the end of one of his lectures and offered to continue his work in this field. Lewis was encouraging, pointing out that she would have to learn Greek. Byatt took the advice seriously, enrolling in an American graduate school, but never got to grips with the subject, later blaming it on the excessive central heating.[49]

Eric Stanley, holder of the Rawlinson and Bosworth Chair of Anglo-Saxon from 1977 to 1991, attended Lewis's series of lectures titled 'Prolegomena to English Renaissance Literature', comprising material that appeared as the introductory chapter of his volume for *The Oxford History of English Literature*, with the rather provocative title 'New Learning and New Ignorance'. Reminiscing about these lectures some sixty years later, Stanley still considered them to be the best he had ever attended. Shabbily dressed, in corduroy trousers and a well-worn M.A. gown, Lewis held his audience rapt with his ability to quote long passages of poetry by heart. While the lectures were fundamentally serious, they were presented with humour, although students did not laugh out loud for fear of missing something important.[50]

George Watson, later a colleague of Lewis's in the Cambridge English Faculty, attended Lewis's lectures in the late 1940s, despite the stern warning of his own tutor, who thought their erudition and scope potentially confusing: 'If I hear you are going to Lewis ... I shall have serious doubts about you.' Watson recalled his surprise at the size of the audience and the appearance of the lecturer, whose short, stocky figure resembled a 'pork butcher of hearty disposition', rather than a celebrated scholar. Also distinctive was Lewis's mode of delivery: he spoke slowly in a booming voice, with a deep, velvety tone.[51]

Marjorie Boulton, later a decorated poet in both English and Esperanto, attended Lewis's lectures in the 1940s, when she was a student at Somerville College. She found Lewis 'lucid' and 'fascinating' and particularly appreciated his dry wit. On one occasion Lewis noted Marlowe's confusion of the four contraries and the four elements, adding: 'But then he did not have the advantage of attending these lectures.'[52] Another lecture is described as 'one long laugh', with Boulton particularly enjoying Lewis's 'screamingly and rather cruelly funny' comparisons between medieval and modern science. The main problem she experienced was in jotting down all the important observations; she also wished she could record his delivery, such as the way he acted out the heated exchange between the husband and wife chickens, Dame Pertelote and Chauntecleer, in Chaucer's *Nun's Priest's Tale*. Lewis clearly relished the opportunity to perform, and his audience lapped it up, leading Boulton to marvel at the amount of recondite knowledge the lecturer was able to impart without his audience being aware of it.[53]

Lewis prepared his lectures by compiling notes that would function as prompts, rather than writing a full script to be read aloud. In this way the event retained a degree of spontaneity and performance.

When he felt that additional material was required, Lewis drew upon a second notebook, containing further exempla and quotations with which he could elaborate and support his arguments. One such notebook survives, with the title 'Thickening' written in large letters on the cover, evidently intended to accompany Lewis's introductory Renaissance lectures. A selection from its list of contents offers an insight into the different directions such elaborations might take; it includes materials relating to the sixteenth-century cosmologist Giordano Bruno, notes on *The Individual and the Cosmos in Renaissance Philosophy* (1927) by Ernst Cassirer, and Nesca A. Robb's *Neoplatonism of the Italian Renaissance* (1935), alongside extracts of source materials by writers such as Campanella, Pico, Cusanus and Paracelsus in the original Latin.

CLUBBING

Lewis's evenings were filled with meetings of societies: events at which papers were read and discussed, and food and drink consumed. The most famous of these was undoubtedly the Inklings – discussed in more detail in Chapter 4 – but other groups that predated their meetings highlight Lewis's commitment to such interactions.

The first of these was an Old Icelandic reading group established shortly after Lewis arrived at Magdalen. The group was the brainchild of the recently appointed Rawlinson and Bosworth Professor of Anglo-Saxon, J.R.R. Tolkien, who took up the chair in 1925. The society was known as the 'Kolbítar', the Old Icelandic for 'coalbiters', a scornful label applied to those Vikings who stay at home by the fireside rather than embark on heroic expeditions. The group set out to read the major literary works of medieval Iceland in the original language: a language that is closely related to Old English, though belonging to the northern rather than the western branch of the Germanic language family tree. For Lewis, this was the realization of a childhood dream, which allowed him to revisit some of the early brushes with 'Northernness' that shaped his youth. Writing to Arthur Greeves, he

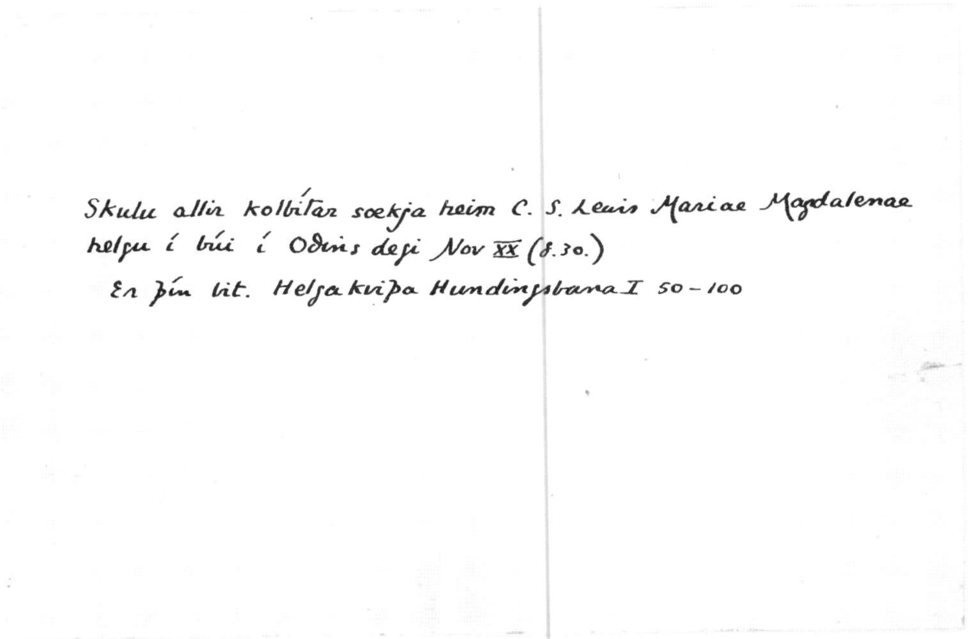

Skulu allir kolbítar soekja heim C. S. Lewis Mariae Magdalenae
helgu í búi í Odins degi Nov XX (8.30.)
Er þín lit. Helgakviða Hundingsbana I 50–100

FIG. 11 Invitation to a meeting of the Kolbítar, written in Old Icelandic, 20 November 1929.

described the pleasure he experienced just leafing through the pages of his Icelandic dictionary: 'the mere name of god or giant catching my eye will sometimes throw me back fifteen years into a wild dream of northern skies and Valkyrie music.'[54]

But the reality of learning to read Old Icelandic wasn't all exultation and delight; there was quite a bit of hard slog too. In February 1927, having received a card noting that the Kolbítar would be reading *Volsunga Saga* that term, and that he had been allocated chapters I and II, Lewis set to work on his translation. Having evidently struggled with the original language, he was forced – like many modern students of Old Icelandic – to consult a crib: 'Began working on it. Felt v. poorly and depressed all morning ... Looked at Morris's translation of Volsunga Saga in the Union.'[55]

The card that Lewis refers to, indicating the section of text he should prepare, would have been similar to one that survives, in Lewis's own handwriting, informing the recipient of the date and location of the next meeting, and setting the required passage for prior translation (see FIG. 11). The card, written in Old Icelandic, calls upon all the Coalbiters to seek the home of C.S. Lewis of Mary Magdalen College on Oðin's day (i.e. Wednesday), 20 November, and informs the recipient that his 'bit' (Lewis apparently did not know the equivalent word in Old Icelandic) is lines 50–100 of the poem *Helgakviþa Hundingsbana I*, 'The First Lay of Helgi Hundingsbane'.

The group brought together an impressive cadre of senior scholars in the university, with a diversity of advanced philological expertise. Regular attendees included R.M. Dawkins, Professor of Byzantine and Medieval Greek; G.E.K. Braunholtz, Professor of Comparative Philology; John Fraser, Professor of Celtic; George Gordon, who had been a fellow of Magdalen from 1907 to 1915 and returned in 1928 as president; as well as Lewis's Magdalen colleagues K.B. McFarlane and C.T. Onions. Lewis was not the only member to find the workload a struggle; John Bryson recalled one senior scholar consulting a printed crib concealed under the table, while feigning to translate the passage unaided.[56]

Other regular meetings with friends and colleagues included a fortnightly philosophical supper with William Francis Ross Hardie, Magdalen's Philosophy tutor (later president of Corpus Christi College), as well as the Cave: a group of English dons who gathered to discuss literary topics and School politics (named after the Cave of Adullam in which David plotted the conspiracy against Saul).[57]

In addition to these commitments, Lewis hosted regular reading groups with his students. Wednesday nights was 'Beer and Beowulf', an Old English gathering for first-year undergraduates.[58] As well as reciting the grammatical paradigms of Old English nouns and verbs in chorus, students read *Beowulf* aloud and debated issues, such as the divine right of kings, while drinking beer drawn from the barrel that Lewis kept in his rooms. Discussion of the text was further enlightened by the presence at some meetings of J.R.R. Tolkien, who introduced parallels from Icelandic sagas and competed with Lewis in blowing smoke rings.[59] In 1928 Lewis referred to a 'great new poem' he was composing in octosyllabic couplets, which would serve as a mnemonic covering all the Old English sound changes and run to a similar length as the *Cursor Mundi*, a Middle English poem on the history of the world in 30,000 lines.[60] It was presumably a similar rhyme about the Germanic sound laws that Ransom composed as a freshman, and that he recites to kill time on Perelandra, or Venus (*Perelandra*, 1943).[61]

Lewis's account of these evenings reveals a more convivial and approachable side to the tutor: 'The actual work is usually done by half past ten: but they are comfortably by the fire and like to sit on and talk – and after all, it is part of one's job to get to know them – so that evening is usually full up till midnight.'[62] This comment highlights Lewis's commitment to the ideal of an Oxford don, for whom the social and pastoral aspects of the tutor–pupil relationship were of vital importance.[63]

Other term-time commitments included Tuesday night's meeting of the Mermaid Club, an Elizabethan drama reading group founded in 1902, of which Lewis was elected president in Michaelmas term 1927. Accounts of their meetings in his diary indicate that Lewis had little sympathy with the other members, or their attitude to the plays. He describes his fellow readers as 'rather vulgar and strident young men', who 'guffaw' at every suggestion of obscenity in *The White Devil*, the play by Webster that they read in February 1927.[64] An entry for the following meeting, at which the group worked through Tourneur's *Revenger's Tragedy*, prompted Lewis to despair of this 'drinking, guffawing cry of barbarians', who ruined the play with the 'continual cackling' which greeted every bawdy reference (no matter how tragic) and every error introduced by a hapless reader.[65]

Alongside his Mermaid Club commitments, Lewis entertained his own students, and any others who cared to join, to a weekly Elizabethan play reading. He began the custom out of a despair that his students would not otherwise get through the considerable number of such works that they were supposed to become familiar with – a fact which prompted him to curse the fertility of the Elizabethan dramatists.

In January 1930 Lewis read a paper on 'Some Problems of Metaphor' to the Junior Linguistic Society, an earnest collection of thirty students who met in rooms on Friars Entry, opposite a sinister-looking hostelry where the notorious Shove Halfpenny Club assembled until it was shut down by the proctors – university officials responsible for student discipline. The rooms were owned by a group of bibliophiles, known as the Broadside Club, who had decorated the walls with pictures of female nudes. Lewis was struck by the bizarre contrast offered by the decadence of the surroundings and the seriousness of the Junior Linguists, who were a diverse and eccentric bunch. Following his paper Lewis got into a lengthy philosophical discussion with a total stranger whom he took to be a lunatic.[66]

Another fortnightly commitment was the Michaelmas Club, an undergraduate discussion group whose members read papers on philosophy and literature. Lewis and the Modern History tutor K.B. McFarlane founded the club out of a frustration with the lack of intellectual life in the college, which otherwise focused on 'rowing, drinking, motoring and fornication'.[67] Lewis feared that, unless students learnt the importance of discussing serious subjects among themselves, the college would never be anything more than 'a country club for the idlest "bloods" of Eton and Charterhouse'.[68] Members took turns to act as host, which involved providing refreshments, to consist of coffee, mulled claret, biscuits and cigarettes. The important role Lewis played in facilitating discussion is apparent from the minutes of the first meeting, at which E.A. Radice read a paper entitled 'Culture and Relativity', following which 'Mr Lewis, in opening the debate, helped greatly to make clear in the minds of the club exactly what issues were at stake.'[69]

On 13 May 1929 Lewis himself read a paper on 'The Personal Heresy' – his term for what he considered the mistaken view that all poetry is the expression of the poet's personality – which would become the basis of a debate with E.M.W. Tillyard in a series of articles published in *Essays and Studies*, and subsequently collected together in a publication by Oxford University Press in 1939. In Trinity term 1931

Lewis presented a paper entitled 'What a Hope', which depicted life as it would be in a Wellsian Utopia, robbed of all religious and heroic motives, and without any incentive to improve the world for the future.

The club also invited external speakers to address them; in Trinity term 1930 Tolkien gave a paper on privately constructed languages, which included examples of 'highly polished philologies of his own', accompanied by readings of poems in those languages. On 21 May 1930 Lewis wrote to T.S. Eliot inviting him to address the society, offering him any date of his choosing before 5 June. Despite expressing a desire that Eliot would be able to come in spite of the short notice, it is hard to imagine that Lewis was in earnest. The animosity Lewis held towards Eliot, which had prompted him to submit spoof poems parodying Eliot's style to the *New Criterion* in 1926, may have contributed to the last-minute nature of this invitation.[70] When the two men finally met, over a cup of afternoon tea in 1945 in the Mitre pub on the High Street, Eliot opened the conversation by commenting on how much older Lewis appeared in person than in his photographs, which did little to soften Lewis's attitude towards him.[71]

Lewis's extensive evening commitments were a considerable drain on his time. In December 1929 he confessed to Arthur Greeves: 'I have too many irons in the fire ... It is very hard to keep one's feet in this sea of engagements and very bad for me spiritually.'[72] This reference to his spirituality appears to allude to a new dimension to Lewis's life, and a new commitment to fit into his already bursting diary. According to his account in *Surprised by Joy*, during the Trinity term of that year Lewis had converted from atheism to a belief in theism, as recalled in a memorable passage:

> You must picture me alone in that room in Magdalen, night after night, feeling, whenever my mind lifted even for a second from my work, the steady, unrelenting approach of Him whom I so earnestly desired not to meet. That which I greatly feared had at last come upon me. In the Trinity Term of 1929 I gave in, and admitted that God was God, and knelt and prayed: perhaps, that night, the most dejected and reluctant convert in all England.[73]

However, Alister McGrath has proposed a revision of this dating, arguing that Lewis's conversion to theism instead took place in Trinity term 1930.[74] This has been confirmed by Andrew Lazo, whose study of an early attempt by Lewis to chart this development in prose makes certain this redating.[75] Perhaps inevitably, Lewis's conversion led to the founding of a discussion group, with Adam Fox, the Dean of Divinity, for pious undergraduates, whose lack of theological knowledge Lewis felt would have shocked an eighteenth-century infidel.

SMOKING ROOM

Lewis's early years at Magdalen were extremely congenial ones; he found the college and its fellows the model of the intellectual life. In an age before the Internet, this was a place where everything could be discovered simply by asking one's colleagues, who always had time to offer some clue as to where the sought-after information could be found: '"You'll find something about it in Alanus…" – "Macrobius would be the man to try…" – "Doesn't Comparetti mention it?"… "Have you looked for it in Du Cange?"'[76] Such conversations would often take place over meals in hall or in the smoking room, where fellows gathered for drinks before dinner, and, on special occasions – following a rather unusual tradition – weighed themselves and their guests and entered the details into the weights book (PLATE 8).

After dining in hall, fellows would repair to the Senior Common Room (SCR) for coffee and dessert: port, pudding wine and an assortment of fruits, nuts and Turkish delight. Lewis's name appears twice in the college weights books, once at the History dinner in 1934, at which he weighs in at 13 stone, and again in September 1954, shortly before leaving for Cambridge, when he is a somewhat more substantial 14 stone 13 pounds: the port and Turkish delight, a weakness which Lewis shared with Edmund in *The Lion, the Witch and the Wardrobe*, had clearly left its mark. In Plate 5 a group of fellows is assembled in the SCR for dessert. As the second most senior fellow present, Lewis is seated to the right of the fireplace, where he is in charge of receiving the decanters sent via the port railway by the senior fellow, occupying the seat to the left of the fire.

Conversation could involve academic debate, college gossip or the solving of crossword puzzles. When arguments got really heated and could not be resolved, fellows took to settling their differences by placing a wager and recording it in a betting book. One such instance records a disagreement between Lewis and C.E. (known affectionately in college as 'Tom Brown') Stevens over whether *eros* appears in Homer's *Odyssey*, resulting in an agreement to stake a bottle of port on the outcome (PLATE 6). A later entry records that Stevens duly paid up; one might have expected the tutor in Ancient History to have known better.

HALL

When the Pevensie children discover the stone ruins at the opening of *Prince Caspian*, it is the layout of the hall that triggers their recognition of their former castle, Cair Paravel. The identification of a terrace as the remains of the dais on which the high table stood reminds them of the great hall in which they themselves had feasted. But it is the presence of a small door at the end of the dais, leading down a set of spiral stairs to the treasure chamber, that makes them certain about the identity. A small door is also located beside the dais in the hall at Magdalen, leading on to a spiral staircase, although in this case snaking up to the roof of the cloisters. This is the route taken by the fellows when moving between the hall and the smoking room, one that Lewis himself would have taken daily on his way to get his meals.

It was in the hall at Magdalen on 7 February 1939 that Lewis and E.M.W. Tillyard conducted a live debate to resolve the controversy between them concerning 'The Personal Heresy'. Despite Lewis's prediction that he would be roundly defeated, John Lawlor, a pupil of Lewis's who became a professor of English at Keele University, recalls that his tutor ran rings around Tillyard, 'like some piratical Plymouth bark against a high-built galleon of Spain'.[77]

OSCAR WILDE ROOM

This room is named after its most famous former occupant, who read Literae Humaniores at Magdalen, graduating with a double First in 1878. On 31 December 1949 Lewis held a lunch party in this room, to which he invited the artist Pauline Baynes, whom he had chosen to illustrate *The Lion, the Witch and the Wardrobe.* Lewis was first attracted to Baynes's work by the illustrations she supplied for J.R.R. Tolkien's *Farmer Giles of Ham* (1949).

Lewis was greatly pleased with her illustrations for *The Lion, the Witch and the Wardrobe*, praising in particular 'the wealth of vigorous detail'. Lewis considered her work to improve throughout the series of Narnian books, especially her portrayal of the animals. On receiving her selection of pictures for *The Magician's Nephew*, Lewis was particularly struck by her depiction of Strawberry the horse, which he considered impressively realistic, whether charging with his hansom cab, growing wings or flying.[78]

The quality of Baynes's submissions led to some difficult decisions about which illustrations to include in the final publication. Only twice did her drawings require correction: once when she had mistakenly depicted the rowers facing forward rather than aft in a picture intended for *Prince Caspian*, and another time resulting in the removal of a shield wrongly placed on a knight's right arm in *The Silver Chair.* That Lewis considered her illustrations to be integral to the success of the books is clear from his response to her letter offering congratulations on the award of the Carnegie Medal for *The Last Battle.* Lewis replied by suggesting that it was 'our Medal' rather than his alone, since the illustrations were surely taken into consideration in the judging.[79]

ADDISON'S WALK

Addison's Walk, or 'Adders' according to the slang of the day, named for the famous essayist Joseph Addison, who was a fellow of the college from 1698–1711, was an important place of refuge for Lewis during a pressing schedule. He typically began the day with a brisk

FIG. 12 Addison's Walk in spring.

canter around the circular walk, before attending the 8.00 a.m. chapel service, having been woken by his scout (a college servant) at 7.15 a.m. with a cup of tea. During the war, Lewis's amiable scout, William Hatton, was sent to work in a local factory; his replacement would wake Lewis at 7.05 a.m. in order to subject him to an unwelcome ten-minute report on the day's weather.

Derek Brewer would often cross paths with Lewis as he rushed towards the chapel, the pair hastily exchanging respective observations about primroses and snowdrops.[80] On warm summer mornings Lewis frequently swam in the River Cherwell at Holywell Ford with the historian A.J.P. Taylor, who lived in the Mill House owned by the college. Max Born, a German physicist who was awarded the Nobel Prize in 1954 for his contribution to quantum mechanics, spent two months in early 1948 at Magdalen when delivering a prestigious series of Waynflete Lectures on 'The Natural Philosophy of Cause and Chance'. Born would regularly bump into Lewis, whom he described as 'a youngish fat little man with humanistic eyes and some wit', when taking a morning stroll around Addison's Walk. On one occasion the two stopped to contemplate the nature of the sun and the earth and to discuss each other's work, about which they were entirely ignorant, as well as the beautiful surroundings and the spring flowers. Their conversation was suddenly broken up when the Magdalen Tower chimed 10.00 a.m. and Lewis 'spurted away to his pupils'.[81]

A post-prandial stroll with Hugo Dyson and J.R.R. Tolkien around Addison's Walk led to Lewis making a major step forward in his acceptance of Christianity. As we have seen, Lewis reluctantly shifted from atheism to belief in a god following a long and lonely battle in his rooms at Magdalen in Trinity term 1930, but he had yet to accept the claims of the Christian religion. In September 1931 Lewis, Dyson and Tolkien were deep in the discussion of metaphor and myth while walking round Addison's, when they were interrupted by 'a rush of wind which came so suddenly on the still, warm evening and sent so many leaves pattering down that we thought it was raining'. The discussion continued in Lewis's rooms, with a satisfying talk about Christianity, and the claims advanced by some that it is the 'true myth', love and friendship, finally drifting back to poetry and books.[82] Tolkien eventually left through the little postern on Magdalen Bridge at 3.00 a.m., while Dyson and Lewis continued their conversation in the colonnade of New Building, finally getting to bed at 4.00 a.m.

Lewis's fondness for Addison's Walk is captured in a poem he wrote titled 'What the Bird Said Early in the Year', a version of a poem called 'Chanson D'Aventure' that was published in the *Oxford Magazine* in May 1938, and that now appears on a plaque that was commissioned and installed by the Oxford University C.S. Lewis Society at Holywell Ford:[83]

I heard in Addison's Walk a bird sing clear:
This year the summer will come true. This year. This year.

Winds will not strip the blossom from the apple trees
This year, nor want of rain destroy the peas.

This year time's nature will no more defeat you,
Nor all the promised moments in their passing cheat you.

This time they will not lead you round and back
To Autumn, one year older, by the well-worn track.

This year, this year, as all these flowers foretell,
We shall escape the circle and undo the spell.

Often deceived, yet open once again your heart,
Quick, quick, quick, quick! – the gates are drawn apart.

THE GROVE

Since Lewis's sitting room in the New Building looked out over the Grove, where the college's deer herd has grazed since the eighteenth century, he had plenty of time to admire and observe the customs of his new neighbours:

> They are erratic in their habits. Some mornings when I look out there will be half a dozen chewing the cud just underneath me, and on others there will be none in sight – or one little stag (not much bigger than a calf and looking too slender for the weight of its own antlers) standing still and sending through the fog that queer little bark or hoot which is these beasts' 'moo'. It is a sound that will be as familiar to me as the cough of the cows in the field at home, for I hear it day and night.[84]

Following a dinner at Exeter College in 1933, the Lewis brothers, Tolkien and Dyson took a stroll in the Grove and admired the deer prancing about in the twilight, with Tolkien greeting them by sweeping off his hat and wittily exclaiming: 'Hail fallow, well met.'

As well as enjoying watching the deer, Lewis cultivated a friendship with a rabbit that he fed with chestnut leaves and that he christened 'Baron Bisket' – using the old spelling of 'biscuit' that Lewis particularly favoured.[85] The rabbit became so tame that it would stand on its hind legs and put its front paws on Lewis's legs, prompting him to pen the following limerick:

A funny old man had a habit
Of giving a leaf to a rabbit.
  At first it was shy
  But then, by and by,
It got rude and would stand up to grab it.[86]

Having been bewitched by his 'lollipop eyes' and the 'twitching velvet nose', Lewis was distressed to find that just a few days later the Baron was shunning him: 'The Rabbit and I have quarrelled. I don't know why, unless I gave him something that disagreed with him. At any rate, he has cut me dead several times lately – so fair and so fickle!'[87] Lewis referred to the rabbit again in a letter to his eleven-year-old godson, Laurence Harwood (see PLATE 11), although by now he has decided that the Baron is in fact a Baroness.

Lewis finally came to resign his Magdalen fellowship in 1954, having accepted a chair at Cambridge. In his letter of resignation to the President, Lewis signs off by hoping that the Bursar will not be too prompt in requesting the return of his college keys, as it is difficult, after twenty-nine years, to envisage 'a Grove-less and Adderless life'.[88]

CHAPEL

Following his conversion to theism, Lewis began attending daily services in chapel (PLATE 7) and remained a regular worshipper throughout the remainder of his time at the college. References in his diary, however, show that he also made infrequent appearances in chapel before his conversion, occasionally reading the lesson.[89] But with his conversion came more regular chapel-going. Lewis made a commitment to attend the 8.00 a.m. service every day during term, which meant cutting back on his extensive evening commitments and going to bed earlier.[90]

The stall that Lewis occupied during these services, nearest the altar on the south side, is now marked with a plaque. Lewis took his seat promptly; as soon as the clock in the Great Tower struck the hour, he rose and the service got under way. Reverend Arthur

Adams, Dean of Divinity from 1949 to 1975, recalled how, as soon as the final 'Amen' was said, Lewis would leap to his feet, make his way noisily down the wooden steps in his heavy brown brogues and bustle through the chapel at a quick march, often 'blowing his nose resonantly' as he left the antechapel.[91] Lewis was not partial to church music so he rarely attended the choral services, including those on Sunday, when he would worship at his local parish church. He made an exception on Ascension Day in 1940, when he was moved by the experience of hearing a full male choir sing an anthem that could blow the roof off the chapel, despite there being just six communicants in attendance.

VICE PRESIDENCY

The Vice Presidency of Magdalen College is an office to which a senior fellow is elected, initially for a period of one year, with reappointment to a second year in most cases a mere formality. The position involves sitting on all college committees, which at that time consisted of the Tutorial Board and its subcommittees, the running of the college's two schools, as well as meetings dealing with Livings (which elected clergy to the college's forty livings and administered tithes), Grants, Refugee Scholars, Fellowships, Sermons, College Servants, the Library, Chapel, Choir and the Bursary, dealing with the college estates, investments and general finances.[92] As one fellow remarked, 'When one contemplates that as one's daily company, it's daunting.' In addition to this punishing committee schedule, the vice president was required to deputize for the president in the chair when he was prevented from attending.

In 1941 the president was George Gordon, whose discussion group Lewis attended as an undergraduate and who had been a member of the Kolbítar. Gordon had struggled with illness since 1935, when he was compelled to take a period of sick leave. His health came under particular strain from 1938 to 1941, when he served as the university's vice chancellor, with the additional stress of the contingency planning required by the onset of war. Shortly after demitting the vice chancellorship, Gordon was diagnosed with terminal cancer.

Vice presidents are chosen from the college fellowship according to seniority, based upon length of service. According to this custom, Lewis was next in line; however, a cabal of fellows, led by T.D. ('Harry') Weldon, a Philosophy tutor, planned to reappoint H.M.D. Parker to an exceptional fourth year in the role, citing the president's absence and the war as justification for breaking with tradition. Lewis had been offered the post the previous year but turned it down. Since it was known that he would refuse the position a second time, the plan was to present Parker as a continuity candidate and thereby hold off the next in line, the powerful History tutor K.B. McFarlane.

But Weldon had met his match in McFarlane, a shrewd operator who took great glee in his powers as an unscrupulous politician: 'Machiavelli couldn't come one over me!' McFarlane recognized Lewis's lack of guile, describing him as 'dead honest and reliable'. His response to the plot against him was to persuade Lewis to accept the position, thereby blocking Parker's reappointment. McFarlane impressed upon Lewis his duty to the college; Lewis preferred to defer to McFarlane himself, but the latter argued that, since he would succeed Lewis following his two-year stint, this would ensure '4 years of "good" government'.[93] In the end McFarlane succeeded in persuading Lewis into holding the fort temporarily and, at the college meeting of 6 November 1940, he was duly nominated, elected and admitted to the vice presidency.

In addition to facing the challenges presented by the war and the president's illness, Lewis was in demand as a speaker and broadcaster. It was in 1941 that he delivered the first of his radio broadcasts for the BBC Home Service, entitled 'The Case for Christianity', which launched his career as a public apologist for the Christian faith. In June Lewis preached the sermon 'The Weight of Glory' in the University Church, speaking from the raised pulpit that was installed in 1827 to ensure that growing numbers of students could hear the preacher, a necessary accommodation given the huge audience that assembled for Lewis's oration. That Lewis was well equipped to occupy such a prominent pulpit – from which John Henry Newman and John Keble preached before him – is apparent from the comments of those who were present. Erik Routley, a Magdalen undergraduate, turned up to find the church packed long before the service began; he remembered the superbly unaffected delivery, the effortless rhythm of the sentences, 'the scholarship made friendly, the sternness made beautiful', combining to produce a stunning effect.[94]

Most demanding, however, was the extensive travel Lewis was undertaking to RAF stations to lecture on religious topics, resulting in his never being at home for more than three days at a time. Lewis was exhausted by the constant journeying in crowded trains, which left him aching all over, as if he had just played a game of football.[95] Addressing the RAF in hangers, Nissen huts, parade grounds, chapels and YMCA buildings took Lewis from Aberystwyth to Norfolk, Cornwall to Perthshire, Kent to Rutland, leading him to quip that a map of his travels would resemble the missionary journeys of St Paul.[96] Lewis used these addresses as opportunities to test out material to be repurposed in his BBC broadcast talks in front of a live audience. The reaction of one 'old, hard-bitten officer' is referenced in the chapter 'Making and Begetting' in *Mere Christianity*, a version of which was first delivered at RAF Feltwell in Norfolk on 18 April 1943, and then again, an hour later, at RAF Methwold.[97]

But the greatest obstacle to Lewis's ability to carry out the demanding role of vice president effectively was his ineptitude as an administrator, a weakness he himself fully recognized: 'I was made Vice President in College and the real President then got ill so that I had all his work to do as well – office work, which as you know is not in my line.'[98] Even McFarlane acknowledged his mistake: 'Lewis as acting-president is troublesome; he is a hopeless failure. It is perhaps a pity that I persuaded him to do the job.' McFarlane privately admitted that he was glad he did not have to take on the job himself, since he loathed the hours wasted in meetings talking in circles.[99] Lewis had a similar antipathy to lengthy college debates, during which he typically dozed off or answered his voluminous correspondence. Despite these significant reservations on both sides, when the time came to renew his appointment for a second year Lewis was duly nominated at the meeting on 5 November 1941. However, the actual admission procedure – in which Lewis would be sworn in as vice president – was postponed.[100]

At the following college meeting, on 3 December, there was a report from the senior fellow, P.M. Benecke, who chaired the meeting in the vice president's absence, that Lewis had decided not to continue in the role, since he was 'prevented by other obligations from carrying out the duties of the office to his own satisfaction'. Instead K.B. McFarlane was nominated and admitted to the vice presidency.

What happened in between the two meetings to change Lewis's mind and to lead to his replacement with McFarlane? While the official account implies that the decision to stand down was Lewis's own, driven by the pressure of a packed schedule, McFarlane's private version suggests that he was pressured to do so by fellows who would not support his reappointment unless he were to give up all his other commitments and devote himself entirely to college business.[101] Such a condition would have been impossible for Lewis, who saw his lecturing and broadcasting as his contribution to the war effort; he kept up his punishing schedule of talks to the RAF and the WAAF until the end of the conflict. Being compelled to choose between service to the college and service to his country would have left Lewis in no doubt that he must resign the position. This was certainly the view of A.J.P. Taylor, who claimed that Lewis gave up the post to free up sufficient time to devote to his writing and lecturing commitments.[102]

Lewis had initially turned the job down; he was persuaded into accepting it by McFarlane, against his better judgement, and only agreed to a temporary period of office. The official line that Lewis had resigned the position because of other obligations is not an attempt to cover up the fact that he was pushed out against his will, but a recognition that, for Lewis, his work as a national apologist took priority over college business. That Lewis was not present at the meeting itself might suggest that he was licking his wounds; but, in fact, he was in Bangor delivering the third of his Ballard Matthews lectures on *Paradise Lost* at the University College of North Wales, subsequently published as *A Preface to Paradise Lost* (1942).[103]

Lewis's final task as vice president was to write an account of the college year in the official register. Where these records were typically a dry prose rendering of the key events of the calendar, typically in Latin, Lewis's contribution was a lively five-act drama in blank verse, with the title 'The Tragi-Comicall Briefe Reigne of Lewis the Bald'.

A central theme of Lewis's drama is his own inability to carry out his vice-presidential duties effectively; in one scene the members of a committee await his appearance as chair of the meeting, only to learn that he had been seen bustling towards the Summer Common Room, where the meeting was to be held, at the appropriate time on the previous day:

> I saw him yesterday, this self-same hour
> Obsequiously attired in cap and gown
> With brow contracted and with lips pursed up
> . . .
> Hasting towards the Summer Common Room.
> You need not doubt he went to take the chair
> At this same meeting, yesterday, on time.

It was the responsibility of the vice president to allocate rooms for meetings and private events to ensure no timetable clashes. Lewis carried a small pocket diary into which he inscribed some such events, but not others, with the result that lecture theatres and dining rooms were often double-booked. On one occasion a high official in the Eastern Orthodox Church, impressively garbed in an embroidered black robe and sporting a gold chain with jewelled cross, arrived for dinner an hour late. Lewis offered him coffee, but the churchman was insistent that he had received an invitation to dine at that time. The confusion turned out to be an error in Lewis's invitation, so that the reluctant vice president was obliged to take the hungry patriarch for dinner at the nearby Eastgate Hotel.[104]

Lewis's unsuitability for the role of vice president is further apparent from his total reliance upon the college secretary, Miss Anderson, named Egeria (from the Greek term for a female advisor) in the drama, who ended up carrying much of the work herself, or referring it to McFarlane. When she appears at the opening of Act IV, Lewis heralds her coming with 'But soft! The fair Egeria', and addresses her in a reworking of Hamlet's famous words to Ophelia: 'Nymph, on thy typewriter / Be all my jobs remembered.' In his letters, Lewis noted how he always referred questions about course documentation to her: 'the idea of anyone sending them to *me* for illuminating comment wd. rouse laughter in Magdalen!'[105]

Lewis's reliance upon the long-suffering secretary during his vice-presidential year is apparent from a scene in the drama where she pleads with him to respond to overdue requests for feedback from unsuccessful candidates for admission, and to look over the agenda for a forthcoming meeting of the college's main teaching committee, the Tutorial Board, known as the 'T.B.' Lewis responds in another Shakespearian pastiche, playing on Hamlet's 'What's Hecuba to him or he to Hecuba?'

> Fairest maid
> I have no time. What's the T.B. to me
> Or it to Hecuba? Make the agenda up
> And set down what you will.

Dismissing the serious business of college governance in this way, Lewis beats a hasty retreat – with the famous stage direction from *The Winter's Tale* 'Exit pursued by a bear' suitably modified: 'Exit pursued by a Secretarie'.

In a later scene, the noble Egeria, 'Never so wearie, never so in woe', like Hermia before her, searches the ominous wood of the Magdalen Grove 'with fix'd intent / To button-hole a lost Vice President', finally giving into fatigue and sleeping. Lewis has taken refuge in this pastoral idyll in order to escape the demands of office:

Here no committees meet. These gentle conies *rabbits*
Know no agenda save to get their kind, *beget*
Nor do the dappled deer.

Lewis's drama is written directly into the vice president's register; this fair copy is based upon a draft version that survives in one of his exercise books. Among these rough jottings we can observe Lewis's first attempts and later revisions; for instance, in this early version we find Hortensius, the estates bursar Mark Dunbar Van Oss, proposing an alternative candidate for vice president in 'Ploughman Charles, incomparable lexicographer': Charles Talbut Onions, editor of the *Oxford English Dictionary* and a fellow of Magdalen since 1923.

A particular focus of Lewis's period of office was responding to directives relating to the war effort. At the onset of hostilities, Lewis and his colleagues were informed that New Building would be required by the government, and so they were required to transport their considerable libraries to the wine cellars in the basement. Having undertaken this onerous task, Lewis then learnt that the building would not be requisitioned after all, and so began the laborious job of returning the books to their shelves.

The wine cellars were, however, used to serve as air-raid shelters in college, being divided into three self-contained sections; two small electric pumps were installed to prevent accumulation of water during the winter. When the air-raid siren sounded, resident students and fellows would assemble in this claustrophobic space. John Simopoulos, a Philosophy tutor at St Catherine's College, who was then an undergraduate at Magdalen, recalled spending a night with Lewis in the cellars, where they engaged in a discussion of recondite literary terminology. Having disagreed about the meaning of one particularly arcane term, the young student was surprised to receive a card from Lewis the following morning conceding that he had been wrong in his definition.[106]

Although New Building itself was spared, the RAF were granted permission to drill personnel on the gravel paths at the front, and to repurpose one of the squash courts as an Officers' Club Room. Their request to set up a miniature rifle range in Longwall Quad, however, was refused.

The regularity with which such injunctions were instantly revoked is mocked by Lewis in his account of his vice-presidential term of office. As vice president, Lewis was obliged to attend the regular meetings of the Air Raid Precautions Committee, tasked with ensuring the college's compliance with the university's detailed directives. There is a scene in the drama in which the college miraculously succeeds in having implemented every regulation; the bursar reports that 'Our petrol pumps and stirrup pumps, our posts / Lamps, oilskins, respirators, whistles, hats / Are perfectly complete'. What's more, all the members of the college – fellows, tutors, demies, commoners, scouts, boys, bedmakers and cats – have internalized some twenty thousand rules, so that not even Momus (the Greek god of criticism) could find fault. But, just as Lewis announces that the best wine will run in the cloister pump until midnight in celebration, a messenger arrives to repeal the earlier directives and replace them with others:

> All is revoked. All orders, minutes, rules,
> Schemes, plans, organisations, policies
> That you have learn'd, all from this moment cease
> And are annulled as though they had not been.
> A wholly new design of A.R.P.,
> Briefly comprised in thirty volumes, each
> An hundred pages long (lo, here the first!)
> Must be engraved, and presently, upon
> Your inner tablets with a style of brass.
> Gentles, tear up whatever you have done,
> And buckle to't. The game begins anew!

The news causes considerable distress among the fellows, especially Lewis, who passes out: 'The V.P. swoons. Look to him' – recalling Osric's 'Look to the queen' at the end of *Hamlet*.

Lewis was also familiar with the directives of the war effort through his service with the Home Guard; he joined up in the summer of 1940 when the Secretary of State for War, Anthony Eden, appealed to all men to enrol in the Local Defence Volunteers. Lewis would typically set out at 1.30 a.m., following a late meeting of the Inklings, eating his sandwiches en route, since he couldn't provide sufficient for everyone and so was too embarrassed to eat them in front of others. His patrol met at Lake Street and then toured the city centre, although he was delighted to discover it included a lengthy period sitting on the veranda of a college pavilion, gazing out over the starlit playing fields. On one such moonlit evening, Lewis pressed upon a fellow volunteer the unlikeliness of the war being the final such conflict, or abolishing human misery for good, prompting the dismayed recruit to exclaim: 'Then what's the good of the ruddy world going on?'[107] On another occasion, Lewis used the opportunity to explain that nature can't have purposes unless it is a rational substance, and, if that's what it is, then it ought to be called God, or the gods, or a god, or the devil. Evidently, an evening's patrol with Lewis was a mental as well as a physical workout, and not always a very encouraging one.[108]

The watch lasted three hours and, although he regretted that it was not as agreeable as Dogberry's in *Much Ado About Nothing*, which involved sitting on a church bench till two and then 'all to bed', he found it quite pleasurable, despite the discomfort of having to carry a heavy rifle and wear a uniform that he felt made him look an 'absolute ass'. Lewis enjoyed the respite from the heat of summer, the owls and bats and the solitariness of the streets, although he noted with surprise that – even at that late hour – he would encounter at least one mysterious and solitary individual roughly every three minutes.

George Gordon died in the President's Lodgings in 1942. When it came to choosing his replacement, the Londoner's Diary of the *Evening Standard* listed Lewis among the likely candidates, alongside McFarlane, J.M. Thompson, another Modern Historian, and Henry Tizard, a fellow in Chemistry at Oriel College. McFarlane discredited the article, on the grounds that Thompson had already been eliminated from consideration, while Lewis had never been seriously considered – the experience of his vice presidency would surely have ruled out any enthusiasm on either side. In the end it was a two-horse race, which Tizard won, leaving McFarlane in the ignominious position of carrying out the duties while waiting for his successor to take up office: 'Drudgery without honour and with precious little reward.'[109]

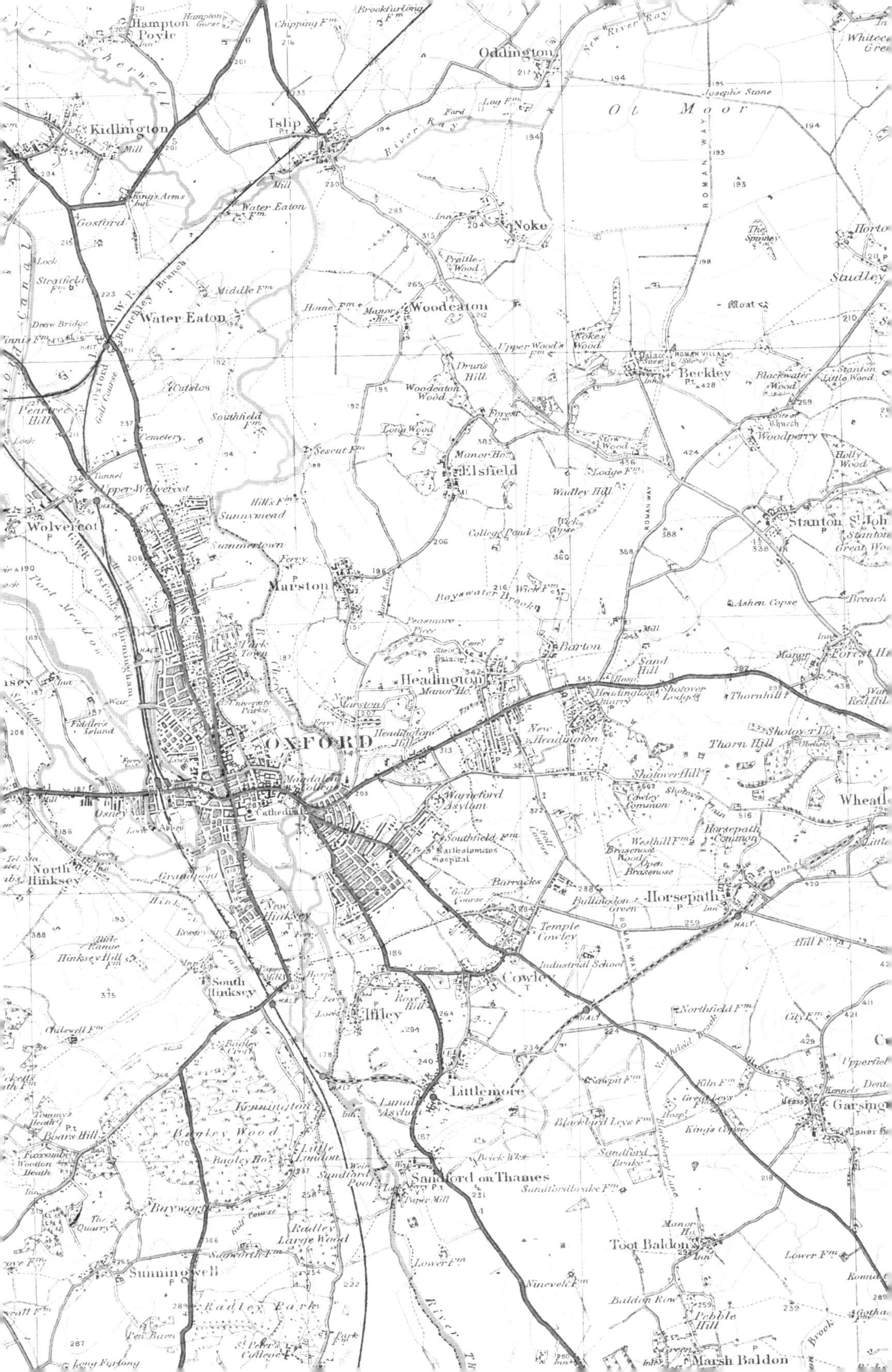
Hampton Poyle
Brookfurlong Fm
Chipping Fm
Oddington
New River Ray
Joseph's Stone
Ot Moor
Kidlington
Islip
River Ray
Log Fm
Gosford
King's Arms
Water Eaton Fm
Noke
Pruttle Wood
Roman Way
The Spinney
Studley
Stratfield Fm
Middle Fm
Home Fm
Manor Ho.
Woodeaton
Moat
Water Eaton
Bletchley Branch
Draw Bridge
Upper Wood's Fm
Noke's Wood
Beckley
Roman Villa
Blackwater Wood
Stanton Little Wood
Oxford Golf Course
Cutslow
Peartree Hill
Drunshill
Woodeaton Wood
Long Wood
Southfield Fm
Cemetery
Forest Fm
Sescut Fm
Stow Wood
Woodperry
Holly Wood
Manor Ho.
Elsfield
Lodge Fm
Upper Wolvercot
Wolvercot
Hill's Fm
Sunnymead
Wadley Hill
College Pond
Stanton St John
Summertown
Ferry
Marston
Port Meadow
Wick Fm
Baywater Brook
Ashen Copse
Peasmore Piece
Barton
Sand Hill
Park Town
Headington
Manor Ho.
Headington Quarry
Shotover Lodge
Thornhill
Forest Hill
Fiddler's Island
University Parks
New Marston
New Headington
Shotover Ho.
Thorn Hill
OXFORD
Headington Hill
Magdalen College
Shotover Hill
Cowley Common
Shotover Plain
Osney
Cathedral
Warneford Asylum
Wheatley
Abbey
Southfield Fm
Westhill Fm
Horsepath Common
North Hinksey
Brasenose Wood
Grandpont
Barracks
Golf Course
Bullingdon Green
Horsepath
New Hinksey
Temple Cowley
Rifle Range
Hinksey Hill Fm
Hill Fm
Reservoirs
Industrial School
Cowley
South Hinksey
Paper Mill
Rose Hill
Iffley
Northfield Fm
Northfield Brook
City Fm
Chilswell Fm
Badley Croft
Littlemore
Sawpit Fm
Kiln Fm
Great Leys
Garsington
Kennington
Lunatic Asylum
Blackbird Leys Fm
King's Copse
Boars Hill
Bagley Wood
Foxcombe
Wootton Heath
Bagley Ho.
Little London
Brick Wks
Sandford Brake
Sandford Pool
Sandford on Thames
Sandfordbrake Fm
Paper Mill
Bayworth
The Quarry
Golf Course
Radley Large Wood
Manor Ho.
Toot Baldon
Sugworth Fm
Lower Fm
Lower Fm
Sunningwell
Nineveh Fm
Baldon Row
Radley Park
Pebble Hill
Pen Barn
Park Fm
St Peter's College
Marsh Baldon
Long Furlong

THREE
HEADINGTON

In 1930 Lewis purchased The Kilns, the house in which he was to spend the remainder of his life. However, his connections with the Oxford suburbs of Headington and Risinghurst date back to 1919. When he returned to Oxford following the war, he was accompanied by Mrs Moore, the mother of his wartime friend Paddy, and her daughter Maureen, who moved into temporary lodgings in Headington. As noted in Chapter 1, according to a conversation overheard by Maureen, Paddy and Lewis had made a pact that, should one of them be killed, the survivor would look after the other's parent. While this explanation may help to explain why Mrs Moore came to live with Lewis after the war, it is not entirely satisfying. After all, it is hard to understand why Lewis would expect Paddy to look after his father if he were to be killed in the war. An alternative possibility, suggested by the secretiveness with which Lewis set up home with Mrs Moore, is that the two were in a relationship.

This second possibility has been given more support by the recent publication of an interview with the late Walter Hooper, in which he recalled having been informed by Owen Barfield that Lewis had a sexual relationship with Mrs Moore. According to Hooper, Lewis put

FIG. 13 OS map showing Oxford and surroundings including Headington and Shotover, 1921.

an end to the affair when he converted to Christianity; his decision to look after Mrs Moore for the remainder of her life was an act of penance for the inappropriateness of the relationship.[1]

Although Headington is now a thriving and popular suburb of Oxford, home to the John Radcliffe Hospital and Brookes University, in Lewis's day it was somewhat quieter. Mrs Moore's first address was 28 Warneford Road; while she lived here, Lewis would visit her on a daily basis, returning to college overnight to fulfil his residency requirements. Lewis subsequently moved out of college accommodation altogether, joining Mrs Moore and her daughter Maureen in a peripatetic lifestyle, driven from house to house by difficult relations with a succession of landlords and landladies.

The properties in which Lewis and Mrs Moore lodged during the 1920s reveal a period of financial hardship and simplistic living. In August 1922 they were offered a month's free rent at Hillsboro, 14 Holyoake Road in Headington, while its owner was abroad. Their finances were sufficiently straitened that they sublet their home on Warneford Road, and, as a further economy, took in a paying guest. Although Lewis was favourably impressed with the house and its garden, he lamented the poor access to gas and the lack of good books.

On returning from a trip to Ireland, Lewis discovered that Mrs Moore had quit the lodgings at Warneford Road and moved into a flat at 76 Windmill Road. Writing to Arthur to inform him of the change of address, Lewis described his landlady as a 'funny old woman'. Looking back on the episode in 1923, Lewis concludes that Mrs Morris, who regaled them with stories of a centaur that used to beg at her bungalow in India, was in fact insane. Since the flat comprised just two rooms, Lewis was compelled to sleep on the sofa.

A further move took them to rooms let by Mrs Jeffrey at 58 Windmill Road, a butcher's shop, where Lewis recalls having been 'bullied and slandered and abused and so haunted by that butcher woman with her stone coloured funny face that D [Mrs Moore] and I dreamed of her for months afterwards'.[2] It was during their stay at this address that Lewis sat Moderations: the public examinations that he was required to pass in order to proceed to the Honour school. Given the disruption of his private life, the First that Lewis achieved in these exams is all the more impressive.

Relations with their landlady became so intolerable that Lewis and Mrs Moore were compelled to leave Windmill Road before alternative digs became available. As a consequence, they packed up their effects and deposited them with friends, and, in desperation, decamped to the Somerset village of Old Cleeve, where they rented a small cottage. After 'the most loathsome and degrading scenes', with the landlord almost becoming violent, they arrived in idyllic surroundings. Although Lewis had not heard of the village of Old Cleeve before arriving there, describing its location as 'not far from the end of the world', he looked back on the four weeks they spent there as among the happiest of his life. The delightful thatched cottage was surrounded by beautiful countryside, with the sea and the Brendon Hills, orchards, streams and banks covered with primroses.

Lewis spent his days tramping the lonely moors and the hills, from which he was able to gaze across the water at the outline of Wales, and specifically the Arthurian country round Caerleon and the Usk. The landscape of rolling hills, deep valleys covered in bracken and heather, as well as dense forests of fir trees, appealed greatly to Lewis. As he sat on the rocks, drinking in the atmosphere and resting in the enormous stillness, Lewis found himself experiencing the longing that had evaded him for almost a year. This congenial setting, with its Arthurian vistas, and landscapes that point forward to those of the Narnian chronicles, prompted Lewis to write the blank-verse version of a now-lost poem on the legend of Merlin and Nimue.[3] A subsequent visit to Old Cleeve was much less happy since it was a cold summer that Mrs Moore was compelled to spend alone while Lewis was 'doing time' in Ireland – a phrase which hints at the sense of unlooked-for duty with which he viewed a return to his father's home.

Their next Headington address was Court Field Cottage, 131 Osler Road, where they lodged with a Mrs Marshall. Lewis describes his landlady as a strange and mysterious character, one needing a whole letter – 'if not an Algernon Blackwood story' – to do her justice.[4] Although he at first found these rooms comfortable, if rather expensive, Lewis subsequently fell out with Mrs Marshall. This was followed by a brief stint at Lindon Cottage in Headington. In the summer of 1921 the pair returned to 28 Warneford Road, the Headington house where they had been happiest during the previous three years.

A particularly intense period of stress came in early 1923 when Mrs Moore's brother, Dr John Askins – known in the family as the 'Doc' – came to stay at Warneford Road, while suffering a nervous breakdown. Askins lived with his wife and daughter in the village of Iffley, just a few miles from his sister's home, having been discharged from the Medical Corps in 1917. Lewis thought highly of Askins, describing him as 'the most unoffending, the gentlest, the most unselfish man imaginable'.[5] The two men shared an interest in philosophy. However, by 1923, Lewis had noticed a change in Askins's demeanour and an unhealthy brooding that were the first signs of his mental illness. This was shortly followed by a complete psychological breakdown, characterized by fits and an obsessive fear of damnation. On the advice of Mrs Moore's other brother, Rob, a medical doctor practising in Bristol, Askins was admitted to a psychiatric hospital, where he died from heart failure on 5 April. Lewis was badly shaken by the episode. In a letter to Arthur Greeves, he confided that the Doc's death had stressed to him the importance of looking after one's mental health by avoiding excessive introspection, and keeping to 'the cheerful & the matter of fact side of things'.[6]

Lewis drew upon this experience in an unfinished novel, thought to have been written in 1927, which recounts the early life of a Bristol doctor, Dr Easley, returning to his native Belfast to help treat a sick aunt.[7] On arrival, Dr Easley finds himself in dispute with a Reverend Bonner about his aunt's emotional and spiritual well-being, in which the doctor warns that the reverend's teachings of the realities of hell are putting her mental health in jeopardy. The argument draws heavily on Lewis's experience of the torment which John Askins suffered, and the severe strain it placed upon Lewis himself. Although the novel remains unfinished and the dispute never resolved, it is clear that the episode had a profound effect on Lewis, leading him to confide to his diary that he has been 'scared off anything mystical and abnormal and hysterical for a long time to come'.[8]

Lewis did not provide his father with details of his irregular living arrangements, instead telling him that he had moved out of college and was lodging with a fellow student. A threatened visit from Albert Lewis in 1921 prompted Lewis to inveigle a friend into playing the part of the fellow lodger in a back room that had been dressed up to look like an undergraduate's digs.[9] As it turned out the effort was wasted; the Lewis holiday party, comprising Albert Lewis and his brother-in-law and sister-in-law, Augustus and Anne Hamilton, stopped in Oxford only to lunch at the Clarendon Hotel and then proceeded to tour the south of England.

THE KILNS

In 1930 Lewis and Mrs Moore were finally able to purchase The Kilns (PLATE 12), a substantial residence with considerable grounds, built in 1922, named after the nearby brick kilns. The house cost £3,300, with an additional £200 invested in building two extra rooms; Lewis's contribution came from the money he and Warnie received from the sale of the family's Belfast home, following the death of his father in September 1929.

Mrs Moore's daughter Maureen, who lived with them at The Kilns, was a pupil at nearby Headington School, an independent school for girls. Lewis visited on several occasions in order to watch theatre performances. In April 1922 he was treated to a scene from *Nicholas Nickleby*, which was sufficiently well acted to have made him recall the 'Wynyard terrors' – that is, the unhappiness of his time at Wynyard school in Hertfordshire.[10] The programme also included Matthew Arnold's *Tristram and Iseult* and Yeats's *The Land of Heart's Desire*, which were very badly performed, although 'even school girl acting could not quite spoil its wonderful beauty'.[11]

Also resident at The Kilns was Fred Paxford (1898–1979), the gardener and handyman, whom Lewis described as 'our indispensable fac-totum'.[12] Having been engaged by Mrs Moore shortly after their arrival at The Kilns, Paxford remained there until Lewis's death in 1963. Paxford took responsibility for tending the house's extensive grounds, managing the orchard and the vegetable plot, cooking, and acting as chauffeur (Lewis never learned to drive). According to Hooper, Paxford's irrepressible pessimism provided the model for the character of Puddleglum, the gloomy Marsh-wiggle in *The Silver Chair*.

The eight acres of garden included an extensive wood, whose trees served as fuel when coal became short, a tennis court (which Lewis considered a blot on the landscape) and a lake, known as 'Shelley's Pond' because of the tradition that the poet used to meditate on its shores, on which Lewis would punt and skate when the water froze over. The Lewis brothers experimented on the ice in January 1933, having purchased skates at Eagleston & Son, Ironmongers. This was their first attempt at skating since their school days; they quickly discovered that they had forgotten the torture – 'no other word is adequate' – to one's shins.[13] Much of the house's original garden is now part of the C.S. Lewis Nature Reserve, managed by the Berkshire, Buckinghamshire and Oxfordshire Wildlife Trust.

On his retirement from the army, Warnie came to live at The Kilns, which he found to be a 'veritable garden of Eden, a lotus island, a faerie land, or any other term which will express sheer loveliness'.[14] Although he greatly enjoyed living there, a dinner invitation to the Dysons' home, at 12 Holywell Street, prompted him to note how clean and compact their house was compared to the 'slatternly and straggling Kilns'. While the Dysons ate off shining silver and crisp table linen, The Kilns had the air of being a 'perpetual picnic'. Although by then Warnie had been resident at The Kilns for fifteen years, he still did not think of it as home; instead it felt like an army billet that he had just marched into and would be quitting in the morning.[15] By 1947 Warnie had come to dislike the house intensely, although this animosity was to some degree bound up with the challenges of living with an elderly and demanding Mrs Moore, whose health was failing.

In September 1939 Lewis and Mrs Moore welcomed a group of evacuees to The Kilns; Lewis was quite taken with the three schoolgirls, whom he described as 'very nice, unaffected creatures and all most flatteringly delighted with their new surroundings'.[16] The children also appear to have taken to the animals; in those days The Kilns was a positive menagerie. In one letter, Lewis mentions having four geese, ten hens, a cat and a dog; in another, he refers to a hamster, a rat, rabbits and a wood full of owls at the bottom of the garden. In 1931 Lewis was given a pair of swans by the provost of Worcester College, which he fed with grain every evening, even during the breeding season when the cob would get quite aggressive.[17] When the cob swan was killed by a fox eight years later, Lewis felt sorry for the widow left alone ('if swans are sensible of bereavement') and regretted that Dan Russell – the name of the fox in Chaucer's Nun's Priest's Tale – had not completed the job.[18] Walter Hooper's recollections of the animals living at The Kilns in the 1960s include an old ginger cat called Tom; Snip, a Siamese cat (which came to the family with Joy and which Lewis referred to as his step-cat); and a boxer pup named Ricky.[19]

Lewis was a lifelong dog-lover, having grown up with a very ill-disciplined Irish terrier called Tim. Lewis recalled how he and Tim would go for walks together, but more as friendly visitors to the same hotel than as master and dog, meeting frequently, passing the time of day, but pursuing an independent course: 'He never exactly obeyed you; he sometimes agreed with you.'[20] In later life, Lewis kept a number of dogs, which he named Poggio, Pat, Susie, Tykes, Bruce and, his favourite, Mr Papworth.[21] Mr Papworth was replaced by a substantial golden retriever puppy, with the 'appetite of a lion, the manners of a hurricane, the morals of a gangster, and an over salivated mouth'.[22] Lewis's reputation for attempting to corral them in stentorian tones became apparent to Warnie when, walking the dogs over Shotover Hill one afternoon, he found himself overtaken by a rabble of boys shouting 'Heel! Tykes' in mocking tones.[23]

The evacuee children made considerable use of the pond, taking it in turns to go bathing due to the lack of sufficient swimming costumes. Their reluctance to come out led to Lewis shouting at them 'Time to come in', only for them to duck back under the water and come up 10 yards further away claiming not to have heard.[24] At other times their lack of resourcefulness was a source of some frustration. Their tendency to regularly ask 'What shall we do now?' prompted Lewis to exclaim to his brother, 'Shades of our own childhood!'[25] The Pevensie children show no such lack of resourcefulness – even when confined indoors by the rain – though, to be fair, they had Narnia to keep them busy (PLATE 17).

Shortly after the arrival of the schoolgirls, Headington experienced its first air-raid warning, at 7.45 in the morning, much to the delight of the children who had been excitedly awaiting such an event. Everyone made it to the concrete bunker that Lewis had directed Paxford to construct in the garden, where they remained until the all-clear sounded, emerging safe and sound, though very hungry and thirsty.

For Lewis the major inconvenience of the war was the blacking out, covering the windows at night to prevent lights being seen by enemy planes. He described his method as a 'most complicated Arthur Rackham system of odd rags', which was quite effective but very laboursome, although quicker than when the children helped out.[26] But the experience of moonlit Oxford nights, when all lights had been extinguished, was a source of great joy for Lewis, prompting him to wish that blackouts would continue long after the end of the war.[27] His wish was fulfilled at The Kilns, since the blackout curtains were still hanging in the windows when Joy Davidman came to live there in 1956; removing them was one of her first tasks when she moved in.

The difficulty of feeding the expanded household was mitigated in November 1939 by the Magdalen home bursar offering each of the fellows a haunch of venison, following a cull of the college deer. Although the resulting meal was enjoyed by all the diners, the smell of the cooking meat filled the entire house; while it dissipated during the meal, it reasserted itself so violently as soon as the appetite was satisfied that everyone fled the dining room immediately.[28]

Lewis commuted between Oxford and Headington by bus or on foot. As a pedestrian he would take a brisk walk down Cuckoo Lane and across the bridges and islands of the Cherwell, which were completely deserted first thing in the morning. This would bring him to Magdalen at the little gate leading into the Fellows' Garden, which joins Addison's Walk at Bat Willow Meadow.[29]

The bus home would take him gradually up the steep Headington Hill from the roundabout near Magdalen College, known as The Plain. It was on one of those slow ascents that Lewis found himself confronted by the need to make a firm commitment to either belief or atheism. Sitting on the top of the bus, Lewis felt himself presented with a free choice between accepting a faith in God or remaining an atheist: 'Neither choice was presented as a duty; no threat or promise was attached to either, though I knew that to open the door or to take off the corslet [a piece of armour] meant the incalculable. The choice appeared to be momentous but it was also strangely unemotional.'[30]

Following his conversion, Lewis used his walks between Magdalen and The Kilns as times for intense introspection and meditation, when he could examine his character and conscience and think through his response to his newly adopted faith. Not all his walks up the hill were so spiritually improving. Dirk ter Haar, a fellow Magdalen don who lived in Headington, recalled one evening after dinner when Lewis suggested they walk home together. A light drinker, ter Haar was surprised to discover that the journey involved stopping for a tipple at every pub that they passed.[31]

One of the hostelries Lewis frequented was the Ampleforth Arms on Collinwood Road. The pub was constructed in 1939 and is said to have been the work of the same master builder who was responsible for Ampleforth Abbey in York. After their marriage, Joy and Lewis visited the pub; in 1958 Lewis records walking with Joy to the Ampleforth Arms after she has spent the morning shooting – 'or anyway shooting *at*' – pigeons.[32] The couple passed their evenings reading, talking and playing Scrabble; they drank draught bitter from pewter tankards, sending Joy's son Douglas to the Ampleforth Arms to have the empty quart bottles refilled.[33]

Another Headington watering hole that Jack and Warnie would patronize having made the steep climb up the hill was the Mason's Arms. After dining in college in March 1948, the two brothers walked home while reminiscing about their childhood – Jack was at that time working on his autobiography – calling in at the Mason's Arms for a pint of Burton ale, where they watched the locals playing bar billiards.[34]

One of Lewis's favourite recreations in Headington was to go walking in nearby Shotover Park (PLATE 13). Originally part of a royal forest, providing a hunting ground as well as timber for the construction of many of Oxford's historic buildings, Shotover was converted into open farmland in the seventeenth century. In the early twentieth century it began to be established as a woodland, a place that can evoke the eeriness of the forest into which Lucy stumbles in Narnia, which is full of spies acting for the White Witch: 'Even some of the trees are on her side.'

Lewis particularly appreciated the excellent views offered by its elevated position, the wonderful colours of its rich store of wild flowers and the concert of birdsong performed by the many summer migrants. On one occasion, Lewis bicycled over Shotover Hill, along its sandy lanes and bridle paths: the name 'bridle path' particularly appealed to Lewis for its suggestion of mystery. The countryside was peppered with barns and haystacks, rabbits and bluebells.

Tramping across Shotover was an opportunity for Lewis to attempt to resolve particular philosophical cruces. In January 1927 he records a walk through one of his favourite parts of the wood lit up by a watery sun and a faint purple mist in the valley below; the silence was emphasized by the occasional chuckling of a bird. This occasion enabled him to think through his current confusion concerning imagination and intellect, in which 'undigested scraps of anthropsophy and psychoanalysis' jostle with orthodox idealism over a background of 'good old Kirkian rationalism'.[35]

Lewis and his brother also enjoyed rambling in nearby Bury Knowle Park. Today a walk past the Bury Knowle library brings the visitor face to face with Aslan, or at least a wooden statue of him, carved by Matt Cave from the trunk of a felled tree (PLATE 29).

HOLY TRINITY CHURCH

Following his conversion to theism, Lewis began to attend services at Holy Trinity Church in Headington Quarry (PLATE 14). The church was built in the mid-nineteenth century to a design by George Gilbert Scott, to cater for the spiritual needs of the workers in the local quarry. Although at that time he was not a professing Christian, Lewis felt it was important to attend services as a way of flying his flag. He had little time for the various components of the church service and for the inevitable social interactions that accompanied them, what he called the 'the fussy, time-wasting botheration of it all! the bells, the crowds, the umbrellas, the notices, the bustle, the perpetual arranging and organising'.[36] Lewis's tendency to leave during the final hymn was well known; it was partly driven by his dislike of church organ music and partly by his antipathy towards small talk.

Lewis typically attended the 8 a.m. communion service, occupying the same seat each week, which now carries a memorial plaque inscribed 'Here sat and worshipped Clive Staples Lewis (1898–1963)'. It is believed that Lewis chose that particular seat because, while he could see the service, he was partially concealed from other members of the congregation. It was certainly not driven by comfort; at an Easter service attended by an especially sizeable congregation, Lewis complained at finding his hip wedged against the pillar and his bottom resting on the angle at the end of the bench.[37] Warnie, too, became a regular worshipper at Holy Trinity, serving on the Parochial Church Council and as an elected churchwarden.

It was at a service at Holy Trinity in July 1940, when Lewis found himself listening to a rather dull sermon, that he was struck by an idea for a book. Provisionally titled 'As one Devil to Another', it would form a series of letters addressed to a novice devil, beginning work on tempting his first 'patient', by an older retired devil.[38] This is the genesis of what became the bestselling *Screwtape Letters*, first published in a series of thirty-one letters in instalments in the *Guardian*, between May and November 1941, appearing in book form in 1942.

Lewis's description of the germ of the idea in a letter to his brother shows a number of distinctive features of the *Screwtape Letters* already fully formed: the reference to the tempted as the 'patient', God as the 'Enemy' and the depiction of the psychology of temptation from the devil's point of view. The example he offers concerning an attack upon the patient's faith in prayer, which shows how both answered and unanswered prayer can be used to undermine the case for divine intervention, is an early version of Screwtape's 'heads I win, tails you lose' argument against petitionary prayer in letter XXVII.

In finding Screwtape's voice, Lewis may also have been influenced by hearing a speech given by Adolf Hitler at the Reichstag and broadcast by the BBC a couple of days earlier.[39] What struck Lewis about the speech was how easy it was, while listening to the Führer speaking, to find oneself wavering just a little. Lewis admits that being persuaded by people who make statements with conviction – even ones that he knows to be false – is a particular weakness of his: 'If a candidate with a bold, mature handwriting attributed *Paradise Lost* to Wordsworth, I should feel a tendency to go and look it up for fear he might be right after all.' But, despite this, it is clear that Lewis recognized in his own reaction a wider human failing, while the confident rhetoric of Hitler's speech gave him a voice through which he was able to ventriloquize the devil.

But, while Holy Trinity can boast a part in inspiring Lewis's novel idea, his fellow churchgoers were no doubt somewhat offended by the cavernous divide that Screwtape highlights between the body of Christ and the 'actual faces in the next pew', comprising a selection of the neighbours that the patient has worked hard to avoid and whose idiosyncrasies – singing out of tune, wearing squeaky boots or odd clothes – can easily be used to convince him of the falseness of their religion.[40] Perhaps Holy Trinity's parishioners drew comfort from Lewis's warning in the preface that not everything Screwtape says should be believed, nor are his depictions of individuals wholly just: 'There is wishful thinking in Hell as well as on Earth.'[41]

Holy Trinity also has a connection with Lewis's Narnian stories, through an etched window with scenes from the books which was installed in the north aisle in 1991 (PLATE 15). It was designed by a painter and architectural glass engraver, Sally Scott, having been commissioned by George and Kathleen Howe as a memorial to their children William (1938–1954) and Gillian (1945–1947), who are both buried in the churchyard.

The Narnia window features a rich constellation of images drawn from the books. The top of the left-hand side carries a substantial depiction of Aslan's head with flaming mane; beneath we see Jill riding on Glimfeather the owl, above the *Dawn Treader*. On the right-hand window Digory and Polly, riding Fledge the flying horse, soar over the towers of Cair Paravel. Both windows are adorned with a collection of talking beasts, including Jewel the unicorn and Reepicheep the mouse, and the gifts given by Father Christmas to the Pevensie children in *The Lion, the Witch and the Wardrobe*.

Holy Trinity Church also provides the resting place of both Lewis brothers and Mrs Moore. Janie King Moore died at Restholme Nursing home, Oxford, on 12 January 1951. At his death in November 1963, Lewis was also buried in the churchyard at Holy Trinity. His grave bears the same inscription that appears on his mother's tombstone: 'Men must endure their going hence' (FIGURE 14). This rather sombre quotation from the end of Shakespeare's *King Lear* was chosen because it featured on his mother's calendar on the day of her death.[42]

Lewis's devoted brother Warnie, who was too grief-stricken to attend his funeral, moved into a rented house on Ringwood Road after the loss of his brother. He initially feared this move would cut him off entirely from Jack, and was relieved to find that he continued to feel his presence in his new digs, although this had the effect of increasing his loneliness. It was not until April 1967 that Warnie felt able to move

FIG. 14 Grave of C.S. Lewis, Holy Trinity church, Headington Quarry.

back into The Kilns, sleeping in Joy's old room as the only one that he had not used during his brother's lifetime. Lewis's increasing fame, especially across the Atlantic, led to a constant stream of visitors to The Kilns, eager to see where he had lived and shake his brother's hand. Warnie feared that on his deathbed he would find himself being stood over by a stranger, lecturing him on some overlooked detail in one of his brother's books.[43] Warnie died on 9 April 1973 and was buried in the same grave as his brother.

FOUR

EAGLE AND CHILD

The Eagle and Child pub, known locally as the 'Bird and Baby', has occupied its current location on St Giles' since 1684; the Oxford historian and antiquarian Anthony Wood (1632–1695) was a regular (see PLATE 20). This Oxford hostelry is best known today for its role as the location for the Tuesday morning meetings of the Inklings, the group of academics and writers who congregated in its secluded back parlour, now known as the Rabbit Room, drinking beer and strong cider, which they called 'bung misery'.

The group was formed around Tolkien and Lewis, who had been meeting in Lewis's rooms since 1929 to read aloud their work to each other for feedback and discussion. The idea for a larger group grew out of a literary society based at Univ, founded by an undergraduate, Edward Tangye Lean, younger brother of the film director David Lean. Founded in the 1930s, the group met to share and critique members' own compositions. Lewis and Tolkien attended meetings of this society as senior members; it was at one of their gatherings that Tolkien read his poem 'Errantry', later published in the *Oxford Magazine*. This literary group was known as the Inklings, which Tolkien explained as 'a pleasantly ingenious pun … suggesting people with vague or half-formed intimations and ideas plus those who dabble in ink'.[1]

The group met in Lean's rooms at Univ, though it may have drawn its members from the wider university. A student of PPE, Lean was not taught by Lewis, but the two may have encountered each other at the Martlets, which Lean joined in 1930, and whose meetings Lewis continued to attend while a fellow of Magdalen. Contributions deemed worthy of preservation were inscribed in the group's record book. The loss of this journal is especially unfortunate, since Tolkien recalled that he acted as its 'scribe and keeper'.[2]

There are some obvious similarities between this group and its more famous offspring, beyond the direct borrowing of the name. In a letter of 1938 Tolkien referred to the Inklings as a 'literary club of *practising poets*'.[3] Reflecting in 1967 on the group's origins, he described it in the following way:

> Its name was transferred (by C.S.L.) to the undetermined and unelected circle of friends who gathered about C.S.L., and met in his rooms in Magdalen. Although our habit was to read aloud compositions of various kinds (and lengths!), this association and its habit would in fact have come into being at this time, whether the original short-lived club had ever existed or not. C.S.L. had a passion for hearing things read aloud, a power of memory for things received in that way, and also a felicity in extempore criticism, none of which were shared (especially not the last) in anything like the same degree by his friends.[4]

When writing to Charles Williams in March 1936 to invite him to attend, Lewis described the group in similar terms, emphasizing its informality, the tendency to write, but adding an additional qualification – the Christian faith.[5] Another key difference between the two Inklings groups is that the latter regrettably had no record keeper and no minute book, so that there are no extant official accounts of their meetings.

An alternative source, albeit a fictional one, is Tolkien's 'Notion Club', whose papers were supposedly discovered in the basement of the Examination Schools by the clerk, Mr Howard Green, in the summer of 2012. Although the group is entirely fictional, its name, a synonym of 'inkling', and its role as a forum for conversation, debate and the discussion of papers, in verse or prose, read by the members, is clearly intended to allude to the famous Oxford writing group. The Notion Club papers represent the group's minute book, containing records of around one hundred meetings of conversations ranging over languages, history, legends and myth. The Notion Club also resembles the Inklings in having no fixed membership, with different numbers of attendees turning up to weekly gatherings.

But, where the Notion Club is peripatetic, assembling in different colleges across Oxford, the Inklings had two set locations: Lewis's rooms in Magdalen College on Thursday evenings and the Eagle and Child pub on Tuesday mornings. On Thursday evenings, members congregated in the sitting room on the north side of the New Building, and then, once everyone had arrived, moved into the south room to begin the readings. The importance of the Magdalen venue for the Thursday night encounters became apparent one August evening in 1940, when the group met at Tolkien's home on Northmoor Road, in leafy North Oxford. Despite staying until 12.45 a.m., Lewis was somewhat underwhelmed by the experience; he noted that, as Tolkien himself often admitted, 'it never feels quite the real thing outside 3 New Building'.[6]

Despite this, in the autumn of 1947 some Thursday night meetings were convened in Tolkien's room at Merton College. Since he was a non-resident fellow – by then he was living with his family in a college-owned house at 3 Manor Road – Tolkien was allocated a single room, located on the second floor of Fellows' Quad, looking south over Christ Church Meadow. He was initially offered the smaller room next door but managed to negotiate a swap with his neighbour on account of his more substantial book collection. Robert Havard, a member of the Inklings, recalled how this setting, with its view over a 'low-lying, fogbound stretch of riverside grassland', provided an effective backdrop to Tolkien's 'unearthly and heroic tale'.[7]

Despite the atmospheric surroundings, the Merton meetings were not particularly well attended. On the evening of 13 November, only the Lewis brothers, Tolkien father and son, and Colin Hardie (who left early) were present. At that meeting Tolkien read his poem on autumn, which Lewis described as 'Matthew Arnold strayed into the world of Hobbit'.[8] At another, C.E. Stevens was proposed as a member; he made his debut on 27 November, when the conversation covered the difficulty in interesting the uneducated in religion, the difference between primitive and savage man, pagan mythology as a substitute for theology, bravery and panache.[9]

Although Tuesday morning meetings were customarily held at the Eagle and Child, beer shortages during the war compelled the group to try alternative hostelries. On one occasion, Tolkien, heading to the Eagle and Child having delivered a lecture, was hailed by a voice from across St Giles'; he turned to find the two Lewises and Charles Williams, 'high and very dry', on the other side of the road. Finding their local pub shut due to a lack of beer, the group had to make do with four pints of 'passable ale' at the King's Arms on Broad Street. On another occasion the Inklings met at the Mitre on the High Street: 'The result was a most amusing and highly contentious evening, on which (had an outsider eavesdropped) he would have thought it a meeting of fell enemies hurling deadly insults before drawing their guns.'[10]

Another venue popular with this group was the Trout at Godstow, which can be reached via a short excursion across Port Meadow. On one occasion, recorded in Warnie's diary, the group drained a couple of pints at the Eagle and Child before taking up Robert Havard's suggestion of adjourning to the Trout, picking up Christopher Tolkien on their way. Sitting and drinking beer in the sunlight, Warnie was struck by the beauty of the scene and its theatricality: 'That nothing might be lacking to show off the warm grey of the old inn, there was a pair of peacocks.'[11] In his memoir, James Dundas-Grant, commander of the Oxford University naval division, recalls how, following Inklings meetings during the summer months, Havard would frequently drive him and Lewis to the Trout, where they would 'sit on the wall with the Isis flowing below us and munch cheese and French bread'.[12] Figure 15 shows Dundas-Grant, Colin Hardie, Havard and his son Peter sitting with Lewis on the wall in the beer garden of the Trout. One Tuesday meeting was diverted to the Trout because of the closure of the Eagle

FIG. 15 The Inklings at the Trout pub in Godstow, c. 1947.

and Child during the St Giles' Fair; the time was spent imagining Dr Johnson's likely views on contemporary literature and discussing the nature of women – a reminder of the group's male-only membership.[13]

Although there was no official membership of the Inklings, a handful of core members attended regularly, while a larger group satellited the inner circle. By 1936 that inner circle comprised Lewis, Tolkien, Warnie Lewis, Hugo Dyson, Nevill Coghill, Lord David Cecil, whom Warnie considered 'the worst reader of his own works in Oxford', and Dr Robert Havard. The last of these may seem the most surprising inclusion, since Dr Havard was a medical physician rather than a doctor of philosophy. Havard was invited by Lewis to join the group because of his shared literary interests and his Catholic faith. He was known affectionately to Lewis and other members of the Inklings as 'Humphrey' – it was in tribute to Havard that the doctor in *Perelandra* was given the same name – and, less affectionately, the 'Useless Quack'.

While his medical skills were evidently disputed, his gift for narrative was not. At one meeting Havard read out his description of a mountain climb he had recently undertaken; despite being an unembellished account, with no particular literary aspirations, Lewis noted that it made his listeners' hair stand on end.[14] Having added a medical man to the group, Lewis observed that, with Adam Fox, Dean of Divinity at Magdalen, Warnie the soldier and Owen Barfield the lawyer, the Inklings now comprised all the estates – 'except, of course, anyone who could actually produce a single necessity of life, a loaf, a boot, or a hut'. As well as being his family doctor, Havard remained a close friend throughout Lewis's life; the second of the Narnian stories, *Prince Caspian*, was dedicated to his daughter Mary Clare.

It was rare for guests to be brought along to meetings of the Inklings; when potential new members were proposed, the protocol was for them to considered by the group in advance.[15] On one occasion, when Tolkien brought along a guest who had not been pre-approved, there was consternation, as recorded in Warnie's diary: 'J and I much concerned this evening by the gate crashing of B; Tollers, the ass, brought him here last Thursday, and he has apparently now elected himself an Inkling. Not very clear what one can do about it.'[16] On another occasion, when Tolkien annoyed the assembled members by inviting Gwyn Jones, Professor of English at the University of Aberystwyth, the unannounced guest turned out to be an excellent addition, reading a humorous Welsh tale of his own composition. Another occasional member was Stubbs, the Siamese cat owned by K.B. McFarlane, whose bright red eyes lit up the room.[17]

Lewis himself introduced a visitor to the meeting of 17 February 1943: the novelist E.R. Eddison, whose *The Worm Ouroboros* (1922) he greatly admired. Eddison wrote enthusiastically in response to the event, where he tasted wisdom as well as good ale, but where 'good discourse made night's horses gallop too fast'. For his own part, Eddison feared his offerings were somewhat preliminary and unconsidered; in a letter of thanks, composed in a pseudo-archaic language in which the two men corresponded, Eddison described his contributions as like those 'a man will write at a first drafting, or with purpose but to flush a quarry & see whose falcon … will mount swiftliest highe enow to strike it downe'.[18]

A lively meeting at the Eagle and Child in October 1944 was interrupted by a tall stranger with bright eyes, a hooked nose and a broad-brimmed hat, whom Tolkien had spotted taking an interest in their conversation, reminding him of Strider, the mysterious Ranger, at the Prancing Pony. Once the stranger had butted in, picking up on a reference to Wordsworth, he was revealed to be the South African poet and critic Roy Campbell, whom Lewis had recently lampooned in the *Oxford Magazine*. Campbell was invited to join the group on Thursday evening, where he entertained them with stories of daring escapades, including rescuing the Carmelite archives from a burning library in Barcelona, and picaresque tales of encounters with poets and musicians.[19]

Over time, some of the core members drifted away and ceased to attend. By March 1940 Lewis had noted that Coghill had become an increasingly rare member of the group; his time was now taken up with the Oxford University Dramatic Society. His absence was apparently not much lamented; Lewis and Dyson confessed to each other that the group got on better without him and despaired of his tendency to accept an invitation and then fail to appear.

Adam Fox left Oxford when his terms of office as Dean of Divinity and Professor of Poetry came to an end, to take up a canonry at Westminster Abbey. Although these central figures were never replaced, new faces were introduced to the group. These include John Wain, a student at St John's College, who was taught by Lewis. Having claimed that any poem that can be understood on a first reading is not poetry at all, Wain redeemed himself by reciting an accomplished poem of his own composition and the first two chapters of a book he was writing on Arnold Bennett, which Warnie considered to be 'absolutely first class'.[20]

At another meeting Wain won a bet by successfully reading a chapter of Amanda McKittrick Ros's novel *Irene Iddesleigh* (1897) without cracking a smile.[21] Norman Bradshaw, a pupil of Lewis's in the 1930s, recalled playing the same game after a dinner in Lewis's rooms with a dozen of his fellow students. The challenge was to see who could read aloud its purple prose – the first paragraph of which gives a flavour of the challenge – for longest before erupting into laughter:

> Sympathise with me, indeed! Ah, no! Cast your sympathy on the chill waves of troubled waters; fling it on the oases of futurity; dash it against the rock of gossip; or, better still, allow it to remain within the false and faithless bosom of buried scorn.[22]

One exception to the more liminal status of these late arrivals was Tolkien's son Christopher (1924–2020), who was formally admitted as a permanent member, independent of his father. Christopher matriculated as an undergraduate at Trinity College in 1942 and was taught by Lewis in Hilary term of the following year. Later that year he joined the Royal Air Force and was sent to South Africa for training. He resumed his studies in Trinity term 1946, switching from Literae Humaniores to English, and was once again taught by Lewis. Since Christopher Tolkien was Lewis's only pupil at Trinity, it is tempting to assume that the arrangement was due to a personal request from his father.[23] One of Christopher's main roles at Inklings meetings was to assume the responsibility of reading the extracts from *The Lord of the Rings*, since he was a far more accomplished reader than his father, whose delivery was famously dry. Not even Christopher's recitation could overcome Hugo Dyson's lack of sympathy for the work; since he was given the right of veto, his arrival would often mean a reading being aborted in mid-flow.

Since there was no fixed membership and no formal business, no official records were kept of the meetings of the Inklings. But we can get a sense of a typical evening from the accounts provided in some of Lewis's letters and Warnie's diary. Writing to Warnie on 11 November 1939 Lewis describes a meeting on the previous Thursday:

> We dined at the Eastgate. I have never in my life seen Dyson so exuberant – 'a roaring cataract of nonsense'. The bill of fare afterwards consisted of a section of the new Hobbit book from Tolkien, a nativity play from Williams (unusually intelligible for him, and approved by all) and a chapter out of the book on the Problem of Pain from me. It so happened – it would take too long to explain why – that the subject matter of the three readings formed almost a logical sequence, and produced a really first rate evening's talk of the usual wide-ranging kind – 'from grave to gay, from lively to severe'.[24]

The books read at this meeting give an idea of the typical range of interests. The new Hobbit book is a reference to its sequel *The Lord of the Rings* (finally published in three volumes in 1954 and 1955). Williams's nativity play is *The House by the Stable*, published in *Seed of Adam and Other Plays* (1948). Lewis's contribution was a chapter from a work of Christian apologetics, written at the request of Ashley Sampson, founder of Centenary Press, for a series titled 'Christian Challenge', which aimed to introduce the faith to non-believers. Lewis's sense of his debt to the group discussions during the writing of *The Problem of Pain* is apparent from his dedicating the work to the Inklings when it appeared in print in 1940. This book also contains an appendix, contributed by Havard, on the observed effects of pain from a medical perspective, which concludes that 'Pain provides an opportunity for heroism; the opportunity is seized with surprising frequency.'[25] Lewis's desire to fully understand the neurophysiological basis of pain led him to consult his Magdalen colleague Hugh Sinclair, who introduced Lewis to a work by another Magdalen fellow, Sir Charles Sherrington, *The Integrative Action of the Nervous System*, published in 1906.[26]

Meetings often included discussions of thorny theological issues. At one event there was a heated exchange about cremation, in which Tolkien and Havard defended the reasons behind the Catholic opposition to the practice:

> At our Thursday meeting we had a furious argument about cremation. I had never realised the violence of the Papist dislike of the practice, which they forbid. Neither Tolkien nor Havard, to my mind, produced a real argument against it, but only said 'you'd find in fact' that it was always supported by atheists; and that a human corpse was the temple of the Holy Ghost. I said 'but a vacated temple' and said it wd. be reasonable to blow up a Church to prevent it being defiled by Communists. They denied this, and said if you destroyed a chalice to prevent it being used for Black Mass you wd. be mortally guilty: for it was *your* business to reverence it and what the magicians did to it afterwards was theirs. I was surprised at the degree of passion the subject awoke in us all.[27]

Following a meeting in March 1946, Warnie's diary includes the disappointingly brief note: 'Interesting discussion on the possibility of dogs having souls.'[28] At a September meeting the assembled discussed communications with the dead, while Warnie read the Duc de Saint-Simon's account of a lowly blacksmith of the provincial town of Salon, who claimed to have been visited by the consort of Louis XIV after her death, with instructions that he was to take to the king at Versailles. A gathering in October 1947 descended into a lengthy argument about the ethics of cannibalism, with Tolkien finding himself alone in considering it to be unjustifiable under any circumstances. The first meeting of 1948 covered the different versions of the Bible and the Collects, followed by a discussion of the ferocity of A.E. Housman's prefaces, and from there to the medieval French poem *La Chanson de Roland*. Three weeks later the Inklings met and debated Mauritius, public schools and Sherlock Holmes stories, over wine and a Kentucky-style brandied cake, which Lewis had been sent by an American admirer. Discussion could also cover more philological topics, such as the various ways of saying 'farewell', unusual place names, surnames and obscenity – the topic arising from Warnie's misunderstanding of the word 'stool' in a verse of the psalms at evensong in the cathedral.[29]

The group met throughout the Second World War. Tolkien described an evening in June 1944 at which Warnie Lewis read a chapter on the system of government in the *Ancien Régime* of France, which, despite the unpromising subject matter, combined with its great length, was very amusing. But, despite this, and a powerful new chapter from an uncompleted romance by E.R. Edison, Tolkien characterized the evening as 'Enjoyable, but no longer amid exams and wars to be taken so lightly as of old.'[30]

A subset of the Inklings would take an annual walking holiday in the south of England during the Easter vacation. Lewis, Owen Barfield and Cecil Harwood formed the nucleus of this group, known as the College of Cretaceous Perambulators – a reference to the geological period in which the chalk downs were laid – while Tolkien was a less regular participant.[31] The group would walk some 15 miles each day, overnighting at local pubs, where they would engage in both serious and whimsical conversation.

When Lewis was unable to join his friends on a walking tour in April 1936 because of examining duties, the others produced a spoof examination paper for him to sit to gain readmission to the college (see PLATE 18). A series of questions referring to previous tours and in-jokes are followed by an English Essay, with a choice of topics from 'The Mechanization of the Walking-tour', 'The Early Start' and 'My Favourite Soaking-machine, and why' – soaking machine being a term coined by Lewis to refer to a seat for 'soaking': sitting idly or 'sleepily doing nothing'.[32] Finally comes Part III, the practical test, in which candidates are expected to show reasonable proficiency in the game of darts and to read a chapter to the satisfaction of a recognized bishop of the established church. A footnote clarifies that it is the responsibility of candidates to make arrangements within their diocese for securing episcopal approval.

Lewis responded to the challenge by supplying a full set of answers, deliberately mimicking the handwriting of his early childhood (see PLATE 19).[33] His response to the requirement to write notes on the word 'caboodle' makes reference to their experiences on an earlier walk over Exmoor: 'A caboodle is a name sometimes given to lavatories. We are told that there was a very beautiful one on Exmoor painted the colour of peacock feathers. Some scholars say it was more the colour of the vault of heaven. Vault = Sky.'

In response to the question 'Why are you the best map reader?', Lewis began by defining the four causes, as described by the 'world famous Aristotle'. While Aristotle may not have been as good a philosopher as Lord Bacon, he should not be mocked, because he lived much earlier, when people were less civilized and when most other thinkers simply wrote down the first thing that came into their heads. By contrast, Aristotle – whose sentences were full of classical allusions – discovered that there were four causes: formal, efficient, material and final. Applying these to the question, Lewis offered the following answer:

> The formal reason why I am the best map reader is because
> I have the best map reading faculty.
> The efficient is because I read it best.
> The material is my brains.
> The final is that we can find the way.

During the period of post-war rationing, meetings of the Inklings were frequently enlivened by the bountiful offerings of an American correspondent, Dr W.M. Firor (1896–1988) of Baltimore, Maryland, who sent substantial food parcels to Lewis. In January 1948 Lewis acknowledged receipt of a package containing plum pudding, chocolates, jelly, chicken, sardines, lard, syrup and butter. Later that same month Lewis wrote again, expressing his astonishment at the receipt of an entire ham. Since ham was in such scarcity, Lewis expected his house to become the focus of attention for every burglar in the district.

Instead of falling prey to the housebreakers of Headington, the ham's fate was to be eaten at a meeting of the Inklings held in a private dining room at Magdalen. The college kitchen supplied soup, sole and a paté dish to accompany the ham, which was washed down with burgundy from the Merton cellars supplied by Tolkien and Dyson, and New College port brought by David Cecil.

The eight members of the Inklings who were present at the event drank Dr Firor's health; Lewis included a list of their names and signatures as a memento of the event with his letter of thanks (see PLATE 21).[34] Dr Firor responded by pledging to send a ham every month, which munificence was met with incredulity: 'Oh golly! A Ham a month? Did you say a Ham a month? If you added a Phoenix-nest and a Unicorn's horn it wd. hardly be more dazzling.'[35] Lewis explained that, to the Inklings, Dr Firor had become a mythological figure: 'Firor-of-the-Hams, a sort of Fertility god'.[36]

Dr Firor's bounty was particularly appreciated by Lewis because of the cut-backs imposed by Magdalen's kitchens. In August 1940 Lewis complained about the decision to restrict dinner to three courses rather than the customary four, while also making Friday meat-free. Lewis described this announcement as 'the most genuinely alarming piece of war news I have heard since the surrender of France'.[37] He was prepared to make his own economies, however; during the war, he and Colin Hardie elected to drink tea instead of Madeira at their regular Dante readings. In general, however, college routines and its luxuries, the candles, wines and saddle of mutton, helped to make the war seem a long way off.

THE COSMIC TRILOGY

As well as sharing excerpts from *The Problem of Pain*, Lewis also used meetings of the Inklings to solicit feedback on his first attempt to write science fiction. The opening book in Lewis's Ransom trilogy, *Out of the Silent Planet* (1938), was begun as part of an agreement with Tolkien in which both would write an 'excursionary thriller'. Recalling the pact in a letter of 1967, Tolkien described it as follows: 'L[ewis] said to me one day: "Tollers, there is too little of what we really like in stories. I am afraid we shall have to try and write some ourselves". We agreed that he should try "space-travel", and I should try "time-travel".'[38] Once the story was under way, Lewis relied upon input from the Inklings for this new departure in his writing. While working on the book, Lewis wrote to Charles Williams and urged him to be at the group's next meeting: 'I have written a thriller about a journey to Mars on which I urgently want your opinion.'[39]

The book was completed by September 1937. Its connection with the Inklings is most apparent in the description of Ransom's return to earth from Malacandra, the natives' term for the planet Mars. Finding himself in a secluded village street, Ransom observes a lighted door leading into a room in which voices could be heard speaking English and from which emerged a familiar smell. 'He pushed his way in, regardless of the surprise he was creating, and walked to the bar. "A pint of bitter, please", said Ransom.'[40] Ransom was home again.

The specific debt to Tolkien is apparent from Lewis's decision to make the book's hero a philologist. When he first discovers that the hrossa (borrowed from the Old Norse word for a horse) he meets on Mars are rational creatures with their own language, Ransom's fear of imminent death is immediately replaced by the 'dazzling project' of making a grammar of the Malacandrian tongue. Possible titles – *The Lunar Verb* – *A Concise Martian–English Dictionary* – flit through the hero's mind, surely a covert joke at the expense of his friend's passion for constructing grammars of imaginary languages.[41]

Tolkien encouraged Lewis to send it to his publisher, Stanley Unwin; Lewis received an encouraging response, with the publisher noting that any manuscript with Tolkien's recommendation was of enormous interest. It is usually claimed that the book was sunk by a single critical reader, whose report dismissed the invented creatures as 'bunk', judging that, while Lewis was quite likely to write a worthwhile novel one day, this was not that novel.[42] But the manuscript was initially despatched to three reviewers, whose reports were somewhat conflicting. While one described the work as a 'remarkable imaginative achievement', another identified both good and bad parts, conceding that, even in the weak sections, it is 'not wholly unreadable, though it can be very tedious'.[43] It was a summary of these reports that Unwin sent to Tolkien, which is cited in *The Letters of J.R.R. Tolkien*, somewhat misleadingly, since it was the 'ethical content', which he considered to be the 'least creditable part', that one reader dismissed as 'bunk'.[44]

In the end no fewer than six reports were commissioned; at the conclusion of this drawn-out process, Unwin remained unconvinced of the book's commercial prospects. He suggested Lewis offer the book to Bodley Head, who had expressed an interest in publishing it. Lewis wrote to thank Unwin for the suggestion, noting that the amount of reading his firm had undertaken on his behalf lay heavy on his conscience.[45] Bodley Head published the book the following year.

The Inklings was an exclusively male group; there are no references to women having attended any of its meetings. But the publication of *Out of the Silent Planet* prompted fan letters from some unlikely sources, sparking long-standing friendships between Lewis and several female writers, in which they discussed their works and their shared Christian faith in a manner similar to the Inklings. Evelyn Underhill, a respected religious writer and author of *Mysticism* (1911), wrote to thank Lewis for the great pleasure his book had given her, praising him in elevated terms: 'It is so seldom that one comes across a writer of sufficient imaginative power to give one a new slant on reality: & this is just what you seem to me to have achieved.'[46] She particularly commended the way Ransom's experience of space challenged his view of a 'black cold vacuity', instead finding it an 'empyrean ocean of radiance ... the womb of worlds'.[47] As a recent convert, Lewis took great delight in praise from a spiritual authority. However, while the idea she singled out was also one of his favourites, Lewis confessed that he had since learned that, far from being beneficial, interplanetary rays in outer space would be fatal.[48]

Lewis also received a letter from Sister Penelope Lawson (1890–1977), a member of the Community of St Mary the Virgin, an Anglican religious order based in the Oxfordshire town of Wantage, founded in the mid-nineteenth century as part of the Oxford Movement. In her letter Sister Penelope praised the book and asked if Lewis had plans to write a sequel.[49] She also sent him a copy of her book *God Persists: A Short Survey of World History in the Light of Christian Faith* (1939), which Lewis read at once and commented on in detail in his reply.[50] This exchange marked the beginning of a lifelong friendship, and a lengthy correspondence in which they discussed the progress of their writings, as well as issues of theology and faith. Expressing his dismay at how few reviewers of his first science-fiction novel had spotted the Christian connections of the story, Lewis suggested that 'any amount of theology can now be smuggled into people's minds under cover of romance' – an observation that seems to point forward to the writing of the Narnian stories.[51]

Sister Penelope's interest in the sequel to *Out of the Silent Planet* prompted Lewis to send her updates during the writing of *Perelandra* (1943), reporting on his progress as well as particular theological or artistic struggles. On completion of the book, Lewis sent her the typescript so that she could provide a report to the Reverend Mother in support of Lewis's wish to dedicate it to the sisters. Consent was duly given, with the instruction to use the nomenclature 'The Community of St Mary the Virgin' or 'C.S.M.V. Wantage'. Lewis, however, insisted upon dedicating the book 'To some ladies at Wantage', a wording that caused some confusion for his Portuguese translator, whose rendering reads: *Para algumas senhoras que aqui faltam* ('For some ladies who are not here'). What might sound like a philosophical paradox is probably nothing more than the result of the translator confusing Wantage with 'wanting'.

Lewis visited the convent in person in April 1942, when he delivered a series of talks to the sisters. Accepting the invitation, Lewis expressed his surprise at 'the odd tasks that God sets us', admitting that his Protestant background left him somewhat anxious of coming across an oubliette or chained skeleton in his gate-house accommodation, adding wryly: 'the doors do open outwards as well, I trust'.[52]

On its publication in 1940, Lewis sent Sister Penelope a copy of *The Problem of Pain*, which she acknowledged with grateful excitement: 'I was beside myself with flatteration at receiving a copy of your book ... I expected to enjoy myself reading it, & I have done so even beyond my hope. It made me bolt my dinner to get more time for it.'[53] It was perhaps because of her willingness to risk indigestion to read his work that prompted Lewis to send Sister Penelope the manuscript of *The Screwtape Letters* for safekeeping, fearing that it was at risk of enemy action. After the war, when she offered to return it, Lewis instructed her to sell it and use the proceeds as she saw fit. The manuscript now resides in the New York Public Library, where it forms part of the substantial Berg collection of modern manuscripts.

END OF THE INKLINGS

Lewis was on his way to a meeting of the Inklings at the Eagle and Child on 15 May 1945 when he called into the Radcliffe Infirmary to visit Charles Williams, who had been admitted for an operation. Expecting to find him propped up in bed convalescing, Lewis had taken a book to lend him; he also planned to convey any messages Williams might have to his fellow Inklings. When he arrived, however, he was dismayed to discover that Williams had died. Lewis walked the short journey from the Infirmary to the Eagle and Child in a daze – 'the very streets looked different' – and, having delivered the shocking news, he had difficulty persuading the others that Williams was dead.[54] Warnie Lewis was similarly stunned – 'I felt just as if I had slipped and come down on my head on the pavement.' Feeling restless and dazed, Warnie headed for the King's Arms on Broad Street, but was reminded of pleasant visits with Williams after they had left Tolkien at the Mitre, 'clearing one [*sic*] throats of varnish with good honest beer'.[55]

Although Thursday-night meetings petered out at the end of the 1940s, lunchtime gatherings at the Eagle and Child continued, even after Lewis's move to Cambridge. In order to accommodate Lewis's new timetable, the meetings were switched to Monday, enabling Lewis to travel to Cambridge directly afterwards. On some occasions they met at the Trout in Godstow to allow Lewis to catch the train to Cambridge from the village of Islip. In a subsequent adjustment the meetings were later transferred to the Lamb and Flag pub, directly opposite the Eagle and Child on St Giles'. In a letter to Roger Lancelyn Green, Lewis noted with regret the decision to break with tradition, which had been driven by the Bird and Baby becoming 'too intolerably cold, dark, noisy, and child-pestered'.[56]

Although the group continued to convene after Williams's death, Lewis evidently felt his loss deeply. This period also coincided with a cooling in his friendship with Tolkien, which led to his becoming an increasingly irregular attendee. Combined with this was a change in landlord of the Eagle and Child: Charles Blagrove died suddenly in the summer of 1948. Warnie missed him greatly, describing him as 'not only a publican, but a friend, and an irreplaceable one'.[57] Warnie especially valued Blagrove for his connection with the Oxford of the turn of the century, when it was common for students to fight a landlord for a pint of beer in the backyard, and for rowdy undergraduates to be literally thrown off the premises.

In 1959 Lewis noted: 'There is still a weekly meeting at the Bird and Baby: but whether you can call it the Old Group when there is a new landlord and Charles Williams is dead and Tolkien never comes is almost a metaphysical question.'[58] To better understand the friendship between Lewis and Tolkien, and their subsequent drifting apart, we need to turn to another Oxford hostelry, the Eastgate Hotel.

FIVE
EASTGATE HOTEL

The Eastgate Hotel was one of Lewis's favourite venues for eating and drinking. It is number 73 on Oxford's famous High Street, known locally as 'The High', at the corner with Merton Street, the location of Merton College, where Tolkien became a fellow in 1945. The Eastgate stands on the site of a seventeenth-century inn called The Crosse Sword, which was knocked down in 1772. This was replaced by another hostelry, known as the Flying Horse, which became the Eastgate Hotel in 1900.

Tolkien regularly made the short walk to Magdalen on Monday mornings during term time; these discussions often ended up at the Eastgate, where they would drink a pint of beer or two. Lewis described this as 'one of the pleasantest spots in the week'. He summarized their usual topics of conversation in the following way: 'Sometimes we talk English school politics: sometimes we criticise one another's poems: other days we drift into theology or "the state of the nation": rarely we fly no higher than bawdy and "puns".'[1] These meetings, and the mutual encouragement they supplied, were extremely important for the work of both men, especially for Tolkien's completion of *The Lord of the Rings*. We get an insight into the reciprocal nature of these encounters from a letter dated 14 May 1944, in which Tolkien records having met with Lewis from 10.45 to 12.30, during which time Lewis read two chapters of 'Who Goes Home?' (the working title for *The Great Divorce*), after which he himself read the chapter 'Journey to the Cross Roads', which became the seventh chapter of book IV of *The Two Towers*.[2]

Tolkien notes with satisfaction that his contribution met with 'complete approval'. He does not record his own reaction to Lewis's offering. However, Tolkien's lack of enthusiasm for the project is apparent from his somewhat dismissive reaction to hearing a chapter of it read to the Inklings the previous month: 'I did not think so well of the concluding chapter of C.S.L.'s new moral allegory or "vision".'[3] At a later gathering Tolkien made the flippant suggestion that the title should instead be 'Hugo's Home': an allusion to Hugo Dyson, although it is unclear whether Tolkien was referring to heaven or hell.[4] By contrast, Tolkien notes with satisfaction that hearing the chapters 'Shelob's Lair' and 'The Choices of Master Samwise' at a Monday meeting at the end of May moved Lewis to tears.[5]

This reminds us that, while the two formidable scholars had much in common, and were greatly sympathetic to each other's tastes, they also had their differences. These contrasts were apparent from their very first encounter, at a meeting of the English Faculty in 1926, shortly after Lewis was appointed to his fellowship at Magdalen and Tolkien had moved from Leeds to take up the Rawlinson and Bosworth chair. Following the formal business, the two men gravitated together for some informal chit-chat. Lewis was positively disposed to his new acquaintance, labelling him a 'smooth, pale, fluent little chap'. But they disagreed significantly on a key aspect of the curriculum: the appropriate balance between literary and linguistic studies. Tolkien was passionately committed to philology; Lewis noted that Tolkien was unable to read Spenser 'because of the forms' – a reference to the artificial and archaic diction in which that poet wrote. Tolkien's belief that the study of medieval literature should have a strong focus on its language was opposed to Lewis's more literary inclinations. It is presumably for this reason that Lewis summed up his description of Tolkien with: 'No harm in him: only needs a smack or so.'[6]

We have seen how Lewis's antipathy towards philology was established early in his undergraduate studies. It is indicative of the influence Tolkien was to have over Lewis that he came to support Tolkien's proposed focus on Old and Middle English linguistics; their combined efforts were successful in moulding a new syllabus in 1931, requiring all students to engage in detailed study of the language of medieval English texts. Lewis described their victory to Warnie as a 'great feather in my cap', characterizing their success as having forced the new syllabus upon the junto 'after much hard fighting'.[7]

But this first encounter between Lewis and Tolkien was significant for much more than syllabus reform; in a later reference to their developing friendship, Lewis records the pair staying up until 2.30 a.m. in his rooms at Magdalen, 'discoursing of the gods & giants & Asgard [the home of the Norse gods] for three hours, then departing in the wind & rain – who cd. turn him out, for the fire was bright and the talk good?'[8] It was quickly apparent that the two were kindred spirits, both deeply affected by the mythology of the ancient North.

By 1929 the two were meeting to share their work in progress. Tolkien read to Lewis from *The Silmarillion* and solicited feedback on a manuscript draft of *The Hobbit*, which he lent to Lewis early in 1933. Lewis's enthusiasm for his writing is expressed in a letter to Arthur Greeves, in which he described Tolkien as the one person who would have been fit to form a third in their friendship group. Lewis found the experience of reading Tolkien's fairy story uncanny, since it so resembled the kind of work that Arthur and he would have wished to write themselves 'that one feels he is not making it up but merely describing the same world into which all three of us have the entry'.[9] In a review of the book, published in the *Times Literary Supplement* in 1939, Lewis elaborated on this idea, ascribing part of the work's success to the way we, as readers, gain entry into a world that seems to have been established long before we have stumbled upon it.

Lewis's direct input into Tolkien's creative writing is apparent from the textual history of 'The Geste of Beren and Lúthien', which recounts the love between an immortal elf-maiden and a mortal man. This was an intensely personal poem for Tolkien, since the idea for the story was inspired by a country walk with his wife Edith through a woodland glade at Roos, in Yorkshire. When Edith died in 1972, Tolkien had the name 'Lúthien' inscribed on the tombstone that marks her grave in Wolvercote Cemetery in North Oxford. At Tolkien's own death in 1973 he was buried alongside Edith and the name 'Beren' was added.

The story of their relationship began life as the poem titled 'Tinúviel' in the summer of 1925; this early version was abandoned unfinished in September 1931.[10] Tolkien sent a typescript draft of the poem to Lewis for comment towards the end of 1929. Lewis records his admiration for it in a letter of 7 December: 'I can quite honestly say that it is ages since I have had an evening of such delight: and the personal interest of reading a friend's work had very little to do with it.'[11] Early in 1930 Lewis sent Tolkien some fourteen pages of detailed comments on the poem.[12] He couched his criticism in the guise of an academic commentary on an ancient text, an amusing conceit which allowed him to mask any barbed judgements as the opinions of the learned yet somewhat austere German critics Peabody, Pumpernickel, Schuffer and Schick. Like a reviewer of any medieval edition, Lewis also assessed the value of alternative readings, as preserved in six imaginary manuscripts, referred to by the sigla *H*, *J*, *K*, *L*, *P*, *R*. This enabled Lewis to offer his own suggestions, usually under the sigla *J* and *L*, presumably standing for Jack and Lewis.

As a result of Lewis's comments, Tolkien made a number of emendations, often adopting wholesale his proposed alternatives. For instance, Lewis's commentary on the phrase 'Meats were sweet' in line 4 of the original draft notes that many scholars have rejected this phrase, and indeed lines 1–8 as a whole, as unworthy of the poem. According to Peabody, the lines were evidently the work of a later hand, probably added to make good a lacuna in the original manuscript. As the openings of medieval poems were prone to loss (since the first and last pages of unbound books commonly became detached from the remainder of the text), scribes and compilers frequently added spurious material in this way. Lewis even supplied his own rewriting of the opening, disguised as the version preserved in a different manuscript, which he suggested may preserve the authentic opening of the original

Geste. It was no doubt this criticism that prompted Tolkien to rewrite the opening; although he did not adopt Lewis's version wholesale, Lewis's 'And in his many-pillared house' clearly influenced the altered line 14: 'in many-pillared halls of stone'.

But not all Lewis's somewhat tart criticisms were accepted by Tolkien. His note to line 68, 'in many a tall and torchlit hall', prefers the alternative reading 'vast', as attested by manuscript *L*, citing Pumpernickel's view that 'The poet of the Geste knew nothing of internal rime, and its appearance (so called) is an infallible mark of corruption.' The original reading was left to stand in the revised version, despite Lewis's clear antipathy for the 'cacophonies' of this rhyme scheme. Tolkien clearly disagreed strongly with Lewis's revision of lines 629–630, which removed a 'half-hearted personification' of the 'dizzy moon ... twisted grey', scribbling 'Not so!!' in the margin and clarifying that the moon's appearance was the result of the tears in his eyes. Nevertheless, the two lines were excised in the revised version.

Lewis's comments were not all critical; his note to lines 88–150 observed simply that 'This is considered by all critics one of the noblest passages in the Geste.' At other points Lewis was inspired to attempt his own imaginary retelling, cited as part of a work known as the *Poema Historiale*, contemporary with the manuscript versions of Tolkien's work. Alongside lines 555–6, Lewis cites an early lyric preserved in a manuscript held in the public library at Narrowthrode (the ancient Nargothrond) which handles a similar conception of 'death-into-life', which he later included, in a revised form, in *The Pilgrim's Regress* (1933).[13]

Having listened to Tolkien father and son intone sections of *The Lord of the Rings* during its lengthy gestation period, Lewis read the entire text in typescript in late 1949. In a letter of 27 October Lewis conveyed his sincere admiration and delight in the work. He characterized the experience of reading through what would become a three-volume epic as draining a cup and thereby satisfying a long thirst. *Uton herian holbytlas*, he exclaimed, a phrase which may be translated out of Old English as 'Let us praise hobbits.' While Tolkien no doubt appreciated the sentiment, he may have cringed somewhat at Lewis's erroneous grammar. Tolkien coined the supposed Old English etymon of 'hobbit' from two genuine Old English words: *hol* 'hole' and *bytla* 'builder'.[14] But, since *bytla* belongs to the Old English weak declension, the plural ought to be *holbytlan*.[15]

Later reflecting on its successful publication, Tolkien acknowledged the importance of Lewis's enthusiastic encouragement in the following terms: 'The unpayable debt that I owe to him was not "influence" as it is ordinarily understood, but sheer encouragement. He was for long my only audience. Only from him did I ever get the idea that my "stuff" could be more than a private hobby.'[16] Lewis would have concurred with this statement; in a letter of May 1959, he noted that 'No one ever influenced Tolkien – you might as well try to influence a bandersnatch.'[17] Diana Pavlac Glyer has convincingly argued that the encouragement that the Inklings offered each other was in fact a crucial way by which they directly impacted each other's writings.[18] Lewis, however, focuses on those occasions on which he had criticized specific passages or suggested changes, most of which were vehemently rejected by Tolkien – '*rejected* is perhaps too mild a word for your reaction on at least one occasion!'[19] Lewis ends this letter on a poignant note, adding 'I miss you very much' and signing off as 'Jack Lewis', a rather formal mode of address given the former closeness of their relationship.

According to Humphrey Carpenter, this coolness was in part the result of Tolkien's lack of enthusiasm for Lewis's Narnian stories – the mythical hotchpotch combined with the speed and facility with which he produced them.[20] Roger Lancelyn Green reported Tolkien's dismissal of such whimsical touches as the titles of the volumes on Mr Tumnus's bookshelf: 'Nymphs and their Ways' and 'The Love-Life of a Faun'.[21] Such reports fit with a comment Tolkien made in a letter of 1964, where he expressed his sadness that the Narnian stories remained 'outside the range of my sympathy, as much of my work was outside his'.[22] This is a puzzling remark, since Lewis consistently expressed the greatest enthusiasm for Tolkien's fiction; perhaps it was intended to help justify a lack of reciprocity for which Tolkien may have felt a tinge of guilt. Holly Ordway, however, has argued that Tolkien's supposed distaste for Lewis's stories has been overstated; recalling Tolkien's description of the tales as 'deservedly popular', Ordway locates his objections in their overt Christian subtext and mixing of mythologies.[23]

The routine of the Monday morning get-togethers was disrupted by the arrival in Oxford of Charles Williams, a figure who played a significant role in the distancing of their relationship. Lewis wholeheartedly embraced Williams's presence in Oxford; we have already seen that it was Lewis who invited him to join the Inklings. Lewis also encouraged Williams to make a third at the Monday morning meetings. Tolkien no doubt resented this intrusion into their friendship; he never quite understood the enthusiasm that Lewis had for Williams and his writings. As a consequence of Williams's presence, those meetings became more literary and less philological than Tolkien would have liked. Musing on one such encounter, Tolkien identified the way in which conversation had strayed into discussion of writers for whom he had little sympathy: 'spent two hours with C.S.L. and C.W. It was very enjoyable. We talked a good deal about "prosody" and (more than I cared for) about C. Lamb: an author that I find no use for, I fear.'[24]

Combined with the intrusion of Charles Williams was Tolkien's disappointment that Lewis, having returned to Christianity, had not entered the church by 'the new door' of the Catholic Church to which he himself belonged. Arthur Adams, a former Dean of Divinity at Magdalen, recalled hearing that the fellows' betting book at All Souls College contained a wager that Lewis would eventually become a Catholic;[25] the bet remained unpaid, since Lewis re-entered the faith by the 'old door' of the Ulster Protestantism of his youth and remained a member for the rest of his life.[26]

But the major event in Lewis's life that was to disrupt his personal and emotional world and his settled relationships was a very different encounter: one that also took place in the Eastgate Hotel.

JOY DAVIDMAN

It was in the Eastgate Hotel that, on 24 September 1952, Lewis first met the American writer Joy Davidman, who was accompanied by her London-based friend Phyllis Williams.[27] They lunched at Magdalen a few days later in Lewis's rooms; Lewis had invited his brother Warnie to accompany them, but, when he was forced to cancel, Lewis asked his former student George Sayer to step in. Sayer described the event in his biography, *Jack: C.S. Lewis and His Times*, recalling his first impressions of Joy as a 'an amusingly abrasive New Yorker', who charmed Lewis with her bluntness and anti-American views.[28] Warnie was similarly struck by her lack of inhibition; he was especially shocked by the way that Joy, in the hearing of several Magdalen dons, asked if there was anywhere in that monastic establishment where a lady could relieve herself.[29] However, George Watson, who met Joy over lunch during one of her rare visits to Cambridge, found her to be a softly spoken woman of letters. Watson was surprised by her portrayal in the *Shadowlands* film, since he found nothing brash in her manner; of the two, Lewis was by far the noisier.[30]

Although these were their first face-to-face encounters, Joy and Lewis's friendship dates back to 1949. Writing to her friend, the academic Chad Walsh, a professor of English at Beloit College in Wisconsin and author of a book on Lewis, *The Apostle to the Skeptics* (1949), Joy mentions that, encouraged by Walsh's assurance that Lewis answers all correspondence – even 'asinine letters' – she had sent 'the unfortunate man five single-spaced pages of personal history and what not'.[31]

Joy's decision to write to Lewis was prompted by her close engagement with his writings; references in her surviving corpus of letters suggest that she and Lewis debated philosophical and theological issues in some depth. In a letter to Walsh, Joy describes an exchange with Lewis in which he 'knocked my props out from under me unerringly'. Far from being humbled or upset to have her theories dismantled so completely, Joy evidently considered this kind of debate to be extremely pleasurable and intellectually invigorating, leaving her marvelling at the

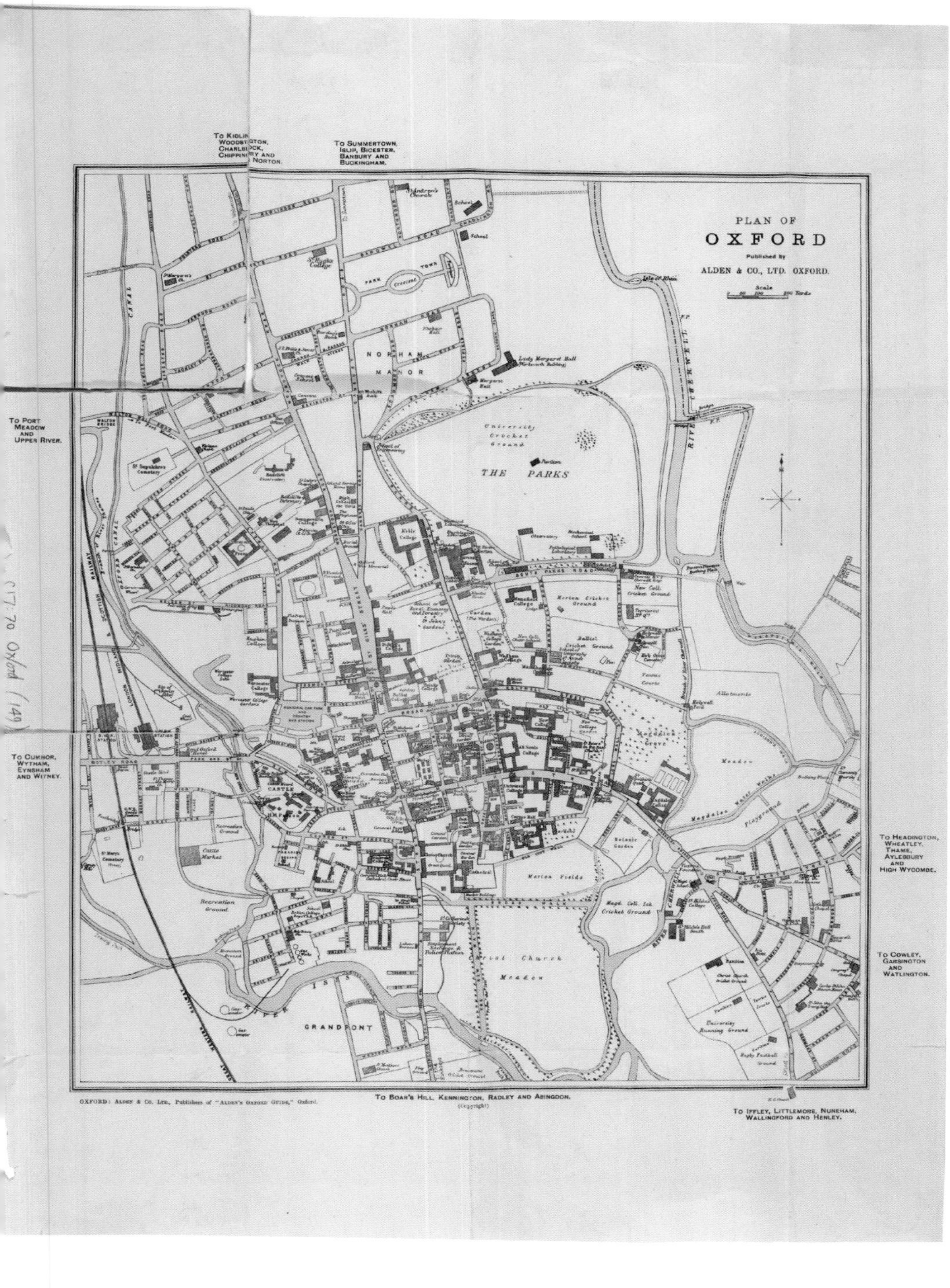

PLATE 1 Oxford city plan *c.* 1930, showing the railway station at the top of Botley Road, Magdalen College and Addison's Walk.

PLATE 2 The New Building, Magdalen College. Lewis's rooms were on the first floor.

PLATE 3 Arthurian murals at the Oxford Union library, painted by William Morris and Dante Gabriel Rossetti.

17

Reduplicating Verbs.

a. Lǣtan – lēt – lēton – lǣten
   Hātan – hēt – hēton – hāten.

b. Healdan – hēold – hēoldon – healden

II.

Orosius, Paulus. Late IVth century Historia adversum Paganos. Which begins with a short outline of geography. Here Aelfred adds much from his own knowledge to the part dealing with Europe and interpolates the travels of Ohthere and Wulfstan wholesale.

Translated by Hakluyt 1589. Paraphrased by Longfellow in Birds of Passage

1. Hlāforde Ohthere presumably in the temporary employment of Aelfred cf 48

3 Norþweardum Adj. agreeing with lande.

þeah. sc. in spite of the fact that he lived further Nth. than anyone

5. Stycce piece (cf germ. stück) mǣlum cf "piecemeal".

8 Legjan, læg, lǣgon, legen V
  > licgan IM.

10. Lǣtan, lēt, lǣten allow > to cause > "to have". Habuit sibi.

Steorbord Steered by a paddle on the right stern wh is hence the steorbord. The helmsman thus faces right and has at his back the bæcbord. Later developments of nomenclature all depend apparently on fact that such a ship cd. not be brought alongside except to a wharf or bank on the left. Hence bæcbord is the lādbord or side you load from: hence by analogy larboard. It is also the port or harbour side: hence port. (v. Oseberg ship. Hmskr. p 580).

PLATE 4 Lewis's notes on the voyage of Ohthere, which he studied as an undergraduate at University College.

Lewis bets Stevens that the word ΕΡΩΣ does not occur in the Odyssey (a bottle of port)

May 14th 46

Paid by Mr. Stevens

PLATE 5 Painting of fellows in the Senior Common Room, Magdalen College, by Alan Sorrell, 1952.

PLATE 6 Record of a bet between Lewis and C.E. Stevens in the SCR betting book, 14 May 1946.

PLATE 7 Interior of Magdalen College chapel.

PLATE 8 Magdalen College weighing scales.

PLATE 9 *(overleaf)* Annotations in Lewis's copy of *Love's Labour's Lost*, the 1909 Arden Shakespeare.

METRE, peculiarities of. pp. 91, 92, 93, 99, 138, 145, 175, 177.
MILTON. gorgeous east. p. 99.
MISPRISION p. 90. I cant understand this place
MONARCHO p. 66 and n. ibid
MOONSHINE IN WATER From Aesop > a thing of no worth > (? according to Hart) mod. "all moonshine"
MOTE p. 94.
MOTH. supposed connection with M. la Motte p. xxiii. (2)
MUSCOVITES pp. xxvi, xxviii.
O'ERSHOT p. 94. Astray in ones aim, wide of the mark
OPINION. self conceit. p. 109.
ORTHOGRAPHY shd regulate pronunciation on Holofernes' view p. 110.
OSTENTATION, apparently = spectacle p. 118.
OUT OF ALL SUIT. Hart "Out of all fitness." Onions explains "suit" = attendance at court of a liege lord; hence "out of all s" = out of all service
PAINTED CLOTH. p. 162.
PARITORS officers of ecclesiastical courts, summoners > person concerned with discovery of fornication p. 55.
PASS. p. 120 "To represēt, take the rôle of" (Hart, on stregth of unconvincing quotation from B. Jonson). Onions the same, queried.
PASSADO. forward lung with foot & sword. p. 28.
PATCH. p. 73 A patch > patch'd or pied coat > wearer of pied coat > fool. (Hart) Fool (Onions)
PATHETICAL 23, 71.
PEDANTIUS. parallel p. 64. v. p xxxvii et seq.
PEN = style. p 84.
PEREGRINATE Adj. = with a travelled air. ἅπ. λεγ. v. sub Armado.
PERJURE WEARING PAPERS Papers set on the heads of convicted perjurers (in pillory?) p. 87
PERSON, pun on. p 78.
PICKED. = argutus, exquisitus (Rider 1589)
PIERCING A HOGSHEAD v. Hogshead
PINN'D ON SLEEVE "to pin wenches" etc. Hart thinks it from pinning the mistresse's favour on sleeve, but his quotations give rather the idea of "tying to ones apron-strings", "keeping in ones pocket" p. 143.
POINT DEVISE here an adj. apparently = picked (q.v.) No explanation in Hart or Onions.
PONEWATER. a large juicy pale apple now lost. p. 71
PRICKET v. Buck
PROMETHEAN Chapman (1594) finds it necessary to annotate the word
PROTESTANTISM [?] "defects Not by might mastered but by special grace" (p. 9.) — "to hearken after the flesh" p. 12 — "in the testimony of a good cōsciēce" p. 71 — "My beauty will be saved by merit — Oh heresy" p. 59 — "Charity itself fulfils the law p. 106.
PRUNING = preening p. 96.
PUTTENHAM dominator p. 13 — voluble p. 32 — passionate p. 42 — vulgar p. 63 — ortography p. 110 — p xl — Translace p. 127
QUIBBLES pp. 12, 21, 26, 37, 39, 49, 56, 67, 76, 77, 99, 123, 124, 132, 138, 141, 145, 163, 164.
QUILLETS. p. 102.
QUOTE. 1. To give the reference to (a quotation) i.e. in the margin as we find in old books (p. 40). 2. To set down for, to reckon as (pp 90, 176)
REASONS = conversations (ragion-) p. 108.
REVELS, DANCES etc. p. 108. This line borrowed in Return frō Parnassus. Also see some nonsense of Hart's ad. loc.

REGULAR ANAPESTS p. 40.
REMEMBER THY COURTESY Ordinarily means "The devil don't you uncover?" (wh. by the bye show[s] semantic history of the surviving courtesy, a fem[ale] bow): but in p 117 Holofernes is already ūcove[red] Malone reads "remember not" (Pray dont both[er] keep your hat off.) Steevens explains "You've forgotten your hat is off (i.e. your courtesy) Ple[ase] put it on again. Hart thinks Hol. is being tol[d] to ūcover (not to Arm. but) at the king's name, [and] cover again
ROSE TRADTN. v. Allegory.
SCHOOL OF NIGHT Hart. ad. loc (p. 100) delirat
SCURRILITY = smut. pp. 75, 109.
SELL A BARGAIN to one = to sell him a pup. p
SEQUENT, a follower. p. 83.
SEVERAL A "several field" >< a common. p. 39.
SHROWS, shrews. p. 125
SIDNEY juvenal p. 18 — arrest your word p. 36 62-63 — p. 108 (v. slight) — thousand years a bo[y] 123.
SISTER p. 123. v. Sources
SINONIMIA. recommended by Puttenham p 77-8. p. 109.
SNEAPING p 8.
SNIP AND AWAY p. 44.
SOURCES No literary source has been found. Fr[om the] facts (a) That Shakespeare nowhere shows the powe[r of] invention in the lower sense & (b) That L.L.L. as a [story] is contemptible; I cōclude that he invented it. Hi[storic]al sources have bin conjectured.
1. Hunter Unfulfilled promise about Armado sug[gests] that S. is following real story. Draws same fro[m] the crown speech & cfs Monstrelet s. an. 1425 — s[ome] negotiations betw. Frãce & Navarre rē 200,000 [crowns]
2. Sidney Lee In 1586 Katharine de Medici — v[ice?] gov. of Frãce for infirm & mentally defective s[on] (cf. p 9. "Decrepit sick & bedrid father) negotia[ted] with H. of Navarre: in whose train were Longueville, de Biron, de Mayenne. Interes[t in] this in Englãd because London sent Navar[re] 1000 men in 1589.
3. Furnivall. Why shdnt. Moth be the Fr. amba[ssador] de la Motte?
4 Hart The sister business (p 123) looks like fra[gment] of real story. The Princess represents Frãce ita[self]
Sum up: Lee has pretty clearly found the so[urce] of the names. The rest is verbiage. (1)
SOWED COCKLE etc p 107. I dont know why [I] indexed this but no doubt there was a good re[ason]
~~[illegible]~~
SPENSER ? p. 123. also p xxv
STAFF = stanza >< verse = line.
STATE = stance p. 96
STATUTE CAPS p. 132 Johnson thought it me[ant] mortar boards. Grey showed that in 1571 wool [caps] on Sunday became compulsory for all except [...] as a measure to ēcourage the cappers. Hart wan[ts] to give an extra pt. to "plain" (also "citizen" in quotatn. from Marston) has ferreted out a 158[.. reg]ulatn. enjoining wool cap for prentices.
STEEP-UP p. 58. Adj. cf Sonnets. But Q & F steep up is just as good.
STOOP p. 90. Adj? (Onions). Hart takes as imperat[ive] "Come down off your high horse.

(1) D.W. argues "LLL was printed under same condtns as Romeo. Romeo had a bad Q. be[hind] it. ∴ LLL had a bad Q. behind it. But most bad Q.'s reproduce earlier plays. ∴ Th[ere] was an earlier pre-Sh. LLL. Q.E.D. (2) Or Nash

6033a

UNG WITH HIS HAIR p.105
GEST(IONS) pp. 10, 175. = Tempt(ations)
ITORS p.67. pron. "shooter."
EAR CUT p. 53 To forswear, give up. p.21 to outswear
id" may be explained in same way, as the ordinary
se of "outswear" has little point here.

THE ARDEN SHAKESPEARE
GENERAL EDITOR: W. J. CRAIG
1899-1906: R. H. CASE, 1909

PATHIZED p.46 = adapted, suitable, appropriate
ions & Hart) The vb. occurs first in Lyly. v. Nashe.
LES p.144 James played on a "table" or board,
h. genus backgammon is a species p. 144
FETA p.132. Accdng. to Hart the pt. here is that
masks are made of taffeta.
IT IN SNUFF. To take it as you wd. take the
l of a snuff'd candle (?Hart) > to dislike > to
uffy or snuffy at. p.123.
HIM AT HIS WORD "To talk to him in his own
" (Hart) p.38
p.84. Not identified (Hart)
RBOROUGH p.11. = Thirdborough or constable (Onions)
SONICAL p.109.
WAT NOVUM p.159. Locus paene desperatus
E DEATH p.131. Apparently only means "until we
NLACER, figure of. Explained from Puttenham p.27
xamples pp. 3, 27, 62, 86.
SLATION (of hypocrisy) p.125. Onions & Hart tac
equidem primus, ut videtur, haereo.
S (sb. pl.) p.136 Threes at dice

LOVE'S LABOUR'S LOST

AND GO p.83. Name of a morris dance (Chappell)
AN, "Trojan" in sense of a "brick," a good fellow.
66, 170.
E-SOD = bis coctus p.73 cf "Double-distilled"
EMING p.36 "Not seeming (to be willing)" ! (On
) Hart tacet.
OOT or upshot = The shot wh. is best or leading
given moment, i.e. until a better is shot (Hart) p.69.
ING. = to lower, hence to unveil p.141 v. Clouds
not a pun on veil p.137
= Forward! > cheer up! (Hart) Onions tacet.
E PENCILS p.124. H's explanation poor.
SHALL BREAK IT WILL p.3. Capells "break it; will
nothing else" Hart nearly inarticulate here
ON. Arte of Rhetorique 1584. Parallel to Arm
s letter p.62 ... insinuation p.72 ... in collection
ynecdoche p.83 —
LD pun on p.115
COCKS = fools p.89.
S p.93. As elsewhere = lovers. Why, I dont know.
HIES (sb. abst. pl.) = excellences p.100.
D p.150. i.e. with the plague (v. Date)

ADDENDA
defends neologisms in -ish p.46 — piercing a hog.
p.78 — Allons! Allons! p.107
p.82. Pun — or aetiological myth?
NAME To miscall, name wrongly (N.E.D.) p.146
NT. Not a whit (Florio) From French? pp. 37, 139.
= nota, branded on criminal p.92 v. Perjure
ERS RATIFIED. p.82 Verses duly measured out.
WARD = wearing wool next the skin p.172.

Text

Furnivall gives — Q1 1598 | F1 1623 | Q2 1631

Hart gives — Actors copy α | Q1 1598; Actors Copy β? | F1 1623 | Q2 1631

Hart thinks β may have contained improvements and that, in any case, F1 printed from its source more carefully than Q1. Furnivall prefers Q1

Textual Places.

I i. 106 (p. 8.) QQFF. New fangled shows
Edd. Various emendatns for rime

I ii 173 (p. 28) QQFF. Shall turn sonnet
Hanmer Shall turn sonneter
Amyot Shall turn a sonnet

III i. 21 (p. 44) QQFF. Do you note men
Hanmer Do you note me.

III i. 171 (p. 54) QQFF. Signior Junios
Hanmer Senior Junior

III i. 181 (p. 56) QQ.F1. Cloak.
FF2-4. Clock.

IV i. 142 (p. 70) Q1. Ath toothen
F1. Ath to the
Grant White O' the to
Rowe A th' to
Dyces O' the one

IV ii 112 (p. 82) QQFF. Apostraphas
Murray in N.E.D. Apostrophus.

IV iii 13 (p. 85) QQFF. Mallichollie
Edd. Melancholy.

IV iii 50 (p. 88) QQF1. Triumphery.
Rowe Triumviriate.

IV iii 56 (p. 89) QQFF. Shop.
Theobald Slop.

IV iii 83 (p. 90) QQFF. She is not, corporal.
Theobald She is but corporal.

IV iii 158 (p. 94) QQFF. Moth ... moth
Rowe Mote ... mote.

IV iii 170 (p. 96) Q1 caudle
F1 candle

IV iii 177 (p. 96) QQFF. Men like men of inconstancy
Dyce Men like you, men of inconstancy.

IV iii 252 (100) QQFF. School of night.
Theobald Scowl of night.
Hanmer Stole of night.

IV iii 355 (p. 106) QQFF. Loves all men
Hanmer Moves.
Mason Leads.

IV iii 380 (p. 107) QQFF. Alone! Alone.
Theobald Allons! Allons

K. A. TAYLOR. (B-) Collection Paper I. Wd. like more than two answers

3. Gower's Confessio Amantis is the work of a very considerable craftsman. It is something more than a collection of tales translated from the standard sources of the fourteenth century. The tales themselves are, with few exceptions, extremely well-told, and even if one is familiar with them from other writers, there is often to be found in Gower's version a novel turn of events, or attitude to the story, which cannot fail to make a good impression. But the original parts of the Confessio are no less interesting. The introduction, the conclusion, & the dialogues between Lover & Confessor which link the tales together form a picture of the mediaeval ideals of love. The lover tells, at one time or another, almost his whole life at court. He describes his mistress, delighting in recounting her excellences, & reveals all the methods which he uses to win her. She is neither cruel nor indulgent, but behaves with the perfect restraint of the courtly lady. He expects little attention from her, and receives little, but is highly aggrieved when she shows signs of favour to one of his rivals, and he then speaks maliciously to her of this rival. [a bit clumsy] By so doing, however, as the Confessor points out, he is more likely to fall than to rise in her esteem. This is one thing which he must not do, & though he admits it, the lover observes that he finds it a very difficult precept to follow. [Sufficient has been said to demonstrate that] this side of Gower's work is [one of no little] excellence. [excellent] ? Wd. it be better with these amputations?

The tales themselves prove that Gower's skill was no less in the art of translating, selecting, & arranging than in conceiving the whole idea of the poem. (There are flaws in this, flaws perhaps as much of the time as of the man, but they will be mentioned later.) The style is simple & straightforward; regular octosyllabic couplets are used; and the language is if anything easier to understand than Chaucer's. The tales are all told to illustrate points of virtue & Christian morality; unlike Chaucer's they do not have to be fitted to any characters, as the Confessor, who tells them is a guiding voice rather than a living being. ~~the~~ Gower thus had perhaps an easier task than Chaucer in writing his work, but he can still claim to be the superior of the two as far as actual tale-telling is concerned. While comparing him with Chaucer, it is useful to comment on Chaucer's words, "moral Gower." The difference between Gower's Tale of Florent and the Wife of Bath's Tale will illustrate the seriousness and virtuous purpose of the one, and the gay attitude of entertainment which characterizes the other. Gower [is this quite the right word?]

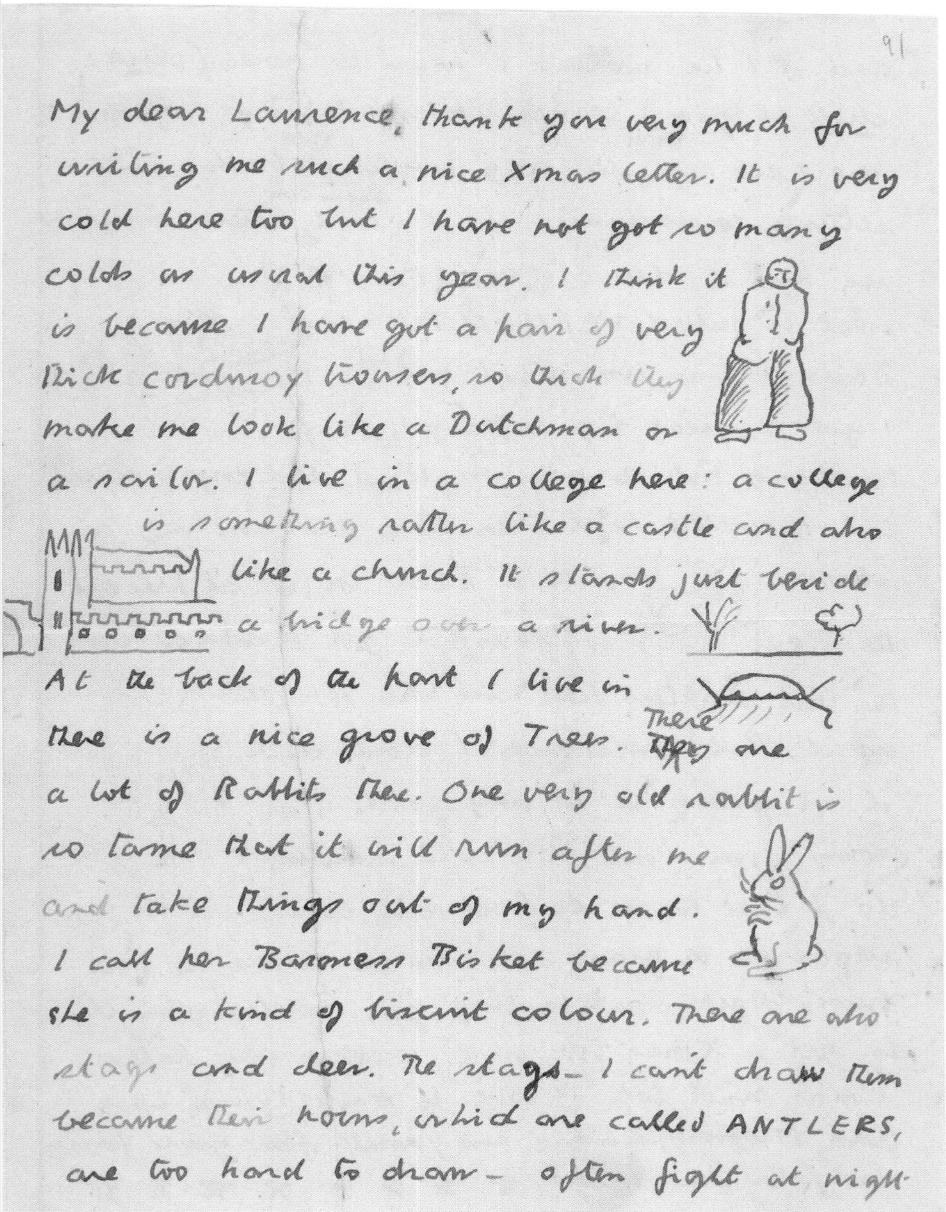

91

My dear Laurence, thank you very much for
writing me such a nice Xmas letter. It is very
cold here too but I have not got so many
colds as usual this year. I think it
is because I have got a pair of very
thick corduroy trousers, so thick they
make me look like a Dutchman or
a sailor. I live in a college here: a college
is something rather like a castle and also
like a church. It stands just beside
a bridge over a river.
At the back of the part I live in
there is a nice grove of Trees. There are
a lot of Rabbits there. One very old rabbit is
so tame that it will run after me
and take things out of my hand.
I call her Baroness Bisket because
she is a kind of biscuit colour. There are also
stags and deer. The stags – I can't draw them
because their horns, which are called ANTLERS,
are too hard to draw – often fight at night

PLATE 10 Examination paper marked by Lewis, c. 1944–47

PLATE 11 Letter to Laurence Harwood, December 1944.

PLATE 12 The Kilns, bought by Lewis and Mrs Moore in 1930.

PLATE 13 Woodland in Shotover Park, Headington, where Lewis walked his dogs.

PLATE 14 Holy Trinity Church, Headington Quarry.

PLATE 15 Narnia window, Holy Trinity Church, Headington Quarry.

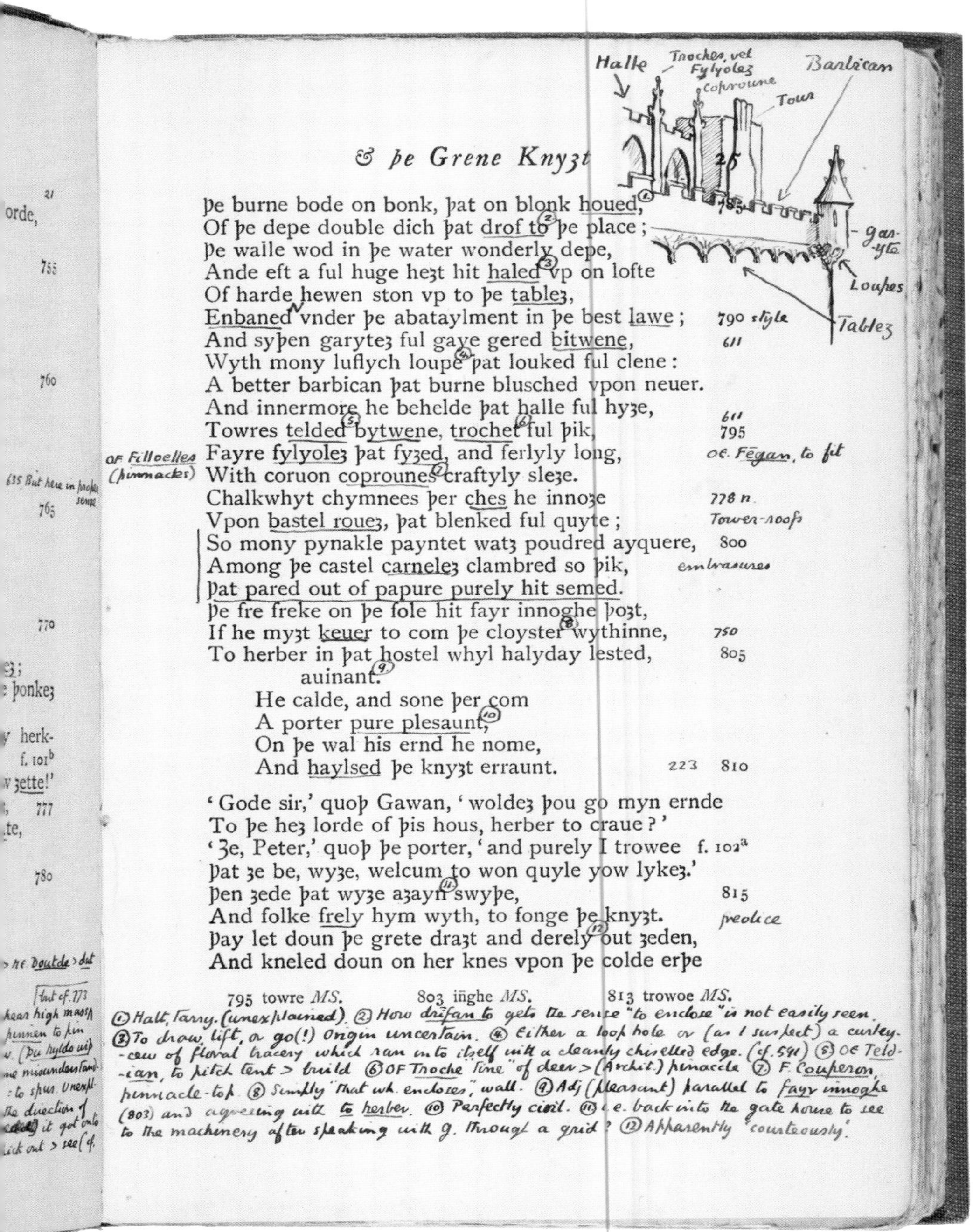

& þe Grene Knyȝt 25

Þe burne bode on bonk, þat on blonk houed,
Of þe depe double dich þat drof to þe place;
Þe walle wod in þe water wonderly depe,
Ande eft a ful huge heȝt hit haled vp on lofte
Of harde hewen ston vp to þe tableȝ,
Enbaned vnder þe abataylment in þe best lawe;
And syþen garyteȝ ful gaye gered bitwene,
Wyth mony luflych loupe þat louked ful clene:
A better barbican þat burne blusched vpon neuer.
And innermore he behelde þat halle ful hyȝe,
Towres telded bytwene, trochet ful þik,
Fayre fylyoleȝ þat fyȝed, and ferlyly long,
With coruon coprounes craftyly sleȝe.
Chalkwhyt chymnees þer ches he innoȝe
Vpon bastel roueȝ, þat blenked ful quyte;
So mony pynakle payntet watȝ poudred ayquere,
Among þe castel carneleȝ clambred so þik,
Þat pared out of papure purely hit semed.
Þe fre freke on þe fole hit fayr innoghe þoȝt,
If he myȝt keuer to com þe cloyster wythinne,
To herber in þat hostel whyl halyday lested,
auinant.
He calde, and sone þer com
A porter pure plesaunt,
On þe wal his ernd he nome,
And haylsed þe knyȝt erraunt.

'Gode sir,' quoþ Gawan, 'woldeȝ þou go myn ernde
To þe heȝ lorde of þis hous, herber to craue?'
'Ȝe, Peter,' quoþ þe porter, 'and purely I trowee f. 102[a]
Þat ȝe be, wyȝe, welcum to won quyle yow lykeȝ.'
Þen ȝede þat wyȝe aȝayn swyþe,
And folke frely hym wyth, to fonge þe knyȝt.
Þay let doun þe grete draȝt and derely out ȝeden,
And kneled doun on her knes vpon þe colde erþe

795 towre *MS.* 803 inghe *MS.* 813 trowoe *MS.*

PLATE 16 Picture of Bertilak's castle drawn by Lewis in a copy of *Sir Gawain and the Green Knight*.

PLATE 17 An early attempt to begin *The Lion, the Witch and the Wardrobe* inscribed on the back of another manuscript.

This book is about four children whose names were Ann, Martin, Rose and Peter. But it is most about Peter who was the youngest. They all had to go away from London suddenly because of Air Raids, and because Father, who was in the Army, had gone off to the war and Mother was doing some kind of war work. They were sent to stay with a kind of relation of Mother's who was a very old Professor who lived all by himself in the country

1. Science & Religion
(a) Miracles
(b) Origins.

2. Evasion of the Ethical.
Yes: from the beginning.
Natural Law.
All re-affirmed by Xtianity

3 Pacifism
(1) Ought we to [illegible] at all.
No condemnation of soldiers. John Baptist.
Nor of Israelite past) Civil magistrate
(Then the other cheek.
i.e. accept [illegible] of Retaliation as real.

(2)

4. Relation to the State.
Demand for martyrdom)(Flight. Honour the King.
Intermarriage.
Pagan Divine parties

5. 2 Ders. II 2. Devil [illegible] the day is at hand
III 4 Dark because [illegible] go quietly [illegible]

E X A M I N A T I O N   P A P E R S

PART I (Time allowed 60 mins)

Candidates must attempt at least four and not more than six questions. All candidates are expected to answer Questions 1 and 2.

1. Write brief notes on SIX of the following:

   (a) Goring Post Office
   ~~(b)~~ The 'warm comfort of the Christian Religion'.
   ~~(c)~~ Exeter Station.
   ~~(d)~~ Bread for the House of Lords.
   (e) Philocasius.
   (f) "He thinks I'm a Financer".
   (g) "If it isn't bacon and eggs, its eggs and bacon!"
   ~~(h)~~ "I hold no brief for Humanitarianism".
   ~~(i)~~ The mystic word 'caboodle'.

2. Why are you the best map reader?

3. Distinguish carefully between a walking-tour and a walking-race.

4. In what sense may a Quirinal be said to be 'lovely'?

5. Describe the principal uses of EITHER (a) the British Camp OR (b) Offa's Dyke.

6. Under what circumstances are billeting areas permissible?

7. Complete the following formula: "And could we, in about ten minutes..."

8. "...centre de Tourisme incomparable!" MAUROIS. Justify this contemporary estimate of Cheltenham.

9. Give the (long) semantic history of the word 'Guiting'.

10. Describe in your own words an imaginary walking-tour lasting not less than 4 days with not more than 4 of the following:

    Lytton Strachey
    Big Bill Thompson
    Percy Simpson
    Father Ronald Knox
    W. Force Stead.
    Mahatma Gandhi
    Lady Oxford
    Sigmund Freud
    G. K. Chesterton
    Professor J.A.Smith
    Benedetto Croce
    Sir William Morris
    King Alfonso
    Mary Pickford
    Lord Olivier
    C. H. Wilkinson
    The Dhali Llama of Thibet
    Edgar Wallace

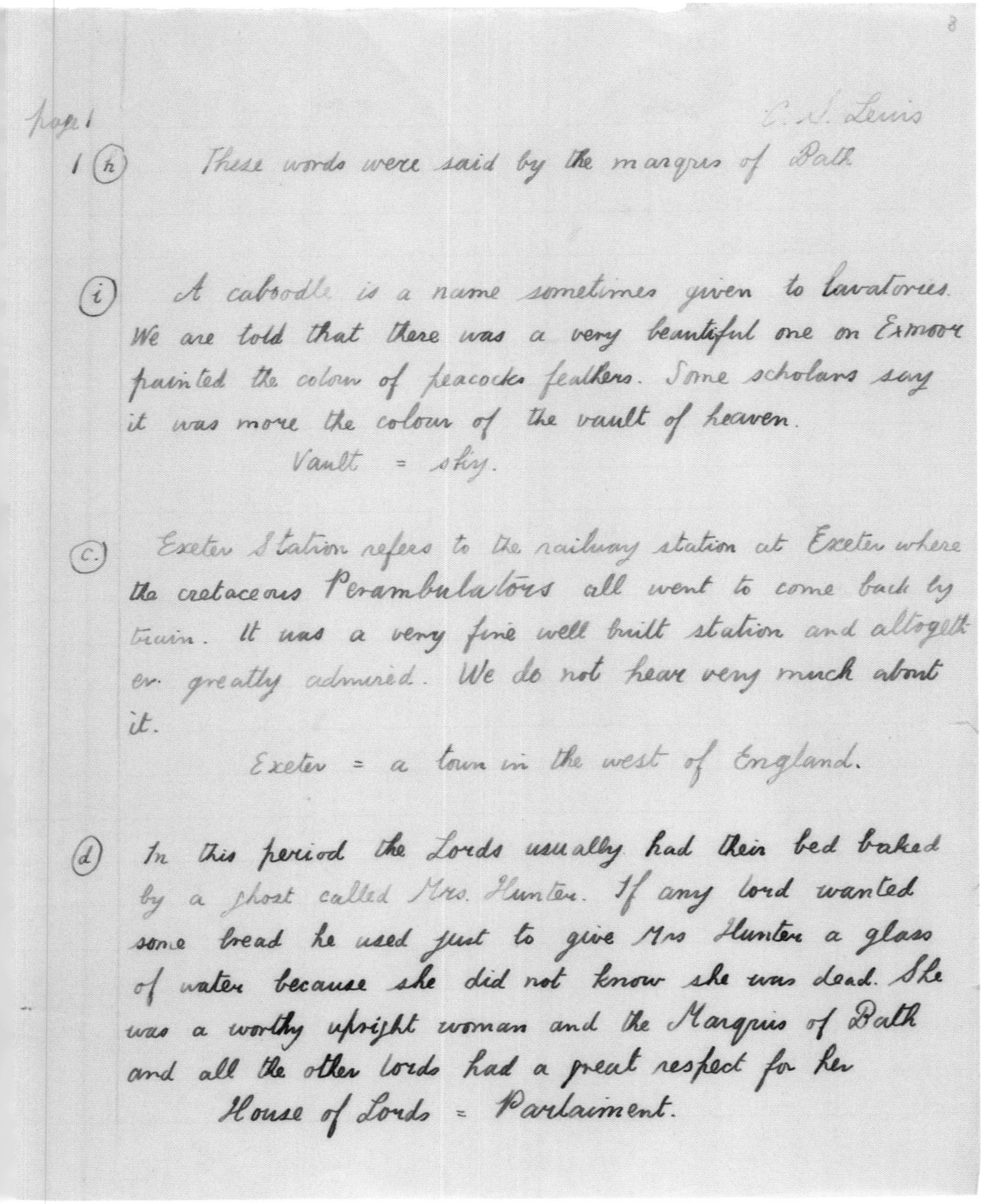

8

page 1 C. S. Lewis

1 (h) These words were said by the marquis of Bath

(i) A caboodle is a name sometimes given to lavatories. We are told that there was a very beautiful one on Exmoor painted the colour of peacocks feathers. Some scholars say it was more the colour of the vault of heaven.

Vault = sky.

(c.) Exeter Station refers to the railway station at Exeter where the cretaceous Perambulators all went to come back by train. It was a very fine well built station and altogeth-er greatly admired. We do not hear very much about it.

Exeter = a town in the west of England.

(d) In this period the Lords usually had their bed baked by a ghost called Mrs. Hunter. If any lord wanted some bread he used just to give Mrs Hunter a glass of water because she did not know she was dead. She was a worthy upright woman and the Marquis of Bath and all the other lords had a great respect for her

House of Lords = Parlaiment.

PLATE 18 College of Cretaceous Perambulators Re-entrance Examination, 1936.

PLATE 19 Lewis's answers to the spoof examination paper.

PLATE 20 The Eagle and Child pub, where the Inklings met.

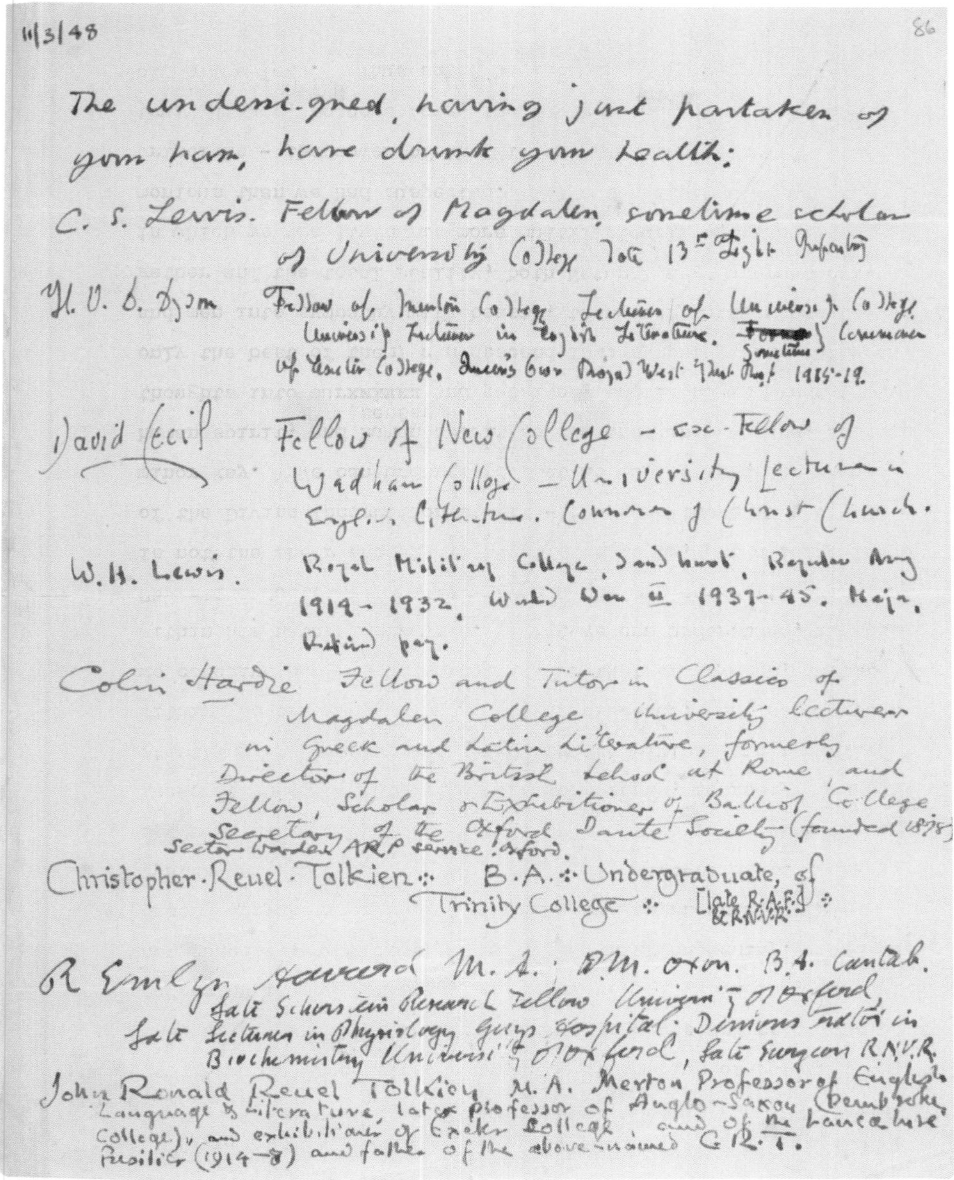
11/3/48 86

The undersigned, having just partaken of your ham, have drunk your health:

C. S. Lewis. Fellow of Magdalen, sometime scholar of University College late 13th Light Infantry

H. V. D. Dyson Fellow of Merton College Lecturer of University College. University Lecturer in English Literature. ~~Formerly~~ sometime Commoner of Exeter College. Queen's Own Royal West Kent Regt 1915-19.

David Cecil Fellow of New College – ex-Fellow of Wadham College – University Lecturer in English Literature. Commoner of Christ Church.

W. H. Lewis. Royal Military College, Sandhurst. Regular Army 1914–1932. World War II 1939–45. Major. Retired pay.

Colin Hardie Fellow and Tutor in Classics of Magdalen College. University Lecturer in Greek and Latin Literature, formerly Director of the British School at Rome, and Fellow, Scholar & Exhibitioner of Balliol College Secretary of the Oxford Dante Society (founded 1876) Sector Warden ARP service: Oxford.

Christopher · Reuel · Tolkien ∴ B.A. ∴ Undergraduate, of Trinity College ∴ [late R.A.F.] & R.N.V.R. ∴

R Emlyn Havard M.A. D.M. Oxon. B.A. Cantab. late Schorstein Research Fellow University of Oxford, late Lecturer in Physiology Guys Hospital; Demonstrator in Biochemistry University of Oxford, late Surgeon R.N.V.R.

John Ronald Reuel Tolkien M.A. Merton Professor of English Language & Literature, late Professor of Anglo-Saxon (Pembroke College), and exhibitioner of Exeter College, and of the Lancashire Fusiliers (1914–8) and father of the above-named C.R.T.

PLATE 21 Thank you letter to Dr W.M. Firor, 1948.

Oxford University

SOCRATIC CLUB

President: C. S. LEWIS, M.A.

This Club has been formed for those who do not necessarily wish to commit themselves to Christian views but are interested in a philosophical approach to religion in general and to Christianity in particular, in a spirit of free enquiry and in the light of modern thought and knowledge.

OPEN DISCUSSION will follow the introduction of the subjects by speakers who will include both Christians and non-Christians.

MEETINGS

Hilary Term, 1946

Jan. 28th. (S. HILDA'S)	**Religion in the Post-War World**	**Mr. SHAW DESMOND** **Mr. C. S. LEWIS**
Feb. 4th. (S. HILDA'S)	**Morals and Religion**	**Mr. D. M. MacKINNON** **Dr. D. FALK**
Feb. 11th. (ORIEL)	**Can Science Provide a Basis for Ethics?**	**Dr. C. H. WADDINGTON** **Dr. A. M. FARRER**
Feb. 18th. (ORIEL)	**Superstition and Faith**	**Prof. L. W. GRENSTED**
Feb. 25th. (ORIEL)	**Reply to Historicism**	**Dr. F. H. HEINEMANN** **Mr. J. M. URMSON**
Mar. 4th. (S. JOHN'S)	**Rehabilitation - and then?**	**Hon. E. PLUMER**
Mar. 11th. (S. JOHN'S)	**Religion and the Evolution of Man**	**Dr. KÖSTERLITZ**

The Meetings are on MONDAYS at 8.15 p.m.
The Papers will be followed by OPEN DISCUSSION.

SECRETARY:
HELEN McGIVERING
(S. Anne's) 'Phone 3780.

Oxonian Press, 29 Queen Street, Oxford.

PLATE 22 Socratic Club term card, January 1946.

PLATE 23 Lewis liked to work in Duke Humfrey's Library in the Bodleian – though he found it more conducive to 'dreaming' than to studying.

PLATE 24 First Court, Magdalene College Cambridge.

PLATE 25 The Lewis family wardrobe.

PLATE 26 Warnie Lewis's typewriter – Warnie typed up his brother's manuscripts.

PLATE 27 Carvings on a doorway on St Mary's Passage, Oxford.

PLATE 28 Door handle of the rectory, St Mark's Church, Dundela, featuring a lion – could this be the inspiration for Aslan?

PLATE 29 Sculpture of Aslan in Bury Knowle Park, Oxford.

PLATE 30 Narnia mural, Belfast.

PLATE 31 Searcher statue, Belfast.

FIG. 16 Joy Davidman and Lewis with Susie, 1958.

superior performance of Lewis the dialectician.[32] That Lewis himself enjoyed her lively and engaging missives is suggested by Warnie, who noted that Joy's letters stood out from the rest of his substantial fan mail for being witty and well written.[33]

The first reference to Joy in Lewis's own correspondence is in a letter of 12 September 1952, when he describes her to Michal Williams, Charles Williams's widow, as an 'old & valued pen-friend', asking her to remind Joy to firm up plans with Lewis for an anticipated visit.[34] This highlights Lewis's enthusiasm for such a meeting, contradicting any suggestion that the impetus was all on Joy's side. At that time, Lewis was trying to settle on a title for the latest Narnian story, which would be published as *The Silver Chair* (1953). Lewis evidently sought Joy's views, quoting her as being in favour of *The Wild Waste Lands*, which was proving unpopular with the publisher.[35]

In December 1952 Joy returned to Oxford for an extended visit, staying with Lewis at The Kilns. Since Lewis's housekeeper was ill and had returned home to Ireland, he was forced to do much of the catering himself: 'the can opener is very much in evidence'.[36] During this stay, Joy received a letter from her husband, Bill Gresham, proposing a divorce, which would allow him to marry his lover, Renée Pierce, and thereby leave Joy free to wed again, should she wish to do so. Joy showed the letter to Lewis, who advised her to take up her husband's suggestion and get a divorce.[37]

In November 1953 Joy returned to England, bringing her two sons, David and Douglas, and taking rooms in a flat in London's Belsize Park. Lewis invited them all to spend three days at The Kilns, 17–20 December.[38] Lewis had little experience of young boys and found the Gresham boys (then aged nine and eight) quite exhausting. Although his reports show that he considered the boys to be delightful, he likened the experience to 'surf-bathing, which leaves one breathless and aching'.[39]

There are few surviving letters from Lewis to Joy, so that it is hard to reconstruct the development of their friendship. That it was founded upon a shared love of fantasy fiction is suggested by a long letter Lewis wrote to her on 22 December 1953, describing his reaction to Arthur C. Clarke's *Childhood's End* (1953), which Joy had encouraged him to read. Having recorded his enthusiastic response to the work, along with a list of minor faults, Lewis seeks Joy's opinion: 'And now, what do *you* think? Do you agree that it is AN ABSOLUTE CORKER?'[40] This direct soliciting of Joy's views on the book, about which Lewis himself has such clearly articulated opinions, shows the extent to which he saw her as an intellectual equal.

As well as valuing her critical insights and observations, Lewis evidently respected Joy as a writer, referring to her published works with enthusiasm to his correspondents. In a letter to Dorothy L. Sayers, dated April 1955, Lewis notes that he is rereading Sayers's own *The Man Born to be King*, as he did every Holy Week, and asks if she has tried Joy Davidman's *Smoke on the Mountain*, which he considers 'really good'.[41]

Lewis's relationship with Joy clearly stimulated his creativity. Most significantly, it appears to have been discussions with her that reinvigorated his plans to write a version of the Cupid and Psyche myth that had stalled, and that was published as *Till We Have Faces* in 1956 and dedicated to Joy. Lewis first encountered this story when he read it at Christmas 1916 in the translation by William Adlington, published as *The Story of Cupid and Psyche by Lucius Apuleius* in 1903. In 1917 Lewis discovered the complete works of Apuleius in the Univ library and was enchanted by their 'brooding magic', combined with 'occasional voluptuousness & ridiculous passages'.[42] In May 1922 Lewis records trying to work on a poem titled 'Psyche' in the Oxford Union with no success; in 1923 his head was 'very full of my old idea of a poem on my own version of the Cupid and Psyche story', which he had made two former attempts to write, one in couplets and the other in ballad form.[43] An unfinished draft of a poem in couplets was preserved by Warnie Lewis in *The Lewis Papers* and later published with the title 'The Tale of Psyche Is Unjustly Told'.[44]

In April 1955 Lewis returned to this work and his personal approach to the story, which adopts the somewhat radical position that 'Apuleius got it all wrong'. Joy described their discussions of this book in the following way:

> One night he was lamenting that he couldn't get a good idea for a book. We kicked a few ideas around till one came to life. Then we had another whiskey each and bounced it back and forth between us. The next day, without further planning, he wrote the first chapter! I read it and made some criticisms (feels quite like old times); he did it over and went on with the next.[45]

In a subsequent letter Joy describes her role as that of 'editor-collaborator', facilitating Lewis's writing and offering him advice, which he apparently considered to be 'indispensable'.[46] Responding to Chad Walsh's review of the published work, Joy complains of the way most critics identify the story as an allegory. Joy dismisses such claims, characterizing it instead as 'a romance with touches of parable', a subtle categorization that neatly captures the work's complex generic affiliations.[47]

As well as *Till We Have Faces*, Joy also influenced Lewis's writing of *Reflections on the Psalms* (1958) and *The Four Loves* (1960). She read a manuscript draft of *Surprised by Joy* before its publication in 1955, offering criticisms and comments, as well as typing it up and checking the proofs. Lewis's portrait of the year he spent at Malvern College was sufficient to put Joy off considering it as a possible school for her two sons.[48] Joy also shrewdly noted that, although a 'first-rate job', the book would be something of a disappointment to those looking for personal details.[49]

Lewis's first recorded reference to his proposed marriage to Joy is a cryptic remark in a letter to Arthur Greeves in October 1955.[50] Lewis had spent the first two weeks of September in Ireland with Arthur, during which time he appears to have mentioned his plans to marry Joy. The reason for this was to enable her to secure British citizenship and remain in the UK indefinitely. The couple were married in a civil ceremony at the Oxford Registry Office on 23 April 1956, with Robert Havard and Austin Farrer as witnesses. The Registry Office was at that time situated at 42 St Giles', a listed building that goes back to the 1760s. It is now a dental practice, although its Lewis connection continues to be celebrated with a copy of their marriage certificate on display.

Even after the ceremony, Lewis restricted knowledge of his marriage to a tight inner circle. Writing to Katherine Farrer, who was helping to move Joy's effects into The Kilns, in October 1956, Lewis authorizes her to share their 'innocent little secret' with his friend Colin Hardie and his wife Christian.[51] But the group of people who were admitted to their confidence did not include Tolkien. Reflecting upon his friendship with Lewis in a letter of July 1964, Tolkien described Lewis as his closest friend from 1927 to 1940. But he notes that they saw increasingly less of each other when he 'came under the dominant influence of Charles Williams' and even less following his 'very strange marriage'.[52]

Shortly after their marriage, Joy fell and broke her leg. She was taken to the Wingfield-Morris (now the Nuffield) Orthopaedic Hospital, in Headington, where it was discovered that she had terminal cancer. Lewis continued to keep up his extensive correspondence, but was deeply shaken by the diagnosis. In one letter he describes being 'all embroiled with affairs arising out of a friend's sudden illness, and v. much distressed'.[53] In another he faces up to the facts as the doctors have presented them: 'Joy is in hospital, suffering from cancer. The prospects are 1. A tiny 100th chance of ultimate cure. 2. A reasonable probability of some years more of (tolerable) life. 3. A real danger that she may die in a few months.'[54] But, alongside this apparent stoicism, appear brief glimpses into the turmoil that he was experiencing: 'I can hardly describe to you the state of mind I live in at present – except that all emotion, with me, is periodically drowned in sheer tiredness, deep lakes of stupor.'[55]

By November, Lewis was planning a full Christian marriage at Joy's hospital bed. This second ceremony took place in the hospital's Mayfair Suite on 21 March 1957; it was carried out by Peter Bide, another former pupil of Lewis's, who was an Anglican priest in the Diocese of

Chichester, because the Bishop of Oxford, Dr Harry Carpenter, had refused a licence.

Lewis remained somewhat defensive about the circumstances of his marriage. Writing to Mary Shelburne, an American poet and long-term correspondent of Lewis's, he rejected her labelling of their union as 'mysterious', noting that he had known Joy for a long time before they married. Although conceding that it is impossible to determine exactly when friendship becomes love, he identifies her cancer as a factor in accelerating his decision to marry her: 'You can well understand how illness – the fact that she was facing pain and death and anxiety about the future of her children – would be an *extra* reason for marrying her or a reason for marrying her sooner.'[56]

Lewis refers to this additional motivation in a letter to Dorothy L. Sayers in June 1957, noting how the approach of Thanatos (the Greek personification of death) as a rival focused his mind: 'We soon learn to love what we know we must lose.'[57] In September 1957 he returned to the development of their relationship in a letter to Dom Bede Griffiths, mapping it onto the various kinds of love that he was to consider in detail in *The Four Loves* (1960), which began as a series of recorded talks broadcast in the USA in August 1958: 'It is nice to have arrived at all this by something which began in Agape, proceeded to Philia, then became Pity, and only after that, Eros. As if the highest of these, Agape, had successfully undergone the sweet humiliation of an incarnation.'[58] Joy herself described the process in characteristically different terms:

> All I really care about is having a bit of life with Jack and getting adequately on my feet for it. He has been growing more attached to me steadily – is now, I think, even more madly in love with me than I with him, which is saying plenty – and give dear Georgie Sentman my love and tell him he was wrong about the intellectual Englishman's supposed coldness. The truth about these blokes is that they are like H-bombs; it takes something like an ordinary atom bomb to *start* them off, but when they're started – Whee! See the pretty fireworks! He is mucho hombre, my Jack![59]

Despite the pessimistic prognosis from the doctors, Joy's health improved such that she and Lewis were able to enjoy a belated honeymoon in Ireland in the summer of 1958, staying at the Old Inn in Crawfordsburn; the hotel now carries a blue plaque commemorating this association. Tragically, just when her recovery seemed complete, the cancer returned in December 1959. The couple were able to enjoy a final holiday together with Roger Lancelyn Green and his wife June, visiting the classical sites of Greece in April 1960. Joy died on 13 July 1960 at the Radcliffe Infirmary in Oxford; her funeral took place at the Headington Crematorium on 18 July, the service being conducted by Austin Farrer, who – according to Warnie's report – read poorly because of the strength of emotion. Lewis had a plaque erected with a poem he composed for the occasion:

Here the whole world (stars, water, air
And field, and forest, as they were
Reflected in a single mind)
Like cast off clothes was left behind
In ashes, yet with hope that she,
Re-born from holy poverty,
In lenten lands, hereafter may
Resume them on her Easter Day.

A GRIEF OBSERVED

His letters following Joy's death reveal the huge emotional turmoil Lewis went through, describing his grief as a 'kind of bewilderment, almost a psychological paralysis. A bit like the first moments after being hit by a shell.'[60] The experience also prompted him to question the divine response to a person in urgent need: 'The moments at which you call most desperately and clamorously to God for help are precisely those when you seem to get none.'[61] In being taken back to the experience of fighting in the trenches, Lewis was also reminded of advice his innocent younger self had given Arthur in 1916, when he counselled that the most effective way of cheering oneself up is to write: 'Ink is the great cure for all human ills.'[62] He now put his own advice into practice, pouring out his grief into four empty notebooks he found lying around the house, which would act as a 'safety valve': 'a defence against total collapse'.[63] He later collected together these observations, revising them into a wider reflection on the nature of loss and grief, in *A Grief Observed*, which he wrote during the summer of 1960.[64]

Lewis submitted the manuscript to Faber & Faber under the pseudonym 'Dimidius', or 'Halved'. The work was accepted for publication by the director, T.S. Eliot, despite the earlier animosity between the two men. Relations between them were a good deal more cordial since they had worked together on the Archbishop of Canterbury's commission to revise the Anglican Psalter; in July 1959 Eliot invited Lewis and Joy to dine with him and his wife.[65] For the publication of *A Grief Observed*, Eliot suggested that a more plausible English pseudonym would be a more effective way of putting enquirers off the scent. Lewis replaced it with N.W. Clerk, with the initials standing for 'Nat Whilk', Old English for 'I know not who' (i.e. 'Anon'), under which he had published much of his occasional poetry. Letters that Lewis received following its publication indicate that some of his readers had guessed at his identity, partly because of its style, but also because of its reference to the earlier loss of a close friend, identifiable as Charles Williams. Lewis also responded to letters sent to him via his publisher, although in one case he mistakenly signed off C.S. Clerk, inadvertently giving his correspondent an additional clue to the book's author.[66]

In *A Grief Observed* Lewis notes that, despite a fear that their favourite haunts – a pub and a wood – would be especially painful places to revisit without Joy, it turned out to make no difference. Her absence was no more felt in those places than any other: 'It's not local at all.'[67] As such, Lewis's response to the loss of Joy differs from that registered in the poem 'Scazons', in which he finds himself shedding tears when passing a cottage where he once walked with friends who have since died:

'Out little spear that stabs! I, fool, believed
I had outgrown the local, unique sting,
I had transmuted wholly (I was deceived)
Into Love universal the lov'd thing'.[68]

Although their life together had been rooted in the Oxford locations they frequented, including the Eastgate Hotel where they first met, Lewis's feelings of loss for Joy were not tied to such places but rather transcended them: 'like the sky, spread over everything'.[69]

SIX

SOMERVILLE COLLEGE

Somerville Hall was founded in 1879 for the education of female students, although its first members were not permitted to attend university lectures, use the Bodleian Library or take degrees. The Hall was named after the scientist and campaigner Mary Somerville; in 1894 it was renamed Somerville College as a marker of its academic ambitions.

THE SOCRATIC CLUB

Towards the end of the Michaelmas term of 1941, Monica Shorten, an undergraduate at Somerville College, complained to Stella Aldwinckle, Chaplain to Women Students, about the lack of opportunity to ask elementary questions about the Christian faith in Oxford. Aldwinckle decided to hold a meeting and encouraged Shorten to call any students who felt similarly frustrated to attend. She put a poster up exhorting 'all atheists, agnostics, and those who are disillusioned about religion' to attend an event in the East Junior Common Room at Somerville.

That meeting was the impetus for the founding of the Socratic Club. While Oxford was well supplied with organizations that were explicitly Christian, its aims were to apply the Socratic principle to the pros and cons of Christianity. Each event began with the presentation of a paper, followed by a formal reply by a speaker chosen to represent a contrasting viewpoint, which was intended to spark a lively and engaging discussion. The first meeting was held at Somerville on 26 January 1942 at 8 p.m.; the speaker was Dr R.E. Havard, who addressed the question: 'Won't mankind outgrow Christianity in the face of the advance of Science and of Modern Ideologies?'

As every university society is required to appoint a senior member to oversee the club's activities, Aldwinckle approached C.S. Lewis and asked him to take on the role of president. As a recent convert and former atheist, with a background in philosophy and a reputation as an accomplished lecturer, Lewis was an inspired choice. Lewis served as the club president from its inception in 1942 until his departure for Cambridge twelve years later. During that time, he was the opening speaker at eleven meetings, while making a major contribution to the discussion on many more occasions (PLATE 22).

Socratic meetings were not debates, in which speakers attempt to score points off each other in an effort to win votes. As Aldwinckle herself put it, the aim was to 'follow the argument in good faith and good temper wherever it went'.[1] Despite this, some who attended have described the atmosphere as gladiatorial. On one occasion, following C.E.M. Joad's paper 'On Being Reviewed by Christians', the secretary announced somewhat forcefully that 'Mr C.S. Lewis will now answer Dr. Joad.' Lewis gently corrected her: 'Open the discussion, I think, is the formula.'[2]

Helen Tyrrell, an English student at St Hilda's College during the war, had tutorials with Lewis, covering Spenser, Milton, Malory, Tasso and Walter Scott. In her end-of-term report Lewis described her as 'extremely fertile and nimble in thought', but warned against oversubtlety and overabstraction in her argumentation. In a report on her tutorial partner, Miss P.A. Scadden, Lewis noted that she frequently found herself at a disadvantage in discussion because of Miss Tyrrell's quicker mind.

With her ready intelligence and confidence in discussion, Helen Tyrrell was well qualified to take on the role of secretary of the Socratic Club, holding meetings in a large, sprawling room at St Hilda's, with as many people sitting on the floor as in the immense armchairs. She recalled the bright lamplight inside the room contrasting strongly with the complete blackout outside. Lewis, having hurried across Magdalen Bridge to preside, struck a genial though somewhat impersonal air, with his bright eyes and ruddy cheeks lending him the appearance of a medieval illustration of a fiery seraph.[3]

Although its initial impulse was to cater for female students, the Socratic Club quickly drew in a large number of male undergraduates. Meetings were crowded affairs, with students finding seats where they could on the floor, perched on window ledges, even under a piano. For George Watson, the attraction was the prospect of a roaring fire during a particularly cold winter, although he came to greatly enjoy Lewis's 'politely merciless' performances, labelling him 'a Socrates with a sense of fun'.[4] Particularly memorable were Lewis's famous rejoinders, such as his response to a logical-positivist student who attempted to undermine Lewis's argument by questioning the entire basis for rational argument: 'How can you prove anything? How can you prove there isn't a blue cow sitting on that piano.' Lewis replied calmly: 'Well, in what sense *blue*?'[5]

Accounts of the meetings were kept by the secretary in the club minute book. They were signed off by the president, who checked them over carefully and added his own comments. The account of one evening's discussion records that 'one member explained fully the existentialist views of assent'; Lewis circled the word 'fully' and added in the margin 'is it possible? C.S.L.'

Lewis also cast his keen eye over copies of the published *Digest*. In issue number 2 there is an account of Lewis's discussion with Professor H.A. Hodges on the subject of 'Philosophy To-day'. In the copy now held in the Magdalen College library, Professor Hodges' reporting of Lewis's claims has been edited, with the words 'as Mr. Lewis says' crossed out in pencil – evidently Lewis did not concur with this statement of his position.

Some of Lewis's most famous theological essays, such as '"Bulverism", or the Foundation of 20th-Century Thought' and 'Is Theology Poetry?', began their lives as papers delivered at meetings of the Socratic Club. Other papers were intended to respond to those presented by visiting speakers. In May 1946 he replied to Professor H.H. Price's 'Grounds of Modern Agnosticism' with his own 'Religion without Dogma'.

Lewis's renowned martial approach to debate is apparent from the minutes of ensuing discussions. Following an account of Father Gerald Vann's address on the topic 'Is Christian Sex-Morality out of date?', the minutes note that 'Mr Lewis opened the discussion in which Father Vann's conception of the moral law was vigorously attacked.' But Lewis was happy to receive as well as dish out criticism. On 15 October 1945 Lewis presented a paper on 'The Nature of Reason' to a packed room. A brave member of the audience objected that Lewis had adopted too safe a position, refusing rational proofs of unreason as well as irrational. The secretary notes of the objection: 'This pleased rather than dismayed Mr. Lewis.'

ELIZABETH ANSCOMBE

The most famous such encounter is undoubtedly the meeting of the Socratic Club on 2 February 1948, where the speaker was Elizabeth Anscombe. Anscombe (1919–2001) was a research fellow at Somerville College who had been a pupil of Ludwig Wittgenstein at Cambridge University, to which she returned in 1970 as Professor of Philosophy. Anscombe's paper, 'A Reply to Mr. C.S. Lewis's Argument That Naturalism is Self-Refuting',[6] was a critique of the third chapter of Lewis's book *Miracles* (1947), in which Lewis argued that, if Nature works entirely by blind chance, then the arguments proposed by Naturalists must also be the accidental by-products of such random events. As such, there is no reason to prefer one argument over any other: 'We may in fact state it as a rule that *no thought is valid if it can be fully explained as the result of irrational causes*.'[7]

The secretary's account of the resulting discussion notes that the opening of the debate was confined to the two speakers, who sought to clarify their positions and key terms. Lewis finally conceded that his use of the word 'valid' was unfortunate; the secretary concluded that 'Mr. Lewis would have to turn his argument into a rigorous, analytic one, if his notion of "validity" as the effect of causes were to stand the test of all the questions put to him.'[8]

Lewis continued to consider these questions long after the debate itself. He published a note in number 4 of the *Socratic Digest*, in which he formally retracted his use of the word 'valid' and instead proposed 'veridical', 'verific' or 'veriferous'.[9] When a publisher proposed to issue a paperback edition of *Miracles* in 1960, Lewis seized the opportunity to rewrite the chapter in light of Anscombe's critique.

This was not the first occasion on which a reader had taken issue with Lewis's argument about the self-refuting nature of Naturalism. Lewis had made a similar claim in his paper 'Is Theology Poetry?', read to the Socratic Club in November 1944. Following the paper's publication, an anonymous letter appeared in the *Oxford Magazine*, questioning Lewis's total rejection of the scientific account of the world.[10] Lewis responded to the writer's depiction of him as either a 'heresiarch' or a 'pioneer' by pointing out that he himself cannot claim to have invented this 'venerable philosophical chestnut', and referring readers to a similar statement in J.B.S. Haldane's *Possible Worlds* (1927).[11]

Friends and later biographers have suggested that Lewis was crushed by his defeat in this debate, which was considered to have undermined a central plank of his Christian faith. Derek Brewer, who attended an informal dinner with Lewis, Dyson and several of his fellow students a couple of days later, recalled Lewis's low mood, writing in his diary:

> He was obviously deeply disturbed by his encounter last Monday with Miss Anscombe, who had disproved some of the central theory of his philosophy about Christianity. I felt quite painfully for him. Dyson said – very well – that now he had lost everything and was come to the foot of the Cross – spoken with great sympathy.[12]

That Lewis was bruised following his disputation with Elizabeth Anscombe is apparent from a letter of June 1950 to Stella Aldwinckle, proposing speakers and topics for the following term's Socratic Club.

Of his eight suggested candidates, Lewis pushed strongly for 'Why I believe in God' by Miss Anscombe, adding that, while she was quite right to refute what she considers poor theistic arguments, she should be prepared to find stronger ones to put in their place: 'having obliterated me as an Apologist ought she not to *succeed* me?'[13]

However, his wish to have Anscombe return to the Socratic Club suggests a desire to engage further with her arguments, rather than to shy away from them. Indeed, Anscombe's own account of the debate portrayed it as a sober discussion of her criticisms, which Lewis clearly thought were justified. Anscombe considered his later rewriting of the chapter to take account of her critique evidence of Lewis's honesty and seriousness. She rejected claims that the encounter had been deeply traumatic for him, suggesting that such accounts, by those who had no interest in the arguments or subject matter, were evidence of projection – the displacement of one's own feelings onto another.[14]

That Lewis was content to engage his opponents in debate is also apparent from the invitation extended to J.B.S. Haldane. Elizabeth Anscombe was a devout Catholic, whose objections to Lewis's arguments were never intended to undermine his claims for Christianity. Haldane, by contrast, was an atheist who had already attacked Lewis's writings in print. A large crowd gathered to hear him deliver his paper, simply titled 'Atheism', and to witness the two men engage in debate. However, having responded to the opening of the discussion by Ian Crombie, Philosophy tutor at Wadham College, Haldane promptly left. According to the account in the Socratic Club minute book: 'The speaker unfortunately had to leave early and ended with an impressive running panegyric of atheism of which the last word was perfectly timed to coincide with his exit.'[15]

DOROTHY L. SAYERS

Dorothy L. Sayers was born in the Headmaster's House of Christ Church Cathedral School on Brewer Lane, Oxford, in 1893. In 1912 she won a scholarship to read Modern Languages at Somerville

College. Sayers was a brilliant student and received First-class Honours, although she was not awarded a degree at the time as women were not permitted to graduate until 1920. In her novel *Gaudy Night* (1935), detective writer Harriet Vane returns to her alma mater Shrewsbury College for a gaudy dinner – one held in honour of former students – but finds herself at the centre of a poison-pen campaign. Although the fictional Shrewsbury College is located on Jowett Walk, it was clearly based upon Somerville College.

C.S. Lewis and Dorothy L. Sayers enjoyed a long friendship that began with a fan letter, when Sayers wrote to Lewis praising his *Screwtape Letters*, especially its handling of love and marriage. Lewis replied in kind in March 1943, congratulating her on the publication of *Six Other Deadly Sins*, which he found to be, within its limits, perfect: 'There is nothing one would wish added or removed or altered.'[16] Sayers responded by sending an advance copy of *The Man Born to be King*, accompanied by a letter, part of which is the work of a devil called Sluckdrib, detailing the unfortunate effects of certain religious plays on atheists, but pleased with the effect of their success on the author's character:

> I have already had the honour to report intellectual and spiritual pride, vainglory, self-opinionated dogmatism, irreverence, blasphemous frivolity, frequentation of the company of theatricals, captiousness, impatience of correction, polemical fury, shortness of temper, neglect of domestic affairs, lack of charity, egotism, nostalgia for secular occupations, and a growing tendency to consider the Bible as literature.[17]

In his reply, Lewis noted that the letter makes no reference to sloth, or to the real threat of getting involved in such controversies: the danger to one's own faith. This is not because of the arguments posed by the devil, but rather those devised by oneself: 'Never do I find a doctrine less credible than when I have just invented and delivered a telling argument in its defence.'[18]

Having got to know Sayers through these initial lively exchanges, Lewis was greatly attracted by 'the extraordinary zest and edge of her conversation'.[19] The two continued to swap letters detailing their various book projects. While Sayers was working on her translation of Dante's *Divine Comedy*, Lewis was writing *The Great Divorce* (1945), which is itself a reworking of Dante's magnum opus. Lewis read Sayers's translation very carefully, sending her his observations and comments (both positive and less so); he wrote to her following its publication to congratulate her on a 'stunning work'. 'The real test is this, that however I set out with the idea of attending to your translation, before I've read a page I've forgotten all about you and am thinking only of Dante, and two pages later I've forgotten about Dante and am thinking only about Hell.'[20] This was apparently intended to be a compliment. Lewis was less enamoured with the Lord Peter Wimsey novels, privately admitting that he didn't enjoy *Gaudy Night* at all, but noting that, since he had no interest in detective fiction, this proved nothing.[21]

Having read the first *Socratic Digest*, Sayers travelled to Oxford to attend one of the society's meetings. She was so impressed that she decided to found a London equivalent. An advertisement for the London Socratic Club, to be launched in October 1944 under her presidency, was placed in the second issue of the *Digest*. When this failed to get off the ground, Sayers became a communicating member of the Oxford Socratic Club; on 3 June 1954 she presented a paper on the subject of 'Poetry, Language and Ambiguity', with Austin Farrer as the respondent.

Lewis's long friendship with Dorothy L. Sayers contradicts the suggestion that he sought out only members of his own sex. Oxford University was a male-dominated environment in Lewis's day, so that it is hardly surprising that there were no female members of the Inklings. But it is clear from their correspondence that Lewis considered Sayers to be an intellectual equal, whose insights and writings he valued highly.

Similarly, his willingness to support the Socratic Club from its inception as a forum for female students wishing to pursue matters of belief testifies to a concern for the education of women in the Christian faith. It has also not been recognized how many students Lewis taught from the women's colleges. In 1941 Joan O'Hare and another St Hilda's student – women were taught in pairs by male tutors – were sent to Magdalen to study Milton with Lewis. They were so intimidated by the prospect that they made a pact to be sparing in their criticism of each other's work; when Joan's tutorial partner broke the agreement, savaging her essay on Milton's prose, Lewis weighed in in her defence.

Joan recalled being struck by the degree to which her termly report was perceptive of her personality – much more so than any other in her three years at Oxford. She must be referring to the report of Hilary term, in which Lewis attributes a perceived flatness to her essays to excessive diffidence and a need of encouragement. It certainly cannot be the report on the previous term's efforts, which simply states: 'Has done a satisfactory term's work.'

Rosamund Rieu and Patricia Thomson, of St Hugh's College, attended tutorials with Lewis in 1942. Both recall the happy mixture of politeness and rigour; Lewis stood for no nonsense and subjected their opinions to the same stern criticism that he applied to his male students. But, far from browbeating them into accepting his views, Lewis encouraged them to formulate their own; Miss Thomson described the process as a weekly spring-cleaning of the mind. Lewis was clearly impressed by both women; his report on Miss Rieu described her as 'Quite definitely a First Class pupil', while Miss Thomson, whose work showed 'considerable penetration', 'ought to have a good chance of a First'.[22] Another St Hugh's student, Mary Gerken, who had tutorials on Spenser with Lewis in Trinity term 1944, was 'clear-headed and diligent', although Lewis added a somewhat backhanded compliment about her readiness to profit from her own mistakes. Lewis recognized the difficulty he experienced in drawing out students who were tentative and diffident in tutorials; he referred to this in a report on Miss Beese of St Hugh's College in Hilary term 1930, noting that she might have got more out of the discussion if she had knitted or smoked, thereby creating a less intense atmosphere – an unusual piece of advice to find in a tutorial report.[23]

It wasn't just female students that Lewis taught who impressed him. Reading an examination essay submitted by Muriel Bentley, an undergraduate of Somerville College, Lewis came across an observation concerning the infernal debate in Book II of *Paradise Lost* which helped him to unlock a particular puzzle about the text that he had failed to resolve after countless rereadings; he acknowledged the importance of her ('unhappily not yet printed') remark in chapter 14 of *A Preface to Paradise Lost*.[24] Miss Bentley graduated with a First-class degree in 1941 and went on to a successful teaching career, including five years at an Anglican theological college in the Solomon Islands; her account of this period of her life was published as *Married to Melanesia* (1974) under her married name Muriel Jones.

SEVEN

ST MARY'S PASSAGE

A specific set of architectural features are often claimed to have been the inspiration behind *The Lion, the Witch and the Wardrobe*. These can be found on St Mary's Passage, a narrow thoroughfare off the High Street that runs between Brasenose College and the University Church of St Mary the Virgin. Here stands a seventeenth-century timber-framed house, formerly the City Arms pub and now part of Brasenose, with a porch that is decorated with two gilded fauns (PLATE 27). Carved into the centre of the wooden door appears to be an image of a lion's head. The Narnian connections are increased by the presence of a Victorian cast-iron lamp post, recalling the one that greets Lucy when she first steps into Narnia, in an area known as Lantern Waste.

The story that is repeatedly recycled by Oxford City tour guides is that, one freezing winter's night, Lewis exited the University Church via the side door onto St Mary's Passage and found himself confronted by the juxtaposed images of faun, lion and lamp post, all covered in a blanket of white snow. This, it is claimed, was the moment that the central features of the first Narnian story came together in Lewis's mind, prompting the writing of one of the best-known children's stories of all time.

However, Lewis's own account of the tale's genesis is very different, pouring cold water on this theory. He explained that in *The Lion, the*

Witch and the Wardrobe he drew upon pictures which he started seeing in his imagination decades before he sat down to write the story. The initial prompt was an image of a faun carrying an umbrella and parcels in a snowy wood, which had been in his head since he was about sixteen years old. 'Then one day, when I was about forty, I said to myself: "Let's try to make a story about it".' Having embarked upon this exercise, Lewis had little sense of how the story would unfold, until – prompted by a series of dreams about lions – Aslan came bounding in and 'pulled the whole story together'.[1]

Although Lewis remained unsure what prompted him to sit down and write the book when he did, it seems likely that it was encouraged by the arrival of the group of schoolgirls who were evacuated from London to The Kilns in 1939. The positive impact their arrival had on Lewis is highlighted by his remarks in a letter to Sister Penelope the following month: 'I am a bachelor and never appreciated children till the war brought them to me.'[2] Since the story begins with four children being evacuated to the home of a professor in the countryside to escape the London bombing, this seems a plausible stimulus (PLATE 17). Although the book was not published until 1950, the initial urge to write a children's novel appears to date back to at least 1948, when he told Chad Walsh of his plan to write a book for children 'in the tradition of E. Nesbit', whose fantasy stories had entertained him as a child.[3]

The landscape of Narnia itself has more in common with Lewis's native Ireland and its spectacular scenery than that of his adopted home of Oxford. Looking back on his childhood in *Surprised by Joy*, Lewis recalls the longing he experienced when gazing from his nursery window to the Castlereagh Hills on the horizon. Although not very far away, they were to him – as a child – quite unattainable and thus an early induction into the experience of unsatisfied desire that is central to his conception of Joy. That same sense of yearning is expressed by Bree, the talking horse in *The Horse and His Boy*, when he describes his longing for his homeland of Narnia to Shasta:

> 'The happy land of Narnia – Narnia of the heathery mountains and the thymy downs, Narnia of the many rivers, the plashing glens, the mossy caverns and the deep forests ringing with the hammers of the Dwarfs. Oh the sweet air of Narnia! An hour's life there is better than a thousand years in Calormen.' It ended with a whinny that sounded very like a sigh.[4]

The landscape described here, with its mountains, rivers, forests, downs and glens, recalls Irish locations such as the glens of Country Antrim and the Mourne mountains in the north, with their generous covering of wild thyme and heather.

Lewis's love of the countryside of County Down is commemorated in a plaque on a bench in the town of Bangor, which occupies one of his favourite vantage points, overlooking Belfast Lough, with an inscription quoting his view that 'Heaven is Oxford lifted and placed in the middle of County Down.' The idea of relocating Oxford to Ireland clearly appealed to Lewis; elsewhere he suggested taking up the city and placing it between the mountains of Donegal.[5]

Lewis's home city of Belfast boasts a rival claim to the doorway in St Mary's Passage as the source of inspiration for Aslan. On 29 January 1899 Lewis was baptised at St Mark's Church, Dundela, by his maternal grandfather, Thomas Hamilton, who was the first rector of the parish until his retirement in 1900; Lewis was confirmed at St Mark's on 6 December 1914. Hamilton lived at the church rectory, the front door of which has a doorknob shaped like a lion's head (PLATE 28). This doorknob would have been head height for the young Lewis, so that he would have stared directly into the lion's eyes while waiting for the door to be opened: some have speculated that the knob is the inspiration for Aslan.

The Lewis brothers maintained an affection for the church throughout their lives. Following their father's death in 1929, they donated a stained-glass window, designed by Irish artist Michael Healy, to the church in their parents' memory. The windows depict the saints Luke, James and Mark – the last being the patron saint of the church. The traditional symbol of St Mark is the lion, an association which might have further linked the church with lions in Lewis's fertile imagination.

But, while the chronicles of Narnia may have allowed Lewis's imagination to transport him back to the countryside of Ulster, they are deeply immersed in the academic world of Oxford. This chapter began with a door that appears to show two fauns accompanied by a carving of a lion's head, claimed by some to be the inspiration for the first Narnian tale. But this misleading story has one further significant objection: the carving is not of a lion at all, but rather depicts a green man, whose face is surrounded by foliage, resembling a lion's mane. The green man is a figure of English folklore, a kind of wild man of the woods, representing seasonal fertility and rebirth.

While this identification further undermines the door's Narnian pedigree, the conjunction of a faun and a green man points towards an alternative Narnian association, albeit one more likely to have been suggested by medieval literary sources than an Oxford doorway. In *The Lion, the Witch and the Wardrobe* the various monstrous creatures that gather at the Stone Table are described as follows:

> Ogres with monstrous teeth, and wolves, and bull-headed men; spirits of evil trees and poisonous plants; and other creatures whom I won't describe because if I did the grown-ups would probably not let you read this book – Cruels and Hags and Incubuses, Wraiths, Horrors, Efreets, Sprites, Orknies, Wooses, and Ettins.[6]

This list draws on an eclectic set of mythical and legendary creatures, reflecting the variety of literary sources upon which Lewis drew in the Narnian chronicles. Efreets are mythological Islamic demons, which would have been well known to Lewis from his reading of the *Thousand and One Nights*. Orknies go back to the Old English *orcneas*, 'evil spirits', from Old English *orc* 'demon' – as found in the epic poem *Beowulf*. *Ettins* are giants, from Old English *eoten*, also found in the name of Ettinsmoor, the land of the giants across which Puddleglum, Scrubb and Pole must pass in *The Silver Chair*. *Wooses* are wild men of the wood (from Old English *wudu-wasa*), familiar to readers of medieval literature from their appearance in the fourteenth-century alliterative poem *Sir Gawain and the Green Knight*, where they feature among the ferocious creatures that the hero must overcome during his lengthy journey from Camelot to the Green Chapel, where he is destined to receive a blow from the Green Knight's axe. During this arduous and perilous journey, we are told that Sir Gawain battled with a range of vicious beasts, including *wodwos*: a transitional form between Old English *wudu-wasa* and Lewis's *woose*:

> *Sumwhyle wyth wormez he werrez, and with wolues als,*
> *Sumwhyle wyth wodwos, þat woned in þe knarrez,*
> *Boþe wyth bullez and berez, and borez oþerquyle,*
> *And etaynez, þat hym anelede of þe heȝe felle*
>
> Sometimes with dragons he struggles, and with wolves also,
> Sometimes with wild men, that lived in the woods,
> Both with bulls and bears and boars at other times,
> And giants, that pursued him from the high fells[7]

This assortment of real and mythical beasts encountered by Sir Gawain bears a number of correspondences with the motley crew gathered at the Stone Table. As well as the *bullez* 'bulls', *wolues* 'wolves' and *wodwos*, there are *etaynez* 'giants' – the origin of the *ettins* that appear in Lewis's story.

Sir Gawain and the Green Knight is a core text in the Middle English literary canon, with which Oxford English students have been doing battle from Lewis's time to the present day. Written by an anonymous poet based in the north-west of England, the poem is constructed using an alliterative metre that looks back to Old English verse. With its provincial dialect, and its Old English poetic vocabulary, the poem presents a linguistic challenge for modern readers, who are more used to the London dialect and rhyming couplets of the Gawain-poet's better-known contemporary Geoffrey Chaucer.

As both student and teacher, Lewis investigated the language of *Sir Gawain and the Green Knight* in some detail, as is apparent from the dense series of annotations found in the margins of his copy of the edition which is now held by the Bodleian Library. As well as adding learned glosses of its technical vocabulary, and cross references to other literary works, Lewis contributed small pictures illustrating some of the key images in the poem and labelled them using the correct Middle English terms: Sir Gawain's armour, the Green Knight's axe and Bertilak's castle (see PLATE 16).

These connections remind us that, while Lewis's imagination may have been influenced by the people he met and the places in which he lived and worked, the fictional creatures and locations that he encountered in his extensive reading were far more influential.

EIGHT

CAMBRIDGE

By the early 1950s Lewis had been a tutorial fellow at Magdalen College for almost thirty years, and the heavy demands of the tutorial system were beginning to take their toll. Prospects for advancement were few. In 1945 Tolkien had been elected to one of two chairs of English Language and Literature at Merton College; but his plan to have Lewis installed in the other was never fulfilled. When the chair fell vacant in 1947 Tolkien supported Lewis's candidacy but also that of Lord David Cecil. In the end the post was offered to Lewis's former tutor F.P. Wilson, with Lord David Cecil being elected to the Goldsmiths' Professorship of English Literature in 1948.

Lewis lacked the ambition and desire to engage in the politicking that such advancement required. When Percy Simpson vacated the Goldsmiths' chair in the 1930s, Warnie hoped that it would go to Lewis, but acknowledged that his brother would not stand in the way of another candidate who needed the job more.[1] Having been invited to Birmingham University in 1934 to discuss a professorial vacancy, Lewis determined not to be considered, instead making the case for his friend Hugo Dyson.[2] In Oxford, it appears that Lewis's commitment to what he himself called 'hot-gospelling', both the method and manner of his apologetics, which drew verbal abuse and ostracism from some colleagues, combined with his self-confessed incompetence as an administrator, had left his colleagues uneasy about his suitability for such a prominent position in the English Faculty.[3]

A further blow came in 1951 when Lewis was proposed as a candidate for the Professorship of Poetry, a position that was founded in 1708 with a bequest from a Berkshire landowner who wished to promote the study of poetry in the university. Election to the chair is by members of the university's Convocation, which consists of all former students and members of Congregation, the body of university teachers. Since until recently voting had to take place in person, the actual number of voters was considerably smaller than those eligible.

During the five-year term of office, the holder must deliver one public lecture each term, as well as an oration at the honorary degree ceremony every other year. In Lewis's day, the lectures were delivered in the Divinity School, part of the Bodleian Library, which dates to the fifteenth century. Lewis first set foot in the room when attending Adam Fox's lecture as Professor of Poetry in November 1939; he was enchanted by it, describing it as 'simply the most beautiful room in Oxford or perhaps in England', singling out the way its stone roof, with vaulting in the perpendicular style, is set off by the black, unpolished oak from which the benches and railings are carved. The lecture itself was less impressive; Lewis considered it 'good but not capital'.[4]

Elections to the post and a list of nominations are published in the *Oxford University Gazette*. Lewis's candidacy was supported by an impressive group of nominators; while many of these were Lewis's close friends, including J.R.R. Tolkien, Hugo Dyson and F.P. Wilson, others included the master of Pembroke College, the provost of The Queen's College, the rector of Exeter College and the principal of St Hilda's College. His opponent was Cecil Day Lewis, who later became Poet Laureate, whose list of supporters exceeded that of Lewis, although it included fewer college heads.[5] Hugo Dyson, who toured the college common rooms canvassing on Lewis's behalf, was not optimistic of the outcome: 'If they offer you sherry, you're done, they won't vote for you: I had lots of sherry.'[6] The election was held on 8 February

1951, with voting taking place between 9.30 and 10.00 a.m., 1.45 to 2.15 and 3.30 to 4.00 p.m. An announcement in the *University Gazette* records the outcome of the contest: 'for Mr. C. Day-Lewis 194; for Mr. C.S. Lewis 173.[7]

According to Warnie, Lewis's supporters were much more disappointed than he was; Tolkien recalled meeting Lewis in the Eagle and Child shortly afterwards and being instructed to fill his glass and stop looking so glum: 'The only distressing thing about this affair is that my friends seem to be upset.'[8]

Lewis consoled himself with the belief that the votes against him reflected an atheist-communist conspiracy to keep a practising Christian from occupying the chair. This view received some support from Dyson's report of a conversation with one don who refused to vote for the author of *The Screwtape Letters*.[9] Lewis's chances of securing the post had been dealt a blow by the withdrawal of a third candidate, Edmund Blunden, who might have split the vote of those who felt the post should be held by a practising poet rather than a critic.

Lewis had also begun to become disillusioned with his Magdalen colleagues, and their propensity for intrigue, mutual back-scratching and lying. As early as 1928 he described the college as a 'cesspool', a 'stinking puddle' inhabited by 'cunning, desperately ambitious, false friends, nodders in corners, tippers of the wink: setters of traps and solicitors of confidence'.[10] Andrew Hegarty has suggested that Lewis's lecture 'The Inner Ring', delivered to an audience of students at King's College London in 1944, warning of the corrupting influence of the desire to be part of the 'in-crowd', drew directly on two decades of dealing with the philosopher Harry Weldon and his circle – whom Lewis referred to as the '*diabolus ipse* and the *succubi*' (the devil himself and the demons)'.[11]

Lewis's satire of college politics in the Bracton College of *That Hideous Strength* (1945) probably owes something to this period of disenchantment. The manner in which members of the college's inner circle, or 'Progressive Element', plot to sell off Bragdon Wood to the N.I.C.E. (the National Institute of Co-ordinated Experiments) is a masterclass in underhand manipulation of a college meeting (including timetabling the discussion under item 15 on the agenda at the end of a full day's debate). To make matters even more pressing, should Bracton not take up this opportunity, the Institute would undoubtedly go to Cambridge. The young Sociology don Mark Studdock observes that such discussions would initially have been lively debates between rival claims of sentiment and progress, but that such traditions have since been abandoned. When the older contingent of the fellowship, or 'Die-hards', come to realize what is happening, it is too late, and they are made to appear ineffective and out of touch:

> Jewel had been already an old man in the days before the first war when old men were treated with kindness, and he had never succeeded in getting used to the modern world. For a moment as he stood with his head thrust forward, people thought he was going to reply. Then quite suddenly he spread out his hands with a gesture of helplessness, shrunk back, and began laboriously to resume his chair.[12]

Lewis felt himself similarly out of touch and out of sympathy with his fellow fellows, but, with no chair to fall back on, he was unable to move college or find relief from the burden of undergraduate tutorials.

However, in 1954 an alternative escape route was offered by an unlikely source in Oxford's great rival: Cambridge University. Having seen Lewis being passed over for the Merton chair, Cambridge spotted an opportunity, creating a new post with a remit that spoke precisely to Lewis's expertise: a Professorship of Medieval and Renaissance English. Given his wide-ranging interests in both periods, and the recent publication of his magisterial survey of the sixteenth century, *The Oxford History of English Literature*, or 'O-HEL', as Lewis referred to a work on which he had slaved for decades, Lewis was eminently suited to such a position.

Where for many scholars the two periods are seen as rigidly separated, Lewis was sceptical of such a division. In Cambridge's Lent term of 1939, he gave a series of lectures entitled 'Prolegomena to Renaissance Literature', at the invitation of H.S. Bennett, a senior figure in the Cambridge English Faculty, who was a member of the appointing committee. In a letter to A.K. Hamilton Jenkin, Lewis explained that the lectures were an opportunity to set out his discovery that 'the Renaissance never occurred', asking whether, given this, he should continue to use the term:

> Do you think it is reasonable to call the lecture 'The Renaissance' under the circumstances? 'Absence of the Renaissance' sounds so odd, and 'What was happening while the Renaissance was not taking place' is inaccurate because, of course, if the Renaissance *never* occurred, then all times were times at which it did not occur, and therefore everything that ever happened happened 'while the Renaissance was not taking place'.[13]

Nevertheless, Lewis's initial reaction to the approach was to politely rebuff Cambridge's overtures, since he considered the idea of uprooting the family at The Kilns an impossibility. The electors were somewhat surprised to receive a response in which his primary reason for declining was an unwillingness to part with his 'general factotum', Fred Paxford.

Cambridge was undeterred and wrote again to Lewis, giving him a fortnight to think over his response. He, however, replied at once, citing again his 'peculiar domestic set-up', combined with his brother's drinking – which he euphemistically referred to as 'psychological health' – which would be impossible to transport to Cambridge. In the meantime, one of the external members of the electoral panel, Lewis's old friend J.R.R. Tolkien, called on Lewis, explaining that it would be possible for him to live in college accommodation in Cambridge during the week and return to The Kilns at weekends. The result of this conversation was that Lewis changed his mind and wrote to the chair of the appointment panel to accept the post. But, in the meantime, Cambridge had moved on and offered the chair to their second-choice candidate, Helen Gardner, Fellow and Tutor in English at St Hilda's College. After learning that Lewis was now minded to accept the position, Gardner turned it down, leaving the university free to offer it to Lewis, who quickly accepted.[14]

For Lewis, the benefits of the chair were first and foremost practical. Writing to many of his familiar correspondents to inform them of his forthcoming move, Lewis repeatedly pointed out the irony that the professorship would mean less work for more money. The new position would see his salary more than treble, and would free him from the grind of reading student essays and holding tutorials. In addition to his Magdalen tutorial stint, Lewis took students from Univ until 1946 and served as lecturer in residence at New College from 1929 to 1934. For Lewis, a typical week would comprise around twenty-four hours of tutorials; the standard stint for a college tutor today is eight hours. The potential tedium of a tutorial is captured by Dr Dimble's response to an especially dull student ringing his bell in *That Hideous Strength*: 'I must go to the study, and listen to an essay on Swift beginning, "Swift was born." Must try to keep my mind on it, too, which won't be easy.' That Lewis had grown tired of the undergraduate essay is suggested by a comment in a letter, where he notes that, while the prospect of change is causing him some anxiety, '29 years of pupils' essays is enough, bless 'em'.[15] Several years into the job, he noted to Arthur Greeves how much he was enjoying the new leisure time it afforded him: 'I've never been so under-worked since I first went to school.'[16]

Lewis's earliest visit to Cambridge was for the Martlets joint meeting with Pembroke College in 1920, at which he read a paper on narrative poetry. In a letter to his father, Lewis recorded his initial impressions of the city: 'Some things – such as King's College Chapel, in which I was prepared to be disappointed – are indeed beautiful beyond hope or belief: several little quadrangles I remember, with tiled gables, sun dials and tall chimnies like Tudor houses, were charming.' Visitors to both university cities inevitably find themselves comparing their respective merits. Lewis summarizes the differences in the following way: 'Oxford is more magnificent, Cambridge perhaps more intriguing.'[17]

Lewis particularly appreciated the sense of being in a small county town. He celebrated the absence of a Lord Nuffield, whose Morris Motors car factory, in the suburb of Cowley, Lewis blamed for the industrialization of Oxford.[18] In 1935 Lewis complained to Arthur Greeves about the expansion of the Morris factory and the invasion of his local countryside: 'Where will it end? If we live to be old there will hardly be any real country left in the South of England.'[19]

By 1927 Lewis was making an annual trip to Cambridge to attend exam boards, which required him to spend a week in the city. Despite the long hours occupied by meetings, Lewis found time to explore the city and enjoy its enchanting setting. He visited King's College Chapel, walked the Backs, and bathed in the river Cam, where he gazed up at 'a pearl-coloured sky simmering with summer river haze from morning till twilight'.[20]

In 1944 he returned to Cambridge to lecture to the Royal Air Force Chaplain's School. The title of the lecture, 'Linguistic Analysis of Pauline Soteriology', does not sound like an instant crowd-pleaser, and the audience took some time to warm to the speaker. According to the commandant, Charles Gilmore, 'a few people shifted uneasily, a future bishop surreptitiously filled in a clue in "The Times" crossword.' But, once Lewis 'struck fire' with an 'intolerable phrase' about prostitutes and pawnbrokers being 'Pardoned in Heaven, the first by the throne', the audience came alive and discussion went on for the remainder of the morning.[21] By a quirk of fate, the RAF School was at that time stationed at Magdalene College, the institution which Lewis was to make his new home ten years later.

MAGDALENE COLLEGE

According to the Oxford University joint appointment scheme, most university positions are advertised with a college affiliation. In Cambridge the successful candidate for a university post is left to search for a college association rather than inheriting one. Since this was a new chair, there was no precedent to draw upon; nor did Lewis have a connection with any particular college. In his letter of appointment, the university's vice chancellor, Sir Henry Willink, encouraged Lewis to write to the master of Magdalene to enquire about the possibility of becoming affiliated with that college. Since Willink was also the master of Magdalene, this was a pretty clear steer that such an application would meet with a positive response. Lewis reacted to this heavy hint by applying to the master, noting that he did so at the suggestion of the vice chancellor, 'with whom, in obedience to the Delphic precept, you are no doubt intimately acquainted'.[22] In the letter Lewis explained that he would particularly like to become a fellow of Magdalene since it would enable him to remain under the same patroness: 'Why should one trouble the celestial civil service with unnecessary change?'

Lewis was very content with his new collegiate home. He thought its architecture beautiful, describing it as a 'perfect little gem' (PLATE 24). He was especially taken with its diminutive size, compared to its more austere and imposing Oxonian counterpart: 'After the old Magdalen it is so small that I feel I'd like to take it to bed with me or have it swimming in my bath!' But Lewis was most struck by the attitude and character of his new colleagues and the general atmosphere, which he characterized as 'Much more old-fashioned and less hard-boiled than Magdalen Oxford.'[23] Despite his sense of the coldness of his former colleagues, not all were glad to see the back of Lewis. According to K.B. McFarlane, Lewis's removal to Cambridge prompted all the 'good men' of Magdalen to go into mourning, although the 'ruling clique' was delighted at this turn of events.[24]

Another reason why Lewis found Magdalene an especially congenial environment is because many of his colleagues were Christians; this prompted him to label it Magdalene 'the penitent' and his former Oxford college 'the impenitent'. The gentle, pious and conservative outlook of his fellow dons led Lewis to suggest that, having been the 'fogey' and 'old woman' of Magdalen Oxford, he may become the 'enfant terrible' of Magdalene Cambridge.[25] Where Lewis did encounter atheists in Cambridge, he found them more militant and more engaged with matters of belief than their Oxonian counterparts, who were 'no more on their toes about it than about their disbelief in leprechauns or flying saucers'.[26] Lewis's positivity towards his new home prompted Warnie to suggest that his brother had taken a wrong turning when arriving at Waterloo back in 1917; instead of travelling to Paddington, en route to Oxford, he should have driven to Liverpool Street Station and thereby gone to Cambridge.

Lewis's college rooms were in the North Range of the fifteenth-century First Court, on the second floor of Staircase 3, above the Parlour and the Old Library.[27] In Oxford, Lewis's Magdalen rooms were famed for their spartan and frugal furnishings, and his Cambridge set was no different. A.C. Spearing, who was assigned Lewis as his doctoral 'supervisor' (the quotation marks are Lewis's and reflect his reservations about his suitability to such a role), recalls how Lewis made no efforts to decorate his enviable rooms,[28] as did Richard W. Ladborough, who attributed their plainness to his treating this attractive space as 'merely a laboratory for his work and his writings'.[29] The only desideratum he stated when applying for a room was book-shelving: 'Inches of bookshelf space is the important factor.'[30]

George Watson recalled entering Lewis's spartan surroundings and being confronted by an ancient battered bathtub standing in the middle of a tiny hallway. The meeting was purportedly an interview for a lectureship in the English Faculty; Watson was somewhat surprised to be offered the position, since in the course of the conversation Lewis made no reference to the post or his application at all.[31]

Lewis viewed the transition to Cambridge as a major uprooting, likening the initial process of moving to 'the preliminary agonies of casting one shell and growing another'.[32] According to Joy, Lewis suffered the anxieties of a small boy starting at a new school – an experience that was particularly unhappy for Lewis.[33] He spent his first days at the new Magdalene looking miserable and muttering: 'Oh, what a fool I am! I had a good home and I left!' As well as missing the familiarity of his Oxford college, Lewis wrote to Joy complaining about the restrictions of his new Cambridge lifestyle, which allowed just a single glass of port after dinner instead of Magdalen's three.

FIG. 17 The Martyrs' Memorial, St Giles, Oxford, in 1922.

The loss to Oxford following Lewis's relocation was nicely captured in a pen portrait by Milton Waldman, who reported a mournful friend likening Lewis's translation from Magdalen on the Isis to Magdalene on the Cam to the removal of the Martyrs' Memorial: 'If they had taken the Martyrs' Memorial it would not have left a bigger gap than "Jack" Lewis will.'[34] The Martyrs' Memorial, or 'Maggers' Memugger' as it was known in Lewis's day, commemorates the execution of the Protestant martyrs Cranmer, Ridley and Latimer, who were burnt in Oxford in 1555. It is a substantial Victorian edifice, designed by Sir George Gilbert Scott, and stands in a very prominent position at the end of St Giles'. Lewis responded to Waldman's tribute with characteristically self-deprecatory wit: 'The bit about the Martyrs' Memorial will carry its full ambivalence only to those who know it as the ugliest thing in Oxford.'[35]

That Oxford did at least miss Lewis the lecturer is suggested by his being invited to give the Chichele lectures at All Souls College in November 1955. Lewis initially planned to title the series of four lectures 'Some Eighteenth-Century Views on Milton', but switched to the less specific 'Milton' to give himself more flexibility.[36]

While Lewis's new position required him to spend his weeks during term in Cambridge, he continued to pass weekends at The Kilns. His pattern was to return to Oxford by train on Saturday mornings, arriving at lunchtime. On Mondays he would attend meetings of the Inklings at the Bird and Baby – moved from Tuesdays to accommodate Lewis's peripatetic lifestyle – and then head to the station to catch the return train to Cambridge. While most commuters resent the long hours wasted in transit, Lewis positively relished the three hours it took the leisurely connection between Oxford and Cambridge – which he nicknamed the 'Cantab crawler' – since it allowed him to read and say his prayers without interruption.

Despite his itinerant lifestyle, with feet in both camps, Lewis threw himself into college life. He attended meetings and chapel services, dined in hall and frequented the Pickerel Inn directly opposite the college, where he drank draught Guinness – a drink which he enjoyed but couldn't spell: 'guinneass (realise the spelling is quite beyond me. Read STOUT!)'.[37] Despite having been appointed to a professorship, Lewis became the junior fellow at Magdalene – since seniority is strictly determined by years of service in Oxbridge colleges. This meant that it fell to Lewis to refill the port glasses in the Combination Room at dessert following dinner. Although the senior fellows tried their best to absolve such an eminent figure from this rather lowly duty, Lewis insisted on observing the tradition.

Lewis enjoyed befriending his colleagues, including the English tutor John Stevens, whom he taught Old English in the evenings, as this did not form part of the Cambridge syllabus that Stevens had undertaken.[38] Although Lewis's chair did not include any requirement to teach college undergraduates, Lewis attended meetings of the English Club, listening to and engaging with the students' papers.

In February 1959 Lewis was invited to give the oration at the college's annual Pepys dinner, or, in his words, 'our great domestic binge'. In preparation for the event Lewis studied *Pepys's Diary* in great detail; the resulting speech was considered to be a great success, although some members of the audience suffered from Lewis's assumption that they would be as familiar with the text as he was. Lewis lent his support to the college's plans to publish an unexpurgated version of *Pepys's Diary*, on the grounds that it was unlikely that there would be a 'perceptible increment in lechery' resulting from printing a few 'obscure, and widely separated passages in a very long and expensive book'. As for the college's fear that it would be brought into disrepute and subjected to public ridicule, Lewis accepted that publication may indeed result in its being 'very malodorous in the public nostril' for a week or two, but that 'a few weeks, or years, are nothing in the life [of] the College'. 'I think it wd. be pusillanimous and unscholarly to delete a syllable on that score.'[39]

It was in response to a challenge issued by the Pepys librarian, Francis Turner, that Lewis penned a hymn on the resurrection. The specific details of the challenge have been lost, but the hymn itself survives in the college archives:[40]

Lords coëval with creation,
Seraph, Cherub, Throne and Power,
Princedom, Virtue, Domination,
Hail the long-awaited hour!
Bruised in head, with broken pinion,
Trembling for his old dominion,
See the ancient dragon cower!
For the Prince of Heaven has risen,
Victor, from his shattered prison.
Loudly roaring from the regions
Where no sunbeam e'er was shed,
Rise and dance, ye ransomed legions
Of the cold and countless dead!
Gates of adamant are broken,
Words of conquering power are spoken
Through the God who died and bled:
Hell lies vacant, spoiled and cheated,
By the Lord of life defeated.
Bear, behemoth, bustard, camel,
Warthog, wombat, kangaroo,
Insect, reptile, fish and mammal,
Tree, flower, grass, and lichen too,
Rise and romp and ramp, awaking,
For the age-old curse is breaking.
All things shall be made anew;
Nature's rich rejuvenation
Follows on Man's liberation.
Eve's and Adam's son and daughter,
Sinful, weary, twisted, mired,
Pale with terror, thinned with slaughter,
Robbed of all your hearts desired,
Look! Rejoice! One born of woman,
Flesh and blood and bones all human,
One who wept and could be tired,
Risen from vilest death, has given
All who will the hope of Heaven.

The hymn links the resurrection of Easter and the redemption of mankind with creation, listing an assortment of beasts bursting into life. The inclusion of such unlikely animals as warthogs, wombats and kangaroos led Helen Cooper, holder of the chair of Medieval and Renaissance Literature from 2004 to 2014, to suggest that the challenge may have involved the inclusion of antipodean animals traditionally omitted from accounts of creation.[41] Although not accompanied by wombats and kangaroos, a warthog features prominently in the account of creation in the chapter 'The Founding of Narnia' in *The Magician's Nephew*, suggesting Lewis had a particular fondness for this rather comic beast. That there were also kangaroos in Narnia is apparent from the children stumbling upon one that had been turned to stone in the White Witch's castle. In 2016 a member of the college choir, Peter Relph, took up Professor Cooper's suggestion that the hymn might be set to music; the resulting piece was performed in the college chapel.

ENGLISH FACULTY

All appointments to professorial chairs in the university are tasked with giving an inaugural lecture, attended by the vice chancellor, other university dignitaries, faculty colleagues and members of the public. Given the mixed nature of the audience these are notoriously difficult lectures to pitch. Although Lewis did not take up the post until January 1955, the inaugural took place on 29 November 1954, his fifty-sixth birthday. Lewis titled his address '*De Descriptione Temporum*', borrowing a chapter heading from Isidore of Seville's *Etymologiae*, and using the occasion to revisit the argument he had first made in Cambridge in 1939 that there was no major division in Western culture at the Renaissance. Instead, he proposed that the more important break is that which separated the current age from that of Jane Austen and Sir Walter Scott. Before that was a single period, which he proposed to label Old Western Culture.

Lewis presented himself as a relic of that Old Western order, reassuring his audience that, 'where I fail as a critic, I may yet be useful as a specimen'. While one would not wish to be lectured on dinosaurs by a dinosaur, if such a creature did 'drag its slow length into the laboratory', wouldn't everyone look back to observe its appearance and behaviour as they fled for their lives? While a Neanderthal man might lack something in his lecturing technique, he would be able to tell his audience so much more than a modern anthropologist. It was on these terms that Lewis offered himself to his new university, urging them to make use of him while they can: 'There are not going to be many dinosaurs.'[42]

The event attracted a huge crowd; in his own inaugural lecture, J.A.W. Bennett, Lewis's former colleague at Magdalen Oxford and his successor to the Cambridge chair, recalled a 'platoon' of Lewis's former students travelling from Oxford and ranging themselves like a *sceldtruma*, an Anglo-Saxon 'shield-wall', ready to defend their liege lord.[43] The widespread reporting of his lecture in the popular press, including a review in *Time* magazine, led to some confusion concerning his central thesis. Lewis found his patience being severely tested by one particularly misguided correspondent: 'You've got it nearly right: the only error being that instead of saying the Great Divide came between the Middle Ages and the Renaissance, I said at great length and very emphatically that it *didn't*. But of course *not* is a small word and one can't get every fine shade just right.'[44]

Despite the obvious similarities, there were a number of key differences between the Oxford English Faculty and the Cambridge equivalent. In Oxford the focus was on the older periods of literature and especially the Middle Ages. The curriculum began with compulsory Old English, or 'Anglo-Saxon'; in Cambridge Anglo-Saxon was an optional subject, and later the province of a separate department of Anglo-Saxon, Norse and Celtic. In Oxford the syllabus stopped at 1830, whereas in Cambridge it went up to the present day.

For Lewis, the principal business of an English course was to convey information about the historical and intellectual contexts within which works were written, whereas in Cambridge the focus was on a literary-critical appraisal of the works themselves. In an essay defending the Oxford course and its focus on Anglo-Saxon, older meanings of words, background and context, titled 'Our English Syllabus', Lewis dismisses the value in teaching students to read contemporary works, which they ought to understand better than their tutors, provocatively likening it to asking for a nurse's assistance in blowing one's nose.[45]

Lewis embarked on his Cambridge mission by lecturing on a variety of medieval and renaissance topics, many of which ended up in published forms. In Michaelmas Term 1955 he gave two lectures a week on 'Some Major Texts: Latin and Continental Vernacular'. These included an examination of why Dante placed Statius in Purgatory in his *Divine Comedy*, which appeared in the journal of medieval studies, *Medium Ævum*, in 1957. In the Lent term of 1956 Lewis delivered a series of twice-weekly lectures entitled 'Some Difficult Words', which traced the semantic development of the words Nature, Sad, Wit, Free, Sense, Simple, Conscious and Conscience. These lectures formed the basis of the book *Studies in Words*, published in 1960 by Cambridge University Press. Although they remained unpublished at his death, Lewis's notes for his lectures on Spenser formed the basis of the book *Spenser's Images of Life* (1967), edited by his former student Alastair Fowler.

Tom Shippey, an eminent medievalist and Tolkien scholar, who was in the audience, describes these as the best-delivered lectures he has ever heard. The material was presented with such clarity (from a seated position since Lewis did not feel sufficiently strong to deliver them while standing) that note-taking became unnecessary; Shippey claims he could have written out the material from memory.[46] In Cambridge, Lewis also reprised the series of lectures titled 'Prolegomena to Medieval and Renaissance Literature' that he had given with great success in Oxford. In 1961 he began writing them up for publication; they finally appeared posthumously as *The Discarded Image: An Introduction to Medieval and Renaissance Literature* (1964).

Despite the enthusiasm of those who attended his lectures, Lewis was disappointed with the response, labelling his Cambridge mission a '*flop d'estime*'. According to his own report, a few dons and fewer undergraduates turned up to hear him speak: 'I've never had such small audiences before. Must be frightfully good for me.'[47] This does not tally with the accounts of those in attendance, such as Simon Barrington-Ward, the chaplain of Magdalene College, who recalled the theatre thronging with undergraduates. Lewis did, however, note that his appearance in Cambridge had ruffled the feathers of 'Orthodox Atheists' like E.M. Forster, who were concerned at the influx of a number of Christian academics.[48]

Lewis's inaugural lecture prompted much lively discussion, both during the sherry party afterwards and in a subsequent issue of *The Twentieth Century*. While many debated the distinctions he proposed, particular unrest was generated among members of the English Faculty by his comments about modern poetry. Lewis had little time for the work of modernist poets, and his disdain for the poems of T.S. Eliot was particularly vehement. At a meeting of the Inklings in 1947, Lewis began reading a poem by Eliot but broke off in the middle, declaring it to be 'bilge'.[49] In the lecture, Lewis questioned the value of criticism of such poetry, where respected scholars cannot even agree about its basic meaning. Expounding further on this view, Lewis explained that he was prepared to believe that an unintelligible picture is a very good horse if that's what all its admirers claim it to be. 'But when one says it's a horse, and the next that it's a ship, and the third that it's an orange, and the fourth that it's Mt. Everest, I give it up.'[50]

Lewis's scepticism towards criticism of modern poetry was focused particularly upon a group of Cambridge critics whom he referred to as the 'Leavisites': the followers of Cambridge English tutor F.R. Leavis. A particular objection towards what he termed the 'rule of Downing' – a reference to Leavis's affiliation with Downing College – was the complete neglect of language study, leaving the subject as purely a school of literary criticism, 'with the largest possible capitals for both words'.[51]

That Lewis's relationship with Leavis had not improved by the end of his time in Cambridge is apparent from his response to the suggestion that a collection of essays by friends and colleagues, known as a *Festschrift*, might be a fitting way of marking his retirement. Lewis responded to this with a counterproposal: 'I suppose the head of F.R. Leavis in a charger wd. be rather too costly?'[52]

As a senior member of the English Faculty, Lewis was approached when the post of Chair of the Faculty (equivalent to head of department) fell vacant. Lewis was quick to refuse the position, referring back to his previous disastrous administrative experience as vice president of Magdalen: 'No,' he wrote,

> It would never do. People so often deny their own capacity for business either through mock-modesty or through laziness that when the denial happens to be merely true, it is difficult to make it convincing. But I have been tried at this kind of job; and none of those who experienced me in office ever wanted to repeat the experiment. I am both meddlesome and forgetful. Quite objectively, I'd be a disaster.[53]

RETIREMENT

In July 1963 Lewis was admitted to the Acland Nursing Home for a blood transfusion but had a heart attack and fell into a coma. Doctors thought he would not survive the attack, but, having received Extreme Unction from Fr Michael Watts, the curate of St Mary Magdalen Church, he recovered. After three weeks in hospital, he was discharged and returned home with a nurse to look after him. Recognizing that he was no longer sufficiently fit to work, Lewis resigned his fellowship and chair at Cambridge and became – in his own words – 'an extinct volcano'.[54]

The master and fellows responded by appointing him an Honorary Fellow, in recognition of his distinguished contribution to the college. Lewis was delighted by the honour and wrote to express his gratitude, noting:

> The ghosts of the wicked old women in Pope 'haunt the places where their honour died'. I am more fortunate, for I shall haunt the place whence the most valued of my honours came ... If in some twilit hour anyone sees a bald and bulky spectre in the

> Combination Room or the garden, don't get Simon [Revd Simon Barrington-Ward, the college chaplain] to exorcise it, for it is a harmless wraith and means nothing but good.[55]

But, while Lewis's ghost may continue to haunt the corridors and courts of his former Cambridge home, he has become a truly global figure. It is to this modern phenomenon of the Global Lewis industry that our final chapter turns.

NINE
GLOBAL LEWIS

As we have seen, Lewis spent the majority of his adult life in Oxford; even when his career took him to Cambridge, he continued to reside at The Kilns. He seldom travelled outside the United Kingdom; apart from a childhood holiday in France and his time in the trenches, his only trip overseas was to Greece at Joy's request. And yet today Lewis is a global figure, whose books are read all over the world and are especially popular in America.

The publication of *The Screwtape Letters* by Macmillan in 1943 brought Lewis to the attention of the United States. The enthusiasm for the book and the rave reviews it received prompted Macmillan to issue the Lewis back catalogue: *The Problem of Pain*, *Out of the Silent Planet* and *The Case for Christianity* (the US title for *Broadcast Talks*). These were followed up by *The Abolition of Man* in 1947, *Christian Behaviour* in 1944, *Beyond Personality* in 1945, *The Great Divorce* in 1946 and *Miracles* in 1947.

Time magazine published an interview with Lewis in September 1947, with the title 'Don v. Devil'. A picture of Lewis featured on the magazine's cover, with a comic image of a devil, complete with horns, elongated nose and chin, and clutching a pitchfork, standing on his shoulder. The choice of illustration is somewhat ironic since, for Screwtape, preserving the essentially comic image that devils occupy in the modern imagination is central to ensuring that no one believes in their existence.[1] Underneath the illustration appears a caption labelling the subject 'Oxford's C.S. Lewis' and naming Christianity as his heresy, a reference to the way the letters present belief in 'the Enemy' as a heresy against 'Our Father Below'. In its obituary of Lewis, *Time* went on to describe him as 'one of the church's minor prophets, a defender of the faith who with fashionable urbanity justified an unfashionable orthodoxy against the heresies of his time'.

Today, Lewis's posthumous reputation in the USA is curated by the major collection of Inklings-related materials held by the Marion Wade Center at Wheaton College, Illinois. The Center was founded in 1974, building on a collection established by Clyde S. Kilby, a literary scholar at Wheaton who had corresponded with Lewis since the 1950s. It is named for Marion E. Wade, an enthusiastic reader of Lewis's works and founder of ServiceMaster, a pest-control and domestic service company, who provided its endowment. As well as bringing together much of Lewis's vast library, the Marion Wade Center is home to many manuscripts, letters and the unpublished Lewis Papers: the eleven-volume account of the family compiled by Warnie in Lewis's college rooms, while his brother took tutorials next-door. The Center also hosts collections of other members of the Inklings, J.R.R. Tolkien, Owen Barfield and Charles Williams, as well as Christian writers who were friends of Lewis – Dorothy L. Sayers – or influenced him: George MacDonald and G.K. Chesterton.

In an adjoining museum stands an ornately carved wooden wardrobe, with the door tantalisingly ajar to reveal a collection of fur coats (PLATE 25). The wardrobe was built by Lewis's paternal grandfather, Richard Lewis, in the 1800s, and is from the family home of Little Lea where Lewis grew up. According to family tradition, Lewis and his brother Warnie, and their cousins, would sit in the wardrobe while the younger Lewis told them adventure stories.[2] The story is perhaps too good to be true; although it is based on the testimony of Claire Lewis Clapperton, one of Lewis's cousins, it was recorded as late as 1979. But, since Lewis went to the trouble and expense of shipping the wardrobe from Belfast to The Kilns, it was clearly an important family heirloom.

The museum's desire to connect with its authors through everyday objects, especially those relating to the writing process, is apparent from its inclusion of the desk that Tolkien used when writing *The Hobbit*, Charles Williams's bookshelves and Dorothy L. Sayers's spectacles; in this company Owen Barfield's chess set is a slightly uneasy fit. A centrepiece of the museum is a desk and chair used by Lewis, upon which a bust of his head, the work of the sculptor Lawrence Reid Bechtel, stands. These objects are witness to a different family inheritance, since they were the property of Mrs Moore, who brought them with her when she came to live with Lewis at The Kilns.

Lewis may seem an unlikely figure to feature with such prominence on a campus where consumption of alcohol and tobacco is prohibited, sharing the site with a centre and museum dedicated to its most famous alumnus, the evangelist Billy Graham. But, during his mission to the University of Cambridge in 1955, Graham sought out Lewis and asked for his advice over dinner. In an interview with Sherwood E. Wirt of the Billy Graham Evangelistic Association, Lewis recalled their conversation and described Graham as 'a very modest and very sensible man'.[3]

Lewis's growing global popularity can be traced in the foundation of societies dedicated to the study of his works. In 1969 the New York C.S. Lewis Society was formed, offering its members access to talks and subscription to its journal; by the end of the twentieth century there were more than a dozen such groups in the USA, Canada, Great Britain and Japan.

One of the largest such associations is the C.S. Lewis Foundation, based in Redlands, California, which has been sponsoring summer institutes to study Lewis's work since the 1980s. The Foundation also owns The Kilns and operates it as a 'quiet place of study, fellowship and creative scholarly work', reflecting the way that Lewis himself used the house when he was a resident.[4] Here the blurring of fiction and reality is perhaps most apparent. The house appears little changed since Lewis's day, although a library has been added for the benefit of visiting academics who spend short periods in residence. This provision recognizes the value Lewis placed upon access to books, as well as conversation and debate. A nod to the importance of the pub to Lewis's scholarly life is found in the Eagle and Child sign which hangs on the wall, having been salvaged by Walter Hooper when the landlord replaced it with a modernized version.

The pub sign is one of the few authentic objects in The Kilns today. This is because, although the house has been appointed to look just as it did when the Lewis brothers were in residence, most of the furnishings are replicas. Of the few items on display that can be linked with Lewis's time in the house is an old typewriter (PLATE 26). Lewis himself insisted on handwriting all his works using a pen that had to be repeatedly dipped in an inkwell, claiming that this was essential for his creativity; the manuscripts were then typed up by his brother Warnie.

An insight into Lewis's growing popularity in the USA is offered by the vast volume of correspondence received by Macmillan Publishing in the late 1980s, now held by the Bodleian Library. These letters were written by children keen to share their love of the Narnian stories and characters with their author, unaware that he had died some twenty-five years earlier. The letters typically involve an explanation of the particular appeal of the stories and the children's preferred book or characters, as well as questions about Lewis's motivation for writing them, where he gets his ideas from, and the origins of the word 'Narnia'. In a world before the Internet, many children are interested in biographical details: is Lewis married, what stimulated him to become a writer, does he have children, is he fond of animals and – the most commonly asked question – what do the initials 'C.S.' stand for?

Many letters enclose photographs of the correspondent, accompanied by illustrations of favourite characters or scenes from the book, as well as poems and stories inspired by Narnia and maps of the Narnian world. Not all are unequivocally positive; one young correspondent expressed frustration at the way every story involves someone trying to take over Narnia, which he found a little tedious. The letter ends with some helpful suggestions as to how to add greater variety in Lewis's future endeavours. Another correspondent admits to having initially ignored the Narnian books, fearing that they might be as long and boring as the works of J.R.R. Tolkien and William Shakespeare, but was finally converted by reading *The Last Battle* – an unusual and somewhat challenging place to start.

BELFAST

It has taken rather longer for Lewis's legacy to be appreciated in his homeland, perhaps the effect of his being so closely associated with Oxford. Today, Lewis's contribution is most prominently memorialized in Belfast in the square named for him, populated by statues of various Narnian creatures from *The Lion, the Witch and the Wardrobe*, created by Irish sculptor Maurice Harron. Here we find a huge and imposing Aslan, a tall and gleaming White Witch, Mr and Mrs Beaver, Mr Tumnus, Maugrim the wolf with a bright red eye and vicious-looking teeth, the Robin and the Stone Table. The square was officially opened by Lewis's stepson, Douglas Gresham, at a ceremony held on 22 November 2016, the fifty-third anniversary of Lewis's death.

A short walk from C.S. Lewis Square is Holywood Arches Library, a highly appropriate location for the 'Searcher statue'. Constructed in 1998 to mark the centenary of Lewis's birth, the statue (PLATE 31) depicts a young man in the act of opening a wardrobe. The statue is the work of artist Ross Wilson, who explains the significance of the wardrobe in an inscription on the back. Wilson observes that, for Lewis, a wardrobe was not simply a place to hang clothes but rather a space in which to bring together ideas of 'sacrifice, redemption, victory, and freedom for the Sons of Adam and the Daughters of Eve'. The ordinariness of this functional, everyday object conceals a revelation that is only apparent on further investigation. The statue urges the onlooker to be endlessly inquisitive, and to remember that 'some of the greatest things can be found in the most ordinary of places'.

An accompanying plaque explains that the statue represents Digory Kirke, who has an apple tree with magical properties made into a wardrobe, 'which helped open a doorway to Narnia and Aslan'. Since

Digory appears as an elderly professor in *The Lion, the Witch and the Wardrobe* and as a young boy in *The Magician's Nephew*, the image of him as a young man is striking. In neither book do we witness Digory entering the wardrobe. The ending of *The Magician's Nephew* makes clear that he was unaware of its enchantment until Lucy stumbled through it into Narnia: 'And though he himself did not discover the magic properties of that wardrobe, someone else did.' It is a further irony that Digory is here commemorated as 'The Searcher', since it was his unbridled curiosity that led to his reckless summoning of Jadis and with it her reign as the White Witch, whom the Pevensie children are tasked with overthrowing. Alongside this is a further plaque which reproduces a letter Lewis wrote to ten-year-old Anne Waller in March 1961, in which he explains the series' deeper meaning, and the ways in which Aslan (whose head peers down at the reader from the top of the wardrobe) symbolizes Christ.[5]

Other sites in Belfast's EastSide that celebrate the city's association with Lewis are the Lamppost Cafe, the entry to which is marked by a Victorian lamp post. Inside, the walls are adorned with illustrations and quotations from the Narnian stories, including – somewhat predictably – Lewis's famous boast that 'you can never get a cup of tea large enough or a book long enough to suit me.'[6] Given his particular fondness for pubs, it is somewhat surprising to find a second cafe associated with Lewis: the Jack Coffee Bar, located in the EastSide Visitor Centre. A tour of Lewis's Oxford can become quite an alcoholic adventure, a pub crawl that takes in Lewis's numerous haunts: the Eagle and Child, the Lamb and Flag, the Mitre, the King's Arms, the Eastgate Hotel, followed by a brisk walk across Port Meadow and last orders at the Trout in Godstow. A C.S. Lewis fan visiting Belfast is at greater risk of becoming excessively caffeinated or overindulging in cake and biscuits.

Beyond the sculptures of the EastSide, Lewis and his creations are commemorated in murals painted onto the sides of buildings in a residential district of the city. On a gable wall on Convention Court on Ballymacarrett Road we witness Lucy's opening of the wardrobe to reveal a snowy Narnian landscape, complete with lamp post, alongside an image of the White Witch accompanied by Maugrim, her chief of police (PLATE 30). Above this pairing of childhood innocence and evil corruption we find the figures of Aslan and Lewis himself, the two creators of Narnia, who seem deliberately intended to resemble each other. Down the centre of the building, recalling the spine of a book, is the title 'The Lion, the Witch and the Wardrobe', with the final letters painted over a door, which is raised above the ground to a similar level as the wardrobe, but which carries a large padlock.

A second mural dedicated to Lewis and the world of Narnia, found on a wall in the Dee Street area of East Belfast, replaced an earlier illustration displaying images of the Ulster Volunteer Force. The painting was unveiled in 2008 by First Minister Peter Robinson, who praised the decision to replace a paramilitary mural with one inspired by Narnia.[7] But, while the Narnian murals successfully overlay a political message with one of more universal appeal, we should recall that Aslan arrives in Narnia as a rebel who plans to overthrow a tyrannical ruler.[8] Perhaps it is rather Lewis's deliberately non-sectarian stance in his apologetic writings that lends his work to such use. In *Mere Christianity* Lewis set out to establish the doctrines that all Christians hold in common, irrespective of denomination. Lewis likened this to a hallway in which various doors opened into different rooms, symbolizing the many churches and traditions: it is up to the individual to decide which room to enter. Recognizing that individuals will make different choices, Lewis emphasized the importance of tolerance: 'When you have reached your own room, be kind to those who have chosen different doors and to those who are still in the hall.'[9]

Another Narnian tribute is found in the C.S. Lewis Reading Room at Queen's University in Belfast. Although Lewis himself had no academic connection with Queen's University, his mother, Flora, graduated with a degree in Mathematics in 1886. The Reading Room is accessed via a replica of the wardrobe used in the feature film of 2005. Inside, the reader is greeted with carpets and a central table decorated with Narnian themes.

These sculptures, murals and replica wardrobes emphasize the difference between Lewis's US and British legacies. Where Lewis's reputation in the USA tends to focus more on his Christian apologetics, in Britain he is best known as a writer of children's fantasy. But neither of these is how the young C.S. Lewis set out to be remembered as a writer. His ambitions were to be celebrated as a poet, although the lack of critical enthusiasm for his collection of poems, *Spirits in Bondage* (1919), and his long narrative composition, *Dymer* (1926), prompted him to change direction. Given this early disappointment, Lewis would have taken considerable pleasure from a recognition that has come rather later. On the fiftieth anniversary of his death, in 2013, a memorial to Lewis was added to Poets' Corner at Westminster Abbey, placing him in the august company of some of his most beloved writers, including Milton, Spenser and Wordsworth. Given the fractious nature of their relationship, it is somewhat ironic that Lewis's memorial was placed next to that of John Betjeman.

SHADOWLANDS

Lewis's global fame was given considerable impetus by the 1993 film *Shadowlands*, which introduced the wider public to the story of his marriage to Joy Davidman and her tragic early death. The film, directed by Richard Attenborough, is based upon the stage play written by William Nicholson, which premiered at the Theatre Royal in Plymouth in 1989, having begun life as a BBC film directed by Norman Stone. In the 1993 film version, Anthony Hopkins stars as the shy bachelor whose life is turned upside down by the outspoken American, played by Debra Winger. There are a number of biographical inaccuracies in the story as it is enacted in the film. After their marriage, Lewis took Joy to Ireland to see his homeland, with the couple honeymooning at the Old Inn Crawfordsburn, between the city of Belfast and the seaside town of Bangor. But in the film they set out in search of the Golden Valley in Herefordshire, the subject of a painting on the wall of Lewis's study. In reality, we have seen that Lewis's walls were adorned with

FIG. 18 Filming of *Shadowlands*, Old Kitchen Bar, Magdalen College, *c.* 1992.

renaissance allegories, which would have made a more challenging basis for a honeymoon trip.

Another significant way in which the film plays fast and loose with reality is with the setting. The couple were married in April 1956, some sixteen months after Lewis had resigned his fellowship at Magdalen College Oxford and begun working at its sister college in Cambridge. Despite this, the events depicted in the film are exclusively located in Oxford, with Magdalen College as the backdrop. In packaging Lewis's biography for a global audience, Lewis's Oxford association was central to the story. The stage play does raise the prospect of a Cambridge chair, but Lewis himself makes clear that he would not consider actually moving there: 'Cambridge is a chilly town.'[10] Former students have also taken issue with the film's depiction of Lewis the tutor, and the manner in which he is depicted lecturing sternly at a group of students. Instead, Lewis's tutorials were individual encounters, structured like a Socratic dialogue, in which he stretched a student's intellectual reach with generosity and forbearance.[11]

LAMP POSTS

Today it is to Oxford that the hordes of tourists flock: to enjoy a drink in the Eagle and Child, to sit in Lewis's pew at Holy Trinity Church, to visit his study at The Kilns and to retrace his footsteps around Addison's Walk.

The desire to locate the real-world inspiration for the places we meet in Narnia is most apparent in the number of claims for the original of the lamp post that Lucy encounters when she first steps through the wardrobe. One claimant is Lewis's old school, Campbell College in Belfast, where the nine-year-old Lewis spent just half a term before being removed on health grounds. Another claim that relates to his schooldays comes from the Worcestershire town of Malvern, where Lewis spent the academic year 1912–13, which boasts numerous gas-fuelled lamps dating back to the Victorian period.[12]

We have already considered the lamp post that stands in St Mary's Passage, but this is only one of numerous Oxford possibilities. Not to be outdone by its academic rival, Cambridge also has a candidate for the original lamp post. This one stands in Skaters' Meadow, situated on the route between Newnham College and the village of Grantchester, which was used as a skating lake in the 1930s and 1940s. Now that the field is no longer flooded to supply Cambridge residents with skating facilities, the lamp post cuts a rather lonely figure, standing in the middle of a field in a way that recalls Lantern Waste, although even its strongest advocate concedes that the evidence that Lewis even knew of the lamp post is slight.[13]

These rival lamp posts testify to our desire to associate the magical and mythical world of Narnia with particular locations, to tie it to

Lewis's biography in a physical way. Lewis himself recognized how fairy tales stimulate a longing in the reader for something beyond the material world, offering a new 'dimension of depth'. Reading about enchanted woods does not make the reader despise real woods, but instead makes all real woods a little enchanted.[14] Perhaps it is this yearning that prompts us to look to everyday Oxford landmarks – lamp posts, doors and wardrobes – for a connection with the magical world of his stories. We become like the young Douglas Gresham in the film *Shadowlands*, who climbs into a wardrobe in the attic of The Kilns in the hope of gaining physical entry into the fantastical world of the Narnian stories. The real Douglas Gresham, by contrast, was relieved to discover that the room in which he slept during his first stay at The Kilns was not enchanted; the violent hammering noise that woke him every morning, which he attributed to a 'malevolent, violent, raucous ghost', was in fact due to airlocks in the iron water pipes.[15]

One further lamp post that might seem to have a particularly strong claim to be the 'real' inspiration for Lewis stands in the grounds of Magdalen College, beside the New Building in which he spent the years during which he wrote the Narnian stories. But this lamp post is further testimony to the attraction of such an association, since it was erected as recently as 2019. Rather than preserving a clue to the Oxford influence on Lewis's writing, it shows how his life and writings continue to impact the city today. Lewis's Oxford is not just the city that made him one of the most influential writers of the twentieth century; it is the city that continues to be shaped by his stories, and those we tell about their author.

Lewis spent most of his adult life in Oxford; even when he moved to Cambridge he continued to live at The Kilns. Despite a substantial following in the United States, and offers of lucrative lecture tours, Lewis never set foot in America. When a journalist quizzed him about the humdrum nature of his existence, Lewis embraced the label, claiming: 'I like monotony.' Perhaps Lewis favoured the stability and consistency of his Oxford life in order to inhabit and explore his fictional worlds more fully.

In his critical writings, Lewis emphasized the importance of atmosphere over character development and excitement. We return to our favourite stories not for tension and suspense, since we already know the outcome, but for a particular quality of the world they describe. It was Arthur Greeves who introduced Lewis to the concept of 'homeliness' in the works of writers like Jane Austen and Walter Scott, which offered an appealing contrast to his more fantastical reading. Greeves used the term to capture a rooted quality in their novels, which linked them to simple shared human experiences: the weather, family, food and neighbourhood. Oxford offered Lewis that same sense of rootedness, enabling him to experience the homeliness that he sought in his reading, and that had been snatched away from him by the death of his mother and being sent to be educated in English boarding schools.

For Lewis, the act of rereading favourite works is like returning to a fruit for its taste or to a familiar place for its particular atmosphere: Donegal for its Donegality, and London for its Londonness. The number of such novels that have been written in Oxford suggests that there may be some Oxonian quality that lends itself to the writing of fantasy. The author of the children's classics *Alice's Adventures in Wonderland* (1865) and *Through the Looking-Glass and What Alice Found There* (1871) was Oxford mathematician Charles Dodgson, who spent most of his adult life as a resident tutor at Christ Church. J.R.R. Tolkien wrote *The Hobbit* and its sequel *The Lord of the Rings* while an Oxford academic.

More recently, the action of Philip Pullman's *His Dark Materials* trilogy shifts between the Oxford we know today and another belonging to a parallel universe. What is it about Oxford that inspires such fantastical imaginings? Pullman has suggested it is an effect of the mists from the river, which 'have a solvent effect on reality'.[16] It may also owe something to the architecture and its associated stories; as Pullman notes, a city in which the Magdalen College gargoyles climb down at night and fight with those from New College is one where anything might happen. But, even though Lewis loved the city and its buildings, his physical surroundings had comparatively little influence upon his writings. As he himself acknowledged, despite a lifetime living in the city, he was more familiar with fictional locations such as the Wild Wood of Kenneth Graham's *The Wind in the Willows*, Hrothgar's court in the Anglo-Saxon epic poem *Beowulf*, and the lunar landscape in H.G. Wells's *First Men in the Moon*, than he was with Oxford.

Despite occupying enviable college rooms, Lewis showed little concern for interior decoration and embellishment; every available surface was piled high with books, leaving visitors struggling to find a place to sit. For Lewis it was his extensive and eclectic reading that stimulated his creativity, so that the university where he studied and taught, with its profusion of well-stocked libraries and bookshops, offered the ideal environment. Also crucial for Lewis as a thinker and writer was the stimulation provided by his tutorial teaching and weekly meetings of the Socratic Club, as well as the feedback and encouragement he derived from regular gatherings with his friends and fellow writers. Friendship was key to Lewis's life; his ideal evening was staying up late in a friend's college room, 'talking nonsense, poetry, theology, metaphysics over beer, tea, and pipes'.[17] Lewis saw true companionship as the discovery of others who share tastes that, until that moment, one believed to be one's unique treasure. In Oxford, Lewis found a group of fellow scholars and writers that prompted him repeatedly to experience what he considered to be the typical beginning of a friendship: 'What? You too? I thought I was the only one.'[18] Such encounters and follow-up conversations were greatly facilitated by Oxford's rich assortment of public houses, college dining halls and senior common rooms.

NOTES

ABBREVIATIONS

AMR *All My Road Before Me: The Diary of 1922–1927*, ed. Walter Hooper, HarperCollins, London, 1991.

B&F *Brothers & Friends: The Diaries of Major Warren Hamilton Lewis*, ed. Clyde S. Kilby and Marjorie Lamp Mead, Ballantine Books, New York, 1982.

CL *The Collected Letters of C.S. Lewis*, ed. Walter Hooper, 3 vols, HarperCollins, San Francisco CA, 2004–07.

SJ C.S. Lewis, *Surprised by Joy: The Shape of My Early Life*, HarperCollins, London, 1977.

PREFACE

1. *SJ*, ch. IX.
2. *CL* I, p. 262.

ONE

1. *CL* I, p. 267.
2. Ibid.
3. *CL* I, p. 527.
4. *CL* I, p. 304.
5. *CL* I, p. 317.
6. *CL* I, p. 318.
7. *CL* I, p. 426.
8. *CL* I, p. 321.
9. *CL* I, p. 324.
10. *CL* I, p. 388.
11. *CL* I, p. 343. Burton's text actually reads: 'Be not solitary, be not idle'.
12. *The Collected Poems of C.S. Lewis: A Critical Edition*, ed. Don W. King, Kent State University Press, Kent OH, 2015, pp. 106–7.

13. Robert Graves, *Good-bye to All That: An Autobiography*, Jonathan Cape, London, 1929, ch. 27.
14. *AMR*, pp. 84, 305.
15. *AMR*, p. 107.
16. *AMR*, pp. 107–17.
17. D.J. Palmer, *The Rise of English Studies*, Oxford University Press, London, 1965.
18. *AMR*, p. 120.
19. *AMR*, p. 455.
20. *CL* I, p. 602.
21. *AMR*, p. 120.
22. On Lewis's essay and his Chaucerian scholarship more generally, see Simon Horobin, 'What C.S. Lewis Really Did to Chaucer's *Troilus and Criseyde*', *C.S. Lewis Society Chronicle*, vol. 6, no. 2, 2009, pp. 20–29.
23. *AMR*, p. 123.
24. See Robin Darwall-Smith, *A History of University College Oxford*, Oxford University Press, Oxford, 2008, pp. 427–9. For a more exhaustive account of Lewis and the Martlets, see Walter Hooper, 'To the Martlets', in Carolyn Keefe (ed.), *C.S. Lewis: Speaker & Teacher*, Zondervan, Grand Rapids MI, 1971, pp. 37–62. Joel D. Heck, 'C.S. Lewis and the Martlets', supplies a valuable history of the society, its speakers and Lewis's contributions; see www.cslewis.com/lewis-and-martlets.
25. *CL* I, p. 430.
26. Bodleian Library MS. Top Oxon d. 95/5, p. 100.
27. For a more extensive account of this discussion group and complete transcriptions of the extracts included here, see Walter Hooper, 'C.S. Lewis and the Oxford English Literature Discussion Group', in Bruce R. Johnson (ed.), *The Undiscovered C.S. Lewis: Essays in Memory of Christopher W. Mitchell*, Winged Lion Press, Hamden CT, 2021, pp. 76–87.
28. *AMR*, p. 189.
29. The minutes are quoted from the notebooks in which they were recorded, which were lent to the author by Walter Hooper.
30. *AMR*, p. 200.
31. Mary C. Gordon, *The Life of George S. Gordon: 1881–1942*, Oxford University Press, London, 1945, pp. 76–7.
32. *CL* I, pp. 535–6.
33. *CL* I, p. 554. The list of prizemen is found in University of Oxford Archives NW 1/15/20.
34. *CL* I, p. 304.
35. Joel D. Heck, 'Chronologically Lewis', entry for 25 October 1922, www.joelheck.com/chronologically-lewis.php.
36. *CL* I, p. 304.
37. Ibid.
38. *B&F*, p. 15.

39. *SJ*, ch. XII.
40. *AMR*, p. 22.
41. *AMR*, p. 222.
42. *AMR*, p. 45.
43. *AMR*, p. 261.
44. *CL* I, p. 629.
45. Trinity College, Oxford, Archive: College Government VIII/HEDB/3/1 Fellowships: 1924 Philosophy. I am grateful to Clare Hopkins, Trinity College archivist, for locating these documents and providing me with scanned copies.
46. *CL* I, p. 628.
47. Ibid.
48. *CL* I, p. 635.
49. *CL* I, pp. 648–9.
50. Darwall-Smith, *A History of University College Oxford*, p. 449.
51. Letter for sale from Peter Harrington: www.peterharrington.co.uk/typescript-letter-signed-to-gerald-brodribb-142922.html.
52. University College Archives UC J7/A2/42. I am grateful to Dr Robin Darwall-Smith for giving me access to these archives and for his assistance and guidance.
53. University College Archives UC J7/A2/40.
54. University College Archives UC J7/A2/42.
55. An image of the first page of this letter can be found at www.univ.ox.ac.uk/news/c-s-lewis-univ.

TWO

1. Magdalen College Archives, letter from President Warren, 4 November 1922.
2. *CL* I, p. 644.
3. *CL* I, p. 645.
4. 'J.A.W. Bennett', in P.L. Heyworth (ed.), *Medieval Studies for J.A.W. Bennett: Aetatis Suae LXX*, Clarendon Press, Oxford, 1981, p. 4.
5. *CL* I, pp. 647–8.
6. *CL* I, p. 650.
7. Ibid.
8. *CL* III, p. 335.
9. English Language and Literature Reports, University of Oxford Archives, FA 4/5/2/2, p. 181.
10. English Language and Literature Reports, University of Oxford Archives, FA 4/5/2/3, p. 60.
11. *An Experiment in Criticism*, Cambridge University Press, Cambridge, 2019, pp. 18–19.
12. Derek Brewer, 'The Tutor', in James T. Como (ed.), *C.S. Lewis at the Breakfast Table, and Other Reminiscences*, Collins, London, 1980, pp. 41–67.

13. 'The Great Faces of Oxford', *Vogue,* July 1950. The identification of the painting is taken from willvaus.blogspot.com/2017/11/c-s-lewis-art.html?m=1.
14. As recalled by W. Brown Patterson in 'C.S. Lewis: Personal Reflections', in Harry Lee Poe and Rebecca Whitten Poe (eds), *C.S. Lewis Remembered*, Zondervan, Grand Rapids MI, 2006, pp. 89–97.
15. Personal communication.
16. 'On Stories', p. 84; *An Experiment in Criticism*, p. 12.
17. *AMR*, p. 401.
18. *AMR,* p. 433.
19. *AMR*, p. 383.
20. *AMR,* p. 437.
21. *CL* I, p. 682.
22. Bevis Hillier, *Young Betjeman*, John Murray, London, 1988, p. 183.
23. John Betjeman, *Ghastly Good Taste*, Chapman & Hall, London, 1933, p. viii.
24. Yale University Library, Gen MSS 675, Box 1, Folder 56.
25. *John Betjeman Letters*, Volume 1: *1926–1951*, ed. Candida Lycett Green, Methuen, London, 2006, pp. 250–53.
26. Henry Green, *Pack My Bag*, Vintage, London, 2000, p. 138.
27. *B&F*, p. 314.
28. Edward Sniders, *Flying In, Walking Out: Memories of War and Escape, 1939–1945*, Leo Cooper, Barnsley, 1999, p. 91.
29. For an account of Richard Morgan's RAF career, see Roger Hutchins and Richard Sheppard (eds), *The Undone Years*, Magdalen College, Oxford, 2004, pp. 212–14.
30. Humphrey Carpenter, *The Inklings*, HarperCollins, London, 2006, p. 214.
31. As reported by his brother Laurence in Laurence Harwood, *C.S. Lewis, My Godfather*, InterVarsity Press, Downers Grove IL, 2007, p. 121.
32. *CL* I, p. 837.
33. *CL* III, p. 1541.
34. *Guardian,* www.theguardian.com/theguardian/2001/sep/24/features11.g21. See also the interview in Stephen Schofield (ed.), *In Search of C.S. Lewis*, Bridge Publishing, South Plainfield NJ, 1983, pp. 3–9.
35. *CL* II, p. 53.
36. George Sayer, 'Recollections of C.S. Lewis', in Roger White, Judith E. Wolfe and Brendan N. Wolfe (eds), *C.S. Lewis and His Circle*, Oxford University Press, Oxford, 2015, pp. 175–6.
37. *SJ*, ch. IX.
38. John Wain, *Sprightly Running: Part of an Autobiography*, Macmillan, London, 1965, p. 138.
39. Bodleian Library MS. 16166/1–2.
40. *SJ*, ch. XIV.
41. *AMR*, p. 380.

42. *AMR*, p. 414.
43. I am grateful to Amanda Ingram, archivist at St Hugh's College, for supplying me with a copy of this report.
44. Sarah Tisdall, 'A Goddaughter's Memories', in Poe and Whitten Poe (eds), *C.S. Lewis Remembered*, pp. 213–24.
45. *CL* II, pp. 314–15.
46. *CL* I, p. 654.
47. *CL* I, pp. 661–2.
48. Alastair Fowler, 'C.S. Lewis: Supervisor', *Yale Review*, vol. 91, no. 44, 2003, pp. 64–80.
49. *Guardian*, www.theguardian.com/books/2013/nov/19/cs-lewis-literary-legacy.
50. Eric Stanley, 'C.S. Lewis and J.R.R. Tolkien as I knew them (never well)', *Journal of Inklings Studies* 4, 2017, pp. 123–42.
51. George Watson, 'The Art of Disagreement', in Poe and Whitten Poe (eds), *C.S. Lewis Remembered*, pp. 77–88.
52. Lewis cites Marlowe's *Tamburlaine* as evidence of how popular usage did not always observe the distinction between 'Humours made of Contraries within us and Elements made of Contraries without us', in *The Discarded Image*, Cambridge University Press, Cambridge, 1994, p. 170.
53. Somerville College, Oxford, Marjorie Boulton Diaries, vols 3 and 4. I am very grateful to Kate O'Donnell, assistant archivist and records manager at Somerville College, for drawing these diaries to my attention and giving me access to them.
54. *CL* I, pp. 675, 701.
55. *AMR*, p. 449.
56. Carpenter, *The Inklings*, p. 29.
57. 1 Samuel 22.
58. *CL* I, p. 732.
59. E.L. Edmonds, 'C.S. Lewis, The Teacher', in Schofield (ed.), *In Search of C.S. Lewis*, pp. 37–51. Martin Moynihan, 'I Sleep but my Heart Watcheth', in David Graham (ed.), *We Remember C.S. Lewis: Essays & Memoirs*, Broadman & Holman Publishers, Nashville TN, 2001, pp. 36–40.
60. *CL* I, p. 765. The first fifteen lines of this poem are printed in *The Collected Poems of C.S. Lewis*, p. 139.
61. C.S. Lewis, *Perelandra*, HarperCollins,London, 2005, ch. 14.
62. *CL* I, p. 732.
63. See further Peter Bayley, 'Good College Man', in Poe and Whitten Poe (eds), *C.S. Lewis Remembered*, pp. 72–6.
64. *AMR*, pp. 444–5.
65. *AMR*, pp. 456–7.
66. *CL* I, pp. 879–80.
67. *CL* I, p. 778.

68. Ibid.
69. Quotations are taken from The Michaelmas Club Minute Book, Magdalen College Archives, O21/A1.
70. *CL* III, p. 1518.
71. Roger Lancelyn Green and Walter Hooper, *C.S. Lewis: A Biography*, Souvenir Press, London, 1988, p. 223.
72. *CL* I, p. 838.
73. *SJ*, ch. XIV.
74. See A. McGrath, *C.S. Lewis: A Life*, Hodder & Stoughton, London, 2013, pp. 141–6.
75. Andrew Lazo, 'Correcting the Chronology', *VII: Journal of the Marion E. Wade Center* 29, 2012, pp. 51–62.
76. *SJ*, ch. XIV.
77. John Lawlor, *C.S. Lewis: Memories and Reflections*, Spence, Dallas TX, 1998, p. 4.
78. *CL* III, p. 511.
79. *CL* III, p. 850.
80. Brewer, 'The Tutor', p. 55.
81. David C. Clary, *Schrödinger in Oxford*, World Scientific Publishing, Singapore, 2022, p. 306.
82. *CL* I, pp. 969–70.
83. For the text of the poem 'Chanson D'Aventure', see *The Collected Poems of C.S. Lewis*, pp. 322–3.
84. *CL* I, pp. 650–51.
85. Lewis described 'bisket' as 'an old and good way' of spelling 'biscuit': *CL* I, p. 864.
86. *CL* II, p. 619.
87. *CL* II, p. 525.
88. Letter to the President, 4 June 1954, Magdalen College Archives.
89. *AMR*, pp. 390, 400.
90. *CL* I, p. 942.
91. Arthur Adams, 'C.S. Lewis and Shadowlands', *Magdalen College Record*, 1990, pp. 51–3.
92. The list of committees is cited from a letter by K.B. McFarlane, dated 18 November 1941. See Andrew Hegarty, 'The Tutorial Takeover, 1928–1968', *Magdalen College Oxford: A History*, ed. L.W.B. Brockliss, Magdalen College, Oxford, 2008, pp. 598–9.
93. Hegarty, 'The Tutorial Takeover, 1928–1968', p. 582. See also the account in a letter by K.B. McFarlane to Helena Wright, dated 6 October 1940, Magdalen College Archives, MC:P27/C1/527.
94. Erik Routley, 'Stunning Effect', in Schofield (ed.), *In Search of C.S. Lewis*, pp. 97–101.
95. *CL* II, p. 504.

96. *CL* II, p. 492.
97. Bruce R. Johnson, '"Answers that Belonged to Life": C.S. Lewis and the Origins of the Royal Air Force Chaplains' School, Cambridge', *Sehnsucht: The C.S. Lewis Journal* 5/6, 2011–12, pp. 81–102.
98. *CL* II, p. 504.
99. Magdalen College Archives P27/C1/585; P27/C1/590.
100. Magdalen College Archives CMM/2/2.
101. Magdalen College Archives P27/C1/590.
102. A.J.P. Taylor, 'The Fun of the Thing', in Schofield (ed.), *In Search of C.S. Lewis*, pp. 117–21.
103. Joel D. Heck, 'Chronologically Lewis', entry for 3 December 1941, www.joelheck.com/chronologically-lewis.php.
104. Hugh Sinclair, 'C.S. Lewis and the Hungry Patriarch', *Magdalen College Record*, 1990, pp. 53–5.
105. *CL* II, p. 637.
106. Personal communication.
107. Lewis describes this encounter in '*De Futilitate*', a lecture given at Magdalen College at the invitation of the president, Sir Henry Tizard. *C.S. Lewis Essay Collection: Literature, Philosophy and Short Stories*, HarperCollins, London, 2002, pp. 261–73.
108. *CL* II, 448.
109. K.B. McFarlane, *Letters to Friends 1940–1966*, ed. Gerald Harriss, Magdalen College, Oxford, 1997, p. 11.

THREE

1. wadecenterblog.wordpress.com/2021/12/08/walter-hooper-interview.
2. *AMR*, p. 252.
3. On this poem, see Fiona Tolhurst, 'Beyond the Wardrobe: C.S. Lewis as Closet Arthurian', *Arthuriana*, vol. 22, no. 4, 2012, pp. 140–66.
4. *CL* I, p. 488.
5. *AMR*, p. 202.
6. *CL* I, p. 605.
7. David C. Downing and Bruce R. Johnson, 'C.S. Lewis's Unfinished "Easley Fragment" and his Unfinished Journey', *VII: Journal of the Marion E. Wade Center* 28, 2011, pp. 5–26.
8. *AMR*, p. 221.
9. *CL* I, p. 563.
10. *SJ*, ch. II.
11. *AMR*, p. 15.
12. *CL* II, p. 213.
13. *B&F*, p. 111.
14. *B&F*, p. 142.

15. *B&F*, p. 217.
16. *CL* II, p. 270.
17. Fred W. Paxford, 'He Should Have Been a Parson', in Graham (ed.), *We Remember C.S. Lewis*, pp. 119–28.
18. *CL* II, p. 307.
19. Green and Hooper, *C.S. Lewis: A Biography*, p.189.
20. *SJ*, ch. X.
21. Bruce R. Johnson, 'All My Dogs Before Me', www.humanesociety.org/sites/default/files/docs/all-my-dogs-before-me.pdf.
22. *CL* II, p. 214.
23. *B&F*, p. 181.
24. *CL* II, p. 273.
25. *CL* II, p. 277.
26. *CL* II, p. 273.
27. *CL* II, p. 413.
28. *CL* II, p. 287.
29. *CL* I, p. 495.
30. *SJ*, ch. XIV.
31. I am grateful to Roger ter Haar QC for sharing with me this anecdote of his father.
32. *CL* III, p. 1000.
33. Douglas H. Gresham, *Lenten Lands: My Childhood with Joy Davidman and C.S. Lewis*, HarperCollins, London, 2003, p. 105.
34. *B&F*, p. 247.
35. *AMR*, pp. 431–2.
36. *SJ*, ch. XV.
37. *CL* II, p. 377.
38. *CL* II, p. 426.
39. *CL* II, p. 425.
40. *The Screwtape Letters*, HarperCollins, London, 2001, letter II.
41. Ibid., Preface.
42. McGrath, *C.S. Lewis: A Life*, p. 23.
43. *B&F*, p. 309.

FOUR

1. This account of the Univ Inklings is indebted to Peter Gilliver, 'The First Inkling: Edward Tangye Lean', *Journal of Inklings Studies*, vol. 6, no. 2, 2016, pp. 63–77. For Tolkien's account, see *The Letters of J.R.R. Tolkien*, ed. Humphrey Carpenter, HarperCollins, London, 2006, p. 388.
2. *The Letters of J.R.R. Tolkien*, p. 388.
3. Ibid., p. 36.
4. Ibid., pp. 387–8.

5. *CL* II, p. 183.
6. *CL* II, p. 436.
7. Robert E. Havard, 'Philia: Jack at Ease', in Como (ed.), *C.S. Lewis at the Breakfast Table*, pp. 215–28.
8. *B&F*, p. 241.
9. *B&F*, p. 243.
10. *The Letters of J.R.R. Tolkien*, p. 103.
11. Quoted from Carpenter, *The Inklings*, p. 209.
12. James Dundas Grant, 'From an "Outsider"', in Como (ed.), *C.S. Lewis at the Breakfast Table*, pp. 229–33, 231.
13. *B&F*, p. 220.
14. *CL* II, p. 405.
15. Diana Pavlac Glyer, *The Company They Keep: C.S. Lewis and J.R.R. Tolkien as Writers in Community*, Kent State University Press, Kent OH, 2008, p. 12.
16. *B&F*, p. 219.
17. *B&F*, p. 246.
18. *CL* II, p. 554.
19. *The Letters of J.R.R. Tolkien*, pp. 95–6.
20. *B&F*, p. 252.
21. *B&F*, p. 222.
22. Norman Bradshaw, 'Impressions of a Pupil', in Schofield (ed.), *In Search of C.S. Lewis*, pp. 17–27. That Lewis played this game with his Univ students is suggested by a letter to Gerald Brodribb responding to a request for the title of this book.
23. Trinity College Oxford Archives Senior Tutor A/9 and D/2. I am grateful to Clare Hopkins for her help with my enquiries about Christopher Tolkien's Trinity career and for locating these records and supplying me with photographs.
24. *CL* II, p. 288.
25. C.S. Lewis, *The Problem of Pain*, HarperCollins, London, 2002, p. 162.
26. I am grateful to Dr Harvey White for this information.
27. *CL* II, p. 358.
28. *B&F*, p. 213.
29. *B&F*, p. 246.
30. *The Letters of J.R.R. Tolkien*, p. 84.
31. Owen Barfield, 'Introduction', in Jocelyn Gibb (ed.), *Light on C.S. Lewis*, Geoffrey Bles, London, 1965, p. xiv, mentions A.C. Harwood, W.E. Beckett, Leo Baker, Walter Field, Colonel Hanbury Sparrow, Tolkien and, on one occasion, Bede Griffiths.
32. The term is defined by Lewis in a letter to Arthur Greeves; see *CL* I, p. 119.
33. The walking tours and spoof examination papers are discussed in Harwood, *C.S. Lewis, My Godfather*, pp. 17–38. See also Owen Barfield's explanation of the in-jokes and allusions: www.owenbarfield.org/wordpress/wp-content/uploads/2022/07/The-Mock-Examination-Paper.pdf.

34. *CL* II, p. 838.
35. *CL* II, pp. 857–8.
36. *CL* II, p. 909.
37. *CL* II, p. 432.
38. *The Letters of J.R.R. Tolkien*, p. 378.
39. *CL* II, pp. 219–20.
40. *Out of the Silent Planet*, HarperCollins, London, 2005, ch. 21.
41. Ibid., ch. 9.
42. Glyer, *The Company They Keep*, p. 2.
43. These readers' reports form part of the Allen & Unwin archive at the University of Reading Special Collections; see AURR 6/1/43–6.
44. *The Letters of J.R.R. Tolkien*, p. 32.
45. University of Reading, Special Collections AUC 53/36.
46. *CL* II, p. 234 n.34.
47. *Out of the Silent Planet*, ch. 5.
48. *CL* II, p. 235.
49. Ibid.
50. *CL* II, p. 261.
51. *CL* II, p. 262.
52. *CL* II, pp. 478–50.
53. *CL* II, p. 449.
54. *CL* II, p. 649; C.S. Lewis, 'Preface' to *Essays Presented to Charles Williams*, Oxford University Press, London, 1947, pp. v–xiv.
55. *B&F*, pp. 206–7.
56. *CL* III, p. 1409.
57. *B&F*, p. 248.
58. *CL* III, p. 1040.

FIVE

1. *CL* II, p. 16.
2. *The Letters of J.R.R. Tolkien*, p. 80.
3. Ibid., p. 71.
4. Carpenter, *The Inklings*, p. 194; *The Letters of J.R.R. Tolkien*, p. 83.
5. *The Letters of J.R.R. Tolkien*, p. 83.
6. *AMR*, p. 393.
7. *CL* II, p. 9.
8. *CL* I, p. 838.
9. *CL* II, p. 96.
10. On the complex history of this poem, which Tolkien rewrote and revised numerous times, see Catherine McIlwaine, *Tolkien: Maker of Middle-Earth*, Bodleian Library Publishing, Oxford, 2018, p. 234.

11. *The Lays of Beleriand*, ed. Christopher Tolkien, HarperCollins, London, 2015, p. 151.
12. Ibid., pp. 315–29.
13. For a more detailed account of Lewis's proposed emendations and Tolkien's revisions, see Glyer, *The Company They Keep*, pp. 110–16.
14. See *The Lord of the Rings*, Appendix F: The Languages and Peoples of the Third Age.
15. The phrase appeared in an earlier version of *The Lord of the Rings* in the correct form but was removed in revision. See J.R.R. Tolkien, *Sauron Defeated*, HarperCollins, London, 2015, p. 47.
16. *The Letters of J.R.R. Tolkien*, p. 362.
17. *CL* III, p. 1049.
18. Glyer, *The Company They Keep*, pp. 46–75.
19. *CL* II, p. 991.
20. Humphrey Carpenter, *J.R.R. Tolkien: A Biography*, HarperCollins, London, 2002, p. 268.
21. Green and Hooper, *C.S. Lewis: A Biography*, p. 241.
22. *The Letters of J.R.R. Tolkien*, p. 352.
23. Holly Ordway, *Tolkien's Modern Reading: Middle-earth Beyond the Middle Ages*, Word on Fire, Park Ridge IL, 2021, pp. 75–80.
24. Carpenter, *The Inklings*, pp. 121–2.
25. Arthur Adams, 'C.S. Lewis and Shadowlands', *Magdalen College Record*, 1990, pp. 51–3.
26. Carpenter, *J.R.R. Tolkien: A Biography*, p. 203.
27. *CL* III, p. 228.
28. George Sayer, *Jack: C.S. Lewis and His Times*, Macmillan, London, 1988, p. 214.
29. *B&F*, p. 273.
30. Watson, 'The Art of Disagreement', p. 86.
31. *Out of My Bone: The Letters of Joy Davidman*, ed. Don W. King, Eerdmans, Grand Rapids MI, 2009, p. 106.
32. Ibid., p. 116.
33. *B&F*, p. 273.
34. *CL* III, p. 222.
35. *CL* III, p. 230.
36. *CL* III, p. 270.
37. *CL* III, p. 275.
38. *CL* III, pp. 376, 388.
39. *CL* III, p. 390.
40. *CL* III, pp. 390–92.
41. *CL* III, p. 596.
42. *CL* I, pp. 304–5.
43. *AMR*, p. 266.

44. *The Collected Poems of C.S. Lewis*, pp. 131–3.
45. *Out of My Bone*, p. 242.
46. Ibid., p. 246.
47. Ibid., p. 306.
48. Ibid., p. 207.
49. Ibid., p. 235.
50. *CL* III, p. 669.
51. *CL* III, p. 801.
52. *The Letters of J.R.R. Tolkien*, p. 349.
53. *CL* III, p. 798.
54. *CL* III, p. 812.
55. *CL* III, p. 808.
56. *CL* III, p. 834.
57. *CL* III, pp. 861–2.
58. *CL* III, p. 884.
59. *Out of My Bone*, pp. 308–9.
60. *CL* III, p. 1169.
61. *CL* III, p. 1188.
62. *CL* I, p. 187.
63. *A Grief Observed*, p. 47. Peter J. Schakel has suggested that this is not a literal account of Lewis's method of composition, but rather a fictional premiss for the writing of the work. See *Reason and Imagination in C.S. Lewis: A Study of Till We Have Faces*, Eerdmans, Grand Rapids MI, 1984, p. 168.
64. George Musacchio has argued that in writing *A Grief Observed*, Lewis adopted a fictional persona reflecting on bereavement rather than his own personal loss. See 'Fiction in a "Grief Observed"', *VII: Journal of the Marion E. Wade Center* 8, 1987, pp. 73–83.
65. *CL* III, p. 1063.
66. *CL* III, p. 1343.
67. *A Grief Observed*, p. 9.
68. 'Scazons' in *C.S. Lewis: Poems*, ed. Walter Hooper, Geoffrey Bles, London, 1964, p. 118.
69. *A Grief Observed*, p. 9.

SIX

1. Stella Aldwinckle, 'Memories of the Socratic Club', in White, Wolfe and Wolfe (eds), *C.S. Lewis and His Circle*, pp. 192–4.
2. John Wain, *Sprightly Running*, p. 141.
3. Helen Tyrrell Wheeler, 'Wartime Tutor', in David Graham (ed.), *We Remember C.S. Lewis: Essays & Memoirs*, Broadman & Holman, Nashville TN, 2001, pp. 48–52.
4. Watson, 'The Art of Disagreement', p. 80.

5. Routley, 'Stunning Effect'.
6. *Socratic Digest* 4, 1948, pp. 7–15.
7. C.S. Lewis, *Miracles: A Preliminary Study*, Geoffrey Bles, London, 1947, p. 27.
8. Lewis's reply was published in *Socratic Digest* 4, 1948, p. 15.
9. Ibid., pp. 15–16.
10. *Oxford Magazine* LXIV, p. 302, 23 May 1946.
11. *Oxford Magazine* LXIV, p. 359, 13 June 1946.
12. Brewer, 'The Tutor', p. 59.
13. *CL* III, 35.
14. Christopher W. Mitchell, 'University Battles: C.S. Lewis and the Oxford University Socratic Club', in *C.S. Lewis: Lightbearer in the Shadowlands*, ed. Angus Menuge, Crossway Books, Wheaton IL, 1997, pp. 329–51.
15. Bodleian Library MS. Eng. c. 7884, Oxford University Socratic Club Minute Book 1, ff. 4–15.
16. *CL* II, p. 564.
17. *The Letters of Dorothy L. Sayers*, Volume 2: *1937–1942, From Novelist to Playwright*, ed. Barbara Reynolds, Dorothy L. Sayers Society, Cambridge, 1997, pp. 410–12.
18. *CL* II, p. 573.
19. *CL* III, p. 1400.
20. *CL* II, p. 997.
21. *CL* II, p. 505.
22. Muriel Jones, 'With Women at College', in Schofield (ed.), *In Search of C.S. Lewis*, pp. 61–75.
23. I am very grateful to Amanda Ingram, St Hugh's College archivist, for her considerable assistance in locating these reports for me.
24. Jones, 'With Women at College', pp. 74–5.

SEVEN

1. C.S. Lewis, 'It all began with a picture...', *in C.S. Lewis Essay Collection,* p. 121.
2. *CL* II, p. 451.
3. Chad Walsh, *C.S. Lewis: Apostle to the Skeptics*, Wipf & Stock, Eugene OR, 1949, p. 10.
4. C.S. Lewis, *The Horse and His Boy*, William Collins, Glasgow, 1988, ch. 1.
5. *CL* I, p. 313.
6. *The Lion, the Witch and the Wardrobe*, ch. XIV.
7. *Sir Gawain and the Green Knight*, ed. J.R.R. Tolkien and E.V. Gordon, Oxford University Press, Oxford, 1967, lines 720–724.

EIGHT

1. *B&F,* p. 184.
2. *B&F,* p. 186.
3. See Helen Gardner's obituary of Lewis in *Proceedings of the British Academy* 51, 1965, pp. 417–28. Lewis recounted the hostility his work as a public Christian

attracted in an address to the RAF. See Bruce R. Johnson, 'Scripture, Setting, and Audience in the RAF Talks of C.S. Lewis', *Journal of Inklings Studies*, vol. 4, no. 2, 2014, pp. 87–113. For Lewis's reference to himself as a 'hot-gospeller', see *CL* II, p. 214.

4. *CL* II, p. 293.
5. *Oxford University Gazette*, 1 February 1951, pp. 450–51.
6. *B&F*, p. 268.
7. *Oxford University Gazette*, 15 February 1951, p. 490.
8. *The Letters of J.R.R. Tolkien*, p. 351.
9. *B&F*, p. 268.
10. *CL* I, pp. 762–3, 767.
11. Hegarty, 'The Tutorial Takeover, 1928–1968', pp. 610–11.
12. C.S. Lewis, *The Space Trilogy*, HarperCollins, London, 2002, p. 364.
13. *CL* II, pp. 246–7.
14. For the correspondence regarding the appointment, see Magdalene College Cambridge Private Papers F/CSL/1.
15. *CL* III, p. 487.
16. *CL* III, p. 900.
17. *CL* I, pp. 511–12.
18. 'Interim Report', p. 230.
19. *CL* II, 160–61.
20. *CL* I, p. 722.
21. Green and Hooper, *C.S. Lewis: A Biography*, p. 207; Charles Gilmore, 'To the RAF', in *C.S. Lewis at the Breakfast Table*, pp. 186–91. The phrase 'Pardoned in Heaven, the first by the throne' is a quotation from 'The Lost Leader' by Robert Browning.
22. *CL* III, p. 484.
23. *CL* III, p. 541.
24. K.B. McFarlane, *Letters to Friends 1940–1966*, ed. Gerald Harriss, Magdalen College, Oxford, 1997, p. 104.
25. *CL* III, p. 521.
26. 'Interim Report', p. 232.
27. *CL* III, p. 550.
28. A.C. Spearing, 'C.S. Lewis as a Research Supervisor', *Journal of Inklings Studies*, vol. 12, no. 1, 2022, pp. 110–17.
29. Richard W. Ladborough, 'In Cambridge', in Como (ed.), *C.S. Lewis at the Breakfast Table*, p. 99.
30. *CL* III, p. 485.
31. Watson, 'The Art of Disagreement', p. 82.
32. *CL* III, p. 518.
33. *Out of My Bone*, p. 235.
34. *CL* III, p. 896.

35. Ibid.
36. All Souls College Archives C/3/199–206. I am grateful to Gaye Morgan, All Souls College librarian, for locating these documents and providing me with scanned copies.
37. *CL* II, p. 331.
38. Simon Barrington-Ward, 'Foreword', 'C.S. Lewis: Personal Reflections', in Poe and Whitten Poe (eds), *C.S. Lewis Remembered*, p. 20.
39. *CL* III, p. 1164.
40. *CL* III, pp. 955–6.
41. https://magdlibs.com/2016/06/24/c-s-lewis.
42. '*De Descriptione Temporum*', in C.S. Lewis, *They Asked for a Paper*, Geoffrey Bless, London, 1962, pp. 9–25.
43. J.A.W. Bennett, 'The Humane Medievalist', in George Watson (ed.), *Critical Essays on C.S. Lewis*, Scolar Press, Aldershot, 1992, pp. 52–75.
44. *CL* III, p. 624.
45. 'Our English Syllabus', in *Rehabilitations and Other Essays*, Oxford University Press, London, 1939; Brian Barbour, 'Lewis and Cambridge', *Modern Philology*, vol. 96, no. 4, 1999, pp. 439–84.
46. Tom Shippey, 'The Lewis Diaries: C.S. Lewis and the English Faculty in the 1920s', in White, Wolf and Wolfe (eds), *C.S. Lewis and His Circle*, p. 148.
47. *CL* III, p. 793.
48. *CL* III, p. 577.
49. *B&F*, p. 235.
50. *CL* III, p. 449.
51. 'Interim Report', p. 231.
52. *CL* III, p. 1379.
53. *CL* III, p. 802.
54. *CL* III, p. 1448.
55. *CL* III, p. 1471. The Pope quotation is from *Epistles to Several Persons: Moral Essays*, Epistle II, 'Of the Characters of Women'.

NINE

1. *The Screwtape Letters*, Letter VII.
2. *C.S. Lewis: Letters to Children*, ed. Lyle W. Dorsett and Marjorie Lamp Mead, Collins, London, 1985, p. 13.
3. 'Cross-Examination', in *C.S. Lewis Essay Collection*, p. 148.
4. www.cslewis.org/ourprograms/thekilns.
5. The letter is also printed in *CL* III, pp. 1244–5.
6. As recounted by Walter Hooper in the Preface to *Of this and Other Worlds*, Collins, London, 1982, p. 1.
7. news.bbc.co.uk/1/hi/northern_ireland/7463800.stm.

8. This point is well made by Rowan Williams in *The Lion's World: A Journey into the Heart of Narnia*, S.P.C.K., London, 2012, ch. 3.
9. C.S. Lewis, *Mere Christianity*, HarperCollins, London, 1955, Preface.
10. William Nicholson, *Shadowlands: A Play*, Samuel French, London, 1990, p. 23.
11. 'C.S. Lewis', *The Canadian C.S. Lewis Journal*, Fall 1996, pp. 8–11.
12. I am grateful to Dr Bradley Wells for showing me round the college and sharing his knowledge of Lewis's time in Malvern with me.
13. This suggestion was first made in M.A. Manzalaoui, 'Narnia: The Domain of Lewis's Beliefs', in Kathryn Lindskoog, *Journey into Narnia*, Hope Publishing, Pasadena CA, 1998, p. 211 n1. Manzalaoui concedes that the evidence that Lewis would have known the lamp post is slight: 'Because the Newnham lamp post was once known to many academics, it is not unlikely that Lewis was aware of it; and if he was aware of it, he had no doubt visualized it.'
14. 'On Three Ways of Writing for Children', in *C.S. Lewis Essay Collection*, pp. 97–106.
15. Douglas H. Gresham, *Lenten Lands: My Childhood with Joy Davidman and C.S. Lewis*, HarperCollins, London, 2003, p. 57.
16. Philip Pullman, *Dæmon Voices: On Stories and Storytelling*, ed. Simon Mason, David Fickling Books, Oxford, 2020, p. 111.
17. Taken from a biographical sketch Lewis wrote for Macmillan; quoted in Green and Hooper, *C.S. Lewis: A Biography*, p. 170.
18. C.S. Lewis, *The Four Loves*, HarperCollins, London, 1960, ch. IV.

FURTHER READING

Carpenter, H., *J.R.R. Tolkien: A Biography*, HarperCollins, London, 1977.

Carpenter, H., *The Inklings: C.S. Lewis, J.R.R. Tolkien, Charles Williams and Their Friends*, HarperCollins, London, 2006.

Como, J.T., *C.S. Lewis at the Breakfast Table, and Other Reminiscences*, Collins, London, 1980.

Duriez, C., *J.R.R. Tolkien and C.S. Lewis: The Story of Their Friendship*, Sutton, Stroud, 2005.

Duriez, C., *The Oxford Inklings: Lewis, Tolkien and Their Circle*, Lion, Oxford, 2015.

Glyer, D.P., *Bandersnatch: C.S. Lewis, J.R.R. Tolkien, and the Creative Collaboration of the Inklings*, Black Squirrel Books, Kent OH, 2016.

Graham, D. (ed.), *We Remember C.S. Lewis: Essays & Memoirs*, Broadman & Holman, Nashville TX, 2001.

Green, R., and W. Hooper, *C.S. Lewis: A Biography*, rev. and expanded edn, Harper-Collins, London, 2002.

Gresham, D., *Lenten Lands: My Childhood with Joy Davidman and C.S. Lewis*, HarperOne, New York, 2003.

Heck, J.D., *No Ordinary People: 21 Friendships of C.S. Lewis*, Winged Lion Press, Hamden CT, 2022.

Hooper, W., *C.S. Lewis: A Companion & Guide*, HarperCollins, London, 1996.

Jacobs, A., *The Narnian: The Life and Imagination of C.S. Lewis*, S.P.C.K., London, 2005.

Loconte, J., *A Hobbit, a Wardrobe, and a Great War*, Thomas Nelson, Nashville TX, 2015.

McGrath, A., *C.S. Lewis: A Life*, Hodder & Stoughton, London, 2013.

McIlwaine, C., *Tolkien: Maker of Middle-earth*, Bodleian Library Publishing, Oxford, 2018.

Poe, H.L., and J. Veneman, *The Inklings of Oxford: C.S. Lewis, J.R.R. Tolkien, and Their Friends*, Zondervan, Grand Rapids MI, 2009.
Poe, H.L., and R. Whitten Poe (eds), *C.S. Lewis Remembered*, Zondervan, Grand Rapids MI, 2006.
Schofield, S. (ed.), *In Search of C.S. Lewis*, Bridge Publishing, South Plainfield NJ, 1983.
White R., J.E. Wolfe and B.N. Wolfe (eds), *C.S. Lewis and His Circle*, Oxford University Press, Oxford, 2015.
Wilson, A.N., *C.S. Lewis: A Biography*, HarperCollins, London, 2005.
Zaleski, P., and C. Zaleski, *The Fellowship: The Literary Lives of the Inklings*, Farrar, Straus & Giroux, New York, 2015.

PICTURE CREDITS

FIGURE 1	E.H. New, *New Loggan series of prints of Oxford colleges, and other prints.* Bodleian Library, G.A. Oxon a.33, fol. 10
FIGURE 2	Reproduced by permission of the Master and Fellows of University College, Oxford
FIGURE 3	By permission of the Warden, Fellows and Scholars of Keble College, Oxford/Bridgeman Images
FIGURE 4	Photo from the *Liber vitae Reginensium* (T. & A. Constable, Oxford, 1922) published by The Queen's College. By permission of the Provost and Fellows of The Queen's College, Oxford
FIGURE 5	Reproduced by permission of the Master and Fellows of University College, Oxford
FIGURE 6	Bodleian Library, OUA/NW 1/15/20
FIGURE 7	By permission of the President and Fellows of Magdalen College, Oxford, O1/P1/1, p. 89
FIGURE 8	By permission of the President and Fellows of Magdalen College, Oxford, FA1/9/2P/3, fol. 11
FIGURE 9	Photograph by Arthur Strong, Camera Press, London
FIGURE 10	Bodleian Library, Library Records c. 1826/© copyright CS Lewis Pte Ltd
FIGURE 11	Professor Andy Orchard/© copyright CS Lewis Pte Ltd
FIGURE 12	Wikimedia Commons/Gagravarr
FIGURE 13	Bodleian Library, C17 (29G) [34]
FIGURE 14	Photo by Leanda Shrimpton
FIGURE 15	Used by permission of the Marion E. Wade Center, Wheaton College, Wheaton, IL
FIGURE 16	Photograph by Michael Peto, © University of Dundee, Peto Collection
FIGURE 17	Alden's Oxford Guide Bodleian Library, G.A. Oxon 16° 107 (10), p. 90

FIGURE 18	By permission of the President and Fellows of Magdalen College, Oxford, O2/1/P8/124
PLATE 1	Bodleian Library, C17:70 Oxford (149)
PLATE 2	Wikimedia Commons/Velvet. Licence: CC BY-SA 3.0
PLATE 3	Wikimedia Commons/Topper. Licence CC BY-SA 4.0
PLATE 4	Bodleian Library, C.S. Lewis Notebook 29, p. 17 (Walter Hooper collection)/© copyright CS Lewis Pte Ltd
PLATE 5	By permission of the President and Fellows of Magdalen College, Oxford, P0325
PLATE 6	By permission of the President and Fellows of Magdalen College, Oxford, Acc. 2023/7/© copyright CS Lewis Pte Ltd
PLATE 7	Photo by David Iliff. Licence: CC BY-SA 3.0
PLATE 8	By permission of the President and Fellows of Magdalen College, Oxford
PLATE 9	By permission of the Master and Fellows of Magdalene College, Cambridge, M.10.18/© copyright CS Lewis Pte Ltd
PLATE 10	By permission of the President and Fellows of Magdalen College, Oxford, P317/MS1/1/© copyright CS Lewis Pte Ltd
PLATE 11	Bodleian Library, MS. Eng. lett. c. 861, fol. 91r/© copyright CS Lewis Pte Ltd
PLATE 12	Image © C.S. Lewis Foundation
PLATE 13	Photo by Leanda Shrimpton
PLATE 14	© Martin Anderson/Alamy Stock Photo
PLATE 15	© Martin Anderson/Alamy Stock Photo
PLATE 16	Bodleian Library, Arch. H e55, p. 25/© copyright CS Lewis Pte Ltd
PLATE 17	Bodleian Library, MS. Eng. misc. c. 1109, fol. 1v/© copyright CS Lewis Pte Ltd
PLATE 18	Bodleian Library, Dep. c. 1104, fol. 6r/© copyright CS Lewis Pte Ltd
PLATE 19	Bodleian Library, Dep. c. 1104, fol. 8r/© copyright CS Lewis Pte Ltd
PLATE 20	Wikimedia Commons/Ozeye. Licence: CC BY-SA 3.0
PLATE 21	Bodleian Library, MS. Eng. lett. c. 220/1, fol. 86r/© copyright CS Lewis Pte Ltd
PLATE 22	Rare Books and Special Collections, Northern Illinois University
PLATE 23	Photo by David Iliff. Licence: CC BY-SA 3.0
PLATE 24	Photo by David Iliff. Licence: CC BY-SA 3.0
PLATE 25	Used by permission of the Marion E. Wade Center, Wheaton College, Wheaton, IL
PLATE 26	Image © C.S. Lewis Foundation
PLATE 27	© Flik47/Shutterstock
PLATE 28	Wikimedia Commons/MrHistorianDude. Licence: CC BY-SA 4.0
PLATE 29	Photo by Leanda Shrimpton
PLATE 30	© Radharc Images/Alamy Stock Photo
PLATE 31	Wikimedia Commons/genvessel

INDEX

Love of Art & Murder

From Mystic to the City of Steeples

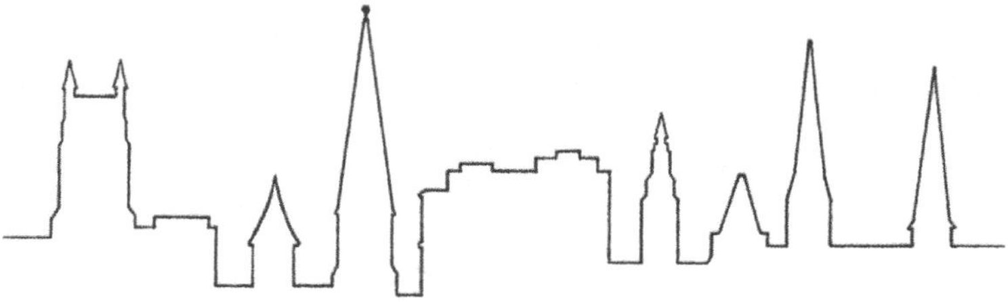

A Novel by

Rose Young

Inspired by a True Art Crime

♥

BestBooksPublish.com

xxxx

Library of Congress Control Number: 2023903160

ISBN 978-0-9988817-6-8 (paperback)

ISBN 978-0-9988817-5-1 (eBook)

Book Cover Design & Steeple Illustration: Cindy Samul, Illustrator

www.CindySamulIllustrator.com

Dedication

This book is dedicated to all creative types: artists, sculptors, performers, photographers, designers, writers, and those who appreciate the fine arts and support them.

Many creative people can be weird and different, and that's cool because they have a back door pass to a different universe than the highly logical types. Being creative can be a spiritual connection, a personal connection to one's art that doesn't need explaining.

The journey of a creative person is a striving one, and often monetary rewards and accolades are intermittent. Artists are innately inspired to create, and when they express their spirit in their art, we may discover they have inspired our creative spirit too.

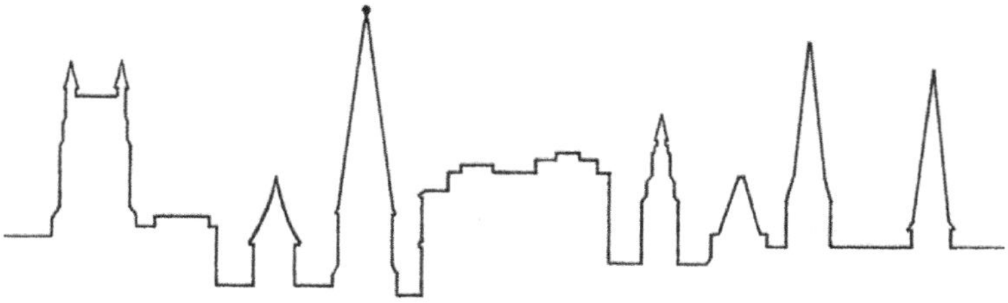

CONTENTS

Love of Art &
Murder

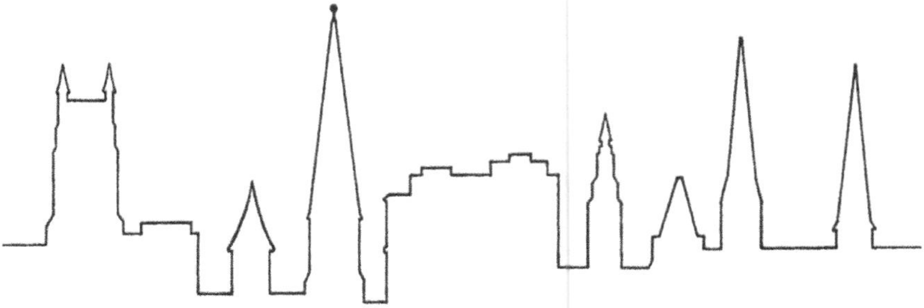

AN IMAGINATIVE ACCOUNT OF A
TRUE ART CRIME
THAT IS STILL UNSOLVED.

CHAPTER 1

Vinho Verde Wine Bar
Friday - 8:00 a.m., August
City of Steeples - New London, Connecticut

The summer morning breeze off the river caught a blonde wisp of Marilyn's hair, touched her cheek, and kissed her hot-pink lips. Yet, her lovely green eyes were frozen by her partner in death, Athena's spear. Her latest sculpture of Athena, whose golden shield has caught the morning's rays, glints toward the street three stories below.

Georgi Algarve sweeps the front sidewalk of the Vinho Verde Wine Bar. Dance music plays from the exterior speakers. The young wine sommelier swings the broom around like a dance partner, and as he bends back in a final move, his upward glance captures an oddity on the third-floor balcony of the Dahlia Art Gallery studios.

He turns to achieve a better view. His beautiful artist friend, Marilyn Maroney, in her vintage 1950s dress, was in a static backbend against her sculpture of Athena - dead. He sees a dark pool of blood on the sidewalk below. Immediately, Georgi lets out a blood-curdling scream. Wildly, he races up and down Bank Street crying for help.

***

Ready to respond to the call at the Dahlia Gallery on Bank Street, Detective Dan Morrison clamps the badge onto his belt, sweeps back his dark hair, and rushes out to his official black SUV.

Officer Demi Acevedo, the police department's forensic photographer, is already at the scene. She looks up from her ground-level vantage point at the gallery's handsome French colonial building and began photographing the staggering image of Marilyn Maroney on the balcony. Any casual passerby would think it was another extreme sculpture at the avant-garde institution. The Dahlia always welcomed dramatic art.

Officer Demi is prepared with her gloves and protection on her shoes to eliminate contamination. She passes the first-floor gallery door and opens a nearby entrance that leads to the six art studio apartments. She climbs a long single run of stairs, and at the top, she passes two apartments, loops through the corridor and ascends the next run of stairs, until she reaches Marilyn's apartment on the third floor. With her camera in hand, she heads toward the death scene.

The forensic photographer takes a deep breath and steps on the balcony to see Marilyn's vintage dress waver in the warm August breeze. She clicks away but suddenly stops with a gasp. Her years of experience in crime scene photography didn't prepare her for this death scene. *Marilyn is part of her sculpture! Has this been staged?* Athena's spear pierced Marilyn's back.

The goddess of war and wisdom was in an action pose. One leg was forward in a lunge, and her right hand held an authentic spear at waist height, ready to jab a rival. Unfortunately, the spear held Marilyn in place.

Slowly, Officer Demi changes her camera angle. She observes Athena's intense facial expression representing the moment of the jab. The sculpture has a distinctively tall helmet and an armored breastplate that brandishes the head of Medusa, the hideous hag with writhing snakes for hair. Through her camera lens, she gazes at Medusa, then at Marilyn, and gulps. The legend of Medusa's stare was that it could turn anyone into stone. Demi whispers, "Rigor mortis." Marilyn was rigid as stone.

Demi continues to use her camera to zoom in, study, and magnify the scene further. Athena's shield was in her left hand. Marilyn carefully had brushed small squares of gold leaf on its surface to enhance the shine of Athena's disc. The morning sun's angle made it glow. This was an aspect of psychological warfare to dazzle a foe with one's weaponry and render them awestruck and fearful. Yet on this fateful day, the brilliant reflection from Athena's shield morosely illuminated the stark scene on the balcony three stories high.

Officer Demi shakes the tension out of her hand from gripping the camera and stares in disbelief at how Marilyn had died. Inhaling deeply, she exhales her breath expressively and gathers her confidence. Standing back she scrutinizes the possibilities of what had occurred. A heel on Marilyn's shoe was jammed into the grated ironwork of the balcony. With her discerning eye, she photographs every angle. This detail made it possible that Marilyn had tripped and fallen onto Athena's spear. *But did she?*

On the street level, Detective Morrison arrives and crosses the police barrier. He sees Georgi sitting on a bench in front of the gallery. The slim, well-dressed young man of twenty-nine years held his head in his hands. His hair, usually coiffed on top with razor-trimmed sides, was noticeably mussed. Concerned, Morrison approaches him. "Georgi! *You* discovered the body?"

The detective's last major case involved the homicide of Georgi's boss. And now, here he was again. Morrison knew him well enough yet, could never anticipate Georgi's sensitive nature. It ranged from demure to a sudden tidal wave of emotions. Today, Georgi's tear-stained face informs him that trauma for his friend has set in.

Georgi responds to Morrison's familiar voice with the exasperation that came from being in shock. "Discovered the body? It's not a body! It's Marilyn! The vivacious, stunning, eccentric Marilyn! The one and only girl I admire so much that if I were a girl, I would want to be her." Georgi's hands went to his heart as he admonishes the detective. "It is not a body! She is Marilyn Maroney!" Exceedingly upset, Georgi proceeds to gasp for air.

"Georgi, take a deep breath," Morrison advises. "Remember what Roxanne has told you? Breathe."

Georgi sucks air loudly and seems on the edge of hyperventilating.

Morrison gulps. "I didn't know the woman was your friend. I'm sorry."

Georgi inhales deeply through his nose, while he fans his face with his hand and attempts to calm himself. He exhales loudly.

Morrison ponders the situation while Georgi pants. *He does not have the constitution for this.* He looks skyward. *Why him again?* He notices sweeping cirrus clouds shaped like exclamation points. *Mom would say, "That's a sign from heaven, Danny."* It was then that Morrison knew whom to call for help. "Stay put, Georgi. I have several things to do. I'll come back around to you." Morrison was now in pursuit of permission to bring in a trusted confidant.

Georgi sat back on the bench and gazed across the street into the eyes of Prince. A large honorary mural of the musician had been painted on the brick wall of the Hot Rod Cafe. Georgi remembered how much Marilyn admired his music. He sunk his head in his hands again and cried.

Just as the activity increases under the gallery's sign, Troy Zaner, one of the artists in residence, burst out the door. "Georgi, what's going on? I just woke up."

"Troy!" Grabbing his arm urgently, Georgi asks, "Can we go inside the gallery? Do you have a key?"

"Sure, I do." Troy unlocks the door. "You look horrible, and you never do. Why are the police here?" He searches Georgi's face for understanding. They each take a seat on two of the twenty black vinyl stools that line the long reception bar of the art gallery.

"You don't know, do you?" Georgi saw in Troy's eyes the innocence of being unaware and wishes he, too, were ignorant of the morbid knowledge.

"Know what?"

With great apprehension, Georgi whispers, "It's Marilyn, Troy." Unable to control himself, he cries, "She's on her balcony...dead!" He folds into a lump and sobs into his already wet shirt.

"No! No, no! That's not possible!" Troy exclaims in disbelief. He leaps out of his seat about to go back outside.

Georgi quickly grabs his arm. "Don't go, Troy! It's a horrific scene, and you can't remember her like that. You can't." Pausing briefly, he whimpers, "It's no way to remember her."

Troy froze, shocked by his friend's words. Images of Marilyn flash through his mind from the previous night when they had a massive party and art reception for the resident artists. Three hundred guests had filtered through the event and the neighboring Velvet Muse performance venue. He put his hand on Georgi's shoulder. "I should listen to you. I've had enough experiences to know I don't need to traumatize myself with an image of Marilyn I will never forget."

He slowly settles his stocky body on a stool. His usual ready smile has vanished. He leans on the counter and reflects in a daze, "You're right, you know. I need to remember her dancing with friends, being full of life, and having fun."

Georgi sighs with relief. "Oh yes, that is the way, Troy. Listen, the detective is coming back. Will you stay in case he has questions about last night?"

"Sure. Let me put the lights on and get us some water." Troy did so and pushes a button for some subtle background music. He extends a bottled water to Georgi from behind the counter that doubles as a bar and buffet during gallery events.

"Troy, I need to call Roxanne. Do you mind? I want to see if she'll come by and sit with us. Her presence is comforting to me."

"Of course. It would be good to have another friend to talk with and keep us distracted. Are you all right if I run to my apartment while you make the call? I want to put on another shirt. I'll be right back, okay?"

Georgi nods as he dials his dear friend.

Troy left the gallery and was escorted to his apartment after he put on shoe coverings. He had lived on the second floor for ten years. His youthful appearance defied his age of mid-forties. Locally, he was a well-known talented artist who had created several city murals.

***

Roxanne Samson is the wife of the fire chief and an expert gardener. Two months earlier, in June, she had found Mitch Stockman, Georgi's boss, deceased in a city garden she tended. The incident bonded Roxanne and Georgi's friendship through muggings, murder, and of all things, a water dunking. She and Georgi sleuthed their way into Detective Morrison's heart via heartburn when they haphazardly uncovered the true villains in the crime.

As the phone rang, Georgi paces the art gallery's floor, his heels click on the polished hardwood. Roxanne answered, and Georgi tried to contain his distress but failed. "Roxanne! You're not going to believe it. My world is ending!"

Startled, she knew it had to be something for Georgi to carry on this way. "Georgi, what happened? What's the problem?"

Roxanne was a sensible woman in her late forties and did not consider herself an embellisher like Georgi. She knew he had a good reason at times to express his enthusiasm or dismay with great extravagance. But this was a surprise.

"This is not a problem—it's a tsunami! Someone has opened the floodgates to hell! Why is this happening to me, Roxanne? Please, can you come down?"

"Where? Where are you?"

"I'm at the Dahlia with Troy, and well, uhh…I don't know how to say this, but ughhh. Marilyn is dead!" Georgi broke down. Through tears, he blubbers, "Detective Morrison told me to stay here."

"I'll be right there, Georgi. Hold on to yourself—don't lose it."

CHAPTER 2

Lethal Sculpture
The Dahlia

Having left Georgi, Detective Morrison approaches Fire Chief Samson, aka Chief Sam, whose first responders work with the police to secure the area. They block the road and detour traffic away from Bank Street. Since it was a weekday with morning rush hour, that took some doing because the major one-way artery needed to be diverted into the labyrinth of downtown New London. When Morrison approached, Chief Sam had just finished communicating with his crew on his two-way radio.

"Chief, did you know Georgi found the victim?"

Chief Sam nodded, "Yes, I heard." He leaned toward Morrison. His six-foot-two stature was intimidating, and his bushy, white eyebrows were raised inquiringly. "Let me guess. Is my wife Roxanne in your next question?"

The chief handled most emergencies well, except for the ones Roxanne was in. Those kept his heart rate up.

Morrison winced. "It's an awkward request, but you understand my dilemma, Chief. Roxanne can keep Georgi calm. Can I utilize her talent while we get through the questioning?"

With a sigh, the chief nodded perceptively. "She'll be happy to assist you, though I am reluctant." Then he steps forward and lowers his voice. "Georgi will be better with her by his side, and it will hopefully make quick work of it for you. Right? So go ahead."

Morrison nods his appreciation. "Thanks, I'll give her a call."

But the chief's following few words were pincers. "They may try to help you in your investigation again. Resist, Detective, resist. I don't trust them, but I do trust you."

"Yes, of course, Chief."

Roxanne was already on her way when the detective phoned her. *Why am I surprised?*

***

Forensic officer Carolena Sanchez had suited up to dust for prints and collect evidence. She very carefully analyzed every inch of the apartment. Her jet-black hair was swept into an informal knot with several thin metal skewers set into her thick bun. Interestingly, they were ready tools for her job. She would grab one, disinfect it with a wipe, and use it to pick up evidence from the ground, lift fabric on a body, or for whatever needed her eagle-eyed inspection.

Speaking informally to each other, Carolena points, "Can you take photos of this cake crumb caught in the balcony's grate, Demi, and another to capture the fire escape ladder?" They notice the escape ladder had been released from its three-story perch. It extended down to six feet above the sidewalk. She dusts it for prints.

Although they seemed in a world of their own at three-stories high, Carolena suddenly notices people on the street gawking. She had called for the privacy sheet to be brought up. *Where are they?* Voyeurs with cameras could see Marilyn from at least a half block away, and common practice was to cloak a death scene from view.

Calling on her walkie, Officer Sanchez asked Chief Sam to extend the cordoned scene farther because she was waiting on a privacy screen.

Immediately, the chief acted. "Push back those onlookers, will you?"

One of his men managing the foot traffic responded, "Yes, sir, and it looks like the press are coming too."

"Hold them back. I don't want them capturing this scene." He radios his crews. "Extend the perimeter and get a sheet screen here, will ya? This is becoming a spectacle. They'll be selling tickets next." He lifts his uniform hat and brushes back his thick white hair. "They always want a view, then wish they never saw it."

***

Medical Examiner Dr. Angela Storm arrives ready to observe, examine, and determine the cause of death. She meets Detective Morrison on the street by Dahlia's neighbor, the Hygienic Art Gallery. They stand below the huge mural of five statuesque women painted on the side of the brick historic building. They look up at Marilyn's sculpture of Athena and her obvious death scene. The detective tries to read Dr. Storm's face. Her golden-brown eyes were serious, yet he detects her surprise.

They had only worked together for two months. Both had over fifteen years of experience in similar but different fields of death. Morrison told her what he knew so far. "Georgi Algarve, the owner of the Vinho Verde Wine Bar from across the street, discovered her. She's his friend, Marilyn Maroney, an artist-in-residence at the Dahlia. That is her third-floor apartment."

Dr. Storm was tall at five feet eight and had a slim athletic build. Her honey-brown hair was clasped into a French twist. She wore a summer-weight navy vest with "Medical Examiner" emblazoned in bold white letters. Mesmerized by Marilyn's dramatic position, nonetheless, Dr. Storm was ready to analyze her up close. She and Morrison covered their shoes and donned gloves before striding up the narrow flight of stairs to the third floor.

Her voice echoes in the tight stairwell. "Detective, did you know that in the 1940s and '50s, the image of Marilyn would have been all over the front page of tomorrow's newspapers?" She turns and whispers, "Her dress fits that era."

Morrison had a small notepad and pen in hand and stopped. "Should I be writing this down?" he jests, and she turns to look down at him. He points his pen at her. "Dr. Storm, I'm not surprised you said that since you have a professional curiosity about death." Tapping his pen in thought, he probes, "Do you have a book of images from that era, Dr. Storm?" He watched eyebrows raise.

"Your deduction is correct, Detective. I have a coffee-table book of them." She waves him up the stairs. "Now, let's get to work."

They reach the long hallway of the second floor and continue upward to Marilyn's apartment. The somberness of the scene settles on them as they study the room.

Dr. Storm notices Marilyn's studio apartment was fashionably decorated. The retro interior was neat and clean. She integrated 1950s furnishings with a contemporary style. A bright pink, retro refrigerator highlighted her kitchen with a cat cookie jar on the counter. At first glance, the medical examiner thought Marilyn's painting style was similar to Georgia O'Keeffe's, yet with a unique twist.

The medical examiner and detective approached the open balcony door. Dr. Storm sighs at seeing Marilyn's backbend position against the spear that impaled her. Softly she said, "If only she didn't add the spear, she would still be alive. Look at the directional impact. Tsk, it's such a shame."

Morrison took it all in. "I hope it was quick," he murmurs. He examines the spear and Athena's lunging position. "This is a Greek tragedy. Her art killed her!"

"Why design a lethal sculpture, Morrison?" She watched a grim expression cross his face as he folds his arms and ponders.

"Unintended consequences," he said with dismay. "I believe she did not intend to design art that would achieve a mortal outcome. She didn't think the spear's height and position could harm someone."

Morrison studies the probability of her fall and moves in closer. Pausing, he gazes at her face; it looked like exquisitely painted porcelain. Her coiffured shoulder-length hair had soft pinup girl curls, and her lips were hot pink and parted in the last gasp for life. The unending stare of her green eyes halts him. Morrison steps back, affected by the terrible loss of her youthful life. Even with years of experience, he had to fight off his astonishment.

Dr. Storm observes the mournful look on his face. "It is bizarre, Morrison, to see a beautiful young woman die like this. Are you okay?"

He pulls himself together. "Yes. I suppose artists want their work to be dramatic, but she took it too far."

"Well, sometimes it's hard to know what too far is…until you've gone too far," she responds knowingly. Morrison gave her a quizzical look, and she continued. "Unfortunately, Marilyn didn't live to learn that lesson, and that is how many of the deceased end up on my examination table."

"The real question is, Doctor, did she fall on her own accord, or is this a homicide?" Morrison was eager to know.

Dr. Storm contemplates the scene before her. "It appears at first glance that she may have fallen. Look at her feet. Her heel is caught in the balcony. All women know the hazard of heels, yet we still wear them." She shook her head in disbelief. "Weegee would have been all over this mortal ending."

"Is that the photographer in your coffee-table book?"

She analyzed the horrific scene while answering. "Yes, Arthur Fellig's nickname was 'Weegee,' and he was notoriously the first to arrive as a press photographer in the forties and fifties. His Speed Graphic camera captured photojournalistic images. The contrast of his black-and-white photos was blunt and powerful. He caught the strange and traumatic ways people died and the witnesses' horror.

"It was common for these vivid scenes to end up on America's front-page news." Looking toward Morrison, she adds, "Of course, that practice stopped when decency and honoring the dead took the place of selling newspapers."

Dr. Storm's gaze went to Marilyn's neck as she looks for any bruising that would depict strangulation. Nothing. Marilyn's summer dress of pink rosettes set against cream was tailored perfectly to her form. Wide straps hugged her shoulders. She scrutinizes the fatal wound and reanalyzes the balcony's grillwork and how she might have fallen. "Hmm. Yes, Detective, it is easy to assume she tripped, but we will factor everything."

"Do you want to speak with our forensic officers?" he asks. "They've been gathering and photographing the evidence."

"Yes, I would like a few specific photos from various heights to calculate if an assailant pushed her."

Dr. Storm gave her instructions, and Officer Demi set off to find a ladder and tripod to position the photos accurately. She would also utilize a drone to take pictures, submitting a different perspective that might reveal more in the overview shot.

"My autopsy starts here Detective, and my goal is to do the best I can for her family and your investigation. I'm sure you have plenty to do. I will determine the time of death and give you as much information as possible."

He looks away from Marilyn. "Yes, I need to get back downstairs to Georgi. Let me know if anything important comes up. My assistant, Detective Peabody, should be here if you need anything."

"Yes, of course." Suddenly, Dr. Storm's attention was caught. "Detective, there are cake remnants. Do you see them?" She nods toward pink and white cake pieces lodged in the balcony's iron grate. Raising Marilyn's hand, she saw pink frosting on her fingers.

He looks around. "Is there more?" He turns and glances over the balcony. Down below, by the curb on the sidewalk, there appeared to be a bright pink napkin from the party.

Dr. Storm inquisitively cocked her head. "Is it possible someone did not like cake, Detective?"

Immediately, Morrison examines the distance of the cake on the balcony from the body, the frosting on her fingertips, and the suspect party napkin below. Considering the trajectory, he squints in thought. A sly knowingness crosses his face. "Ahh, it does seem there could have been two people on this balcony last night, Dr. Storm, and possibly, one did not like cake. Thank you for pointing that out."

Enthused by a possible clue, Morrison left to examine the sidewalk below for evidence. As he descends the stairs, he recalls the medical examiner plaque Dr. Angela Storm had outside her office:

Let conversation cease, let laughter flee.
This is the place where death delights to help the living.

The detective considered the words with confidence. *With Dr. Angela Storm, the angel of death on my side, I have an excellent chance of solving this case soon.*

CHAPTER 3

Was This an Accident?
9:30 a.m.

Roxanne made her way to the fortified scene on Bank Street. Her petite frame of five-foot-two, blonde pageboy hairstyle, and teal top with khaki shorts contrasted in the scene of dark uniformed police and emergency responders. An officer was about to deny her access when Morrison spotted her and hollered, "Let her through." Welcoming her with heartiness, he was relieved to see her sweet face. "I knew I could count on you, Roxanne. Poor Georgi has had quite a shock."

"Detective, was this an accident?" she asks, drawing in close.

"It's hard to tell." Morrison's eyes told Roxanne it might not be. "Look, I'll give you a few minutes with him and Troy before I start questioning them. Go on in." He held the door for her.

She enters the gallery. Her two friends, Troy and Georgi, were huddled in conversation. Upon seeing Roxanne, they rose to greet her. She gave them each a firm hug, and they sat at the long counter. "I'm so sorry for you two. What happened? Do you know?"

Troy shook his head, and Georgi tried to tell his story but cups his mouth and cried. "I can't get the image out of my mind!"

Roxanne hugs him and gently cautions, "Be careful now. Calm down. You don't want to get upset and pass out."

He took a deep breath and sniveled. "It might be better than the sight of Marilyn."

Roxanne glances at Troy. He was unshaven and wearing navy skate shoes, sweatpants, and a fresh T-shirt that displayed a colorful creature. Saddened, he said, "Georgi warned me not to look. I'm glad I didn't."

Georgi fans his face anxiously. "And now I have to answer Detective Morrison's questions. He may grill me again since I'm connected to another death on Bank Street." He looks at Roxanne. "Remember how unkind he was the first time?"

"Now, now, don't you worry, Georgi. The detective likes you. Look at all we did to help him catch those nasty people in the wine business. He knows you are honest and true. You just happened to be the unlucky bystander who discovered her."

Georgi swipes the tears from his cheeks and sweat from his forehead. "I know we left on his good side. But why? Why does this keep happening? I'm overwhelmed." Sniffing, he grabs a napkin and daintily blew his nose. Grabbing another, he swats the air with it. "I don't want to be unlucky," he whines.

Roxanne patted his hand. "All we can do right now is try and help them find out what happened. That is all. Okay?"

Georgi straightens up in his seat and takes a deep breath. He held Roxanne's hand. "Thank you. You're my muse of comfort and wisdom."

Troy watched as this played out and withdrew within himself, pondering Georgi's words: *My muse of comfort and wisdom.* It made him a little curious, and he realized, *I need a new muse.* Even though Roxanne couldn't read his thoughts, she gazed at Troy with empathy, and he gratefully felt it.

Detective Morrison walked through the door. His dark slacks, badge on his belt, blue oxford shirt, no tie, black hair, and piercing blue eyes were all business. But on moving into their scene of sorrow, he softened. He knew them all well enough. Troy Zaner had been on the board of directors for the Dahlia in the past, and Morrison was aware of him through the many art openings, receptions, and parties, though sometimes rowdy, that had occurred over the years.

"Troy, I'm sorry about your friend. Do you know who she was with last night?"

"Ugh," Troy groaned. "Detective, our art opening and reception party started at six o'clock last night, and the music in the Velvet Muse got going around seven-thirty. There must have been three hundred people between the Dahlia Art Gallery and the Velvet Muse. Marilyn was everywhere.

"The blues band The Night Shakers and local hip-hop rapper Suave-Ski performed until nearly ten o'clock. She was in the gallery but went outside when a DJ took over the stage. He had electronic dance music and a multicolored laser light show. By then, the fog had rolled in from the Thames River, and the atmosphere had turned surreal, it was hard to see anyone clearly. The light show reflected off the mist that billowed around the dancers.

"Throughout the night, all the resident artists mingled with patrons and sold art. Marilyn was our main attraction because her work has become popular in the past year at major galleries." He paused. "Come to think of it, I saw her before eleven, so it must have happened to her afterward."

"That's good, Troy. Then we need to know who was here with her after eleven. This must be treated as a possible homicide until we can prove it differently. I hope you understand." Troy nodded, and Morrison asked, "Did anyone seem suspicious to you?"

"Suspicious? Hey, if you come to any of our events, you will always see someone suspicious. Hmph! You must know what I mean. We're free-spirited here and have our quirks and eccentricities, but that makes us creatives."

Troy collected his thoughts. "Look, some get drunk at these parties or are in a bizarre mood. How can you tell if they have malicious intent? Maybe you can." Troy rethought his comment. "Detective, I can suspect almost anyone, but how can you really tell? Isn't it all about motive?"

Morrison answered thoughtfully, "It depends. Is there a guest list or suggestions of who we should question first?"

"Ophelia Starr manages the gallery and can help you with our email list and social media followers, but you must realize people show up and walk in until we meet the maximum occupancy. There are a few of us who can look at the lists and try to recall who was here after eleven."

"That will narrow our suspects." Morrison was glad to have willing help.

Roxanne asked Georgi, "Were you here last night?"

"Yes, of course. I was behind the bar serving wine with Marco. We're a good team, and I like helping the gallery out. It's my donation to bring in some decent wine and bartend for the night." Taking a deep breath, he exhaled to try and maintain control of his emotions.

Roxanne kept her hand on his back for comfort. She was relieved he was doing better than she expected. He had been very distraught when his boss died. Then it occurred to her that he was probably in shock.

Georgi continued, "Marilyn came by the bar several times. We chatted about her vintage dress and her pink pumps. She told me about some of the artwork she'd sold. She said she had an offer to show her work in New York and arranged to meet with a curator when she returned from her show in Iceland."

Roxanne glanced at Detective Morrison, who was absorbing Georgi's details. "Did you notice anyone out of place, Georgi?"

"Who didn't fit in? That's impossible to determine at a Dahlia art event. Like Troy said, Detective, I don't think I can be of much help. We were busy serving people all night."

Roxanne schemed. "Georgi, how about if you and I stay busy together? What do you think about planning to open the doors of your Vinho Verde Wine Bar in the next few days to anyone who knew Marilyn? It might help you and everyone by being together." She continued to measure Morrison's reaction.

Considering her idea, Georgi said, "Hmm, Marilyn would like that, I'm sure." As he thought of everyone who loved her, he wanted to honor her memory. Taking Roxanne's lead, Georgi added, "It would be good for us to support each other. What do you think, Troy? What should we do?" Georgi bit the edge of his fingernail.

"I think our artist community needs to be together at a time like this. I can ask Ophelia to help us organize a list of whom we should contact first." The three began talking all at once, agreeing with the idea, when a high-pitched whistle froze them like a theatrical tableau.

"Okay, cool your jets!" They switched their full attention to the detective. "Don't get too far ahead of yourselves. I have an investigation to run and people to question. Do you really want to plan a get-together? This is highly irregular."

Roxanne sheepishly raised her hand. Morrison nodded to her. "Yes?"

"Detective, isn't it a good idea to have as many people who were at last night's event or who knew Marilyn easily available to you? We can do this right across the street. We're willing to help you." But just as the words fell out of her mouth, Morrison's one eyebrow raised, and those steely blue eyes looked at her incredulously. She held her breath.

"Mrs. Chief, I do not want a replay of our last murder-solving escapade where you and Georgi could not stop yourselves from being helpful. I cannot be responsible for your shenanigans. So, let's make this clear…." Georgi tried to hide behind Roxanne, figuring the detective's ire would hit her first. "…I'm in charge. Do you all agree?"

"Yes. I'm glad you're in charge," Troy said with relief.

Georgi popped out from behind Roxanne. "Yes, sir, and you can use my office to talk to people privately. If it's okay with you, we could arrange it for this Sunday afternoon. By then, we should be able to let everyone know."

Morrison fixated on each of them, then relented from his position. He nodded, "Alright, Detective Peabody and I will have members of the police force on hand in case anyone has information." He pointed his finger at Roxanne and Georgi. "But no funny business or sleuthing on your own. If you hear of anything, report it to Detective Peabody or me. Got it?"

"Got it!" they said in unison. Georgi looked behind Roxanne's back to see if she had her fingers crossed. Hers were not. His were.

Morrison continued, "Okay then, you can tell people about Marilyn, and that an inquiry is underway to determine the cause of her death. We'll start at one o'clock Sunday. It should give most people time to hear from you and try to make the event. You call it a get-together, and I'll call it gathering details."

Instantly, Troy and Georgi pulled out their phones. They texted some friends to call as soon as possible.

Morrison watched them and thought, *This is the most unconventional way of launching an investigation*. At that moment, his mystery-loving Irish mother popped into his mind. *See, Danny, just like Agatha Christie, you bring people together in one room and learn more about everyone. It just might work.* But Morrison thought differently from his mother. This was more serious than a fictional tale. "I'll see you all Sunday at one o'clock."

Troy and Georgi nodded without looking up from their phones while Roxanne stood between them, a pillar of support like the goddesses on the giant mural at the nearby Hygienic Art Gallery. Morrison left to scrutinize Marilyn's apartment again.

Troy contacted Martina Shaw, the Dahlia Art Gallery's board of directors' president. He then would call Ophelia Starr, the gallery director who coordinated the art reception and music with the Velvet Muse. Next would be the resident artists: Cora, Teddy, and Bruce. Together, they would devise a way to let everyone know about Marilyn and the Vinho Verde Wine Bar gathering.

Marilyn's Apartment

Upstairs, Morrison watched Dr. Storm complete the examination of Marilyn's wound. She informed him, "It looks like she's been dead for maybe seven hours or more. That would bring the time of death around one o'clock in the morning because the rigor has set in solidly."

"At least I have a timeframe to work with—" Morrison was interrupted as two men with a gurney entered to assist Dr. Storm.

"The three of us will release her from the spear now, Detective. Stop by my examining room when you have the chance." Then she whispered, "There was no cake in her mouth."

He nodded slowly. "Okay, I'll be there later today." Morrison left, wondering what it meant that there was cake everywhere but in her mouth.

CHAPTER 4

Marilyn - Before Her Fatality

Galleries, national magazines, and art collectors worldwide had finally recognized Marilyn's art and sculptures. Her work was all the buzz as fresh, dynamic, and worthy of investment. Yet her home base remained in New London with easy access to large East Coast cities by train. The quick ride to Hartford's international airport made this creative waterside location in the City of Steeples, her little slice of heaven.

Troy had encouraged Marilyn as an art mentor during her teenage years. Her imaginative first works were shown at the Dahlia Art Gallery with her high school art class. She then volunteered at the gallery and learned different mediums and methods to create art. She attended the Rhode Island School of Design, and through art experimentation, she emerged with her own style.

Now, after years of experience and turning thirty, she was achieving popularity. Galleries were scheduling her a year in advance.

***

Marilyn was wearing tight jeans cuffed at the ankles and black flats. Her pink cotton blouse fit loosely and flowed about as she placed and adjusted her newest sculpture on the balcony over Bank Street. Her development of a sculptural medium made of lightweight fiberglass formed and shaped over high-density polystyrene foam was successful. It was a flexible combination that allowed her to make additions or changes, and once hardened, it was unbreakable.

As Marilyn anchored the sculpture on the balcony, she recalled the school trip where she first saw a statue of Athena. It was at the Slater Memorial Museum, just minutes away, in the city of Norwich. The museum's world-renowned plaster collection represents thousands of years of masters' sculptural works. She loved many, but Athena became her muse of feminine strength.

She had a second encounter at Boston's Fine Arts Museum. As she ascended the grand staircase, to her surprise, the original stone sculpture of Athena was looking down at her. This had her search for more images in museums worldwide for inspiration. She found many forms of Athena as the goddess of handcrafts, victory, wisdom, and protection. The animals that accompanied her were either a snake or an owl. Yet most depictions were of her poised in her armor, holding a spear and shield.

Marilyn had considered Athena's many attributes, but ultimately, she thought, 'what would a buyer want?' She decided her heroine in action would be unique and dynamic. This was when she formulated the lunging pose with the spear.

She worked for many months to complete Athena, then added the shield, burnishing it with gold leaf. She stood back to observe and was pleased with Athena's surreal appeal of beauty and strength in action. Yet Marilyn's last dilemma was how to create a believable spear. Time was running out. She stared at Athena and delved through the options in her mind. Suddenly, she remembered Georgi's friend Marco and resorted to asking him for help.

Marco's antique and restoration warehouse had many items of décor for various applications. His clients ranged from the average homeowner looking for architectural details to movie houses and event planners who needed props.

After calling his many contacts, Marco serendipitously found Marilyn an authentic antique spear in an estate sale. Unwanted, it sat in the estate agent's warehouse. Upon examination, Marilyn purchased it and was thrilled with her luck. Carefully, she slid the sharp lance into the slot she created in Athena's gripping hand. With the spear set, she stepped back to observe her finished work and was overcome with pride. It was her most important piece of art to date.

CHAPTER 5

The Value of Death

Martina Shaw arrived at 10:30 a.m. to find Troy with the detectives. Her youthful motherly vibe jived with her long silver-gray braids and Jamaican floral dress. Her vivacious persona hid the fact that she had entered her sixties.

Immediately, Martina approached Troy with a hug and a hint of a lilting accent, "This is a disgraceful tragedy. It's good you called me right away." She looked him over to see how he was handling the stress. Troy had known her for at least twenty years, and with a few tears forming, they took a moment to compose themselves for the detectives.

Morrison knew her and introduced Jack Peabody, his assistant. "I'm sorry for your loss, Martina. This must be devastating for you." He paused a moment as she nodded and swiped a falling tear quickly. "Please have a seat." She sat next to Troy on a stool. "Martina, if you don't mind, I have a few questions that can't wait. What can you tell me about last night? Troy and Georgi said you were all here for an art opening and reception party."

"Oh yes, I was helping with the drinks behind the bar with Georgi and Marco. Marilyn came and went by us all evening. It does seem odd not to have seen her after eleven because she usually helps us clean up. I assumed she had an interested buyer, Dan." Martina pulled on her long braids and curved them around her hand with concern.

"Did you notice anyone suspicious before, during, or after the event?" Morrison proceeded.

Martina spread her arms wide to encompass the room as she explained, "Oh my, it was a sea of souls, Detective. It was bustling all night. Drinks were flowing, and the beat of the music filled the air. We always attract an eclectic crowd. I didn't notice anyone with nefarious intentions. If you know what I mean. It was a party! Everyone was happy."

Peabody held his chin and asked, "What else goes on at these art receptions? Do the artists sell their work on the spot?" Peabody had his phone for note-taking and leaned against a column. He was Morrison's assistant and was in his late twenties. His first homicide case was two months ago, covering the death of Georgi's boss.

"Yes, we were showcasing Dahlia's resident artists and Marilyn to the New York buyers who often don't attend our functions. We also combined our art event with the Velvet Muse's outdoor music venue. Our doors lead to their garden park with the stage. We thought that if we merged our guest lists, it would be a more significant event, and it was.

"To answer your question about sales," Martina continued, "each artist has multiple works on the walls and pedestals. Since we have four gallery rooms on the first floor plus the basement, everyone moves around between the spaces. If artwork sells, the sale is handled here at our counter. We often place a red sticker by the title and mark it sold, and it remains in the gallery. If the artist has more artwork in their studio, they may let the buyer take home the piece, and the artist replaces it with another."

Troy added, "During a show if we have a very interested buyer, we may offer to bring them upstairs and show works from our studios that are not on display. Most of us do that, and Marilyn did too."

"Troy, are you aware of how Marilyn's studio looks? If something is missing or out of place, would you notice?" Morrison asked.

Troy smiled slightly. "My apartment is so full that it would be hard to see something missing. But Marilyn keeps her place incredibly neat. If there is a vacancy on the wall, I will know."

Martina nudged him. "My dear Troy, you have organized chaos. Your studio is packed, yet you still know where things are, plus your cat doesn't go missing." She smiled, and Troy held her hand warmly.

He answered Morrison. "I visited with Marilyn yesterday, and she showed me several pieces she was planning for another show." He caught himself as a wave of realization hit. "It's tough to grasp that she is gone." His hand went to his head. "This is so hard. I'm trying to keep up with reality right now." He inhaled deeply and sighed.

Martina placed a hand on Troy's shoulder. "It's a blessed mess, hon. We're all feeling unsettled. Reality becomes surreal when we must deal with a passing. Especially one like Marilyn's, God rest her soul." Turning to address the detective, she asked, "Do you have a clue to what happened, Dan?"

"We hope to know very soon, Martina."

She nodded. "Is there anything else we can do? I probably should contact people right away."

"Yes, we can let you both go for now. Peabody and I must return upstairs to Marilyn's apartment. I will speak to you later. Call me if you think of anything that will help." Morrison turned to Peabody. "Are you ready?"

Unexpectedly, Troy asked, "Can I go with you, Detectives? I want to keep busy, and maybe I can help."

Martina left, and the three men went upstairs. As they did, Peabody asked, "Do you know Marilyn's family, Troy? We need to contact them."

"That's the weird thing. It's been a long time. Once she started college, they left for an around-the-world trip. That was more than ten years ago. There was no mention of them after, and I didn't want to pry."

"I'll find them," Peabody nodded. "I'm sure my skills and the internet will locate them."

Troy gulped as they opened the door to Marilyn's studio. He inhaled her scent of white lilies that still lingered. Gingerly, he scanned the room as if walking on hallowed ground. He admired her colorful oil paintings above the sofa anew and heaved a sigh. He felt like she was still in the present.

Seeing nothing out of place yet, Troy advanced to her storage closet. He had built her a sizeable vertical box with slots to store paintings that were not on display. Immediately, he noticed a vacancy.

"Detective, she had a pair of large lotus flowers floating on water. They were unframed on canvas. Each one was about thirty-two inches wide and eighteen inches high." Troy hesitated. "I suppose it's possible she sold them last night. Maybe a buyer came up, but I...I don't know. She was pretty attached to them. You see, that's what happens to us. We grow attached to our favorite works. I would be surprised if she sold them."

Peabody's brown eyes flashed a questioning look. "What do you mean attached?"

"Our work is an extension of ourselves or our spirit. It's like selling you my favorite pet. I don't want to. It means too much to me. I don't want something so meaningful to me to become a memory." Troy eyed Peabody to see if he understood.

Peabody's eyes narrowed. "I'm a logical thinker, Troy. I'm not likely to veer off into deep or esoteric thoughts."

Morrison watched the two, absorbing every aspect of their perspectives. Each case was a new experience, an exploration of someone's story. A metaphorical puzzle that he would piece together in his mind's eye. Every case included another set of unique details to learn. Therefore, his job was never dull. He unwrapped a stick of cinnamon gum. "So you think she was attached to these lotus paintings?" He folded the gum into his mouth.

"She either sold them last night or something else." Troy wasn't sure and didn't want to speculate, though it gave him a funny feeling in the pit of his stomach. "It seems weird, Detective. Maybe they stole them after she died."

"Why would they want these paintings, Troy? There are so many here." Peabody asked.

"Possibly, they liked those the most," Troy explained. "Once news of her death gets out, they will be worth a bit more today than they were yesterday. Her death will cause the price to go up. The value of an artist's work can increase prices by a hundredfold. And the longer they're not sold, the higher the price goes because of the buzz."

"Buzz?" Peabody asked as he made notes and tried to catch up. "Do you mean people talking about her work?"

"Yes, talking about her oeuvre, which is her body of work throughout her life. Really what they are doing is positioning themselves." Troy paused. Peabody rested his chin in his hand and listened intently.

"It becomes like a feeding frenzy," Troy continued, "among art dealers, collectors, and merchants. It's as if a sound wave goes out, and it can be heard around the world. If your work is known well enough, and you have a good body of it, then your agent will be approached. Soon, his phone will be ringing off the hook."

"And what happens when they approach the agent?" asked Peabody.

Morrison leaned in as he, too, was captivated by the unfamiliar details of dealing with art on a world-sized scale. The scent of a motive was in the air, and both detectives had caught a whiff.

"He'll be approached to sell privately, create a collection, or have a large auction house create an even bigger buzz. Contemporary art is all the rage. Then print galleys of her work may be created. Of course, there are the current owners of her past work. They will be approached to see if they want to sell. It's a crazy piranha tank of buyers, sellers, and middlemen."

"Wow!" exclaimed Peabody as his hand went to his temple, then flared open in the air. "This is all news to me." He asked Morrison, "Isn't it time to find out who her agent is, Boss?"

"I can help you," Troy offered. "Marilyn has his card here." He pointed to a painting over her desk. It was a closeup of a glowing white lily; the pistil glistened with nectar and was surrounded by dark orange stamens. "She mentioned him advertising her work. It paid off with great gallery placement.

She claimed he made her popular." Troy approached the painting. "She slips his card into the back of the canvas."

Morrison stopped him. "Troy, here." He whipped gloves out of his pocket. "Put on these first."

He obliged and found the name card of the agent, Garfield Feinberg. "He's on the Connecticut/New York border." Heaving a sigh, Troy suddenly felt exhausted, "Detectives, if you have enough information, I think I need a break. I'm now hungry and sad. For me, that's not a good combination. By the way, Ophelia texted and said she would be here around one o'clock to give you the guest list and the RSVPs from last night."

"You've been more than helpful, Troy." Morrison and Peabody shook his hand. "Peabody and I are available if you think of anything. Give us a call."

Troy descended the stairs to his apartment in a cloud of grief. He had watched Marilyn's progress to success, and now it devolved into a ride for investors' profit.

He rustled some food together and, while munching, concluded, *I'll lose myself in the realm of color and create a painting while I think of her.* Then it dawned on him, *Marilyn will be my muse! I will paint for her!*

CHAPTER 6

Murder Follows Me
Vinho Verde Wine Bar

Roxanne and Georgi had left the Dahlia Art Gallery at 10:30 a.m. She told him she would meet him in fifteen minutes at the Vinho Verde. They were to start planning for Sunday's gathering to remember Marilyn. When the door chimed, he was comforted to see her return with a special delivery from Muddy Waters Café: apple tarts and Columbian spiced cocoa.

"We need a boost," she said.

"Roxanne, you know what I like," he cooed. "Come, let's sit out on the back deck."

Perched a story above street level, they overlooked the Thames River. The morning sun was intense. The low-lying mist had dissipated from the river but was still in the harbor. Far off in the distance, a foghorn sounded. Georgi said, "That's a mournful sound today. My dear Marilyn, a friend of my heart, is gone, and I feel dreadful," he sniffled. Roxanne patted his arm.

They sat silently for a moment. He continued, "We tried to meet for lunch weekly, and she would call me when she was far away on an art trip. She'd come to my apartment at least twice a month. We'd have food delivered and watch vintage movies like *Philadelphia Story*. I loved Cary Grant and Katherine Hepburn." He reached for a napkin to dab his nose, "I don't know how much more of this I can take. Two months ago, I lost Mitch, and now Marilyn! How am I to reckon with these emotions?"

"To lose a boss and a friend so close together is a tragedy. It's good to release these feelings." Roxanne patted his back and gave him a sturdy hug. She knew words were not as good as just being there and listening. She had learned from experience that silence could heal a heart better than her talking. Several moments passed.

He took a deep breath and wiped his tears again. "How did this happen? Did someone murder Marilyn? And why?" His face contorted.

Roxanne didn't want him to go any further into a tailspin. "Let's remember, Georgi, this is just as easily an accident. It is possible she slipped in those lovely pink pumps you mentioned. Maybe she fell off balance. It happens."

He pounded on the deck rail adamantly. "I doubt it very much!"

Shocked, she asked, "But why?"

"Because…" he whispered strangely, "*Murder* follows me." He looked over his shoulder.

"Georgi!" She lightly shook his arm. "That is not happening. You are one of the sweetest, smartest, and luckiest guys I know."

"I am?"

"Yes, look at how you have succeeded thus far. You are one of the youngest sommelier wine experts at age twenty-nine. Your mind, nose, and taste buds can summarize the details of a wine, even the year it was produced. You're also the best-dressed young man I know. And look at how we helped solve that last case with Detective Morrison. You were determined and brave, even though it was hard.

"Georgi, it was you that made the connection to the conniving killer. Neither of their deaths had anything to do with you. So don't think for one second that you are unlucky or grasp onto any other superstitious mumbo jumbo."

As Roxanne listed his attributes, each compliment was like a little puff of air filling his self-confidence balloon. Slowly, he sat up a bit taller and breathed a little deeper until finally, he inhaled a great deep breath and let go a big sigh. "Roxanne, only you could know all the right things to say to me. It's not me or bad luck. It's just life and bad people."

"Accidents are possible, Georgi, and they can happen in the weirdest ways. I nearly hung myself trying to clip a tree from a second-story deck."

His eyes popped. "You did? How is that possible?"

"I had the electrical cord to the clippers wrapped over my shoulder in such a way that when I lost my balance by leaning too far over the deck railing, the cord slipped. It wrapped across my neck but kept me from going over the railing. Simultaneously, that cord saved me but almost killed me. I had a hell of a time getting back on my feet, and I had a cord burn on my neck for a week. It was embarrassing."

Georgi chuckled as he imagined her escapade. "I'm sorry, Roxanne. I can only laugh because you are standing here. Better embarrassed than dead."

"Yes. See? Anything can happen." Roxanne was glad to deflect his sorrow, if even for a moment.

"Let's see what we can do to prepare for Sunday's event, shall we? It sounds to me that you only need to imagine what Marilyn would like, and we'll go from there."

"Okay, let me think." Georgi tapped his chin with two fingers. They gazed out to the sparkling water and watched a ferry depart toward Long Island Sound while tilting sailboats passed by from the fresh breeze. A passenger train clicked across the rails below them and announced its arrival with two loud blasts of its whistle. Roxanne and Georgi jumped.

"Whoa, that jolted me," she said, and they giggled. "The train is on its way to Mystic. Why don't we take it some time, just for fun, instead of the car? We can walk around downtown."

"I'd like that, and maybe Marco would too." On uttering his name, Georgi had a realization. "Oh! Marco! He'll know what to do. Let's call him over here and ask for his help. The three of us will pull this event together."

Marco was one of Georgi's best friends. His design and organization skills had come to the rescue on many occasions, and, at this time, his friendship would be a comfort.

***

Before entering the Vinho Verde, Marco went immediately across the street to talk to Detective Morrison. The detective watched him approach. Marco hugged his slim, five-foot-eight frame as his jet-black hair hung in his tearful eyes. Presenting his wrists to Morrison, he whimpered, "I provided Marilyn with the spear!"

"Did you kill her?" The detective's hands were on his hips, but he was ready to draw his cuffs.

Marco's arms flailed. "No! No, the spear did! But I sold it to her."

Morrison's hands went to his head. "That's not enough to arrest you, Marco! Didn't you leave with Georgi at twelve-thirty?" Marco nodded vigorously.

"Look, you're admirable to come forward, but Georgi is your alibi, and since I know you through Georgi, I know how to find you. Go across the street to the Vinho Verde and commiserate with Georgi, okay? Thank you for coming by and telling me about the spear, buddy. I'm sorry for your loss."

CHAPTER 7

Privacy is Priceless
The Dahlia - 1:00 p.m.

Morrison was in Marilyn's apartment, painstakingly going over the crime scene. He sent Peabody to collect video footage from businesses and neighbors on the surrounding streets.

He was on the balcony when he saw a thirty-something blonde woman approach the officer on duty. He looked at his watch, 1 p.m. He advised the officer to let whom he assumed was Ophelia into the gallery.

When he walked in, Ophelia was already at the computer. A blue dress wrapped her small, slim form. Dove-white skin matched her stylish hair, which was like radiant corn silk. A forlorn expression overtook her sprite-like appearance. As he approached, she turned toward him, and he saw her bright hazel-green eyes shadowed in shock.

"Excuse me, Ophelia Starr? Troy told me you would be here. I'm Detective Morrison." He sat across from her workstation at the end of a live-edge wood counter.

"Yes." She held out her hand to shake his. "I'm very sad right now, Detective. Troy told me about Marilyn and said you needed information. I came in to help by printing the email guest list from last night. I was unaware of Marilyn's death since I stayed with friends last night." Ophelia hooked a length of her hair and swiped it behind her ear. "What happened?" she asked in despair.

"We're trying to find out. Do you know who Marilyn was with last night?"

Ophelia shook her head, and tears fell. She wiped them swiftly and reached for a tissue. Dabbing her eyes, she said, "My boyfriend was helping me all night while I managed the event. I last saw Marilyn dancing with a group of people. I didn't see her after the music stopped around eleven-thirty. We were here cleaning up. It had become very foggy. I guess that's why they call it pea soup because we couldn't even see across the street. We left sometime after twelve-thirty."

A printer made predictable noises and spewed out pages of the guest list. She organized them, then stopped. Her eyes, stained red from sorrow, looked directly at Morrison. "How did she die? I want to know if I'm safe here. Am I, Detective?"

Her honest question was sobering, and Morrison always felt this was the most challenging part of his job. "We are trying to determine if it was accidental, but we need to know who was with her last. This list will help. I don't have enough information right now. I suggest that until we have more facts, you do whatever you need to make yourself feel safe and comfortable. I'm sorry you've lost a friend, Ophelia."

She softly said, "I didn't know her well. She regularly traveled for art shows. But I am scared, so the sooner you know what happened, the better." She stapled the pages and handed them over. "Is there anything else I can do?"

"Yes, do you have any cameras or video footage we can review?"

Ophelia thought a moment. "Well, it is possible there is some footage from the art reception and the Velvet Muse. Several people were using their phones to take photos and videos. We don't have security cameras on the building walls, if that's what you mean."

Morrison was surprised. "Why not?"

"It may be typical in your line of work to have video cameras everywhere, Detective, but most people, especially free-thinking creative types, don't want their every move laid out in the digital universe. Unless, of course, we place it there ourselves. All of us here at the Dahlia agreed to no surveillance cameras. Privacy is priceless." Morrison nodded.

"Detective, Troy told me you spoke about gathering at Georgi's place this Sunday. I have been in touch with our members from the board of directors already, and I came up with a draft of what we could send in an email and text message to invite everyone. I'd like you to hear what it says if you don't mind." Ophelia read the brief statement aloud.

A Get-Together for Marilyn

We have the sad task of informing you that our dear artist friend Marilyn Maroney has gone to heaven. She was an angel among us.

Please come to the Vinho Verde Wine Bar on Sunday for a gathering of her friends and those who attended her art opening as we remember our love for her. There will be food and drink from 1 p.m. to 4 p.m.

Detective Morrison and his team will be available if you have any information to help with the investigation of her passing,

Sincerely, The Dahlia Art Community

"Detective, I hope your department cares enough to respect our raw feelings. A safe and friendly community is important to me. Right now, my life feels upside-down."

"Yes, I will see to it. And know that I want this solved more than you, Ophelia. That's how much I care."

She nodded with relief. "I will see you Sunday. Here's my phone number if you need anything. I'm going to stay with friends now. It's very depressing to be here." She handed him a beautifully designed business card.

He placed it in his shirt pocket and watched her leave. The work in front of him and his team, to interview possibly three hundred attendees, was daunting, yet his desire to determine the circumstance of Marilyn's death was motivating. He needed to confirm if it was an accident. It would quell the imminent scandal of a death in the downtown region. Looking at his watch, he knew it was time to check in with his right-hand man, Jack Peabody.

CHAPTER 8

A Decline in Politeness
Police Headquarters

By 2 p.m., Peabody had yet to locate the next of kin for Marilyn Maroney, yet he was determined to find them. While he searched, Morrison approached his desk.

"This type of death is maddening, Peabody. It is tabloid fodder for the masses. Word spreads faster than ever with social media. Countless calls have come in from the press as far as California. They all want the scoop on Marilyn's death. How strange is it that, on the one hand, people abhor violence, death, and injustice? Yet, on the other hand, they gobble up sensational news as if they arrived at an all-you-can-eat buffet.

"An old woman dies at home by tripping over her Persian carpet, and they yawn at the discovery. But a beautiful young woman in the glow of her achievements dies by her sculpture on an open-air downtown balcony, and it becomes a nationwide story. Everyone wants to be the first to report results.

"It must be a slow news cycle today because they're clogging our phone lines. The shame is she lived for attention, and now that she's dead, she's getting plenty of it." Morrison checked his pockets and found his nicotine antidote, a stick of cinnamon gum, and folded it into his mouth.

"The public may not have known her, but now they want to know her. What a way to become famous or infamous, as in this case. My Irish mother would say, 'Most people are all for gossip until it is about them!'" He chewed his gum. "I suspect if psychologists inspected societies' fascination with death, they would find morbid curiosity scintillates gossip. Peabody, a decline in politeness has peaked in our society."

Peabody stopped his multiple searches on the computer, and asked, "Have you had this conversation with Dr. Storm?"

"Why would I?" Morrison asked, gazing down at him.

"Because she has a point of view that is close to death. And she may have an insight or two on people fascinated with death."

"I can't do that," Morrison said matter-of-factly.

"Why not?" Peabody thought it was an obvious conversation to have.

"Because she is one of those, preoccupied with death, and I may not want to know her answers."

"Well, excuse me for asking, Boss, but isn't it obvious she is exactly the one you should ask? Who could know better?" Peabody was entering unchartered waters.

Morrison rubbed his chin. "Since when did you get so smart? You're the greenhorn around here."

"I heard her comment about the photographer, Boss. The one who would capture accidents and crime scenes just after they happened. I looked him up, Weegee. He made the newspapers rich, and they paid him highly too."

Unnerved, Morrison gave him a stern look. One of his eyebrows was raised as if a question mark had formed. *Could he trust Jack Peabody?* Morrison adopted a gruffer tone. "You must realize there is a fine line between professionalism and eavesdropping, Peabody. The former requires investigation; the latter embodies the word busybody. Keep your detective work away from my private conversations with Dr. Storm. Understood?"

Taken aback, Peabody did not realize he had strayed into the "don't touch that territory." "Yes, Boss, but don't we depend on the busybodies for information?"

Morrison walked toward the hallway exit and turned to respond. "I consider myself informed." Peabody rose out of his seat to follow him but was halted by his boss's raised hand. "Stop right there. Do some research on Marilyn's family. Typically, they are overcome with grief and annoyed at the coverage. Find out why they haven't called us."

"Where are you going?"

Morrison's voice echoed from the hallway. "It's a need to know, Peabody, and you don't need to know. Put those listening skills you have honed into your job."

"Yes, Boss." Peabody's head lowered as he sat at the computer.

Morrison stepped into the men's room to wash his hands. He looked at his reflection and talked to himself. "I know why people are fascinated with death:

"First, they survived when others have not. Second, they want to understand why someone died and how they can avoid death. Third, death is a mystery, and they wonder if they are going somewhere or nowhere.

"Fourth, and the most intriguing reason, is that people are fascinated with death because they are alive. That is why murder and horror are interesting. It entertains their mind, and they feel better about their own life when someone else's is worse, as in dead. And now they think, 'I don't have it half as bad as that guy.'"

Drying his hands, he thought of Dr. Storm. *I wonder which of these drew her to become a medical examiner. Was it a complicated past? A question of life after death? Or maybe she's the fifth element: a geek about the details and the science of death.*

Perhaps Peabody's suggestion to check in with her was a good one. His stomach rumbled as he fixed his hair in the mirror. *I'll stop for lunch first.*

CHAPTER 9

The Inner Sanctum of Dr. Angela Storm
Late Friday afternoon

Morrison jumped into his official SUV, grabbed a quick bite to eat at the Washington Street Coffee House, then traveled to the outskirts of New London to visit Dr. Storm. He approached the medical examiner's office, which met the needs of the southeast region of the state. He looked at his watch. It was three-thirty when he arrived. The office assistant saw him on the video camera and buzzed him in immediately. The detective gave her a nod and dashed by to the sterile morgue.

Dr. Storm had spent the day focused on Marilyn's autopsy, and with her assistant, they had finished. She was sitting on a rolling stool; her protective gear had been removed. After she cleaned up, her standard garb was a white lab coat covering her street clothes. She was expecting Morrison, and upon hearing him enter, she glanced up from her paperwork. "You're on the ball, Detective. We just put Marylin in refrigeration. Would you like to see her?"

"No, your current findings are all I need, thanks."

"Have a seat."

He scanned the examination room and glanced at a stainless-steel table, the only surface between them. "I'm not quite sure I should sit on this." He pointed to the table.

"Oh," she chuckled, "my apologies. Come this way into my inner sanctum." Dr. Storm stood and motioned toward her office.

He followed and asked, "By putting Ms. Maroney in the fridge, does this mean you have finished the examination?"

"Yes, I am for now. We may continue once I receive more information from your forensic team."

They moved into a professional yet cozy twelve-by-fifteen-foot room that reminded Morrison of a Victorian library. Behind a large antique oak desk was a vintage credenza with a colorful landscape painting above it and bookcases on either side. Her doctor of pathology degree was framed above lateral file cabinets that lined the wall to his right. To his left was a single massive window with mullions. A giant hanging fern took advantage of the natural light, and a blossoming pink begonia overflowed on a pedestal.

Morrison took a seat in one of the traditional Hitchcock armchairs and found the bowed back a comfortable fit. He noticed file folders were organized in several neat piles across the credenza behind her.

"Have you discovered anything I can work with, Doctor?"

Her eyes narrowed with seriousness. "As you know, rigor mortis starts at death, but after twelve hours, it begins to reverse as muscle tissue breaks down. It then disrupts the determination of the time of death. Based on body temperature, rigor, etcetera, she had been dead for at least eight hours, possibly nine, when I initially examined her at eight-thirty this morning. I've noted a one-and-a-half-degree change in body temperature per hour after death. I figure that brings it to midnight, give or take."

He leaned forward. "Marilyn was seen by many until eleven o'clock. Your findings match what I'm hearing from people at the event. So would you say we have an hour of play either way?"

"Correct. As you may also know, once a body is in the morgue, we have a protocol to follow. I may want to go directly to the injury I can see, but I don't. We first search for scars, previous suicide attempts, or anything that could account for mysterious blood from other parts of her body. None was found. I can tell you she was alive when she came in contact with the spear."

"How do you know?"

"Because her heart was still pumping. Remember the scene and the pool of blood on the sidewalk below? During the autopsy, we found her heart was empty of blood, which indicates she was alive."

"I'm glad you've confirmed it, but to be honest, it did not occur to me that she might have been purposely placed there after death. That would have been truly morbid and slightly impossible to achieve, considering how her heel was stuck in the grate."

"Yes, you're quite right. We know she died on impact." Dr. Storm looked over her file. "I also did not find any identifying marks on her to say she was pushed. There was no indication of bruising from someone's hands on her. What I do know from my autopsy is that her liver and right lung were pierced at a one-hundred-thirty-degree angle, and she died instantly. With your forensic team's data, I believe we can prove the spear could not have penetrated as deeply as if she fell on her own. That will determine if it was an accident or homicide."

Morrison nodded. "All good information. I will have them send their data right over." He leaned forward in his chair to watch her expression as he said,

"Dr. Storm, as much as I would like for this to be an accident, my gut says otherwise."

"I can't go on my gut, Detective. I can say she did have cake in her stomach and wine in her system but not in excess. She had frosting on her fingers but none in her mouth, and there was remaining cake on the balcony. So was it dropped or flung? And was she alone?"

"Hmm, yes. Was she alone? It doesn't seem likely, does it? A beautiful woman, a successful artist, and an art opening reception with three hundred guests, artists, and patrons. Hmm, not likely."

He leaned back in the chair and looked out the window to consider the eve of Marilyn's death. In halftone, he asked, "Did you know there was a dense fog last night? It started to come in around nine o'clock."

"I'm familiar with that part of Bank Street where the fog settles off the water. I drove through once when it was heavy. I felt transported to the London tales of Jack-the-Ripper. Mischief is easily cloaked in a foggy night."

She observed Morrison as his forehead creased and the corner of his mouth curved.

"Yes, it does, Dr. Watson," he replied. "You do know you have stated the obvious?"

"Quite sure I have." She added emphatically, "And you can depend on that because I will continue doing so." She gave him a smirk and returned to her commentary. "It does not seem likely Miss Maroney was alone. I'm sure you will discover suspects, lovers, and thieves among the crowds of people. But did any of them mean to kill her? Was it accidental? Or was it the perfect crime, planned and executed on a dark and foggy night?"

Morrison smiled. Her voice was smooth and effective. "It sounds like a novel, but I need to consider all those possibilities in this case." A little weary, he leaned back in the chair and sighed. "This inner sanctum of yours, Dr. Storm, is oddly my first moment of peace since we found Marilyn Maroney today."

"That may be an honest admission, Detective Morrison, but it is the morgue. Everyone here is at peace." Whimsy flashed in her golden-brown eyes.

"Ha! That's another obvious fact, Doctor." He stood. "And with that, I shall leave you with your peaceful companions." A glint of humor remained in his inflection.

"A laugh at times like these is healthy, Detective, especially at death. While we still have life, our laughter lets death know we will not take it too seriously. I believe not one person on the other side takes death seriously because they are too busy enjoying their next adventure." She stood and added, "I'll let you know when the tests for the exact time of death come back."

"Thank you, Dr. Storm. You have a unique perspective. It's refreshing." As he was leaving, he glanced back at her. "Have a good day now."

"You too, Detective." She nodded, curious of the imprint of intrigue he left on her.

CHAPTER 10

The Artists of the Dahlia
Saturday - noon

Detective Morrison had asked Ophelia to gather the resident artists from the Dahlia to meet with him and Peabody for questioning. On their arrival at the Dahlia Gallery, they found a room ruled by sorrow. A collective line of tear-stained faces sat on stools at the long reception bar. These artists in residence were part of the Dahlia Artists Cooperative team. Their goal was maintaining a safe, healthy, and inspiring environment to make art and hold events. But now, it didn't feel safe.

"Hello, everyone, I'm Detective Morrison, and this is Detective Peabody. We met Ophelia and Troy. Could everyone else say their name and tell me how long you have known Marilyn?"

A tall, slender woman with cropped, black hair raised her hand. "Hi, I'm Cora. I've known her since I moved here two years ago."

A tall, muscular young man responded, "I'm Teddy. I've known Marilyn for four months."

"And I'm Bruce." He had broad shoulders and thighs like an NFL football player. "I've been here a year, and that's how long I've known Marilyn."

"Detective Peabody and I are sorry to put you all through this right now, and I thank you for taking a few moments with us. We are not immune to the grief you are feeling for Marilyn. Please understand we must ask you a few questions in case you may know some detail that will help us find out what happened."

The group nodded.

"Did any of you see Marilyn after eleven o'clock last night, or do you know who she was with after eleven?"

Everyone shook their head.

"We were all working, Detective," Troy answered.

Suddenly, questions were flying at Morrison. "Did she fall?" "Was she pushed?" "What do you think happened?" Peabody's head retracted from the onslaught.

Morrison put his hands up. "We are trying to find that out. We are hoping there was a witness. I need to know if there was someone suspicious we should be questioning."

While Morrison spoke, Peabody analyzed their body language, determining whether any of them knew more than they were saying. Each appeared authentically concerned and sad.

Troy knew Marilyn the longest of the group, so he asked, "What would Marilyn tell us if she were here? I can't think of anyone she would complain about. Can you guys?"

"I live in the apartment across the hall from Marilyn," Bruce said. "She seemed happy. I never heard her complain. In fact, I could hear her singing, often along with her music."

"Somebody has to know where she was after eleven o'clock," Troy said. The group fell into a solemn stare, peering at the floor. If only an answer would rise through the seams.

Cora, the willowy agent of art, spoke up. "She'd tell us, 'My work is going to be damn famous now. Too bad I had to die first!'" They all nodded. "Then she would say, 'You better figure it out. I don't deserve to be an unsolved murder case on some ID channel!'"

They knew it was true that Marilyn would make a wisecrack. Cora raked her hands through her short hair. "Did someone do this to her? I think she tripped on those gorgeous pink pumps. Occasionally, she could be a little klutzy." They nodded again.

Morrison took back control. "Does everyone here have someone who can vouch for them until twelve-thirty yesterday morning?"

Each said yes.

He scanned their faces. "Does anyone here have a key to her apartment?"

"I do," said Troy. "And she had a key to mine."

"May I have it, please, Troy?" Morrison asked.

"Of course." He pulled out his keyring, removed it, and handed it to Peabody.

Morrison could tell it was time to finish. "Look, we'll be across the street tomorrow afternoon at Georgi's wine bar get-together. If you think of anything at all, come see me. Here is my card. Detective Peabody and I will be in touch with you again."

The detectives left and crossed the street. "We will give them a little time, Peabody. Memories can come back after a grieving period. So far, they seem to have alibis and are too sad to pressure with lots of questions. Let's focus on the work in front of us and set up for our interviews."

Sunday at the Vinho Verde Wine Bar

Georgi's get-together for Marilyn was about to start. Everything came together nicely with Roxanne and Marco's help arranging the room. The downtown businesses provided the finger foods he ordered, and two couples who often volunteered, Shatana and Jason with Aaron and Marguerite, arrived early with homemade desserts. Troy and Martina met them at the door and helped with the setup.

Fortunately, Georgi's part-time staff also came to assist with the refreshments. Georgi hoped this big gathering would comfort the mostly youthful group. He found that being with friends and keeping busy staved off his deep heartache.

A long buffet table lined one wall of the spacious, historic room with wood beams, granite and brick walls, and wide plank floors. Tall warehouse windows showcased the water view. Light jazz music subtly played over the speakers. The welcoming décor of the Vinho Verde was now prepared for an afternoon of mourning.

As the guests arrived, they were asked to see the detectives if they had any information that might help the investigation. Morrison would use the business office for more private conversations, as Georgi had suggested. Four officers were ready to assist.

By one-thirty, most of the room was filled with a diverse group who mingled, hugged, and cried. Double doors to the outdoor deck beckoned the grieving to seek comfort in their memories as they sat under large umbrellas and gazed out at the sparkling water of the Thames River. Georgi and Troy overheard a woman say, "Marilyn's soul is now like one of those sparkles. On its journey into the great ocean beyond."

The group seemed willing to help the investigation with their recollections of Marilyn that evening. Although this setting was uncharacteristic for police work, standard questions had been formulated. They were asked one by one what time they last saw her. An officer would determine who should talk to the detectives. Morrison would then sit with them in conversation and Peabody took notes on a laptop in addition to using a voice recorder.

Morrison asked, "Do you know Marilyn's friends? Did she have any romantic interests? Who were those in her past relationships, and are any of them unhappy with her? Have any of them been here recently? Has anyone been noticeably jealous of Marilyn? Do you know any of her work contacts? Were any of her customers or gallery representatives troublesome?"

Peabody typed away, keeping pace with their answers.

Morrison's questions continued. "Can you tell me if she was stalked or harassed by anyone? Do you suspect someone? How much alcohol did she drink? Did she take any drugs that you are aware of? Please list everyone you recall in conversation with Marilyn that night."

Shatana and Jason were the last to be interviewed. They worked as volunteers in the gallery on the night of Marilyn's death. He had been an artist-in-residence for three years at the Dahlia, then they moved into their own loft apartment six months ago. Shatana's ebony face shone from the tears that fell onto her lemon-colored sundress. Her hands interlaced with Jason's. Her soft voice described what she remembered. "I helped with the art sales and replenished the appetizers; I saw her come and go all night. Marilyn and I have been quite friendly for months."

Shatana gracefully nudged a tear away. "It was still busy after eleven o'clock, and Marilyn came by for tonic water. I saw her go out the gallery door and thought she had dashed to her apartment, maybe to bring down more business cards or flyers. One of her sculptures of a lily flower was in the main gallery; there was lots of interest in it." Shatana leaned against Jason's shoulder and murmured, "That's the last time I saw her." He wrapped his arm around her.

Jason was distraught. His head dipped, and he wiped the tears he could not hold back. "I didn't see her after ten o'clock. I was busy talking to visitors about the art in the basement gallery. I've known Marilyn for three years. I don't understand what happened. Did she fall?"

Morrison delivered his standard response. "We are still investigating. A few people are offering us video footage from their phones, so we have a lot to review. It's still too early to tell." He thanked them for their information, and they left.

"Peabody, what did you piece together from the interviews?"

"I've sorted it by a list of facts and a smattering of gossip, Boss. The known boyfriends were Brad in California, Josh in England, and Roberto in Italy. They were always long-distance relationships. She told friends it kept life simpler so she could focus on her work, and it kept them more interesting to her." He looked at Morrison. "That seems like wise advice."

"Follow up and collect their contact information. We want to talk to everyone."

Peabody was fussing with details on the laptop. "Okay, Boss. No one was aware of any jealous person. She wasn't a heavy drinker usually—two glasses of wine with water in between. Her friends never saw her take drugs and highly doubted she ever did.

Peabody tapped away on the keyboard. "I created a 'persons of interest' list, Boss, and it is more like a soap opera."

Morrison leaned against the door frame. "Hmm, you will soon discover that soap opera types are the people we usually deal with in our line of work."

Grasping the thought, Peabody gave him a look of understanding. "Well, we have several to contact, and some seem random. One person mentioned that the shopkeeper down the street is weird. Do we card him for weirdness?"

"We need to find out where they all were Thursday night, Peabody. Look, it's four o'clock, and it seems we've spoken to anyone who knew something about Marilyn. What we don't have is a solid witness to her death or a hard motive for it. Let's continue this in the morning. I'm tired and feel like this must be what speed dating is like."

Peabody's head snapped wondering if his boss had been speed dating. "What do you mean?"

"We just managed speed interviewing. We should receive a plaque or trophy for the most in one afternoon."

"Boss, you do have to admit Roxanne's odd idea, and Georgi's willingness to host, did make short work for us." Morrison put his fingers to his lips. "Shh, don't let them know."

The detective glanced over his shoulder. "Come on Peabody, let's thank Georgi and we'll continue our investigation in the morning."

Little did the detectives know that Roxanne's idea and Georgi's hosting skills for the event had provided the perfect cover for an incognito character to lurk among the grieving guests.

CHAPTER 11

Juggling Data
Monday

It was eight-thirty in the morning at police headquarters, and Morrison paced the floor.

"Listen to this, Peabody. Here is our bland statement. 'Marilyn Maroney, female Caucasian, artist, sculptor deceased. Lived in New London, CT. Cause of death yet to be determined.' And yet, before us, we have images of her life in online news from across America: New York, Chicago, and San Francisco. Headlines reading, 'Fabulous, superbly talented, magnificent artist!'

"Look at these photographs of her. She could be Marilyn Monroe's sister." Morrison held up eight-by-ten glossy pictures of her at art receptions pulled from her apartment. "Marilyn recently had events with celebrities, politicians, and buyers at these art installations. This woman had a successful career. She floated among some very influential people in the last six months. So what happened? Or should we ask, what's missing?

"Listen to this national tabloid that came out today." Morrison read the teaser to Peabody.

Darling Artist Impaled!

> A strange series of events led to the death of artist and sculptor Marilyn Maroney on Friday, August 14. Questionable circumstances have left the investigation in limbo. Was it a homicide or an accident? Watch this space as we keep up with the police department's reports.

"Give me a break. It's sensational and puts more pressure on us."

"It's online news fodder, Boss. They're just trying to capture people's attention. It should say, 'Don't wear high heels on an open grate balcony.' At least that would be educational." Peabody pointed to himself. "I'm always thinking of safety, and it really looks like she tripped and fell backward. It's a perfect death, accidental landing-on-a-spear." Knowing it sounded like another tabloid headline, he shrugged.

"Or the perfect murder, Peabody. Every time I see a dead body, I think of murder. It's in my DNA. I can't help it."

Peabody shook his head and mumbled, "Sure, but people should be more careful." Speaking more audibly, he said, "I'm always looking at safety conditions, Boss. Maybe that should be considered."

Morrison leaned on Peabody's desk and looked at his computer screen. "What are you saying exactly?"

"I dated a girl who didn't pay attention. She put me into a panic. She wouldn't look when she crossed the street, walked away from the stove when she was cooking, filled the bath, and left the room until it was so full she couldn't get in. I was constantly worrying, so I ended the relationship. I couldn't take the stress."

"I see what you mean, but my gut says someone else was on the balcony because of the cake remnants we found. I'm not letting that go."

Officer Demi Acevedo walked in with her laptop displaying forensic photographs. "Officer Sanchez sent me right over to show you these, Detective. You were right. This cake on the balcony has a tiny corner pressed down. Look!" She showed him the blowup of the cake. "See? She could not have been alone. Someone stepped on the cake."

Morrison looked at the photos closely. "Hmm, my one dilemma is it's not clear if she dropped the cake, stepped on it herself, then fell backward. We need a little more evidence than this."

"There's more," she added. "A tiny amount of frosting is on the threshold into the apartment, sir. And as we examined further, there was a tiny amount on the floor near the closet. Someone tracked it into the apartment. Carolena, I mean Officer Sanchez, said it would take all day to verify the details. We just wanted you to know we are working in this direction."

"Fantastic! Keep at it and let me know when you have something more definitive." Morrison pondered the information he had. He knew more about Marilyn but not what had happened on the balcony.

"Boss, we have a lot of nothing. Peabody complained. "These interviews haven't added up to anyone suspicious yet. Neighbors and people at the party didn't see anything happen to Marilyn, mostly because of the fog. Where do we go next?"

"It takes persistence, Peabody. Start working on the street camera video footage that's been collected. See who can be identified and the time they left the party. Let's have Officer Acevedo give you a second set of eyes. Her expertise in video technology and imaging will benefit us. She can clarify the details if they are grainy or out of focus. Watch the entire evening and note what happens after eleven."

Peabody smiled. "Okay, I'd like her help."

Morrison looked at him suspiciously. "She's too smart for you, kid. Don't get any ideas."

"Maybe she'll teach me something. I won't mind learning from her." Peabody gave his boss a wily wink.

"Listen," Morrison flashed a stern face, "don't put yourself in an awkward work-related position of you trying to date her. That's a no-go."

Peabody hung his head. "Yes, sir." He was about to ask, *What if she likes me?* But when he looked up at Morrison, he could tell the question was already expected. Peabody kept quiet, swallowing his hope with a gulp.

***

Peabody had videos from multiple locations ready for viewing, but only a few seemed viable: a couple of restaurants, a bar, and a bank. In the historic City of Steeples, small businesses were family-owned and had not invested in exterior cameras. The city had not added them into the budget, mainly because the voters didn't want them.

He was set up in a small room when Officer Acevedo came by, ready to analyze the digitized results. "How many do we have?" she asked.

"Quite a few, but it looks like three have the right angle to capture what we want. Here is one; it's down the street. The angle encompasses the front of the Dahlia, the street, and the stores across from it. We will cover from 6 p.m. to 2 a.m. Are you ready, Officer?"

"Yes, I am, and please call me Demi. We don't have to be formal, Jack, since we'll be working for hours." She leaned back in the chair, put her hands behind her head, and relaxed. "I'm ready to observe the footage, Jack."

He inhaled her subtle scent of jasmine perfume, delighted with his task partner.

After much time was spent on the first video, Demi and Jack saw an immediate problem. The fog descended after nine, thick as lather, and the camera did not capture the balcony.

"Well, I don't see how we will get anywhere with identifying someone," Jack announced.

"Just a minute," Demi said. "I can adjust the contrast for a better resolution." She did so, and the clarity improved, but it was more of an outline in high contrast rather than details. "We'll go through them again. There may be other filters I can apply, but let's start here."

Many people came and went, crossing the street. But it was difficult to see who they were. At 11:25 p.m. on the video, Jack finally exclaimed, "Well, looky here. Do we know who that is?"

A woman in a large-brimmed hat, mid-length raincoat, and heels crossed Bank Street and entered the alleyway heading toward Water Street.

"She's carrying a big rectangular case," Demi whispered and leaned forward. "It must be an art portfolio case." She replayed the image again and again, then said, "Hola, señorita, por favor, what are you doing?"

Jack smiled, enjoying her accent on all the right syllables, whether they were Español or English.

"This one goes in the keeper file, Jack."

"Si, señorita." Jack could not help himself.

Demi judged him suspiciously. "Are you making fun of me, Assistant Detective, the new boy on the block?"

"No, Officer Demi, por favor. Mi appreciates you." His face became rosy, hoping he did not offend her.

"It's okay, Jack. I won't beat you up. Let's see what else we can find on these other videos around 11 p.m. and later."

Jack hummed a tune called 'Señorita' by Camilla Cabello and Shawn Mendes. Demi gave him a glance and smiled to herself.

CHAPTER 12

Unnecessary Death

Roxanne called Georgi on Monday at 9:30 a.m. and found he was moping.

"I'm exhausted," he muttered, "and depressed. I saw Marilyn practically every week. She would wave from her balcony or stop in to say hello for a quick chat. I miss her so much."

It was understandable that he was not his normal, upbeat self, so Roxanne thought he needed a change of scenery, and she had an idea. She asked him to meet her at the fire department's headquarters.

They climbed the stairs to her husband's office on the second floor to say hello to him. Chief Sam had a calm demeanor, and Georgi liked his company because he accepted him as he was. He was also grateful the chief had forgiven him for secretly taking Roxanne to Long Island two months ago, which had ended in a big fiasco. They each took a seat.

Georgi looked around the tiny office. On the wall behind Chief Samson were his plaques touting accomplishments and photos of fully involved structure fires. Wide-eyed, Georgi said, "I don't know how you do it, Chief. You are around tragedy all the time. How do you deal with the drama? I would be a nervous wreck every waking hour."

"It starts with wanting a job that is filled with excitement. It's a sense of pride and accomplishment to know you can help people at their worst times. Then you discover that you feel great after combating a fire, maybe saving someone's life or house, and then you are hooked. Yes, you have tragedy, but it's balanced by the adrenaline rush that allows you to go to the extreme with big fires and yet help folks in their time of despair. Then I have the wonder of the job. It helps me deal with the tragedy."

"The wonder of what?" Georgi asked. Sam smoothed his handlebar mustache. His kind eyes and mellow disposition put Georgi at ease.

"When you enter the scene of a structure fire, with flames all around you, it is a surreal experience. The fire dances and swirls, and you see things just melting off the walls. It is dangerously beautiful in its own way. Yet managing a fire is extremely challenging, and you must have the stamina and the right character for the job. I understand why it doesn't interest you. I know men that quit in the middle of their training. Others come on board, and their next big hurdle is dealing with injury and death. All firefighters are trained in CPR. We learn how to bring someone back to life after they've died, and there is no feeling like it." Sam paused, watching as Georgi's gaping mouth turned into a grimace.

Sam nodded. "It's hard for most people. It's in your cells, Georgi, or it is not. We learn to file the scenes we don't like and keep the ones we do in the forefront of our mind."

Georgi huffed, "It's definitely not in my cells. I don't like breaking a sweat, never mind being in a fire. And you know I would crumble under the weight of the gear, for sure."

Sam and Roxanne's eyes locked with a knowing smile.

Georgi hesitantly asked, "Do...do you know anything new yet about Marilyn?"

"No, nothing yet, but if I hear anything certain, Roxanne or I will let you know." He glanced at Roxanne; she nodded, understanding that he couldn't say some things even if he knew. They had honed their own secret language of facial expressions, nods, and hand signals. They even had word cues and coded messages for when they wanted to leave a place or person.

"Georgi, I know Marilyn was your friend, and you miss her. I've found it's best to fill your time with the things you like to do and put aside thoughts that try to haunt you. Because they will; I've been haunted by many. It isn't easy, but strength of character and maturity come from learning to accept the things we can't change. Focus on your happy memories with her, funny times. Think of her warmth and love for those around her. Eventually, you can enjoy life again by holding onto the good memories. It's important for your well-being and peace of mind."

Georgi's hand went to his heart as he absorbed Sam's words. "Thank you," he murmured.

Roxanne winked at Sam and changed the subject. "Sam, do you mind if I give Georgi a tour of the fire station? It's one of the reasons I met him here. I knew he would enjoy the unique experience."

"Not at all, but if a call comes in, get out of the way. There will be men and women sliding down the pole, donning their gear, and as quick as a flash, they're gone with sirens and air horns blasting."

Georgi pressed both hands to his cheeks, imagining the scene. "Uhh, if a call comes in, leave someone behind to give me CPR. It's way too much excitement for me."

Roxanne and the Chief laughed, and Sam said, "You mean cardiopulmonary resuscitation, Georgi?"

Roxanne whispered, "That means you'll be kissed by a firefighter." His eyes grew large. "Come on," she took his arm, "I'll show you around."

They left Sam in his office and walked down a narrow, railed passage that overlooked the fire trucks parked below.

"These trucks are even more impressive from up here! Look at all the dials, hoses, and handles." While pointing, movement caught his eye, and he grabbed Roxanne's shoulder. A group of firefighters were at work on a piece of equipment. He whispered, "Oh, look at those muscular men." He fanned his face to emphasize his delight. Roxanne shook her head and grinned.

As they were about to go down the staircase, Roxanne stopped him. "I want to show you something over here." He willingly followed.

Suddenly, he gasped and halted abruptly. "Oh no, I don't want to." He looked down a gaping hole.

"You will love it." She coaxed him toward the edge of a tall brass pole.

"I was raised to avoid unnecessary death."

"Georgi! Most death is unnecessary. This, however, is completely safe." Roxanne stood by the opening of the fire pole. "Loosen up. Leave all your worries behind. Consider this a new beginning. You'll feel brand new when you slide down. I'll be right behind you. It's fun!"

Georgi looked Roxanne squarely in the eyes. "You sound like a mythical creature luring me to death with sweet words of delight. Do you really think I will feel different or better from doing this?"

"Yes, if you leave your worries at the top and let them go. Remember, you have cojones!"

With gravel in his voice, Georgi made a fist and said, "Balls of a bull, Roxy! Here goes nothing!"

"No, here goes everything! Let your worries go!" Roxanne urged.

A few firefighters looked up wondering what the commotion was about.

Georgi wrapped his legs around the pole and slid down with a squeal. His five-foot-ten slim body landed in a squat on the floor. Four uniformed men looked down as he blinked up at them. "Well, hello, fellas, I'm Georgi. Can you help me up?"

The men smiled and lifted him by his shoulders.

Roxanne ceremoniously slid down the pole with one hand out to the side.

"Hello, Mrs. Chief!" the men chimed.

"Hi, guys. I'm just giving Georgi a tour." She winked impishly.

"An initiation is what it looks like," said Cody with a broad smile. "And, once again, breaking the chief's rules about that pole."

"I forgot about that." The expression on her face said otherwise.

The guys grinned. Cody added, "Well, Georgi, I can tell you've never ridden one of these before."

Georgi turned beet red. "The only thing I have to say is it was thrilling. You've truly made my day!" He restrained himself from bowing or doing an expressive twirl.

"Since Roxanne is giving you a full tour, you can try on some of our gear. Have you ever put on a firefighter's helmet?"

Although Cody was teasing, he was inadvertently ticking one of Georgi's fantasies of dressing up as a firefighter. His expression of glee was priceless.

Roxanne stepped forward. "I think we've initiated him enough for today, guys. Time to go, Georgi. We have that thing to do."

"What thing? Is there a thing that is more important than this mojo moment? Seriously?" Georgi was perplexed because he was having fun.

Roxanne grabbed his arm. "Come on; we're going for an iced coffee to cool you down. Bye, guys!" she sang.

"Bye, Mrs. Chief," they called back. "Thanks for the morning entertainment," piped Cody.

Georgi turned and waved as Roxanne yanked his arm.

CHAPTER 13

Silent but Deadly
Monday - 11:00 a.m.

Detective Morrison returned to the scene of Marilyn's demise. He preferred to revisit her apartment alone and without interruption. It allowed him to run different scenarios in his mind of what may have occurred. As he scanned the apartment's interior, he wondered if it was Marilyn or someone else who went to the closet and left behind the tiny cake crumb of evidence on the floor.

Suddenly, he heard quiet footsteps on the staircase. *Who's crossing the crime scene tape?* he wondered. He stepped into the kitchen alcove and waited to see if a tenant or culprit had returned to the scene. An unlawful entry attempt could be an admission of guilt.

The old floorboards creaked. Morrison saw the edge of a shadow move across the floor toward the balcony. He leaned out to catch a glimpse, but the intruder was out of sight and on the balcony. Hedging forward, Morrison planned to block the door to keep them from escaping. He slowly peered out and saw the emblazoned initials, 'M.E.'. "Oh, it's you, Dr. Storm."

"Yes. Peabody told me you would be here, and I wanted to look at a few things myself."

"Be thankful it's me here and not another officer. You might have been pounced on as Cato did to Inspector Clouseau in the *Pink Panther*."

Finding him amusing, she responded, "It wouldn't be the first time someone tried the *Pink Panther* pounce on me. I assure you my reflexes would have had him off this balcony in one second flat, and I'd have another guest in my morgue."

"I thought you might be the silent but deadly type," he joked, then asked, "What draws you back to the scene? Is there anything new you've discovered?"

"Well, yes. It's what I call a SWAG."

"What? What kind of swag?"

"In my profession, it's known as a Scientific Wild Ass Guess." Morrison laughed, and she continued, "We carefully take the details of the scene, observe the person's body, and if we guess the matter of death, that's a SWAG. As we proceed with the autopsy and lab work, we prove our SWAG correct or a busted theory. It's secretly a medical examiner's challenge to surmise the cause of death ahead of proving yourself right or wrong. You see, Detective, you need to keep your sense of humor in my field of work. It allows you a clear perspective as you move toward the factual proof of your SWAG. And that is the reward for your hard work."

Morrison was intrigued by her pathway to discovery. "But my understanding of the original word is that swag is a pirate treasure. Which, in our case, means you found something I can use. Could our diverging terms of SWAG be meeting under a new listing in the dictionary?"

Dr. Storm gazed at him. "Traditionally, you are correct. It was pirate booty in the 1800s. But my friends who attend opening nights at art museums know it as a goodie bag, Stuff We All Get, aka SWAG. It's presented at the door in return for their generous private donation. These are gifts that make the event memorable and keep them coming back. But I digress."

He continued to play. "Do you have a treasured result that is booty for me? A goodie of information."

With a twinkle in her eye, she said, "I do, but before I tell my results about Marilyn, tell me why you're here?"

"I like to return to the scene and imagine what happened. Sometimes I can almost hear gunfire or yelling. With any homicide investigation, I start with the victim and work my way outward. I ask myself, 'Was she with someone? Did she know them?'

"Usually, I consider a small circle of people and expand it as I eliminate them as suspects. They either remain in the investigation, or they're out by way of an alibi or documented evidence." Morrison placed his hand on his chest. "In my heart, I am the hunter of predators, a hound dog on the scent of a wolf. I won't stop until I have the person who crossed the line and committed the murderous crime. I care for the victim. Because other than you, Doctor, who else will find the truth?"

She nodded at his sincere determination.

Morrison added, "In this case, several people saw her all night. She moved around a lot. She left and came back to them until she didn't. Tracking the timeline down to the last minute, to the last person who saw her alive, has been difficult. I'm eager to see what you have found."

"Good. I have something to show you that will put you on a clear hunting path. Meet me at my office at three o'clock."

***

At 3 p.m. Morrison entered the medical examiner's building. He was greeted by the assistant and unceremoniously escorted into the morgue. Dr. Storm stood over Marilyn Maroney, whose body was covered except for her face. Snapping off her gloves, she lifted her protective eyewear and motioned. “Right this way, Detective.” They approached a large monitor. She clicked the keyboard and brought up a visual representation program.

“We bought this software when I was in New Haven. It was made for a case such as yours. It has helped me have confidence in my SWAG. I didn’t want to interrupt your investigation until I could input the data from your forensic officer, Carolena Sanchez.”

Before them was a virtual reenactment of Marilyn’s fall. “With this software program, I’ve determined the velocity, rate of pressure, and the angle required for Marilyn to have been pierced by Athena’s spear and not survive.

“Yes, she may have slipped and fallen onto the spear. But did she? Once I performed the autopsy, I saw several indicators. To reenact her fall with multiple outcomes, I entered the data from my autopsy and Officer Acevedo’s forensic photographs into the program. What came together is the only indicator of what I believe occurred and can determine how she died.”

Morrison was captivated as he watched the screen in this virtual reenactment video. The imagery of Marilyn on the balcony was before them, and the sequence played out in slow motion while Dr. Storm narrated. “You see, if she had slipped, she might have been injured like this.” The video showed her tripping and falling back. “But it would not have killed her immediately. Marilyn would have been able to cry for help. See here? The spear could not have gone in as deep as it did. The velocity is off. Now, look at this one.”

Morrison watched the reenactment scene change. This time, another person was on the balcony, facing Marilyn. Dr. Storm hit the play button, and they watched the person push her.

“The velocity makes all the difference, Detective. I played out dozens of options. This is the only one that creates the injuries I see here on her body. She would not have these fatal wounds from slipping. Her death was instant and only because she was pushed. It pierced not only her spinal cord but her liver.”

“Can you replay that?” he asked. They watched the scene. “Again, please?”

After several silent reviews, she could see he was convinced. “Right? It seems obvious when you see it play out like this, doesn’t it, Detective?”

As he stared at the final image, Morrison's hand was over his mouth. It dropped when he asked, "And your autopsy backs this up? By simply falling on her own, the spear would not have touched her liver?"

"Yes, Detective, it required not just a push but a mighty shove. This is definitely a homicide. Granted," she paused, looking toward Marilyn's placid face on the table, "it could have been an accidental death. It's possible the person did not intend to harm her, just to push her away. But since they left the scene, that makes it manslaughter. Correct, Detective?" She eyed him, awaiting his response.

"You really think that is also possible?"

"Sure. The person could have been entirely shocked that Marilyn fell upon the spear and ran off. It's like a hit-and-run driver who panics and leaves the scene."

"I can see how that might happen." Morrison pondered for a moment. "Someone was invited to her balcony to see the Athena sculpture up close. That was her point of placing it outdoors—to draw potential buyers from the street. She then escorted them to the balcony. Unless someone came up the fire escape ladder, we'll have to look at the surveillance footage again." Morrison's thoughts churned in several directions. "I've come up with one outcome that I am sure of."

"What's that?" she asked.

"You've done it again, Dr. Storm. You've taken the case in a new direction, just like our last one. This is fantastic. The advanced software is precisely what we needed to classify this as a homicide. We'll work on our suspect list if you send your autopsy results and this data to my office."

"Certainly, we'll do that right away." She extended her hand and shook his. "Good luck, Detective. Now that you know the case is murder, it's all yours."

CHAPTER 14

Dazed, Drunk, or Drugged
Tuesday - morning

Troy parked his hatchback at 10 a.m. on Bank Street. The car was full of art supplies, and he felt lucky to have nabbed a choice spot in front of the residence door at the Dahlia.

He hauled several armloads of hemp canvases and painting materials upstairs for his next series of work.

Returning to the car for the rest of his art materials, he heard screeching brakes and a woman shrieking, “Help her, for god’s sake!” Men driving by were gawking. Troy looked in the direction of the commotion to see a tall, young woman in underwear with a blanket on her shoulders. She was stumbling and dazed, drunk or drugged. Shocked, he realized it was his neighbor, Cora Swift. He raced over and covered her with the blanket, then supported her. He steered her toward the gallery’s entrance. The door was locked, so he leaned her against the building, found his key, and unlocked it. He guided her to sit at the counter.

“Cora, what happened?”

She stared at him blankly.

Martina had been working downstairs while the gallery was closed and came up when she heard Troy speak. She rushed to Cora’s side.

“I just found her like this. She needs help. I’m calling Ophelia to bring down some clothes.”

Martina grabbed an orange juice from the fridge and sat beside her. “Sip some of this, sweetheart. You may need the sugar.” She looked Cora over for injuries. “Are you hurt, dear?”

Without speaking, Cora took a sip of the juice before guzzling it.

“Should we bring you to the hospital? I’m concerned for you.”

She shook her head.

Ophelia arrived with clothes. She slipped a skirt over Cora’s feet and helped her pull it up around her waist, then helped her put on a top.

Troy leaned toward Martina and said quietly, “I’m calling a friend who will know what we should do.”

Holding Cora's hand, Martina asked if she was hungry. Cora nodded. Ophelia agreed to stay with her while Martina went across the street to Muddy Waters Café. Troy went outside to make the phone call.

"Roxanne, it's Troy. Can you help us? We're at the Dahlia. Cora seems to have been drugged. I just found her in the street without clothes on. This isn't like her, and I'm really concerned with what just happened to Marilyn. What should we do?"

"Oh no! I'll call Sam, and he'll have the paramedics check her over. They're only two blocks away. They'll be right there, and so will I."

Martina returned with the food and placed it on the counter in front of Cora. "Eat something, dear. It will make you feel better." With her head resting on her arm Cora ate.

Martina was deeply concerned. "Are you in pain anywhere?"

"I don't think so," Cora mumbled.

"Well, we are all here for you until you feel better."

Fire Chief Sam arrived with the emergency medical responders. They attended to Cora. When he saw Roxanne arrive, he met her on the sidewalk. "They're checking Cora's vitals now," he said. "I called Morrison and told him to come down to question her personally. She seems to be doing better with liquids and food. We are waiting to see if she will go to the hospital."

"Troy just stepped out before you," Roxanne said. "The poor guy is quite upset. He went upstairs to rest and give the paramedics privacy with Cora. It's all too much for him, this, and Marilyn. I told him to come for dinner tonight."

"That's fine. I'll fire up the grill, and we'll eat in the backyard."

Morrison pulled up in his SUV and got out. "Okay, what's happening as far as you know?"

The chief told him, "The paramedics are with her now. She seems dehydrated. Let's give them a little more time, and then you can question her. We want to be sure she's stable."

"Sure thing, Chief." He turned and gave Roxanne a quizzical look. "Roxanne, is the universe plotting a reunion from our last case?"

She pursed her lips in thought as her hands gestured up and outward. "I'm involved whether I want to be or not. You might pin that deputy badge back on me from the last case. It looks like I'm on this one before you today." She enjoyed teasing them both.

The detective and chief leaned toward each giving a sideways look. Sam murmured, "Here we go again, Morrison. She's on the scent. The game is afoot."

Morrison took the cue. "You know you are banned from helping me, Mrs. Chief, or should I call you Mrs. Unpredictable?"

The chief nodded in agreement. "That's more accurate."

Giving him an amused look, Roxanne asked, "And who told you that?" Her head snapped toward Sam, and she stared at her six-foot-two husband from her five-foot-two stance. "I speak for myself, and here's my report: Troy called me first. He found Cora staggering across the street, dazed and confused, in her underwear with only a blanket. She appeared drugged, and he didn't know what to do. I called Sam and the rest you already know."

Reconciled, Sam said, "We can't change fate, Detective. She knows everybody."

"Well then, I have some news you both should know. The case with Marilyn Maroney has been designated a homicide. It's no longer considered a possible accident. We are pursuing inquiries in that direction now."

"Wow!" Roxanne exclaimed and watched her husband as he nodded at Morrison realizing his wife would stay involved because of Georgi and Troy.

Chief Sam said, "You're going to be busy, Dan, especially if this incident with Cora is related. I can't imagine a local doing this. An outsider may be using our little city for their havoc. If so, they're giving our City of Steeples a bad name. This crackerjack won't get past you. The cases you have under your belt would curl hair. They'd be cold cases in most departments. You'll get it done."

Dan Morrison felt humbled. "Thanks for your faith in me, Chief."

"I don't need faith," Chief Sam said. "I've seen you in action for over fifteen years. You're the man for the job. You're a bloodhound."

Roxanne asked, "Can I tell Georgi it's a homicide? I think I should."

Morrison responded, "Better you than me, Roxanne. You are close friends, and besides, he shouldn't read it in the paper tomorrow."

"Okay, I'll see him now and tell him about Cora too." She made her way across the street to the Vinho Verde Wine Bar.

"Your wife has courage, Chief. I don't want to give Georgi bad news. Next to smoking, he might be my kryptonite." Both men smiled, knowing she was the woman for the job.

Through the glass picture window of the gallery, the chief saw that the paramedics were finishing up with Cora. "Do you want to ask her a few questions, Dan?"

Morrison went inside and sat on a stool. Cora appeared alert, and Ophelia and Martina sat next to her.

"Please tell me what you recall, Cora."

She spoke softly. "I woke up inside a van in just my underwear with a blanket. Thankfully, Troy found me as I made my way here. I was near the train tracks on Water Street. I met with a gallery representative from New York in the afternoon yesterday, around four o'clock. I prepared a display of artwork upstairs in my studio. His name is Mario Corinthian. He was very encouraging and seemed so interested in my work. He suggested we go to dinner to discuss a contract so he could represent me at a gallery in New York City.

"We went to the Café La Ruche. It was amazing. I felt like a princess and was excited to be recognized as a professional artist. We ate dinner, then he ordered a bottle of champagne, saying we should celebrate my being discovered. I don't remember anything after that…until I woke up in the van." Cora realized she had been fooled. "I'm so embarrassed." She covered her face and wept quietly.

Ophelia and Martina hugged her, wishing they could take away her sorrow. Morrison was sympathetic. "Cora, I don't want you to feel bad because this is not as uncommon as you might think."

"What?" Cora wiped away her tears.

"You're not the first young woman to be fooled by a man who compliments and promises to promote her work," he explained. "I have too many stories to tell, but I'd like to ask if you would be willing to do something for me?" Morrison paused. "Could we have a sample of your saliva? We can test it to see if the drug is still in your system."

Secretly, Morrison was testing Cora. He wanted to know if she was willing to provide a sample. If she had something to hide, this would be a time for her to say no. Marilyn's death was only days prior. Was she connected to it? Or was there a perpetrator pursuing artists? The more leads he could garner, the quicker he could solve Marilyn's case.

Cora readily answered, "Yes."

"If there are any similar cases, it can help us develop a profile of the person who uses this drug. Did anyone see you with him?" Morrison asked.

"There were plenty of people at the restaurant, but not anyone I know. He must be from the art world. He knew what he was talking about. I believed him. He dressed very well and treated me to an expensive dinner and champagne. There were no red flags. I'm not that gullible." She wondered what other details might be essential or perhaps there was something she overlooked. "I can sketch you a picture of him," she suggested, feeling better that she might be helpful.

"That's fantastic, Cora. Your talent is a bonus." Gently, he said, "I'm going to let the paramedics check your vitals once more, and we can talk again when you have the drawing for me. Okay?"

Cora nodded and thanked him.

Morrison pulled a female paramedic aside and asked if Cora might have been assaulted. The paramedic asked Cora, but she did not know and agreed to go to the hospital to be tested. Morrison was relieved he might get some evidence to work with.

He was told that Cora had lived at the Dahlia for two years. She was another up-and-coming artist, following in Marilyn's footsteps. Her artwork was mixed media: a collage of crepe paper, watercolor, and ink. It was ethereal, pastel, and abstract, leaning toward landscapes, unlike Marilyn's work. She had shown her work in different galleries too.

Is this connected to Marilyn? he wondered. *It's too much of a coincidence. There must be a correlation somewhere.*

CHAPTER 15

Who is Mario Corinthian?
Noon

Ophelia scoured the internet at the Dahlia gallery with Jason, a former resident, and Marilyn's friend. Their mission was to find evidence of Mario Corinthian. They thought they could track him down if he posted comments on Cora's social media sites. She had recently left for the hospital with the paramedics but had told Ophelia he referred to galleries in Greenwich, Norwalk, and Westport, Connecticut, where she had shown her work. They called them all with no results.

After much effort, Jason bit his lower lip with concern. "I wonder if my girlfriend, Shatana, could be duped too."

"Jason, how can we know when someone leads us down a primrose path? Everything sounds so wonderful, and you're encouraged to promote your work, but then it's all a literal mess. That damn monster hunted her down to offer her a golden opportunity. He took her to dinner; everything seemed nice, and ta-da! You're drugged and in your underwear. It's just horrible."

She held her forehead and forced back tears. Expelling a breath of air, she groaned angrily, "Ugh! He had to have planned this tragedy, and for what? How can we know when we've entered an *Alice in Wonderland* delusion?"

"Maybe you need to verify who they claim to be," said Jason, "or have a friend nearby when you meet with a stranger. Troy and I will do that for you, Ophelia." Her shoulders relaxed. "Thank you, Jason," she whispered.

Street sounds entered the gallery space as Georgi and Roxanne walked in. "I saw the ambulance drive off," exclaimed Georgi. He gave them a hug. "You both met Roxanne at the get-together."

Ophelia took her hand. "Yes, Troy told me he called for your advice since your husband is the fire chief. We need all the help we can get right now."

"Please tell us, what has happened?" Roxanne asked. "I'm worried for you all."

"We're trying to find this guy who abducted Cora," Ophelia stated. "He is a supposed art agent from New York City named Mario Corinthian. We've called galleries and searched everywhere on the internet, including Cora's public feeds. We found no obvious leads and surmised the guy who targeted her must be an imposter." She turned and grabbed a piece of paper. "Look,

Cora drew a quick sketch of him. We made copies." Ophelia handed one to Georgi and Roxanne.

Jason said, "Well, he wasn't very smart because he didn't know Cora's talent for sketching faces." Georgi studied the drawing of a handsome man with an angular nose, dark hair with a prominent widow's peak, and piercing eyes. He wore a suit jacket over a polo shirt. "What's odd is this guy is familiar. Wait! Uh! I saw him at the event for Marilyn!"

"I don't recall him," Roxanne said, "but if this character knew your keen eidetic memory as a wine sommelier, he wouldn't have risked being in your establishment."

"I was focusing on my friends," said Ophelia. "I don't remember him."

Georgi passed the copy back to Jason. "You don't remember him?"

"Now that you mention it, I did see him. He was standing in the corner by the deck doors. He wandered around by himself. Right, Georgi?"

Georgi stomped his foot and raised his arms. "Yes, this is the guy! But why was he at the event for Marilyn? Was he scoping out Cora?" Exasperated, he pressed his temples then his hands flared out as he said, "Did this man murder Marilyn?"

Roxanne asked, "Why would he be there? He must have known Marilyn. And if not, who is this guy? Detective Morrison needs to check this out!"

Ophelia's hand went over her mouth as she gasped in shock and murmured, "Uh, a predator has invaded our fun in the art world."

"I'm going to find Shatana and let her know," Jason said. "Will you tell the detective that we didn't find much on the internet, Ophelia?" She agreed and hugged him. After he left, a silence settled on them.

Georgi proposed, "Roxanne knows the detective well. Would you like her to call, and you can tell him what we know?" He figured Ophelia needed a nudge. He glanced at Roxanne. She gave him a wink of agreement.

"Thank you, I would like that." Feeling supported, she smiled softly.

Roxanne asked for Detective Morrison, but Peabody took the call. She put him on the speaker to let him know that Georgi and Ophelia would inform him.

"Detective, Jason and I searched everywhere online," said Ophelia, "and there are no clues as to who this man is. We think he's a fake. We can't find a reference for him. Cora said he made the appointment with her on Saturday morning by texting her through an online app she was comfortable with. It seems he must have used her website to become familiar with her work and art shows at galleries because he mentioned them to her. I'll send you a list of the galleries we called. None of them have heard of Mario Corinthian."

"Thank you, Ophelia, for your effort. It helps us move forward, and we'll investigate the record of the text messaging app."

"But Detective Peabody, we have some helpful news too," Georgi interjected. "I recognize the man in Cora's sketch, and so did Jason. We saw him at our event for Marilyn. Don't you think this means it's all connected?"

"Georgi, this incident is so close to Marilyn's, of course, we'll investigate. I'll let Detective Morrison know. Pass the sketch around to see who else might remember him."

Georgi felt desperate. "But is there anything else we can do? We really want to help."

"Just keep your eyes and ears open for tips or gossip, and let me know if anyone else recognizes the guy."

"Okay, will do." They ended the call, and Georgi grabbed copies of Cora's sketch while his eyes darted to Roxanne. She wondered what he was thinking.

Roxanne took notice of Ophelia's nervous energy of swirling a length of hair around her finger. "Let's take you to lunch, Ophelia. I think you need a break."

Before she could answer, Georgi and Roxanne each took an arm and gently lifted her from her seat. She went along without hesitation, flipped the gallery's sign to closed, and locked the door shut.

CHAPTER 16

New London Ink

After lunch with Ophelia, Georgi locked his arm into Roxanne's elbow and whispered, "Come along, we have a mission."

"What do you mean we have a mission?"

"Didn't you hear? We were given permission to listen."

"By whom and to what?"

"By Detective Peabody. He told us to listen for any tips or gossip and to let him know if we hear anything. So we need…" he motioned air quotes, "team members."

Georgi gently pulled Roxanne along Bank Street. "Right this way, please." He took a sharp right into New London Ink, a tattoo parlor. Roxanne quickly became overwhelmed with the unique establishment's sounds, colors, and art. She noticed each artist had a personal section, with a table, tools of the trade, and a tall wall displaying their art or art they loved.

The receptionist greeted them, and Georgi asked if Elise was busy.

"She just finished lunch. Let me see if she can say hi before her next client."

Soon, Elise came forward, smiling. Roxanne was awed by her Rasta dreadlocks of blonde hair woven and swirled atop her head into a tall bun. She had a relaxed, warm, friendly presence. Roxanne noticed an intricate collar tattoo of woodland flora and fauna.

"Hey, Georgi, what's new?"

"Hey, Elise, this is my friend, Roxanne. I may have mentioned her to you."

"You certainly have. Your last escapade on the ferry from Long Island with a villain! You're famous, Roxanne, at least in Georgi's mind." She chuckled. "It's nice to meet you."

Wide-eyed Roxanne glared and pointed at Georgi accusingly for his storytelling. With a turn, she said to Elise, "I'm in awe. I've never been in a tattoo artist's studio. But honestly, Georgi hasn't told me why we are here." She nudged him. "Are you getting a tattoo today?"

He gave Elise a weak expression and cringed.

"I haven't touched you, Georgi. Stop acting like you're in pain." Elise squeezed his upper arm gently. "He's afraid, Roxanne, but that's okay. I have plenty of clients who aren't." She smiled at him. "But may I tousle your hair?"

Georgi feigned worry and put his hands over his head. Roxanne laughed, knowing perfect hair was his weak spot.

"Okay, Georgi, let's get down to business. Why don't we step out on the sidewalk for a minute, and you can tell me why you're here?" Relieved, he held the door for them.

Elise was a classically trained artist who had attended art college in Old Lyme, a town famous for the Florence Griswold Museum and its well-known artist colony. She became a popular tattooist, finding inking skin a great way to express her creativity and make a good living too.

"Listen, did you hear what happened to Cora this morning?" Georgi asked as Elise lit a cigarette.

Her expression was full of concern. "I did. Troy texted to let me know and said to be careful. It's just terrible. I can't believe these things are happening. Do you know what's going on?"

"I spoke to Detective Peabody, and he said we need to listen for any gossip or tips about what happened to Cora and Marilyn." He pointed to her. "You and I are around lots of locals and tourists. We may hear things that could help catch this guy." Then he whispered, "and find out why it's happening."

Roxanne handed her a sketch. "Here's the drawing Cora made of him. He called himself Mario Corinthian."

Elise scrutinized the drawing and inhaled another toke of nicotine. "He does look familiar."

"Right, he was at the event for Marilyn. Do you remember him there?"

"That's it. Yes, that must be where I saw him."

"Ophelia has more copies," he continued. "Can you spread the word to your coworkers to listen for anything suspicious and to be on the lookout for this weird guy hunting women?"

Elise nodded firmly while blowing smoke away from them. "Absolutely, Georgi. We hear all kinds of strange stuff while people are in our chairs or on the table. Often, it's just fun talk of bizarre things."

"Oh, sure, like the story you told me about Jack Dracula?" Georgi asked, and Roxanne's eyes widened.

"Exactly. A tragic love story." Elise explained, for Roxanne's benefit, "I saw a photo of him. He was awesome. Tattoos were all over his body like a Māori tribe member from New Zealand. Detailed and intense ink. He had a tattoo parlor right here on Bank Street and was in love with a woman who became so jealous that she drove her car into his storefront. Not only did she put him out of business, but that's when the mayor closed all the tattoo parlors in New London. At least, that's how I heard the story. It was forty years before the parlors could come back." Elise tapped the ash off her cigarette. "It's what crazy jealousy will do."

Roxanne reasoned, "Which means it's possible someone was jealous of Marilyn or Cora, right?"

Georgi was energized. "That's why we need a listening team. Somebody around here must know something."

A final puff of smoke left Elise's lips. "Georgi, if we find him, I'll guide the dude into a dark alley full of righteous men. Afterward, we'll turn him over to the detectives."

Roxanne laughed as if it was a joke, but Georgi reached out and hugged Elise. "I'm so glad you're my friend because I know you meant that."

Elise smiled at Roxanne, whose eyes grew wide. "I'm just kidding. It's just how I feel when people I love are wronged."

Considering her words, Roxanne realized how true they were. "I believe their freedom is only temporary because when the justice of karma kicks in, they'll get what they deserve."

"Yes! Karma's their payback," Elise agreed. The receptionist knocked on the window and waved at her. "I must go. Georgi, I'll get people on our team."

"Thank you, doll. You know I appreciate it."

Roxanne said, "And I'll tell the firefighters to come to see you for a tattoo." Elise waved goodbye.

Georgi hooked onto Roxanne's arm again. "Okay, let's go to our next shop."

"Well, you're just full of ideas, aren't you, Mr. Algarve?" She winked at him and her formality. "Well, I know where there are some familiar faces. Let's go to Muddy Waters and have an iced coffee."

"Yes, missy," Georgi teased. "Did I discombobulate your comfort zone by bringing you into a tattoo parlor?"

"Hmm, only for a second. New experiences are fine as long as I feel safe." She squeezed his arm. "We've had many odd things happen to us this summer. Let's keep life simple and be good listeners this time. The secret agent tack wore on Sam when we were nearly killed going to that vineyard in Long Island two months ago. We have to tone it down. Okay, Georgi?"

"I'll do my best, Roxy, but I can't promise I won't look into something if I need to."

She poked him. "Don't call me Roxy, Mr. Algarve! You know I don't like that nickname."

Grinning impishly, he steered her into Muddy Waters. "Yes, Mrs. Chief."

CHAPTER 17

The Wolves in the World

After Morrison completed his report on Cora's incident at police headquarters, he had Peabody organize another knock and talk with the neighbors on Bank Street with Cora's sketch in hand. Peabody was to collect any surveillance camera footage that might have caught her with the man.

Morrison decided his next stop was a visit to Dr. Storm. Calling ahead, he gave her a quick overview of what had taken place with Cora and said he wanted to identify if there were any connections to Marilyn's case. But Dr. Storm caught him off guard with a request. "If you haven't eaten yet, why don't we meet at Fred's Shanty and talk about it while we have lunch?" His silence encouraged her to justify the invitation. "We have to eat, Detective. Besides, fried clams, coleslaw, and lobster rolls are always better by the water. Don't you agree?"

Morrison did agree but struggled against crossing any professional lines with the new medical examiner in town. She had only been in her regional role for two months. He liked being cautious yet agreed. He was hungry.

At Fred's Shanty, they carried their seafood baskets to a table with an umbrella that overlooked the busy Thames River boating scene. The mild August weather fit in with Dr. Storm's work habit of keeping her long hair tied up. Today, it was in a bun. Morrison noticed she wore little makeup, but none of that took the magic out of her golden eyes.

He started with a work question to maintain his boundaries. "With all your experience in New Haven, I imagine you have thoughts about what happened to Cora. We have saliva samples being tested, and I had the samples sent over to you. I want to find out if there were any drugs like this in Marilyn."

"I did send Marilyn's blood samples for an in-depth toxicology report. I'll compare the results and dig deeper if needed." She dipped a whole belly clam into tartar sauce and took a moment to enjoy it. "After you called, I began thinking about Cora as an artist. This man, posing as a gallery agent, has the typical modus operandi of a smooth operator. Sometimes, an older man promising success is a standard ploy. They've learned they can't just ask a young woman for a date because they would be rejected. Therefore, any independent young lady concerned about her career is a perfect target. I've encountered a few of these."

Morrison listened intently. "Smooth operators or young women in trouble? And do you mean personally?" He ate a few fries and took his turn at dipping his fat clam into tartar sauce. While waiting for her answer, he noticed she was staring out at the water. *Is she pausing or pondering?*

"Young women are taken advantage of like this too often." Glancing at him, she asked, "And you know why this happens, Detective?"

"You tell me."

"Vanity and hope, but usually, it's hope. Because most young ladies are hoping someone likes them, likes their work, and has faith in them. Because it's likely they don't have faith in themselves yet." Her gaze returned to the water. "They are the typical quintessential babes in the wilderness of the world with no knowledge of the creatures lurking behind a posh suit, a fresh smile, and the sweet scent of success. So they take a chance, a risk, and believe an older, wiser man or woman will help their career.

"Look at the Ghislaine Maxwell and Jeffrey Epstein case, for instance. They played this game strategy. These smooth operators targeted young women going to art school in New York. They'd say things like, 'Your art is good, and I can help you,' or 'You're great! I'll make you successful.' How can a vulnerable young woman discern this to be potentially harmful? And as you know, young men can be just as susceptible to these ploys."

Morrison had not thought much about a woman's perspective like this. "I think you've got something there. I investigate the villains, but maybe I don't look enough at a victim's vulnerability to those who will take advantage. I suppose our education system doesn't prepare the youth for the wolves in the world. It would be helpful if they could learn situational awareness and critically analyze an opportunity carefully. But…" he murmured, "I imagine that's wishful thinking."

"Yes, it's worth exploring," she said, surprised he was receptive to her viewpoint. "You interview victims and explore possible theories to catch the perp. My victims no longer have a say, so it's up to me to explore the evidence that tells the story.

"Poor Cora and maybe Marilyn were victims of this commonly played hand by expert poker players. Those who can read your face and swiftly stack the deck against you. She was set up. But, Detective, when did it start? Yesterday? Last week? Last month? How long has he been tracking Cora? And for what cause? If it is not sex or money, what is it?"

Dr. Storm looked to the sailboats in the water and took a bite of her lobster roll. Suddenly, a big grin came over her face.

Morrison wondered aloud, "Yes? Those were deep questions and gray conclusions you were painting. I had a turbulent cloud of possibilities descend on me, and now you're grinning. What's up?"

"Mmm, the lobster. It's divine, and the view of the water is fantastic. I don't think anything makes me happier."

The cloud disappeared from Morrison's forehead.

Lowering her voice, she said discreetly, "I don't want to get all dark on you again, but I will." She took a sip of iced tea and glanced around to see who was nearby. "Detective, these smooth operators have no concern for their victims. They crush cheap quaaludes or some other elixir into a drink. That will make normal people do strange things. Once drugged, the victims have no memory of what happened and therefore nepenthe! They cannot account for their lost time. The evidence is the situation they wake up in and the drugs in their system."

Morrison leaned in and asked curiously, "Nepenthe? I'm not familiar."

"The Greek poet, Homer, told of this elixir used in *The Odyssey*. Helen, daughter of Zeus, drugged the wine with nepenthe 'to quiet all pain and strife, and bring forgetfulness of every ill.' In other words, Helen delivered the drug so they would forget what the gods delivered or did to humans."

Morrison wondered, "We've taken a saliva sample, but would a blood test identify the drug more accurately?"

"Blood never lies, Detective. And let me know if your people can't get the test done fast enough. I have connections in New Haven." He nodded, and she continued. "I also have a friend from work there who has invested in art. His art dealer may know if this Mario character is truly involved in the New York art scene."

He pulled a folded paper from his back pocket. "Here's the sketch Cora drew of him. Please ask your friends to show it around."

She looked at the drawing carefully. "He's handsome and dangerous. That's a volatile mix." She folded the paper. They continued to eat their food and watch the boats.

"Lunch was a good idea, Doctor. I rarely take a minute to stare out at the water."

"I'm glad. Because I believe fresh air is the healthiest free drug available. I try to get a daily dose." She inhaled deeply with her eyes closed. She tilted back her head and smiled softly. "And now and then, Detective, you can call me Angela if you're comfortable with that."

She can read me like a book, he thought. "I think I'll stick to Dr. Storm for now. But you can call me Morrison—everyone else does." Feeling a need to explain, he added, "Decorum is everything in our profession, or else people digress into gossip. It's a small town where everybody knows you." He hoped she would grasp his restrained formality.

I knew he would say that. She nodded. "I understand. It's important to keep the village content." She smiled, and he lightly chuckled.

"But in our village, Morrison, you have Marilyn and Cora's cases, which seem intricate. I suppose you feel this guy, posing as a gallery scout from New York, has a more devious plan. How old did Cora think he is?"

"Cora guessed forty, but she wasn't sure. The poor kid was so embarrassed."

"Morrison, I learned some advice from my mountaineering friend, Scottie. He said, 'You must be your own mother. Watch out for yourself. You can't depend on others.' Scottie climbed the tallest peaks on every continent, including Mount Everest. He survived a fateful climb when several in his rope team did not.

"When he told me the story, I came up with my own motto: 'Death makes life more real.' And now I've gone all dark on you again."

"Well, hence your profession, Dr. Storm." He peeked at her for a reaction.

"Yet, I remain lighthearted. Otherwise," she hesitated purposefully, "I would look like Morticia."

Morrison laughed aloud as he imagined this beautiful honey-brown-haired woman sitting across from him, instead, with pale skin, black hair, and gothic clothing. He teasingly wagged his finger. "You got me with that image. My Irish father would say, 'You led me down a tattered path to twist my mind and garner a laugh.'"

"Congratulations, Morrison! That's the first time I've seen you truly lighten up. I was starting to wonder if changelings got hold of you when you were young."

Morrison's eyes popped. "That's something my Irish mother would say. God bless her soul." He shook his head in near disbelief. "Hmm, yes, it's rare to hear a laugh from me. It probably has to do with the fresh air and down-to-earth company. I don't come across many people who think like you, Doctor." The detective's tough exterior melted like ice cream on a summer day.

"That's because you don't know people with the experience of laughing in the face of death, Mr. Morrison."

"You've certainly got that right!" *My mom would have liked her.*

They collected their napkins and plates as a popular song played over the speakers, "Sittin' on the Dock of the Bay" by Otis Redding. The smooth tune fit in with their scenery. They both took a moment to watch a schooner swiftly sail the center of the Thames River, skirting past the towering stacks of buildings where submarines were built. Dr. Storm sighed into the moment.

Yet, the detective was perplexed. He wondered how he could feel so agreeable with a woman he barely knew.

CHAPTER 18

Is This a Game?
Tuesday - 3:30 p.m.

Jack Peabody had informed his boss that Georgi recognized the man in Cora's sketch. Morrison decided to stop by the Vinho Verde Wine Bar to see if the friendly wine server had any other details.

The door chimed when he entered, and Morrison walked by a vintage coat rack. He halted suddenly and loudly called out, "Georgi! Where did you get this hat and coat?"

Georgi rounded the corner quickly. "Why are you disturbing my peaceful shrine to wine and food, Detective?" His arms were spread wide in the air.

"Bring me a trash bag," Morrison demanded. "I'm confiscating these items now!"

"What?" he squealed and reeled back. Then he strutted forward with his hands on his hips and looked the detective up and down. "What has gotten into you? I'll have you know I like that hat and coat, and you can't have them, especially to throw them away again!"

Morrison raised his hand for calm. "Please bear with me. Where did you get these?"

"Outside in the bin behind the building," he sniffed, agitated by the question. "I took out the trash, lifted the lid to the bin, and there they were—this beautiful, large-brimmed hat and gold leatherette raincoat. I put them on, and they fit me well enough. So, you can't have them."

"I know what I'm doing. These belong to my investigation."

"Huh? I don't get it." Georgi raised his arms. "It's obvious someone didn't like them because they threw them away!"

Morrison considered his dilemma. He did not want a repeat of two months earlier when he was standing right there, in the Vinho Verde, telling Georgi, "You are a suspect for your boss's death." It didn't turn out so well. Georgi wailed and nearly passed out from hyperventilating over the possibility of going to jail. The detective chose his words carefully but was firm. "I'm going to ask you some questions. Can you please answer them quickly and to the best of your ability?"

Georgi looked at his fingernails, then leaned on one hip and tilted his head. "Is this a game?"

Morrison pressed his lips with impatience, "No, it isn't. Tell me where you were after 11 p.m. last Thursday when Marilyn was last seen, and who were you with?"

Morrison was serious. "I was there," Georgi pointed across the street to the Dahlia gallery, "until maybe twelve-thirty. And—he counted on his hands, "I was with Martina, Ophelia, Troy, Jason, Shatana, Cora, and Marco." He crossed his arms and sported a gallant pose of being above question. "I have nothing to hide."

"And when did you find this hat and coat?" Morrison prodded.

"Saturday afternoon when I was here," he pointed to the floorboards and stomped them with defiance, "because I was preparing this place for you on Sunday." He pointed at Morrison. "So that you could have people to interview." Georgi took a deep breath and demanded, "Now don't you dare tell me I'm a suspect, Detective!"

He pointed to the sky and emphasized, "Don't forget your last case. Roxanne and I risked our lives helping you catch a killer. By the way, your department *finally* returned the blackmail money I put up. Ten thousand dollars is nothing to sneeze at, and remember, that was a favor to you because you don't have prop money in your line of work for some reason."

Morrison's stern exterior weakened with the memory, and a snarky grin emerged. "You and Roxanne practically did everything wrong, and somehow it ended up right. Yes, you have been helpful, and I'm asking if you can do so again." Morrison was secretly relieved Georgi confirmed he had an alibi for Thursday night and would avoid the suspect list.

Georgi was baffled and displeased. "Detective, you perplex and confuse me." Tapping his foot rapidly, he tried to think of what to say next. He was so bewildered that he waved away his attachment to the clothing. "Go ahead, take the hat and coat. It must be important to your case."

Inhaling another deep breath, Georgi softened his tone. "You know, it's a nice leatherette. And the big, brimmed hat, in that shade of yellow, is divine." His hands were in a pose of prayer. "When you're done with them, think of me."

He spun on his heels. "Now, let me find you a *proper* bag." He strutted toward his small office.

Georgi brought a green Vinho Verde tote and presented it to the detective by holding it open. He waited for him to fill it.

Morrison pulled a pair of gloves from his pants pocket and snapped them on to his hands.

With eye-popping wonder, Georgi exclaimed, "Oh my! You are official."

Morrison could not share that Marilyn was last seen wearing this clothing. The hat and length of the coat seemed like the street camera video he'd seen. The silhouette of the clothes would be compared to the footage of her walking through the fog on Bank Street. But it caused another question: Why did she throw them in the trash bin of the Vinho Verde?

Georgi was miffed. "Well, aren't you a man of mystery? Don't you have anything to say? You come in here all gruff and demanding. I answer your questions, and you take my clothes."

Keenly aware of Georgi's feelings, Morrison carefully folded the raincoat into the bag and placed the hat on top. "I'll take good care of these. And Georgi, you can put your mind at ease because you are not a suspect this time."

"I better not be!" Georgi's hand went to his chest with a perturbed look.

"By the way, I stopped here because Peabody said you recognized the man in Cora's sketch."

"Yes, I remember seeing him here during the event for Marilyn. He stood out to me because he wore gray Sperry boat shoes."

Morrison smiled to himself. *Yes, shoes would impress Georgi.*

"But also, I didn't see him conversing with anyone, and he was here for an hour. Uh, I almost forgot! Elise at New London Ink and Jason saw him too. But that's all I know."

"Excellent, Georgi. Thank you for the bag and the clothes and for being helpful." Morrison nodded, turned, and left. The door chimed behind him.

"At least I'm not a suspect," Georgi sang. He sashayed to his sound system to play his favorite up-tempo dance tune. It was called "City Boy" by Kyven. Georgi's friend Steven was the co-composer and one-half of the duo group. Turning the pulsing music to a loud volume, he danced out his anxiety and sorrow for his friends.

CHAPTER 19

Bad News Sells
Tuesday - 5:00 p.m.

Karl Rubens drove home from his job as the director of the Mystic River Fine Art Museum. He heard the updated news report on the radio about the death of Marilyn Maroney. Rarely did Karl react to anything, but this news disturbed him. Usually, he couldn't care less about people. His pale blue eyes often had a gaze of haughty indifference yet told of his delight when a fine work of art turned his dial. His stiff body language became expressive, and his hands exuded enthusiasm. However, news of this rising star's death threatened his latest business plans.

At the age of fifty-six, Karl was a seasoned conservator. He was well respected for his refurbishing skills on priceless fine artworks worldwide. Previously, his career of thirty years had been with the Boston Fine Arts Museum, the BFA. A year ago, Karl earned his new prestigious position in Mystic. Yet, his Beantown coworkers would say it was due to his "meticulous and annoying way of being fussy and addiction to having his way."

Karl had moved to his mother's grand Mystic home for many good reasons. A new career, the historic scenic location, and the refined tastes of Mystic all lured him, as did his relationship with his mother. She was his cherished confidant. The shared home was close to the center of Mystic and work.

Karl had planned for a grand reopening of the Mystic River Fine Art Museum for six months and was secretly ecstatic he was able to loan fine art from the BFA for the event. It was a favor to him for having worked there most of his life. Finally, he was ready to impress the region, which was happening in a week.

Marilyn's death had overtaken the local news and interrupted his extravagant marketing expenditures. The press was fixated on the unfortunate dramatic homicide at the Dahlia Art Gallery. Karl's selfish concern was that they were receiving the attention he wanted for his museum's reopening. And so, when he arrived at their home on Mason's Island, he complained unabashedly to his mother about people's fascination with New London's art scene.

"Oh, Mother, why did she have to die? It attracted the press and everyone to the Dahlia Gallery. It's extremely inconvenient when I'm planning my grand reopening."

"Bad news sells, darling." The cosmetically restored Isadore sipped from her favorite porcelain teacup in the conservatory. Her mid-length dark hair swept to one side and contrasted with her colorful outfit, a decorative kaftan dress. She waved her hand and exclaimed, "Just another obstacle to overcome, and you will, my dear. In a week, everyone will be grateful to take their mind off her and put their full attention on your big event at the museum. Don't worry, my love; all the attention will be on you."

Karl pressed his lips. "Pff, that reminds me of my next big dilemma. The fine wine server pulled out today. He double-booked, lost some of his staff, and says he must prioritize his function in Westerly, Rhode Island, ahead of mine. He canceled with me, Mother. Can you believe his disrespect?"

Agitated, Karl pushed his fingertips against his forehead. "This is too much pressure at the last minute." He looked at her. "The man recommended a wine sommelier named Georgi Algarve, who runs an exclusive wine dinner and event business. My reluctance is he's from New London too."

Isadore admonished him. "Can't you get past your issues? Just because you see it as competition does not make it so. You are overly fixating for no good reason. Besides, friends of mine have thoroughly enjoyed wine dinners hosted by Georgi Algarve. I think you should stop brooding and go on their recommendation." She lay back in her seat and sipped her tea. "Darling, you don't have another option."

Isadore Rubens' deceased husband left her a fortune. Her first investment was to beautifully maintain her face with plastic surgery, light therapy treatments, and potions most women could not afford. She also invested in art, as she had with her husband, but more so, enjoying the benefits of her art connections from New England to Europe. Her energy and spunk were contagious for a woman of seventy-eight who looked sixty. Because of her name and philanthropy, she was invited into posh societies wherever she went.

Yet for Isadore, her supreme adoration was for her son more than art, fortune, or fame. She was thrilled he had moved from Boston to be with her as she aged and delighted to share him with her friends in social settings. Now she wanted him to be the next famous man in town.

Karl took his mother's advice and called to make an appointment with Georgi. He was impressed with Georgi's changing of his schedule to accommodate the museum's grand reopening event. They arranged to meet in the morning.

9 a.m. – Wednesday

When Georgi arrived at the Mystic River Fine Art Museum, he noticed Karl's thick, blond hair was smoothed straight back with hair product. He had piercing light-blue eyes and was exceptionally tall and lean in his blue linen suit with a yellow pocket square and neck scarf.

Karl had a haughty demeanor that contrasted with Georgi's flamboyant nature, so Georgi decided to tone down his mannerisms and act as reserved as possible to get this choice job and further his career.

"How do you do, sir? I'm Georgi Algarve. My family is originally from Portugal, yet I have come to this area via New York City." Georgi bowed slightly, guessing Karl would appreciate the added politeness and respect.

Karl nodded. "Very good to meet you, Mr. Algarve. I go by Karl Rubens. We are extended from the Rubens of the Netherlands, modern-day Belgium. You may have heard of Peter Paul Rubens, the great fine artist, a Flemish Baroque painter. He is a distant relative from the seventeenth century, and we have been proud ever since of his success as an artist and a businessman. I came here via Massachusetts, but my parents originally met and lived in New York City. Therefore, we have that in common, Mr. Algarve."

"You may call me Georgi unless you want to keep the formality." While waiting for an answer, Georgi was secretly pleased that his observation skills helped him connect with his new prospect. He straightened his five-foot-ten frame but felt diminished by Karl's stature and height of six-foot-two.

"Please, call me Karl." He presented the tips of his fingers to grasp the ends of Georgi's for an inferior handshake. He grabbed a handkerchief from the top pocket of his light-blue linen suit coat and generously wiped his hands. His gold cufflinks glimmered in the museum's lighting. Georgi's eyebrows raised at Karl's seeming obsession with cleanliness. "Georgi, I would like to know what kind of wine you would serve with an Italian painting from the fourteenth century?"

Caught off guard, Georgi stammered, "May I…may I…see the painting?"

Karl was impressed with his response because it was correct. "Why, yes, of course. If I showed you a painting of a courtesan, it would be an entirely different wine than if I showed you a painting of a pious priest." Karl gave him a bemused smile.

Georgi acknowledged the test by keeping his head slightly downturned in deference while looking up at Karl. "May I suggest a way to raise the drama of your event?" Georgi offered. "I believe we can elevate it to a high level and become the talk of the town."

Standing stiffly with his hands behind his back, Karl nodded.

Georgi maintained his refined tone. "I know a fine gentleman who can assist you with staging the museum in high fashion. For example, he has antique architectural columns, tall theater draping, and classic urns for flowers or potted palms. He can create a memorable and classic grand reopening."

Since Karl seemed open to the idea, Georgi asked, "May I continue?" Karl nodded. "I suggest a fine gardener who can select the most sophisticated plants."

Karl analyzed Georgi with curiosity. "I am quite intrigued by your suggestion for architectural columns, urns, and plants. It could be quite fitting with the theme of the curated art from the BFA Museum. Can you make the calls and see if they would be available to complete the look for next week's opening?" Karl was not usually intrigued by anyone, but he was with Georgi. *This young man presents himself quite well. Mother was right again.* Karl's worries dissipated, and his spirits lifted.

Georgi withheld his internal excitement as Karl requested wines from Italy and France and left it up to Georgi to make appropriate selections. He then showed him the kitchen, which had been refreshed for catering, and where Georgi would place the cases of wine. Karl next presented the new fifteen-foot, crescent-shaped, movable bar that would be placed in the museum's grand hall. It even had a name: Four Kisses.

Georgi wondered if his hour with Karl was long enough for him to be at ease. "May I ask, why the name Four Kisses?"

Karl was pleased to explain. "We have a great sponsor for the event, and she asked if she could name the bar. I was hesitant, of course, but she is my mother, Isadore Rubens, so how could I not? I'm told it's a French expression that mother had with father."

"That is delightful," Georgi cooed. His hands went to his heart. He observed that Karl's hard exterior melted just a little then too. They said their goodbyes, and Georgi clicked his heels when he left the entrance. *This was magical*, he thought. *I have a fantastic event to plan, Marco will elegantly dress the museum, and Roxanne will adorn it with lovely plants inside and out.* Before stepping into his car, Georgi let loose with a dance move like John

Travolta in *Saturday Night Fever* to burn off his excitement before driving home.

Little did he know, Karl was watching out the window, wondering why his new hire was dancing next to his car. Having forgotten how to express simple pleasures, a small smile cracked Karl's typical, serious expression.

CHAPTER 20

Go as a Man
Wednesday - 11:15 a.m.

Morrison made a call to the Vinho Verde. "Georgi, Morrison here. We have not located any of Marilyn's family. Do you know why?"

"Well, she didn't know where they were. Her parents left on holiday around the world when she went to college at age eighteen. They never came back. Eventually, they wrote and said they were living in the Himalayas in Bhutan to help an orphanage. They gave her enough money to live on and pay bills. That was ten years ago. Marilyn was an only child and said she had no other relatives, Detective. She was embarrassed they abandoned her."

"Okay, now that makes sense." Morrison rubbed his chin. "Has anything else come to your attention?"

"Well, I noticed Cora's incident is in the newspaper and online. They've made it clear to everyone that the Dahlia artists are troubled, the cases are unsolved, and it doesn't look good for the City of Steeple's reputation. But what's worse, Detective, is that you're calling me for information. I want to hear what has come to your attention. Have you no new information on Cora being abducted or Marilyn's death? Do you think they are connected? How come this is happening to my friends? What's going on, Detective?"

"I'd like you to remember I don't report to you, Georgi," Morrison informed with an even tone. "I called to see if you learned anything new. We are investigating both cases. I am taking them very seriously, and my whole department is looking into them. I thought I would give you the courtesy of a call."

Georgi sat down and sighed. "You are very nice to me and have a horrible job. Well, maybe it's not horrible to you, but it is to me. Anyway, I've got nothing. But I'll keep my ear to the ground and listen and watch." His gaze wandered to his schedule on the whiteboard that laid out the week in advance.

"Hey, by the way, I may have an opportunity for you. I'll be doing a wine tasting at the Mystic River Fine Art Museum next week, and all the artists, patrons, and everyone in the region will be there. Maybe you should go. That Mario guy could be there, or you could meet people and get some leads. But on second thought, you can't go as a cop. You must go as a man…I mean, a guest." Georgi snickered. "You know what I mean, Detective. You always seem to be working."

"Hmm, I understand. You see me as the law, and I am always working."

For one moment, Georgi felt Dan Morrison was a regular guy.

"You may be right. I'll attend as a guest and see *you* at work, for once, serving wine."

"Yes, from five to seven o'clock, the affluent patrons will be there for an early viewing. Then it's an open reception for the public from seven until ten o'clock. I expect I'll see you after seven."

"Yes, you will, but if you hear anything before…."

"I know, I know you miss me, and I will call you," Georgi joked.

Morrison chuckled, "You got me there."

They ended the call, and the detective recognized that in just a couple of months, Georgi had been a victim of loss twice. In June, he lost his boss, and now he lost Marilyn. Dr. Storm had told him that many people are grieving when a person dies.

When Georgi put down his phone, he thought of Marilyn and felt sad, so he called Roxanne to tell her about his conversation with the detective.

She could tell he was spiraling downward emotionally, so she came up with an idea. "If you have an hour, I want to take you somewhere special. Are you free to go?"

"If you mean now," he looked at his watch, "it's eleven-thirty. Well, yes, I can take an early lunch."

"I'll be right there," she said and ended the call.

She pulled in front of the Vinho Verde Wine Bar, tooted the horn, and waited in her black gardening truck. She watched Georgi run out the door, noticing his dark orange jeans, brown leather tennis shoes, and green Vinho Verde polo shirt.

He swung open the door to her truck and stepped into the extended cab. "Is this really an adventure?" His eyes gleamed.

She grinned. "Yes! I'm going to surprise you so you will be inspired to tell me about dessert wines. Do you want to wear a blindfold?" She waved a bandanna at him.

"No! That will make me carsick."

"Never mind then. You'll be surprised anyway."

Roxanne drove under the I-95 overpass, through Hodges Square, and beyond the Coast Guard Academy, then straight toward the countrified area by Connecticut College and into the Lyman Allyn Art Museum. Giant sculptures in the garden surrounded the stately, historic building once owned by the daughter of its namesake, Captain Lyman Allyn.

Georgi exclaimed, "Oh! I've done wine tastings here for fundraising events. It's magnificent, like a treasure box."

"Have you been here recently?"

"No, but my favorite exhibit is the Tiffany gallery. I was here for the opening, and they had a gorgeous cake that looked like a jeweled Tiffany creation."

Roxanne noticed Georgi's mood had lifted. "Well, I brought you here to see a new exhibit that is just as colorful."

They entered between the Doric columns under the grand pediment of the granite structure. Roxanne asked for the sweets exhibit at the desk. The volunteer pointed to the staircase and said, "It's on the second floor in the opposite wing from the *Tiffany in New London* permanent collection."

Georgi whispered, "Let's look in the reference library first. It's here on the left." The room featured a high ceiling with paneled wood beams and books lining the walls between tall windows. A lovely white marble sculpture of a nymph with a butterfly was lit softly in the center of a large reference table. The room was big enough for a musical trio, and the rich wooden floors were perfect for dancing.

"Ooh," Roxanne cooed, "I love it here: the books, the scent, the light."

"We've held events here with appetizers, lemonade, and wines. It's a lovely space for a party." Georgi took Roxanne's hand and gave her a twirl. "Okay, now that you've seen the library, let's go upstairs." They passed a large-scale model of a captain's sailing ship along the grand staircase.

At the top of the stair, they took a hard right. Roxanne stopped Georgi. "Now close your eyes, and I'll walk you to the doorway." He did so, and she guided him. "Okay, open your eyes."

And pow! There was the most oversized donut Georgi had ever seen. A frosted chocolate one, over three feet with sprinkles, all gooey and yummy, suspended on the wall. "Wow, my head will fit inside the hole," he exclaimed.

The artist/sculptor, Peter Anton, had fun recreating sweet confections of every kind down to the most minute detail. Children and adults would recognize big boxes of exquisite chocolates, massive cupcakes, popsicles, lollipops, ice creams, and German chocolate cake. A rainbow confetti cake was six-feet-wide, and a slice looked ready to eat.

"Oh, I love it here." Georgi slowly turned. "It's so, so happy."

The vast desserts appeared to be completely edible. They watched a family round the corner who became delighted to see the beautiful sweets. Stunned and wide-eyed, there was a moment they seemed spellbound by the size and quantity of the sugar. One child squealed, breaking their suspension, "Mommy, look!"

In one of the gallery rooms, huge, candied hearts read, "I Love You." Roxanne and Georgi went through the four rooms of the exhibit three times, and finally, they were ready to fulfill their dessert craving.

"Shall we peek into the Tiffany gallery before we leave?" Roxanne asked.

"Of course, we can't come here and not see it." Georgi waved her ahead of him.

The alluring entrance had a stunning wall-sized mural of a Tiffany decor with a dragonfly.

"This is candy of another kind," Roxanne whispered.

"Yes, eye candy to decorate your home or to wear." Suddenly, Georgi halted and took Roxanne's elbow. He watched a tall man walking behind an older woman. "Wait," he breathed. "I think I know him."

The couple turned into a room with Tiffany stained-glass windows. "Uhh, it's Karl Rubens," he said into her ear. "He is the one hiring us for the Mystic River Fine Art Museum's reopening. Shall I introduce you now?"

Roxanne looked down at her clothes and eyeballed Georgi. "It might be better another time when I have my act together. I want to dress up more. They look very formal."

Georgi nodded. "We don't want to blow our big chance. Let's wait until we are fancied up to present our grand ideas." Together, they practically tiptoed out of the gallery and gently tapped their way down the stairs, giggling.

Once they were in the main foyer, she asked, "Is a scarf fancy enough, or do I need to wear a dress? I don't wear dresses, you know. It might have to be a pantsuit or maybe just a nice top. What do you think? Why am I asking you? You told me you insure your shoes—"

"Shh, Roxanne," Georgi interrupted. "You'll know what to do, honestly."

"Okay, never mind. I'll figure it out."

Georgi wrapped his arm around her shoulder as they walked out the door. "Don't worry, gorgeous. You are beautiful inside, and it shines on the outside."

CHAPTER 21

Troy's Musings
Thursday - 1 p.m.

Marilyn and Troy had been close friends even though their ages differed by fifteen years. He had encouraged her since high school, taught her paint-mixing techniques, and showed her how to design large-scale murals for buildings. Because of her recent success, she had made plans for a joint show with Troy to help him promote his work to her new clientele. It was all about being seen, so he was excited to be introduced to her cultured clients, where he could improve his visibility and hopefully earn a better living. He anticipated high-end gallery showings nationwide, which would produce a good income. But now, that dream was over.

Troy had found it challenging to be discovered as an artist and win financial comfort. For him, it was depressing because when a client didn't pay on time, he would internalize the stress. He figured his clients never went hungry, and they didn't understand that the money could determine his next meal.

To counterbalance his meager art earnings, Troy created a vintage typewriter business. He would buy them inexpensively, refurbish them, and give them a creative custom paint job. This combination of repairing and tinkering was mind-absorbing. Yet, at this moment, he was overtaken by his sadness about losing Marilyn and his concerns for Cora, so he wasn't in the mood to tinker.

Troy began to sketch ideas for his next piece in his studio. Next to him was a large wax block he created. Troy developed the artistic skill of carving, much like traditional wood-cut engraving, but he carved wax since it was renewable. From his finished carvings, he would create monoprints on canvas and paper. Each was unique in color and detail.

One coping mechanism was to bury himself in his artwork, but as he tried, Troy's thoughts traveled along to his worry about his lot in life. He was making a reasonable wage at his sideline job with the typewriters, but he was tired of waiting for his art to earn the lion's share of his income.

His reliable cat, Matt, sat nearby on the windowsill, a willing listener. "My worries haunt me, Matt. It seems I was born worrying. It has stayed with me my whole life, and I feel stuck in a worry slot." Matt mewed a response. Troy stroked the cat's back, then continued to sketch on the large pad of paper. His thoughts voyaged to a childhood photo of himself that looked like Auguste Rodin's sculpture, *The Thinker*. "Hmm...even as a child, I was trying to solve the reason for being. Why am I here? Maybe these were my original wonders and worries, Matt. What do you think about that?"

Matt reached his paw toward Troy for a pet, and with no response, he cried, "Meow."

Images began to emerge from his drawing. They became defined shapes of giant bees and flowers. Troy recalled the various spiritual beliefs he examined as he became older, some saying his many lifetimes of karma had brought him to this point and place. *Sure, so that I can deal with worry.* Yet here he was, older, working hard, and still worrying about how to earn a higher price for his art.

Troy paused to stare out the second-story window. Blue skies had broken through the clouds, and the day was getting brighter. It made him think of the brilliant skies in Ethiopia and his philanthropic work there, teaching young artists. He had developed a new series portraying sunshine over the Ethiopian landscape. When he returned home to New London, the landscape series of work became a show at the Dahlia. Troy softly smiled at the memory.

A cloud swept over the sun. The shaded garden below his window brought up thoughts of odd jobs. One was cleaning street drainage traps from leaves and debris, and another was card dealing long hours in a smoky casino. He did these jobs to survive as an artist. *All for the passion of creating.*

To make money with his art, he tried everything. Yet the prominent outdoor art shows under tents, had high entrance fees, as did juried shows, art agents, and dealers all wanted a cut. Most galleries required significant percentages of his sale. Therefore, being busy didn't always add up to making money.

Troy had done it all for over twenty-five years: experimented, collaborated, helped with fundraisers, assisted nonprofits, and painted murals on significant city buildings. He was on NPR radio, in glossy magazines, and in newspaper articles that featured his work. Yet his worry about money still ticked like a pendulum in an antique clock. His worry had a rhythm, a beat. It knocked on his door and rang in his head.

His thoughts swung in another direction. He remembered learning that karma meant his attitude or habit of worry was part of his earthly karma. "It's annoying to know I have to work on this, Matt." The cat pushed his nose against him.

Troy sketched, deciding to play with the idea of worry as a disparate being. He thought of the zombie movies he liked, possibly because zombies were far worse off than he was. *You can't kill a zombie; they're already dead. Is my worry about money like the undead? Can I ever be free of worry?*

Troy moved to his workbench, where his thick block of wax was ready. He smoothed his hand over the four-foot wax rectangle. The talented artist pulled out his many tools and started carving a new design. Shavings gathered under his hand, and he blew them aside as he imagined cutting away his worry about money and sadness for Marilyn and his concern for Cora.

CHAPTER 22

Magnets for Danger
Thursday - 3:30 p.m.

Georgi, Roxanne, and Marco planned to meet to discuss ideas for the Mystic River Fine Art Museum's reopening event the following week. Georgi was told they would meet in Roxanne's backyard. Once through the gate, he found her in the shade of her Japanese-inspired garden. A tray of iced tea was on the café table. He took a deep breath and sighed expressively. "This is a little sanctuary. I am rarely in a setting that allows me to relax."

"Good, I planned it that way." She gave him a glimmering smile.

While waiting for Marco, they sipped the tea made with lemon balm leaves from her garden. Roxanne noticed Georgi gratefully sink into his seat and gaze around the garden. The day was slightly humid, and a hosta flower fragrance from "Royal Standard", wafted into the air. It caught Georgi's attention. "Mmm, I could compare that sweet scent to a wine. Maybe a Riesling."

A soft green mound of moss lay below the hosta where a snail inched along. Georgi spied it and was bemused. Then a dragonfly swooped by him, and he jerked. "Whoa, what was that? I'm not sure I can handle this much nature." He clenched his hands under his chin, terrified. Squinching his nose, he pursed his lips, then yelped. "There's a bee near me!"

Roxanne leaned over and swatted his shoulder, making him jolt. "Will you calm down? He's on a flower, for god's sake. He doesn't care about you. He's in the honey business. How long have we been out here? Just five minutes. I think you have to give nature a little more time."

Georgi was a city boy. Roxanne planted his flowerpots and window boxes at the Vinho Verde. He watered them, that's all. Yet, when he was young, he had helped his grandfather with his home vineyard. But somewhere along the way, he stopped putting his hands in the soil. The profession of a sommelier had his brain preferring the mental exercises of viticulture and wine knowledge. Georgi found that he liked his nails manicured and to wear fine clothes.

Trying to be kind, Georgi said, "I love nature from a distance." He held his saucer and teacup and delicately sipped his tea. "Their honey business makes this tea delicious."

He eyed the bees buzzing from flower to flower and stuttered, "I… I just don't like sitting this close to them. Bees have stingers." Suddenly, he looked perplexed. "On second thought, why is it such a paradox?" He cocked his head like a bird. "Why would you create a honeybee with a stinger? Is that a God joke?"

Roxanne shook her head. "I can't imagine what it's like to live in your brain. Never a dull moment, I'm sure. You are either singing and dancing, managing multiple vintages of wines for tastings, or wistfully wondering about honeybee stingers and God." She squeezed his arm. "You're a wonderful enigma."

Georgi was pleased. "I like being an enigma, thank you."

"And that is why we are here in my back garden." Roxanne waved her hand across the yard. "We are in nature, under the shade tree, by the koi pool, in my tiny Japanese-inspired garden so you can develop a new skill." She looked at him elfishly. "Let's see who will surprise us next."

Smiling, Georgi skipped the part about learning a new skill and asked, "There's a surprise?"

Looking around, he noticed the creatively pruned pine tree reflected in the koi pool. His eye moved along and caught movement in the greenery. "What's that?" He pointed. "Over there in that shrub. It's creeping!" He went stiff in his seat. Roxanne followed his stare.

"That's one of my friends." She walked over to the Hinoki cypress and reached out her hand. A four-inch green thing walked onto her arm. She returned to the café table. Coaxing Georgi, she said, "See? She's friendly."

He recoiled in his seat. "What is it? A bug?"

"Here, see for yourself." She brought the insect closer for him to inspect.

"Oh no, that's close enough." Georgi's eyes were like saucers, his chin was tucked in, and he looked like he wanted to escape. So, Roxanne backed off and sat in her seat.

"She is harmless to us and good for the garden. She is a great hunter who helps farmers by eating moths, mosquitos, and aphids. See how sweet she is? Look at her face. She's called a praying mantis."

Georgi watched as the insect moved from one of Roxanne's hands to the other. Since she wasn't afraid, he inspected it closer. "Her face is curiously pretty and heart-shaped. Look at those antennae. She does look like she's praying, doesn't she? I wonder if they use them in the vineyards for aphid management?"

Once he connected the praying mantis to growing grapes, Roxanne knew she had him. "When you're afraid of something in nature, be still and watch it. When you observe it long enough, you'll realize it is in its own world and doesn't care about you. Be mindful of their business and feel comfortable knowing nothing is out here to harm you. Just don't surprise them. That's a nature secret and how I work next to bees and bugs in the garden."

Georgi's arm was next to Roxanne's, and the praying mantis inched onto him. "Okay, I'm initiated into the wild world of your garden, but I'm still reluctant." He watched the bug gently walk about until he had a thought. "Hey, when Marco is here, don't say anything, and let's see if he notices the praying mantis on me."

They heard Marco arrive through the back gate. "Hello, Roxanne?" He joined them at the table. Suddenly, seeing the bug on Georgi, he kicked back in his chair and flipped. Marco's arm splashed into the koi pool. Georgi laughed while pulling his arm out.

"I take it you don't like bugs," Roxanne grinned. "I'll get you a towel."

Georgi put the praying mantis back on the shrub, and Roxanne handed Marco a towel. "That's it for my nature training. You guys have to get out more." They smiled at her sheepishly.

Pouring Marco some tea, she announced, "We have a job to do. Let's get to work on our undercover mission and the decorations for the Mystic River Fine Art Museum event." She raised her eyebrows twice for significance.

"What undercover mission?" Marco asked, raising his voice.

"It's never a dull moment with us," said Georgi.

"What are you two up to now?" Marco shook his head in disbelief. "You're impervious to being cautious." During their last escapade, Marco had played a small part in helping Georgi to drop off a blackmail payment of ten thousand dollars to entrap a villain. "My thoughts are telling me we are already heading for trouble. You two are magnets for danger. I don't know if I can be a witness to this."

"Don't worry. You don't have to witness," Georgi coaxed. "You can be a team player."

Marco's mouth dropped in astonishment.

"Listen," Georgi placed his hand on Marco's shoulder, "the man who fooled and abducted Cora? Well, he could be there, and if he is, I will spot him because he was at the event for Marilyn. See? Here is the sketch Cora drew. He calls himself Mario Corinthian, and we'll take him into custody."

Marco observed the sketch, pursed his lips, and squinted at Georgi. His voice rose with each word. "*You*–will take him in?"

Georgi corrected himself. "Well, not me or we, really. I mean Detective Morrison. He'll be at the event. He will arrest him for Cora. This guy may also be connected to Marilyn's death."

"I didn't know Marilyn was murdered! I felt so terrible because I found the spear for her sculpture." Marco's hands went to his face as he moaned, "This has been torture. The balcony seemed like a safe place, away from the public. I wish I had found a plastic, fake, dull spear instead of dangerously sharp."

"Marco, it's not you. It's an evil man!" Roxanne felt for him.

"Marco, look at the sketch. Do you recall seeing him?" asked Georgi.

"Yes, I do! I can't believe he showed up at the get-together. You think this man killed Marilyn?"

"Wait, wait!" Roxanne held up her hands. "We must stop and remember we don't know it was him. We surmise this man solicited Cora with sweet promises, then drugged and dumped her."

"But he might have," Georgi surmised.

Roxanne's voice became smooth and monotone. "Yes, that's true. Marilyn might have been fooled too."

Georgi and Marco sat in grief. As they stared at the ground, the scent and sounds of the contemplation garden encompassed them in an atmosphere of reverence for Marilyn. A blue butterfly flitted by and surprised Marco by landing on his teacup. Wide-eyed, he whispered, "Could this be a sign from Marilyn?"

Roxanne smiled, "Why not?" she murmured.

He welled up with tears, releasing his pent-up guilt. Roxanne and Georgi each held one of his hands.

"Wonders can occur when you sit in nature," Roxanne said softly. "Think of it as her way of letting you know she's okay." Georgi and Marco each took a deep breath and were unusually quiet.

"So now, gentlemen," Roxanne attempted to change the mood, "we are in a garden of good…" she held out one hand, "but we must also venture into the garden of evil." She held out her other hand. "We must be alert and wise to our surroundings while at the museum event. We know what the guy looks like, so if we spot him, we must have a plan. I'm glad the detective will be there; he'll handle everything if we see the guy. This time, we won't get in trouble with

Detective Morrison by trying to solve it on our own." She eyed them both. "Which will also save my marriage."

Georgi and Marco chuckled, knowing Roxanne's trouble streak for being helpful.

"I'm glad that's settled," Marco said. "I thought Georgi had a new undercover job, and he would arrest the guy."

Georgi smiled coyly. "Wouldn't that be fun?"

"No!" Roxanne and Marco chimed.

"Huh, I would love to throw some handcuffs on him. Why not?" Georgi exclaimed. He took a breath to compose himself. "Look, no matter what, I'm glad we are doing this job at the museum together. We have something to keep us busy, and I won't think about Marilyn every second. I'll be thinking of catching that bad man instead. Now, let's plan the décor."

Marco had decided on Italian garden statues for the exterior entrance. Roxanne would complement them with potted Mandevilla vines and oleanders for color, tall grasses for softness, and topiaries for structure. For the interior, Marco suggested simply providing sheer reams of fabric to soften areas of the room with draping techniques and adding columns of various heights so Roxanne could top them with ivies and ferns. They would all meet with Karl in the morning to discuss their ideas and pricing.

Marco and Georgi left, and Sam returned to find his wife with tea at the café table in the contemplation garden. *Ah, all is right in the world*, he thought. *My wife is relaxing in the garden instead of scheming to catch a killer.*

CHAPTER 23

Barbeque & a Bear
Thursday - 4:30 p.m.

Roxanne sat in the garden of good with concern for Georgi, Marco, and Troy. She didn't like seeing her friends grieving. She relaxed in her seat and closed her eyes. Soothing sounds came to her attention. The garden hummed with crickets, and the small water feature trickled. The thought of making a concoction of borage flowers and honey for her friends came forward. It was an old-time recipe for heartache.

She imagined mashing the blue star flowers with a mortar and pestle, mixing it with honey, then giving each of them a jar with instructions: take one spoonful to relieve grief and heartache. Her image ended when she heard Sam.

"Honey, what would you like? Steak or chicken on the grill?" He was standing on the raised deck off the back of their two-story house.

"Steak, dear." *Maybe steak will give me stamina for the days ahead.* Packing up her tray with teacups and the empty pitcher, she went indoors and made a big salad of mixed greens, vegetables, and herbs from the garden. Colorful peppers were cleaned and cut, and she put them on the tray with paper plates and utensils.

Sam had the grill hot, and he put the steaks and peppers on as she set the table. He looked over at her several times. "You're very quiet. Are you going to tell me what you're thinking? Or do I have to withhold food until I find out?"

She gave him a meek smile. "Well, I was wondering, how did she die, exactly?"

"I suppose you mean the Maroney girl?"

"Yes, and Georgi said she was thirty, so she's not a girl. Well, technically, she is, but you know what I mean." Roxanne attempted to amend his thinking.

Sam smiled. "Yes, dear, and you know I don't mean anything by it. According to our paramedics, it appears Ms. Maroney fell on the spear in her sculpture. But as you know, Dan has confirmed it's a homicide. He must have irrefutable evidence."

"And the spear killed her?"

"No, the person who pushed her killed her. The spear happened to be there. They could have pushed her over the balcony."

"Oh, that's horrible." She winced.

"I feel bad for my friends. Marilyn was one of Georgi's best friends, and poor Marco provided the spear, and then Troy tutored her since high school."

"You didn't tell me Marco provided the spear!" Sam was surprised by the news. "Does Morrison know?"

"Oh!" Roxanne's eyes darted. "Yes, Marco told him right away. You don't think he could be a suspect, do you?"

"Everyone is until they aren't. I'm sure Morrison is keeping one eye on him."

Sam finished cooking, and they sat to eat. For a few moments, they were quiet, enjoying their meal. Then Sam said, "With the cases we've had over the years, Morrison has always come through. It often starts as a mystery and ends as a sad story or a joke."

"What do you mean by joke?"

"Remember when someone called about the bear struck by a car in the Neptune Beach neighborhood?"

"Tell me again."

"It was a dark October night around eight o'clock. At that time, Dan was Officer Morrison with a beat and was the first on the scene. The bear was lying on the side of the road beside a parked car. He pulled over, had his emergency lights flashing, and waited for animal control to arrive. The bear started to rouse; he must have been hit hard enough to knock him out. Now concerned, Morrison didn't want it to take off into the neighborhood because, as you know, these houses are tight against each other.

"He got out of the vehicle to keep an eye on it. With his hand on his weapon, he watched the animal try to get up on all fours. Morrison decided to draw his gun just in case. Finally, the bear was on all fours when the animal control truck came around the corner. The truck's headlights streamed across and caught a full view of Morrison with his gun drawn in front of the bear. But it wasn't just any bear; it was a brown bear.

"Joey said to Hank, 'Whoa, what's a brown bear doing around here, Hank? We don't see that kind, ever.'

"Hank said, 'Geez, you got me. It looks like a young one, too, doesn't it?'

"Joey said, 'It doesn't matter. They're just as dangerous. Grab that tranquilizer gun, Hank! This officer needs help!'

"The two jumped out of the truck, and the bear stood on its hind legs. It was then that the headlights caught a full view of this creature. All the men were stunned.

"Hank yelled, 'For Pete's sake, it's a bear costume! What the…you got to be kidding me!' They put down their guns and advanced on the guy.

"It was Willie Washburn. The silly kid thought it was hysterical to dress up in a bear costume and scare his neighbors by roaming around their houses. He began crossing the street on all fours but apparently couldn't see well because of the bear's head. The driver of the car didn't see him emerge, and he was struck. They brought him to the hospital, bear costume and all. Boy, did those guys laugh. He did have a concussion, but the doctors said the extra padding in the costume saved his life."

"So, Willie Washburn's joke went wrong." She shook her head and chuckled softly, imagining Morrison's surprise.

"Oh, I didn't tell you," she remembered. "I picked up a new job for pay. Tessa and I will do up the Mystic River Fine Art Museum with plants inside and out for their grand reopening next week. We will donate the money we earn to the New London Beautification Committee for the fall plantings."

She reached out and touched his hand. "Make plans for a date night next Thursday. Georgi is serving the wine, and Marco will add decorative flair to the interior. A special visiting exhibit from the Boston Fine Arts Museum will be there. It should be fun."

"Will there be food?"

"Yes, Georgi says it will be catered."

"If there's free food, I'll be there." He smiled and ate the last bite of his steak. Spotting a shift in Roxanne's demeanor, he asked, "And…is there more to this story of a date night at the museum?"

"Just a tiny detail," she admitted, her brow furrowed with anxiety. "There happens to be another reason we will be there. It's a guy."

He jutted his head forward to hear her answer, "What kind of guy?"

"The suspect, Mario Corinthian," she whispered. "The one that attacked Cora and maybe harmed Marilyn."

He leaned hard onto the picnic table and gave her a look of disbelief. "What…are you…up to now?"

Squirming, she said, "It just so happens that Georgi, Marco, and Jason all recognized him from Cora's sketch. And so, we figured since he went after artists, he might scope out people at places like this event at the museum."

Sam raised his hand. "Okay, give me a second. I'm trying to catch up to the fact that you're sleuthing again. You can't help but get involved, can you? I can't look away for one minute before you're all Miss Investigator. I—"

"Let me explain, let me explain," Roxanne interrupted. "I...I didn't get involved; I am involved. These are my friends. I can't ignore everything going on. I happened to get this job at the Mystic River Fine Art Museum, and it happens to be the type of event with people this guy might hang around as he lurks on the sidelines. We're not going to do anything but keep our eyes peeled. And by the way, Dan Morrison is going to be there. If anyone sees the guy, Morrison will be ready to grab him. That's all, and there's nothing else, I promise." She held up her hand like a Girl Scout.

He laughed, unable to hold in the humor he saw in her trying to reassure him. "Look, Miss Goody Two-shoes," he raised two fingers, pointed them at his eyes, and then back at her, "I've got my eyes on you. I know that the next clue that appears, you're going to jump on it like the last drop of water in the desert, like a monkey on a banana, like a shark on tuna. You can't help yourself. You're fixated. What's that thing they call some people? Obsessive-compulsive! Anyone who has it thinks it's a good thing. Ask them. But..." he raised his tone, "...it's a disorder, dear!"

He wiped his brow. She was about to speak, so he raised his hand again. "The weird thing is that anyone who lives with someone like that must accept it. It's just the way their brain works. It's not a bad thing. It's just, well, annoying sometimes. Guess what? That's what a psychiatrist says, and you know why? Because they can't fix it! So, I'm going to say one thing: don't do anything dangerous. What was that line your grandfather said? 'If you can't be good, be careful.' That's all I can ask because I've given up. You're going to do what you want anyway."

Roxanne's elbows were on the table, and both hands were over her mouth. She didn't like seeing him so concerned and realized she had pushed a button. "I know you're concerned because of the escapades Georgi and I were in two months ago. All we wanted then was to be free of a murderer. I think you're overly worried about me. I'm sorry, dear. I really do promise I won't go near anyone dangerous." She patted his hand and held it.

"Hmm, I'm going to hold you to it. If I hear you have outlandish plans, I'll call the detective to borrow one of those ankle bracelets and have him put you under house arrest."

They laughed. She leaned over and kissed him. "Does that make me your prisoner?" she whispered. They laughed more.

CHAPTER 24

Big Fire on Belham
Friday – a week since Marilyn's fatality

The sirens rang, and the fire station speakers crackled before the dispatcher's announcement, "Fully involved structure fire at Belham Street. Engine one, engine three, truck one, and A-100 responding.

At 4:20 p.m., Fire Chief Samson and his crew bolted into action. Down the pole, into their boots, donning turnout gear and helmets, the driver and lieutenant took their seats in the apparatus as two others slid into the jump seats behind the cab. While the truck was rolling toward the fire, the crew in the jump seats put their arms through the straps of the seat-mounted Scott Air-Paks. All the trucks maneuvered through traffic with sirens blaring. The ones equipped with an Opticom Emergency Vehicle Prevention device mounted on the front turned traffic lights green on their approach, helping them to proceed through cleared intersections safely. The chief followed in his department-issued SUV.

Belham Street was only a few blocks from headquarters, so firefighters arrived in minutes to the structure fire, already wearing the Air-Pak masks with rubber straps taut to their faces. As units took over the street, the firefighters pulled two-and-a-half-inch lines attached to the truck's 500-gallon tank. Engine 1 laid a five-inch line to a hydrant, dressed it, and cranked the bolt on top to release the water and resupply the tank on the engine. Each engine company supplied at least four lines to accommodate the master stream to the tower ladder.

The two-family house was fully involved. Chief Sam sized up the scene and directed Engine 1 to approach and attack from the rear. The firefighters took a Halligan bar to the front door. The bar consisted of a claw, blade, and tapered pick, which is especially useful in quickly forcing open many locked doors. Knocking down the initial blaze at the entry, Private Cody and his team advanced slowly, watching the fire spreading across the top of the water. He forged forward with his buddies, holding the hose behind him. If not manhandled correctly, the water pressure in a two-and-a-half-inch line was difficult to maneuver. He circled the nozzle to create a pocket of moist air around him in the blaze.

Chief Sam noted that the fire was fierce, and the spread was unusually intense. He knew a typical fire burned at eight hundred degrees, but add an accelerant, and a fire could reach fourteen hundred degrees.

Slowly making headway, the firefighters plowed ahead, trying to knock down the fire while conducting a preliminary search for victims. Communications were over two-way portable radios, positioned in their top left coat pockets. Once the room was somewhat under control, they all heard Private Cody's radio message. "Chief, it looks like we have two fatalities: man down, first-floor kitchen and female down, back room."

The chief called dispatch and requested the medical examiner. Sam entered the building while the firefighters continued working on hot spots. "You're going to want to see this," Private Cody said as he brought him to the first victim. The chief observed the surroundings and recognized clear signs and patterns of an accelerant.

Carefully, Chief Sam approached the first victim and immediately noticed that he recognized the man and that his injuries were not consistent with being overcome by fire. Shaking his head, he said to Private Cody, "This is Nick Strongback. He was a good man." They moved to the second victim, a female. "This is a shame." The chief called in the fire marshal and detectives from the police department as he stared in disbelief.

In short order, the detectives arrived with their homicide team. "What's going on, Chief?" Morrison asked.

"Sadly, this is the home of Nick Strongback and his girlfriend."

"Nick? Ugh!" Morrison's hand went to his chest. "This is terrible." Gathering his thoughts, he asked, "What do you know so far?"

"I'd call it the volatile combination of a murder and arson cover-up," the chief answered.

The sounds of firefighters watering down hotspots created background noise as smoldering pockets continued to occur. The strong scent of various burned and melted materials filled their nostrils. And in a solemn state, the men stared at the charred debris around them while thinking about their comrade. Their somber moment was duly interrupted when the medical examiner arrived.

Sam said, "Dr. Storm, I'm glad you were on call. Unfortunately, the detective and I know the victims." The chief escorted her and the detectives to review the casualties, and he stated the obvious. "As you can see, these are not fire-related fatalities."

Reviewing the wounds, the charred bodies were severe to observe. Dr. Storm was deftly aware of the delicate situation of the men knowing the victims. She felt their grief.

"Gentlemen, this is quite a scene." She put down her examination bag and bent over the man. "Yes, I'm sorry to say it looks like he was beaten." With sympathy, she frowned at her inspection. "Good thing the firefighters arrived when they did; otherwise, the fire could have destroyed the evidence. It makes my job easier to be on-site to observe the scene firsthand."

She turned to Detective Morrison. "Once the homicide team photographs and completes their investigation, I'll proceed with the pre-autopsy inspection and verify the manner of death in my examination room. Smoke inhalation would be evident if they were still breathing when the fire was set. Yet it certainly looks from their appearance and the pool of blood that they were bludgeoned."

Chief Sam added, "The fire marshal is collecting samples for the lab now. Detective, let's walk into the kitchen. I have something to show you regarding the charred spread." They stepped over the destruction and viewed what was left of the room. "See the well-defined floor pattern and this severe alligatoring on the walls?"

Morrison nodded. "Yes, doesn't that indicate intense heat in a quick burst?"

"You got it right. An accelerant created this blaze." The two men sharply analyzed the scene; the burnt odor, the blackness of char, and the imperceptible blobs of melted objects were all evidence that held their attention. They knew Nick's reputation as a beloved handyman, carpenter, and artist. Always good-humored and enjoyable to have around. He even rebuilt the popular local bar called The Sail & Anchor from floor to ceiling after it was consumed by fire. He was indeed a pillar in the community.

Morrison shook off the grief. "Let's keep things moving and get the person who did this. Was there anyone on the upper floors?"

The chief responded, "No, it's all clear, but they're still knocking down hotspots. I'm sure the crowd of neighbors outside can tell you a thing or two."

Jack Peabody observed from the doorway his first fire fatality and homicide. "Peabody, talk to the neighbors and take Officer McNamara with you."

"Sure thing, Boss." As a young assistant detective, he was willing to learn yet wondered if this new situation was more than he had bargained for. His unique experiences with death were unexpectedly adding up. He walked out the door of the scorched building, took in a breath of fresh air, and swallowed a gulp of determination. He found McNamara, and they went to work questioning the neighbors.

After hours of knocking down the fire, Chief Sam checked on the firefighters' status and left the engine company at the scene to secure it for the night. The street would remain closed, and he would be back in the morning.

***

It was nearing 8 p.m., and Roxanne was waiting for Sam's arrival with a hot meal of shepherd's pie. Sam wolfed down the food with a hearty appetite. She was quiet. Every fire had a story, and she waited to hear the news. Sometimes, it wasn't good, and it was best to let the story trickle out. She learned to sit by and be patient because she did not know what he saw or how bad it was.

"It was a sorry sight." He shook his head. "It was our friend, Nick Strongback, and his girlfriend. It's a shame, but someone did this to them. It's a homicide." Sam drank some lemonade. "He was the nicest guy. I can't imagine how it escalated to that point."

Roxanne's hands went to her face in shock. "I can't believe it! I saw him last week. He finished painting the carousel horses at Ocean Beach Park. This is terrible!" Her hand held her forehead. "He generously gave his construction skills to help rebuild the boardwalk too. So good-natured and always ready for a laugh. I'm sorry, honey. That must have been awful." She held Sam's hand.

"It was," he admitted. "I'll take a shower, and maybe we can find a show to watch before bed. It will help put this event out of our minds for a while."

"Okay. I'll get some dessert together. What would you like?"

"Hmm, how about that ice cream combo we had last week? That was tasty."

"Hot fudge on butter pecan ice cream and whipped cream coming up." She knew the ritual. Let go of the details for the night. Relax and don't dwell—repair emotions. Sleep and take care of things in the morning. That was the way to handle trauma. Some folks had few traumas, but a firefighter could see multiples in a month, all depending. They had to learn how to adapt and take care of themselves in whatever way worked best.

CHAPTER 25

Before the Fire
Friday

Reginald Crumberton, known as Reggie the Crumb on the streets, sat on his usual bench by the Little Chicken Pantry. It was his lucky spot for handouts or fried chicken, especially when he did not feel like going to the food pantry. Reggie was six feet tall and well-fed, even though he was homeless. He purposely left his hair long and messy to keep people away. A couple of his teeth were missing, but it didn't bother him.

After a full stomach, he routinely picked up cans for the deposit money. He would section off city blocks and collect in various neighborhoods.

As he moved through the streets, his sturdy build and broad shoulders always carried a knapsack with a roll-up bed, blanket, and bare necessities. His other essentials were good shoes. He could pick them up at Ms. Zelda's homeless hospitality center. She ensured she had his size because he didn't want anything else from her, even though she offered to help him out on many occasions. There was also the promise that anytime he was ready to move off the streets, she would be there for him.

"All I need is shoes," he would mumble. "I don't want anything else." Reggie knew it was important to protect his feet with his daily survival routine. He learned this in Afghanistan throughout several tours of duty. An infection, fungus, or even wet feet causes one to become miserable. It was also where he developed PTSD, post-traumatic stress disorder.

Reggie made his long circular route through the city blocks using a large plastic bag for can collection. He headed down Belham Street and spotted a couple of discarded cans next to a building. Suddenly, he heard an odd, loud *Whoosh!* Instinctively, he braced himself against the building. His body shuddered uncontrollably with a flashback memory of Afghanistan.

When able, he darted behind a large rhododendron shrub against a traditional duplex. He camouflaged himself and watched from his position on high alert. The sound was undeniable and unique; he had heard it during his tours of duty. Across the street, he watched two people run out of a building. They yelled at each other to hurry, and both entered a car and sped off. At that point, a loud explosion blew out windows on the first floor, and fire burst and enflamed the interior. Reggie was stunned by the blast. He grabbed his bag of cans and ran to a neighboring porch, yelling, "Fire! Fire! Call nine-one-one!"

The neighbor looked out and immediately saw the flames. The first floor was engulfed with waves of fire licking up to the second floor. He called it in.

Reggie muttered to himself, "I can't get away from it! What am I going to do? This is making me crazy." As fast as he could, Reggie walked to the historic Old Town Mill and a wooded spot beyond it near the Interstate 95 overpass. Nervously pacing, he couldn't get peace. He sat by the mill's churning waterwheel.

Reggie had learned to let the sound of the water overtake his thoughts. It rippled through him and calmed his nerves. It was the reason he slept close enough to hear the water run every night. He called it his lifesaver because it could mask the noises from the war that reverberated in his mind. After an hour, he settled down and slept directly behind the mill for the night.

Saturday

Reggie went to breakfast the following day at the hospitality center and sat near the director. "Ms. Zelda, can I tell you something?"

"Reggie, we've known each other for two years. You can tell me anything. What's on your mind?"

"I witnessed an arson on Belham Street yesterday. I believe I saw the people who lit it." He stroked his unkempt beard. "You know I don't like to get involved with people, but I can't put this aside. I figured you would know the right person to call, and you'd vouch for me."

"I heard about that fire! Geez, I know Fire Chief Samson. He's a decent guy and the one we should talk to."

"Will you call and ask if he can meet me here?" Reggie asked.

"Of course. I'll call him right now." She dialed as he went to the bathroom to clean up. Reggie usually came across as shy to her, but on the streets, he would play-up being an outright curmudgeon to keep people away. Ms. Zelda knew what unsettled him was his reintegration into a peaceful society. Once she heard his war history, she understood his preference to remain remote. The director had tried to get him off the street and provide housing, but he didn't want anything but shoes and food.

Once he received the call, Chief Samson raced out the door. Ms. Zelda led him into the empty dining area of the center. "Chief, this is Reggie Crumberton. He witnessed the fire."

The chief nodded and assessed Reggie's disheveled appearance, with hair matted and a wild and woolly beard. He had a few missing teeth, and his clothes were dirty. It was hard to tell his age. He guessed possibly mid-forties.

"It's good to meet you, Reggie. Were you in the armed services?"

"Yes, sir. I served five tours in Afghanistan."

"Ah, I see. That's a tough place. What was your position?" the chief asked.

"I was in Army Special Forces, sir."

"Thank you for your service, Reggie. I'm sure you've seen a lot, and I appreciate you stepping forward to tell me about this Belham Street fire. Did you see someone at the scene?"

"Yes, sir, I did. I believe they set the fire," Reggie answered. "I was on the street making my daily rounds of collecting cans, and I heard the loud whooshing sound of an accelerant catching a flame. This tall, young fellow, looking mighty drunk, and an older lady ran out of the building. As the flames erupted, the windows blew out on the first floor. These two jumped into a Ford Fiesta, taking off as if the flames were on their tail. I yelled to the neighbors to call nine-one-one, then I left. I get flashbacks, you see, and that was a powerful trigger. I hadn't had one in a while."

"Do you consider it PTSD from your tours?"

"Yes, in my last year, my body was acting on its own accord. I couldn't stop it from being triggered. I guess it's a nervous system thing. I also lost some men and could not perform to the speed and requirements for the job, sir."

"I understand. We lost two fine people in that fire, Reggie. I'd like to have the homicide detective come by and ask you a few questions. Are you willing to file a report?"

Reggie looked at Ms. Zelda. "Yes, I am."

Ms. Zelda interjected, "Chief, would it be okay if we met in a couple of hours? It will give Reggie and me some time to prepare." She knew interacting with people needed to be done in small doses for Reggie. Spacing out the meetings would help. Reggie nodded.

"Okay, I'll be back with the detective in two hours. Your eyewitness account will allow me to file this as arson Reggie. I'm grateful."

Reggie confided, "Ms. Zelda, my military training and discipline has kept me sane, but I could use some help. I've been surviving long enough. Let's start planning my transition off the streets." She gave him a winning smile.

10 a.m.

The chief told Morrison of Reggie's military tours and to be prepared for his unruly appearance. When they arrived, Ms. Zelda escorted the men into a private living room. "Reggie will be right in," she said, raising her eyebrows mysteriously.

Soon enough, a man walked into the room and Ms. Zelda said, "Detective Morrison, I'd like to introduce Reginald Crumberton. He goes by Reggie."

Chief Sam did not immediately recognize him and was stunned at his clean, new look. Not only had he showered, but his brown hair, beard, and mustache were also shorter and trimmed. He wore a fresh blue oxford shirt, black jeans, and gray canvas sneakers.

Reggie grinned, and said, "Your face says it all, Chief. Ms. Zelda has quite a stash of ready-to-wear clothing and even had prepackaged temporary veneers for my teeth. I think they are my favorite part of this transformation."

The chief was in disbelief. "You look great, Reggie." They shook hands.

Of course, Morrison had not seen Reggie's scruffy side, but the chief had described a man utterly dissimilar to the one before him. "Good to meet you, Reggie." He shook his hand. "Thanks for coming forward to help us out." Morrison laid out photographs on the coffee table. "Do you see anyone you recognize that was there yesterday?" The photos were of people in the neighborhood.

"That's them right there." Reggie pointed at the culprits.

Morrison looked at the chief. "Well, what do you know? They live upstairs."

A few more questions were asked and answered, and Dan told Reggie he would be in touch once the two felons were picked up. An APB was immediately sent out to police officers. In no time, the mother and son team were caught, found in a nearby motel, having spent the previous night playing the slot machines at one of the casinos. They attempted to get rich quick and keep running.

CHAPTER 26

Seven Deadly Acts
Saturday - 2 p.m.

After managing the manhunt for the Belham fire, Morrison interviewed the killers and immediately asked for their whereabouts on the night of Marilyn's death. The mother and son team had unshakable alibis, but the detective pressed on and asked them about details of the night surrounding Cora's abduction. Again, he hit a dead end.

Morrison heard Dr. Storm was finalizing the paperwork on the fire victims and stopped by the morgue. She handed him a file. "Chief Samson was correct. The evidence points to them being beaten before the fire burned their bodies. It appears it was a blunt object, possibly a baseball bat."

Morrison had a few of his details to share. "The young man we arrested is twenty-nine and said he had been drinking yesterday since morning. It's a shame. He was not remorseful and casually described what he had done.

"The guy said his downstairs neighbors were complaining about his loud music, so he decided to fix their ears with his baseball bat. He lives upstairs with his mother. She is a piece of work too. It was her idea to grab the gasoline can from the shed and douse the place to hide the evidence of their bodies.

"The man said, 'Seemed like a good idea at the time.' Pretty poor reasoning when he'll likely spend the rest of his life in jail."

Dr. Storm shook her head. "Well, let me tell you something about my line of work. Men are often unaware they are drawn to death like a moth to a flame."

"How do you mean? Like a death wish?"

"No, not that. The stats are that thirty-five thousand males from youth to forty die each year from accidental death because they enjoy risk-taking. And why is that? Because they don't think through the outcome of a decision to consider the consequences.

"Then, when we add that young men are most vulnerable due to high testosterone, male risk-taking from ages fifteen to twenty-four amounts to three out of four deaths—also, factor in the macho aspect of driving fast and early conditioning of laughing at stupid acts.

"Regarding this case, Detective, twenty percent of Americans aged twelve and older are binge drinkers. Men are eighty percent more likely to die of homicide and ninety percent more likely to commit a homicide than women.

This mother and son have probably been drinking most of their lives, which discombobulated their brains and decision-making abilities. The son committed the murder, and his mother tried to protect him by telling him to burn the evidence. Quite a pair!"

With a sideways glance, she concluded, "Since I can spout all these facts no one wants to know, I might write a textbook for high schoolers. I expect it could be a thriller."

Morrison grinned, "What will you call it: *The Angel of Death Reveals How to Avoid It*?"

"Ha-ha, not bad, but I'm a little surprised."

"By what? That I called you the angel of death?"

"No, that you weren't more creative. I've been called that nickname from day one of my work. Plus, someone already has a book with a similar title. My working title is *Lessons from the Morgue - Seven Deadly Acts to Avoid.* It will be geared for ages thirteen to thirty."

"What are the seven deadly acts? Can I guess?"

"Go ahead, Detective. I'm going to enjoy this."

"Okay, well, alcohol, you already said. Risk." She held up two fingers to keep count. "Murder, suicide, accident, and.... What are the others?" he asked.

"The combination of alcohol, drugs, and risk is number six, and health, nutrition, and pandemics are seven. What do you think?"

"I think they'll be intrigued coming from you, besides parents need all the help they can get about sobering truths to keep their kids alive. But I must get back to work."

Morrison headed for the door. "Oh, one more thing, we caught the mother and son because a homeless veteran came forward. He was in the neighborhood collecting cans when the mother and son ran out of the building. We got lucky. I need more luck with the Maroney case."

"You don't need luck," she said. "You need a witness. Maybe one will come forward. There must be more to the story. Hey, when you get the lab results on Cora from the toxicology department, can I see them?"

"Of course." He nodded. "I planned on it."

"And where is the homeless veteran now?"

"The New London Hospitality Center. They're finding him a permanent place to live. I think he's taking a step in a good direction. Why do you ask?"

"My cousin was in Afghanistan and didn't come back." Her eyes shifted to the floor.

"I'm sorry to hear that. Chief Sam told me Reggie was in Afghanistan for five tours. I don't know how anyone can do that. It must change you."

"Yes, but at least he's still alive. I hope he realizes it's better than dead."

"Certainly. Well, thanks for the education. I'm leaving here a little bit smarter." He waved goodbye.

"Good day, Detective. I'll catch up with you on the other side of Sunday."

***

Back at headquarters, Morrison was anxious to hear more about Marilyn Maroney's case. Peabody reported they had more people to interview, and every lead, so far, had turned up nothing.

"We need to find this Mario Corinthian fellow, and we need a motive, Peabody. In the past, I would have called in all of Dahlia's resident artists and questioned them again with an officer present, one that looks intimidating and growls. They would feel the heat to have their memories jogged. McNamara could cross-examine them individually while I observed behind the glass mirror.

"We would interview them in succession and have them all wait in the boardroom where we have a video camera on them talking to each other. It usually works in a tight community. They'd either stick together or go at each other's throats if someone was guilty." He rubbed his hands together. "It gets interesting when the claws come out!"

Peabody scratched his head. "I haven't been to one of those yet. Do I get protective gear for a claw convention?"

Morrison laughed. "No, just ensure your badge is visible, and your brow is furrowed. They would be afraid of you."

"Are you sure?" Peabody wasn't intimidating and knew it. His was a face you'd bring home to your mother.

"The badge is the one advantage you have and all the protection you'll need inside police headquarters. But be assured, outside these doors, you can't always count on that."

Even with all his training, Peabody was shy and polite, not apt to take advantage of the authority of his badge. For the first time, the rookie realized people could be afraid of him. Morrison liked that about him; he chose him because he could mold him, and he used his brain.

"The Dahlia residents all have an alibi, so what troubles me most, Peabody, is the timeline. How could Marilyn walk away from her apartment with a portfolio case at eleven-thirty but be back on the balcony and dead around midnight?" He paused for a moment. "Maybe Dr. Storm has the time of death wrong. It could be much later when no one was around. Heck, someone may have returned with her to her apartment after midnight, and that's when it happened. We are within an hour of her time of death, but we need more to work with." Morrison's hand went to his forehead. "This is frustrating!"

"Boss, I agree. We verified what the Dahlia artists knew and who they were with. Let's face it; they would have told us if they saw her or someone suspicious after eleven-thirty. I can investigate more of the video footage we haven't seen. You know it takes time. At least we now have Cora's description of the guy. I'll try more street cameras."

"Have Acevedo help you review the videos if she's not busy working on another case. Include anything you can find on the municipal parking lot and the back of the Dahlia."

"Boss, we could canvas the neighborhood for more footage now that people use those doorbell videos for security. It's possible one of them captured some evidence we can use."

"Good thinking." Morrison was hoping for any recordings of the back of the building where the exterior staircase went to the second-floor locked entrance. Jason and Shatana verified that Marilyn used the back stair during the art show to take people up to see more of her work.

The forensic officers had collected and identified every print, yet Morrison still needed more evidence. "I wonder, how else could someone access her apartment on the third floor?"

"There is an artist named Aaron Goshen, Boss. He's an acrobatic parkour specialist. They're roof jumpers, and I heard he frequents the area. We can investigate him." Morrison whistled. "Do it, Peabody. See if he has an alibi."

CHAPTER 27

A Backward Miracle
Sunday - 3 p.m.

Ms. Zelda had a stack of *The Day* newspapers from past weeks in the corner of the hospitality center's sitting lounge. Reggie's broad hands grabbed a handful of the papers and carried them into his temporary private room. His typical daily disciplines of finding food and a place to sleep were settled. His next mission was to reintegrate into society, and the newspapers were the first step.

Reggie's living on the fringe of society was a strict discipline that he honed as a survivalist. It had kept him alive in a foreign country and this one.

He laid the newspapers on his bed by the window with a view of birds pecking at feeders in a tree. Reggie leafed through the papers to familiarize himself with recent events when the news heading of Marilyn Maroney's death caught his eye. The report said she was discovered after the night of heavy fog. Reggie sifted through the subsequent papers to see if the case had been resolved.

He sought out Ms. Zelda and found her at her desk. "Do you know about this case on Bank Street where a woman was found speared by her art sculpture?"

"Yes, it's been the talk of the town. Why do you ask?"

"Thursday nights, I sleep near there because Friday mornings, there's a free breakfast at the Elks Lodge with Whalers Helping Whalers. I was walking by the Dahlia that night after eleven."

"Well, how about we tell Detective Morrison? You may know something helpful."

"Yes, ma'am. I'd like to. In my experience, we never take an opportunity for granted. I imagine the detective feels the same."

Morrison and Peabody arrived at the hospitality center within the hour and met him in a private room.

"Reggie, you said you were downtown the night the Dahlia artist was murdered. Where were you around eleven?" Morrison asked.

"I was walking through the municipal parking lot and headed toward the Dahlia through the alley. I occasionally sleep near the water. That way, I'm close by Friday mornings to eat breakfast at the Elks Lodge."

Morrison nodded, intrigued by Reggie's ability to care for his bare necessities.

"When I walked past the Dahlia, there were a few people in the back garden, but the fog made it surreal."

"How many people?" Morrison asked.

"Four but two sat in the garden. The light show from the Velvet Muse bounced off the fog, creating weird shadows. I saw a woman in a dress in front of a tall person. I couldn't tell the gender, but these two figures were silhouetted as they went up the back staircase. It was as if they rose out of the mist, which became slightly thinner the higher they went. Then they suddenly disappeared. I assume, into an entrance. That's why I remember it."

Peabody asked, "And can you describe the person behind her?"

"At least six feet compared to her, but not heavyset or a big girth. It could have been a slim man or a woman. I didn't notice a dress like the first person. It was only a moment when I passed by." Reggie gave a tug on his newly trimmed beard.

Peabody asked, "How can you be sure it was around eleven.?" He handed him a photo of Marilyn in a similar dress. "And do you recognize this woman?"

"The church clock said eleven. It must have been five or ten minutes later. And it's too hard to tell if that was her, but I would say the dress style seems similar."

"Okay, that's a helpful piece of information." Morrison was relieved to finally have an observant witness after all the people they had interviewed. "If anything else comes to mind, please contact me again, Reggie. You are a man about town, aren't you?" They both grinned at the double meaning.

"Ms. Zelda is planning to set me up with a permanent place to live," Reggie informed. "I'll be around but not as much on the streets. Next, I'll find a job if anyone will take me."

Peabody asked, "You were in Army Special Forces?" He was curious about this homeless veteran living on the streets.

"Yes, sir. I was lost when I came home. I didn't find a place to use my skills and had nightmares and flashbacks. They've subsided, except on the occasion of an explosion, like that fire on Belham."

"It's good to see you can accept the help being offered," Morrison said. "I'll be back in touch." They shook hands. "Have a good day, and thanks for your help. We need to do more for you guys during the transition."

Reggie nodded, and Peabody shook his hand too.

***

Morrison had a gleam in his eye as they sat in his SUV, "This is good, Peabody. No one else noticed these two going up the back staircase. We'll call Troy and have him contact his neighbors. Maybe we can find out if Reggie is ready to interact with a few more people. We'll do a reenactment; he can help us verify the height and build of this mysterious agent."

"This is like a backward miracle, Boss."

Shooting him a perplexed look, Morrison asked, "What are you talking about?"

"If those two nut cases, the mother and son, hadn't burned down their home to hide evidence of a murder on Belham, and Reggie hadn't witnessed it, we wouldn't have him telling us he walked by the Dahlia at that very moment the person walked up the stairs to possibly kill Marilyn. That's how a backward miracle works. Something bad or wrong must happen first for something good to come out. Those are some slim chances, Boss. He's the first to mention this stranger going up the back stairs."

"Peabody, you've got some odd thinking knocking around in that brain, but I like it."

"Thanks, Boss, that means a lot." He smirked. Jack Peabody was pleased to get any compliment from his boss, even backhanded ones.

"Give Troy a call, and let's find out when we can do this. I'll call Ms. Zelda and Reggie. Let's see how he does when he meets with Troy and go from there. I don't want to overwhelm him too soon, but I'm impressed with his military resume, and we could use his help. Those guys are above tough. Heck, they run into buildings with live gunfire. It boggles my brain that he's been on the street for two years after five tours. We have to do better by them."

"I agree with you, Boss. He has my respect."

Monday - 11 a.m.

Reggie agreed to go to the Dahlia. Troy buzzed them in through the front door, and they climbed the stairs to his second-floor studio. Morrison introduced Reggie, and they all took a seat in his dual living and workspace.

"Would you like something to drink? I have Mexican Coke that I mix with sparkling water."

Reggie accepted the drink, and the detectives did not. They sipped the sweet, iced beverage.

Morrison asked, "Troy, can you tell us who uses the back stairs entrance?"

"Well, all of us residents."

"Does anyone else have access?" Peabody asked.

"Martina Shaw and the board members have a key, but they don't come up here unless we call with a problem. We have an agreement about it. We also keep the gate locked to the back garden. Of course, when there's a big party, people can hold the door and let someone in. But the back stairway is just for residents and their guests."

Morrison explained, "Reggie was walking through the alley by the back garden after eleven o'clock and saw the silhouettes of a woman in a dress and a person behind her going up the back staircase. He didn't get a good look because of the thick fog and lighting. Do you know who they could be?"

"It must have been Marilyn." Troy's face shifted toward angst as he thought of her. "Unless Cora...no, she wasn't wearing a dress." He paused again. "Ophelia wasn't either."

"Do you know where the residents, Teddy and Bruce, were during that timeframe?"

"I do. They were with me. It had to be Marilyn with another person." His heart sank. "That means she knew who killed her. Ugh."

"As Detective Peabody told you, we'd like to experiment to have a clearer idea of the person's height and stature for Reggie to identify. Who is in the building now?"

"I told Teddy and Bruce you were coming, and they want to help. I'll tell them to meet us in the back garden." Troy put down his drink.

Teddy grew up in New London. His family was originally from the US Virgin Islands. Bruce's family came to New London via Puerto Rico when his grandfather took a job at the New London Sound Lab with the Navy. Both young men's ethnic heritage was incorporated into their art. Bruce created large, colorful, surreal paintings that included family members. Teddy was a wood sculptor and had won awards for a sculpture of a giant muscular man releasing himself from chains. Each link in the chain was in the shape of a human.

Reggie and Peabody stood in the alley, about thirty feet away from the stairs. Morrison told all three guys, "We'll have you each walk up the back stairs, and Reggie will watch us from the alley side of the garden gate where he walked by that night. He can tell us how he thinks the person differs in size from you. Marilyn and her guest ascended the stairs with slow, even steps, so don't rush."

Teddy went first. He was six-foot-one in height with a slim, muscular build. Reggie tried to recall the night from a week ago as he watched him ascend. Bruce took his turn. He was five-foot-eleven with a broad girth, wide shoulders, and hefty thighs like a football player. Then it was Troy's turn. He was five-foot-nine and not as broad as Bruce. Reggie asked Peabody to have Troy and Teddy go up the stairs again. Troy went first. Then all the men came together in the garden.

"Detectives, the second person that night, was as tall as Teddy but much slimmer, nothing like Bruce or Troy in build. Troy seems more like Marilyn's height—is that true?" Reggie asked.

"Yes, she is only an inch shorter than me," Troy commented as if she were still alive.

Reggie continued, "I cannot say if the second person was male. It was quick."

"That's good," Morrison said. "So now, guys," he looked at all of them, "does anyone come to mind? Peabody, in your videos? Troy, Teddy, Bruce, anyone that would go upstairs with Marilyn of that height and slim build at that time of night?"

No one spoke up.

Peabody pulled out Cora's sketch of the man she had dinner with, Mario Corinthian. "Have you seen him, and if so, does he match this description?"

"I didn't see him that night," said Teddy.

"Me neither," Bruce added.

Troy shook his head as Reggie examined the sketch. "No, I didn't see him."

"Okay, how about Aaron Goshen, the roof-jumping parkour artist? What do you know about him?" Morrison asked.

Troy spoke, "We all know him and his girlfriend, Marguerite. Why?"

"He could gain access to Marilyn's balcony, right?" Morrison probed.

"Oh no, it's not him," Troy responded, and Teddy and Bruce agreed. "I've known him for years. He wouldn't do anything to Marilyn or Cora. Besides, he was helping us here by volunteering. He and I talked in the back garden when we took a break." Troy recalled Aaron balancing on the fence rail above him.

"Even though he fits the description of thin and tall, he was with us that night and then with Marguerite and his parkour friends until late. We discussed it. They also helped at the Vinho Verde get-together."

"Okay, well, at least we verified Marilyn went to her apartment with a guest around 11:10 that evening. If anyone remembers anything else, call me."

Morrison motioned to Peabody to leave and said, "Reggie, let's give you a ride back."

Once they were in the vehicle, Peabody confirmed, "Boss, that's the same information we were told when we questioned Aaron, Marguerite, and their friends. They were together the night of Marilyn's death."

"There must be evidence somewhere in this maze of data, Peabody. Somewhere between the Dahlia, the Velvet Muse, and the Vinho Verde. We know this perp, Mario Corinthian, was cocky enough to be seen at the Vinho Verde."

Reggie entered the conversation. "Detective, from my experience in the Special Forces, when a crook attends a function in broad daylight, it is usually before they've committed the crime. From what I've heard from you, he doesn't fit the description of the person on the stairs with Marilyn. But since he was seen at the Vinho Verde, it could mean he was the next guy called into work.

"So, I see two choices," Reggie continued. "He either followed up the crime on Marilyn, with the crime on Cora or the two are unrelated."

Peabody's hand was locked onto his chin while he listened to Reggie. He turned to face Morrison with raised eyebrows and waited for a response.

A grin slowly formed on Morrison's face. "Peabody, this is the type of thinking head I like to have around me. One that knows how to look at and dissect a problem. Unravel it and get to its core elements."

He turned in his seat, "Thank you for the clarification, Reggie. Sometimes three heads are better than two."

Reggie nodded. "Just offering up an observation, Detective."

CHAPTER 28

Morrison's Review
Tuesday

At Police Headquarters, the detectives compiled the latest data. Additional images and brief videos were from individuals at the Dahlia art reception, including the surrounding buildings and the Velvet Muse. Some of the images showed Marilyn coming and going out of the scenes. Peabody watched her dance happily with friends. Her vibrancy emanated through the computer screen. With each viewing, Peabody became more connected, invested, and attached to solving the case.

The sketch of Mario Corinthian brought more people forward who confirmed they had seen him at the Vinho Verde event for Marilyn. Therefore, the detectives determined that the incidents with Cora and Marilyn must be connected. Additionally, the restaurant staff at Café La Ruche claimed Mario and Cora left with her leaning on his shoulder as they walked out.

The van on Water Street that Cora woke up in was swiftly recovered by the police. Upon a detailed inspection, they found it was a utility van with dealer plates from New York City and had been reported stolen. Morrison had the highway camera footage analyzed with digital software enhancements. They found the vehicle with the same license plate. It traveled up the coast of Connecticut during Monday morning's rush hour traffic. The highway surveillance cameras showed two men who seemed to be wearing disguises: baseball caps and Groucho glasses with the built-in nose and mustaches.

Officer Sanchez's forensic team inspected and tested the vehicle from top to bottom. Cora's prints were found all over the van, and a strand of her hair, but no identifying marks from her abductors. Sanchez had said, 'It was as if they wore clean room suits to mask their presence.'

Morrison was aggravated and ran his hand through his thick black hair as he paced the conference room. "Peabody, these perpetrators were prepared professionals. The Union Train Station is within a block of the van. Are they on the video footage at the train station or platforms?" He motioned with his hand impatiently. "Give me something."

Peabody looked over his computer at him. "Sorry, Boss, there are no cameras on Water Street. Mario is nowhere to be found in the train station videos. We see white vans come and go in the city, but we have no obvious hits on the two random men that drove the van. So far, they are indescribable. I'm bleary-eyed searching for them."

Morrison paced with his hands on his hips. "Either some idiot is playing a stupid game and getting very lucky, or there's a master plan behind this fiasco. It doesn't look like a mad boyfriend scenario. These women were targeted with a deliberate and coordinated effort.

"Mario Corinthian was at the Vinho Verde on that Sunday. Two men drove from New York to meet him and assist with Cora on Monday evening." Morrison searched his pockets for gum. "We have three men. Did one of them kill Marilyn?"

Peabody added to the brainstorming. "Mario Corinthian is an alias because I can't find him anywhere. And maybe the two goons took the train back to New York?"

"Or east to Rhode Island or north to Boston," Morrison inserted. "And if that's the case, one of them had a personal vendetta or a mission. But why? Add to that the result of Cora's medical review. She had two drugs in her system. The first, simple quaaludes, and the second, a heavy dose of sleeping pills that kept her knocked out, disoriented, and unstable when she did wake. There was slight bruising on her arms, possibly from being handled while unconscious."

"Well, Boss, it comes down to what you always say," Peabody added, "What's the motive? It's unclear, isn't it?"

"Let's list some. Was someone angry with the artists, and this is revenge? Was the Dahlia Gallery the real target, maybe to discredit it? Did Marilyn and Cora have a common enemy? Or was Marilyn accidentally killed, and the person ran off? But why Cora? The evidence points to maybe three men and New York."

"Boss, you always say to follow the money. I don't see the money in this list."

Morrison stood back and held his chin. "Yes, Troy told us Marilyn's work is worth way more today than the day before her death. What happened with her agent after we spoke to him? Did he give us any leads?"

"No, I told him to freeze all sales of her artwork. And he was supposed to forward us a list of known owners of her previous work so we could track them."

"I haven't seen it. Did he? And what's his name?"

"Garfield Feinberg, and no. He said he would do it but was very distraught over her death. He kept crying. He said he would put a hold on all her works in galleries or storage, but it was difficult to track down private owners. He said that when rich people want an investment, a privately owned art piece can be sold quickly and multiple times. That's because these clients have art dealers and agents to buy for them. The artwork can be sold over and over due to Marilyn's popularity.

"It's like an art stock market, Boss. Art is a currency being traded over the internet. Plus, these buyers can be anywhere in the world. That would create a lot of motivated people if the price tripled overnight because she's dead."

Morrison pulled on his collar, suddenly feeling a need to call Interpol.

"But remember, Boss, we were busy working on Cora's case and the Belham Street arson fire. We've been straight out without a break." Peabody then mumbled, "It's been nuts."

Morrison paced the room again. "Okay, the toxicology report on Marilyn showed no drugs were found in her system, just wine. She either knew or met the killer, maybe the buyer, at the art party with three hundred guests. We know from Reggie that a person at least six feet slim was with her, ascending the exterior stair to the rear second-floor door. No one else recalls seeing them together.

"We also have the grainy video from after eleven that evening of what looks to be Marilyn crossing the street. We still don't have the DNA results from the coat and hat to verify she wore them last." He took a deep breath.

Peabody added, "Troy said two of her lotus flower paintings are missing. If the killer stole the paintings, that could be a motive. Did Cora see something related to Marilyn's death, and she doesn't know that she did? Maybe they asked her questions while she was drugged, and she doesn't remember.

"Peabody, get on the phone with Marilyn's art agent, Feinberg. Tell him he's done mourning. I need all he has on Marilyn, and I'll bring him in here if I must, or even better, I'll be visiting him."

"I'll get right on it, Boss."

"I have a mission of my own. I'll be visiting Francisco Milano's office if you need me. He's an old friend and a neighbor of the Dahlia Gallery. He and his wife, Poppy, oversee the Helios Art Association."

Morrison could have walked, but his SUV served as his traveling office with a computer. He drove the few blocks from police headquarters to Francisco's photography studio.

CHAPTER 29

Crazy Fetish Nights

Francisco's street-level office/studio had an expansive window for display. It was filled with photos of many recognizable people: Nathan Lane, Lin-Manuel Miranda, Meryl Streep, and Michael Douglas. These photos were taken by him at the famous Eugene O'Neill Theater Center in nearby Waterford when he was their principal photographer.

The detective entered the front office of his old friend, and Francisco came out from behind a walled partition with a store-bought coffee in hand. Morrison exclaimed, "Wow, you updated your window. I'm a little bowled over by the people you know."

"It's a retrospective of my work at the Eugene O'Neill Theater. These folks come with the territory. It's been well-known for transforming American theater since 1964."

Morrison teased. "You must be famous just for knowing these people." Francisco shook his head. He and Dan had grown up in town, and both came from simple beginnings.

The photographer offered Dan a seat. He could see the various photography equipment, tripods, and light-enhancing umbrellas in the back studio.

"Francisco, we are both aware of the checkered history that our city has had over the decades. We've seen alcohol-fueled disagreements and controversy over extreme art, but these are two incidents at the Dahlia within five days. With your knowledge of people downtown and the neighborhoods, do you think there is someone who has it out for the Dahlia Gallery or these artists? I don't think the old story with sailors and ladies of the night applies to this case. I need to determine whether locals have generated these incidents and how this character Mario Corinthian is connected."

Francisco's friendly demeanor turned grim. "Dan, I haven't heard anything about this guy until Cora. We're a tight community. Several of us planted seeds for the arts to flourish in the city, and they have rooted and grown strong. We provide a space for the artists' independent expression."

Francisco took a sip of coffee. "Hey, decades ago, the city of New London had wild nights and rabble-rousers but of a different crowd. You may recall the stories of El 'N' G, just around the corner, where we had art events before the

Helios had its building. Crazy fetish nights with naked people playing music, such as the Impotent Sea Snakes, and people doing all kinds of debauchery downstairs.

"They had Rick Derringer playing and the Spin Doctors, excellent bands. The whole local music scene thrived. We had New Johnny 5, The Reducers, Paisley Jungle, and Cat Fang. Bands came back together to do these live shows with the original players. It was like a little Woodstock because people came from around the world. We live-streamed it, and it was watched from everywhere. There were more artistic happenings in these few blocks than ever, but we didn't have this type of stuff going on with Marilyn and Cora."

Morrison understood what he meant. These recent acts were specifically nefarious.

"Dan, this concerns me deeply." Francisco gestured to his heart as he spoke. "It has sucked the life and motivation out of everyone. We enjoy collaborating with the Dahlia Gallery and all the local businesses. These are two successful women. Marilyn's death and Cora's incident are completely out of the left field. If I had a clue, I'd share it with you." Francisco shook his head in dismay. Silently, the friends pondered the dilemma.

Morrison broke it. "Francisco, keep your antennae up, and let me know if you hear anything new." He stood to leave, then remembered an additional question. "Hey, are you going to the reopening of the Mystic River Fine Art Museum this Thursday night?"

"Yes, Poppy and I will be there. I'd like to see what this new director Karl Rubens has done with the place after being in Boston his whole career."

"Good. I'll be there looking for this man in Cora's sketch, Mario Corinthian. I'll see you there, buddy."

"That reminds me," Francisco added, "I told Peabody I'd send you a copy of my recent photos from that night at the Dahlia and the Velvet Muse. Maybe I captured him in the crowd."

"Excellent, and by the way, Francisco, cameras are being installed on the exterior of both places. It seems wise after all that has happened because I might have had someone in custody by now, and this case would be solved. He gave him a crooked smile that meant, 'if only,' and grabbed the door handle. "I'll see you Thursday in Mystic."

CHAPTER 30

Ask All the Worst People
Wednesday

Detectives Morrison and Peabody reached out to other art organizations in the city in case information or connections to the Dahlia Gallery and the artists who lived there had been missed. They spoke with locals associated with the art councils, cultural coalitions, art centers, museums, colleges, and galleries. From there, they branched out farther. Since nothing new came forward, Morrison felt he was at a temporary dead end until he thought of Marilyn's art agent Garfield Feinberg.

"Hey, what's the deal on Feinberg, Peabody? Did you talk to him?"

"Sure, he emailed me a list of Marilyn's art in galleries and storage, and he placed all sales on hold. The list includes the value of the work before her death. He also noted that her privately owned artwork has been trading heavily on the open market, and he's tracking the sales. His office assistant is compiling a paper trail from the last year and a half with Marilyn as his client. Feinberg says he's so depressed about her death that he's staying out of the city. He doesn't want to be harassed by all the dealers who want Marilyn's pieces. He's taking time off from work and grieving by the pool at his home in Fairfield."

"Does he mean New York City?"

"Yes, Boss, everything else is a borough, a glen, a town, a village, or a name like Norfolk. When you live near it, it's the only city. There is no other like the NYC."

Dan Morrison smiled at his young protégé. Jack Peabody was dead right. "Did Feinberg respond to that sketch Cora made of Mario Corinthian? Did he call all his art contacts and pass the sketch around? If this guy who attacked Cora is from New York City and fooled her with his suave art knowledge, he must know someone in the art world. Make sure Feinberg gives us names in the underworld of art. If he scoffs, tell him to ask the people he typically doesn't deal with, all the worst people from his point of view, the underground art agents. Let's see what turd floats to the surface."

Peabody swiftly caught on. "Yeah, the underground's underbelly of squirmers who only work at night."

"Do you know any of those, Peabody?" Morrison smirked.

"No, Boss, I'm just going with the turd theme you offered up." Peabody raised his chin with an upward nod, signaling he knew what Morrison was talking about.

"Listen, I'm taking you out tomorrow night. We're going to the Mystic River Fine Art Museum. I'll pick you up at six-fifteen."

Peabody looked over his shoulder, wondering whom he was talking to. No one was there. "What do you mean, Boss? What if I have a date?"

"Do you?"

"Maybe. Is this a work thing? Am I getting paid?"

"Of course. I'm not wasting your time," Morrison answered.

"Okay, I'm free."

"Are you saying you don't have a date?" he queried.

"I'm going to say what you said to me: that's a need to know, Boss." Morrison gave him a deadpan expression, thought about it, and looked away.

"Wear something that doesn't look like you're at work. We are going incognito."

Peabody sat up straight. "What do you mean? Do you want me to wear a disguise?"

"No, be either more casual or more formal. Can you do that?"

"Which one? I'm confused."

"Go for casual. It's a museum. Look nice, but not out of place, and not like you're a detective. Can't you figure it out? And you can call me Dan tomorrow night, not Boss."

Jack Peabody scratched his head and mumbled, "I'll be up all night trying on clothes."

Morrison shook his head and left the room. He thought about the Mystic River Fine Art Museum's event. *It could provide some answers or, even better, a suspect. They all move within the swirl of the art world crowd. I need to know it better. I need to advance this case.*

***

The Dahlia Art Gallery Director, Ophelia Starr's centurial roots were established in New London in 1664, likely descendants of Comfort Starr, who landed on the shores of Sandwich, Massachusetts, in 1635. Her ancestors had seen witches and women wrongly hung at the infamous Gallows Hill site. And now Ophelia, too, could say she lived where history would record the strange murder of Marilyn Maroney.

Starr Street was just a few blocks away from her Dahlia studio apartment, and it was there that she connected with her family's historical past. The lanterned street was lined with Greek Revival homes and appeared as it did over a hundred years ago. On moonlit or foggy nights, Ophelia was enticed to walk there and seek advice from her ancestors about her future. The quiet, moody lane and architecture made her relatives feel close enough that she could hear the whisperings of their guidance.

Yet on this summer day, Ophelia needed to break away from the City of Steeples and chose to spend time in nature at Harkness State Park in Waterford. She wandered the fields toward the brackish tidal zone of the bird's nesting sanctuary for the materials of her next art piece.

Ophelia's connection to nature was her touchstone to tranquility. When she could lose herself in creativity, it was her meditative contemplation. To cultivate this, she attended a yearly multiday event called Burning Man, organized by a nonprofit art community of nature lovers.

The "Burners" participated within the guidance of ten principles: radical inclusion, gifting, decommodification, radical self-reliance, radical self-expression, communal effort, civic responsibility, leaving no trace, participation, and immediacy. Ophelia gravitated toward these principles and found they freed her artistic expression.

Her creations further developed and were delicately crafted with natural materials such as beeswax, cotton, mohair, leather, shells, or wood. Her artwork spanned the ethereal range of beauty, nature, and spirit, all woven together by her hand and heart. Sometimes she would think of someone and secretly place a memento within the paint, such as a lock of their hair.

After collecting a few natural materials at Harkness Park, she placed them in her car and wandered toward the mansion gardens on the Harkness estate. A long oval path encircled the original formal flower garden. Visitors and wedding parties would use it to promenade past the colorful, scented beauties as they also overlooked the expansive lawn that led to the sound's shoreline.

Ophelia entered the sanctuary, and laughter caught her attention. She saw her friend Katlyn conducting an outdoor painting class with children.

She approached her friend and the mini-Monet students. Colorful flower paintings were on easels in front of them. Katlyn gently coached and guided them as bright pink, yellow, and orange paint was dabbed on the bristles of their brushes. They were happily expressing zinnias, dahlias, and daisies on their canvases. Katlyn's natural disposition was delicate, and her voice was like a wisp of mist, encouraging the children with kind, sweet words. Ophelia could see that each child was blissfully creating their artwork.

Katlyn was also a friend of Marilyn and Cora. She had an art studio in New London as a well-known artist in her own right. When she saw Ophelia, she hugged her and offered her a seat at an easel to paint. Gladly, Ophelia took a brush and sat among the flowers and children to escape her worrying thoughts about Cora and Marilyn. Like most female artists in the city, even on a nice day, she wondered: *Am I next?*

CHAPTER 31

The Lust in Their Eyes
Thursday

Marco arrived at the Mystic River Fine Art Museum by 8:30 a.m. to prepare for the grand reopening. He had two men to help unload a box truck full of architectural décor, including sculptures, urns, and freestanding columns. Roxanne arrived with Tessa an hour later in her black pickup truck. It was full of plants, bagged potting soil, and tools to implement their interior and exterior garden design work. They all completed their displays by 2 p.m.

Karl's approval was important to Georgi, so he invited him to review the decorative installation by starting outside at the museum's entrance. The gardens were refurbished with pink flowering 'Fairy' roses and blue flowering caryopteris shrubs. Flanking the museum's doors were large decorative urns with tall, graceful potted palms and red anthuriums at their base.

Inside the museum were three-foot sentinel urns holding four-foot fragrant, oriental rubrum lilies that towered over maidenhair ferns at their base. Georgi glanced at Karl's lean, six-foot-two height and noticed the flowers were taller. Karl sniffed their perfume, which seemed to calm the Kraken-like control freak within him.

From room to room, Georgi pointed out Marco's perfected decorating style. Long lengths of sheer white fabric hung from the high ceiling in key locations and swathed around antique columns. Romanesque sculptures highlighted the spaces grandly, and Roxanne's elegant bouquets of exotic flowers dramatically affected each gallery. But Karl was unnervingly quiet as he nodded his head at every turn with hands taut behind his back.

After all the long hours of hard work everyone had applied, Georgi wanted Karl to vocalize that he was pleased.

Little did Georgi know, Karl's main concern was not the flowers, plants, decor, wine, or food. It was the art. The BFA Museum paintings for the opening arrived at noon. Karl unpacked them and was now ready to hang them. The museum was to be closed off, with the service workers confined to the kitchen and back entrance where the food and wine were to be delivered. He would have all the tradesmen out of the galleries and no one near the priceless works. Essentially, he didn't trust anyone. But at this moment, the often-rude Karl was unconventionally respectful to Georgi by remaining silent.

While they walked, Karl finally spoke and revealed his vision to Georgi. "I decided the Mystic River Fine Art Museum would be an amalgamation of art for sale and show. I feel this is a winning combination that is not generally offered. Don't get me wrong—museum stores are nice, but they have copies and prints of the original works. Mugs, calendars, T-shirts, and the like are my pet peeve. Yet, I recognize they are necessary attractions to a museum.

"I love art books because they educate the public, but trinkets are not my style. So, I prefer and vowed to sell local and national artists' works while featuring a display of priceless art that is not for sale from all over the world." Karl waved his hand across the room. "This, Georgi, is my dream job."

They entered a gallery room with contemporary fine art for sale between $8000 and $125,000. "I can tell when someone loves a work of art. They may try to hide their rush of excitement and the surge of their temperature rising, but they cannot hide the lust in their eyes."

Karl's index finger slowly landed below the corner of his right eye as he looked into Georgi's. "You see a twinkle emerge in a buyer's eye, and once you see that, you know they are hooked. Gently and slowly, you reel them in without letting them know that you see the lust in their eyes.

"When the sale is final, I'm satisfied because the $40,000 painting will provide funds for the museum and a celebration dinner for two of Chilean sea bass with a side of langoustine and French champagne, *oui*?" Karl breathed on his ring, polished it on his jacket lapel, then sighed, luxuriating in the winning glow of an imaginary sale.

Georgi was amused at the unexpected view into the museum director's personality. He was nearly thirty years older than Georgi. "Are you always so successful, Karl? Have you ever experienced a loss of confidence?"

Karl hummed. "I know my way around art, and I'm proud of that. I was a conservator at the BFA Museum for fine art paintings, and I've traveled the world and fundraised for museums. It's a job well done, so why should I make excuses for that?

"I've learned that wealthy people enjoy being separated from their money; otherwise, they wouldn't come to me for advice. They know I will attract fine art collections to a museum or find them excellent art to invest in. A million dollars is just the beginning bid for some of them."

"Oh my! I never thought of it that way," Georgi exuded. "Do you really think they enjoy being separated from their money?"

"Of course! When you have too much money, what else will you do? Be bored. Why be bored? There is no point in that. They seek out extravagant ways to spend their money for a thrill. Yet some also want it to be an investment—one they can easily justify. That's the difference with rich people, Georgi; they only care about making more."

Karl leaned in and spoke into Georgi's ear to put a fine point on it. "Many rich people don't care about anyone else. Otherwise, their money would help a neighbor, a community development center, or even a small village with the millions they have."

Georgi found the closeness and the topic disconcerting, so he moved to give distance to both. Karl straightened his stance and pulled on his vest. "They may be able to fund such things, but they don't want to because it's not instant gratification. They might say to a fundraiser for charity, 'Maybe next year after I review my earnings report.' I assure you they know what they have.

"Some could provide water for a small country, but do they? No! Because they don't give a hoot. And that is why they see me, the art expert so that they can make an arousing investment. You'll see it tonight, Georgi. We'll make a fortune, and they'll feel good about giving us their money."

Georgi felt increasingly disturbed. He hadn't examined wealth in such a stark light. A queasy feeling came over him. "Karl, please excuse me. I just realized my staff should be at the back door."

Karl waved him off but called out, "Handle your staff, Georgi. I have plenty to do. I'm going to place the art on the walls, then run home to freshen up for the evening. And by the way, tell Marco and Roxanne I am pleased. The museum décor and plants will highlight the art very well."

Georgi headed straight for the kitchen, grabbed a can of ginger ale, popped it open, and guzzled. A burp came over him, and he ran out the back door to eject it. Fanning himself, he felt hot and sweaty. The realization of extreme greed greeted him severely.

He strolled across the lawn toward the Mystic River and sat on a bench. A few more belches overcame him, but he remained unsettled. Finally, he returned to the kitchen, met with his staff, and organized the setup of wines and drinks at the Four Kisses Bar.

CHAPTER 32

Karl's Trajectory

Karl's mother, Isadore Rubens, selected their family home on Mason's Island in 1988 as a summer getaway from Boston. It was just a short hour by train and an easy hop from their Brownstone in the Back Bay to the shoreline in Connecticut. She moved to Mystic permanently in 1990 and enjoyed her community with its clockwork routines of daily cocktails at 4:30, weekly dinner parties, and monthly private soirees at stately homes.

She adored helping others acquire art and delighted in donating some of her own. On occasion, she arranged a fundraising gala when a rare piece of fine art was desired for a collection at the BFA Museum, where Karl worked. The combination of her late husband's fortune, her expensive art collection, and their ancestral family name of Rubens opened many doors.

Her husband, Saul Rubens, was from a traditional wealthy family. Saul didn't need to work, yet he studied architecture, became a model maker, and freelanced for several architectural firms in Boston.

When he met Isadore, who loved art and architecture, they traveled and toured the world, visiting as many museums and cathedrals as possible while collecting art.

The couple purchased a large Brownstone in the Back Bay of Boston near the Ritz Carlton, Shreve, Crump & Low, and Winston's Flower Shop. She frequented Bonwit Teller and the curated shops on Newbury Street. And every Sunday after church, the family had a ritual of visiting museums and mansions.

When Karl was seven, he claimed a portrait in the Raphael Room of the Isabella Stewart Gardner Mansion drew him in. He felt lured as if the painting pulled him across the room. The image was of a young man wearing golden armor over red underclothes; he held a sword in his right hand. He had a casual pose and stared at young Karl, who returned the gaze.

Karl wondered why the painting so entranced him. Was it the brilliant colors of red and gold, the tiny faces on his armored knee plates, or his eyes that seemed to follow him? He studied the young warrior and his unchanging expression. He peered at other portraits and found a similar sensation of enjoyment because their unending stare remained serene and beautiful.

As a boy, he thought his mother was beautiful, but unlike a painting, she didn't stay that way; she changed. In still photos, she was gorgeous with her stunning angular face and dark brown hair swept up to the side. But he found she could be ugly when she scolded him. If he didn't follow her strict rules, she would grimace. A fierce line would cross her forehead, and a deep crinkle would fold in her brow. Her lipstick, a perfect shade of peony pink, became distorted as she pursed her lips.

During their mansion visits, young Karl eventually inched closer to the refined oil paintings. He noticed the brush strokes glistening in the soft light. He wanted to touch it. He began to learn the quality of the linseed oil mixed with raw powdered pigments from the era of the painting made them beautiful. And also, the conservator's restorative cleaning kept the colors fresh.

Encouraged by his interest, Karl's parents bought him the mansion's collection catalog, then he asked for more. They visited the Boston Public Library, where he checked out art books of his choosing by the armloads to study the pictures, paintings, sculptures, and artists. Karl would sit in their home library at a table near his father and sketch. His father would read in a winged leather chair with a drink and a pipe, slowly drawing air through the embers and puffing the spicy smoke. They were silent together while classical music lightly played in the background.

By the time Karl was fifteen, he had volunteered at the BFA Museum and decided to be schooled as a conservator in fine arts. When he was sixteen, his father died of a heart attack. This was when Karl found that a museum's ambience, fresh floral bouquets, fine art, sculpture, and music, comforted and reminded him of his father. The peaceful sanctuary of Isabella's mansion became his church. He could relax, stare at a painting, and feel contentment wrap around his shoulders.

***

The Mystic River Fine Art Museum was finally ready for the grand reopening. Karl locked the doors, set the alarm, and drove home to clean up for his splendid evening. He traveled from the west side of Mystic, near the famous Mystic Pizza and Bank Square Books, and crossed the Bascule Bridge over the Mystic River. He whizzed past the Sea Swirl food shack and Mystic Market's prepared delights, then turned toward Mason's Island. His lifelong career had led him to this moment, and he felt exhilarated.

Dressed and ready, Karl stood by the open front door in a newly tailored blue summer silk suit with a yellow shirt and paisley tie. "Don't be late, Mother," he called out. "I'm counting on you to do the idle chitchat so I can maintain my professional position."

"Yes, dear," she returned. She was adept at seeking donors who might line the museum's coffers, then introduced them to Karl. He would lure them in with exquisite words. "Your fine donation could bring in a distinguished collection from across the world," he would say. "We'll mention your name in print as a contributor." This allowed the patrons to feel exclusively needed for funding a fine art show. In a short year, Karl and Isadore had become astute fundraisers for the museum.

Isadore was the type of energetic woman who needed to remain relevant. At seventy-eight, she felt fifty and looked like sixty by investing in herself. Her elegant, model stature of five-foot-ten in stylish designer clothes enhanced her alluring demeanor. She had the look and attitude of a quick-witted beauty, ready to state her opinion and knock you over with it if she had to.

One might say Isadore had a fear of missing out, or FOMO, an actual psychological term designated to those with this specific anxiety. For her, it was mostly a fear of being bored.

Dressed in a gold-trimmed white kaftan and high heels, she eagerly took her seat in her classic Jaguar, revved the engine with excitement, and motored into her son's refreshed future.

CHAPTER 33

Mystic River Fine Art Museum

Dr. Angela Storm arrived at 6 p.m. with a colleague from New Haven for the museum's reopening art event. The $250 per person exclusive preview fee allowed them to see the exhibit before the public. Servers floated trays of appetizers: Kobe beef sliders and lobster with garlic aioli on a brioche bun. Georgi's selections of Italian and French wines were displayed next to non-alcoholic options for the guests. He was stationed with two bartenders and stood at the apex of the Four Kisses crescent-shaped bar.

When he saw Dr. Storm step forward, he used his hip to bounce one of the bartenders out of the way so he could wait on her. At first, the bartender was stunned to be bumped off, but giggled when he saw Georgi knew her. Angela introduced her friend, Ethan, and they both requested a glass of the extravagant French champagne, Château Angelus Saint-Émilion Grand Cru, 1927.

"I see you know your wine," he said with an approving glance. He poured the bubbly into two fluted glasses.

"It's you who knows champagne, Georgi. However, did you acquire this vintage?" Angela asked.

Georgi dramatically covered his mouth with one finger, then showed his smile. "These are secrets that stay in the vault." He winked and swooped his hands gently outward as he said, "My sources are my superpower." Then placed his hand next to his mouth and whispered, "It's what keeps a guy like me in business. Besides," he leaned forward, "I have to keep this client, Mr. Karl Rubens, on the verge of glee for him to invite me back."

Angela and Ethan hummed under their smile and clinked their glasses. Coyly, Angela whispered, "Where is he, Georgi? I'll be sure to tell him I'm impressed."

"Oh, thank you, my dear, and mention the décor too." He spotted Karl and motioned with his head. "There he is—tall, lean, and blond."

They made their way over. Karl was pleased to have the approval of two new donors and escorted them to the six BFA paintings on display.

At 7 p.m., Detectives Morrison and Peabody arrived. "Jack, we are looking for Mario and anyone trying to fit in or looks like they have an ulterior motive. We have now entered situation awareness mode. Watch for someone who can blend into conversations while they read the room. They spy on where each pawn is in their game, and when they put their plan into action, it is usually by creating a diversion. So, stay alert. Plus, we have others working the room."

"Who do you mean, Boss? I mean, Dan," asked Jack.

"The artists from the Dahlia will let us know if they see Mario. We also have Georgi and Marco keeping an eye out, and Francisco is taking photos of the event so tomorrow we can see who attended." The two men noticed Marco arrive with several friends. They headed to the cash bar.

Georgi whispered to Marco, "Keep your eyes peeled for Cora's predator. Detective Morrison is here too." Quickly, Georgi excused himself when a patron asked for a description of an expensive wine.

Artists Ophelia, Katlyn, Elise, Shatana, and Jason arrived together ahead of Roxanne and Sam. All of them were happy to view the exclusive art and look for Mario Corinthian.

Roxanne and Sam found a moment to say hello to Georgi. He came forward and gave her a peck on the cheek. "You look lovely, my dear. Here you were all worried about what to wear." She was graced in orchid slacks with a floral top and sandals. Sam smiled at her, knowing she would prefer to be wearing jeans.

Georgi whispered, "I haven't seen anyone who looks like that guy in Cora's sketch yet. But I did see Detective Morrison here."

Sam's tall height had an advantage. He could see the detective across the room, so he excused himself.

Roxanne admitted, "Sam is perturbed and doesn't want us to get involved. I told him Dan would be here, and we would only point the guy out to him. So don't get me into trouble, okay?"

"Don't worry. I won't. But there are many people here. We all need to stay on high alert." Roxanne nodded in agreement.

Georgi looked over his shoulder. "I must get back to work. I'll see you later." He slipped behind the bar and resumed serving the patrons. Roxanne moseyed over to the private collection of fine oil paintings from residents of Mystic.

Sam approached Morrison. "Dan, you don't look like yourself in a room full of paintings."

Morrison offered a meek smile. "Well, you know why I'm here. It could be a long shot, but worth a night out to see what this art world is all about. And to be honest with you, I like photographs. I guess this isn't my thing, Chief."

"You don't need to explain to me," Sam reassured. "I'm here for the free food and to keep Roxanne out of trouble. If I don't watch her, she'll peel off and be gone. Then we'll find out she's on a boat trying to follow some guy to Long Island."

Dan laughed. "Yes, it's a fact. She can't help herself, and Georgi eggs her on. They're a pair."

"I already told her they're a pair of nuts, and I want her to cut it out. The problem is that I understand because it's connected to her friends. I can't stop them. They become emotionally invested, so I hope you get a lead tonight."

"Of course, me too," said Dan. "Hey, is that Dr. Storm over there?"

Sam looked above everyone's heads. "Yes, it is, and she's all dressed up. Remember when she caught you off guard at the memorial service for Mitch Stockman? That was funny." Sam checked him on the shoulder. "Good luck, buddy. I'm going to find Roxanne." Dan's mouth was left hanging open.

Before he knew it, Angela Storm's voice was behind him. "Excuse me. I didn't expect to see you here, detective."

Morrison gave her a cowering look and said, "I'm here on art business."

It dawned on her what he meant, and she nodded. "Oh, yes."

He was surprised to see her in an elegant Japanese-inspired cocktail dress and high heels. The sunset shot through the windows, setting her aglow. Her honey-colored hair fell on her shoulders stylishly, and her unusual golden eyes were lit. At that moment, Peabody stepped in. "You look nice, Dr. Storm."

"Call me Angela, Jack. We're not at work." Morrison felt the sting of his professional rapport.

Jack smiled. "Right, we're not at work." He glanced at Morrison and realized he better leave. "Excuse me. I'm going to grab a drink."

"We're looking for the guy in Cora's sketch," Morrison said. "I already saw several artists. They are keeping an eye out too. So far, he hasn't been spotted."

"I'll keep a lookout too, Detective. If you'll excuse me, I should find my friend. He's here somewhere. I'll see you at work."

Morrison felt another sting, but this time it stung his heart. Perplexed, he spun on his heel and headed for the bar. Georgi saw him coming and was ready. "I'm sorry, Detective, you better stick to homicide. I think she's too much for you."

"Georgi, give me a beer. I have to pretend I'm not working."

"Yes, sir." He poured a beer into a glass and handed it to him. "I don't think he's here."

"Who?" Morrison looked around the room and saw Angela with a tall, dark, handsome man.

"The guy we are looking for, Detective."

"Oh yeah, I haven't seen him either." His eyes were stuck on Angela.

Georgi could see Morrison was distracted. "Have you been out to the back patio by the Mystic River yet? You look like you could use some fresh air."

"Maybe I should. Ah, Jack, there you are." His partner approached the bar. "Let's step outside and see if this guy is around."

As the men prepared to walk away, Georgi said, "Good luck with her, Detective." Morrison pretended he didn't hear. Two good lucks in ten minutes were too much for him.

Troy, and his friend Rick, joined the party atmosphere in the museum. Immediately, Troy saw his friend Aaron, the acrobatic performer who was also an artisan woodworker from New London. Aaron regularly volunteered at art events and did the same for the museum tonight.

Aaron advanced toward Troy and Rick, stepping away from his station of guarding a BFA painting. "Hey, guys," he whispered, "you've hit the jackpot. The director has gone all out with the appetizers. Check out the trays of food the servers are strolling around. It beats the cheese and crackers at the Dahlia receptions. This is a royal meal, dude."

"A level we'll never reach," chuckled Troy.

"Yes, it's a slice of heaven. Cloud nine, my friends. Hey, I must get back to my station before Sir Director sees me out of place."

"Is Marguerite here?" asked Troy.

"No, she has a deadline and is working on an installation at the Lyman Allyn Museum. They are representing local artists next month, and they like her technique for fabricating textiles and collaging them into 3-D art. I gotta go." Aaron gave a wave as he left.

A tray of food came by, and swiftly, Troy and Rick reached for a napkin and a royal snack. They both munched gratefully. "How about we see the art that's for sale first?" Rick suggested. "I bet they're not as good as yours. Maybe one day your artwork will be on these walls."

Troy considered the opportunity. "I'll find out if the museum director is interested. I haven't met him yet. I wonder if he would like my work. It could probably go for double the price here."

A classical music trio of violin, viola, and cello filled the gallery with a grand air as the patrons moved through the numerous rooms to view the art.

The main attraction was the six paintings from the Boston Fine Arts Museum.

The Sower by Jean-François Millet – French, c. 1850 (Dimensions 40 x 32 ½ in.) A peasant strides down the hill of a tilled field, casting seed. In the distant background is a man covering the seed on an ox-drawn harrow. *The Sower* is prominent in the foreground in the dim light of early morning. The bag of seed, draped over his left shoulder and held tight by a fisted hand, looks full of grain. Millet is ennobling *The Sower* to the status of hero with dignity, a food provider to a stricken country after the French Revolution in 1848.

Grainstack (Sunset) by Claude Monet – French, c. 1891 (Dimensions 28 7/8 x 36 ½ in.) Color, light, and form of a grain stack at sunset in rural France are elevated by Monet's application of this Impressionist style. Monet may have us consider things we take for granted, such as where our bread comes from. Typically, it is from silent laborers. A painting can be a window to a message the artist presents to a viewer. It is up to the viewer to be awakened.

Fog Warning by Winslow Homer – American, c. 1885 (Dimensions 30 ¼ x 48 ½ in.) This image shows the arduous task of a fisherman's life. A man in his dory has caught two large halibuts in Prouts Neck, Maine. Although he has successfully made a catch, his concern is to get to the distant ship before the approaching fog descends upon him and leaves him lost at sea. The waters are choppy, the waves high, and he's rowing with force against the wind. Homer leaves you to ponder, *Will he make it?*

Picture Gallery with Views of Modern Rome by Giovanni Paolo Pannini – Italian, c.1757 (Dimensions 67 x 96 ¼ in.) Here is a splendid view of modern Rome's iconic buildings, fountains, and monuments, including sculptures of Michelangelo and Bernini. The Duc de Choiseul commissioned Pannini to commemorate his time in Rome as the French Ambassador to the Vatican. This beautiful tribute also exemplifies how artists create propaganda in history for the wealthy. The duke is in the center of the fantasy art gallery.

Monsieur Returns the Gaze - In the Loge by Mary Stevenson Cassatt – American, c. 1878 (dimensions 32 x 26 in.) At the opera, a man in the foreground peers across from his balcony box seat at a woman in the distance who is gazing at him through her opera glasses. He tips his hand toward her. She is a voyeur, yet so are many in the room, as we see from the painter's view. This recently discovered painting is a companion to *In the Loge,* her most famous work, of a woman in black with her opera glasses. It was the first of her Impressionist paintings to be displayed in America.

Postman Joseph Roulin by Vincent van Gogh – Dutch (worked in France), c.1888 (Dimensions 32 x 25 ¾ in.) Van Gogh applied sensitivity with painterly strokes to portray his friend's gaze as he looked directly at the viewer. He modeled the face with care and enhanced the beard with wispy details. Masterly, he depicted the postal uniform with a rich, dense blue, intense gold buttons, and flourishes of embroidery on the cuffs. Most artists paint with an emotion in mind. Van Gogh's works show love, sensitivity, wonder, and more.

At 8:30 p.m., Karl approached a microphone to give a short presentation. From his small, boxed stage, he could see his mother in the white silk kaftan, waltzing through the room, mingling with patrons, and making new friends.

Karl chimed his champagne glass with a spoon into the microphone to capture everyone's attention.

"I am so pleased to have you all here at the Mystic River Fine Art Museum's grand reopening." Everyone clapped loudly. "This is a new beginning, and with your kind attendance, we have filled the rooms. I already feel that together we have made this a success."

The clapping took over again. "Your donations have made all this possible. Also, the BFA Museum has allowed us to borrow this spectacular exhibit for a short two weeks. From the age of sixteen, I worked at the BFA Museum and became a conservator of fine paintings until I arrived here a year ago. I am honored that they allowed us to show these stupendous works of art here in Mystic for our fundraising efforts." The audience clapped with vigor, and a few hoots rang out.

"As you know, we have one last construction project to finish: the rooftop garden and café for outdoor functions. It will open soon but only with your donations. So, give what you can, my friends, and we'll have events with the sunset view over the Mystic River." He raised his glass, "Here's to you." The crowd gave him rousing applause.

By 9:30 p.m., Roxanne and Sam stopped to say goodbye to Georgi. "Did you buy anything?" he teased.

"Yes, the Monet is mine," she jested with a smile.

"Did you enjoy yourself, Chief?"

"I did because there was no agenda. We meandered, ate, drank, listened to music, and sat by the water. What's not to like?"

"Good! I'm glad nothing else happened, and everyone had fun."

Morrison approached with a beaming Peabody. "I think Jack had the most fun. He has the phone numbers of three young ladies."

Jack fanned their business cards with a smile and waved them under his chin. "I had no idea museum events could be like this. They might be my new hangout."

Dan put his hand on Jack's shoulder. "Before the prince turns into a frog, we'll get going. This was a unique experience for me, and since nothing out of the ordinary has happened," Dan summed, "it could be that the connection to Mario has taken another route. We'll say goodnight so we can resume our work tomorrow."

Roxanne hugged Georgi for a job well done, and she and Sam walked out to the parking lot with their friendly undercover detectives.

The museum event ended by ten o'clock. Georgi and his staff cleaned up with the volunteers, who had a few drinks, but they all left by 10:30 without seeing Mario Corinthian or any suspicious behavior.

Isadore helped Karl lock up. All they had to do was set the alarm and walk out. Karl was ready, but Isadore suddenly remembered she wanted to bring home some of the leftovers in the fridge for lunch the next day. She stopped by the maintenance closet to find a tote bag.

"Go home, dear," she said. "I'm right behind you, and I'll set the alarm."

"Okay, I'm tired. See you at the house." Isadore had locked up numerous times over the past year, so Karl was not concerned. The parking attendant for the lot was still on duty, so he knew she would be fine.

CHAPTER 34

Dead Tide
Friday – Two weeks since Marilyn's fatality

At seven the following morning, Detective Morrison called Karl at home. "Mr. Rubens, I'm sorry to bother you, but one of your volunteers from last night, Aaron Goshen, has been reported missing by his girlfriend, Marguerite. As a courtesy to me, I've had the Mystic police check the municipal parking lot. His car is still there. It seems he never left. Do you have any information about him or where he might be?"

"Why no, Detective. The place was empty when my mother and I left last night."

"Thank you, Mr. Rubens. You see, this would normally be out of my jurisdiction, but we have had a few odd things happen to artists in New London, and I am extra cautious these days."

"I understand, Detective. Hold on a moment, and I will ask my mother." Karl muted his cell phone as he called out, "Mother, did you see a young man when you left? His name is Aaron Goshen, and he volunteered last night."

"No, dear," she returned, "but he was helping us out all evening."

"Sorry, Detective, we haven't seen him. I plan to be at the museum at 8 a.m. I will call you in case I find anything out."

"Very good, Mr. Rubens."

When Karl arrived at precisely eight, Morrison was already there. The detective had spoken to the parking lot company and the man on duty, and they reported that nothing unusual had occurred.

Morrison introduced himself, and Karl said, "Good morning again, Detective Morrison. I don't expect Aaron to be inside wandering around. We have a state-of-the-art security system."

"It's my job, Mr. Rubens. I'm sure you understand the protocol."

Karl unlocked the museum door and turned off the alarm. They both wandered from room to room. "All seems peaceful from my perspective, Detective. You're welcome to look around. I'll be in my office."

Morrison scanned the familiar spaces from the night before, then went to the back of the building and opened the double doors to the patio that faced the lawn and water. He searched the surrounding grounds for any clue of Aaron's whereabouts, then walked toward the large dock that stretched into the Mystic

River. The blue stillness of the water drew him to the end of the pier. A peaceful mood descended over him as he watched the current and noticed the river was in a slack tide.

Across the water on the opposite shore were numerous boats in the seaport marina. Various crafts took advantage of the river's ten-foot draw for their rudders and traversed into Long Island Sound to its terminus, the Atlantic Ocean. To his left, Morrison could see downtown Main Street and the Bascule Bridge's 230-ton concrete counterweights suspended in the air.

Morrison peered into the water at a school of minnows swimming near one of the pier posts. He turned back toward the museum and observed the newly constructed roof patio. It had a wing that cantilevered away from the museum's primary structure and jutted near the water. It would soon offer patrons a broad view of the waterway once completed.

Walking back to the museum, Morrison eyed some floating debris rising from under the dock close to the riverbank. It looked like a bubble of fabric at first glance. He bent down and pulled, but it was caught and would not dislodge. He stooped to his knees to get a better look.

In the meantime, Karl walked through the museum and into the main gallery that housed the paintings from the BFA Museum. He admired each one as he strolled in front of them: Monet's *Grainstack*, Homer's *The Fog Warning*, and Millet's *The Sower*.

But with one simple glance from afar, he saw something odd and peculiar across the room. He began to twitch and then ran toward the painting. Looking at the others and back again, he discovered Mary Cassatt's *Monsieur Returns the Gaze* was all wrong! Once reality pounced on his thoughts, a guttural roar sprang out of Karl's mouth, and he raced to the back door. He cried out to Morrison in a near shriek. "Detective, we have a major problem." Morrison was already strutting toward the door. "A Boston Fine Art painting has been stolen! And an appalling replica is in its place!"

"You have a much bigger problem than that, Mr. Rubens."

Karl tugged on his vest. "That, my dear sir, is entirely impossible!"

"I just found Aaron Goshen under the dock."

"What the hell is he doing under there?" Annoyed and confused, Karl yelled.

"He's dead."

Karl's tall form staggered and landed against the doorframe. He slowly leaned back inside the museum with his hands gripping his forehead. "My lovely life is passing before my eyes," he whimpered. The interior wall provided support for his weakened body. Feeling dizzy, Karl took a deep breath. Suddenly, another emotion leaped forth, and he burst out angrily, "This is sabotage! Who is doing this to me? How else can I have two catastrophes the day after my grand reopening?"

Morrison was caught off guard by Karl's personalization of the incidents. "Mr. Rubens, I would imagine it has to do with the expensive paintings from the BFA Museum and not you."

The detective immediately contacted Mystic Police and informed them of his discovery, including the identification he found in Aaron's back pocket. When the call ended, he told Karl, "Please don't touch anything, Mr. Rubens. Be prepared to close the museum until the investigation is completed. It will be days to at least a week or more."

Karl became like a pillar of stone in his tailored suit and bow tie as he considered the word *closed*.

Wondering if he was about to topple, Morrison suggested, "Have a seat, Mr. Rubens. I know this is a lot to take in right now."

The proud museum director haltingly stepped into the gallery toward a bench. His head tilted back as he sat. Catatonically, he stared at the ceiling. The always firmly-in-control Karl was now out of his element with a multimillion-dollar insurance policy competing for his thoughts against the museum being closed due to a dead man on the grounds.

Morrison leaned against the threshold of the exterior door and carefully observed Karl. Sirens could be heard in the distance. Karl moaned, and Morrison said, "Stay right here, Mr. Rubens, and please think of who was here last night near the end of the evening."

Karl's mind jolted to attention, *Mother!* Then he realized he didn't want to put the spotlight on her.

The entourage of first responders, EMTs, and police entered the museum parking lot. Morrison greeted Detective John Hanniford of the Mystic Police and walked him to Aaron while sharing details about how his body was discovered.

As the investigation proceeded, Morrison excused himself to make a call. "Meet me down here, Peabody. We have another incident with a New Londoner." While he waited, Morrison stood by and surveyed the scene. They pulled Aaron farther up onto the lawn. He was face down. The local detectives examined the back of his head. The coroner would soon be on the scene to take over.

Peabody arrived and asked Morrison, "Is it possible Aaron may have seen the culprits steal the art, and they took him out?"

Morrison stared ahead as he answered. "We need evidence. Inside, outside, and from his injuries."

"He could have helped them steal the art," Peabody continued, "and they took him out."

"You can guess all you like, Peabody. We have to wait for the facts."

"Could this be connected to the other artists?" he asked.

In a low tone, Morrison answered with conviction, "It may not be connected at all. Will you please stop?" Morrison folded a stick of cinnamon gum into his mouth and offered one to his partner. "Do me a favor and use this to plug the hole that keeps asking me useless questions."

Peabody obliged and somberly watched the examination of Aaron's body.

Previously Karl had hired contractors to dredge the river area for the newly installed museum dock. It was to attract boaters, making the water near the shore deeper too. Aaron's body had been lodged under the pier during high tide. Morrison found him within minutes of the tide's ebb out to sea.

The coroner arrived and noted a big gash on Aaron's skull. "This laceration is deep. It appears he was struck with a heavy implement or thrown against the dock edge. See how this incision appears to have an angle to it?" They nodded and murmured their assumptions. The coroner looked to Hanniford. "I'm ready to transport the body straight to Dr. Storm's examination room."

"Package him up," Hanniford agreed. He then pulled Morrison aside. Mystic Police had partnered well with Morrison over the years, so Hanniford welcomed the news on the recent cases with New London artists. "I've got the BFA Museum art theft to deal with here, Morrison, so let's work together on this one. We need to know if this kid from New London is involved with the art theft or if he was an innocent bystander."

"You bet. My case with Marilyn Maroney may not be connected, so I appreciate our departments working together, Hanniford." They shook hands and left.

Peabody followed Morrison's SUV out of the parking lot, onto the interstate, across the Gold Star Memorial Bridge, and back to police headquarters. Morrison was sitting at his desk reviewing paperwork when Peabody came over.

"Boss, you know what is weird about you finding Aaron Goshen?"

"No, what?"

"It was a dead tide."

Morrison became still, turned his head, and gave Peabody an empty gaze. Finally, he asked, "Are you joking? I haven't encountered the term dead tide, only slack tide."

"No, Boss. When the water is between high and low tide, there is a twenty to thirty-minute lull when the tide is neither going in nor out. You hear it called slack tide all the time, but it is also called a dead tide. That was when you found him. The tide was about to pull him out into Long Island Sound. He could have been gone without a trace. So you know what that means, Boss?"

Morrison had looked away and was half-listening. "That I found a dead body at dead tide?"

"It means you're a lucky dog!" Jack Peabody grinned like he had discovered luck was Morrison's superpower.

The detective's steel-blue eyes sternly fixated on Peabody. "No! It is deduction; it is persistence and determination. I am rising early because I can't sleep, and I want this case about New London artists solved. Luck has nothing to do with it."

Eyeing Peabody as if his brain had left the room, he continued, "I am fully aware that the marijuana laws have changed, and if you are hitting the hooch, that makes a perfect explanation for your fantasy world. Just lay off my methods of detecting. It all boils down to hard work and keeping your mind clear and your head on straight. Don't mess with my internal instincts and methodical research, okay?"

"Yes, Boss, but—"

Morrison held up his hand. "Stop talking and start thinking. Think on the inside, not the outside. I don't want to hear your every thought. That is a youthful, naïve approach. Think things through internally, and when you have arrived at a sensible outcome, you can share it with me. Otherwise, it's just noise. I want less noise and more knowledge. Comprende, señor?"

"Si, comprende, Boss." Peabody went to his desk, thinking about his job and his lead detective. *He must be feeling the pressure because that's when he gets extremely serious. I better get my act together if I want to stay here.* Jack Peabody set to work finding Aaron's family contacts.

CHAPTER 35

Escape to the Slater

Karl sat at his desk while the police interviewed him. He reported on the previous evening's events and answered their specific questions. Detective Hanniford also required the passwords for the museum's security system files and video catalog.

Karl then called the Boston Fine Arts Museum to report the theft; their insurance company would also cover the painting under an "All Risk Policy" and investigate the crime. This was a standard policy that art museums carried for traveling exhibits. Consecutively, he called his museum's insurance company. Both would be involved as more details of the crime came forward.

"Mr. Rubens, we have all we need for this moment," Hanniford informed. "You've been very cooperative and can go home now. We'll contact you if we have more questions or anything to report. And please do not leave town."

Standing, Karl straightened his jacket and adjusted his bow tie. "Detective, I'm here until you find that painting. If you need me, I'll have my phone with me but send a text as I will have the ringer off. Please understand that I don't want to be bothered by the press. The phone ringing will only make me more upset than I already am."

Hanniford noticed Karl seemed tired, but then, something else happened. *Why are his hands shaking?*

The museum director's face contorted. "Sir, I want that painting back!" his pent-up anger spewed out, and his fist pounded the desk. "My reputation is on the line. You cannot imagine what a blow this is to me. I was entrusted with these priceless paintings based on my reputation alone!"

Karl pulled out his pocket square and dabbed his forehead. Composing himself, he softened his tone yet remained firm. "You see, I installed a top-notch security system six months ago. This system has performed flawlessly. It was a requirement before I showed these works of art, some of the most priceless in the world.

"Detective, I don't know if this kid Aaron was involved in the theft, but it's too coincidental for him not to be. He looks like a rat, smells like a rat, so he must have rat friends."

"Now, now, Mr. Rubens, please bear with me." Hanniford attempted to alleviate Karl's tension. "We are confident we'll find the answers because of your fine security system. We are also working with Detective Morrison in New London. He is interviewing Aaron's friends and family and handling that end. He is very thorough. You have two detectives working on this case. My team will analyze all your security footage, and we will get to the bottom of this; I promise you."

Karl left in a state of combined morosity and annoyance.

John Hanniford pondered the situation. There had not been a high-profile homicide case in Mystic's recent history, and this one coincided with grand larceny. His reputation could be negatively impacted, just like Karl's. This made him realize he must find evidence quickly because he soon would be contending with the BFA Museum's fine art insurance investigator arriving on his doorstep. He set his team to work.

Karl truly felt his career was ruined as he was the guardian of the paintings. Now, Aaron's death on museum property made him appear damningly suspicious. Karl's gilded vision of the future was fading. *I can't believe this is happening to me. My dream was for our museum to be the art headquarters of the region. This is a disaster!*

Karl slipped into his sleek car and decided he was too upset and shaken to go home and deal with his mother. When he started the engine, a Haydn symphony filled the air of his black Jaguar XJ-S. He slid on his black leather driving gloves, gripped the steering wheel, and drove.

Traveling circuitous roads was one way to escape his thoughts. He drove through Mystic into Norwich while gazing at architecturally grand homes that lined the route to his destination. These were the original neighborhoods of the famous city called "The Rose of New England."

He turned off Washington Street and sighted the six-story, red-brick tower of the Slater Memorial Museum. Rapunzel could easily be imagined letting down her hair from this fairytale turret that highlighted the magnificent Victorian building. Karl heaved a long sigh of relief because he was about to enter a historical past and step into a portal that could momentarily disconnect him from the present.

In his mind's eye, Karl fantasized about visiting a Duke in a castle full of wondrous treasures, and they were. Famous plasters of sculptures from around the world were housed in the museum on the Norwich Free Academy campus.

Facts: Slater Memorial Museum

Norwich Free Academy (NFA), built in 1846, has always followed the philosophy of its founder John P. Gulliver to "return to our hamlets and our homes its priceless freight of youthful minds, enriched by learning, developed by a liberal culture, refined by the study of all that is beautiful in nature and art, and prepared for the highest usefulness and the purest happiness."

The Slater Museum, built in 1884, was a gift to NFA and was designed by a Boston architect in a style known as Richardsonian Romanesque. In 1888, the principal of NFA, Dr. Robert Porter Keep, persuaded Slater to attain 227 plaster casts of classical and renaissance sculptures from around the world as an additional contribution. They are the finest representations of the original stone works and can be viewed online on a 3-D virtual tour.

Karl strode across the modern atrium entrance between the Norwich Free Academy and the Slater Museum. He rode the elevator to the second-floor gift shop and put a substantial donation into the collection box, then passed through the massive double wooden doors into the historic sphere of the museum.

Karl nodded his approval to the first room with an ornate fireplace, once the library, and continued to the great hall. In 1888, a museum curator from Boston antiquities selected which ancient sculptures should be cast into plaster for the Slater. Of course, the connection gave Karl a fond affinity toward the grand gesture and enormous effort to replicate world treasures.

He walked into the quiet room full of giant sculpted gods and goddesses, mythical beings, and ordinary humans. Karl's gaze rose the three stories to where sunlight streamed down from several eyebrow-shaped windows. The numerous ivory-white figures were luminous against a rich wood-paneled gallery.

Karl sighed at the wonder of these silent giant companions who gave him solace. Above him was the magnificent, winged Nike. He turned, and Aphrodite gazed down at him. He beheld the massive centaurs from the Temple of Zeus at Olympia, and being among them all, he quickly lost himself and entered their alternate reality where his life of mayhem, theft, and death did not exist.

Yet when he came upon the Laocoön, one of the most famous sculptures in the world, the icon of suffering made Karl feel differently. It was a dramatic, larger-than-life scene: a Trojan priest and his sons, all muscular, naked men, were being attacked by sensationally giant snake-like sea serpents.

The sculptor emphasized the dynamic squeezing, writhing, and tightening grip of the creatures upon the suffering men. Karl connected with the tableau, and the impact compelled him to take a step back. *This is how I feel. Out of control, desperate, and unable to win my freedom from tragedy.*

He left the room for something more serene and came upon the youthful sculpture of David, the slayer of the giant Goliath. The fifteenth-century original by Verrocchio was in Florence, Italy, and Karl had seen it in person. David's smug expression was warranted. He had a small slingshot in hand, and at his feet was the head of Goliath. Karl felt inspired and thought of himself as David. *I need to lop the head off my goliath problems.*

One of Karl's favorite pieces was on the balcony of the lofty gallery. Sunbeams flowed around Michelangelo's brilliant sculpture of a tender moment with Mary and Jesus. Mary held him after his death, and Karl had been to see the original at St. Peter's Basilica in the Vatican.

He appreciated Michelangelo's depiction of draped fabric in stone and the skillfully portrayed emotion of a mother's care for her son. It warmly reminded Karl of his mother. Isadore told him she thought of him as her little miracle when he was born. As he grew, she often pointed to famous paintings of Mary and baby Jesus, telling Karl they were paintings of her with him. At first, he was in awe at how many there were, and then, with age, he realized her sweet fib.

Although she was often strongly opinionated and had an annoying way of directing his life and career, he wondered if she could help him salvage it this time. His life was about to worsen with the anticipated publicity of both incidents after his grand reopening. He knew his mother would squelch the gossip among her friends, but might she help redirect the negative energy from the situation and keep the museum and his reputation from ruin? *Maybe, she could rally her influence.*

Feeling calmer, Karl felt his art therapy session was complete, and a gnawing feeling of hunger took over. He might have called a friend to join him for a late lunch if he had any. His ways were so particular that he found he was generally disturbed by people. His peers in Boston would say that for forty years, he was only known to have colleagues, not friends. Therefore, Karl decided to enjoy one more comfort alone before tumbling back into his dilemma of an art heist and a dead young man.

He made a reservation for a private table at Captain Daniel Packer Inne in Mystic. This curator's goal of hiding out in the refined, old-world charm would allow him to avoid his future a little longer.

Facts: Captain Daniel Packer Inne

> Built in 1756, the building was a home, then became an inn for fatigued travelers between Boston and New York. The inn's guests would gorge, guzzle, and be entertained by Captain Packer's tales of sailing the high seas.
>
> Back then, a rope ferry carried folks across the Mystic River. To this day, the stone with the iron ring is still on site. The elegant dining above and historic ground-level pub are well-noted for their charm as a gathering place.

***

While Karl was enjoying his meal at the inn, the police arrived at Isadore's home on Mason's Island to question her about the previous night. Hanniford was respectful of her age and slowly told her about Aaron and the stolen painting. He attempted to query her, but she was overly concerned for Karl. "Where is my son? Why isn't he here with you?"

"He has been occupied, Madam, by the activity and our questioning at the scene. I'm sure he will contact you very soon."

"Detective, this is a disaster!" She pulled a floral handkerchief from her pocket and sniffled into it. "How was the painting stolen?" Her voice rose. "How did poor Aaron end up dead and in the water?"

"Madam, please tell me what you saw and when you left last night," Hanniford pressed.

Waving her handkerchief, she explained, "The museum was empty by ten thirty, and Karl left before I did. I stayed to collect leftover food to bring home. I assume Aaron left with all his friends. We didn't see him."

Once he had her story, he felt she knew very little, so Hanniford left to pursue more leads and review the security footage from the museum. This would help him verify her and Karl's accounts.

Isadore called Karl and left a message. "Please call me, darling. The detective came by and told me what had happened. I'm worried about you, dear."

***

By the afternoon, the detective discovered evidence while reviewing the museum security footage. At 11:30 p.m. the night before, he saw that the closed-circuit exterior camera caught two men wearing police uniforms when they approached the museum's back entrance. One of them carried a large satchel. Hanniford watched as they tapped the keycode into the security system and accessed the museum.

Interior cameras captured the men as they proceeded to a closet. A moment later, the security feed went black. The system went back online fifteen minutes later, at 11:45, seemingly having been re-armed. The men came out of the closet and left with the satchel. The BFA Cassatt painting was seen on the wall before and after, but Hanniford understood it was the replica they left behind.

Hanniford was disappointed that he could not see where the thieves came from or the direction they had left. The cameras had a limited scope and only captured the doorway, so the lawn down to the river was a blind spot. The security company still needed to complete their camera installation due to the exterior roof construction project. It would capture the back lawn, dock, and any boats tied up.

Karl Rubens had told him the security company was tasked to add those cameras after the grand reopening. Hanniford couldn't believe the bad luck. There had to be an inside man at the security company. Quickly, he and two officers sped off to question the company and interview their security officers and employees.

CHAPTER 36

Heads Together
New London, Friday - afternoon

Aaron and his girlfriend, Marguerite, had collaborated with Troy a year ago on a large art installation between the Dahlia and the Velvet Muse. It was created for the week of Sailfest when the famous tall ships were on parade in New London Harbor and the Thames River. Every year, the City of Steeples was crowded with tourists, and the artists wanted to attract them to their gallery and the outdoor park of the Velvet Muse.

Marguerite, an excellent artist, helped Troy with a large mural of a ship and sea captain for the outdoor stage. Then throughout the Velvet Muse, Aaron used his creative woodworking and construction skills to make standing characters of extravagant lobsters, mermaids, and pirates for family photos. It became a popular stop that brought people into the art gallery where Marguerite, Aaron, and Troy had their works for sale. They had become good friends and helped each other from that day forward.

When Troy found out Aaron was dead, he was devasted. And with a BFA painting stolen on top of that, he immediately called Roxanne and Georgi. They met at the Washington Street Coffeehouse.

They ordered lunch and huddled into a booth. "I feel so helpless," Troy moped. "Why is this happening to my friends? And poor Marguerite, she must feel shattered."

Both Roxanne and Georgi put an arm around Troy. "It's a good thing we have each other," Georgi consoled. "Roxanne knows I would be a basket case without her."

"I appreciate you guys, yet I'm confused. Georgi, you were there last night after we all left. When did you see Aaron last?" Troy asked.

Georgi stirred his iced tea slowly and spoke in a soft tone. "He was in the kitchen having a few drinks with the other volunteers while my staff and I were packing up. I thought they all left together. We cleared out soon after. I don't know what could have happened. I now wish I had paid more attention. Have you heard anything, Roxanne?"

"Sam called this morning and said to hold on to my seat because there was another death of a New Londoner, and a BFA painting was stolen too!" She sighed. "We had such a nice time last night at the museum, but we didn't know a plan was being hatched the whole time. I'm in shock."

At that moment, their food was delivered. She took a bite of her Caesar salad, and Troy and Georgi chomped on their shared sandwich. They quietly ate and stared at the table in a daze of grief.

Breaking the silence, Troy asked, "What is going on? Why are Marilyn and Aaron dead? Why did Cora meet an art agent, then find herself drugged and in her underwear? Do we need to worry about who's next? This is so strange. How do we find out what's happening?"

Georgi sprang to attention. "You're right, Troy. Let's be proactive. I have an idea. Let's get our heads together with some of our art friends and launch our own covert reconnaissance mission."

Roxanne slowly reached out with both hands. Troy watched as they moved toward Georgi's neck. Troy's eyes bugged out. Georgi peered over his shoulder and saw her coming. "What? I can have ideas," he exclaimed.

"You…" she pointed her finger at him teasingly, "you got us in hot water last time with your ideas, so hold your horses, Mr. T, for trouble. We must be careful, logical, and smart in whatever we do. Not spontaneous like before. Do you agree?"

Roxanne quickly rethought her statement. "Who am I kidding? You cannot be tamed. You have a windup toy inside you that once you release it, it goes running about wildly." Roxanne put her elbow on the table and leaned on her fist to gaze at Georgi with resignation. "What were you going to say?"

"I think if a few key art friends and some local art groups put their heads together, we could make a more concerted effort. Hey, Aaron must be linked to the painting somehow. It all happened in one night. Maybe we can find the connection, and there might be a reward. There always is, right?" Georgi nudged her. "See? That isn't such a bad idea."

"Sounds reasonable to me, and money is always great." Troy's incentivization rose. "We can start right away. Aaron worked regionally and helped organize youth artistic and parkour performance events with me. Let's include local organizations like Spark Makerspace, Cultural Coalition, and the New London Arts Council. We can find out who knows what within our art network."

Roxanne was now grinding her forehead with her hand. "I'm not sure we should be doing all this. Our Detective Dan Morrison might find out and become upset with us. He may have evidence he's working with, and besides, I don't see anything that relates this to Marilyn and Cora."

"Please let us try," Georgi pleaded. "What don't you understand about covert? This is an exploratory gathering of information for the detective. He needs us, though he may disagree. People will talk to us before they talk to him. Come on, Roxanne, you know I'm right. Relax! Troy and I will do all the planning and contacts, and you know nothing."

Her shoulders relaxed. "Good. I'm just a friend, and that's my story." She smiled and continued eating.

Georgi explained, "Troy, she knows the detective will tattle to her husband about her." Roxanne nodded and he continued. "We don't want the detective against us. He can be adamant about how his investigation should run."

"He's not that bad," Roxanne defended Morrison and tapped the table for Troy's attention. "We can't go off after a lead like we did last time and have a killer after us. That makes him angry. And don't even try kidding around when he's being serious."

Troy's head bopped between his two friends, trying to interpret their messages on dealing with Morrison. "So, you're saying be cool, don't say too much, and don't make him suspicious. Look, I'll just put my hands up whenever I see him. Then I'll be covered." He demonstrated the action. They snickered but became serious again.

Troy offered, "Why don't you both come to an art event on Sunday, and we can chat with some local artists? Ophelia and a few of us will be at The Red House. It's north of here. We'll be selling our artwork outdoors at a pop-up sale. We can hash out some theories. By then, we may all know more."

"I'll check with Sam," Roxanne said. "He may go."

"We can go together. I'll drive," Georgi offered. "It will be a nice ride, and if we all put our heads together, we may come up with a clue. Our biggest frustration is not knowing what has happened." Troy and Roxanne nodded.

CHAPTER 37

Karl's Dilemma
Friday - 3 p.m.

When Karl returned to their Mason's Island house, he was exhausted after the whole day from the theft of the painting, the death of Aaron, and being questioned. His search for peace at the Slater Museum and a quiet lunch was just a momentary reprieve.

Isadore ran to meet him in the garage. "Where were you? I've been so worried! Why did you leave me alone to be questioned by the police? You know I needed you here."

"Listen, Mother. I'm tired." Karl was disheartened. "I know you mean well, but I have my worries. I'm about to be roasted by the press because my grand reopening ended with a man dead and a painting stolen. They'll probably enjoy it. I feel my neck should be in a guillotine operated by the BFA Museum for losing their precious painting. Let's face it. I'm ruined. I see no other way around this situation."

Isadore trailed him as Karl took long strides toward the living room. Her full-length outfit, a blue floral kaftan, moved about her. "My darling son," she pleaded.

"Seriously, Mother!" Karl motioned for her to stop. "I'm trying to figure this out and how it happened to me." He paced the smartly decorated room to expel his nervous irritation.

Isadore became tired from watching him parade about, leaned against her Steinway piano, and exhaled impatiently.

"Mother, there were too many unsuitable bystanders at last night's museum reopening. I believe people from the City of Steeples are trying to sabotage our success here at the museum. Aaron was from New London, and his art friends probably had something to do with the theft." He halted and raised his index finger with a realization. "They must have made that horrible forgery to replace Cassatt's elegant painting of the opera house." Spinning another theory, he added, "I believe they took the artwork to ruin my reputation and fund their careers. What am I to do? My reputation is all I have."

Isadore straightened her stance and calmly stated, "Darling, we shall do what we always do—we'll figure it out together. You know that there is nothing we can't resolve." She moved gracefully to the sofa to relax and gaze out the window at the expansive view of Poggy Bay. She fingered a long strand of pearls about her neck.

"I've been thinking while you tied yourself into a knot of frustration. We should post a reward before the day gets away from us. One that will let the press and everyone know how serious we are about recovering the painting and discovering what happened to Aaron. In fact, let us call Detective Hanniford and tell him now. He plans to address the local news stations and media press this evening. He said he needs to curb gossip and let everyone know his team is working to solve this case quickly."

Karl stopped in his tracks. "He's going to address the news stations?" The blood drained from his face.

"Sit down, dear. You're making me nervous, and I don't like how frazzled you look. Have a seat in your club chair, put your feet up, and I'll make us some tea and bring out those nice desserts the caterers left behind from last night."

A defeated Karl sat in his chair, and Isadore moved toward the kitchen, her kaftan fluttering around her. "This is all going to work out. You did nothing wrong. We are the victims here! The Mystic River Fine Art Museum's board of directors knows this is true, the BFA Museum knows it, and the detectives know. You need to settle down and let everyone else do the work for you."

Karl put his hand to his forehead, leaned back in the chair, and murmured, "Yes, Mother." He shut his eyes and sighed, "She could be right."

Isadore returned from the kitchen, wheeling a beautiful antique tea cart. She traversed the lengthy oriental rug and placed a tray on the small table between them. Sitting in the opposite club chair from him, she poured the tea, added honey and lemon, and handed Karl his cup and saucer. She remained composed and said, "No one questions your honesty and dedication, my dear. Everyone saw how hard you worked to make this museum reopening the best it possibly could be. Last night was a grand success. Everyone understands it was due to you."

Karl sipped his tea and watched her with genuine appreciation.

"What do you think about what I said? We shall offer a handsome reward for useful information to the detectives." Her manner was quite comforting. "We will show everyone we are doing our best, considering the appalling situation. That is all we can do, my son." Holding a tea biscuit, she emphasized, "And it *will* save your reputation."

Karl took a deep breath and sighed again. He knew she was right; he could always depend on her cool-headed thinking. "Okay, Mother, let's offer a huge reward, so they know we mean business. We'll get everyone's attention, especially the thieves and their compatriots. One may betray the others just for the reward and amnesty."

Isadore raised her teacup. "Karl, my dear, let's offer $250,000 and blow the socks off this community! This reward will polish your reputation."

A crack of a smile formed on the corners of Karl's mouth. He leaned in and clinked her teacup with his own.

Before taking a sip, her eyes flashed with a realization. "My dear, you could never get this kind of publicity for the museum, no matter how many ads you placed. The theft of the Cassatt will likely go international!"

Karl was caught off guard. *Could it be true? Our misfortune, plus the reward, may bring the museum international attention?*

Isadore's personal motto was coined from an advertisement: "Avoid disappointment and future regret." She stroked her pearls and comforted herself, knowing Karl was feeling better about their circumstance and that the reward may fix his future.

CHAPTER 38

Fingers Crossed - The Public Address
Friday - 5 p.m.

A small, temporary stage with a podium had been purposely erected at Mystic River Park, a charming green zone by the river. The area offered plenty of room for the substantial crowd now standing in front of Detective John Hanniford. The scene behind him framed a picturesque view for the television cameras posed to capture the attractive storefronts on Main Street and the counterweights of Mystic's 100-year-old Bascule Bridge.

Hanniford was keenly aware of the interest from the media, online, in print, and news stations. He gripped the podium with both hands and spoke authoritatively into the microphone. The detective issued the facts of the tragedy and reported the joint investigation between Mystic and New London police departments.

The detective cleared his throat and continued, "It is too soon to tell what exactly happened, folks, but we are following the evidence to determine Aaron Goshen's death and the theft of the priceless Cassatt painting on loan from the BFA Museum."

He paused to survey the crowd, raised his fist, and thumped the podium loudly to capture a moment of full attention. The audience was hushed. "Folks, I've been told of a new development that may help our case. Mr. Karl Rubens of the Mystic River Fine Art Museum is personally offering a reward of $250,000!" The crowd gasped, and he raised his voice while leaning into the microphone. "This substantial reward is for any information that leads to the arrest and conviction of the perpetrators. The seriousness of this case cannot be overstated. You know where to find me. Good day."

The press immediately peppered the detective with questions hounding him for more information. Without answering, he held up his hand, waved, and left the podium.

Hanniford could reveal no more. He was still collecting video evidence from surrounding buildings, reviewing footage from the museum party, and the forged painting was being forensically examined. Currently, the top suspect on his list was a yet-to-be-named employee from the security company. Hanniford felt someone on their payroll could have assisted in the theft and contributed to Aaron's demise.

***

Roxanne and Sam watched Hanniford's TV press conference from Mystic. Afterward, they ate dinner outside on their back deck. Roxanne blurted, "Two deaths combined with Cora being bamboozled and drugged does not make a coincidence."

Sam felt her anxiety and reached out for her hand. "But I want you to do me a favor, and please be a bystander this time."

"I'll do my best." It was a temporary stay that she knew might be broken, so she crossed her fingers on the other hand under the table. Somehow, she reasoned, crossing her fingers was a way of skirting a lie, one that may never occur. Yet she knew from years of experience that circumstances can change.

Sam held her hand tighter. "You may have to consider something else."

She slowly gazed up from her food as various scenarios ran through her mind. "What do you mean?"

"Consider the theory that Aaron may have been an unsuspecting witness to the art theft, and the thieves killed him. Then his death would be unconnected to Marilyn and Cora."

"Wow, honey, my little gray cells are firing. So while Georgi, Troy, and I had our radars up to find Mario Corinthian during our lovely evening at the museum, poor Aaron could have been caught in the middle of their operation and not part of it at all!"

Sam added, "And with our detectives, Dan, and Jack, right there when an art heist was in the making. But that's hypothetical. They still must prove if Aaron had a part in the theft or if he tried to stop them and died for it. Only time will reveal the truth."

"Ugh, I feel terrible. I'm sure Aaron was just in the wrong place at the wrong time. He was a good guy, according to Troy and Georgi." She took a deep breath and gazed at her Japanese contemplation garden. Her eyes focused on the foliage and wandered down the path to a bench under their cedar tree. *It's hard to be calm when all this chaos is going on!*

Sam interrupted her thought. "It reminds me of that young man, Harry Daghlian, another New Londoner who died trying to do the right thing."

"Was that the twenty-four-year-old guy who was a smart, young nuclear scientist on the Manhattan Project? Didn't they make a movie about it with Paul Newman?"

"Yeah, it's called *Fat Man and Little Boy.* In 1945, he saved a laboratory of scientists from a nuclear explosion by putting his hand into the reactor to pull apart the nuclear components. He died twenty-five days later from the nuclear radiation. He's one of the few I would call a true hero."

Sam had repeatedly voiced to Roxanne that the word hero was thrown around too often and was becoming as common as grilled cheese on rye.

Sam stopped reminiscing and said, "Let's hope Aaron was on the right side of this theft. Maybe he was trying to stop them and be a hero. Not for nothing; no one wants to be right and dead."

Roxanne mused, "Hopefully, the reward will grab the attention of anyone who knows or saw what happened to Aaron. And what about the insurance for the painting?" she asked. "Do they send someone?"

"Yes, usually an insurance investigator will come in right away. The Boston Fine Arts Museum must have trusted Mr. Rubens completely to ship these paintings for his opening."

Roxanne pondered, "Well, from my experience of working around Mr. Rubens, I can tell you he's all business and follows his pecking order protocols with meticulous attention to detail. I imagine this has devastated him."

Sam confided, "Since Morrison is working the case on the New London side of the Thames River, he'll be questioning all of Aaron's friends and the artists again to see if they heard any rumblings before the theft."

Roxanne shook her head. "Dear me, they have been through enough already. We need a clue."

Sam cleared his throat. "Dan Morrison does not need Roxanne Samson's help."

"Okay, honey, don't worry." She patted his hand. She rose to retrieve dessert, a pineapple-upside-down cake. Back at the table, she asked, "Are you busy Sunday? There is an arts center called The Red House that is having an art tent event. Do you want to go?"

Sam thought a moment. "I'd prefer to relax in front of the television. Do you mind?"

"Not at all. I'll ask Georgi to pick me up. It will be a nice ride."

"Sure. Maybe you can find some early Christmas gifts for the family there." Roxanne smiled knowingly with her fingers crossed behind her back.

CHAPTER 39

Odd Stakeout

Morrison did not waste any time investigating Aaron Goshen's life and death. Already, he and Peabody had interviewed Aaron's family, his girlfriend Marguerite Santa Maria, and several friends. The detective then called Francisco and asked for digital copies of his photographs from the museum event. He hoped for a clue.

He took a new tack and said, "Peabody, I have something for you to do. Go home and get some rest. I'd like you to work tonight from six to midnight. You and I have a secret mission."

Spinning around in his desk chair, Peabody's chair halted with a jerk. "We do?"

"This will be on-the-job training for you. It's time you gain more experience."

"It is?" He visibly gulped.

"Yes, so go home and be back at eighteen hundred hours, ready to work in your casual street clothes."

Jack Peabody was learning not to ask so many questions, but one popped out: "Is there anything else I should know?"

"Bring your laptop. We'll use an unmarked car to go between these five locations throughout the night. They are all connected to Aaron Goshen." He handed him a folder with the details, names of the persons of interest they had interviewed, and a list of others they should watch. "We are looking for out-of-the-ordinary activity regarding the stolen painting because they will have to move it. And if any of them created the forgery? Be prepared to work past midnight. Do you understand?"

"Yes, sir." Peabody stood. "Thanks, Boss." He left.

Morrison's brow smoothed with relief as he watched his protégé leave without a second question.

When Peabody arrived for their undercover work, they chose a 2010 Chevy Impala, their incognito vehicle for the night. "We are just two guys out cruising for some action. You'll want to tune into your observation skills, Jack."

"Sure thing, Boss." Peabody went through some papers. "I have the addresses from our checklist that we'll rotate through to watch for suspicious behavior. I'll keep track of the time and each location.

First, they drove under the Gold Star Bridge to the river, where many youths hung out. "I was told Aaron fished here often," said Morrison. With no activity, they drove past the Old Town Mill.

Peabody checked his list. "Okay, next is Riverside Park. The city revitalized it after our last case with JJ's death, and it's another spot he frequented." They entered the green oasis by the Thames River and found a couple of boys shooting hoops. Otherwise, it was vacant.

Next, they positioned the car near Marguerite's family home. Visitors were stopping by to offer their condolences. Jack leaned back in his seat and set his phone on video to record them. Morrison pulled out a snack of caramel popcorn with peanuts. After fifteen minutes and a few handfuls, he took his turn recording and passed the Cracker Jack mix to Peabody.

When it began to get dark, they drove to a warehouse where Aaron practiced his parkour performance and athletic gymnastics. Morrison stepped out of the car and peered into a window. All was still, with no lights on, so they left to circle the homes of people who had known him.

By 10:30 p.m., they approached a location where Morrison had hired a retired officer to keep watch on friends of Aaron's who were persons of interest. Peabody muttered when they rounded the corner, "You've got to be kidding me. He's not incognito." The man was leaning against a lamp post and cut quite a silhouette in profile: a big guy, broad shoulders with a rotund stomach, a long torpedo cigar, and a baseball cap. A glowing ember from the stogie flashed his location like a lightning bug.

"That's CG undercover," Morrison said sarcastically.

"Is that how you guys do it?" Peabody slowly lowered his window. "What are you doing, CG?"

CG was in a smoke bubble that hovered around him like a specter. A grumble passed the lips gripping the soggy end of the stogie. "I'm on a stakeout, you rookie nitwit. What does it look like?" CG puffed further on his tobacco stick, and the cinder shone. His task was to watch this apartment complex of Aaron's questionable friends. If they left, he was to follow them.

With the confidence of Morrison behind his back, Peabody whispered, "You've got to be kidding me, man. You're under a streetlight, for Pete's sake. You might as well put a flashing blue light on your baseball cap. And don't call me a nitwit."

Stepping up to the car, CG growled, "If no one knows I'm on a stakeout, then they won't be suspicious of me. But you're blowing my cover, you moron. Now get out of here. You're ruining my aloof presence in the neighborhood."

Morrison leaned forward so that his face lit up. "Hey, CG. You're just enjoying a cigar, if anyone asks. Right?"

"Hey, Morrison, I didn't see you there. I'm just out for an evening stroll and stopped to enjoy my cigar. I haven't seen any action yet."

"You've got my number if you do." He closed Peabody's window and slowly drove away, turning down the next street.

"That guy is ridiculous, Boss. That can't be how you do it, puffing away, staring down the front door, and looking up into the windows."

"Maybe being obvious will get him beat up," Morrison smirked, then shook his head.

Peabody chuckled. "That image cheered me up. Let's retake our loop downtown. Maybe we'll see activity this time around."

"Sure, but before we do, why don't I give you a little stakeout training."

The rookie bolted upright. "Really? Okay!"

"I'm doubling back to park behind the apartment building that CG is watching. Stay here and see what I do." Morrison kept to the shadows, moved behind a shrub, and perched himself on the building's gas meter. Grabbing onto an exterior pipe, he climbed to the second floor, peered into a window, watched for a while, and climbed down.

In the car, Morrison reported, "Aaron's friends have a tough exterior, but they're chilling at home, playing video war games, as young men do when they don't take part in a real war."

Peabody gawked, impressed by Morrison's boldness. "Well, that's good to know."

"Listen, you don't need to waste your breath on CG," Morrison advised. "Let him enjoy his cigar. It's up to him to realize he can be identified by the guys he's watching. People often don't listen. You can tell someone how or what to do, but it doesn't mean they'll do it. They do what they want."

"Why not? You're his boss?"

"Simple. They either think they know better, or they don't respect you. I've seen people's eyes glaze over when I'm talking to them. I know when they aren't listening to what I'm saying."

His rookie partner cocked his head, wondering if he said he was psychic. Morrison caught his eye. "Hey, you have to learn how to read people. The strange thing about two-way communication is that you never know if it's taking place unless you are paying attention. You could be pouring your heart out to someone or giving a coworker information they need, and they are just out there in la-la land, tuned into the channel of their thoughts. They could be thinking about what they're going to have for lunch.

"When I see the eye glaze, I change the conversation to test them, and guess what, Peabody? Some don't even notice.

"I may say, 'Hey, what are you going to have for lunch?' If they don't catch on, I change the subject; I know they live in a small, small world. You don't have to create an issue because you are now informed that you can't depend on them, so you find someone else. So far, Peabody, you're doing alright, and now you have a better idea of what I am looking for in a detective."

Morrison rubbed his chin with a fresh idea. "I wonder how Reggie Crumberton, the veteran, is doing. I'll have to check in on him. He has skills."

Peabody nodded in agreement with the idea. "He seems like a good man."

The detectives did two more rounds of all locations. Each was less fulfilling than the first. Even CG was still under the lamppost, with the Alfred Hitchcock-type silhouette, puffing away on his cigar as an undercover dragon. The yawning detectives called it a night.

***

On Sunday, Morrison made an appointment to visit Reggie at the hospitality center. They sat in the outdoor garden.

"Good to see you again, Detective." Reggie shook his hand.

"I just thought I'd stop and see how you're doing."

"Well, thank you. Ms. Zelda has found me a small apartment, and I'll be moving in this week. I'm doing all right, considering."

"That's excellent. Have you found any job opportunities yet?"

"Not yet. I am planning to investigate an experimental drug called MDMA. They say it assists in relieving the war trauma of PTSD. It naturally helps to rewire the brain and stop the trauma response. It's worked for others. We'll see."

"That sounds promising." Morrison pondered his next thought. He wanted to know Reggie better but didn't want to pry. "I imagine you lost a few friends in Afghanistan."

"I lost many, too many to count in five tours. I have seen things no one should see in a foreign land, yet it is meaningless to everyone here. For the past two years, I hid from the world. I felt I could not relate to anyone because they did not know my sorrow. They could never understand.

"When we relive the sorrow, the emotions stay too raw, creating a trigger. And I paid for it. I felt my reputation had been ruined for living this way. I had a repeating thought that kept me there. 'I've been broken, branded, and burned. I've been shredded, sullied, and scorned'.

"You see, as a homeless person, I became a nobody–it's worse than non-existence because you must live with the downward looks, the upturned nose, repeated harm by opinions and judgments by others. No one offers a cure for your sorrow or a kind word. They only offer disdain and looks of distrust. And that is why I hid deep in the shadows and corners of life where no one could access me.

"Eventually, it seemed I did not exist to them because they would no longer see me in their world even when I was there. And strangely, that is the wonder and magic of disappearing in plain sight. It was where I became free. I used my Special Force skills. I purposely created a dirty, rough version of myself without care to keep people away. And sometimes, I elicited feelings of sympathy, so people would bring me food or give me a coin. I didn't care anymore."

"But you have re-emerged," Morrison said.

"This is only a disguise. These shiny teeth are false, the clean clothes and shave will let me move through this world again, but I will always be who I was on the streets or in war. Those experiences last, like a brand or tattoo. They may become blurry with age and distorted, but you can never remove the memory. You only adapt. And so, I have permitted myself to let the extreme memories live in the past, forgotten for now. I believe I will make those memories my friend one day because they are chapters in my book of life.

"That's a wise way of looking at it. I admired you."

"So, I have a new repeating thought, 'Every second, I am creating a new present moment.' When I fully realize that idea, I will have won the battle with myself and the past."

"That sounds good. You've already come a long way, Reggie. Let's stay in touch. I could use someone with your attention to detail as a consultant occasionally. Once you're settled, give me a call, would you?"

"Yes, sir, I may just do that. Thank you. I appreciate you recognizing I might have something to offer."

"Keep in touch. I may have some work for you." They shook hands.

Morrison walked to his vehicle with plenty to consider: three cases and a lack of answers and evidence.

CHAPTER 40

Lucky Charm
Saturday - morning

Since Karl could not cross the crime scene tape at the museum, he became so irritable that Isadore proposed they visit the Mystic Seaport Museum. She knew the change of scenery, maritime history, paintings, and wooden boats would keep his mind occupied. They could spend hours at the compound, a recreated seafaring village from the 1800s consisting of sixty historic buildings on nineteen acres.

Mother and son left their home at 10 a.m. and arrived at the museum's entrance within ten minutes. Isadore took her son's arm as they walked.

Karl welcomed the diversion. He had not visited the museum in several months, and a new J.M.W. Turner art exhibit was installed that interested him. He also knew the whaling ship Charles W. Morgan was docked on the river. The circa 1841 vessel had been restored at Mystic Seaport, and Karl was looking forward to going aboard.

"I've been thinking, Mother, of calling Detective Hanniford to ask if I may take the train to Boston. I feel it is necessary to meet with the BFA Museum's board of trustee president on Monday. He must hear that I am serious about my responsibility for the Cassatt painting. I can also meet with the department that handles theft and insurance. I wish to follow their instructions to the letter. They need to know I will be available and involved as much as possible." Karl's quiet desperation was evident.

"Darling, you should go. They already know you are dedicated by putting up the reward, yet your arrival will show them you are also devoted. I would hope the detective sees how important it is." She squeezed his arm. "Maybe you should call him now so you can make a plan."

They found a bench, and he made the call. He explained his idea of visiting Boston, and Hanniford said he would let him know in a few hours. Karl took a deep breath and tried to focus on the serene surroundings along the Mystic River as swans, kayakers, and paddleboarders passed by.

He hooked Isadore's arm again, and they continued their promenade to their first stop inside the museum. The J.M.W. Turner exhibit, curated by the British Museum, boasted ninety-two watercolors and four oils. The Seaport

Museum was the only American museum to show these works, which thrilled the mother-son duo to have them so close to home.

Isadore smiled at her twofold success: she diverted Karl's attention, and they luxuriated in the presence of Turner's immensely famous paintings.

Saturday - 1:00 p.m.

The detective gave the green light for Karl to go to Boston. He had been in contact with the Fine Arts Museum and reported his efforts to recover the stolen painting. Currently empty-handed, Hanniford figured allowing Karl to make the trip to the BFA Museum would show his department's cooperation with the institution. He told Karl to be back by Monday evening. In the meantime, he had his hands full with interviews, videos to review, and the hunt for evidence.

Meanwhile, in the City of Steeples, Detective Morrison felt like he was trudging waist-deep in mud as he slogged through mounds of paperwork, photographs, videos, interviews, and stakeout reports on three cases: Marilyn's homicide, Cora's abduction, and Aaron's death. The specter of New London's unfortunate events was in the newspapers, television, and online. Morrison felt a strong internal drive to resolve at least one of them.

"Peabody, my gut keeps telling me intruders have infiltrated our fair City of Steeples and are giving it a bad rap. We need some evidence to prove my gut is right." Tapping away on the computer, Peabody looked up. "Boss, is that like women's intuition?"

Morrison thought of his Irish mom, who believed in it. "Yes, and one day, when your gut tells you it's suspicious, and the end result of a case proves your gut was right, you'll know how it works."

The phone rang, and Peabody took the call. "Boss, the medical examiner's office is working overtime and wants you to stop by." Morrison gratefully left his paper load behind and took off. He was hopeful the autopsy of Aaron could provide some conclusive results.

Dr. Storm's assistant escorted Morrison into the morgue. A sheet covered Aaron on the examining table. Dr. Storm lifted her protective eye gear and moved away from the body toward the detective. She launched into her observations about the state of Aaron's body.

"Morrison, I examined the blunt force trauma to Aaron's head, but you know my protocol. First is preservation and refrigeration to halt decomposition before the autopsy. Second are the measurements of the organs to quantify length, weight, and volume to describe the amount of blood the victim lost.

The third is collecting body fluid for toxicological testing. And fourth is the internal examination.

"Detective, I've completed all of these, and my determination is Aaron was not hit over the head with a blunt object. His internal injuries are far more complicated— they depict falling from quite some height. In Latin, we say, '*Quoniam res ipsa loquitur*.' That means, 'The thing speaks for itself.'"

"He fell! Did he drown?"

"No. His lungs were clear. Which means he was dead before he landed in the water. Does the museum's second story come close to the water?"

"Well, yes, but...." Morrison imagined Aaron falling off the unfinished rooftop patio and hitting the lawn or the dock. "Hmm, the fall would not have landed him in the water." Perplexed, he realized there was more to review at the scene. He needed to contact Hanniford. They might have video footage of the incident. "Is there anything else?"

"Yes, his organs were a mess, his spleen was ruptured, and his right shoulder and pelvis were broken. All indications of a fall from possibly twenty feet in height. He landed in such a way to cause these injuries." Dr. Storm rolled the protective gloves off her hands and washed them in the sink while her assistant finished with Aaron. Morrison was deep in thought, imagining all the possible scenarios. Dr. Storm turned from the sink and said, "But there is more."

"There is? What else have you found?" He anticipated a helpful clue to ease the search in the swamp of information.

"Well, we must wait until next week, but we will soon find out." She watched the disappointment pass over Morrison's face.

"What am I waiting on?" he asked eagerly.

"The toxicology report will tell us if he was drunk, drugged, or high. It will also help you determine if the fall was an accident or a homicide. You see, his injuries only inform us he fell from some height. Hopefully, you will find that video evidence. The results here tell you he did not walk into the water." Behind her, the assistant wheeled Aaron into cold storage. Dr. Storm continued to remove her implements of protective gear; her scrub cap and hairnet were next.

Morrison leaned against a stainless-steel counter and pondered. "Yes, a video could tell us if he was pushed off the roof. Either way, his body was moved into the water. But why? Can these results be rushed?" He winced. "Waiting is not my strong suit."

"Yes, I can tell." His disclosure of the obvious amused her. "Let me make a few phone calls, and I will find out how fast I can get results. I may have a connection or two if you want me to fast-track this one."

"That would be wonderful." His spirits lifted. "I'm always waiting for lab results, which drives me crazy."

"I suppose that means it doesn't matter what the case is. You will always want me to call in a favor. Right?" Dr. Storm tilted her head and smiled. All the extra protective gear was gone, and she looked like herself again, a natural beauty.

"Of course, I would always want that favor." He traced his finger along the edge of the counter as he said, "Doctor Storm, if you can pull a favor for the lab tests on this case, I will find a way to return the favor." He glanced up to see her response.

She laughed. "I'm just teasing you, Morrison. I have plenty of people who owe me favors. No worries, you're good. I'll let you know how soon we can get the lab results on Monday. Deal?" She held out her hand.

"Deal." He took her hand and smiled. "I have plenty to keep me busy between now and then." He turned to leave, pleased with the results of his visit. "I'll wait to hear from you Monday. Thank you, Dr. Storm."

Morrison read the sign she had placed near the entrance of the building.

"Let conversation cease. Let laughter flee.
This is the place death delights to help the living.
Medical Examiner Motto, Giovanni Morgagni

He tapped the sign. *This is my new lucky charm.* He remembered the Kennedy silver dollar in his pocket that his father had given him and patted it. *It's okay, Dad. No harm in having two lucky charms.* His Irish dad's voice came to mind. *Danny boy, there's no getting by the fact that the real charmer is that pretty angel inside the morgue.*

Morrison smiled as he climbed into his SUV.

CHAPTER 41

Train to Boston
Sunday - 8 a.m.

Karl anxiously tapped his foot on the train platform of the Mystic station. A quick look at his watch proved it was late by five minutes. He heard a distant whistle which meant it was passing through downtown on approach. Karl heaved a sigh. He disliked lateness, no matter the cause. His eternal impatience was that the world didn't run by his watch.

Once aboard the train, Karl felt the relief of leaving behind the drama in Mystic. His heartbeat slowed. Karl selected his favorite seat by the window in the dining car, facing the oncoming views. Soon, the shoreline water inlets and salt marshes zoomed by. He felt propelled into his future. *I'm homesick for Boston and our old Brownstone in Back Bay.*

The train whistle announced the next stop: Westerly, Rhode Island. Peering down the branching streets, he remembered walking downtown with his mother. They ate lunch by the river, strolled in the park, and slipped in and out of the handsome historic buildings that housed specialty shops.

The clicking sounds of the wheels on the tracks resumed. The rocking of the train lulled Karl. His eyes closed, and a memory of a childhood misadventure came forward.

***

When Karl was eight years old, his mother stopped to buy him a pumpkin at a country farm. Karl saw a sign for a corn maze and asked if he could go in. She refused. When her back was turned, he raced into it. Running in a cornfield was freedom compared to the confines of their Brownstone in Boston.

Spreading his arms wide, he raced through the cornstalks, touching the leaves on either side of the path. He raised his eyes to the sun and inhaled the fresh air of greens and soil. Then ran straight into a dead end. Doubling back, he went through hairpin turns and reached another dead end. Little did he know, the maze was giant, and adults were meant to accompany children.

Sweat and thirst caused him to slow his racing for an exit. Karl jumped, but the green wall was too high. He yelled for help, thinking the staff would come running, but no one responded. Squeezing between the stalks made him too claustrophobic. His face brushed against the corn-silken cobs, and the sweet scent made him think of his mother.

In 1974, this multiacre farmstead created the corn maze for families, but the owners still needed to determine what to do when someone was lost. Isadore realized Karl had disobeyed when she couldn't find him. She became frantic on the outskirts of the maze, shouting demands and ordering the staff to find her son.

A bird's-eye view would have shown Karl was in the middle of the maze. The farmstead offered maps, but Karl hadn't taken one. Hopeless and exhausted, he moped and sat. Peering into the cornstalks, he hugged his folded knees.

He rested his head, closed his eyes, and thought about his favorite place: the Isabella Stewart Gardner Mansion. It, too, was like a maze of sorts. The rooms were large, and one could easily get turned around. Yet his father had taught him how to use the map and not become lost. Karl would always first go to his favorite painting in the Dutch Room.

It was of a youthful Rembrandt. He wore a cap with a tall feather and a pale cloak with a gold chain. The self-portrait looked directly into Karl's eyes. At the age of twenty-three, Rembrandt had portrayed himself with the gentle face of a refined young man.

Soon, young Karl fell asleep in the maze, and his memory became a dream. He was staring at Rembrandt, who winked at him, then stepped out of the painting and held out his hand. Karl clasped it, and together they raced into the great Tapestry Room where banquets and fine dinners were once served. Proceeding to an open window, the two peered down into the multistoried atrium garden. Palm trees and ancient sculptures flanked its Roman mosaic floors. Orchids, lilies, and pots of cascading jasmine filled the courtyard with floral scents.

The giggling adventurers ran the length of the heavily decorated room to their target, a grand fireplace. They each grabbed a fire iron and played a mock duel. Laughing, they dropped their pretend swords and escaped into a narrow wood-paneled passage. Karl entered a room rich with religious icons, but Rembrandt didn't follow. Karl caught sight of Mary and baby Jesus, and his mother came to mind.

In the corn maze, she called out his name. He woke from his dream. Leaping, he grabbed her waist. "I will never, never leave you again, Mother."

"Never?" Isadore asked. Her concerns melted away as he was only lost and not taken.

"Never, Mother," he promised, wiping his tears on her dress.

Later, his mother told him, "Your father and I will show you many kinds of mazes and how to use a map so you will never be lost again."

During the family's world travels, he sought the mazes and labyrinths. They existed in churches, gardens, courtyards, and palaces. All had intricate, unique designs of their own. He learned labyrinths usually ended at a central goal, whereas mazes were often complex, concealed courses with dead ends.

When Karl was an older teenager, Isadore taught him not to be bothered or bullied by people and to think like an adult.

"You can create a labyrinth in people's minds to gain favor. You only need to feed them candy such as gifts, compliments, dinner, or a grand gesture now and then. But even your enemies, Karl, must respect you, even if they don't like you. Eventually, they will turn their face to you and their back on your enemies. And for the enemies you dislike, build them a golden bridge."

Karl's mouth dropped open. "Why, Mother, why would I build them a bridge of gold?"

"Listen," she said, "if they are bad enough, and you don't want them around, then build them the best golden bridge you can. A glittering edifice of promises that leads them away from you. You find them a better opportunity or a better pawn than you to achieve their means or mean games. They will be grateful to cross that metaphorical bridge, and you will have led them out of your life. They will think it is kindness, but for you, it is liberation."

It was at this moment that Karl knew his mother was wise. These were nuances of the human mind he had never considered.

"Remember," she said, "don't underestimate anyone. You must be your own man and protect yourself at all costs. Your career in the fine arts world will depend on holding your head high."

***

Karl drifted from his dreams and memories and opened his eyes. His recollection of this conversation confirmed his feelings about his mother. Even though she was bossy, challenging at times, and a little rude, he could count on her to help him through trying times.

Glancing out the train's window, he could see the beautiful Boston skyline. "I'm back!" he whispered.

The taxi waited while he entered his room at the Boston Park Plaza hotel. He dropped off his bag and promptly took the cab to his place of adoration, the historical Isabella Stewart Gardner Mansion.

CHAPTER 42

Isabella's Mansion
Sunday - Boston

Karl's arrival at the mansion felt monumental as he imagined walking in the footsteps of its creator, Isabella.

Yet as he did, his thoughts drifted to his workplace a few blocks away for nearly forty years as a conservator at the Boston Fine Arts Museum. His duty was to protect the art's cultural heritage and to preserve the artist's original intent. His professional specialty was artworks from the thirteenth to fifteenth centuries. Karl now craved to restore his reputation.

Trained in chemistry, his examination required a series of scientific processes to restore and rehabilitate paintings. He also collaborated with museums from around the world. When Karl had a strict deadline, he would work late into the night, particularly on a painting he loved. He often took a long lunch and walked the two blocks to Isabella's mansion to be inspired by her selected art.

Worldly excursions during Isabella's time in the late 1800s and early 1900s proved that art and antiquities were not only available but affordable and discoverable, especially for the wealthy. Karl was enamored with her achievements and collections, and he would daydream about joining her on a buying trip in Europe. *If only I were living then.*

Karl heaved a sigh. Pushing away his thoughts, he focused on his well-worn routine of roaming in Isabella's mansion. His first stop was the multistoried atrium courtyard, a formal layout filled with flowering plants and sculptures. The ambience of her indoor garden captured his senses. He took a deep breath of the floral aroma and let his tension drop by a fraction. He closed his eyes and imagined Isabella standing beside him. This gave him comfort.

With hands clasped behind his back, the art expert strolled across a hall to the Spanish Cloister. Here he admired a painting that was so large it appeared to be a performance in another room. A tall flamenco dancer was poised in a dramatic move. Her grand gestures were echoed by dancers succumbing to the joyous Spanish rhythms. In addition, expressive musicians strummed guitars and sang passionately. Karl imagined Isabella had placed *El Jaleo,* one of her John Singer Sargent paintings, near the entrance for one reason: to alert every visitor that this was *her domain and her choice of art.*

Karl, impressed by Isabella's confidence, wished he had some for his visit to the BFA in the morning. *I expect to be disgraced.*

To divert his thoughts, he examined Sargent's dynamic technique. Karl's keen eye knew the secret. It was the high contrast of colors and tones. The white of the flamenco dancer's flowing skirt juxtaposed against the image of her shadow on the wall and the black garments of the musicians. A splash of red in a dancer's dress on the right connected the eye to a smidge of red on the left. This was part of Sargent's brilliance, the art of directing one's vision across an enormous painting. He knew how to coax the eye and hold the viewer's interest.

Karl purposely moved to the Yellow Room to swipe away the haunting thoughts of Aaron's death and the stolen painting. Temporarily, he was alleviated by gazing at the famous paintings by Turner, Matisse, Degas, and Whistler. One of his mother's favorites was *Love's Greeting* by Dante Gabriel Rossetti. And in the Blue Room, he admired an original manuscript by Ralph Waldo Emerson, and a painting called *The Omnibus,* from 1892 by Anders Zorn, of a young lady traveling alone. She was an example of a new trend, the independence of unchaperoned women. A theme Isabella had emphasized her entire life.

The Blue Room gave Karl many memories of his childhood visits with his parents. And yet, a painting that reminded him of his kind father was gone, and it shot pangs into Karl to not see it on the wall. *Chez Tortoni* by Édouard Manet was stolen in 1990. It depicted a gentleman with a mustache and top hat looking up from writing a letter.

Karl stopped in the Gothic Room to stand before Isabella's portrait. He stared at her striking subdued beauty. The neckline of her black dress created a heart-shaped décolletage. She wore a pearl choker with a ruby pendant. Around her tiny waist was a double strand of pearls. Her hands gently came together, creating an oval frame for the pearls.

John Singer Sargent finished the painting in 1888 when Isabella was forty-seven. Women were not to show their strength of character at the time. The image received much controversial press, and her husband refused to have it viewed publicly. It was not seen until 1925, after her death.

Karl felt the opinions of cruel people and art critics who relished demeaning her, unfortunately, influenced her husband. Yielding to their pressures, he banished her painting.

Karl continued to stare at his infatuation, Isabella. He whispered to her, "Isabella, you were a creative artist, a world traveler, a deep thinker, and a desirous friend with some of the most famous artists in the world, and I wish I were your friend."

Though they were nearly one hundred years apart in age, Karl decided Isabella was the only woman he could have loved. They both learned that art and travel took away the painful memories of grief. She had lost a child; he had lost his father when he was sixteen.

He also imagined Isabella felt like him about great artists who could capture light and air on canvas and bring heaven down to earth. They would also agree that a painting enjoyed with a loved one created happy memories. The images he and his father loved were Vermeer's *The Concert* and Rembrandt's *The Storm on the Sea of Galilee.* Both were stolen with others in 1990, but his memory of them brought him closer to his father. He silently wished he could hear his wise counsel and be unburdened.

Karl left his beloved Isabella's mansion at closing. The typically cocky and confident man was grappling with feelings of self-doubt. For the first time in his life, he felt inferior. He had no control over his misfortune. His judgment would be handed down in the morning, and he felt much like a man going to the gallows. His reputation and profession were hanging on the line.

Facts: Fenway Court

Isabella Stewart Gardner purchased land in the Fenway section of Boston after her husband, John (Jack) L. Gardner's death in 1898. The building's design was fashioned after Renaissance homes in Venice. It was made to house the fine art, furnishings, and collections she and Jack had acquired while traveling the world.

In 1903, she opened it to the public as a museum called Fenway Court and held a grand celebration on New Year's Day with a performance by the Boston Symphony Orchestra. In her words, Isabella created an endowment in her will to support the museum in perpetuity "for the education and enjoyment of the public forever." It became known as The Isabella Stewart Gardner Museum and was gifted to the city of Boston in her will after her death in 1924. The museum is on the National Register of Historic Places.

CHAPTER 43

The Red House

At noon on Sunday, Georgi drove his burgundy PT Cruiser down Ocean Avenue to pick up Roxanne. He swung into her driveway, tooting his horn with excitement. Roxanne bounded down her front stairs and opened the passenger door. "Hi, Georgi." She could see Marco in the back seat. "Hi Marco, I'm so glad you could come along."

"Me too! I haven't been to the countryside recently, or The Red House, so this is a little adventure for me."

"Yes, on both counts. Sam asked me to look for gifts for the family, and Georgi said it's next door to an ice cream stand, so we'll have fun." She gave her friends a twinkling smile.

"But don't forget the real reason we are here." Georgi sang, "We are organizing a reconnaissance mission."

"Georgi!" Marco swatted his head, and Roxanne pinched his arm.

"Ow, owww!" Georgi cried. "Alright, you two, we are here for art, here to shop, and here to chat! Is that better?"

"Yes!" Roxanne and Marco agreed.

Georgi drove for twenty minutes, heading north out of New London, and came to Darling Road. He passed the ice cream stand and arrived at the driveway of The Red House Cultural Arts Center. The long, narrow avenue of trees created a shady canopy entrance.

"Ooh, I feel like I'm entering another realm," Marco cooed.

"Yes, nature's realm," Roxanne said softly.

The one-story Red House was revealed at the end of the lane. The owners generously offered a gallery and gift shop for local artists and artisans to display their work. They made a low percentage, so the artists kept most of the money.

Hopping out of the car, the three spotted a dozen artists' tents in the art center's yard. "There's Troy," Georgi said, pointing. "Ophelia and Katlyn too!" He headed toward their tents to say hello when he noticed K.C. "Hey, my fine friend." He hugged K.C. "Show me your work."

K.C. led him through the tent, where he had set up sculptures and original paintings. "My favorite pieces are your puppets," Georgi complimented, "but I also love your monster-themed chess sets." Suddenly, Georgi jolted with enthusiasm. "I have an idea. Can I hire you to do a pair of puppets? One of Marco and one of me. I think it would be a great surprise for him at Christmas."

K.C. gave him a broad smile. "Of course, making you into a puppet will be amusing. Marco can operate it and tell you what to say." He nudged Georgi jokingly.

Georgi put a hand on his hip. "You're teasing me?" The artist gave him a wry imp-like smile. "But K.C., I want my puppet to be handsome, and you can make Marco's puppet look like a monster." K.C. rolled his eyes. "I'm kidding," Georgi sang, "he wouldn't like that." Just then, a pair of customers approached K.C.'s tent. Georgi stepped aside.

Roxanne and Marco talked to Troy, Ophelia, and Katlyn near their art tents. Each had colorful and dynamic work. Georgi joined them and whispered, "Does anyone know who was with Aaron last Thursday night?"

"I spoke to several of the volunteers who were with him," Ophelia replied, "and they said he stayed behind to go to the bathroom just as they were leaving."

"Does anyone here think he was involved in the art theft?" Roxanne asked. Everyone shook their head.

"There is no way," said Troy. "I told Detective Morrison that Aaron and Marguerite were too sweet to be caught up in this. Since we all think Aaron is innocent, he might have snuck up to check out the rooftop patio. We all know how much he liked parkour training on rooftops. He was always practicing downtown, jumping from one roof to the another or balancing on the edges."

"What if he saw the thieves, and they killed him?" Ophelia guessed.

"I think our goal is to ask around our art community," Troy offered. "What if someone heard about the painting being forged? Any news about that or Aaron would be helpful."

"It doesn't seem connected to Marilyn and Cora, does it?" Katlyn asked. "None of us saw the man from her sketch at the museum that night."

Troy shared, "I think some of Marilyn's paintings were taken when she was murdered." The group audibly gasped. Katlyn's hand covered her mouth, and Georgi's went to his forehead.

"We hadn't heard this!" Ophelia's hand went to her heart. "Oh my, Marilyn's paintings are worth a lot more now! Were any of Cora's paintings taken?"

"No," Troy answered. "I don't think Marilyn and Cora are connected to Aaron or the Cassatt painting being stolen."

Georgi crossed his arms in frustration. "None of this makes sense. But maybe, just maybe, we can set a trap."

"What?" Marco whipped his head toward Georgi. "You cut that out, Mister Wanna-Be Detective."

"He's right, Georgi," Roxanne persuaded. "This is out of our league. I'm concerned for all of you. We must wait and see what the detectives come up with. They have lots of technology at their fingertips. Let's gather information and leave it at that. Look, it's time we enjoy the day now."

"Sorry, everyone. I think I've transitioned from feeling extremely sad to seriously mad," revealed Georgi, "and I don't want to be either of those. I want to be active, to feel like I'm helping."

Troy nudged him. "We're all in this together. Don't put all the weight on your shoulders."

The friends scattered. Georgi and Marco roamed the grounds visiting various artist tents while Roxanne walked into the store to admire the creative selections. Artists presented jewelry, scarves, books, handbags, sculptures, and artisanal crafts. She knew she could find all the gifts needed for friends and family.

One artisan had sculpted life-like animals from felted wool, mythical unicorns, and characters reminiscent of children's storybooks.

Kim, the owner of The Red House, saw Roxanne inspecting the felted works. She was slim and stylish with short-cropped hair. "That's Lori's work. Isn't she talented? She also teaches felting classes on how to make them."

"They have a presence as if they'll come to life," murmured Roxanne. "My nieces would love them. And are you an artist too?" she asked.

"Pottery is my thing. Those are my vases and bowls on the shelves." The elegant pottery was showcased prominently in shades of white, blue, turquoise, green, and warm brown glazes.

Roxanne selected one and then admired the fine art paintings. "These works are exquisite. Are the frames custom too?"

"They are handmade by my husband, Barry. He's a woodworker. One of his many talents."

"What else does he do?" Roxanne asked, enjoying the quiet conversation.

"He loves wine, and he's done a few successful wine and art auctions. He's a bit of an aficionado."

"He must meet my friend Georgi. He's a wine expert too."

Kim waved to Barry, and Roxanne found Georgi. A friendly man with a trimmed gray beard and glasses approached. Barry greeted them, and Roxanne blurted, "Georgi, Barry is a wine aficionado like you! And he has hosted wine and art auctions! Isn't that a wonderful idea?"

The two men spoke sommelier. Soon, Kim and Roxanne realized they couldn't keep up with the wine lingo, so they wandered off.

Georgi was thrilled to discuss his passion with someone new. "What are your favorite wines, Barry?"

"Reds are my favorite, but where should I start? Off the top of my head, I'll tell you what is in my wine cellar. If it's Italian, then a 2015 Banfi Brunello di Montalcino or the 2016 Antinori Solaia. But if it is French, Chateau Talbot Saint Julien. Or Portuguese; I love the 1985 Graham's Vintage Port. And don't worry; I have American and Australian wines too."

Georgi was brimming with glory. "Oh, my heart! You know your wine. But tell me how to host a wine and art auction." Barry explained the detailed process to raise funds for the artists and nonprofits.

"Barry, if I create an event like that, would you be willing to assist? We'll brainstorm together, of course."

"Just let me know when and where, and I'll see what I can do." They shook hands and were interrupted by a patron.

Georgi found Troy and whispered, "I have an idea brewing in my brain. Can we meet for lunch this week?"

"Sure, buddy. You're buying. Right? I'm unsure how much I will make today, and I have bills to pay."

"Of course, Troy. My business is a little more constant than yours. Lunch is on me. I will text you late morning with the time and place. I think you're going to like what I'm dreaming up."

Troy watched him suspiciously, then smiled. "Whatever you're dreaming up must be more interesting than what I have going on. Bruce and Teddy have been working on a new multicultural mural for downtown, so I'm practically alone at the Dahlia residence. Ophelia has been staying with friends, and Cora is at her parents.

Georgi nudged him, "Death changes everything. We need to appreciate each other. We may be a big dysfunctional downtown community at times, but we all have one goal: to thrive. So, I will scheme and dream our way through this situation of mayhem if it's the last thing I do, Troy."

Chuckling, Troy added, "I should put you and Roxanne on my speed dial for instant pep talks."

CHAPTER 44

Marguerite

At two o'clock on Sunday afternoon, Marguerite Santa Maria walked along the river by the Mystic River Fine Art Museum. She stopped at the crime scene tape, which was still taut around the dock, where Aaron, her year-long boyfriend, had been found. The short train ride from New London made it easy for her to visit the place Aaron's spirit had transcended into the light.

Sitting on a nearby bench, Marguerite gazed into the river's current and watched it slowly move toward the sea. She wanted to place her aching heart, her broken spirit, into that current and disappear into deep waters. Only then would she hurt no longer.

With her head in her hands and heartbroken, she cried. Her long dark hair was a sponge for her tears.

Nearby in the parking lot next to the museum, a woman placed a garment bag in her car. She spotted Marguerite in distress and wandered over and asked why she was crying. Marguerite told her about Aaron. The older lady said she knew of the incident and wanted to comfort her, so she invited her to tea at a nearby café.

She ordered a traditional British delight of scones with jam and clotted cream. "There's nothing better than strong tea for the spirit and sweets for the heart," the woman gave her a pleasant smile. Marguerite was grateful to share her grief with this friendly stranger. The lady listened while the tea steeped in its pot.

When Marguerite briefly excused herself to use the restroom, the woman poured each of them a cup of tea. She pulled from her handbag a small brown vial. "This will help comfort the poor dear," she murmured. Discreetly, she squeezed a brown tincture into a teacup and stirred. Upon Marguerite's return, she asked, "How do you like your tea, dear?"

"Milk and sugar, please." Just then, scones and cream arrived.

After an hour, the woman saw that Marguerite's emotions and state of mind seemed to improve. Her mood was lifted from the tea, food, and conversation. Gazing out the window, Marguerite's voice lilted dreamily, "I'd like to go for a walk by the water. I feel so much better now. Thank you for spending time with me. Please tell me again. I've forgotten your name."

"It's Mrs. Leonardo, my dear. I'm so glad you're feeling better." And they parted ways.

Marguerite sauntered past the shops downtown, feeling strangely removed from her grief. As music emanated from a convertible playing a smooth beat, Marguerite hummed the tune and swayed her skirt to the rhythm.

She strolled across Main Street and walked away from the bustling town center to explore the residential neighborhoods along the Mystic River. It brought her to the quiet rural area where nature and the river became one.

On this sultry August day, Marguerite felt lighter, as if peace and harmony rested on her soul. Sensing a breeze, her skin tingled with a unique effervescence. Her upsetting reality had morphed into surreal tranquility. She gathered wildflowers and was surprised that colors from nature began to rise into the air and swirl. She followed a path that led into the salt marsh.

Once on the river's edge, she thought to lay her flowers as a memorial for Aaron. Her sandals automatically slipped off her feet. She then placed her small purse on the shore. Slowly, in dreamlike fashion, she stepped forward into the warm summer water carrying her wildflower tribute. The soft sand oozed a web between her toes, and she heaved a sigh of comfort from the sensation.

The nearby cattails, purple loosestrife, and pink rugosa roses perfumed the air. The sweet scent became intense and soothed her heart. She felt encouraged to wade deeper to cast her bouquet, so it might drift.

Pausing, she clutched the flowers to her chest and whispered a prayer for Aaron. The cicada's summer mating song joined her murmured appeal, rang in her ears, and reached a crescendo like the chanting of Tibetan monks. In awe, she gazed around her and watched as poplar leaves, lifted by a breeze, clapped in approval to her prayer and the song. Marguerite felt nature was healing her heart.

Soon, a pair of swallows swooped about her and skimmed the glassy water mirror. Their beaks broke the surface for a drink, and her dreamy world of nature rippled, rippled, rippled.

Inhaling deeply, Marguerite thought, *Aaron must be gloriously peaceful in a place like this.* She stepped forward, into the warmth of the water's embrace. It rose to her lavender sundress, and she absorbed the reflection of the puffy white clouds and blue sky above. Impulsively, she slipped in to float on the mirror of the sky with her bouquet in hand.

Her long dark hair, lovely face, and sundress floated on the surface as if in a watery frame. The dress glistened like the gossamer wings of dragonflies that dived and dipped around her.

Bringing the flowers to her chest, she imagined Aaron, and her tears melded with the tidal waters. Curious minnows gathered, attracted by her ever-so-slow traverse, and they followed as she drifted along. A mourning dove cooed when she passed below a willow's weeping branch of silvery fronds. And without any thought, Marguerite, in a dreamlike trance slowly descended below the waterline toward her love.

***

Sunday evening, Marguerite's family members called the New London Police Department, stating she had not arrived for a planned dinner and was unreachable.

CHAPTER 45

Karl's Reckoning
Monday – Boston Fine Arts Museum

An opulent white marble staircase beckoned Karl into the main entrance foyer of the BFA Museum. Reverently, he ascended, and as he did, he felt the Greek and Roman statues stationed on each side of the stairs judging him for his negligence and mocking him for the loss of the Mary Cassatt painting. Flanking his procession to the rotunda were giant stone Doric columns.

The awe-inspiring space typically brought Karl upliftment, but today, he felt diminished by the magnificence. He glanced at an oval fresco overhead depicting a tribute to the arts. Two golden-winged sphinxes were below the fresco. The sentinels protected a two-foot gray urn. Karl imagined it housed the ashes of famous artists, and if he didn't do well with his meetings, he would need an urn of his own.

The board of trustees' president had told Karl to meet with the museum's director first. They did so in the wood-paneled board room with seating for thirty people. The director, Charles Whittemore, and Karl had known each other for years. They shook hands, and he welcomed Karl to have a seat. Charles informed Karl that the investigation so far, determined that the Mystic River Fine Art Museum's security system had failed on several counts. The BFA held this top-notch security company responsible. Karl felt a slight relief.

Charles remained standing. He pointed to a large screen on the wall. "I'll play the video we received from the Mystic Police Department." Captivated, Karl watched the footage from the evening of the theft. The director commentated as the events played out on the screen.

"It was discovered that the security system went down twice during the evening, once at ten thirty-five and again at eleven-thirty. In both cases, the backup system failed. It gave no indication of failure, no alarms, and no warning. Therefore, the security company was not alerted, and there was no video feed to reference.

"Here is the last image as Isadore goes into the maintenance closet at ten thirty-five. The system revives when she leaves the closet at eleven o'clock. If we only watched her image and didn't look at the time stamp, this easily could have been missed. You told us you left the museum before ten-forty, but we did not see you because the cameras were down.

"Approximately twenty-five minutes are missing, but the good news is that when the video image returned at eleven, you can see the original Cassatt painting was still on the wall. Here is when Isadore exits the broom closet, picks up her bags, and sets the front door alarm to leave. The parking lot attendant acknowledged that she had left at eleven o'clock.

"But here is what happens when the thieves arrive at 11:30 p.m. The museum's back door camera catches them as they enter the code into the keypad. Soon after, the video screen turned black, and the whole system is disarmed."

Charles paced back and forth with his hands clasped behind his back, then stopped. "Karl, we believe the security company had an inside man or woman who hacked the system. Possibly, they tested it at ten thirty-five while you, Isadore, and Aaron were still inside. More on that later. The operation's mastermind possibly hired these uniformed characters to steal the painting. But you know what really boils our blood?"

Karl's fingers were pressed against his lips. He lifted them to say, "What could be worse?"

"We received this video last night. Detective Hanniford obtained it from the marina across the river from the museum. The camera is at least two hundred feet away. The footage is dark and grainy, but we can see two things. Watch this."

Frozen, Karl stared at the video. From a different angle, it showed an old lobster boat slowly approaching the museum's dock, and two figures secured it to a piling. When they disembarked, one carried a flat rectangular shape that looked like an art portfolio case to Karl. Once on the museum lawn, they suddenly stopped, dropped the case, and gestured wildly at each other. To Karl's horror, they pulled on a body-sized image and dragged what he now knew was Aaron into the water. Unceremoniously, the two continued across the property and opened the door to the museum with the case in hand.

The director advanced the footage to show them returning with the exact case less than fifteen minutes later. One entered the boat, and the other untied the dock line. The thieves puttered down the river, leaving no wake.

"As you will see in this video string, various business and home cameras caught their slow escape until they entered rural areas and the open waters of Long Island Sound.

The museum director exclaimed, "They made it look easy! They escaped by water. And we caught something else that was first missed." By now, Karl was as white as a sheet. "Look at this." An earlier scene was displayed from the same distant camera across the river. "Although we have improved it, this is very grainy." He pointed. "Watch here, on the museum's rooftop patio. We believe this is Aaron."

Suddenly, a lone figure emerged at the patio's edge and mounted the parapet. Karl gasped. The person walked along the perimeter. "You can see this oak tree obscures our view of him temporarily." They watched the action for over a minute. The figure continued balancing on the edge until suddenly, he seemed distracted. He wobbled, lost footing, then fell twenty feet to the ground. The impact could not be seen in the dark.

Karl covered his face. Through his hands, he said, "That was Aaron, wasn't it? How was he up there?"

"We believe we know the answer." Karl's mouth hung open as Charles brought up a different video. "Here we are in the museum at 9:55 p.m. All cameras are rolling; the security system is on. We see the bartenders and catering company cleaning up. We see Aaron in the kitchen with the other volunteers. It seems they've had a few drinks. Who knows when they started?

"He mixed his wines and so forth. We see his friends head out the door, and he is right behind them until he decides to go to the bathroom. They leave. Once out of the bathroom, Aaron seems disoriented and walks into the maintenance closet. We never see him leave because the cameras went out. Maybe he passed out. Is there anything he could have slept on?"

Stunned, Karl thought. "Well, the space is about eight by ten. We have cleaning implements, the vacuum, a floor polisher, and a stack of drop cloths in the back corner."

"Yes, he probably used the drop cloths to lie down. Look here, and we see Isadore go in and out of the closet for tote bags, and then she goes into the kitchen and packages up food. The system went down at ten thirty-five. While it was off, Aaron must have woken and made his way upstairs."

Karl held his head. "I'm sorry I wasn't aware of any of this." He thought of Isadore. "Mother could have been harmed!"

Charles thought Karl seemed genuinely shocked. He offered him a reprise. "At this time, the evidence indicates the security company is at fault, Karl. If someone was inside the museum, you should have been alerted. The system failed you, and they will be held accountable.

"When someone entered unlawfully, you and the authorities should have been warned immediately. We are extremely disturbed that the Cassatt painting was stolen. Our art insurance investigator is on the case, as are the police and the FBI's art crime team. The thieves may have crossed state lines while in

Long Island Sound. We are tracking every possible avenue, and the painting may still be recoverable with any luck."

Karl dabbed the sweat from his brow with his pocket square. He felt small and humiliated. He wished to vanish into one of Isabella's Botticelli paintings and never return. Nothing could be worse than the BFA Museum regretting having loaned him the paintings.

"Karl, you worked here for most of your life and have an excellent record. It would have helped if you left with Isadore, considering our valuable paintings were under your care. But this institution has known her for over fifty years as a longtime donor, and the video footage recorded the original painting was still on the wall after you both left that evening.

"We can all see it looks like Aaron was drunk and went up to the rooftop before Isadore left. It could be a strange coincidence that he was there before the theft, but we have not determined that yet. Possibly, he was meant to give them a hand. As you saw, the thieves dragged him into the water to remain undiscovered until later. This indicates a ruthless determination to follow through with their plan, undeterred by his death. It is highly likely they are professional thieves hired for this job."

Karl tried to decipher all the information. His mind replayed the evening: he had watched the video footage, and his ears heard the facts, yet he felt off balance. *How could I have been so unaware? The security system went down, Aaron was in the building, a theft was planned, the river made access easy for the getaway.* Karl's awareness returned to the room. "I will do all I can to assist you, Charles."

"Thank you for making the trip to meet in person, Karl. It shows us that you are just as concerned as we are. We have no reason to doubt your allegiance because of your cooperation and the reward you offered for the painting's return. We view you as a pawn in this theft."

"I never should have left the building before my mother, though it is unlikely a contributing factor to the theft. I admonish myself daily for doing so. It's a small relief to see the painting was on the wall after we both left and that Aaron had not disturbed it either, poor soul. How distressing to learn he was still in the building and the security system was not working. I'm appalled that the security company, so well-known and exorbitant in cost, failed us miserably. What more can I do?"

"Nothing currently, Karl. We will be in touch to let you know when we need you. Excuse me while I brief the board president, and he will see you. Please wait here."

The director reviewed his meeting with the president, who had been secretly listening to their discussion. Both men agreed Karl appeared innocent, but they would continue the covert security detail they had placed on him and his mother since the theft.

Karl tapped his foot nervously. An office assistant peeked in, gave him a tepid smile of sympathy, and withdrew. Within five minutes, the director was back with the board president, Joseph Cragin. He had known Karl for over fifteen years. "Karl, I am sorry we are meeting under these conditions. But I want you to know that the esteem of your family, professionalism and work ethic keep our relationship with you in good standing. The security company has much to answer for, the least of which is negligence," the president stated.

He took a sip of water and eyed Karl. "Since the paintings were vulnerable, we had the Mystic Police Department place an around-the-clock watch on the Mystic River Fine Art Museum. Our people are packaging the remaining paintings to return to our care as we speak. All I can ask is that you continue cooperating with the insurance agency and the authorities involved."

With absolute contrition, Karl responded, "I am grateful, Joseph, to not have fallen out of grace with you and the institution. I am dreadfully sorry this has happened, and I will be available at a moment's notice, day and night, as you see fit."

They shook hands, and Karl left feeling completely wrung out. At a slow pace, he proceeded to the museum café to unwind. He sat with a pot of tea, a croissant, and jam. He reviewed the sequence of events in his mind. *Someone must have planned the theft after I advertised that the priceless exhibit was coming from the BFA Museum.*

Karl was haunted by the video of Aaron on the museum rooftop patio and the lobster boat arriving with two people. The museum's cameras, meant to face the water, were due to be installed in another week. Current construction had held up the adjunct to the current system.

In that short time, no one considered theft would occur via easy access to the river conduit, to open waters, into the sound, the ocean, and who-knows-where. The escape possibilities were endless.

I should have been thinking like a thief. What have I done? I'm an idiot to have left before Mother. It wouldn't have mattered; they would have accomplished it anyway. Zounds! I relaxed my obsessive nature for one second, and look what happened. I should never have hosted the art in my small museum. I should have known better than to put those paintings in jeopardy.

My excitement to exhibit them outweighed my good sense. I know better. I should have done better.

Karl left the café downtrodden but was relieved at their absolution of his guilt. When he trod down the grand stairs, he overheard two women commenting on the new Dutch and Flemish art gallery. He glanced at his watch. It told him he had time to view the gallery before catching his train home. Although he was exhausted from the meeting, art was his lifeline. He determined that wandering among the great masters could be precisely what he needed to revive himself.

It was like going home when he regarded his favorite art works by Rembrandt, Peter Paul Rubens, Anthony van Dyck, and Frans Hals. For Karl, disassociating from reality was what he had done as a conservator. He lived with and repaired centuries-old paintings, and they were his companions. Their friendly, motionless faces, landscapes, and still-life oil paintings were his welcomed escape.

CHAPTER 46

Road Trip
Monday - 8 a.m.

Dr. Storm called Morrison. "I'm taking blood and tissue samples from the examination of Aaron Goshen's body to New Haven. I've received permission to fast-track them at a privatized lab. Their reputation for identifying unusual toxins and solving difficult cases, with their cutting-edge technology, is known far and wide in the state. They may give me the results today."

The last thing she said rang in Morrison's head, so he jumped on the possibility. "I would be interested in seeing the lab and hearing the results firsthand. Would you mind if I went along for the day?"

She considered the dynamics and reviewed her options before answering. "As long as you don't mind me driving. It's my old stomping ground, and I know all the best parking spots."

"That's fine with me." Morrison imagined the thick traffic on I-95 and was relieved not to drive.

After ending the call, he asked Peabody to keep him abreast of any new findings. "Check Francisco's photos for anyone that looks suspicious or like Mario Corinthian." He packed his laptop, and Peabody smirked. "How long will you be gone, Boss? A couple of days?"

Morrison lifted his eyes. "You know full well this is a day trip. I'm looking forward to meeting the forensic doctor and lab specialists."

"Boss, you're encroaching on Dr. Angela Storm's territory now. Who knows what else she'll find for you to do? You may be busier on 'this case' than you realize." He motioned air quotes. "Once they get a good look at those samples, you may need to stay overnight." His mischievous crooked smile appeared.

Unmoved, Morrison scanned his face. "Give me a break, Peabody. Go find some drama of your own and leave me be." He swung his jacket over his shoulder. "Call one of those ladies you met at the museum. You must have a half dozen women on your 'want to date list'." Morrison shook his head and strode out to his SUV.

Dr. Storm suggested they meet at the crematory next to the I-395 on-ramp. He pulled in and looked for her black Audi. Not seeing it, he mentally sorted through the facts of Aaron's case until he heard a knock at his window.

"Are you ready?" she asked.

"Of course. I didn't see your car." Morrison grabbed his laptop bag, locked his car, and turned to see her standing by a midnight blue Aston Martin DB11. He gawked at the latest European twin-turbocharged engine that went from cruiser to sports car with the push of a button. A long, low whistle escaped his lips while he thought, *Wow, she's full of surprises!* His father's voice kicked in. *She's showing another side of herself, Danny boy. Loosen the tight wrappings you're in and enjoy the ride.*

"This car drives better on the highway," she said matter-of-factly.

"If you say so." He approached the vehicle. Peabody's sly smile flashed in his mind's eye. A fancy car on a long drive with a beautiful woman, while on duty and not the one in charge, had him feeling a little out of his element. He placed his laptop bag in the back and planted himself in the wide plushness of his seat. "How long have you had this?"

"They delivered it yesterday."

"Am I your first passenger?"

"It's the first time I'm driving it," she answered, looking to see his reaction.

"Well, okay then. What can I say? You've got my attention!" He watched the dashboard panel light up.

Angela put the car in gear and entered the ramp to I-395. "Let's see how well it handles on the highway. The stats say it goes one hundred ninety-two miles per hour, but I'm told I must wait until the engine has one hundred miles on the odometer."

Morrison's forehead wrinkled under the force of his raised eyebrows. "Yes, I agree to wait…, and you probably shouldn't have this passenger with you either."

She smiled. "You bet, Detective, and I really don't drive fast. You see, I don't want to end up on one of my tables." He visibly relaxed. She chuckled and tossed her head to the side. "I thought that might ease your mind."

He noticed how nice she looked with her golden hair released from the bindings of her profession. Finally, he caught on. "You're giving me a hard time, aren't you?"

"How else am I to know what you're made of?" she chuckled.

"Ha!"

"Hey, if you take things too seriously or personally, then I'll know I must treat you with kid gloves. But if you have a sense of humor, then at least I know I can work with you."

"Work with me? Don't you already?" he countered.

"Well, I mean *how* to work with you. If you enjoy your work, it usually means you can have fun while working."

"Are we having fun?" Morrison asked. "Because I feel like I'm the mouse, and you're the cat."

His eyes squinted at her, so she knew he was teasing. "Look, I work with dead people," she quipped. "They're mute. I have to get my conversational fun from somewhere." She glanced at him and began to speed up.

"When you put it that way, you make perfect sense," he laughed.

"I'm glad we understand each other because now I want to see how this car feels." Crossing into the high-speed lane from behind someone traveling sixty miles per hour, she pressed harder on the gas pedal. In two seconds, her car was going eighty miles per hour. She held it there.

"That's it?" he complained in jest.

"I thought you would never ask," her voice lilted. She hit ninety-five miles per hour on a straightaway with no traffic ahead. The Aston Martin purred. Slowly, she took it back down to eighty, then seventy-five miles per hour. "Detective, have you ever been in an Aston before?"

"No, ma'am, I haven't. Nor have I driven ninety-five miles an hour with a medical examiner. That's many firsts in a span of fifteen minutes. You're putting me in a spot."

"How's that?" she asked.

"Well, now that I know what you're made of, I'll have to come up with a list of firsts for you someday." Morrison had caught the rhythm of his father's message. His parents were jovial characters, and he realized he was missing their lightheartedness.

"Being a medical examiner has me ahead of you already on things you've never done. So don't stress yourself out. Besides, it's not a competition. We both want to know the results of these samples from my colleague. I've worked with Dr. Lin for many years. His experience and equipment should tell us something about the evidence in just a few hours if we are lucky."

"Anytime you have something from one of my cases for Dr. Lin, just let me know. I'll go along for the ride," Morrison offered.

Smiling, she said, "Glad to hear it, Detective."

"When I consider the video evidence," he recounted, "it showed that Aaron fell off the roof while doing balancing tricks. It doesn't tell us if he was involved in the theft. The museum footage shows him entering the maintenance closet and appearing quite drunk. He should never have been up there in his stumbling condition. But I wonder what startled him on the roof. He seemed to be walking the edge okay until he lost focus and fell."

Morrison pondered a bit and added, "But just like Marilyn's death, if I make assumptions, as I have seen others do, you usually find what you are looking for, so I have to keep an open mind to all the options."

"Seeing your assumptions is a phenomenon called pareidolia," Dr. Storm offered. "It's a tendency to have an incorrect perception of something seen. Especially if someone is invested in the outcome, they tend to apply their opinion or belief to an idea. Or it can simply be making something out of nothing, such as seeing the image of a face in a loaf of bread."

"Are you saying pareidolia means seeing what you want?"

"Yes, like shapes in clouds, faces in inanimate objects. You find what you are looking for."

Morrison laughed. "My Irish mother always pointed out cloud formations as a sign to take heed. But as you say, if others don't find the evidence, then it's not science. People gladly give their opinions, but what is their point of view? People who are jealous of Marilyn would say she attracted the killer. And someone without the facts might think Aaron committed suicide."

The Aston Martin purred along. "Well, in our professions, we must be wary of those trifling about the significance of a person's worth. Telling tales about someone's life once they're deceased is questionable and just plain nasty."

Morrison saw her serious expression. "You seem quite definite in that opinion. But you realize it's these opinions and feelings from people that are my fodder, and they bring me the information I can use to find out about someone's habits, discover motives, and solve a homicide case."

"Morrison, I can make jokes about death in general, but I won't make light of someone's death personally. They have a mother, a father, and a family. You know me—I work with facts only. Respect the dead is my motto."

"We can agree on that," he nodded. "Too often, I have to deal with the seedy side of the living to help the deceased and their family obtain justice and closure."

The exit ramp to New Haven came into view. In under an hour, they had arrived. Dr. Storm pulled up to a tall downtown building and parked underneath in the garage. Morrison followed as she showed her medical examiner badge at the access point and said hello to familiar colleagues along the way. Entering the anteroom to the secure lab, they waited.

Forensic Pathologist Dr. Ethan Lin came forward. Right away, Morrison recognized him. *He is the man who escorted Dr. Storm to the Mystic River Fine Art Museum.* After greeting one another, she handed over the samples from Aaron's autopsy and asked him to first test for common substances that would impair a person's judgment. Dr. Lin told them it would take several hours and that he would call with the results.

As they left, Morrison said, "I thought we would stay."

"Their schedule is their own, Morrison. In the meantime, I have a few things I thought we could do while we are here. Are you game?"

"Sure," he shrugged, "I'm at your mercy."

"Good! Let's go around the corner to a museum, the Yale Center for British Art."

"Really? I don't frequent museums much. You'll have to be my guide."

"No worries, I used to go there all the time. You'll be surprised how much you learn about yourself and others."

"I don't know what you mean by that statement."

"You will soon enough." She opened the door, and they stepped into the bustling downtown of New Haven.

CHAPTER 47

Morrison's Art Lesson

Dr. Storm and the detective walked down Chapel Street and into the Yale Center for British Art. In the center of a large hall, they came upon a stone sculpture called *Father Time*. The artist depicted an older man with a long beard and wings. He held an hourglass in one hand and a sharp scythe in the other. He foretold impermanence.

Morrison walked around the finely chiseled white marble figure. "I suddenly feel mortal."

"Yes, every day in the morgue, I realize my finite time on earth. When you think of life as an hourglass and grains of sand measuring out your life cycle, it becomes real. That's why it's important to find some happiness, so you have no regrets."

The doctor proceeded to the main gallery as he lingered on her advice. *Enjoy the ride* came to mind. He caught up and met her stride. In a low tone, she said, "I'll tell you a little secret that most people don't realize about museums. Once you understand why you visit a museum, you will go more often." She surveyed him to see if he was interested.

"Okay, why do you go?" he challenged. "I'm not sure museums are my thing, but I can have an open mind." They walked side by side.

"When it's a museum I've never been to, I pace myself, and in the quiet hallways and galleries, I observe the art with anticipation. I want to see what attracts me in each room because I know sooner or later, I will be surprised."

"Surprised by what exactly?" said Morrison.

"Sometimes, it's a slow surprise, and other times…it's a snap…like a bolt of lightning. I can be shocked, amused, or even dismayed. Great art, an image, a painting, a sculpture, or even jewelry can elicit a feeling that emerges from my core, leaps up and punches my heart, then tantalizes my brain. It tells a story or signifies something I either relate to, hope for, or may even dread. But it reaches right inside and grabs me.

"Of course, you can't look away; you must pay attention, and that, Detective, is fine art. Art, I will visit again and again. And that is why I go to museums."

"Whoa!" Morrison's face showed his stunned expression. "I had no idea art could make anyone feel that way. I'd be interested in finding art that just captured my attention. I don't think I will ever have the reaction you described."

A hint of laughter hummed in her throat. "Good! This should be fun. We don't have to spend much time reading plaques or staring at art. Just wander, and you'll figure it out."

Angela approached an average-sized oil painting. "I always stop to look at this one by Peter Paul Rubens. It's called *Peace Embracing Plenty*, completed in 1634. I love it because it exudes hope." She pointed and her finger drew in the air. "See these bright peach and gold draping garments and the swirl in the cornucopia of fruit? Look at the genuine eye contact between the two figures. They hold your attention."

"Your eye continues to gently move within the frame from one region to the other, and it circles back again. This is how a good composition works. Beauty is man's connection to the divine, as in a great painting like this. One that I will visit and never tire of because I feel hopeful when I gaze upon it."

"Hmmm. And do you know that Rubens is Karl's last name, the curator of the Mystic River Fine Art Museum? I heard he fancies himself related to a famous artist. Is it likely this Rubens?"

"Quite right, Detective. Of course, Karl mentioned it when we spoke at his function because he couldn't help himself. It's an ancient family connection. His mother beat that drum and drummed it into his head. I suppose touching the cloth of fame through their genealogy makes them famous too. I think that makes them a little touched by self-importance."

"Why do you say that?"

"I noticed her at the museum event. She exudes an unyielding nature to me. I try to stay away from women who are that headstrong. They give me a headache." Morrison nodded. "Come along. There is plenty more to see."

They moved from room to room until Morrison stopped at a painting and said, "This one is pleasant." It was a peaceful landscape scene of a blue water bay and white cliffs. A young boy was on shore with a rope line to the boat his father was in. It was by John Brett, from 1884, and illustrated the coast of Dorset in the United Kingdom. "It's not punching me in the gut, but I like it." He grinned, waiting for her comment.

"That's what I call a slow surprise. It softens you because there is something there you relate to. Would you say that is true?"

"Yes, it reminds me of my father and grandfather. We used to take a small boat out. And the scene is relaxing."

"See? You are getting the hang of it."

They continued their slow pace through the galleries, had lunch in the café, then continued to search for their next art revelation. "Morrison, here are two very moody paintings I love. Look at this one. It's a night scene called *The Blacksmith's Shop* by Joseph Wright of Derby from 1771."

Morrison observed. It was as if he were gazing through a window. A blacksmith's fire flared in the dim light of evening. Many figures were gathered around. The swing of the hammer had struck white-hot metal against the anvil.

"Can't you almost hear the ringing sound of metal on metal?" she asked. "And look at the reaction on the faces lit by the firelight of the boys and men."

"Yes, I see," he murmured. "It's easy to wonder what it's like to stand there and to hear the stories they must tell each other."

She confirmed, "When art is good, we want to be inside the scene. It adds something to us, maybe a new awareness, and we can benefit from it." She smiled. He was genuinely amused.

She took a few steps to another painting and said, "Now, this one is slightly scary. It's called *The Wish*."

Morrison observed the large painting of a young woman whose torso filled the frame. In her hands, she was gracefully shuffling fortune-telling cards. The gaze of this dark beauty was slanted downward. Her long, brunette hair was in stark contrast to her glowing white bodice. A pearl pendant hung over her cleavage. The 1841 painting was by Theodor von Holst. "She is mysterious," he murmured.

Angela pulled out her phone. "Based on this painting, a young and not-yet-famous artist named Dante Gabriel Rossetti wrote a chilling poem called *The Card Dealer*. Here, check it out. It reveals that her game is death."

Morrison took her phone to read the first line. "Could you not drink her gaze like wine?" Suddenly, the doctor's phone vibrated. He handed it back to her. It was a call from the New Haven Forensic Lab. "Hi, Ethan! Do you have the results? Okay, we'll be there within the hour." She hung up, raised her fist, and whispered, "He found something! Sempre Avanti! Always forward!"

Facts: Yale Center for British Art

was founded by alum Paul Mellon from the class of 1929. It holds the largest and most comprehensive collection of British art and culture, not in the United Kingdom, from the fifteenth century to today. Mellon was a great art collector and philanthropist. His love for British culture came from his English mother and his childhood visits to her homeland.

CHAPTER 48

The Tribulations of Aaron & Marguerite

Together Morrison and Dr. Storm returned to the forensic lab, and Dr. Lin handed her the results. "The tests show a high percentage of alcohol and psilocybin, the psychedelic mushroom, in his system. I hope this is a result you can work with." Grateful for the fast turnaround, they left for New London.

"I imagine you are surprised about the psychedelic mushrooms," she asked while driving.

"Somewhat. Aaron seemed to work all night without an issue. Granted, we know he mixed his alcohol and was drunk after work, but when did he take the mushrooms? I will need to question his friends and coworkers who volunteered with him that night. I'll also ask Karl and Isadore what they noticed. If you'll excuse me, I'll call Peabody now."

"Certainly. Go ahead." She drove along a stretch of interstate between Branford and Guilford and admired the historical seaside towns until her thoughts took over. *The effects of the mushroom undoubtedly disoriented Aaron. If he's a parkour professional, his common sense should have stopped him from balancing on the edge of a building while hallucinating.*

Morrison put his conversation with Peabody on speaker. "Boss, I was going to call you. Aaron's girlfriend, Marguerite Santa Maria, is in the intensive care unit at a hospital in New London. Kayakers discovered her in the Mystic River last night. She came in as a Jane Doe. Her family identified her just moments ago."

"Do me a favor, Peabody. Have the doctor in charge call Dr. Storm as soon as possible with toxicology information. And call Karl Rubens and his mother. Tell them I want to meet with them, say tomorrow at one o'clock. I have a few more questions."

"Yes, Boss. Marguerite came in unconscious and had to be put on a ventilator and an arterial line. The doctor said all indications show she is brain-dead."

"Okay. I'll be in touch, Peabody." Morrison turned to Angela, "Brain-dead? That means dead, doesn't it?"

"Yes, An accepted legal criterion for death is *brain-dead.*" Her words were matter-of-fact. "Some people request, either verbally or through a living will, not to be kept on life support. Often, it falls back on the family to decide to pull the plug. The machines keep them alive until the decision is made. No one will recover from a brain-death condition.

"But oddly, since your heart is still beating, are you legally dead? The legal answer and scientific answers are yes because your body requires brain support for its systems to continue living. If a body cannot maintain itself independently, it is not alive. You are only a biological membrane being kept alive by machines." Morrison held his chin with concern. *Not another artist!*

Angela continued, "What's interesting is that while the heart is beating, despite the person being brain-dead, organs can be donated before the plug is pulled. Viable organs—heart, kidney, liver—can be transplanted quickly to many other people who need them to live.

"Since Marguerite's heartbeat does not constitute life if her brain has no activity, we need to confirm if she's brain-dead. They will need to do an EEG, an electroencephalography."

"I am constantly learning," Morrison mumbled. "What does that do?"

"By attaching electrodes to Marguerite's scalp, they will be able to determine whether there is any *macroscopic activity* on the surface layer of her brain. Doctors use it to diagnose epilepsy, sleeping disorders, coma, and brain death. It's been around since 1924 and has been a godsend for those pronounced dead when they are 'only mostly dead but not all dead'."

"What? Are you quoting Miracle Max from *The Princess Bride*?" Morrison snickered.

"Quite right, Detective! You know that one!" She chuckled with him. "And guess what?" she added. "Marguerite can hear what is being said if they find macroscopic activity."

The detective was perplexed. "She can?"

"Yes. We call this a *locked-in* syndrome. It paralyzes the nerves in the body. She can appear *brain-dead*; but is not. The mind remains normal, but she is locked in the shell of her body and cannot move. If she is in a locked-in state, she will eventually snap out of it. Mistakes have been made when you don't take the time to do the EEG test. It all depends on the trauma."

Morrison recalled people who were buried alive by mistake in the 1800s. Bells were placed above ground and attached to a string within the coffin so those who awoke could ring for help. It was a miserable thought until he remembered Marguerite could be alive. *If she woke up, she could tell me what had happened.*

Dr. Angela returned Morrison to his car, and he raced to headquarters. Immediately, he read the details of how Marguerite was found in the Mystic River on Sunday afternoon.

> Two male kayakers saw a young woman walk into the water from afar. She had flowers in her hands as she waded fully dressed into the river from the wetland edge. They were curious and watched when she moved to a floating position. They became concerned when she seemed to disappear. Paddling swiftly, they urgently wanted to know if she was okay.
>
> As the kayakers drew closer, their paddling became frantic. The bouquet was dispersed, and she couldn't be found. One paddler ditched the kayak and dove in. He searched under the water. *Where was she?* A shimmering glint caught his eye. He took a gulping breath of air and swam toward it. Her arm was raised in her descent. Her bracelet gleamed. He grasped her arm and pulled her up into the air. His companion hauled her onto his kayak.
>
> Thankfully, these two young men were experienced in water rescue. They began mouth-to-mouth resuscitation with chest compressions, then rolled her onto her side. She finally coughed out the water she inhaled. But she did not regain consciousness. Immediately, they called 911 for help. The emergency crews brought her to the nearest hospital as a Jane Doe.
>
> Her sandals and small purse were found on Monday, so it appeared she had floated away after placing them on the riverbank. Her family was called to identify her.

Morrison finished reading the report and turned to Peabody. "I'd like to see everyone die of old age. I hope this is not a suicide. Murdering yourself is sad, Peabody. What we need to know is if this was an accident or another homicide?

"Plus, the crux in these cases is too many artists are connected. The incidents do not add up to where I can put my hands around someone's neck. Marilyn's death was a homicide, and we think Cora was abducted by the people connected to Marilyn. Aaron's death still looks like an accident. The issue is that the thieves moved him. Marguerite is still alive, but it seems like grief brought her to the river. I see no connection to Marilyn with Aaron and Marguerite except they are New London artists."

"Well, Boss, here's something that just came out in the news from The Mystic Report, the daily online newspaper." Peabody handed him a piece of paper.

> **The Mystic Report** breaking news: Ms. Marguerite Santa Maria, 23, of New London, was found floating among the cattails just days after her boyfriend, Aaron Goshen, 28, of New London, was found dead by the docks on the Mystic River at the Mystic River Fine Art Museum. Both incidents are suspicious yet could be accidental. Suicide is being considered.

"Suicide has not been mentioned!" Morrison thundered. "The journalists should stop surmising outcomes. It fries me that they put that word out there. Suicide should not be written until the facts are established." Morrison growled and clenched his fist. "Boy, that irritates me." Peabody watched Morrison's fist relax before he punched something.

"Boss, I called and spoke to Isadore Rubens." Morrison was still grimacing but listened. "I told her you wanted to meet with them. I set the appointment for one o'clock tomorrow. She said Karl was returning tonight from Boston after a debriefing with the BFA Museum about his side of the story on the painting."

"Excellent. The Mystic police have been dealing with them regarding the painting, but I am suspicious, and hold them responsible for their volunteer. The very least they could have done was inspect the premises for stragglers. I blame them for mishandling a high-valued event, Peabody. They relied solely on the security system and didn't staff the event properly with professionals."

"Maybe they were trying to save a dime," Peabody said as he swiveled in his desk chair. "I like being economical, plus they were still raising funds for the rooftop construction. But then, Boss," his index finger raised with the thought, "it's a case of penny-wise and pound-foolish. A volunteer like Aaron doesn't have a vested interest. It was like a party night. Why didn't they have armed guards with those top-quality paintings?"

"You're thinking like a detective, Peabody." Morrison pondered his question and answered with a question. "Was their risk assessment ill-advised, and were they blindsided? And therefore, 20-20 hindsight has them saying, 'woulda, coulda, shoulda'? Or..." he held up a finger, "...was the event *intentionally unsecured* so the thieves easily entered and exited with their prized treasure?"

Morrison tapped his pen on Peabody's desk. "When my adrenaline is overly stimulated, the not knowing is supremely aggravating." Morrison pointed his pen at Peabody, then himself. "Remember, you and I don't stop.... until the whole story is revealed."

CHAPTER 49

Unexpected Fortune
Monday - Evening

When Karl returned from Boston, Isadore was waiting for him in the living room, lounging on the sofa with the French doors wide open to the sea breeze. "Darling, Detective Morrison will be stopping by the house tomorrow to ask us questions about Aaron."

"Mother, I saw Aaron today on the video footage from the security cameras at our museum on the night of the theft. It caught Aaron drunkenly stumbling into the maintenance closet." Karl was perturbed. "The flawed system went down for nearly a half hour. It turned off before we left.

"When the cameras came back online, the original Cassatt painting was still in place, you locked up, and the parking lot footage caught you going to your car. It was obvious you were unaware of what happened. Did you see Aaron after I left?"

"Of course not, dear. I would have told you and the detectives if I had."

"It is certainly suspicious that the cameras went down before the theft. The BFA Museum believes it was an inside job within the security company. I wonder if it was a routine system update that shut it down. You didn't see anything?"

She rose and crossed the room to make a drink, saying, "I was busy packaging up all that leftover food. I won't leave behind shrimp cocktails and expensive canapés for the help when we can eat them."

Karl knew that was normal behavior for his mother. He thought of the exterior video from the marina across the river. "I saw a video of Aaron on the rooftop patio."

Isadore spun around in her kaftan dress in shock. "You did?"

"It was very grainy and difficult to see, but he was balancing on the parapet's edge. We designed that short wall so patrons could enjoy the view. No one anticipated someone would be foolish enough to walk on it. This buffoon jumped right up and balanced on it like a tightrope."

"Did you see him fall?"

"Yes, Mother. It was horrible!" Karl's hands twitched against his pant legs. He stared at the floor while the sickening scene replayed in his mind. He eyed her for empathy. She knew he didn't handle death very well.

"Was there anything else?" Her thoughts raced as she pictured the scene.

"It seemed something had startled him. He lost his balance, wavered, then fell. A half-hour later, this lobster boat slowly came up the river from the direction of Long Island Sound. It tied up at our dock, and the two thieves exited the boat."

Isadore was transfixed. "You could see all that?"

"Yes, you could barely tell, but one carried a large art portfolio case. I was shocked when they stopped and unceremoniously pulled Aaron's body across the lawn into the water. The brutes casually went to the rear door, and that's when our museum camera caught them. But we couldn't see their faces because of their caps. They were dressed as uniformed police officers. Can you believe it?" Isadore turned to collect the ice for her drink.

Karl continued, "They punched in our passcode, entered the building, and soon the whole system shut down again. They went about their business unseen by our cameras, and voilà, they stole the Cassatt painting and left a forgery. Now that I think of it, why didn't they steal more?" Karl looked to Isadore for an answer. He narrowed his eyes and wondered.

"Darling, we don't know why people do what they do. That one painting is worth a fortune. Whoever has it is filthy rich if they can sell it." She waved her hand, banishing his question. "It is done with. Let the police do their investigation. They know everything from seeing the video footage. Poor Aaron fell on his own accord from our rooftop, and the thieves got away." She dropped several ice cubes from the bar fridge into her glass and poured herself a bourbon.

Karl considered her words and nodded. "I'm so fortunate everyone at the BFA was kind to me today. My dedication to the museum left a lasting impression. And they mentioned you, Mother. I believe our long-standing philanthropy was on their mind. I hope they can catch the thieves and recover the painting so my museum's reputation can be restored."

She swirled her ice cubes and lifted her glass to him. "Don't worry, my love, anything is possible....it truly is."

She smiled and sipped her drink while eyeing him. "Look at it as an unexpected fortune that the whole world knows about you and the Mystic River Fine Art Museum now."

CHAPTER 50

Brain Power Equals Life
Tuesday - 8 a.m.

Dr. Nichols was overseeing Marguerite's care at the hospital. He called the medical examiner's office at 8 a.m. Dr. Storm answered his call. "Hello, Dr. Nichols. I want to share the toxicology report from Marguerite's boyfriend, Aaron Goshen. Besides plenty of wine, he had psilocybin mushrooms in his system. I'm sure Detective Morrison updated you on how he was discovered Friday morning."

"Yes, Dr. Storm, I am aware. Marguerite's family is very close with Aaron's, and they have informed me of the circumstances in Mystic and her grief. They have permitted me to share information regarding her condition with you in case there are similarities. I will have tests done for the psilocybin. Some people don't handle those psychedelic highs very well."

Dr. Storm knew psilocybin was successfully prescribed medicinally, but only under controlled therapeutic conditions. It was proven helpful for depression, PTSD, and other clinical issues. Although it was not approved for recreational use, some people used it to achieve a high. She was told they claimed a feeling of unity with nature and humanity.

Dr. Nichols continued, "All indications show that Marguerite has not responded to any stimuli since Sunday evening. Her eyes, nor her nervous system, and she is only breathing with assistance. As you know, these signify brain death."

"Have you performed an EEG, Doctor?"

"The hospital staff has been hectic, and they'll be performing the electroencephalography this morning. Once they do, we will have the results in an hour. The family will contact the detective with any news."

"Thank you, Dr. Nichols, and please be sure to inform the family that if her EEG returns positive, it indicates Marguerite can hear them. I have known this to be true. Patients have stated they heard every word."

"I've not encountered this condition myself, but I'll let them know."

Without hesitating, Dr. Storm called Morrison to inform him of her conversation with Dr. Nichols. The hospital was performing the EEG that morning.

Morrison called the family and asked if he could visit her. They agreed.

Standing at the side of her bed, he spoke gently to her. "Marguerite, this is Detective Morrison. You are in good hands, and I am here to find out what happened to you and Aaron. If you can hear me, you hang in there. We are going to help you."

The family watched Morrison deliver his message and were touched by his genuine concern and belief that Marguerite could hear him.

Nurses arrived and wheeled Marguerite to the room where the test would be performed. Dan, the man, had empathy for the family, but Morrison, the detective, had anxiety about his case. Once in the waiting area, he repeatedly looked at his watch, hopeful to learn if she might awaken. Soon, he would know if she was alive.

The nurse applied electrodes to Marguerite's head and carefully explained to the unconscious patient what was happening. Once they were all attached, the attending doctor nodded for them to begin. The EEG machine underwent routine scans for an hour to read if any electrical activity was apparent in Marguerite's brain.

Dr. Storm had told Morrison that if Marguerite were brain-dead, she could not survive brain death without machines. Her family would need to decide how long to wait before they were ready to let her go and whether to donate her organs. She had explained that the heart was the most-prized organ, and usually, a person was waiting for a transplant. Even once unplugged and legally dead, the heart continued to beat for two more minutes because it had its own independent bioelectric power source.

Morrison had been intrigued by her point that a heartbeat did not legally constitute life; only the brain's ability to operate the body independently determined life.

Once the scans were completed, Dr. Nichols told the family, and they asked him to inform Detective Morrison. "Detective, her brain activity is weak, but it is entirely there. She is alive, and she will recover."

"This is tremendous news!" Morrison's hand swiped the sweat from his forehead. "Is there anything else? Were you able to do a lab test for suspicious drugs?"

"Yes, since Dr. Storm had the psychedelic mushroom identified in Aaron's system, and you gave us the drug in Cora's incident, we focused on those and have a result. It is confirmed: that Marguerite had the psilocybin mushroom in her system. It doesn't mean someone drugged her. But they both had the psychedelic hallucinogenic in their system."

The detective shook the doctor's hand vigorously. "Thank you for informing me. Please let me know when she wakes up." He then placed a call. "Dr. Storm, the results are in. Marguerite is alive!" he exclaimed.

"It's so nice to hear good news." She sensed his elation. "What a blessing that she will recover! *And* you don't have another dead New Londoner."

"Yes, that is true, but I have a question for you. Dr. Nichols confirmed she had the same type of mushroom in her system as Aaron. How exactly did it affect them?"

"The effects are sensory, visual, and auditory. The mushroom can alter one's relationship with space and time. For Aaron, he was in a no-win situation by teetering on the edge of the museum parapet while high. As we have covered, taking risks is a common youthful mistake. But he was seen at the museum all evening, so he must have taken it at the night's end.

"You told me Marguerite wandered into the water. Once she awakens, you can find out why she did it and whether she was alone. Did she intend suicide? If the drug had been in her system long enough, it would have altered her perception of reality, and her near-drowning may have been accidental. She might have taken the mushroom to forget about her sadness. Was she heartbroken enough to want to meet Aaron on the other side? These are all possibilities."

"Thanks. You're making my job easier, Doctor. The mushroom is a common element between them, and Mystic is the common location. About how long before Marguerite recovers?"

"That's very hard to determine because every case is unique. But the hospital staff and doctors are all working toward that goal. I'm sure they are giving her plenty of IV fluids, electrolytes, et cetera. She could wake up in hours or days."

"Doctor, I can honestly say your help has been timely, knowledgeable, and entertaining."

"We enjoy our work, don't we, Detective? Good luck with your case."

Morrison put the phone down and noticed his heart raced, but not because of the case. Angela lingered on his mind more than any other woman.

He heard his father's Irish proverb. *Danny boy, A little fire in the heart that warms you…is better than a big fire that burns you.*

CHAPTER 51

Patterns of Criminal Intent
Tuesday

Roxanne received a call from Georgi before 8:30 a.m., asking to have coffee with him. She stopped by the firehouse on her way to Muddy Waters Café to see if Sam wanted her to bring back any goodies. Striding up the stairs to his office, she saw his crew below, "Hi, guys!"

The firefighters were washing down a truck and glanced over their shoulders. "Hello, Mrs. Chief!" They waved.

Sam was pleasantly surprised when Roxanne appeared in his office. "What are you up to? Do the window boxes need refreshing?"

"Not yet. We'll do the seasonal change with the New London Beautification Committee later. I'm in town to meet Georgi for coffee. Do you want something from Muddy Waters for lunch?"

"No, I'm good. Cody has decided to fire up the grill and cook hot dogs today. I have a stash of those specialty dogs in the fridge."

"Firehouse cooking at its best!" Roxanne chimed.

He motioned to a chair. "Could you shut the door and have a seat for a second?"

Roxanne did and eyed him curiously from across the desk. "What's up?"

"You know the young lady called in by her family as missing Sunday night?"

"Yes, Marguerite, Aaron's girlfriend. Did they find her? Is she all right?" Roxanne leaned forward in anticipation.

"They did, and she is at the hospital in ICU. She was rescued from the Mystic River by two kayakers. They identified her yesterday afternoon. That's all I know right now."

"I'm so glad they found her. Is it okay if I tell Georgi?"

"Sure, it's not confidential. Ask him to check with his friends. I'm sure Morrison would like to know anything at this point."

"Okay, I will do that. Georgi's always willing to help."

"Yes, I know, but nip it right there. Don't encourage him to get involved any more than that."

"I know, I know. Stay out of trouble and be a good doobie. Don't rock the boat or fly too close to the sun. You do know that being cautious can become very boring. We've behaved, sat on our hands, gritted our teeth, and bitten our lips. If we hear anything or find evidence that Dan Morrison can use, by golly, wouldn't he be tickled?"

Sam gave her a look, then surprised her. "Okay, Wonder Woman. Yes, I have been impressed by your constraint. At least this time, I know you are not the target like you were in Dan's last big case. If you quietly find things out the way you do by talking to people in the community, there is no harm in research."

Roxanne jumped up with glee. "Yes, sir!" she saluted in jest.

He laughed. "Don't get too excited. Where's that restraint?"

"Yes, I know. Be good, be careful, don't get into trouble." She batted her eyelashes. "I'm good. Can I go talk to Georgi now?"

"Go ahead, but don't be late for dinner."

She gave him a peck on the cheek. "Thank you, dear." She scooted out the door, and instead of turning left toward the staircase, she took a right.

He yelled out her name. "Roxanne, don't you dare!"

But before he finished his words, she was down the firepole and running out the garage bay door. She could hear the crew laughing behind her as she jumped into the front seat of her truck and took off.

***

Roxanne and Georgi walked into the popular coffee shop, ordered their iced coffees and pastries, and settled on the expanded outdoor deck with a view of the Thames River.

"Sam just told me they found Marguerite, and she's in the hospital," she whispered. "Did you know?"

"Yes, Ophelia called me. They say she is in the ICU because she is unconscious. I hope she's going to be all right. Marilyn's gone, Cora's been humiliated, Aaron is gone, and now Marguerite."

Roxanne patted his shoulder. "There, there now, don't worry. She's in good hands, and we have Dan on these cases. He'll get this man, Mario Corinthian, or whoever. I know he can't bring back your friends, but you can be there for the ones who are still with us."

They looked out to the river's edge. The Coast Guard's tall ship, the Barque Eagle, was proudly docked at the City Pier, and nearby, the water taxi loaded tourists traveling to the opposite shore to climb the stony point of the Fort Griswold obelisk where one could see a grand view of New London

Harbor. Silently, they watched the water scenes and ate their favorite scones and tarts.

Suddenly, Georgi bolted upright in his seat. "What is that tugboat guiding?" He stood and leaned for a better view. "Oh, I see it." He pointed. "It's a submarine!" The sleek, black metal hull was just above the waterline, and two dozen sailors stood on top. His interest was piqued. The ship typically left the Naval Submarine Base in Groton for a journey to the deep ocean waters of the world. "That's awesome. I'll never tire of that sight." He squinted and peered a bit more. "Hey, wait a minute. Are they waving?"

Georgi began jumping and waving a napkin. "Hello, officers!" he yelled. "Come back and see me. I'm at the Vinho Verde, and your first drinks are on me!" He heard a sharp whistle from the crew, so he kept waving his napkin as they glided forward. Finally, he flopped into his chair. "My, my, Roxanne," he used his napkin to fan himself, "that's the best thing that could have happened to me. I needed that."

"Georgi, whatever floats your boat." She chuckled. "Don't end up in the water this time, okay? Remember, you can't swim." Memories of his last encounter in Long Island Sound bobbed in her head.

"I'll depend on them to save me if I accidentally find myself in the water," he sang. Clutching his chest, he delighted in being saved by a handsome Coastie or Sailor. Coyly, he waved his napkin at her with a smirk.

She squeezed his arm. "Don't you dare make me worry about you doing something ridiculous. I swear I won't do your window boxes or planters."

Georgi crossed his heart and raised his hand. "I promise not to make you worry…because I won't tell you what I'm up to."

"Good. I don't want to know about your wily ways. And now that you are perked up by coffee and sailors, let's talk about Marilyn, Cora, and Aaron. Listen, we want to look for patterns of criminal intent connected to art. Remember, the painting was stolen the night Aaron fell."

Georgi's eyes popped. "We're back in business?"

"What?" she asked evasively, pretending not to understand his question, though her expression gave her away.

"Okay!" He rubbed his hands together. "What are you thinking? Ms. Pretend-we-are-not-sleuthing."

She tipped her head and grinned. "Patterns, Georgi, we are looking for patterns. I always see them in nature: leaves, trees, animals, birds, and insects. I can tell when an animal has walked through my yard because I see its tracks, skat, or where it has rubbed against a tree. In nature, I watch for repeating patterns of activity. Like when crows make a big commotion, a hawk is probably after their eggs or young. Patterns require further inspection.

"We can find that in human behavior too. Twice is interesting, but thrice starts a pattern. Three artists seem to have been woven into a web of mysterious activities, all related to art. Even if it seems secondary." She pointed at Georgi. "That, my friend, is a pattern of possible criminal intent!"

Georgi gawked at her as if she had antennas. "How do you know all these things?"

"Because I pay attention. The more you pay attention to details, the more experience you gain. And I was reading a book about it too." She raised her eyebrows twice, as the character in *Magnum P.I.*, that Tom Selleck played.

"Well, that's cheating! Reading a book about it." They both laughed. Admiringly he said, "I think your mind catalogs experience different from the average bear. I know this because my mind catalogs wines, grapes, and vineyards more than the average sommelier."

"You can always twist something into a wine reference," she teased.

"That's how you make wine. You crush the essence out of the grape and get to the heart of the juice. We will do the same—distill these happenings down and progress until we find the mean-hearted culprits." Georgi suddenly fussed with his shirt, rolled up his cuffs, popped his collar, then glanced at his manicured nails, ready to sleuth. "So, Miss Spyglass, you're saying all these incidents with the artists are part of a pattern."

She smiled broadly. "Let's call it suspicious. Don't you think?"

"We need to know why Marguerite was in Mystic."

Roxanne gazed out to Ledge Lighthouse and the horizon. "We need to know if she was alone, Georgi. Can you find out through her friends?"

"Yes, of course, but wouldn't Detective Morrison and his team know that?"

"We don't know what they don't know," she sang.

"The idea of someone after artists makes no sense to me." Georgi laid his hand on his forehead.

"But that's just it," Roxanne inserted. "It must make sense to someone like Mario Corinthian. We know the incidents with Marilyn and Cora are related. All four are from New London, and two live above the Dahlia Gallery. Aaron and Marguerite were always volunteering there too. Maybe that's the tie-in, the Dahlia! Some see coincidence, but I see patterns."

Georgi nodded as he took a bite of his apple tart when, suddenly, Roxanne grabbed his forearm and attention. "Georgi Algarve, if you are willing to accept it, our mission is to scrutinize all the common elements between these people."

He took a sip of coffee, cleared his throat, made musical sounds, and drummed the table to the *Mission Impossible* theme song. Roxanne laughed and rocked to the beat in her seat. He finally raised his hand. "Mission accepted! Now, is something going to melt or go up in smoke like on TV or in the movies?" They both giggled. "What's next?" he asked.

In thought, Roxanne tapped her index finger against her lips. "Let's see. All four knew each other, and many people knew all of them. But what is unique to this equation?"

"I know," Georgi caroled. "Mystic is unique. Together, none of them has a connection to Mystic."

Roxanne's head snapped toward him. "You're right! So, who do we know in Mystic who may have answers?"

They gaped at each other and said in unison, "Karl!"

"Oh my gosh, I forgot something," Georgi exclaimed. "Marilyn said the curator at the art museum in Mystic was trying to meet her and see her work. This was before I knew who he was. I wonder if Karl ever did contact her."

Roxanne lit up. "Can we meet with him? Ask him to tea or something. Maybe we can find out about Marilyn and Aaron from him."

"I'll see when he is free. He trusts us now." Georgi answered.

CHAPTER 52

The Black Cat Bar & the Cool Cat Lounge

Troy was in his art studio. He had whittled a design into the surface of his flat wax block. His bucket was now full of the filings from his scoring. An image of Marilyn had emerged in the foreground. She walked on a winding cliff path that overlooked an ocean view. The final intricate details had been carved. He had engaged in the journey of his muse, much like a vision quest into the imaginative realm where she resided.

He would produce prints from this original in colorful or muted tones for his finished work. But Troy's muse began whispering another vision to him. A new series of paintings formulated in his mind, so he pulled several stretched canvases from his pre-made stash.

He imagined Marilyn in broad landscapes and wanted to produce a collection quickly. The wax-cut process was time-consuming. He started by painting the canvases with an acrylic base of gray paint. Once dry, he sketched and laid out blocks of color. The details for each canvas came to him quickly.

In one painting, she gazed into a colorful sunset on the horizon, transitioning to stars above and the universe. Another depicted her on the peak of a mountain, looking into the paradise valley of Shambala. And a third, she was on the bow of a great ship, facing the horizon, heading out to sea towards a distant light. She was looking away from the viewer in all three paintings, disengaged from this reality. Troy desired to make them brilliant and hopeful. He believed her soul continued to exist, and now she was on her ever-evolving spiritual journey.

***

It was late Tuesday morning when Troy received this cryptic text message from Georgi: **Meet me at the Black Cat Bar at 2 p.m. today—the last stool on the left. Don't tell anyone.** Troy had heard this recent artsy addition to downtown was described as far-out. The artists loved it as a hangout.

When Troy approached the entrance of this new bar, he laughed out loud. He had heard about walking into a cat's mouth, but seeing it in person, was a delight and surprise. Creatively sculpted, the black cat's mouth yawned wide, teeth and all. Troy stepped into the dark interior to find the door lit with a mini disco ball. At first, he felt like a mouse about to be devoured, but his mood changed when he heard the music, a whimsical tune with a metronome circus-like beat.

The door of the Black Cat Bar slowly closed behind him, and Troy immediately admired the unique, eclectic setting. The walls were matt-black but painted over with large florescent leaves and vivid flowers. The marvel was that blacklights illuminated them, and the flowers optically popped off the walls.

Troy's attention was then taken to the surface of the bar. The thick transparent plexiglass was lit from within to enhance colorful beverages. The drinks glowed, such as golden Manhattans, brilliant pink cosmopolitans, bright yellow RumChata Limóns, green Midori melons, and orange creamsicle daiquiris. Troy snickered. *This place is tripping me out. I don't even need a drink!*

He said hello to two friends as he made his way to the end of the long bar. Reaching the deeper interior, he spotted Georgi at the last stool on the left. "This place is wild, Georgi. Is this your first time here?"

"Oh, no. Marco and I have been a few times on Saturdays after 11 p.m. for the dancing. They have a fabulous DJ who plays nonstop, and we don't leave until 2 a.m. It's our exercise." Georgi took a sip of his virgin piña colada. "Do you want a fruity drink?"

"Uhh, I'll have a cranberry juice with tonic water and lime, no alcohol."

After Troy's drink arrived, he noticed a small neon sign in a far corner. It beckoned those who would enter the Cool Cat Lounge. The allure reminded him of movies by Quentin Tarantino or the Wachowskis. "What's going on in the Cool Cat Lounge? Is it for private parties?"

"Yes and No. It's for cool people who want to wear daring clothes and meet up with like-minded friends."

"What do you mean by cool and like-minded?"

"You know…Coool cats who have the same agenda." Georgi snapped his fingers with both hands.

"Is it a jazz lounge, a beatnik club?" Troy wondered.

"No, us coool cats, like Marco and me," he said, with a twinkle in his eye, "You know, the rainbow clan."

"Oh, I get it." Troy laughed at his naiveté, and Georgi gleamed.

"It's for those who feel they are different. It's just a bit of fun for the rainbow community to have a place to hang out, meet, and feel safe."

Troy raised his glass. "I'll drink to a safe place in New London for my rainbow friends." Troy clinked Georgi's glass. "As an artist, I know what it's like to be misunderstood. I want to be free from the judgment of my point of view. No one wants to lose their freedom."

"That's why I love artists," Georgi reflected, "because you accept everyone from nerdy to eccentric. That's why Marilyn was such a dear friend. We loved each other like siblings." He suddenly remembered to ask Troy, "Have you heard about Marguerite?"

"Yes. It's upsetting that she's in a coma. The family asked if our community knew anything. We all thought she was with them because of Aaron. I hope she comes out of it soon. I want to tell her I appreciate her and Aaron's friendship."

Georgi nodded, "Yes, and that's why I wanted to talk with you." Georgi glanced from side to side to see if anyone was within earshot. Whispering, he said, "I have a secret plan to discuss with you before I talk to anyone else. This is just between you and me. I want to surprise the Dahlia resident artists with a nice dinner. It will be held at Dev's Bistro. What do you think?"

"I think that's amazing. Everyone will love it. I'm the only person you've told?"

"Troy, we've been neighbors for two years, and I value your opinion. You know everyone, and I don't want to overstep my bounds during these difficult times we are all going through."

"Thanks, it would bring us closer and help us feel better about all that has happened. But don't expect it to go perfectly."

Georgi held his drink midair, waiting for Troy to drop the shoe.

"Raw emotions may also be present," Troy forewarned. "Georgi, you are almost *always* optimistic, but life is messy. It would be best if you weren't disappointed. That's all."

"If I can take the sting out of what we've been living through, that's all I want. I won't expect too much. I'll immediately call Candace at Dev's Bistro to let her know my plans."

Georgi glanced over his shoulder to see who was nearby, "Do you know how expensive it is after you die?" Troy shook his head. "Way more than you can imagine."

"I can imagine a lot," Troy admitted.

"Thousands!" Georgi said in a continued whisper.

Troy shook his head. "Geez, never mind life, I can't even afford death! Do me a favor, Georgi. Feed me to the fishes. Then I'll go back into the ocean."

"Oh no! Don't talk that way."

"That's why I work hard," Troy explained, "so I can forget the things I can't afford. Most artists live on the edge until they become discovered, like Marilyn. That's why we often live in our art studios and why I need to go back to work now."

"Your time will come, Troy. You are excellent. A wise old woman once told me, 'Life is for learning about being grateful.' That was my great-grandmother, and she lived to be one hundred one. She would say, 'Don't worry or wonder why—that's a waste of energy. Just be grateful for every little thing, and you'll do all right.'"

Troy's mouth curved into a smile. "That's beautiful. Now I know why you are so upbeat." Troy finished his drink. "Hey, let me know if you need help."

Georgi stood. "I will not because this is my gift to you and my friends at the Dahlia."

Troy grinned, feeling somehow lighter than when he walked in.

Georgi called Candace at Dev's Bistro to discuss his last-minute idea. He hadn't told Troy his true secret—it was a fundraiser. Candace agreed to host the event, reviewed the menu with Chef Rachel, and selected libations with Georgi. She arranged to close to the public and hold the event on Friday evening.

Georgi's talent for serving wine dinner parties at the Vinho Verde allowed him to tap his long list of patrons and friends. His popularity encouraged them to attend the impromptu dinner fundraiser. Soon enough, he had one hundred confirmed to donate $200 each for the event. His dream was to lift everyone's spirits and, possibly, add a little sunshine into their lives.

***

At the Dahlia, Troy met up with Ophelia and revealed that Marilyn had become his muse for a series of works. The idea inspired her, and she thought to create an art piece for Marguerite. A sculpture to represent her coming out of her unconscious state and back into consciousness. Ophelia hoped this new work of art could help her discharge her whirling emotions and angst.

With shears in hand, she began her new art piece. She cut two-inch slits into a white bed sheet, then ripped it with all her strength, one long strip after another. The pulling made her feel strong and in control, yet the fabric-tearing sounds were like the screams she had pent up inside, wanting to come out. Instead, tears rolled down her cheeks. The task helped to release her grief and anger over her friends' destinies.

After destroying two sheets dampened by her tears, she set them aside and began the next phase, utilizing wire to shape a female form. Her idea was to represent Marguerite's journey from leaving the grips of death to returning to the world of the living.

CHAPTER 53

Cemetery Hopping
Tuesday - morning

Morrison went down his checklist. The team had reviewed Francisco's photos of the night at the museum in Mystic, and currently, no identifiable persons of interest had surfaced. At one o'clock, he and Peabody were meeting Karl Rubens and his mother. He sighed. "We've got to catch a break."

"Hey, Boss, the Cedar Grove Cemetery called about a package left in the drop box at their gate. It's addressed to them but in the care of you. There's an attached note saying it must be hand-delivered."

"Come on, Peabody, let's go."

The two detectives arrived in five minutes to find the cemetery director meeting with a couple to arrange a burial. The director ended the conversation when she saw Morrison standing by her door. She excused herself and closed the door. Handing him the manila envelope, she quipped, "Detective, this is the first time I've received your mail. Do you think someone is buying you a plot so they can bury you?"

Morrison returned a sly smile. "You'll be the first to know or never know if you go before me." He pulled out his gloves. Her eyebrows raised. He swiftly put them on, grabbed the envelope, and ripped it open. Inside was a crumpled paper with a scrawled note in black marker.

Go to Elm Grove Cemetery in Mystic for a key to your case.

"What the...? Let's get an evidence bag, Peabody." They quickly thanked the director and said goodbye.

Once in the SUV, Morrison said, "Call the superintendent of Elm Grove Cemetery, Peabody."

He put the call on speaker. Once the super answered, Morrison asked if an envelope or something else had been delivered with his name.

"Huh? Hold on, Detective."

Peabody tapped his fingers on his leg as he waited for the result. He could hear the superintendent moving papers around.

"Yes, I do. It's a manila envelope left in the night drop box."

"Please don't open it. I will have to check the contents for fingerprints. I'll be right there shortly."

The super immediately dropped the envelope back in the mail basket.

Morrison sped across the Gold Star Bridge, and Peabody put on the lights and siren. They took the Mystic exit, and within a quarter of a mile, he slowed for a hard right. A tall granite archway and elaborate wrought-iron gates flanked the prestigious entrance into one of the original cemeteries on the banks of the Mystic River.

Weaving his way through the narrow, tree-lined road, the SUV approached a mansion-like stone building. The two detectives strode in, and the super met them in the foyer.

"Detective, do you often get mail at a cemetery?"

"Today, I do, sir. I just had a similar conversation at Cedar Grove in New London."

Pointing to where the envelope was left, the super stepped aside. Peabody took pictures of the envelope. Morrison donned his gloves, then ripped open the seal. Again, on crumpled paper was a message written in black ink.

Ask for the key to the Avery Chapel at the
Colonel Ledyard Cemetery of Groton.

Morrison held up the note for the superintendent to read. "Can you help me?"

"Well, that's an unusual request. They are closed, but I have a copy of the key to the gate. I'll have Mr. Philips, the sexton, meet you there. He oversees the care of the cemetery and the restoration of Avery Chapel. They're trying to refurbish it, and construction and storage materials are scattered around inside." He handed him the gate key. "I'll give him a call now. It's on Mitchell Street."

"Got it. Thank you, sir."

The two detectives raced back to the SUV. "Let's hit it, Peabody, and call Detective Hanniford."

On their way, Peabody made the call, and Morrison spoke. "Hey, Detective, we have a tip on our dual case. Can you meet us at Colonel Ledyard Cemetery? Someone is playing a game with us." He reviewed the details.

They drove through the central gate and toward the chapel in the far corner of the ancient cemetery with tombs from the 1700s. Once the detectives were out of the vehicle, they could hear the sirens in the distance.

"It sounds like an entourage of blue light specials, Boss." Peabody tingled with excitement and adrenaline. *This must be why Morrison loves the job.*

The sexton, Mr. Philips, arrived. He was taken aback by the interest in the cemetery. He led Morrison and Peabody to the building. A hefty padlock hung from a chain on the double doors to the entrance. With a key of his own, he wrestled with the lock. "You're sure in a hurry, sir. These dead people aren't going anywhere fast." Try as he might, the sexton couldn't unlock the door. Finally, he looked at Morrison in disbelief. "Someone must have switched the lock. Maybe it was the contractor."

Hanniford, and multiple police cruisers, arrived. All the noisemakers went quiet, and Hanniford asked, "What's happening?"

The sexton answered, "It seems the lock has been changed."

Hanniford yelled an order to an officer, who pulled an extreme-sized bolt cutter from the trunk of his vehicle. The tool snipped through the heavy lock, and the thick wooden doors creaked open. Multiple officers stood outside as the sexton and the detectives peered into the timeworn Gothic chapel built in 1934. Morrison lit his flashlight and could see footprints in the middle aisle in the dust. Keeping to a side aisle, they strode in.

The dim realm was illuminated by sunlight through the nine stained glass windows where spiderwebs hung in every corner. Chestnut beams supported the high peaked single room of sixty-feet by thirty-feet. Eight hand-carved wooden pews stood firm in the forlorn space. Although the chapel lacked repair, it still had an alluring appeal and was in good condition for its age.

The detectives carefully maneuvered around the construction debris that cluttered the impressive slate floor.

Peabody noticed a stone archway that denoted the altar with an antique pulpit. On inspection, he discovered behind it a thin rectangular package. "What's in the brown paper, Mr. Philips?"

The sexton stepped forward with curiosity. "I don't know," he reached toward it.

Morrison quickly stopped his hand. "We'll take it from here, sir." A pair of latex gloves were pulled from his pocket, and he snapped them on. Hanniford came forward with his latex gloves. The package was approximately two-feet by three-feet, flat and slim.

"Morrison, you said notes were written to you, and they directed you here. What the hell is going on?" Hanniford slanted the package forward. A manila envelope was stuck to the back. He carefully removed it. Detective Morrison's name was printed boldly on it. Hanniford handed it to him, and he ripped it open. Another bold message emerged on crumpled paper.

Aaron was dead when we arrived.

Hanniford's officers outside had now huddled by the door to listen in and observe the discovery. Intrigued, Morrison looked at Hanniford and said,

"Does this package look to be the size of the stolen framed painting?" Hopeful, Hanniford said, "It couldn't be, could it?"

Peabody offered, "It could be!"

Carefully, Hanniford pulled at the brown paper wrappings and revealed bubble wrap. Grabbing a corner, he slowly folded it back. Carefully, he lifted and glided the object out of its wrappings.

The painting of the well-dressed man at the opera house emerged, *Monsieur Returns the Gaze - In the Loge.* The reveal elicited a simultaneous gasp from the group. Exclamations and questions reverberated in the raftered room of the sanctuary.

Detective Hanniford announced, "Alright, everyone, don't get too excited. Someone is behind this ridiculous method of grandstanding. They've sent Morrison on a wild chase for this discovery. It may appear to be the BFA Museum painting, but it could be another spoof. Therefore, the first order of business will be to authenticate the painting."

Hanniford immediately contacted the BFA museum director and had him on speakerphone. Everyone listened. Upon hearing the news, the director asked for the measurements. Hanniford looked to the sexton, who readily grabbed a tape measure from the construction equipment. Stretching the tape across height and width, he announced, "The painting is twenty-six by thirty-two inches."

The BFA director answered, "That is accurate. And I will send my authenticator by train immediately."

Hanniford's team let out a spontaneous whooping cheer.

"As you can hear, director, we are relieved," Hanniford explained. "We have been searching for this painting and the thieves nonstop, sir." The director spoke, "I love your enthusiasm, but we need to verify this is the Cassatt. Let's hope for a miracle."

Mr. Philips said, "Director, it was found in our chapel. I'm the sexton. I'll put a request into the angels for you." His eyes looked upward as he said a silent prayer for the painting to be authentic and added a few avaricious thoughts. *Hopefully, a providential discovery inside our chapel will help donations soar! Our beautiful Avery Chapel may be restored after all!*

Morrison returned to his vehicle and handed over the evidence bags with the manila envelopes to Hanniford. They would dust for fingerprints and process to determine any connection to the art heist.

"I'm not sure what these jokers are up to, Hanniford. If that is the painting, what was the point of stealing it? Was it too hot a commodity, and now they think they're off the hook because they returned it?"

"You're right, Morrison. It's only been days since it was stolen. Possibly their buyer bailed because of Aaron's death, and these thieves didn't have a backup. They may have expected to unload it quickly, but it became too hot to keep. Our success often comes when criminals don't think things through. Yet, we still don't know if Aaron was part of the plan.

"They found his body on the lawn and hauled him out of sight, but maybe Aaron was supposed to open the door or assist them. And maybe, Aaron provided the forgery."

Morrison offered, "I've interviewed Aaron's friends, and you've spoken to the other volunteers from that night, but neither of us has yet uncovered a viable suspect. But listen, we have Aaron's girlfriend, Marguerite Santa Maria, and I was informed this morning that she would recover from the near drowning. She may be our source about Aaron, the forgery, and the theft."

"Good!" Hanniford put his hand on Morrison's shoulder, relieved to hear this news. "Maybe we are getting somewhere, although slowly. I have the forgery being forensically examined as we speak. They are looking at the paint, and anything in it, brush bristles, dirt, etcetera, that can tell us where it was painted and by whom. This makes me wonder if the girlfriend felt guilt for the crime and grief for her boyfriend, then tried to end her life."

"Hanniford, the doctors found she was also high on magic mushrooms when she went into the water. Both had an altered reality when they met their outcome. We don't know if Aaron died from terrible judgment or because he was a thief.

"Even the homicide of Marilyn Maroney coincided with two of her paintings being stolen."

Hanniford scoffed, "It's unlikely her paintings and this world-renowned BFA theft are related." He looked toward his police unit. "Hey, we could speculate all day, but we each have a job to do. Hopefully, this painting will be confirmed. We'll finish processing this scene, Morrison. See you later."

"Sure thing. I'll check back with Elm Grove Cemetery and see if they have any video of who left the envelope for me. There's evidence out there…and we need to find it."

"Absolutely." They shook hands and parted.

Morrison walked away thinking about what Hanniford said: 'It was unlikely Marilyn's paintings were related to the theft of the BFA Museum painting.'

"Hmm, I'm not convinced yet," he murmured and made his way to Peabody.

Hanniford shook his head and wondered, *Did these perps think they were off the hook because they left a note saying Aaron was already dead?*

These suspects were guilty of abuse of a corpse. It was written law that a person could not legally change the location of a body. It must be left where found so the investigation can accurately determine the cause of death.

Back in his SUV, Morrison looked at his watch. It was nearly 1 p.m. He asked Peabody to call Karl. The meeting with the Rubens would have to wait until another day. They had more pressing concerns.

After the call, Peabody was full of questions. "Boss, who would go to all that trouble and choreograph the delivery of those envelopes to the cemeteries? Have you run into this kind of cat and mouse before?"

"It's always cat and mouse when there is a homicide. But this person, or more likely persons, is bolder than usual. I don't think it's a fluke that Aaron died the night a priceless painting was stolen. That would be an odd coincidence."

"Yeah, well, coincidences don't exist in this case. Right, Boss?"

Morrison chuckled. "You're getting the hang of analysis. We'll try to prove that and head back to Elm Grove Cemetery now. They're likely to have video cameras on site. Then we'll check in with Cedar Grove. Why don't you call them both so they will be prepared for our visit?" Morrison smiled to himself. *A thinking greenhorn who pays attention is worth every penny.*

***

Mystic's Detective John Hanniford was top billing on the five o'clock news Tuesday evening. He proudly reported to the world that the BFA Museum's priceless Cassatt painting had been returned unharmed. An expert authenticator from the Boston Fine Arts Museum examined the painting with the tools of her trade, verifying that *Monsieur Returns the Gaze - In the Loge* was the original painting by Mary Stevenson Cassatt.

CHAPTER 54

From Mystic to the City of Steeples
Wednesday

The Mystic River Fine Art Museum closure was lifted after the Cassatt painting was discovered, and Karl was gratefully reinstated to oversee his domain. He was expecting Roxanne's visit to care for the plants and Georgi's conversation to be just what he needed for a fresh restart. At 10 a.m., the duo arrived in the grand gallery, and Karl stepped out of his office to greet them.

"Karl, I am so pleased to hear the painting was recovered," Georgi congratulated. "Roxanne and I heard on the news last night that they released the investigative hold."

Karl stood in his traditional pose with his hands behind his back, but he also tipped up on his toes with glee. "Yes, a miracle has happened, a sheer and brilliant miracle. Everything has come together at once. I am so grateful the detective allowed me to reopen today. I no longer need to fret. The angels have given me the gift of a lifetime. I hardly can believe it."

Roxanne and Georgi's mouths gaped at the transformation in Karl's personality. He appeared…happy.

"Just yesterday, the painting was found in an old cemetery nearby. After the BFA Museum examined it thoroughly, it was returned to Boston last night. My mother and I are over the moon. My reputation might be tarnished, but it's not ruined."

"Oh no!" Georgi exclaimed. "Your reputation did not falter, Karl. You had the most fabulous party that impressed and pleased everyone. No one thinks less of you or the museum because of it. The nasty thieves are the villains."

"Why do you think they gave it back?" Roxanne wondered.

"It may be that their buyer backed out of the deal with all the international publicity. The Cassatt painting could only be sold on the black market, and they may not have had the connections. If they kept it, they would have been hunted for the rest of their lives."

"Do you think Aaron was involved in the theft?" Roxanne asked, hoping for helpful information.

Karl surprised them by looking over his shoulder as if someone could be listening. They were alone, yet he answered in a hushed tone. "At first, I did.

But no, Roxanne, I honestly don't. I reviewed the security tapes from several locations around the museum, and a video caught Aaron alone on our rooftop patio. He was balancing on the edge. I understand he did parkour roof jumping acts and performance art. The video captured when he fell, and it was before the thieves arrived."

"Oh no, you saw it happen!" Roxanne grabbed Georgi's arm, and he became suddenly uncomfortable and looked for a seat. Karl led them into the office, where they both took a chair.

"I'm very sorry, Georgi. I didn't know you knew him too."

Roxanne spoke up. "Georgi knew him through volunteering at the Dahlia Gallery. But since you believe it was a true accident, that narrows our thoughts on what happened to Marguerite."

"Who is Marguerite?"

"Aaron's girlfriend. She was found nearly drowned on Sunday in the Mystic River, poor dear. As far as we know, she's still unconscious in the hospital."

"My goodness, I'm sorry to hear this. Georgi, do you need a glass of water?" Karl's forehead wrinkled with concern. Georgi nodded while holding his chest. He felt overcome by the image of Aaron falling to his death.

Roxanne pulled a small vile from her purse. "Here, this will help you. It will activate a calming effect on your nerves. It's called Rescue Remedy and is a flower essence for stress and distress." She added four drops to his glass of water.

To purposely distract Georgi from his grief, Roxanne asked Karl, "Have you ever had a theft happen at a museum before?"

Karl seemed to be caught off guard and hesitated before answering. "Well, yes. I was at the BFA Museum when a theft occurred. It was a Rembrandt. When they found the painting, it was under a woman's bed. I was appalled. How could anyone disgrace a priceless painting in such a manner? The thief had to be desperate not to hang a Rembrandt," Karl scoffed.

Roxanne noticed that Georgi was attentive to Karl's story.

Karl continued, "Then the most shocking theft in the world happened right next door to the BFA Museum at the Isabella Stewart Gardner Mansion. You might have heard of this infamous art heist back in 1990. This was devastating to me. I've been visiting there since I was a small child, and on hearing the security was disarmed and the priceless works were swiped, well I was heartbroken. It's still a mystery to this day."

Karl paused. He wondered if he should reveal more of himself to his friendly acquaintances. "I must admit, Isabella, the art collector, has my adoration. She perfectly put her pieces together in a grand mansion, a real palace she designed. She was my inspiration." Karl gushed uncharacteristically, and Georgi was amazed to see his humanity.

"I read her biographies and found her like a strong tea. You become steeped in her knowledge and wit, love of art and architecture. Like the tea, you are awakened, refreshed, and enlivened by her wonderous affection for all things rare and beautiful. That's how I feel whenever I visit her mansion.

"Did you know, according to legend, the word *museum* is from the Greeks, 'place of the Muses?' Isabella is my muse."

Georgi, now sitting upright, was enraptured by the tale and said, "That's wonderful, Karl. I love hearing about what inspires people. I will have to go sometime and see this palace you love so much."

"I can take you there by train one day, Georgi. You will be my guest of honor in Boston."

"Wow, why thank you, Sir Karl Rubens. You must be the Earl De Luxe in Boston society!" Georgi gave a flourishing wave from his forehead to the floor to give a whimsical lift to Karl's status.

Suddenly, Karl looked as though he might sneeze, his nose squinched and eyes tilted upwards. But then he laughed with a funny sniff while his shoulders shook. It was a peculiar snicker that made Roxanne and Georgi giggle with astonishment, realizing they found where his funny bone was hiding.

Roxanne was pleased the two were content and excused herself to check the plants and see if any needed watering. After ten minutes, Karl and Georgi joined her outdoors.

"Roxanne," Karl asked, "Georgi has made a good suggestion, and I would like to know if you are interested in creating a labyrinth garden for me? I have wanted one all my life, and finally, I have enough land. Georgi said you could design one."

"Really?" Roxanne lifted from her plant inspecting position with excitement. "I would be honored, Karl."

"Once things settle," he said, "I will have you over to the house."

"That sounds wonderful, Karl. But before we go, Georgi, didn't we want to ask Karl about our friends?"

Georgi picked up the hint and remembered their mission. "Karl, did you know Marilyn Maroney? She was a dear friend of mine, and I just wondered...."

"If you mean the young lady from the Dahlia, no, I didn't know her. But I heard from people in the art world that her work was outstanding, and I should include her in a show. They encouraged me to meet her since she lived so close by. I did contact her, but she was busy with her travel schedule. Again, I'm sorry for your loss, Georgi." Karl was empathetic and added, "I was planning a Rising Star exhibit here sometime in the future. I would have considered her work."

"Hmm, that would have been nice," said Georgi. "I wish you had met her. She was very vibrant." Gazing across the museum gallery, he asked, "Did you consider Cora Swift too?"

"Why, no, I haven't. Who is she?"

"She is an artist who lives above the Dahlia Gallery as well. Four days after Marilyn's death, she was fooled by an art agent, drugged, and abducted. It was just devasting for everyone."

"My goodness, I did hear about it, and it sounds like a few undesirables are in the neighborhood."

Roxanne responded swiftly, "No, that's just a bad rap often repeated about New London. Infiltrators enter our City of Steeples. This man is supposedly from New York. His name is Mario Corinthian. Have you ever heard of him?"

Karl's brow furrowed and huffed, "Corinthian is an order in ancient Greek architecture. It is not a family name."

"Yes, I was curious about the name," Roxanne acknowledged. "It has other meanings, like a swaggering adventurer or a yachtsman."

Karl shook his head. "It must be an alias. Besides, would a criminal give out his name?"

"Unlikely," said Roxanne. She realized their mission of gathering information was complete. "The garden looks good, Karl. There has been enough rain, so Georgi, if you're ready, we can go if you like?"

"Yes, I'm ready. Thank you, Karl, for taking the time to meet with us. We do feel that knowing what happened to Aaron is helpful. And oh! I nearly forgot, we are having a little fundraiser for Aaron's family and the other artists at Dev's Bistro this Friday night. Are you available?"

"Sorry, we won't be, but I'll give you a monetary donation. I'll write you a check now." Karl walked to his office, and Georgi followed him. "Georgi, is a thousand dollars acceptable?"

Georgi's hands went to his heart. "That's quite fine, Karl. You're very generous." Karl gave him a sincere, rare smile and walked them to the door.

Roxanne and Georgi headed toward the car. "How do you think that went?" Roxanne asked.

"I'm reassured hearing Aaron most likely had nothing to do with the theft. I'm more impressed with Karl. We know he wasn't familiar with Marilyn, Cora, or Marguerite. I believe the Mystic connection is now zilch. The rooftop patio tempted Aaron, which seemed like a bad accident. What do you think?"

"I agree. Mystic isn't part of the pattern of criminal intent with the artists. Aaron and Marguerite seem to be separate and unfortunate incidents. We need to move on with our research. Hopefully, our trusted detective will figure it out." Georgi nodded, and Roxanne's tone changed. "On a different note, I did like seeing Karl's lighter side. He seems transformed. And what a check! I think he is better for knowing you, Georgi."

"I am very grateful, but remember, you'll be designing a labyrinth garden! How exciting is that?"

"We'll stop for another brief adventure if you don't mind. Are you ready?" Roxanne asked.

His eyes sparkled. "I was born ready."

In Search of Labyrinths

Roxanne and Georgi hopped into his burgundy PT Cruiser, and she directed him to turn toward Main Street and pointed to a grand building, "This architectural delight is our destination." An ornate pediment crowned the entrance.

"This extravagant mansion?" They walked across the lawn.

"No, it's the Mystic & Noank Library. A famous sailor, Sea Captain Spicer financed this brick and granite edifice across from his house in 1893. It's filled with materials from around the world: Italian mosaics, African marble, and stained-glass windows. Come on, let's go inside."

"While we are here, I want you to see a special room." Roxanne pulled him along.

They wound their way up a magnificent staircase. On reaching the second floor, Georgi whispered, "Wow, the wood beams and vaulted ceiling make it feel like a sailing ship, but upside-down. The craftsmanship is superior! Can we lie on the floor to stare up at it?"

Roxanne giggled and walked him to the end of the room. They grabbed chairs and sat by an impressive brick fireplace. Leaning back, they looked up at the antique woodwork.

Leaving him there, Roxanne searched and found the book *Labyrinths & Mazes: A Complete Guide to Magical Paths of the World* by Jeff Saward. She returned, and they leafed through the book together. "I'll enjoy this research for Karl's garden." She hugged the thick volume, "I can escape into a secret, treasured realm."

Georgi squeezed her hand. "Gardens and books for you, food and wine for me. By the way, isn't this a fine place for a party? I wonder if they rent it."

She elbowed him. "Why should I be surprised, Mr. Sommelier? Your radar is fine-tuned for places of enjoyment."

Arm in arm, the duo left the library blissfully unaware they were being followed. A quiet man had been watching them through the library stacks and listening to their conversations. When Georgi's PT Cruiser left, so did the covert operator's SUV.

He followed them on their route from Mystic to the City of Steeples.

CHAPTER 55

Deceit and Decadence
Wednesday

Finally, Det. Jack Peabody's research into the video footage from the cemeteries bore results. A livery driver had dropped the first two manila envelopes off. He met Peabody in New London so he could answer questions.

"Why yes, Detective, I delivered the two manila envelopes Monday night. I met up with a man in the parking lot by Denny's restaurant at eight o'clock near the I-95 highway. Neither of us got out of the car; he just drove up and handed me the two packages. He wanted them delivered that night and gave me two fifty-dollar bills. I was happy to take his money."

"Did he show you any identification or give you a name?" Peabody asked.

"Yes, his name was Mario Corinthian, and he said he had two burials to pay for immediately. He told me to put the envelopes in the cemeteries' overnight drop boxes, so I did."

Eagerly, Peabody pulled out Cora's sketch. "Did he look like this?"

The driver carefully considered it. "It could be him."

"Did he have a phone number or anything else?" Peabody asked.

The livery driver swiped through his phone. "Let me see here…no, I can't help you. It was one of those numbers that come up as private."

"I'm sorry, sir, but I need to confiscate your phone to determine which cell tower the call pinged from. If you'd like, you can follow me to police headquarters, and we'll do it right now." This was the first lead that connected the cases, and Peabody was eager.

"Yes, sir, I can do that. Whatever you need."

Peabody triangulated the calls and located pings, one out of Mystic and then New London. The caller likely used a burner phone and destroyed it. Sharing the news with his boss, Peabody excitedly told him they had verified the brazen Mario Corinthian operating in New London and Mystic. Morrison was intrigued that the villain didn't seem to care that they knew.

His first step was to make a call. "Hello Hanniford, this is Morrison. We have a lead that a person using the name Mario Corinthian stole the painting in addition to abducting Cora Swift. Our cases have come together."

Hanniford was intrigued. "Let's broadcast the sketch of Corinthian on TV, print news, and social media. Maybe that will trigger a response."

"I'll do that, and we heard from Marilyn's art agent, Garfield Feinberg. He said there are rumors of a rogue group of art purveyors operating among thieves. Supposedly, works of art are traded and auctioned underground to wealthy buyers. Can you ask the FBI to investigate this for us?"

"Sure thing. This case is finally moving. We'll talk soon."

Morrison considered his plan of action. He had learned from Dr. Strom that Aaron was most likely a casualty of bad behavior. He surmised that Marguerite was a likely victim of grief, so he regrouped his efforts and focused on Mario and his accomplices. His team would put Mario's mug everywhere and revisit New London's public places with the sketch. Georgi's event organized with Candace at Dev's Bistro for the Dahlia artists was on his list to peruse.

Friday evening - Three weeks since Marilyn's fatality

Georgi arrived at Dev's Bistro early to assist with the final setup of the surprise fundraiser dinner. Bunny graciously greeted him at the hosting podium. She had a short, chic hairstyle and wore a black fitted dress that shimmered when she moved. Bunny was Candace's mother and a "hostess with the mostest" when it came to entertaining the patrons in the restaurant.

Georgi leaned in and gave her a peck on the cheek. "Hello, darling," he said. "I'm glad you could be here because you always put people at ease. My friends adore their conversations with you, but mostly your sense of humor."

Bunny was fashionable, in her seventies, and as lively as ever. She wrapped her arm around his shoulder. "I wouldn't miss this, Georgi. I love seeing people be surprised by love. They will have a real treat tonight with the evening you planned."

"Can I see your decorative pin of the night?" he asked. Slowly, she turned and sashayed away. Her back shoulder showed off a delicate hummingbird pin. She dramatically turned and swayed back toward him to present the pin up close.

He smiled. "You wear it so well. Tell me again, why the placement on the back shoulder?"

"It leaves a lasting impression when I walk away. It's an unexpected flourish, a curiosity. For instance, when I'm speaking to a smart, handsome man and leave his table, I look over my shoulder to see if he's still watching. If he is, I'll circle around for more conversation." Bunny cupped her hand and whispered, "When I return, I may tease him and say, 'Come up and see me sometime. I'll have nothing on but the radio.'"

Georgi's eyes grew wide. She reminded him of his idol, Mae West. "You are a tease," he laughed. "I love it."

"If I get a smile," she continued, "I know the man has a sense of humor. If he doesn't, then I can't be bothered. I won't waste my time with a man who doesn't know how to laugh. Life's too short, Georgi."

"You inspire me."

"Here, come and see what has been done for tonight."

The lovely space exuded elegance with candlelit lanterns glowing, flower vases, and a charming, old-world coffered ceiling. The long wooden bar had fine choices of champagne, all resting on ice. Very soon, the bistro would be hopping with activity, and the guests of honor had no idea of the secrets soon to be revealed.

By 7 p.m., the house was full of people, and the room was abuzz with conversations. Candace and Georgi inconspicuously walked to the front of the room to stand atop a small stage. Behind them was a large, paned window, and through it shone historic streetlights and the marquee of the Garde Arts Center in the distance. Georgi smiled, glanced over the audience, pulled out his small bell, and rang it gently into the microphone. When he'd caught everyone's attention, he handed the microphone to Candace.

"Tonight," she began, "we are here to surprise our guests of honor, the Dahlia artists in residence: Troy, Cora, Teddy, Bruce, and Ophelia, the director. We are all here to offer our condolences and much more. Mr. Georgi Algarve and key anonymous donors have paid for the meals and drink this evening, so one hundred percent of your two-hundred-dollar donation will go directly to the artists who have been affected.

"The funds raised will provide five thousand dollars to Marilyn's estate and Aaron's family, who are here in name only, and two thousand dollars to each artist. The contributions will assist them directly as they go through these trials of grief. It will help with rent and art supplies. We ask, 'What do artists need or want?' Good food, a place to create, and supplies to make their art. We will help provide that tonight!"

The crowd erupted in cheer. They clapped and carried on as all like to do at Dev's Bistro events. The honorees were stunned.

Troy, with his artist friends, enjoyed this unexpected gift, a break from their world of woes. They cried and laughed and were amazed by the generosity of the community. Troy noticed Cora, Ophelia, Teddy, and Bruce were smiling and relaxing. They had heard Georgi put on a good party, but this was the first time they would witness his sommelier finesse in a wine dinner presentation.

Georgi, the master of ceremonies, stepped to the microphone. "My dear friends, Chef Rachel has prepared an exquisite variety of decadent delights for our special event. Candace and I have paired champagnes to perfect your experience. Let me start with a little wine education, and if you know me, you know I like to call it 'Vino Veritas,' also known as 'Wine Truths,' about these fine champagnes.

"We shall first serve a bottle of romantic champagne called Perrier-Jouët Grand Brut. In 1811, Pierre-Nicholas and his wife, Rose-Adélaide, founded this champagne house with their famous blend. Your mouth will bask in the energetic effervescence and flavors of the pinot and chardonnay grapes. It is excellently paired with oysters, caviar, or a robustly flavored main course."

The guests sipped along with Georgi and murmured their approval.

"Tonight, we are classically pairing this incredibly versatile champagne with Blue Point oysters, fresh from our own Long Island Sound waters. The oysters are served three ways on the half shell. First, we have black truffle crème fraîche. Next is freshly shaved horseradish, and thirdly, a mignonette of shallots marinated in champagne vinegar, salt, sugar, and crushed white peppercorns."

A team of servers appeared and passed around the platters of various oyster delicacies. The group tasted, humming their satisfaction, and sipped the exquisite champagne.

After twenty minutes, Georgi stepped up to the microphone and announced his next offering. "Okay, my dears, if you have not yet realized it," he held one finger in the air, "then you shall know it now." He whispered into the mic, "You are in a den of delicious decadence."

"Oooh," murmured the patrons in unison. The artists giggled to see Georgi in sommelier action. This show was different from his serving wine at the Dahlia art receptions. They loved it.

Georgi made a presentational wave toward the kitchen. Trays of food appeared. He proclaimed, "May I present white sturgeon caviar atop buckwheat and Yukon Gold blinis."

A train of servers marched to their table positions and lowered the trays simultaneously in a performance art fashion. The guests clapped with vigor.

"With this divine caviar, I bring Veuve Clicquot, a gold-label champagne." Placing a finger by his nose, he said, "This is a well-known wine among those in the know. This Veuve is the Grande dame of French champagne and is always welcome to a party. Yes, there are others, but taste this loveliness and dispute it if you dare." Everyone sipped. Georgi put his hand to his ear and listened. "What did you say?" The patrons nodded in agreement. He smiled like an imp and exclaimed, "I hear no challenge!"

"It's delicious!" called out a guest. "Superb," said another. Georgi left the small stage with a twinkle in his eye and mingled with the Dahlia artists. After another twenty minutes, he received the sign from Candace and went to the microphone to jingle his bell for attention.

"Coming your way, diners of the delectable is a French rainbow trout caviar on toasted brioche, topped with shaved black truffle. As you take your time to enjoy another sampling of either of the two champagnes presented, please meander through the room and mingle."

Georgi stopped by the kitchen door to check on Chef Rachel and her team, who were preparing the next round of gastronomic sensations. Candace gave him a nudge. "A busboy says a gentleman is asking to see you at the back door. Do you want to be disturbed?"

"Oh, it must be the man with another case of champagne. I will go." He quickly descended the stairs and opened the exterior door to the rear of the building. A solitary lamp shone on a person whose face was hidden by shadow.

"Hello, do you have the champagne?" Georgi asked.

"No, Georgi, it's Detective Morrison." He changed position, and the light illuminated him.

"What are you doing out here?" He jokingly added, "Are you trying to crash my party?"

"Not exactly. I found out you were holding this event and wanted to look around. Can you let me in?"

"Let you in? Ha-ha, you are crashing my party!"

"Georgi, I'm looking for a certain person of interest. I believe he could be hiding among your guests."

Clutching his chest, Georgi cried, "Dear me, you can't be serious. A villain among our guests?" His hand went to his forehead as he carried on with another distressed pose. "I do declare, Detective, you have rattled my nerves." He grabbed Morrison's arm. "You must come in now. I'll feel safer with you here." He pulled him in and shut the door.

As usual, Morrison was amused by Georgi's antics, but his biggest concern was that another incident might occur, which made him ever watchful, and even a little twitchy.

Suddenly, Georgi noticed the detective's attire. "What are you wearing?" he exclaimed. He stood back and looked him over, providing commentary. "Nice jeans, leather loafers, and an open-collared shirt. Detective, you look different, and I like it."

"I'm in off-duty clothes. You saw me dressed casually at the museum. Come on, let's go." Morrison smoothed his hair as he followed him up the stairs to the lively crowd.

Talking over his shoulder, Georgi said, "You must eat something, Detective, or you'll look out of place." They entered the room.

Candace recognized the detective right away and raised her eyebrows. He whispered in her ear, "Incognito tonight." She nodded.

Georgi checked in with the kitchen and proceeded to the stage to make his following announcement. "My sweet and generous friends, I can bestow a fine, rare champagne for our event. It is from the collection of my former boss, Mitch Stockman; God rest his soul. He had a case of Piper-Heidsieck Cuvée Rare. People who know this champagne will say, 'Wow.'

"It's a 2006 champagne that radiates an iridescent yellow-green gold and is delicate and dynamic. Its bubbles glisten in flaxen brilliance. It has a honeyed nose and dried apricots on the palate with sweet spices, citron lime, and accents of sweet pastries."

Dan Morrison, the handsome, single, off-duty detective, moved among the people like a guest as Georgi spoke. He kept his distance from the artists and managed to stand where he could discreetly observe the room. Was the man in Cora's sketch lurking here? Now that he had the lead from the livery driver about Mario Corinthian, he wanted to be everywhere.

Morrison's gut told him to search high and low because someone must have seen him. This fundraising party might enable these goons to show up, skulk among the crowd, and scout for targets.

Thankfully, he had the help of two natural observers, Bunny and Candace. Being in the people business all their lives, they could spot someone out of place like a gnat on a steak. Neither was shy to shut down an unsuitable patron, kick them out, or call the police. "Not in my house!" was their motto.

Morrison's monitoring was interrupted by Georgi ringing his bell for the diners' attention.

"Approaching you now, my guests, are platters of fine finger foods." The servers paraded through the room and offered the selections as Georgi described them. "We present a variety of savory delights. They are rosemary and parmesan encrusted lamb lollichops; Kobe beef cheesesteaks with truffled fontina cheese on toasted brioche buns. We also have sea scallops topped with a salty drizzle of creamy pressed caviar sauce on potato pancakes; crispy potato galettes with roasted garlic, rosemary, and shredded asiago cheese."

The artists were overjoyed with the food and the love being showered upon them. It was one thing to lose someone, but entirely another to have continuing stressful events as it had been over the last few weeks. The community outpouring rejuvenated their well-being, and the revelry warmed their hearts.

Morrison ate a lamb lollichop and licked his fingers. Candace brought him a glass of water. "How are you doing?" she asked softly.

"I'm fine. I'm looking for unscrupulous types, a man with dark, short hair. He could be in disguise and around six feet tall. See anyone like that?"

"Yeah, him." Her chin pointed to a well-known local philanthropist. "Is that your man?"

Morrison smirked. "No. The guy I'm looking for is a supposed New York art dealer, a stranger to these parts. Here, you saw this sketch, didn't you? This is my suspect." He handed her a folded drawing of Cora's sketch. "Please show your staff again. It will refresh their memories."

Candace glanced at it. "Georgi showed it to me. I don't think he's here. I recognize almost everyone." She spotted a waitress coming from the kitchen with a full tray. "Have a Kobe beef cheesesteak while you're here. I'll show this around discreetly and text you if we see anyone suspicious." Candace went into the kitchen.

Morrison resumed his people-watching until a woman in her mid-forties rubbed against him as she passed by. She halted and said, "Excuse me," then looked him over. "Do I know you? You look familiar." Without waiting for an answer, she asked, "Why are you standing here all alone? Come with me, handsome." She grabbed his arm and pulled him along.

Suddenly, Morrison felt like a piece of meat. *This must be what it's like for a woman to get unwanted advances.* Gingerly, he slipped from under her hold and walked toward the men's room. A tray of Kobe beef on a bun passed him, so he captured one.

"Hey, where are you going?" the lady called out. It looked like he was heading for the restroom, but he went down the stairs and out the back door.

In peace, he sat in his personal vehicle, a gray Range Rover with darkened windows. He munched on the beefsteak and sighed. "I need to start eating better food. This is delicious." While Morrison waited for a text from Candace, he called an officer who was showing the sketch at the local hotels and bed and breakfast inns. So far, the night had nothing to offer but good food.

CHAPTER 56

Common Thread
Tuesday

Morrison met with Hanniford in a conference room at police headquarters in Mystic, where they spoke privately and informally. "Hi John, what's up?"

"Dan, have a seat." Hanniford began pacing the length of the spacious room. With pen in hand, he clicked it rapidly with his thumb. "I've been thinking. It is not clear that Aaron Goshen's death is linked to the theft of the painting. We're still squeezing the security company for more data.

"The latest on the forensic inspection of the forgery is they have discovered it was painted in New York. Pollen was found in the paint from a Gingko biloba tree near Central Park. We have a location now, we need the painter, and the FBI is helping us track them down.

"So, Mario Corinthian is our common thread between the artists in New London and Mystic's stolen BFA Museum painting. We have another New York link because of the van they used to abduct Cora Swift. But as you stated, all appears to have started with the murder of Marilyn Maroney. I know you said paintings were missing from her apartment, but if it is a ring of art thieves, could you imagine they stole her art, but her death was unintended? You said Marilyn was popular. Maybe she caught them stealing. What do you think?"

Morrison smoothed his hands across the surface of the conference table and took a deep breath. "My gut says to follow the art. I read the newspaper clippings and online buzz about Marilyn. Her friend Troy said her death would skyrocket the prices of her work. It's also possible that Marilyn was purposely killed so that her art would rise in price.

"A painting worth fifty thousand dollars could double or triple in price. It's easy money to a heartless thief. Do you recall the Irish bloke who stole a Vermeer painting to raise funds for guns in the Irish Republican Army? Paintings are considered a golden ticket to some of these groups."

Hanniford stopped clicking his pen, grabbed the back of a chair, and sat. "I see. Stealing for a cause gives someone plenty of motivation." He leaned forward with interest. "They had time to plan it and create a forgery. And these tough guys discarded Aaron's body without hesitation." He placed his pen on the table and folded his hands.

Morrison leaned forward and offered his details, "Marilyn's art agent, Feinberg informed us that her work has been hot since her death. The art dealers, gallery owners, buyers, and sellers are all clamoring for a deal. They want to negotiate. Feinberg has a hold on all sales of her work. But her art in the private sector is selling for top dollar."

Resting his chin in his hand, Morrison added, "According to Feinberg, the hold he has on her work is only making the prices go higher. He's white-knuckled while waiting for the go-ahead to sell. I told him he had to hold until we knew who killed her, and he also needed to wait for the family to come forward to read the will."

"Where is her family?" Hanniford asked.

"Her friend, Georgi Algarve, claims she lost contact with her parents, and he knows no other relatives." Morrison leaned back in his chair. "John, has the FBI talked with Feinberg about that art ring theory?"

Hanniford nodded. "Yes, the FBI is talking to him and working this case hard because of the BFA Museum and the connections into New York. They're investigating the forgery too, but no hard evidence yet. They are tracking anyone associating with Karl and Isadore Rubens too. I have a list from the FBI of people they've encountered since the theft. This fellow you mentioned, Georgi Algarve, is on it with Roxanne Samson. They were the first to visit Karl Rubens when the museum reopened last Wednesday." He handed Morrison a printout with fifteen names and addresses.

Morrison felt a twinge of dread when he saw Georgi and Roxanne's names at the top of the list. He tempered himself to remain neutral. "Yes, I know these two. I'm pretty sure they are innocent bystanders. Both assisted with the reopening of the museum. Roxanne Samson is Fire Chief Samson's wife and installed the museum's flowering plants. Georgi Algarve was the wine aficionado at the museum and organized the bar and servers. He also discovered Marilyn Maroney and was her friend.

"I can practically vouch for them, but I will ask them why they visited Mr. Rubens and tape my conversation with them for the record."

Hanniford looked over his reading glasses with a deadpan expression. "You know this makes Georgi Algarve a viable suspect. He is a connecting link between both cases in New London and Mystic. I trust your instinct, Dan. I'll have the FBI's special agent call you so you can inform him of these two and why they are in touch with the Rubens."

"That's fine, John." Morrison leaned back in his chair. "There are many cogs, but they are on one wheel. If it's a gang of art thieves, it makes some sense."

"Well, the return of the Cassatt painting was monkey business, not divine providence. A lot of effort for what? I don't like being a pawn in some bozo's game." Hanniford pounded on the table. "I can't wait to get close to this mastermind, so I can poke my finger in his eye."

"I'm in lockstep with you, John. I plan to squeeze Karl with questions and his mother about Aaron. Approach them from another angle. Much has occurred since my initial interview with Karl. I want to apply some pressure. We'll see if anything new comes out of it."

"Hey, have at them," Hanniford agreed. "Everyone is a person of interest until they're not."

"Changing the subject," Morrison said, "Marguerite is still unconscious. Both she and Aaron had hallucinogenic mushrooms in their bloodwork. It was isolated in the lab using gas chromatography, and the toxicologist told us the specific substance. That might have been what induced their risky activities and bad decisions."

Hanniford's office chair rocked as he nodded and thought about the ramifications. "Fascinating, Dan. Much to consider if they were taking drugs. We both have plenty to do, my friend." He stood and reached to shake Morrison's hand. "I'll be talking to you very soon."

***

As he considered returning to New London, Morrison had his two amigos on the FBI's list in mind. He wondered if locking them in a police van and driving them around for an hour would get their attention. Instead, he made a call from his vehicle to the one man he knew would understand him. "Chief, this is Morrison. Your wife and Georgi are on my naughty list."

"What do you mean?" Fire Chief Samson drew his hand over his white handlebar mustache with concern.

"They've been fraternizing with Karl Rubens, and the FBI has him and his mother under surveillance. This is just between you and me. I know they have nothing to do with the art theft, but the FBI is watching everyone encountering the Rubens. Roxanne and Georgi were the first to visit Karl at the museum on Wednesday after the police tape came down and it reopened. Can you believe it?"

"This is nuts." The chief cleared his throat. "Well, you know they are benign. Roxanne wanted to check on the plants and was most comfortable having Georgi along. But those two won't waste an opportunity to find out more. They are notoriously crafty at sleuthing.

"Roxanne just wants to help Georgi, who is looking for why bad things have happened to his friends." Sam tugged on his chin. "Question them and rattle their bones a little, Morrison. Hammer home the fact that the FBI is on their tails. That should wake them up and encourage them to keep their hands in their pockets for a while."

Morrison chuckled. "Rattle their bones? I can do that. Thanks, Chief. As you know, I'm keeping you in the Roxanne loop."

"Yes, thanks for the heads-up. Roxanne doesn't tell me everything, and in a way, I'm glad I don't know the half of it."

They chuckled and said goodbye.

***

Morrison stopped by his office at police headquarters. Detective Peabody dashed in behind him. "Boss, you're not going to believe it!"

"Try me," he said dryly. "I'm the type who will believe just about anything. I've seen a lot."

"Mr. Garfield Feinberg has a life insurance policy on Marilyn Maroney. He could be the guy who hired the thieves!"

"Did you retrieve the records from the insurance company?"

"Yes, sir. They're incriminating! The policy is for four hundred fifty thousand dollars and is only six months old!" Peabody had a handful of copies of the policy in hand. Waving them in the air, he darted enthusiastically to a table to splay them out and show his boss the new lead.

"Call him in here immediately, pronto, no excuses. I want to see him ASAP." Morrison felt the urgency. Perturbed, he swiped his hands through his hair while thinking he had been misled.

"Yes, sir." Peabody took off to make the call.

While he waited to hear the outcome, Morrison called Marguerite's doctor, who updated him on her condition. "Marguerite is not awake yet, but her vitals are strengthening. Her family and friends are constantly by her side since they know she can hear them. They're reading to her and trying everything to bring her back from the locked-in state that her body is in."

"That's good to know," said Morrison. "Hopefully, it works. I'm looking forward to talking to her."

He made another call to the angel of death, Dr. Angela Storm. "How are you doing with your cases?" she asked.

"I have nothing to go on. I believe Marilyn was the only murder victim. All I have is what we see on the video and what we can surmise. Aaron was doing a balancing act while drunk and high on mushrooms. Marguerite nearly drowned due to her grief while high. I don't see a villain there?"

Dr. Storm asked, "Detective, it's your case, but my instinct is telling me this villain is unusual. Youths are attracted to risk. You said he appeared drunk on the video, but who led Aaron up to the rooftop? And when Marguerite wakes up, I wonder who she was with last. You may discover the mushrooms are a clue if they both didn't take them intentionally.

"Since Marilyn was pushed, I sense something sinister is going on. Your skepticism toward a guilty person in Aaron's death or Marguerite's near-drowning might keep you sane, but it won't necessarily be correct. They may have had access to psilocybin mushrooms, but what if they didn't?

"If you ask the right questions to a devious person, they may sense a threat and even escalate and eliminate someone else. It could even be you. I've seen strange things in my profession. I'm just saying not to take any pieces off the game board yet."

Taken aback, Morrison queried, "Are you saying someone might threaten me? Ha, I doubt it." He was dubious of her reasoning.

"Go ahead and laugh. I've seen the evidence of their playbook. They'll eliminate anyone who threatens their well-being. I've taken down crafty sociopaths with a microscope and a lab test." She hit the mark of his mockery. "It may be my intuition, but it has served me well on many occasions." Abruptly, she was interrupted by her assistant. "Sorry, Morrison, I've got to go. We'll talk later."

Morrison was left with a quizzical feeling. *Mother always said, "Don't question a woman's intuition.*

Peabody zipped in to say Marilyn's agent Garfield Feinberg was willing to arrive in the morning but asked if he and his lawyer could have a conference call within the hour to clear up how art agents operate in the industry. Morrison agreed.

"Mr. Feinberg, you are on a conference call with New London Police's homicide department, and we are being recorded. Do you agree?"

"Yes, Detective, and I'd like to introduce my lawyer, Simon Rufus, who is on the call with us. He will confirm what I say because he writes my contracts for all the artists I represent."

"Mr. Rufus, do you agree to this conversation being recorded?" Morrison verified.

"Yes, Detective."

"Mr. Feinberg, you have a life insurance policy on Marilyn Maroney, do you not?"

"Yes. I insure any artist I feel is flying in the right direction regarding popularity, profitability, and overall ability to wow people. Let me tell you why.

"As an agent, I make a pittance of a commission compared to the artist, art dealers, gallery owners, and future buyers who become sellers. After you've been in my business long enough, you realize everyone else is getting rich. So, the only way I can secure my future is to pay on a policy just in case the artist dies prematurely. I know it sounds unique, but I'm technically insuring the effort and energy I invest into an artist's career. Mr. Rufus has written many similar contracts for thirty years, and I warrant the right to take out life insurance policies on the artists I sign."

Morrison asked, "Mr. Rufus, can you confirm all that Mr. Feinberg has said?"

"Quite right, sir. We have a standard boilerplate contract with artists, but my client has creatively added protection for his investment. I can send you a dummy contract and the one Marilyn signed. My client has nothing to hide. This is the first time we have submitted a claim on such a young artist. Twenty years ago, we had another artist die, but he was sixty-eight," Rufus explained.

"Mr. Feinberg," Morrison said, "I want you to know you are a person of interest because of the life insurance policy. In fact, Sir, you just moved to number one. You see, you have a viable reason to see her dead. And you DID NOT offer this information to us initially, even though you spoke with Detective Peabody and the FBI." Morrison then heard a peculiar sound. It was Garfield Feinberg sobbing.

"She had so much promise," he croaked, sighed, and sniffled.

"Mr. Feinberg, Detective Peabody, and I will notify you about what will happen next. Do not leave the country. Mr. Rufus, as his lawyer, please make sure your client follows all protocols as a person of interest." Morrison signed off.

"Peabody, I'm calling Detective Hanniford to have the FBI investigate the deaths of artists who have contracts with Mr. Feinberg. Mario Corinthian may be in cahoots with him. After that, we're driving to visit my number two persons of interest, the Rubens."

CHAPTER 57

Shocked into Silence
Tuesday - Mystic

Karl prepared for a new exhibit to replace the Boston Fine Art paintings at the museum. His most important task was to verify that the security company had installed the backup alarm, the extended-view camera system, and enhanced internal protocols. He felt reassured they had the incentive to bolster the security system fully since they faced a lawsuit for the failure during the theft of the Cassatt painting. After a productive day, he settled in at home to relax, yet worrying thoughts haunted him of whether people would be frightened away by the museum's misfortune.

At 6 p.m., Isadore heard a loud rapping on their door. She wasn't expecting anyone and was surprised to see two detectives standing there. "Oh, Detective Morrison, I wish I knew you were coming. I would have made my famous dinner of mushroom soup and Salisbury steak. Please, do come in."

He nodded at her pleasantries. "This is Detective Peabody, and we are here to talk to you and Karl about the night of Aaron's death."

"Yes, you did say you would reschedule. Kindly wait here in the living room, and I'll find him." Isadore drifted away in one of her floating kaftans. "Karl," she called out, "Detective Morrison is here."

They heard her footsteps fade into another end of the house. Peabody and Morrison eyed each other as they waited in the elegant living room with a view of Poggy Bay.

Isadore returned, gliding down the corridor toward them with Karl's lanky form following in long strides. "How do you do, Detectives?" he asked. Then he stepped forward to shake Morrison's and Peabody's hands. "We have not seen each other recently. I'm sad Aaron found his way to our rooftop patio, and I'm grateful the painting was returned due to your efforts. You were both at our reopening event that night, weren't you?" Karl hoped his delicate schmoozing had the desired effect. Peabody stood by with his notepad.

"Yes, Mr. Rubens, we were there because we were concerned that the culprits might try something at other art venues such as yours after Marilyn Maroney's death and the theft of her art. Oddly enough, they did. You also had a theft and a murder on the night of the reopening. It looks as though our suspicions were correct because Mario Corinthian was involved in both. This appears to be an art theft ring, and those in the way are murdered."

Karl and his mother simultaneously sunk to the sofa with gaping mouths. "Why, whatever do you mean, Detective?" Karl asked. "Aaron wasn't murdered. I understood it to be an accident. I saw the video footage from the marina across the way." Isadore vigorously nodded in agreement.

Peabody scribbled on a notepad attempting to keep track of every word while simultaneously observing Morrison's assured approach.

"You don't seem to have all the evidence, do you, Mr. Rubens?" Morrison countered. "You see, Aaron was high on mushrooms and drunk. If we had not discovered the substance in his system, we might have called it an accident. But now we have evidence and can state—he was drugged. Since you saw the videos, you know we have twenty-five minutes of missing time on the museum's cameras. Plenty can happen in twenty-five minutes, Mr. Rubens, don't you agree?"

Karl caught himself about to nod but stiffened his back instead. He cocked his head like a bird, and his eyes shifted about. He didn't know what to say or do.

So, his mother took over. "Who could have drugged him and why? I was there," she said. "I didn't see anyone. He must have found his way to the rooftop and stupidly fallen off. Karl and I had nothing to do with it. Why are you telling us he was murdered?"

Karl sat up a little straighter, feeling bolstered by his mother's response. Peabody's head bobbed between each person as Morrison used his interrogation approach.

"Mrs. Rubens," Morrison added, "I know you were there after Karl left. He may not have known Aaron was inside, but you may have. You were there during the missing time on the video and when Aaron went to the roof. You left after he fell." Accusingly, he pointed at her. "You may well be an accessory or worse to his murder!"

Karl gasped, then jolted to his feet. "Detective! How dare you accuse my innocent mother! She had no reason to see him deceased. She did not know of him being there after we closed! This is ridiculous! You are fishing because you have no leads, so you come here to harass my mother. How dare you!" he repeated. "I want you to leave our house immediately! You are not welcome here, and if you wish to see us again, request our lawyer." Karl pointed toward the door. "Good day, sirs!"

Isadore remained seated and stared at the detective. Peabody caught a glimpse of her and cringed as he folded his notepad.

"Let's go, Peabody," Morrison murmured.

Wiping sweat from his brow, he followed him, and Karl trailed close on his heels. Once they reached the door, Morrison stopped. "Mr. Rubens, I suggest you ask your mother about psilocybin, a hallucinogenic mushroom. It was found in Aaron's lab tests. Do you see how it looks? She was likely the last one with him. I would call it a convenient diversion for Aaron to die on the night of the theft. Why don't you ask her about that too?"

"Good day, Detective!" Karl growled and slammed the door behind them. Yet Morrison had planted a tiny seed of doubt that began sprouting in Karl's mind. He turned on his heel and yelled, "Mother!" as he marched toward her.

The detectives climbed into the official SUV and drove the narrow tree-lined lanes through Mason's Island. Reaching into his pocket, Morrison clicked off his voice recorder and exhaled.

Peabody blurted, "What was that all about? You came onto them with guns blazing, Boss. I was shocked into silence!"

"That's the way it's done, Peabody. I've got nothing, but if I lead them on and make them believe I have evidence to press charges, they may start acting differently. Since the FBI is still tailing them, I'll submit my recording of the encounter, and their activities will be scrutinized.

"The security company is cooperating with the FBI; so far, there is no evidence showing the security company had an inside man. That's why we do the guns-blazing thing. When we are on a case, there is no fooling around. You must be firm. You need to be strong and act with conviction. They must believe everything you say is true. That's how you get things done. Now we must wait."

The young detective sat back in his seat and stared at the road absorbing the shock of the new experience. "I learn something new every day, Boss."

CHAPTER 58

Full Impact
Wednesday

Ophelia Starr had made progress with her sculpture. A coiled wire frame in the shape of a woman was finally completed. It stood on her workbench, and she prepared the next step in the process.

A mix of a milky-white concoction was on the floor in a big plastic bin. She stirred the slimy, viscous liquid and added the strips of ripped sheets into the brew. While she slowly wrapped the wire form, her muse was in her thoughts.

Ophelia's vision depicted Marguerite resurfacing from the waters of the unconscious realm. It was a hopeful symbolic sculpture. With each dripping strip of fabric applied to the wire frame, she imagined reaching toward Marguerite and lifting her into the world of the awakened.

***

Morrison started his day by following through with his rattle-their-bones agreement with Chief Samson. He called Roxanne in the morning and asked if he could meet with Georgi and her at the Vinho Verde at noon for official police business. She agreed to his unexplained request and quickly called Georgi to say she would be arriving.

She and Georgi sat at a high-top table when the bell on the door of the wine bar announced Morrison's entry. They looked toward him and noticed his stiff stride and stern face. Their smiling expressions slowly slackened to sullen. Georgi grasped Roxanne's forearm and braced himself. Morrison's expression became graver.

"Did someone else die?" Roxanne asked grimly, wondering about Marguerite.

Morrison put his hand on his belt where his badge was secured and forcefully asked, "Do you know why I wear this badge?" He moved toward Georgi and glared into his eyes. "It is my business to know everything everywhere regarding a questionable death. My force and I have been combing the streets, going door-to-door, turning over every stone, looking for the person who killed Marilyn and abducted Cora. Jack Peabody has called every art dealer and connoisseur from here to New York, Boston, and beyond to solve this case."

He pointed at Georgi, "Upon your recommendation, Mr. Algarve, I ended up in Mystic at a museum party. But what do I find?" He crossed his arms and looked stern. "The next morning, I find another dead body and discover a priceless painting has been stolen."

His voice echoed in the old brick and granite structure as he paced the wide plank floorboards. "Why did this happen, I ask myself. Within days, I am on a strange wild-goose chase across the region from Cedar Grove Cemetery in New London to cemeteries in Mystic and Groton. All for what? To have the painting returned, or was it really to disguise something else? What exactly or whom am I chasing after Mr. Algarve? Is it you?"

A gasping sound issued from Georgi's throat as he sucked air. He cowered against Roxanne and whined. "I don't understand. Why are you saying these things?"

"You see, the common denominator is you, Mr. Algarve. You knew Marilyn. You might have taken her paintings for the money." Morrison wove his finger and poked the air toward Georgi as he enumerated each point. "You had her raincoat and hat in your possession. You claimed you found them in the trash. But did you? You might have been in contact with these nefarious art-dealing characters and arranged for Cora's abduction as a diversion. And then where does this mysterious man in Cora's sketch end up the next day?" "Here!" he boomed and pointed to the floor. "At Marilyn's get-together, hiding in plain sight."

Roxanne and Georgi gawked as Morrison ranted and paced the floor like an ominous pendulum.

"You see, Mr. Algarve, you have been leading me down a twisted trail, tripping down lanes and avenues, leading me on, but I have ended up where?" His finger darted toward Georgi. "Here, in front of you."

Georgi put his hands to his face to hide his welled-up eyes.

Roxanne took one look at Georgi and raised herself tall using the footrail of her high-top chair. She portrayed an unusual height and emphasized her outrage by facing her palm to halt Morrison's accusations. "That's enough!" she bellowed. "What has changed for you to come to these conclusions? We have done nothing but cooperate and try to help your investigation, Detective Dan Morrison! We are on your side!" Her voice echoed to the rafters, bounced off the brick wall, and ricocheted against the tall windows of the historic mercantile building.

Georgi's fingers curled against his mouth as he watched his world fall apart.

Morrison persisted. "You two have no idea, do you? What you've construed as helpful has landed you on the FBI's watch list." He pointed at the two of them. "They have made it their business to be in your business, and I am answering to their top investigators."

With a sinking feeling in her stomach, Roxanne descended back into her seat.

"Both of you were at the Mystic River Fine Art Museum last Wednesday morning as soon as the police department allowed it to reopen, and you were meeting with Karl Rubens. Aaron's death was the previous Thursday night at the museum. Don't you see? You returned to the scene of the crime. And don't forget Mr. Algarve; you were one of the last ones there the night of Aaron's demise and the theft too."

Georgi's face morphed as it stretched, his eyes bulged, and his mouth hung in a silent wail. Meanwhile, Roxanne realized the weight of the detective's accusations.

Morrison took a deep breath, exhaled, and continued, "You were also at the same event and in the same building where Marilyn died. You, Mr. Algarve, are a person of interest to the FBI. And, by the way, so are Karl Rubens and his mother. Can you see the evidence that guides the FBI to your involvement?"

He turned his focus to Roxanne. "Your only saving grace is that you are married to the Fire Chief. But don't rest on your laurels because you are consorting with persons of interest. You see, Roxanne, this is a serious situation. The FBI doesn't give a rat's ass or offer you a pass because of your husband."

Roxanne's hands went against her cheeks. They slid down, and she gripped Georgi's hand. In shock, she bleakly whispered, "We are in serious trouble."

Morrison walked along the windows that faced the Thames River. He was disturbingly quiet. As a Long Island ferry backed away from the docks, air horns blasted to announce its departure. It shattered the silence in the wine bar. He noticed Georgi shudder. Turning to face them, he could tell they finally felt the full impact of the circumstances.

"You must believe us. We had nothing to do with this," Georgi's voice warbled. "I didn't know I looked suspicious. I was only trying to help." He began to sob and took hold of a cocktail napkin to blow his nose. Sniffling, he pleaded, "Marilyn was my friend. I promise you I'm innocent."

Morrison's demeanor softened. "The two of you must understand that my job is to look at everyone connected to a murder. In most cases, anyone can be a possible suspect. Are you guilty? I don't think so. But the FBI doesn't know you as I do, nor does Detective Hanniford in Mystic. Can you see it? When they look at the facts, they think you are involved. To them, maybe you are accessories, or maybe you are the masterminds. The fact is they don't know you."

They both wilted in their seats. Roxanne was so mortified that her ashen face appeared gray as fog. "Does Sam know this?"

"Yes. I told him I needed to inform you of the FBI's view concerning the case. He wanted me to ensure you understood every detail so you would make better decisions.

"I also spoke to Detective Hanniford and the FBI agent on this case." They leaned toward the edges of their seats. "I told them that I know you, I could vouch for you, and it was circumstantial that you were there. I mentioned Georgi was friends with the victims and connected through work by these common locations. I told them you were more like informants, confidants, and advisers to me, not criminals."

"You defended us?" Georgi yelped. He leaped out of his chair, ready to rush at the detective and embrace his protector. Morrison raised his palms to stop Georgi's advance, prohibiting a potential tackle. Georgi braked on his heels and meekly put his hand forward to shake one of the detective's upright palms. Giving in, Morrison shook his hand.

"Thank you, thank you, thank you, Detective," Georgi said as he pumped Morrison's arm. "I am forever in your debt. I thought you would arrest me and put me in jail." While he continued his grip on the detective's hand, he then waggled his head. "You know I wouldn't survive jail."

Morrison nodded his head, knowing it was true. He put his free hand on Georgi's arm to stop him from pumping it like a slot machine handle.

Roxanne ran to hug Georgi. They wanted to hug Morrison and squeeze him with gratitude, but they knew that would break his bubble of personal space and the protocols he demanded as an officer of the law. They gleefully squeezed each other instead.

"Okay, here is our agreement." Morrison was now amused but kept his voice firm. "You report to me. If you do anything that brings you in contact with Karl, Isadore, or any other characters that could make you look bad or involved, you must report it to me. Otherwise, go about your business as usual. Do you understand?"

Roxanne and Georgi clicked their heels and saluted. "Yes, sir!" they said in unison.

The right corner of Morrison's mouth turned up. "Is that a smile?" Georgi asked. "Because I could use one right now."

The slight grin remained. "That's the extent of it today. I have other business to attend to, so keep me informed. Then I will apprise the FBI and Hanniford of your activities."

"We will, Dan," Roxanne said with contrition, "and thank you. We can see your point of view, and we're both sorry we put you in a tough spot. Aren't we, Georgi?" He nodded vigorously.

Morrison walked toward the door. "Okay, let's have a better day." He waved and was gone.

After the bell on the door stopped ringing, silence ruled the room. Roxanne and Georgi let out a big sigh and rested their heads on the table. Several moments passed before they became animated, then they started speaking on top of each other. "Can you believe it?" "Oh my god!" "I thought I was going to jail." "He was so angry!" "But he spoke up for us, didn't he?"

On and on they went until they started laughing and laughing because they were so relieved.

Later in the afternoon, at the Vinho Verde

Georgi was mostly recovered from the Morrison scare. He was preparing the evening's wine-tasting and appetizer event for twenty when he received a call from Karl Rubens.

"Hello, Georgi. I heard your fundraiser at Dev's Bistro was successful, and it sparked an idea. I told Mother how dreadful I felt about your artist friends, and she suggested we could help by offering another opportunity to the art community, but on a grander scale."

Morrison's words echoed in Georgi's head: '*anything that brings you in contact with Karl...you must report it to me.*' "You have my full attention, Karl. What do you have in mind?"

"Mother has a painting she purchased ages ago for a minimal price, and it no longer holds her interest, yet it's now worth a good sum. She suggests you have an art auction and use it as a catalyst to involve others in a big art event."

Georgi considered Karl's offer while remembering the detective's chiding remarks. "Karl, I have a Las Vegas-sized imagination. How grand are you thinking?"

"Mother realized that since both of our communities have been through so much, it would be helpful if we sponsor a special event commemorating New London's arts. Don't you have a wonderful, large venue that could host a city-wide event? One that allows for stage performances?"

"Yes, the Garde Arts Center. It's a nonprofit institution with many available options." Georgi felt his excitement brewing.

Karl explained, "To be completely frank, Georgi, the painting my mother plans to donate was acquired over forty years ago at a low cost. Today it is worth at least three hundred thousand dollars. What do you think? Are you interested?"

Georgi mouthed the word, *Wow*, but Karl only heard tapping sounds. "Are you still there, Georgi?"

"Are you kidding? Can't you tell? I love the idea. I am tap dancing!"

Karl was pleased and encouraged him. "We feel you're the man who can pull this off. Mother and I will assist in funding the party, but we want you to organize it. We figure it will be a win, win, win for everyone. Mystic and New London will garner accolades and help the arts. Will you do it?"

"Yes, Karl! This is my dream come true to plan an event of this size. When do I start?"

"Immediately. You are running the show. Tell me the costs as you go along, and we will have a grand affair."

"Absolutely! We can call it Celebrate the Arts! And Karl, thank you for your faith in me."

"You're welcome. I believe you can do anything you set your mind to. I'll let Mother know you are on the job."

Georgi was over the moon imagining a grand vision but came down to earth and called to the police headquarters to report the event and the details of his conversation with Karl. Morrison informed Hanniford and the FBI.

CHAPTER 59

Sister City

Georgi had just hung up the phone when he heard a loud horn bellow, *Ahooga*. He popped his head out the door of the Vinho Verde and saw a familiar bright red bus pull up. JoJo and Gio jumped out and greeted Georgi with an Italian-style crushing hug and kisses.

The duo ran a tourism business that traveled through New London every two hours. They transported tourists to popular sites from city to shore. Giovanni, known as Gio, drove the bus, and his sweetheart, JoJo, hosted and announced. Gio had transformed a regular bus, painted it red, and added rooftop seating. He figured that since New London, Connecticut, was a sister city to London, England, the bus would fit right in.

Georgi invited them into the Vinho Verde for a cool lemonade on the deck, where he revealed his newest project, Celebrate the Arts. They were both excited and offered to decorate their bus with a banner. After their chat, they left the Vinho Verde to give their next tour.

Gio drove the short block down Bank Street to pick up their next group in front of the historic Union Train Station. This prearranged tour was for Coast Guard officers who had recently arrived in New London. They had just completed a tour of the construction site of the new National Coast Guard Museum on the river behind the train station.

Quite unexpectedly, another ten paying patrons asked to join the specialized tour for the guardsmen. JoJo graciously welcomed everyone aboard since there was plenty of room on their double-decker bus.

Yet secretly among them was a man in disguise, sporting a mustache and a black Scottish flat cap. He sat away from the group by a window and had his phone and binoculars ready.

While in front of Union Station, JoJo explained that New London was sometimes coined the "City of Steeples," and they would see several. She pointed up State Street. "See there is one of our architectural giants that reaches an exalted height. The magnificent 1850s Gothic steeple is made of gray granite and crowns our city center. It belongs to the First Congregational Church."

As Gio drove forward, the incognito man took videos of the route and spied on various access points to the streets. The bus arrived at another 1850s historic gem. JoJo informed the tourists, "This is the impressive Brownstone steeple of St. James Episcopal Church. It houses a fantastic stained-glass collection. Among them are beautiful Tiffany windows." The group was enticed from the bus to visit the mammoth sanctuary.

The antique interior lulled them into a hushed reverence. The enormity of the wood and stone sanctuary was brightened by sunlight kissing the panes of the colorful windows. A vibrant aura filled the nave and enhanced the spirit of the sacred space.

JoJo, adept in photography, took pictures of the group with cameras and phones, but the man with the mustache kept his black cap low on his forehead and stayed behind her.

Back aboard the bus, Gio drove past the Garde Arts Center, and the nefarious man used his binoculars to scope out travel routes for his next mission. They passed several art murals, and JoJo announced, "We have a *Mural Walk* in New London, and you will see a few of these beautiful building-sized paintings as we go." She pointed out a huge mural with sperm whales and a giant squid called *Whaling Wall* by the famous artist, Wyland, and next a thirty-foot mural called *Hard Hat Painters* that Troy designed and painted collaboratively with another artist. It colorfully depicted a surreal underwater scene of divers in brass bubble-headed suits.

They passed by three more towering church steeples, and JoJo explained that wealthy and philanthropic sea captains of whaling and merchant ships funded them, each competing for their faith to be represented in glory.

One of the destinations to show off was Fort Trumbull, the Coast Guard's original academy, in 1915. Gio parked near the water with a view of New London Harbor. The covert operator utilized his binoculars again to scope the waterway, inlets, and byways while JoJo was inspired to tell a tale.

She spread her arms wide and used them to express her words as she emoted. "Be careful, my friends, the waters look calm, but mermaids reside beneath the blue. When you swagger to your car with too much drink, their siren call will woo you into the river deep." Intrigued, an officer said, "Tell us more!"

"In 1979 a Coast Guard officer who left a pub went missing. After six months and much searching, a well-known local psychic, Pat Gagliardo, told the police of her vision: He was in a *watery grave* by the ferry docks.

"With no other leads, it prompted the detectives to investigate. They sent a dive team to search the murky depths, and he was found in his car, where she said. They realized he drove straight into the river, unable to distinguish it from the road. And the docking of each ferry vessel repeatedly flattened the car and driver into the silt below." JoJo used her hands to demonstrate the flattening of the driver, and her eyes were wide with his ominous descent. The group groaned.

Gio drove the tour forward while JoJo launched into a lyrical sea shanty warning of the mermaid's seductive song. The group joined in and ended with rousing applause.

Gio stopped the bus at a broad overlook of the harbor and Long Island Sound. JoJo pointed out four lighthouses that could be viewed from this one location on Pequot Avenue: Avery Point Light, Ledge Light, Race Rock Light, and New London Harbor Light. Emphasizing their popularity, she touted that the local Long Island Sound ferry cruises were the best way to see twenty-one bold beacons in the sound.

With his mission in mind, the cagey tourist photographed and videoed the shoreline for spots to land a watercraft for a getaway. The bus moved along. While smirking, he caught his window reflection and smoothed his mustache flat.

Gio circled past Ocean Beach Park, and JoJo commented on the popular destination with a long crescent beach and tidal pools. Gio turned around, and soon she directed the group to a picturesque 1870s steeple nestled among trees. She noted that inside Pequot Chapel's beautiful high-beamed interior were two exquisite Tiffany stained-glass angels in iridescent tones that were worth a future visit.

Gio motored ahead and finished the bus tour on Bank Street in front of the city's most famous mural. JoJo informed, "These five scantily clad women, the famous *Hygienic Ladies,* are in the classic style of Greek and Roman statues draped in fabric mimicking stone. These giants are nearing twenty feet tall and highlight the Hygienic Art Gallery's building."

The group gazed upwards at the grand ladies, each atop a pedestal, and with their arms raised, they appeared as columns supporting the building's roof.

"Please browse their contemporary art gallery, and here is a flyer and map of all the downtown art galleries, studios, and shops. Thank you for joining Gio and me today. You have been a wonderful group. Our tour is now complete." Gio tapped the horn, and it rang out, *Ahooga!*

The group applauded their driver and tour guide. The mysterious man off-loaded and strode boldly up to the Vinho Verde Wine Bar window and paused. He watched Georgi preparing for the evening's wine tasting and dinner. He snickered at the ease of nonchalantly striding the area where he started his pursuits.

This quick bus tour had acquainted him further with the City of Steeples and spurred his imagination for his next opportunity. He fussed with his hat pulling it low over his forehead and eyes. With this minor mission accomplished, he boarded the train to Mystic.

JoJo's handout on little-known facts about the Hygienic Diner turned Art Gallery.

Once called the Hygienic Diner, it was established in the 1920s when service, cleanliness, and food quality were of utmost importance in America.

In 1938, the popular 24-hour restaurant provided Franklin D. Roosevelt dinner when his presidential yacht arrived on tour in New London Harbor.

In the 1970s, displays of original art hung on the walls. Local and New York artists such as Barkley Hendricks, a celebrated African American, were among the first to show his artwork at the Hygienic Diner.

The last art show was in the mid-1980s when the diner's doors were closed. The building sat vacant for years and was about to be demolished in 1996. Local friends and artists petitioned the state to save the building so they could renovate and rejuvenate the art scene in New London.

Since 2000, the eclectic gallery has displayed modern and fine art with one theme: No Censorship. The Hygienic's Art Park venue is multi-functional and hosts performers, musicians, playwrights, and more.

CHAPTER 60

Visions of Fancy Dress
Friday – four weeks since Marilyn's fatality

Georgi had established the date for the Celebrate the Arts event. It was just over a week away on a Sunday at the Garde Arts Center. The activity kept him busy while he constantly thought of his friends. He was bolstered by Isadore and Karl's donation of fine art as it would raise funds for artists citywide in one significant event. With so many tasks to complete, an important one was securing an auctioneer. And the only viable option that came to mind was Karl Rubens. He gave him a call.

"Karl, will you please do me the honor of managing the auction of your mother's painting? I know nothing about auctions; your expertise is needed to acquire the top dollar bid. Your presence will elevate the event to the high standard it deserves. I can't imagine anyone else for this important job."

When Karl agreed, Georgi added, "I must thank you again. I want to create an exuberant and bold event and celebrate my friends in how they lived—outrageously courageous. Artists pour their heart and soul into their work without the guarantee of a sale. They work on faith that their creativity will pay off. This event will boost the city and all the artists in town."

Karl considered his words. "Georgi, what you say is like stories of many famous masters, such as Van Gogh. They died poor, and their works were popular only after death. Many artists are not as fortunate as my distant relative, Peter Paul Rubens. Maybe it's time I consider living artists with more regard."

Georgi was pleased he could influence Karl. Maybe, just maybe, a little ray from his sunshine was finding a way into Karl's heart.

When his call ended, he remembered Morrison's warning and called to update him on Karl's involvement and told the detective the event may lure the villains to attend if he didn't capture them first. Georgi's hopeful mind floated two competing thoughts: Morrison's capture of the villain and the visions of a fancy dress party.

Next, Georgi focused on all the activities he wanted to implement for the art event and fundraiser.

Georgi's List for Celebrate the Arts:

Attire: fancy dress or creative costumes for a lively atmosphere

3 p.m.: A parade from the Parade Plaza to the Garde Arts Ctr.

4 p.m. - 6 p.m.: events throughout the Garde

- suggested donation of $5 to $100+ for the arts in New London
- gallery show of local artwork for sale in the grand lobby
- authors and musicians with tables to sell their books and music
- silent wine and art auction in the Oasis Room
- pre-program slide show of artists' work in the Performance Hall

7 p.m. - 9 p.m.: local performers on stage

9:15 p.m.: Auction of the fine art painting donated by the Rubens.

9:45 p.m.: Grand finale auction ends.

Georgi hoped to have the fourteen-hundred-seat Garde theater look like a celebrity fundraiser. He would be ready to hand out a flamboyant scarf, boa, or hat for those who needed encouragement to dress up and make the event look lively. To amuse himself, he imagined how smashing Detective Dan Morrison would look in an Elton John outfit with a bowler hat, star-shaped glasses, and a glittery jacket.

Once the news was out, the word spread quickly with the help of the Celebrate the Arts banner on JoJo and Gio's red tour bus. Georgi only had to mention the event to crucial art organizers for everyone to get involved. Even the local colleges and museums focused on the city's artists with a vested interest. Flock Theater wished to showcase their larger-than-life puppet creations in the parade, and the region's newspaper, *The Day*, offered to cover the event.

The thought of a party gave a resurgence of energy to all in New London's art community. Local artists, including those at the Dahlia art studios, were invited to submit their work for the silent auction. The money raised would be available to any artist or art group who submitted a sincere request for need.

Roxanne happily began posting flyers for the event around town. This was a welcome diversion. It kept her occupied now that she and Georgi were firmly warned off from assisting with the detective's case. But she was unable to comply completely. Secretly stashed in her backpack were copies of Cora's sketch of Mario Corinthian. She handed them out to everyone she met while her eyes searched for him on the city's streets.

Marco, Georgi's right-hand man for décor and pomp, joined him in the preparations. While they looked for themed items to display, their discussion turned to how strange it was that the citywide artist fundraiser came about because of devastating deaths. "I hope the detectives find this Mario Corinthian and lock him up before our event," announced Georgi.

Marco had a boa around his shoulders as he leaned on a human-sized, lightweight replica of Michelangelo's *David.* He shook his head skeptically and waved the end of his boa at Georgi. "Corinthian is not a name. It's a Greek column!"

"That's what Karl said." Georgi raised his feather boa in the air. "It's a consensus. We all think the villain Mario, has a made-up name. But we don't need to worry. The police have a sketch and will catch him if he shows his face while we will be busy throwing a fabulous party!" With a dramatic throw, he placed his boa about *David's* neck, put his arm around him, and nodded to Marco. Together they lifted *David,* and with a tango strut, they danced to the end of the room.

Once *David* landed, Georgi said, "I think Marilyn and Aaron are shining down from heaven over the event coming out of their tragedy. I find it remarkable that Karl and Isadore are generously donating their expensive painting and paying for the use of the Garde Arts Center."

"It seems Karl's rough exterior is beginning to melt," Marco sang. "Maybe he noticed he feels better when he collaborates with people like you."

"Yes, and speaking of collaboration, Ophelia has planned poetry readings on Saturday at the Dahlia Gallery from the book *Sky Break.* She says it's a love letter by a celebrated European writer to New London and America."

Georgi expanded his arms wide. "Then Ophelia added a cherry-on-top and arranged for the Velvet Muse to add a Saturday night performance of the play, *Solace,* by our local playwright, Michael Bradford. Marco, this will be a weekend to remember!"

***

Karl had assumed his mother would accompany him to the Garde Art's auction of her painting, yet when he asked her what she would wear; she responded, "I'm not in the mood, darling. I'd rather stay home."

"Mother, you must! You're the one who wanted to donate the art! It's a grand event. You'll meet people and have fun. And if you don't, purse your lips and bear it. I've seen you do that quite well. Consider it a well-practiced performance. Besides, you said, 'Our reputation will grow from our philanthropy.'" She waved off his comment. "Mother, I'm only following through with your brilliant idea to put our reputation first and our lovely museum on the map. We will look like heroes when the money comes in on this auction. You really must be there."

She gave him a coy smile of pride for using her words to coax her to go. "My dear, you were meant to be a monk, yet you chose art. I'll support you any way I can."

"Good! You will accompany me, and at the end of the night, you can look forward to coming home to your velvet slippers, a drink, and your magnificent collection of art. Remember, it's all about keeping up appearances and the name Rubens on their lips."

Isadore had all she needed: a lovely home on an affluent island near a quaint Franciscan monastery and her famous son. Of course, she would do this for him and their reputation.

She threw him a kiss, "Yes, darling."

CHAPTER 61

The Golden Rule
Saturday

Marguerite was awake!

Morrison's opportunity to speak to Marguerite was refreshing news. He had been frustrated that nary a lead had appeared since Tuesday. A lead could send his team running again.

He invited Dr. Storm to join him, anticipating her knowledge may help.

Once the family met Dr. Storm, they encouraged her to visit Marguerite with the detective. At her bedside, the detective introduced himself and said he was happy to meet her.

She nodded and stared at his steely blue eyes against his tan skin and dark hair. "I remember your voice," she said softly and smiled.

"I'd like to introduce you to Dr. Angela Storm. We work together."

The doctor stepped forward. "Marguerite, I'm so happy you are okay."

Morrison asked, "May I ask you a few questions?"

She nodded. "You have a calming voice."

Dr. Storm noticed him blush. "Oh my, dear, don't give him any compliments. He truly doesn't know how to handle them."

Blushing further, Morrison interrupted her ribbing. "Please tell me, what do you remember?"

"I remember taking the train to Mystic to visit where Aaron was last." She sighed, looking away and out the window. "I was depressed and sat on a bench by the water. I, I met a nice lady. We had tea." She held her forehead. "I recall flowers by the water. It seems like a dream. Nature began to swirl with colors, light, and sound. I waded into the colors. Then I woke up here."

"Who was the woman who took you to tea?" Morrison asked.

"I don't know, but she was kind."

"Can you describe her? Or recall where you had tea?" he asked.

"She was my grandmother's age…around sixty. I don't know where we went." Marguerite's locked-in state and physical weakness had her struggling with her memory.

"Do you know how long you were with her and the time of day?"

The patient appeared perplexed to Dr. Storm, so she interrupted the questioning. "You will remember things later, dear. It takes time, and you have all the time in the world." Gently, she changed the subject. "Are you hungry?" Dr. Storm glanced at Morrison, and he understood his questions were over for today.

Marguerite nodded.

"Your family is here. Shall I send them in so they can order you a meal?"

"Yes." Marguerite reached out to take their hands. "Thank you."

"Marguerite, I have one question," Dr. Storm said. "Did you or Aaron try hallucinogenic mushrooms?"

"No, never," she whispered.

Dr. Storm believed her. "I appreciate your honesty. Now you need to rest."

Morrison's heart melted for this beautiful, dark-haired young lady. He smiled at her before leaving the room with Dr. Storm. They spoke to the family and asked if she was known to use any drugs, specifically psychedelic mushrooms. They claimed she wouldn't because she was conscious of eating cleanly and taking care of her body.

As they sat in Morrison's SUV, he said, "I wish I could have asked her more questions. But I feel more assured she had not intentionally taken the mushrooms."

Dr. Storm added, "Her memory may improve."

"It means someone could have drugged her and Aaron, but why?" Morrison wondered. "Especially since they were both influenced by the drug during a weak moment. It means Marguerite did not intend to drown, and Aaron did not intend to fall. Neither was a suicide."

"Yes, this seems to be true."

"But why were they slipped a mickey? As a joke or with criminal intent? I need to investigate this further." Morrison pondered, "I need to investigate where she had tea and with whom? And should this be compared to Cora's incident?"

They ruminated the events in silence as he drove. Dr. Storm decided to discuss a new topic. "Are you going to the fundraiser at the Garde next week?" When he nodded, she said, "Then I will see you there. Will you be bringing your date, Detective?"

Her question caught him off guard, and he scrutinized her with a quizzical look.

"You know, Detective Peabody," she teased.

There was an unmistakable glint of whimsy in her expression. "No, I'm going stag. Besides, Peabody doesn't count as a date, does he?"

"Hmm, I guess not," she responded, then paused as a bright idea came to her. "Then I shall help you out! But I must break my golden rule."

"What's your golden rule?"

"To not date someone I work with. They always turn out to be deadbeats." She glanced at him with mocking seriousness. "You're not a deadbeat, are you, Detective?"

He joined her game and smiled at her play on words. "No one's accused me of having a deadbeat personality, certainly not as dead as the people you work with." He secretly thought, *That is my golden rule too.* He realized if he was to date Angela Storm, there would be repercussions from his dictates to Jack Peabody. *Can our golden rule have a compromise?* he wondered. "How about I escort you to the event?" He offered. "We will go as friends, which helps me apply an undercover appearance while I keep an eye on people."

"Wonderful," she responded. "Because I don't like getting all dressed up just to go alone."

"Good. That's why friends accompany each other to avoid being wallflowers."

"Yes, Detective, we think alike."

He was intrigued by her twisting ploy to join him, and it made him wonder if she didn't get out much. *I don't get out much.* "Then it's a deal. We'll go to the event together." His thoughts went to Peabody. *He's going to have a field day with this.*

"If you don't mind, I like driving my new car," she said. "Humor me, and let me pick you up."

"Okay." He nodded. *I think she just picked me up!* He knew this was a time to apply his father's advice, not to ruin the moment when a woman makes a move. "I have one more addition to our agreement," he said.

"I'm listening."

"You should call me Dan outside of work."

"Agreed, and you can call me Angela outside of work."

Without looking at each other, they both smiled.

CHAPTER 62

Money to Burn on Beauty
Wednesday - noon

Malcolm Freeman was an art agent from Mystic and a friendly acquaintance of Troy. They met on the second-story deck of Sift Bake Shop in downtown Mystic. They were having coffee while waiting for their food.

"It seems I have to be dead for my art to make money," Troy complained. "It's depressing that Marilyn's death has caused a bidding-war buzz for her work. I know she would have rather had the money when she was alive, and so would I."

Malcolm was a stylish man with a short afro and wore a navy sports jacket with a colorful, open-collared shirt. He was known as an artist's career-maker because of his extensive network of clientele, investors, and high-end gallery owners. At the age of fifty-two, Malcolm had the Midas touch. It didn't hurt that he was handsome, with a cheerful round face and the friendliest brown eyes.

"Troy, your dedication to your art is self-evident. I know you pursue perfection." Malcolm's sincerity shined through his eyes. He leaned in. "I believe your work will be considered collectible and worth ten times more one day. But can you produce double the quantity or create a process that isn't so labor intensive as your wax-cut monoprints?"

Troy felt Malcolm's idea could not apply because he enjoyed the slow progress of his wax block engravings. He felt time improved his art. In his mind, the hourly equation should make his art valued in the many thousands.

"Creating multiple originals may sound simple to you, Malcolm, but as you know, my process is what it is. The good news is, I hear you, and I'm painting more. Marilyn has become my muse for a series of I'm finishing. I'll have one in the silent auction this weekend at the Garde. Come see it."

"I'm intrigued. Yes, I'll be there." Malcolm took a sip of coffee. "Look, Troy, here's the rub. The stats are that over ninety percent of artists don't make enough money to live on from their art. The best way for you to become known is if you hire me.

"When I come across an investor who loves to buy new art, the person often wants to know where you've shown, who bought your work, and what the critics say. They want to see a provenance that you've been in salon shows, certain galleries, and ritzy magazines. But…" Malcolm held up his finger to pause himself.

"…then there are the opposite buyers, who want to discover you, be your patron, invest in you, manage you, and sometimes own you. It is a demanding lifestyle to balance as an artist because you don't want to feel like a prostitute.

"My advice to you as an agent is to market yourself and your art endlessly. Why? Because you want to own your identity, fight for your way of being, and remain autonomous. If you don't, you can end up uncelebrated."

Troy slumped. "I wasn't looking at my art business from that point of view. You know I have difficulty marketing myself." Troy's debts made him waver between wanting a patron who would sponsor him and being independent. He toyed with the idea of having a respected agent like Malcolm. He teetered between independence and worry. *Could he trust someone to help him become famous?* Procrastination was often the result of his wrestling with anxiety.

Malcolm continued, "Troy, I know you've seen the rare artists who had one great show with a catchy theme and won accolades. Then they take that theme and make it commercial, turning it into graphic prints and hiring amateur artists to create factory-like originals of their ideas. Some make a killing. Those are the artists who can make you jealous. Don't give them any attention."

Troy nodded.

"On the other hand, some art investors will never risk their money on a living artist. They prefer prestigious auction houses with bidding at the million-dollar level."

"You mean they prefer dead artists?"

"Some auction houses and investors consider living artists an unpredictable investment. That's cold, I know. What if the going rate of their work goes down due to something the artist recently created? I'm sorry to say it's not about the art with these wealthy buyers. It's about the value of the investment. Art accrues in value based on the exclusive hands through which the artwork passes over time. When an artist dies, it's only the seller and the middlemen making money, unless I make prints of the original, when I keep the copyright."

A moan escaped Troy's mouth. "Once I sell my work, it is no longer mine. If it accrues in price, I don't get the benefit except that I can sell my future work for more money, or prints, etcetera."

"I want your work to be sold to someone who loves it and allows the price to appreciate. Art is beauty. That is what I am dealing. But not everyone needs original art, Troy. It is a luxury to many, not a necessity. Therefore, your work must sell to those who have expendable funds. Money to burn on beauty."

This realization of dealing with the rich was a bit depressing to Troy. "There's a vast space, Malcolm, between my meager way of living and those who treat money like water."

"Your work speaks for itself," Malcolm encouraged. "It needs no explanation because it stirs a feeling and creates a gut reaction. When buyers see your work, they know in their hearts that they must own it. Let me be your agent. I'll charge you twenty percent of every deal I bring in. I'll raise your prices, present your work, and convince the galleries and buyers to invest in you. While I'm on the road of suggestions, why don't you consider moving into a loft space in Mystic?"

Troy shook his head.

Malcolm's arms widened with his grand idea. "What's the big deal? I'm trying to elevate your image. I can fancy you up for gallery showings. I'm sure people will purchase your work, maybe even a whole series. I will introduce you if you allow me to be your agent."

"I am who I am, Malcolm. My introverted tendencies and the casual way I dress are me. I'm not abandoning New London; I like it. It's quirky, like me. It's known for fresh art, independent thinkers, and creative types. Honestly, I can't afford to live in Mystic. I have cheap rent.

"Your deal may sound good to you, but it's not for me. Twenty percent to you and forty percent or higher to the high-class galleries means I'd end up with not enough. I would have to mainstream my sideline business. Physically and financially, I can't make that work. I'm between a rock and a hard place. For me, creativity is the essence of life. Yet I can't pay you if I don't make enough."

"Okay, I give up." Malcolm raised his hands in defeat. "If you change your mind, let me know. In the end, money is the game, and artists and their art are the pieces on the board, though sometimes they are the kingpin. We all play to survive."

"I appreciate your faith in my work but have faith in me and where I am right now. We'll table this discussion until we can change the game or come up with contracts where artists are paid royalties every time their art changes hands in a resale. That way, we can be in the winner's circle too."

Malcolm nodded and spoke gently. "I understand. I'm only trying to offer you a perspective of the selling and buying side that I know so well. Your work is excellent, and I will represent you when you're ready."

Their food arrived, and as they ate, they watched sailboats motor by toward the sound. Something Malcolm said made Troy wonder. *Some art buyers only invest in dead artists. What if Marilyn was indeed killed for her art? Is her art agent in on this with Mario Corinthian? They knew the price would skyrocket.*

The Lobster Boat – Thursday

The FBI finally tracked down the lobster boat used for the Mystic art heist. Videos captured it from several locations along the Mystic River. Although they lost track of it at the mouth of Poggy Bay and Long Island Sound, they did find the fisherman who owned the vessel. "I'm sorry. I thought the guy was kidding when he offered me a fair price to rent the boat for the evening and return it by eight o'clock in the morning.

"His story was that he owed a friend a favor to help him pull up his traps past Stonington Harbor at dawn. He claimed the motor had died on his lobster boat. He gave me the keys to his Mercedes as collateral, and I agreed. He paid me two thousand dollars."

"Did he give you a name?" the agent asked.

"Oh, yes, Mario Corinthian was his name. A friendly guy. I had no concerns, and his money was green."

The FBI followed through and reported the information to Hanniford. Upon receiving the news, the Mystic detective called Morrison. "We have information regarding the lobster boat, and guess what? The name of the man who rented it was Mario Corinthian. The sketch of him was also confirmed. This ghost has his hand in everything."

Morrison whistled. "Well, I'll be. What about Garfield Feinberg? What did the FBI find on him?"

"Interestingly, they found another artist he represented who met an untimely death. The life insurance company did not pay him because the death was an undetermined suicide. The FBI is investigating the details. Feinberg is under suspicion; let's see if we can connect him to this Mario character."

"Okay, we have a few things cooking now, including this art function at the Garde Arts Center this weekend. The Rubens are donating a work of art. I wonder if these thieves will be hanging around looking for opportunities. It's a big venue; we could use the staffing if the FBI can provide it. I will be on duty but appearing as a guest. What do you think?"

"I think it's a good call," agreed Hanniford. "Let's set it up."

CHAPTER 63

Celebrate the Arts - Event Day
Sunday

Early in the day at the Garde Arts Center, Georgi, and Barry, the wine connoisseur and co-owner of The Red House Cultural Arts Center, met in the Oasis Room. They had arranged the silent wine and art auction together. They stepped back to observe their work.

Georgi recounted their activity. "Okay, Barry, we have thirty works of art on the walls and easels, and I couldn't be more thrilled. A patron donated one of Marilyn's flower paintings to help the fundraiser. Once it arrives, we'll place it on this easel." Georgi waved to the anointed spot and moved along to name off a few key pieces.

"These are works by my friends at the Dahlia art studios. This one is Troy's piece of Marilyn looking out to sea, 'The Eternal Gaze.' And here is Cora's collage and watercolor, 'A Sanctuary Garden.' Jason's metal sculpture of windswept grasses called, 'Winds of Change'; Ophelia's white enigmatic sculpture, 'Miraculous Survivor'; Bruce's painting of a magical world called, 'Celebration of Life;' and Teddy's wood masterpiece, 'The Tick of Time,' with face-like cogs on the wheel of life. Doesn't the art make the room look lovely?"

"Yes, I agree it's opulent, Georgi." They proceeded to the wine tables to ensure each display was perfectly set. Barry confirmed, "I have two dozen bottles from my connections, plus we have two cases from the cellars at the Vinho Verde. We have a list of wines from around the world and their descriptions. An auction sheet is by each wine. I believe our choices will tempt people to bid. Do you have a favorite?" Barry asked the tricky question Georgi had posed when they had met.

"Aha, when you're in the wine business, you cannot choose a favorite." Georgi's hand gracefully moved through the air as he expressed himself. "Each wine is like a mood. You may be happy and choose the German wine Peter Lauer 'Barrel X' Riesling, 2019. Yet, if you are contemplative, the French, Domaine Dominique Mugneret Echezeaux, 2005, or the Portuguese, Graham's Vintage Port, 1985. Do you understand me?"

Barry nodded. "Of course, great minds think alike. And it depends on what accompanies the wine; if it is steak, I may have the Melville Pinot Noir Sandy's, 2014."

Georgi gave a flourishing wave toward the display of wines. "I must say, Barry, we have made an excellent pair. If all goes well, we should make a habit of wine and art auctions."

The Parade

On this warm September Sunday, crowds gathered at the Parade Plaza in the city's center to prepare for the short procession to the Garde Art Center. The starting position was at the Soldiers' and Sailors' obelisk-like monument, with a woman on top representing peace. The plaza's expansive location could hold hundreds of people and was the perfect spot for Georgi's planned event to begin. Traffic had been redirected by three o'clock, and the streets and sidewalks were full of onlookers.

Local artists had designed a parade float on a pull-along flatbed for announcers and performers. It was decorated with the theme "Water on Land." The edge of the float had a construction of undulating blue waves topped with foaming white caps of sheer voile fabric.

Georgi's good friend, Father Frank, was ready to bless the procession. He was grandly dressed in his finest vestments, priestly cap, and an ornamental scepter with a golden orb. He was known as a beloved minister with an excellent sense of humor and always put Georgi and his nervous tensions at ease.

Flock Theater actors arrived on the stage in fine Renaissance fashion. They were dressed in period-style frocks. They raised a quartet of long ceremonial horns with decorative banners to announce the parade's beginning. *Toot, Doo, Doo, Doooo!*

Father Frank ascended the stairs slowly. From the audience's view, it seemed like he had emerged from a foaming sea. The crowd cheered, and he waved. He spoke into the microphone. "I'd like to welcome you to our Celebrate the Arts event."

The boisterous and well-costumed crowd cheered loudly.

"As you know, we are here to ascend out of sadness," he began. "Our dear friends, Marilyn and Aaron, will be with us in spirit as we honor their lives and celebrate their talent throughout today's events. They now exist in the heavenly realms where they can see and know all. And what do they see? They see our love for them and the love we share for the arts in our city. I want to start this parade with a blessing.

"May the Holy Spirit protect our event, keep us from harm, and grow in our hearts the seeds of good-naturedness, so we can help each other when in need, heal, and become stronger together. May those who see separations be the glue to bring people together because, in the end, we are all part of the human experience, which is to learn about love. May those with plenty to give do so from their heart, and those who need funds receive what they deserve.

"On this beautiful day, may God bless our parade, and may these blessings be with you all." Father Frank raised his arms with the scepter and golden orb high in hand. A sunbeam shone across the sphere sparking a glimmer out to every eye. "Ohhh," roared the crowd as the glinting flash of light made its way into their hearts.

"The Firefighter's Pipes and Drums will now lead us. Let the parade begin!" The grand master and pipe major started the parade's march with bagpipes, piccolo, snare, tenor, and bass drums. They were all dressed in full tartan regalia.

Flock Theater added to the procession four giant-sized puppets that seemed to levitate above the crowd at nearly twelve feet. Following them were throngs of artists and locals who wore creative fashions ranging from ethereal to comical. Intermixed were dance groups, youth bands, and acrobat performers. JoJo and Gio's red double-decker bus was next, with costumed revelers and giant colorful balloons on the top deck.

The parade concluded under the Garde's marquee entrance, and it was at this very moment that Troy's plan took effect. He had been inspired by Victor Hugo's character Quasimodo in *The Hunchback of Notre Dame*, who he thought the greatest happiness came from the bells of Notre Dame.

Troy had requested and organized four churches to ring their steeple bells simultaneously as a tribute to Marilyn, Aaron, and the City of Steeples. When the celebratory ringing began, the echoes and reverberation bounced off the buildings. The parade revelers gawked and gazed upwards, spellbound by the marvelous crescendo resounding through the streets and city.

The hosts welcomed everyone into the Garde Arts grand lobby. Although it seemed unassuming from the outside, the Garde revealed its treasures once inside. Warm tones of a Moroccan-inspired interior were of burnished oranges and yellows, with touches of blue and brilliant gold. The performance hall had Juliet balconies with lacey ironwork flanking the velvety red-maroon stage curtains. The ceiling towered sixty feet high, with a massive crystal chandelier.

For over ninety years, many had walked through the doors of this 1920s cinema palace's glorious décor. In fact, one might sense the friendly presence of past performers or workers who sprinkled a vibe of goodwill. Often, with eyes squinted in the dim light of the stage's ghost lamp, one might see the happy, sparkling energy left behind by audiences of the past.

It's been said that depending upon one's own kind heart, the ambience in the Garde offered the sense of a warm cuddle because volunteers had saved her from the wrecking ball. In the refurbishment, they had rubbed love into every square inch by reinstating the former glory of the magnificent jewel box.

As Georgi had planned, the large lobby became a place for local books, music, and art sales. The guest also climbed the grand staircase to the second floor, where the vibrant interior had a sitting area that mimed a Moroccan lounge. A hallway from here led to the Oasis Room, where the silent wine and art auction was set up with Georgi's bar. The room was large enough for 150 people to mingle and peruse the offerings for sale.

Ophelia's recently finished sculpture drew attention as people filed into the Oasis Room. They admired the white four-foot female enigma on a pedestal. The sculpture's surface glistened, and wisps of fabric flowed away from the form, suspended by the stiffening mix Ophelia had applied. The mysterious sculpture appeared to have risen out of the water, as in Marguerite's case, to defeat death and live again.

Ophelia stood by her work in case there were questions about her creative process. Yet, when a slim, dark-haired young woman came forward to say hello, Ophelia didn't recognize her at first. She was a wisp of her former self. But Marguerite's smile indicated who she was.

"Oh! Oh! It's you!" Ophelia hugged her, knowing she needed to be gentle, for even though she was better, Marguerite was still recuperating. They sat nearby to catch up and were brought to tears from their shared experience. Ophelia told her of her art piece. She explained how she poured her love into *Miraculous Survivor*, hoping her effort might help Marguerite rise and return to the world of the living. They knowingly embraced as Ophelia's outpouring appeared to have worked.

While the young women chatted, Barry and his wife, Kim, were in wide-eyed wonderment about the excellent results underway in the wine and art auction. They came upon the surprise entry to the silent auction—the painting by Marilyn Maroney. It was a three-foot by four-foot oil named *Helen Elizabeth,* referring to the Oriental pink poppy with a rich deep purple center. It became the hottest work of art in the silent auction and already reached a bid of $35,000. A notice read: Donated by an anonymous citizen for the fundraiser.

Several bars were located throughout the Garde, but Georgi tended the one in the Oasis Room. It was stocked with many local wines and beers to celebrate the region. When he finished pouring a black currant hard cider from Holmberg Orchards, he saw Detective Morrison enter. Georgi was startled. He quickly appointed a server to be in charge so he could leave the bar.

"Ooh, Detective," he fawned. "You are transformed in this blue silk and linen summer-weight suit. I never imagined you with a pocket square and a matching dress shirt. Look at you! You are quite dashing if I'm allowed to say."

"No, you're not!" Morrison said sternly but quickly smiled and elbowed Georgi. In a lower tone, he said, "Don't mess with my tough reputation, Georgi."

"Oh, oh, I get it. You're joking with me." Unexpectedly, a beautiful woman emerged from behind Morrison. Georgi froze. His eyes glanced from side to side to see if there was someone else with her that he had not seen. Then he realized she was with Morrison. "How do you do, Dr. Angela? You're a vision to behold."

"Hello, Georgi." She presented her hand. He bowed and took it gently.

"It's lovely to see you here with Detective Morrison!" He leaned to whisper in her ear. "You help soften his image."

Morrison gave him the hairy eyeball. "If you are talking about me, I will find a way to lock you up."

"I never know where I stand with him," Georgi complained to her so Morrison would hear. "I always feel like I'm in trouble, even when I give a compliment."

She smiled. "That seems to be a detective's prerogative. You never know where you stand and are always under suspicion."

Morrison thought that could be taken several ways. To distract them, he asked her, "What would you like to drink? I'm having a beer."

"I'll have a tonic and lime, please."

Georgi called over one of his waitstaff and gave the order.

New London's mayor stepped in to say hello to Morrison. "Can you talk for a quick minute, Detective?"

Morrison politely asked, "Will you both excuse me a moment?" They nodded.

This gave Georgi another opportunity to speak with Angela. "I must say, your Versace knock-off is stunning!" he whispered. "You look superb in that shade of peacock blue and the broad straps." With purpose, he inhaled. "And your perfume is just lovely!"

Angela winked. "The dress is not a knock-off, and I made the perfume."

"Huh?" Georgi's mouth hung open. "Well, we all moved up in the world with you in the room, darling!" A couple near the bar suddenly took his attention. "Please, excuse me and enjoy your evening." He clicked his heels and was off.

Roxanne and Sam had arrived and already had a pineapple spritzer for her and a beer for him. Georgi gave her a long approving look. Roxanne's matching top and Capri slacks were in a soft melon tone, and her blonde hair was in a French twist. Tiny bluebirds dangled from her ears. Sam was in a dapper suit without a tie.

"My, my! I'm starting to get used to this newly polished Roxanne without the jeans and T-shirt look!"

She gave him a gentle jab and motioned at her outfit. "This all goes away at midnight."

He viewed her thoughtfully, then shook Sam's hand. "Chief, you look more relaxed out of uniform. Would you care for a feather boa?"

Laughing, he said, "Not ever, Georgi! I can't outshine Roxanne!" He gave a wink. "But I must say you have done a fine job. I'm glad to see the community come together like this. Yet I expect you and Roxanne to have other things on your mind." He monitored his wife's reaction.

They both gave in to his accurate assumption. Roxanne admitted, "I can't hide anything, even when I try, Georgi. He knows me too well."

With quiet urgency, Georgi responded, "There is an excellent chance the dirty culprits are here tonight! We have to remember," he pointed to the floor, "this is their type of crowd, so we must keep our eyes peeled for any dissidents, whether they be collectors, art dealers, art agents, or who knows? Someone could be disguised as a weird janitor."

Sam and Roxanne both laughed. "Weird janitors!" exclaimed Sam. "You both are up to no good."

"We only do good!" they chimed.

Sam's head swiveled between them. "You are two peas in a pod."

Georgi squeezed Roxanne's arm. "How about two birds in a bush or two bees in a bonnet?"

"More like two squirrels up a tree!" Sam chuckled softly.

"I think he means we're nuts," Roxanne whispered.

"That's okay. At least we are fun and nutty!" Georgi flared his hands and winked. "But remember, Roxanne, keep your eyes on the lookout. We are undercover operators tonight." He raised his eyebrows high, twisted his torso, and waved. "I'll see you later. I must return to work."

He stepped behind the bar, grabbed a bottle of German Riesling, and poured a glass for a gentleman in an impeccably tailored baby blue suit with a pink bow tie. He reminded Georgi of Randy Rainbow, who had recently performed to a packed house at the Garde.

Roxanne glanced up at her husband. "Don't worry, Sam, honey. I'm just here to relax with you and enjoy the evening."

"You just lied twice in one sentence," he said, knowing her ploy. "You don't know how to relax, and I'm second to the sole purpose of your mystery-hunting mind. But I love you anyway because those oddities are part of the package that makes you the most interesting person here. Let's enjoy ourselves, shall we?" They meandered through the room and said hello to the many people they knew.

Bunny, from Dev's Bistro, looked beautiful with a fresh hairstyle, sparkling earrings, and a designer dress. In addition, she wore her signature decorative pin on her left shoulder, this time a dragonfly. As she moved through the Oasis room, Bunny saw a woman near her age in a beautiful long, designer silk dress. Being openly friendly and feeling she was among friends in the community, Bunny put her hand on one of the lady's arms. "Darling, we're the only ones here with good taste."

"Darling, you've got the wrong lady. I'm upper class, and you have none." Isadore Rubens took Bunny's wrist, lifted it off her arm, and waved her off. She lifted her dress to the sides and swooped away.

Bunny was left in the wind of the woman's heady perfume. Taking a quick turn around the room, she found herself behind Isadore. She placed her heel on the edge of her exquisite silk dress. When Isadore moved forward, Bunny held her foot down and waited to hear that satisfying sound. *Rrrip!* Bunny let go, turned, and wove between people to avoid detection. The only identifier would have been a glimpse of a dragonfly pin.

At the bar, Bunny whispered to Georgi, "You see that old bag over there? I know her kind. You'll never see her drink water. She needs to maintain her acidity."

"Oh my! Do you know who that is?" Georgi asked but answered quickly. "It's Karl's mother, Isadore. She provided the painting for the big auction tonight!"

"I've been in the people business for years, Georgi, and I can sniff out a wicked woman a mile away. Watch out! She sizes you up for what she can take when she looks at you. If she sees nothing, she discards you like her daily trash.

But if she senses your coin, comfort, or celebrity, she'll do anything to use it to advance her image or agenda."

Georgi was pouring a wine spritzer. "Now, now, Bunny. How well do you know her?"

"I just barely met the witch."

"Well, you can't judge a book by its cover!"

"I've read that book a dozen times over, Georgi! Keep clear of her because she's bad luck."

"Yes, ma'am. I believe you know better than I do."

And with that, Bunny moved on to find her friends, completely satisfied with her intentional destruction of Isadore's dress.

Isadore clenched a wad of her silk dress in her fist. She held it close to her hip to hide the gaping tear that would expose her hindside.

At 6:55 p.m., the houselights flickered to announce that it was time to take their seats for the beginning of the evening's music and dance performances in the main hall.

Morrison had verified with the police force and FBI that officers were stationed throughout the building. Several times, he made the rounds to scope the audience and see if anyone there was suspicious, including Mario Corinthian. Peabody continued roving. All seemed peaceful.

CHAPTER 64

Art Revelations

The house lights dimmed, and Steve, the executive director of the Garde Arts Center, came to the stage with his violin in hand. He played a light and lively tune before he welcomed the crowd. Knowing him well, everyone clapped heartily. It felt like a significant family event.

"We have come together tonight to honor our friends in the art community and celebrate the arts. This city has a big heart, and you can see it here tonight with our full capacity of 1420 of our closest friends and neighbors. We are live-streaming this event into people's homes, and on local-access TV, so everyone can watch the fundraising show with options to donate too."

Whoops, whistles and cheers came from the tip-top of the balcony to the floor seats.

"This community event," he continued, "came together because many people saw a need to show our love and respect to the family and friends of the artists we have recently lost, Marilyn Maroney and Aaron Goshen, and all others affected by the tragedy to our art community."

The room was silent, and the stillness was thick with reverence.

"Funds have already been raised for the families of Aaron and Marilyn and our artist friends who reside above the Dahlia Art Gallery. The show you will see tonight has been brought to you by local and regional talent, and everything we raise will go back into our art community to support individual artists and programs in New London.

"After tonight, we will become known far and wide as an Art City, from modern and fine art to sculpture, dance, music, and theater; we are on the map in Southeastern Connecticut.

"What a great show we have for you tonight. Music from the New London Community Orchestra will now accompany a slideshow of art by local artists. Afterward, the New London Talent Show will have an amazing group of performers who will surprise you. We also have a music video filmed in our city by award-winning artist Billy Gilman with his song "Say You Will." An intermission follows this.

"Last is our grand finale: a live art auction." The image of the auctioned painting emerged on the big screen. "This fine art painting from 1615 is worth at least three hundred thousand dollars," the audience oohed, "and it has been donated by our neighbors and friends Karl Rubens, the director of the Mystic River Fine Art Museum, and his mother, Isadore Rubens, from their private collection. It's the main event for our fundraiser."

Steve picked up his violin. "Without further ado, let the performance begin!" He presented his bow, moved it across the strings, and played a quick ditty as he walked off the stage. The audience applauded as the St. James Episcopal Church's magnificent interior appeared with the New London Community Orchestra on the big screen.

***

Backstage, a police officer stood in the wings, and Karl peeked from behind the curtain to locate his mother. He motioned for her to join him, but when Isadore spied him, she grimaced through her peony-pink lipstick and shook her head. He could see she wasn't having a good time for some reason.

Karl had widely publicized the auction of the painting and was confident the floral still-life would do well. Doubting anyone local would be interested, Karl hosted a simultaneous online auction to ensure an excellent bid.

At 9:00 p.m., after the dance and music performances and the intermission concluded, Georgi stepped onto the stage for the auction to begin. "Welcome, welcome, welcome! Seeing so many friendly faces for a cause dear to my heart is a pleasure. Marilyn was one of my best friends, and Aaron was a friend to many of us.

"It is with great pleasure that I introduce Karl Rubens and Isadore Rubens from Mystic. They are here to help us through tough times by donating the art being auctioned tonight." Since Isadore wasn't with Karl, Georgi motioned to where she was seated. She stood clenching the rip in her dress but smiled and waved to the audience.

Even from afar, Karl could tell his mother was out of sorts. Her lips were twisted into an insincere smile. As he walked across the stage, the audience gave them warm applauses.

Georgi added, "Please see your program for the Rubens' full bios. Yet, as you may know, they have recently been through a few of their own trying times. I am very grateful to Karl and Isadore for initiating tonight's big fundraiser. It all started with the donation of this magnificent painting and grew into this fine event. I now give you Karl, who shall commence with the auction."

Roxanne smiled as she noticed Karl's formal demeanor and starchy appearance contrasted with the boisterous party atmosphere of the flamboyant, boa-wearing audience.

On stage next to him was an easel with the rare still-life being auctioned. The painting of doves, pears, and roses appeared on the giant projection screen for everyone to see. Karl spoke. "My mother purchased this work at a very fair price over forty years ago. When I was cleaning it years later, I verified its identity as a lost original by the great Dutch painter Ambrosius Bosschaert. He only signed his work with his initials, and I found them hidden under hundreds of years of dirt.

"This painting is thirty inches tall by thirty-eight inches wide. Two white doves are in a large, elegant birdcage, gazing at each other. On a table is a delicate vase with a bouquet of demure yellow roses and an iridescent beetle. Plump green pears are on a decorative plate with a small paring knife.

"The excellent use of composition and color—chartreuse, yellows, and shades of white—carry the eye across and around the highlights in the painting. The line of the paring knife directs you to the roses while your eyes rest a moment on the little beetle.

"This Baroque painting, exquisitely and carefully executed, is of fleeting beauty captured in a still-life."

Karl paused to look around the audience. "The still-life art form became a prevalent genre in the sixteenth and seventeenth centuries because of Ambrosius Bosschaert. He created a lucrative business and dynasty by teaching his children and family members to become painters too."

Karl nodded to his assistant; he was standing nearby to field the online bids on a worldwide auction site. "And now we shall start the bidding at one hundred fifty thousand dollars." An audible gasp resounded across the Garde's audience. "I ask that the room stay quiet until we finish the auction, please."

Immediately, the first online bid came in, and his assistant announced, "One hundred seventy-five thousand dollars."

"The bidding has begun," Karl announced.

The audience felt the drama. Most could not relate to the art auction's price, the art's description, or the concept of it being a wise investment. Yet the enthusiasm for a bidding war was undeniable.

A person in the audience held up a placard and bid $200,000.

The crowd sat entranced.

"Two hundred thousand dollars to the gentleman in the center row," Karl called out.

Georgi, who stood in the far back of the audience, started jumping up and down. Karl put his hands above his eyes to cut out the glare of the lights. "Georgi, is that you in the back? Do you intend to make the next bid?"

"Oh no!" Georgi squealed. "I'm just so excited. I'll stop jumping."

The crowd laughed, enjoying his high-tension zeal.

The assistant scanned his computer screen. "Two hundred twenty-five thousand dollars from New York." Then another. "Two hundred fifty thousand dollars from Germany."

The audience was humming, which disturbed Karl's auction etiquette. His eyebrows raised at the interruptions, and he used his hand to hide a sour expression.

Then suddenly, the assistant called, "Two hundred seventy-five thousand from New York. Three hundred thousand from California. They're rolling in now. Three hundred twenty-five thousand from Spain."

Still standing in the rear of the audience, Georgi could not control himself; he was jumping again. Ron, the Garde's house manager and Georgi's friend, stepped toward him. He placed one hand on his hip, shifted his weight, then pointed with the other hand admonishingly. "Mr. Georgi Algarve, what do I have to do to make you behave?" Ron scolded as he presented the teapot pose. Admonished, Georgi froze yet was wide-eyed with the wonderment of the auction. Ron, a big brother to him and a fabulous hairstylist, too, placed his hands on Georgi's shoulders to prevent him from jumping.

A bid of $350,000 came from the gentleman in the center row. The audience uncontrollably gasped at another in-house offer.

While the tension built, Ron was called backstage through his earpiece. Nimbly, he entered the back hall and passed by the famous "Signature Wall" of worldwide performers and then the star's dressing room. A police officer joined him before he went downstairs to the performer's green room, where an unidentified person was sighted. Seeing no one, they returned up the stairs.

A cloaked figure had heard Ron and the officer approach and so moved into a dark corner backstage. He waited for them to pass, but Ron stayed behind the curtain and stood next to the policeman. They were caught up in the excitement, watching and listening to the auction and the audience. People were on the edge of their seats as large amounts of money were offered for this single work of art.

The auction stalled for a moment, and Karl asked, "Do I have anyone for three hundred seventy-five?" He waited. "Going once. Going—"

"Three hundred seventy-five thousand from the Netherlands," the assistant interrupted.

"Woo, woo, woo!" The audience could not contain themselves any longer. The sound forced Karl to brace himself against the podium. He was perturbed but composed himself with a weak, prim smile.

The bidding seemed to end. A hush fell over the room. The assistant shook his head. No further bids were coming forward.

Karl called the bid. "Going once for three hundred seventy-five dollars." He waited. "Going twice." He looked to his assistant, and he scanned the audience.

A placard went up. "Four hundred thousand dollars," said a woman inside the great hall. Everyone looked for the top-dollar bidder. Morrison did the same, but his jaw went slack when he turned to his right. There, with her right arm raised, was Dr. Angela Storm.

A murmur traveled through the crowd but stopped when Karl announced, "We have a bid for four hundred thousand dollars. Thank you, mademoiselle." He nodded to her and looked at his assistant, who indicated that no bids were on his screen. Again, Karl made the call. "Any bids?" He waited. "Four hundred thousand going once. Four hundred thousand going twice." He took a long pause and glanced at his protégé. When he shook his head, Karl's hammer came down hard. "SOLD! For four hundred thousand dollars to the lovely lady in blue."

At first, the room was stunned into silence, then exploded into a rip-roaring cheer. People jumped out of their seats. Karl motioned for her to come to the stage to accept the painting.

Morrison turned his entire body toward her. "Who are you, and why are you sitting with me?"

With an amused smile, she whispered, "I am your continual mystery." She tipped her head to look into his deep blue eyes.

"Wow," he mouthed.

Roxanne and Sam were standing and clapping while watching the room. They saw Georgi with his friends and Dan Morrison gawking at Angela Storm. Roxanne beamed a smile at Sam. "She has more going on under her hood than we would have guessed."

Sam chuckled at her car analogy. "Yes, and this will be an entertaining car show to watch. I believe Dan discovered she's a custom Tesla when he thought she was a premium Audi."

"You got a 1970s VW van in me," she smiled, "and I have a classic 'Super Eight' Buick in you. I have the better deal."

"I don't mind," he said.

Now that the audience was standing and chatting, Georgi bounced over to them. "Would you like to join me in the Oasis Room to see how the silent auction went?" Roxanne and Sam agreed and followed him. Sam had noticed the two were so swept up in the event's excitement that they seemed to have forgotten their sleuthing mission. He was relieved.

Once out of the performance hall, they walked through the double doors to the thirty-foot hallway leading to the Oasis Room. A young guard exited the restroom located in the long hallway and followed them. They entered the room just as an emergency exit door to the stairs was closing.

"Huh? Where's Marilyn's painting?" Georgi squealed, noticing the vacancy on the easel.

The young guard who followed them immediately went to the exit door and looked down the stairwell. "Hey," he yelled down. The stranger did not respond. Flustered, the young man turned to Sam, Roxanne, and Georgi. "I don't know who that was, but I think he took the painting. Something was wrapped in a black cloth." The guard's perplexed expression said it all.

"Where's your in-house phone?" asked Sam.

"There on the wall," the guard pointed. "I'll call the emergency to the front lobby. They will catch him on the street."

"Good. I'll get one of the police officers stationed here in the hall." Sam raced off while the young guard called for help.

Roxanne grabbed Georgi's arm, opened the stairwell door, and said, "Let's go!" While they raced down the three flights of stairs, they saw the street-level door close.

Sam returned with an officer, but Roxanne was gone. "Where did she go?"

"They went down the stairwell," the guard answered. "I'll stay with the paintings."

Sam and the police officer took off.

While Roxanne and Georgi were racing up and down the sidewalk, they met officers and the undercover FBI. "Where did he go!" yelled Georgi with arms in the air. Sam arrived, and Roxanne was puffing. "We didn't see where he went or how he got away. He must have jumped into a waiting vehicle."

Georgi flailed. "I can't believe it. The bandits have struck again!"

An officer told Sam, "We saw a police van pull up. A uniformed officer with a covered object jumped into the side door. We now know it was a ruse. They're hunting them down."

All officers were alerted to mobilize a search, and an APB went out for a suspicious person with a painting covered with a black cloth. One officer joined

Roxanne, Sam, and Georgi to document what had happened. Georgi was frantic. "How could this happen? I thought this place was covered in cops!"

Roxanne whispered, "Shh, give them a chance, okay?"

The rare painting on stage was safe on its easel. Backstage, Ron, the house manager, held his position with the police officer standing nearby. When the officer received information in his earpiece of the theft, he was distracted and whispered to Ron, "There's been an incident in the Oasis Room."

Ron was about to leave, but a cloaked figure with a mask suddenly emerged from the shadows and raced toward the rare artwork. He calculated he could not grab it and get away, so he bolted toward the loading dock door. Ron and the officer ran across the broad backstage after him wondering how the area had been infiltrated.

When they pressed on the door to the loading dock, it was jammed shut from the outside. The officer radioed the police team and reported the suspicious person. The back of the building had become unsecured when all officers focused on the theft at the front of the building. Ron had visions from *The Phantom of the Opera* playing in his mind. Like a ghost, the cloaked figure was gone.

In front of the packed house, Angela Storm walked across the stage toward Karl, who presented the painting to her. Unaware of the incidents, they waved to the cheering audience and exited stage left. Two police officers were waiting to escort them.

Morrison made his way backstage, and Angela emerged with her escorts. He was pleased to see them but concerned when he heard about the cloaked figure. "I would feel much better if you placed this painting in a locked vault for the night."

"Do you have one?" she asked.

"I know of one." He turned to the two officers, "Let's place the painting in the evidence vault at headquarters. It is protected in this hardcover case Karl has provided, so it is safe from damage. We'll escort Dr. Storm and show her where her valuable purchase will be secured."

"It's not mine," she claimed, catching him and the officers off guard. "It belongs to Dr. Ethan Lin. He couldn't attend the auction, so he asked me to bid and told me the amount he was willing to spend. He'll collect the painting tomorrow."

"Okaay." Morrison glanced at the officers. "Let's go. We are parked on State Street."

"One more thing, Detective," an officer said. "A painting appears to have been stolen from the Oasis Room. There was a momentary hole in our watch when a younger, uniformed guard took a restroom break."

Internally, Morrison was reeling. This news meant someone had started the merry-go-round again on his nonstop case, and a short-lived evening of enjoyment caught him unprepared. Externally, he remained calm. "Alright. Do you have officers on top of that situation?"

"Yes, they are handling it now."

"Then, while they take care of the theft details, we'll secure this painting and escort Dr. Storm home."

He walked her to her car. "Do you often surprise people like this?"

"I didn't expect to bid on the painting," she confessed. "He gave me a cutoff amount. Since it was a worldwide auction and the painter was so famous, I expected the bidding to exceed his price. If it passed his limit, no one would have ever known I was bidding on it for him."

"Actually," he said, "everyone thinks you are the buyer, and that makes you susceptible to the thieves, hence the vault for the painting and an escort."

"I guess you're right," she agreed. Silence hung between them.

"If you don't mind me asking, how high was he willing to go?" Morrison raised his eyebrows with his question.

"Four hundred thousand and one dollars," she said with a smile.

Morrison laughed out loud. "Well, you sure saved him a dollar!" They both chuckled. "You mean if someone had bid four hundred thousand dollars, you would have added one dollar above the bid?"

"More is more." She giggled and sighed. "Thank you, Dan. I'm glad we can put the painting in the evidence vault. I am slightly unsettled after hearing about the character backstage and the theft in the Oasis Room."

Morrison confided, "Confidentially, I've been suspicious of Karl Rubens and his mother because of Aaron and the BFA painting theft at their museum. But after what happened tonight, I don't see a motive that ties them to these incidents. The FBI is investigating a New York art theft ring, and Marilyn's art agent looks more like the connecting link to the operation. We need to tie him to this Mario Corinthian character definitively."

Grateful for his presence, she gently placed her hand on his arm. "Thanks for telling me. I would never have imagined that I could be part of this strange case because of the auction. We both know these thieves disregard life."

"Yeah, but I know you're used to dealing with deadbeats." They laughed again.

"I'll be returning to the Garde and working late tonight," Morrison said. "Are you going to be all right at home?"

"I have good security at my condo," she answered. "I'll be fine on the third floor. I'm not worried. And Ethan is picking up the painting tomorrow. I want to see it go into his hands."

After safeguarding the painting at police headquarters, Morrison had the officers escort Dr. Storm to her condo. When he returned to the Garde, the officers immediately notified him that Roxanne, Georgi, and Sam had discovered the theft of Marilyn's painting, which had garnered a $55,000 bid in the silent auction.

Once Detective Morrison was briefed on the backstage behavior of the cloaked character, he believed their ultimate plan was to steal Karl's rare painting. *Good thing Ron and that officer spooked him.* Morrison unwrapped a stick of cinnamon gum and pondered the situation. *That would have been a windfall for these thieves.* He shook his head at the debacle. *It looks like Mario Corinthian has struck again.*

CHAPTER 65

A Mad Idea
Monday

Drs. Angela Storm and Ethan Lin retrieved the fine art painting at police headquarters from the evidence vault. Karl was to meet them at 11 a.m. for tea across from the Garde Arts Center at the exclusive Thames Club to finalize the sale. A member had invited Karl to be his guest and use the location to make the expensive transaction.

The pair arrived with the painting and met Karl in the historic club. They entered an elegant room with a plaque stating that the Thames Club was established over 150 years ago.

Ethan told Karl he was pleased with the painting and that it would soon be hanging in his mother's living room. By noon, the ownership documents for the art were finalized. Drs. Storm and Lin left, and so did Karl.

He was about to enter his Jaguar when he heard someone call his name.

"Karl! Hi, it's Troy. I'm one of the artists at the Dahlia. What a nice event we had last night. Thank you for donating that painting to support artists." He noticed Karl was wearing a suit, bowtie, and even driving gloves on this warm day.

"Oh, hello, Troy." Karl recognized him and analyzed his appearance. Troy's clothes were slightly crumpled. "Yes, the event went well, and mother and I were glad to assist, considering all that has happened with the artists. How are things at the Dahlia?" He wanted to know how his non-competitor gallery was doing.

"We still want Detective Morrison to solve the case with Marilyn, especially with another one of her paintings stolen. In fact, he asked me this morning to view a foggy security video of her leaving the Dahlia the night she died. It was weird to see her. After I left, I wondered if it was her in the video. It wasn't how Marilyn walked. She had a certain sway that the person in the video didn't have. It makes me wonder if it was her killer. Maybe a person in disguise is carrying her portfolio case."

"You think so? Maybe the fog distorted the image?" Karl offered.

"No, I know her walk. It's unique. Have you ever seen a beautiful woman move with grace across a room in a way that captures your attention?"

Karl looked at him blankly. "I can't say I have."

"It defines who they are. Just think of an iconic movie star, a woman like Marilyn Monroe. You can't deny they have their own sway. It embodies their essence. Each motion of the hip is their personal signature. Like sweet perfume, they affect the room. Men's heads turn to watch her pass, and their eyes longingly pursue her."

"I might imagine Isabella Stewart Gardner's sway," Karl stated.

Troy made a face of bafflement. "Can't you think of someone you've seen…alive?"

Karl's thoughts took a sharp turn. "Like RuPaul?"

"I'm not sure you like the same women as I do. Anyway…it wasn't Marilyn in that video. I'm sure of it. It was more like a guy who's never worn heels."

"Is that so?" Karl looked at his watch as though he had grown tired of the conversation. "Oh! I forgot I have an appointment. I need to leave, Troy." Tiny beads of sweat had formed on his brow.

Troy observed that he was way overdressed for this weather. *No wonder he's sweating.* As he watched Karl speed off, Troy remembered he had deadlines. Two typewriters he refurbished needed to be finished: one with green racing stripes for a car enthusiast and another with a floral design and pink luster finish for a gardener.

***

Once Troy finished his work, he shipped the typewriters and took a nap. He woke up feeling grumpy. Thoughts of Marilyn, Aaron, Marguerite, and Cora haunted his dreams. Leafing through the local newspaper made his dreamtime dismay turn to frustration. The theft of Marilyn's painting was on the front page, and the price of her artwork in private collections was still skyrocketing.

Troy knew well of this phenomenon. Keith Vaughan was a modern British painter whose 1957 work *Bather* initially sold in 1970 for $350. Seven years after his death, it was valued at $60,000. The value difference between when he was alive and dead gave Troy so much angst that he decided to hatch a plan. *But I need an accomplice.*

There were a few hours left of daylight to do some touch-up work on the huge city mural Troy had created with another artist. He had texted Jason, his artist friend, asking him to stop by. They had known each other for over a dozen years, and both were managing the struggle of earning a decent living.

Troy stood with his brushes and paint on a scissor lift they had rented for the mural work. It brought him to six feet high. "Hey, Jason, how's Shatana?"

"Good. She's working on a fashion show with a friend. How are you doing?"

"I've been thinking. You know how we are always discussing the way artists become famous?"

"Yeah." Jason watched Troy dip his paintbrush into an azure blue.

"Well, I've come to think that the only way to make money is to be dead. That's when you become famous, and the price goes up."

Jason followed Troy's brush as it swirled around seaweed. "Yeah."

His response was a thud. Different from what Troy was going for. "Did you hear what I said?"

"What did you say?" Jason looked up at Troy on his perch.

Gesturing with passion, he repeated, "I said the only way to make money is to be dead because then the price of your work goes up ten-fold! Maybe I should be dead."

Jason almost lost his balance and grabbed the scissor lift. "Are you talking about suicide, Troy?"

"Of course not. Give me a break! The dilemma is that you can't collect when you're dead. But everyone else who has your work does collect. As an artist, I'm complaining because it's not fair. I'm being tortured. Artists have barely enough money to live on during their life, yet after their death," Troy's fists punched the air, "Boom! Pow! Bam! Someone gets rich off their deaths!" The lift swayed with his movements. "This makes me upset, that's all. Thoughts are spinning around in my head, so I devised a plan." Troy wiped his paintbrush with a rag. He brought the scissor lift down and stepped off.

"What are you talking about, buddy?" Jason was concerned for his friend.

"I think I should mess with this reality. Will my work go up in price if people think I'm dead?" Jason's eyes popped, and Troy continued, "I know this won't sound very sophisticated, but what if I staged my death so I could benefit from it? If people believe I died, I predict my work will finally sell at a price I think it is worth. So why don't I disappear suspiciously? Then we'll find out. It's the curse of an artist to be most popular after death!

"If my work exponentially increases, we'll make a point. An artist's value should be recognized while they're alive! We need to make a living too! Hey, we can spin this story into big news if we succeed. We'll expose the insanity and bring recognition to living artists like you, me, and our friends. The people handling the work make the most money from the artist's talent."

Troy began pacing. "Jason, the nature of art and money is surreal. When you're alive, people like your artwork, but they vacillate when it comes to buying because they are indecisive and picky. Once they hear you're dead, bam! They can decide now, and boom! They're ready to pay top dollar and pow! Money is in the pocket of everyone but the artist."

Jason's mind began to whir. "Like Vincent Van Gogh, the greatness of his work was discovered postmortem. I understand the challenge. If you're serious, you'll need a place to stay."

"Yes, I will, but this is just between you and me. You must promise, Jason."

"I got you, dude. Hey, how about my family's cabin in Vermont? You could stay there. I have the key!"

"Good, but I have more favors. Can you watch over Matt, the cat, and take care of my art sales?"

"Of course, but what's my percentage?"

"Ten percent."

Jason scoffed. "If I get you a good price, be fair and give me twenty percent."

"That's why we're starving!" Troy protested. "I thought you would like the challenge more than my money. Remember, you're not the one presumed dead. I'll give you fifteen percent, but only if you get top dollar."

"Aww, alright. It'll be fun."

"Jason, this is our experiment to show how fickle the art world business is. They don't support an artist's talent when they are alive, yet are happy to buy their work when they're dead. It's sick. What's that phrase? The fickle finger of fate. I will make my fate!"

"But why will people think you're dead?" Jason asked.

"I've got a plan, and I don't need a body. You see, I will be lost at sea in the currents of Long Island Sound." Troy waved his arms. "My beach stuff will be on the sand. It will look like I went for a swim and never came back. With all that has gone on with Marilyn, Cora, and the others, I'm just another dead artist."

Jason rubbed his hands together. "I'm all in for fifteen percent. Let's hope your wild idea works."

Troy felt a rush of adrenaline. He was no longer worrying. In fact, he felt more alive, having the plan to die. But there were details to iron out. "Are you ready for people to ask a lot of questions?"

"Not a problem. Your secret is safe with me. It's in the underground, the bat cave, the fortress of my mind," Jason laughed. "I'm going to enjoy this thoroughly. Playfully, he punched Troy's shoulder, and they chuckled at the mad plan.

"Just keep a record of who wants to buy what, stall them a little, then sell. I need my work to sell for high prices before I return." Troy was thrilled Jason was on board.

"But what happens when you come back? Won't you get in trouble?"

"No, I'll just make something up."

Troy was eager for his plan to work. He had been sad and mad, and now he was glad to go into hiding. Maybe he'd come up with a new series of artwork. It would be a vacation. He also knew the wealthy ear of the art world was always held to the ground, waiting for the next artist to drop, then they would pounce on their next art investment. Troy was banking on it. But first, he had a small mission: the charade of his death.

***

At dinner that evening, Karl told his mother about the finality of the painting's sale from the auction and that the money was put into escrow. It would be distributed to New London artists and the art community. Then he shared the news he'd heard earlier in the day.

"Troy saw a video today. It showed a person with a portfolio case leaving the Dahlia building the night Marilyn died. He said it was very foggy, but he didn't believe it was Marilyn because of how the person walked. He thought it could have been someone in disguise, maybe the killer. I wonder if anyone else thinks like him." Karl watched his mother's reaction.

Isadore pursed her lips. Then a smile slowly relaxed her mouth. "Darling, why don't you tell Troy about the Rising Star event you are planning at the museum? Tell him Marilyn was your first choice, but since she is gone, maybe you could discuss a show with him. Ask him to bring his laptop so you can see his work. He may be good enough for this future show."

"Mother, why would I do that?"

"Come now. Flattery will get you everywhere. Don't you want to know what he knows? Besides, he may have access to some of her artwork. It would be a good investment."

"I hadn't thought of that." Karl gave her a warm smile. "Mother, you're always thinking ahead."

Isadore pranced into the kitchen. "Let's invite him for dinner tomorrow. He will be more comfortable if we shower him with hospitality and a good meal. We can ask him then."

CHAPTER 66

Dinner is Served
Tuesday

"I need this vacation." Troy was muttering aloud while packing a small art case and a knapsack with his laptop, clothes, and snacks for Vermont. He had also filled his calendar with appointments for the following week. That way, people would miss him when he didn't show up. Jason would blast the rumor of another missing Dahlia artist, and they would fear another New London artist had met a lethal outcome.

A ringtone strummed on Troy's phone and interrupted his preparations. "Hi, Karl. Did you say you want to see my work? Sure, I can bring my laptop. Yes, I can meet you at the museum today at five-thirty. Thanks, Karl!" This was an unexpected request, and Troy was pleased with the chance for future advancement. *Good! Another coin in my pocket and espresso in my cup.*

Continuing his covert plan, Troy grabbed a canvas duffel bag for the beach. It was packed with a towel, sunblock, sunglasses, and sandals. Inside, he placed an old wallet with his business cards. He now had everything he needed.

Jason followed Troy's car to Pequot Avenue. Troy parked where the Thames River met the mouth of Long Island Sound. He left his phone in the glove box and went to a less frequented beach. Stretching out a towel, he placed his sandals, sunglasses, and duffel bag on it. *A good place for drowning*! He hummed as he looked around.

He walked into the water until he was ankle-deep, strolled through the lapping waves, and came out near a dock at the opposite end of the beach. He was pleased with himself. "You were a good ol' boy, Troy: a radical art dude and painter of life. RIP.... Ha! I'm writing my obituary."

Jason drove him back into town. Troy grabbed his backpack and took the train for his appointment with Karl in Mystic.

On arriving, Karl informed Troy that his mother had made other plans. "I tried to stop her," he said, "but my mother made us dinner. Do you mind if we look at your work there? Then I'll drive you back to the train."

"That's fine. I must be back in New London before nine, however. I'm meeting a friend, and we will work late tonight." Troy was planning to catch the 9 p.m. bus to Vermont.

He slipped into Karl's luxury Jaguar XJ-S. "Wow, this is a nice car." Karl gave Troy an amused glance. They continued the short distance through Mystic to the causeway that bridged Mason's Island. Karl entered the suburban tree-lined setting, passed the guard shack, and meandered down the narrow road. The view opened to an expansive lawn and house overlooking the water. Stepping out of the car, Troy felt noticeably relaxed. He filled his lungs with the fresh, salty air and took in the broad vista.

He followed Karl into the traditional home with refined décor, oriental carpets, and coffered ceilings. Troy's eyes wandered. To his amazement, he spotted a Sandro Botticelli painting hanging above an antique sideboard. The famous artist painted *The Birth of Venus*. Old-world wall sconces were on either side. On another wall, antique fresco panels acted as a window into an Italian vista.

"Karl, you live in a museum. Every wall is covered in fine art. I've never been in a home like this."

This encouraged Karl to lead him into the sitting room. Troy carefully observed a wall of Baroque art and another of Renaissance art with his artistic eye. They passed through into the living room. Classical sculptures and extravagant vases of exquisite porcelain were among plush, antique furnishings.

Having overheard his comment, Isadore said, "Thank you, Troy." Startled by her voice, he turned to see her elegance enter the room in her monogrammed velvet slippers and a wispy kaftan of beach-glass green. An ornate white coral necklace contrasted with her dark hair. To Troy, she had the look of a classic movie star.

She continued, "The collection is from around the world. As you can see, we enjoy acquiring art." She moved gracefully past him. "Please, come into the dining room. I know you and Karl are on a schedule."

"Oh, uh, Mrs. Rubens, it's a very fine collection," Troy stuttered. He combed his hair with his fingers and straightened his casual shirt.

Karl noticed his mother was being surprisingly sweet. He called it feigning friendliness. Such behavior and niceties were usually reserved for her wealthy neighbors. He also saw it used to acquire art such as Marilyn's. If Jonesy from New York recommended her work, his mother wanted it.

"Please call me Isadore, Troy, and come right this way. I've set the table in the formal dining room." She sashayed away, but Troy stopped short and looked up.

"Is that an original Rubens painting?" His mouth hung in awe.

She leaned on a Queen Anne chair and waved her hand. "Why, yes, that one has been passed down in our family. Karl's father's inheritance. We are direct descendants of Peter Paul Rubens. Do you like it?"

Troy's hand pressed against his chest. "Of course! He was a great master and so prolific. Every painting he did was magnificent. Is this one related to his *Feast of Venus?*"

"My goodness, you are well educated," Isadore cooed. "It is considered an unidentical mirror image with varying details, possibly for his own house. His wife, Helene, is one of the young maidens cavorting with a satyr. As you can see, the magnificent landscape surrounds Venus. She is adorned with flowers and surrounded by a multitude of cheerful cherubs. Isn't it lovely?"

Karl watched his mother suspiciously. *What is she up to?*

In wonder, Troy examined the priceless painting meant for museums and answered, "It is magnificent."

They proceeded into a spacious dining room with a crystal chandelier over the table that could seat a dozen guests. "We rarely eat here, but I thought it would be nice for you," she motioned to a chair for him. Three place settings were already laid out with ornate dinnerware, silver utensils, and fresh flowers.

"My, this is beautiful, Isadore." Troy laughed nervously. "You didn't need to go all out for me. I'm not used to fancy things."

"Oh no, dear, this is nothing. Have a seat, please. You too, Karl. I'll bring the food out on the tea cart."

Karl asked Troy about his art and his artistic methods. While he explained carving a wax block for his unique monoprints, Isadore returned with dinner. She had prepared a meal of mushroom soup, Salisbury steak, asparagus, and red bliss potatoes with gravy.

"Mmm, this is delicious," Troy remarked.

Isadore was pleased, but it was time to get to the point. "Troy," she glanced at her son, "I heard from Karl that you knew Marilyn, the poor dear. Could we purchase her art at this time?"

Entirely surprised by her interest, Troy answered willingly. "It's all tied up with her art agent until the case of her death is closed. I told Karl yesterday I watched a video of her on the night she died. It dawned on me after I left the police station that it just couldn't be her. It was not the way she walked."

"Well, who do you think it was?" Isadore took a bite of steak.

"I don't know, but I'm sure it wasn't her. The walk was all wrong."

"Have you told the detective yet?" she asked.

"No. I've been too busy, but I will."

He continued eating until his bread sopped up every bit of gravy. Then he sat back and patted his stomach. "Thank you, Isadore, that was a fine dinner. It's been a long time since someone made me a home-cooked meal."

Isadore enjoyed the flattery, though she expected it. "Thank you, Troy. You are too kind. Why don't you tell me about the art you plan to place in the museum's contemporary exhibit? I'd love to hear all about it." She noticed his eyes starting to droop. "Are you okay, dear?"

"I'm suddenly feeling tired. I guess it's your good food. You know how you can take a nap after you eat?" Troy looked up at the chandelier. Its cut crystals were sparkling with pinpoints of light. "Wow, that chandelier is awesome! I've never seen one that could shoot rainbows." His head swayed as his eyes followed what he saw.

Karl watched quizzically.

"Whoa, I feel a little dizzy." Troy placed his hands on the table to stabilize himself. "Do you have any ginger ale?"

Keeping her eyes fixed on their guest, Isadore said in a monotone, "Karl, dear, why don't you get Troy a can of ginger ale? I think we have some in the fridge."

Still trying to figure out what was happening, Karl went for the ginger ale. A loud creaking sound echoed through the house while he was in the kitchen. His back went stiff. He recognized the sound and dashed around the corner. They were gone.

From below his feet, he heard her distant voice. "It's right over here, Troy. I want to show you my art collection." Isadore spoke kindly, but to Karl, it was the dreadful kind like a spider to a fly. With horror, he suddenly realized the gravity of the situation. She showed Troy their private art gallery; no one had been there before.

Racing to the hallway, he saw the oriental carpet had been peeled back from the floorboards, and the trap door was open, revealing the underground staircase. This was when Karl's dread became real. He leaped down the stairs and entered the gallery. Angrily he glared at his mother. Approaching her, he hissed into her ear. "Motherrr! What are you doing?"

She smiled sweetly and placed a finger to her lips. "Shhh." Karl stood perfectly still, clutching the cold can of ginger ale. A rippling chill ran up his arm and down his spine as he watched Troy slowly sit on a cushioned bench.

"Wow, this room is far out, Isadore. All the colors are moving together." Troy swayed and swiped at nothing but air. "The colors are everywhere!"

It was then Karl realized Troy was tripping on a psychedelic high!

Blissfully, Troy sat and stared at the long gallery of art that seemed to tunnel yet with a weaving warp and weft effect. He watched as the framed paintings undulated.

Isadore had created an elegant gallery with cream walls, crown molding, beige carpet, navy leather benches, two club chairs, and a small table. The beautiful artwork gave the room ambience.

Karl looked from Troy to his mother in a gawking manner. He saw little hope in repairing what she had done. Although Karl was not tripping, he felt his world was crumbling in slow motion. His future passed before him in flux, like the surreal painting of melting clocks by Salvador Dali called *The Persistence of Memory*.

Suddenly, a gurgling growl rose out of Karl's throat. "Motherrr! What have you done?"

Startled by the sound, Troy threw his arms out as if trying to balance himself. "Whoa, what was that? Are you all right, Karl?"

Ignoring him, Karl grabbed his mother's arm. "What are you doing, Mother?" He snarled, sweat beaded on his brow, and his eyes bore into her.

She brushed him off and stepped away. "Everything is going just as planned, dear. Don't you worry. I have it all figured out."

Karl was fuming. "All what figured out? He can't be a witness to the art on these walls!"

Troy slowly descended from sitting to resting his head on the cushioned bench, then closed his eyes. "He can't stay here! What happens when he wakes up and realizes what he saw and where he saw it? We will be doomed, Mother!"

"My dearest," she cooed, "don't you see this is just another ploy to misdirect the investigation away from Marilyn's death?"

"But, Mother," he pleaded, "everything was accidental."

"No one knows that, really, dear. This is how we control the narrative and let them think there is a serial killer. When Troy disappears, it will seem obvious there is some vendetta toward New London artists."

"But I don't understand." Karl searched her face. "How does this end?"

Troy was now snoring loudly.

"It's time for your career to crescendo. We can't have Marilyn's death disrupt it. Nor the popularity of New London's avant-garde artists overshadowing us. It is our time here in Mystic to live happily ever after, and we have the perfect cover. No one will ever suspect us when Troy disappears because he will blend in with all the other incidents. You see, a killer is on the loose."

Karl absorbed the shocking situation, recognizing a dead end. With no way out, he felt desperate. "Explain what happens next, Mother!"

Isadore remained nonchalant. "Don't you remember, dear? We have a crypt. Once the combination of poisonous mushrooms in Troy's soup takes effect, we'll put him next door below your father. We do not need to go above ground since it is adjacent to the underground gallery. No one will ever know he was here. It's only a matter of time."

Karl stared at her, wishing he was the one having a psychedelic dream. "But what if someone knows he is meeting with us?"

"We saw him, fed him, he met with you, and left." Her hand gestures implied that this was just that easy.

"You mean to say you planned this all out and decided not to tell me?"

"I couldn't take the chance," Isadore began to explain. "When you said he suspected the person in the video wasn't her, I knew it was over. I couldn't have you be incriminated. What if he told the detective?"

"Motherrr! You don't know that he would have! You never tell me anything! This is just like Boston! I can't stay here and watch this!" He headed toward the vault door in a huff.

She voiced her appeal to his back. "I didn't want you to worry! Don't worry. It's done…it's all done!"

Karl stormed out of their subterranean gallery. He left the house to walk off his frustration and followed the single winding road of their island neighborhood, passing established homes on acre-sized lots. Distant seagulls called out from the shoreline as they haggled over Poggy Bay's feeding grounds of mussels.

Karl shook his head in hopes of waking up from his nightmare. *She did it again. She's taken away my choices and affected my life.* In his mind's eye, he saw the trajectory of the situation that led to Troy's presence in their home. He groaned loudly, "Ughh." *I should have known. If I had kept my mouth shut, this would not have happened. I should never have told her what Troy said about the video the night Marilyn died.* Karl tried to reason that his mother always wanted to protect him, but she did so in the most selfish ways.

Boyhood Karl tried reasoning with adult Karl. *Look at all she's done to help you. You wouldn't be where you are without her.* Adult Karl felt weak. *How can I blame her? She only wants to protect me and advance my career. But she's imposed her will and captured Troy! What am I to do?*

His agitation and long stride urged him across the causeway to the Franciscan chapel on Edgar's Island. It was a charming structure that was part of the monastery's compound. Emotions of anger and empathy were dueling within him. Entering the small chapel, he knelt, lit a candle, and gazed into the flame. A brief prayer came easily to him. *Help me accept the things I cannot change.*

A glass box against one of the walls held a relic from a saint. The cherished artifact was a mummified bony hand. He spent some time looking at it. *I could be gone tomorrow, and I will be forgotten. The saints, artists, and writers are the only ones remembered with reverence. Those artists are Vermeer and Rubens or the sculptors Bernini and Michelangelo. I will be forsaken.*

He pondered his misfortune and good fortune. *Can I trust her? Can she work this out? How does poisoning Troy make my problems disappear?*

His thoughts flashed back to the horrible night of Marilyn's death.

CHAPTER 67

The Past – Marilyn's Last Art Reception

Karl had been trying to arrange a meeting with Marilyn Maroney for a month. He wanted to view her artwork in person to consider her for his Rising Star series, which would showcase eight contemporary artists. New York and California contacts had told him to book her, but meeting her and seeing the art in person was the only way he would know if he should.

She was absorbed in her current show at the Dahlia Art Gallery and had been putting him off due to her schedule. Although she didn't have time for Karl, she was willing to meet him if he would come by the Dahlia the night of the opening reception. This would be his only opportunity as she would be leaving the following day for a show in Iceland where her artwork and sculptures for the show had already been shipped. Marilyn instructed Karl to enter through the back garden gate, and she would meet him in the garden at 11 p.m.

Karl found it very inconvenient and complained to his mother. "The only reason I am going is Jonesy from New York has told me I must. He says she will bring attention to our museum. I hate chasing people. They should all chase me for attention."

"I agree, my dear, but don't miss an opportunity if Jonesy has suggested it. We must bite our tongue for fame."

"Oh my, that is so beneath us," Karl murmured.

"I'll drive you. We'll be in and out in no time and have a nice cognac when we return." Her voice lilted with enthusiasm. "Shall I be your chauffeur?"

"Of course, Mother." He kissed her forehead. "Will you wear your chauffeur hat?" he baited. In his teens, after his father had passed, she played the part of his chauffeur now and then to make him feel special.

"If you like, I will. I always enjoyed pretending the part. I may even wear the whole outfit." Her eyes sparkled as she gave him a knowing smile.

Sure enough, when she drove her Silver Sand Jaguar XJ6 Vanden Plas out of the garage, she was in her black cap, gloves, and black suit with a white shirt and black tie. Karl sat in the back. When they crossed the Gold Star Bridge, he said, "Look how the fog has rolled in. I can see why they call it the City of

Steeples. I see at least six from this view on the bridge, rising above the mist." Once they arrived in the city, the fog had grown thick enough to mask the buildings from view.

Isadore teased, "I like fog. It's moody like you." She glanced in the rearview mirror for a reaction and saw none.

"My mood fits my attitude of going below my standards. I'll make this as brief as possible. Once I have an agreement with Ms. Maroney, I will leave." She dropped him off near the side gate of the Dahlia Gallery and found a parking spot on Water Street to wait for his call.

Earlier in the evening, the fog had drifted in from the Thames River, rising like a soft gauze. Quietly, it lifted above the docks and stole the shore. The vapor gently advanced across the cobblestones, slinking past Water Street and rising above the inclined alleys. It grew thicker, then spilled into Bank Street's every nook. The silent, evocative mist progressed until it rolled up the buildings and reached two stories high.

The laser light show from the Velvet Muse reflected colorfully off the vaporous particles, creating a glowing orb-like bubble around the entire art reception party. Hazy images of people mingling and dancing to electronic music were surreal in the brumous light. Karl walked through the open gate and into the illuminated fog in the back garden of the Dahlia.

Marilyn noticed Karl because he stood out like a tall, straight line among the revelers. "Please, this way, Mr. Rubens." She held a wine glass and cake on a napkin and escorted him up the exterior stairs and through a door. They took the stairway to her third-floor studio apartment and its 1950s retro décor.

"Mr. Rubens, I'm so glad to meet you in person finally." Karl stood with his hands behind his back in a stiff pose. He had instituted a habit of wearing his leather driving gloves due to his aversion to unfamiliar places. He bowed slightly. "It is my pleasure, Miss Maroney."

"Please call me Marilyn." She giggled.

"Why, yes, Miss Marilyn. I am happy to."

He is certainly a skinny giant, she thought. *And so formal.* "Are you foreign? European? You make me think of someone from the Netherlands."

Karl was flattered. "That is the homeland of my relatives, but no, I am from Boston. I spent time between the Isabella Stewart Gardner Mansion and the Fine Arts Museum. Maybe their fine works brushed off on me." That was as close to being witty as Karl would ever come.

Marilyn found him to be a towering enigma and thought. *He's a bit over-refined.* She pointed to her laptop. "I have some of my work here on the computer. These will be in my Iceland show." She placed her wine and cake down and scrolled to her latest sculptures. She expanded the screen so he could see the detail. "I've often been to the Slater Museum to study the master's plaster casts on display. I love it there."

"Yes, I agree," he said. "The Slater has magnificent treasures. I'm impressed you have studied them. Most people seem unaware of their collection of fine works." He leaned in toward the computer's screen to examine the various photos. "Your work is quite dignified, Miss Marilyn. Do you also have paintings?" He glanced around her apartment.

"Yes, right here." She gestured with her wine glass to the wall. "Above the sofa, there are several pieces from last year. Of course, all my current paintings are downstairs in the gallery, in Iceland, or with my agent."

Marilyn had varied styles from what he could see: large fluid landscapes, still life paintings in oil, small to mid-sized watercolors, and large abstract flowers. Karl squinted, moved in close, then backed away slowly.

Marilyn had an amused expression as she eyed him quizzically. *Does he enjoy my work, or is he about to dissect them?* She sipped her wine and waited.

"I quite like these paintings. You have the range and knowledge of classic techniques, yet you bend the rules with abandonment. You have confidence." Karl peered back at her with an analytical gaze. "Do you feel confident?" he asked.

"Umm, it all depends." Marilyn felt it was more a personal question than a professional one. She wanted to avoid more probing questions, so she suggested, "Why don't you come and see my sculpture of Athena on the balcony? Maybe she can answer that question for you. Follow me."

She picked up her cake and napkin, moved gracefully through the door to the balcony, and placed the cake on a café table. The heavy fog below them created a distinctively surreal ambience for her sculpture. "Here is Athena." She smiled and motioned to her beautiful golden statue with a shield, helmet, and spear. "How do you find her, Sir Karl?" She felt like his formality granted him the title of sir.

Athena entranced Karl. He almost ignored Marilyn's glamour, golden locks, and flowered sundress. They were lost on him. Instead, he scrutinized the Goddess of War and Wisdom, Athena. He zeroed in on analyzing the details of Medusa's head on her breastplate shield and the technique of gently applying tiny sheets of gold foil to the shield.

"I think you will find her more interesting than anyone at this party tonight, Sir Karl," Marilyn teased him, thinking he didn't seem to care much for people.

"She's magnificent," he murmured. "You have captured the essence of the goddess. The intensity of her body lunging forward is reflected in the molded folds of cloth draping her form. It defines her as a warrior with this authentic weapon. How did you come across the spear?"

"Through a collector of historical armament." Marilyn took a sip of wine and a bite of her cake.

Karl changed his position to observe Athena from farther away on the balcony.

The artist watched his eyes rove from Athena's helmet to the spear in its thrust position. Hoping he would be interested, she explained, "This is a prototype. I want to cast her one day in bronze if I can receive the funding."

Karl nodded at her suggestion, knowing it was possible with the right benefactor.

Marilyn offered, "Would you like some cake, Sir Karl?"

Without looking at her, he shook his head. He couldn't take his eyes off Athena.

Amused, Marilyn swiped her finger through the cake's frosting and moved forward between Athena's spear and his gaze.

"Sir Karl," she said playfully. Her whimsical curiosity wondered if his persona was as hard as a rock.

Karl looked at her perplexed because she disturbed his trance. "Yes?"

She pointed the tiny sword of her finger at him and was about to ask if he liked frosting. But instead, she naughtily stuck her frosted finger into his mouth when he said, 'Yes?'

Karl reacted swiftly to the invasion of his personal space, and with horror, his reflexes forcibly shoved her away. The immediate reaction repelled her backward, her heel catching in the iron grate of the balcony, and she was thrust lethally into Athena's spear.

Aghast, Karl stared at her contorted body in a backbend against the spear. She died instantly. Her face froze with her last breath. A moment ago, she was so full of life. Time seemed to stop as he stood alone on the balcony. The electronic dance music pounded in his ears. Slowly, he backed into the apartment and watched the foggy cloud from below waft upwards and gently swirl around her form. Transfixed, he pulled on his chin in anguish. *I can't fix this.* He drew in a deep breath. *Uhh! I can't fix this!*

As a conservator, Karl would scrutinize a torn and tarnished relic of a painting and know the rarity could be renewed with his time and effort. But Marilyn could not be restored. Karl was not in control.

Suddenly, he realized the urgency. *I must get out of here! I can't be seen.* He peered past Marilyn and Athena and saw the fire escape ladder on the balcony's edge. Quickly, he leaped toward it and released the ladder, which dropped with a clang into the depths of the cloud cover. The sound made him bolt back into the apartment. He feared someone might have heard it over the dance music emanating from the Velvet Muse. His hands jerked to his head as he searched his mind for an answer. His mother would know what to do; she always knew. Karl made a call to his goddess of war and wisdom.

"Mother, I'm in a situation. Marilyn's dead!" he whispered into his phone.

"What?"

"It's my fault. It's just terrible. I pushed her, and she fell on her spear."

"A spear! You pushed her?" Isadore gripped the steering wheel.

"She made an advance, and I didn't like it. I shoved her. She fell, and it impaled her." There was silence on the other end of the phone. "What should I do, Mother?"

"Has anybody seen you there?"

"Uh, no."

"Is there something you can use as a disguise? Anything?"

Frantically, he raced into her closet. "I see her clothes."

"Put them on!" she demanded.

"What?"

"You must, my dear. Like when you were young, we played dress-up with hats and shoes. Do it! Go out the front door and walk toward the train tracks. I'm on Water Street. I'll be waiting for you. Now hurry!" She hung up to prevent any hesitation. She knew her son.

He slipped into Marilyn's leatherette raincoat, squeezed into a pair of her open-toe backless sandals, and then rolled up his pant legs. Seeing a portfolio case in the closet, he opened it and placed his shoes and socks inside. A few of her finished pieces were also in the closet, and Karl nabbed two of the canvases and carefully placed them in the case. Finally, he put on a wide-brimmed hat, descended the front staircase, and stepped outside.

Dense night fog instantly cloaked him as he crossed Bank Street. The alleyway toward Water Street was straight ahead, and his heeled sandals tapped against the cobblestone ramp, echoing on the granite walls of the Vinho Verde Wine Bar. Coming across a trash bin under the deck, Karl stuffed the hat and leatherette raincoat into it. His mother's Jaguar was just a few steps away. He opened the back of the vehicle, placed the portfolio case inside, and lay across the seat trembling.

CHAPTER 68

Dante's Purgatory
Tuesday Evening

Karl cringed from his haunting thoughts of Marilyn's dead stare. He walked back home from the Franciscan chapel and shook his head several times to clear it, but it didn't remove Troy from their hidden gallery. He returned to the house to face his mother and her actions. Isadore was in the living room, and upon seeing his tormented face, she knew he was still angry that she had abducted Troy.

"Mother! Are you attempting to stomp through every level outlined in Dante's *Purgatory*? For god's sake, you have been lustful with desire and gluttonous with demands. You have acquired what you do not need, except for your need to have it, then claimed it. You move on to the next item when you own it, almost dismissing the last.

"You have coveted others' property, and you are slothful. You are deficient in appreciating any kindness toward you. You are wrathful toward others and angry about their successes. You are descending, Mother! Do you see? Are you aware of your decline? It is I, watching your descent!"

Karl turned to walk away but reconsidered, his anger keeping him going. "Just because I speak my concerns aloud does not mean you should consider them directives! I did not instruct you to capture Troy!" He pointed at her. "You are so obsessed that you cannot distinguish want from need. You cannot stop until you have your desire without regard for mine. Your descent into purgatory will land me in a cell!" He pointed at his face.

Isadore sipped her tea. "My son, my son, I exist for you." Adjusting her posture, she set her porcelain teacup upon its saucer and gently emphasized with both hands extended toward him. "I exist for you! God gave me no other need for me to be. I am devoted to you. What is wrong with that? I am like a single pomegranate." She cupped her hands together. "When its interior is revealed," she opened her hands, "you see, each ruby seed is meant to nourish you. I have a hundred ways I can assist you, and I will use them all for your success." Her endearing tone was like a sweet syrup.

Karl held up his hand. "Stop, Mother. Just stop! Your impetus for action is unnecessary. I was doing well, and, yes, because of you. But stop now and enjoy your success, our successes. You have achieved your desire. Don't you see it? We are accepted! We do not need to push; we can relax. For god's sake, you are nearly seventy-nine. What more could you need?"

Isadore waved her napkin. "Don't mention my age. It is meaningless. I have an eternal combustion engine. I will not quit. I want to see you in *The New York Times*, *The London News*, and the *World Wide Web*, but for reasons of greatness, not the theft of a painting. You are my glory, my protégé descendant."

"Mother, I have succeeded. I have been recognized by *The Boston Globe*, *The Herald News*, *The Paris Spire*, *The Italia Prestigio*, and Spain's *Exultant*. Settle down and relish your retirement. Father would bemoan your desires and rush you to the Louvre or the Vatican to view Michelangelo, Botticelli, Dürer, and Caravaggio to distract you. That's it—you need a diversion!"

Secrets Underground

Isadore purchased her Mason Island home in 1988 and was determined to create a hidden vault for art. She researched and learned that The British Museum, circa 1753, was the first national public museum in the world to house the Parthenon Sculptures from Athens, Greece. But these 2500-year-old Classical Greek works had to be dismantled during World War II and held underground by the rail stations in London for ten years to protect them from the bombing raids.

The example of a dingy tunnel would not do for her, so she convinced Karl to visit England's subterranean lair of the London Silver Vaults for posh design ideas. He found the fancy realm had the best in unique construction and secure accommodations for a gallery. Karl added to the design. The contractors were told his father's burial vault was to be adjacent to their elaborate hurricane shelter with a restroom and shower.

Wednesday morning

After twelve hours, Troy woke in a dark room with a massive headache. A low hum could be heard from a distant location. If one could see Troy from above, he was lying on a large gray tarp, his feet facing a wall. When he moved, the tarp rustled. "What the…? Where am I?" He rubbed his head. Motion lights went on, and he was blinded. "Ugh," he moaned, turned on his side, and noticed the room. It seemed to be an art gallery, expansive and glamorous.

Troy felt a piercing pain in his right temple. A dizzy, woozy feeling swept through him when he attempted to get up. He sat still, fighting the spinning motion in his head. There was a door in the center of the room. Slowly, he crawled on all fours toward it and reached for the knob. It opened! As it swung, another motion light lit the small room. To Troy's relief, it was a bathroom.

Lurching for the toilet, he threw up until he only had dry heaves. He lay on the cold marble floor and passed out. Hours later, he awoke feeling slightly better. He rose to his knees, grabbed the sink, and hoisted himself to his feet. Splashing cold water on his face, he cupped his hands and drank.

Although he still felt a pinging through his skull, it was nothing compared to his earlier migraine and discomfort. He continued to drink lots of water. When he left the bathroom, he sat on one of the cushioned benches. Rubbing his head, he wondered, *Why am I sick?* He looked around. *I'm in a gallery with no windows. It's so quiet. Where am I?* Observing the numerous works of art on the expansive gallery walls, he found them confusing. *Are my eyes playing tricks on me?*

Abruptly, a sound echoed throughout the room. At first, it was like a machine clicking. Suddenly, he was startled by an invisible panel door creaking open. Isadore entered the room and was startled to see Troy awake. She reacted loudly, "Ohh!" and nearly fell back. Troy had not died from her psychedelic and poisonous mushroom soup concoction. She quickly feigned concern. "Why Troy, how are you feeling?"

"Isadore," Troy laughed nervously, "what are you doing here?" He looked around. "Where exactly am I?"

"Why, my dear boy, I'm helping you. I found you passed out, and I took care of you. Are you hungry? I'll make you some food, and then I'll bring you home." She quickly slipped out of the room through the opening in the wall.

Once shut, Troy could barely see that a door had been there. He heard a succession of clicks. *Did she lock me in?*

Troy assessed his situation. At the far end of the room was a tarp on the floor. *What's going on? How long have I been here? Where's Karl?* He recounted his steps. *I was at the beach and planned to go to Vermont after I took the train to Mystic. I met Karl at the museum; then had dinner with him and Isadore.* A sinking feeling came over him. *Am I in their house?* He looked at the gray tarp on the floor and clutched his head. *Did they drug me? I need to get out of here!*

"Karl! Karl!" he hollered. "Can you hear me?" The sound-absorbing, subterranean gallery deadened Troy's voice. Fear crept toward him, much like the zombies in the movies he liked. His mind was in a battle between disbelief and desperation.

***

Isadore was set aflame by finding Troy alive. She had hung all hope on her poisonous mushroom soup blend. Scheming again, she began to rifle through her kitchen cabinet for ingredients, then opened the fridge.

Finding his mother out of sorts, Karl asked, "What are you doing?"

"It didn't work!" she said with venom.

In two long strides, he was beside her. "What do you mean? What didn't work?"

"He's still alive!" Grabbing his arm, she spouted, "My recipe didn't work! I must try again!"

Karl steadied himself against the marble counter. "Why did you think this was a good idea?" Her words had made him dizzy.

She pounded the counter. "I usually can make someone tipsy or forgetful. When I alter their reality, they make their own mistakes and endanger themselves." She pulled out the vegetable stock, seasonings, and toxic mushrooms. "I have to make another batch."

Karl's memory of Detective Morrison's accusations toward his mother regarding Aaron suddenly came to mind. "How many other people have you drugged?" He towered over her with arms crossed.

Fully conscious now that she had revealed her wicked ways to her son, she softened her tone, "I only tried it out a few times on people who needed coaxing or to forget about things." She hustled her ingredients together.

Karl's hand landed flat on the counter's surface in front of her. "And what makes you think Troy is going to eat another bowl of your mushroom soup? Stop this right now!" Having startled her, he changed his tone. "We need another plan." He gently placed his hand on her shoulder. "We're not killers, Mother."

She took a seat at the kitchen island and wrung her hands. "It's too late. This plan only goes one way."

He shook his head. "Listen, Mother. We have time on our side. We will keep our alibi going. I will go to work, and you will meet up with friends and go shopping. For today, pretend he is not here. Have lunch with your friends and resume a normal life. When I come back, we will have figured out a new plan. Okay, Mother? Can you do that?" Taking her hands in his, he looked into her eyes. "And don't worry, we will find a way to keep our hidden gallery a secret."

Isadore left her ingredients on the counter, walked toward her luxurious bedroom, and considered her options. *When I return, I'll make a potent batch.*

CHAPTER 69

Rude Awakening

Karl paced inside his Mystic River museum's grand gallery. His hands were clasped stiffly behind his back. His many attempts to occupy his mind weren't working. He inventoried art in storage between visiting patrons, but his mother's nefarious mission with Troy wouldn't leave him alone. This was a side of her he didn't want to acknowledge.

He replayed recent revelations from the night Detective Morrison and Peabody had accused her of knowing about Aaron and the stolen BFA painting. It couldn't be a coincidence. Morrison said it was suspicious that she was alone in the museum during the missing time on the video feed.

Karl had defended his mother and had ordered the detectives to leave, but Morrison had planted a seed of doubt about his mother in Karl's mind. He now recalled the image of her giddy behavior when he returned to the living room that night.

Karl's Memory

She glided towards him with her arms extended. "I'm so proud of you, darling. You handled Detective Morrison superbly. You were simply magnificent." She attempted to hug him, but he sidestepped her and strode to the end of the room.

When he turned to face her, he was feeling defiant. "Mother, tell me what exactly is going on here? What kind of dangerous game are you playing?"

She pulled an e-cigarette from a side table drawer, injected a cartridge, and puffed.

"What are you doing? You don't smoke." Karl's hands were in the air.

"I'm too old to hide it from you anymore." She shook her hand at him. "Once in a while, I've had a cigarette, darling. I hid it from you because it's a habit I never wanted you to have. Besides, I only have one a couple of times a month."

With hands on his hips, he asked, "So why are you smoking now?"

"You're irritating me." She dramatically took another puff.

"I'm irritating you! That's rich, Mother. Give me a break," he groaned. "All I wanted was the focus on my museum. Look at where we are now—the detective is making accusations about Aaron and calling it a murder." Karl's fists went to his forehead. "Mother, what...what happened? What happened...after I left? Did you see Aaron?"

"I went in and out of the maintenance closet to find tote bags for the leftover food I was bringing home. I didn't see anything out of the ordinary in there, nor did I see him. The next thing I knew, he popped out of the closet. I imagine he had found a place to sleep in the back corner on the drop cloth. I must have made enough noise to wake him."

Karl stared at her dumbfounded.

"I recognized him for helping with the event, but he was drunk. I invited him into the kitchen, made him my favorite tea, and fed him cookies. He told me he was a performance artist who did acrobatics, parkour, and balancing acts. Since I knew he liked heights, I happened to mention there was a great view on the rooftop patio. Well, the rest is history. All I had to do was leave him alone, knowing he wouldn't be able to resist balancing on something up there. Temptation is usually deadly, my dear."

"Yes, and you used it against him." Karl crossed his arms and scowled at her. "What exactly happened, Mother?"

She ignored him, took a drag on her vape pen, then blew an obnoxiously long stream of mist. The minty scent filled the room and further annoyed Karl. He opened the French doors wide and waved out the odor.

"I took the elevator up and peeked to see if he took the bait. You see, I couldn't have him hanging around. Sure enough, he was balancing on the parapet and was very good. I called his name when he was on the side of the building with the dock and water below. I was wearing the white kaftan with the gold trim and raised my arms. A breeze lifted the fabric, and in the dim light it startled him. I must have looked like a ghost. He lost his balance, then plop, there he went. I didn't say anything because it would have ruined your big night, so I wiped my fingerprints from the elevator and kept quiet."

Karl tried to follow his mother's reasoning, but Aaron was dead.

"Besides, by morning," she explained, "his fall made it look like he could have been in on the theft of the painting. This distracted the detectives from the fact that he fell while I was there."

Karl was aghast and visibly shuddered at her admission. She drew on her vape pen. "You see, I killed no one. Aaron fell on his own accord and became a perfect decoy within the detective's investigation. Besides, we couldn't have Aaron in the way of your big night."

"What is wrong with you?" he shouted. "How can you be so callous? They are human beings, not objects. You can't play with them like toys!"

"Hush, dear. Every day has been busier at your museum since the BFA painting was taken and returned. Yes, you were known internationally for your conservation of rare paintings, but that simple theft and its return made the Mystic River Fine Art Museum famous, which, of course, rubs off on you. That painting put you on the world map again.

"People will forget you if you don't keep up appearances like your famous relative Peter Paul Rubens. Because of me, you and the museum received international press."

Karl was pacing in front of the open doors to Poggy Bay when he stopped short and fully heard her last claim. Swiftly, he turned toward her and gasped loudly.

His voice rose. "Wait a minute, Mother! You said the museum received international press because of you! Did you set up the theft of the Cassatt painting? If they had caught you, they would have blamed me! Nothing to worry about, my god! Did you jeopardize my career? All for your selfish, selfish self?" Karl waited. The more he waited and watched her puff on her vape stick, the more he knew she didn't care about him. She only cared for herself.

Karl scrutinized her, and his realization spread. "Did you put the mushroom powder in Aaron's tea too? Was it the psilocybin mushroom the detective mentioned? He said it was found in his system. You purposely used him as a distraction, didn't you? I thought he was involved in the theft!"

"Oh, darling, don't be so dramatic! I arranged for the painting to be stolen. I hired a man behind the scenes in the art world: Mario Corinthian and his men from New York. I had a cheap forgery made to put in its place, and the Cassatt was returned without harm. I love that painting of the Monsieur looking across at the woman in the distance. I can imagine sitting at the opera house and spying on the room with him there. Mary Cassatt captured the mood perfectly.

"My dear, I ordered the counterfeit painting to be made once you confirmed that the BFA painting would arrive at our museum. I arranged for a man to fiddle with the security system's electronics. He was an expert, of course, and knew how to splice into the system so it would not go on alert. The switch was installed and disguised in the maintenance closet. When it didn't alert the security company that night at ten thirty, I knew the plan to steal the Cassatt painting would work."

Karl's hands held his cheeks as he stared at her.

"You must remember," she declared, "everything I do is for you! I planned to keep the painting, but I returned it once I saw how you would benefit. You were in the newspaper and on the TV news! Bad news has brought you good press! They think Aaron was an accomplice to stealing the painting or a drunk druggy who died from the fall.

"It all worked out in the end, and he became a diversion, just as Cora did."

Karl stiffened up again. "What do you mean?"

"It's like the ploy I planned to keep the heat off you regarding Marilyn. I had Mario help me arrange Cora's incident to misdirect the detective's case away from you and Marilyn's death. Remember, this is how I use my technique of a golden bridge, in this case with misinformation, to lead people away from us.

"As I improvised, it became a better plan." She rose from the sofa. The sea breeze from the open doors caught the loose fabric of her printed kaftan.

Karl could imagine clearly what she had done. Her bravado toward Cora's incident and Aaron's death overwhelmed his senses. "I can't believe you! Is this another symptom of your age? Is this what happens to women as they get older? Are you losing your mind? I thought what you did in Boston was the end, but maybe you've always been this way, and now you don't care anymore, and you're showing me all your cards."

Salty air swooped past them from the open doors. "Darling, one gets bolder as one gets older, or you die of weakness. And yes, I don't care anymore. I am who I am. Take it or leave it. Just like Isabella!"

"Oh no, don't you pull Isabella into this!" Karl stormed off, grabbed his leather work bag, and slammed the door behind him.

"He'll be back," she said to the sea.

He drove his Jaguar to Edgar's Island and parked in the lot of the Franciscan monastery. Karl walked to the water's edge beyond the rose gardens tended by the brown-robed monks. The sun had lowered to the horizon, and Karl sat on a stone bench to stare at the sunset. A hollow feeling had formed in his gut. He tried to identify it. *It is dread. She is an unsolvable problem.*

After some time, a monk walked by. "How are you this evening, brother?"

"I don't know anymore, Father. I feel more lost than I ever have." Karl felt trapped and needed a way to settle his conscience. His arms were folded tight across his chest.

"May I join you?"

"Yes, of course." Karl made room and slightly rocked back and forth in his seat. The monk knew this movement was a way to soothe oneself.

"I have found that there are two reasons people are in despair," the monk said.

Karl looked at him with the hope that he might impart a valuable grain of wisdom. "What are they?"

"Acceptance and forgiveness. We can't change people or conditions, but we can change ourselves. Instead of the vices of revenge or anger, we tend toward, we must work with virtues."

"But what if I can't forgive someone?" Karl visibly squirmed as his conflict wrenched his insides.

"Then it is only you who suffers. They aren't suffering. Do you want them to suffer?"

Karl folded his hands and placed them under his chin. "No, I guess not."

"See? You're already on your way to forgiveness." The monk smiled at Karl and put his hand on his shoulder. "Would you like to come inside and have a meal with me? We have plenty of food in the kitchen from an earlier dinner." Karl agreed. Heaving a sigh, he followed the monk into the parsonage.

The monk's timely counsel allowed Karl to forgive her. Besides, she was his mother.

After the detective's accusations, Isadore had easily convinced Karl to donate their rare Baroque still-life painting to enhance their image by raising funds for the arts in New London. Karl naturally agreed to ask Georgi, his one friendly acquaintance, to organize the event at the Garde Arts Center. Her conniving ideas rerouted Morrison's attention away from her and her son.

Isadore had Mario Corinthian and his illicit men steal Marilyn's painting from the Oasis Room at the Garde. The diversion of the cloaked man backstage was Mario's idea to confound and further deflect the detective's investigation. If his man had been able to steal the Baroque painting from backstage, it would have also been a worthwhile conquest.

Karl wondered if his mother was related to a mythological beast. Like the Minotaur, she lured others into her mind's labyrinth. She had refracted the investigations in multiple directions. It gave the press fodder to chew on and improved their standing in the community. Mario Corinthian was her golden bridge that led everyone away from them, and so was money. All felt better with cash on the table from the Baroque painting, and they felt favorable toward her and Karl. Her game was like that in Rossetti's poem, 'The Card Dealer.' *Every play, each twist, and turn advantaged her.*

***

Karl was now vexed with these recollections of his mother. He grasped the lapels of his jacket and tugged with annoyance at her devious ways of choreographing events for the sake of his reputation. And now, she had raised the bar higher by abducting Troy and poisoning him too. He bit his manicured nails. *I must gain back control. There has to be a way I can release Troy. I don't want to go to jail.*

***

In the meantime, Troy's stomach pains were lessening, yet the dull headache stayed with him. He began to reason why he was there. *They abducted and poisoned me. But why? I'm not worth anything. No one will pay a ransom for me! They don't need money!* Then a worse thought came to mind. *Jason thinks I'm in Vermont!* He looked around while holding onto his head. *I'm a prisoner in a fancy gallery. How do I get out of here?*

He plodded to the bathroom and observed the modest linen closet and walk-in shower. *I'll stay alive by only drinking water from the faucet.* Slurping water with his hands, he decided to move his body. Troy forced himself to walk the length of the room. He guessed its size was sixty feet long by twenty-five feet wide with an eight-foot ceiling. He observed four benches, two club chairs, and a small table. Tiring, he pushed two of the upholstered benches together and rested on his back.

"These people are nuts," he muttered while staring at the white ceiling. The air flowing into the underground room kept it at sixty-eight degrees Fahrenheit, the perfect temperature for fine art. Troy closed his eyes and listened to the sound of the hum through the tiny ventilation ducts. The low-toned sound helped him drift and visualize the night of the Dahlia Gallery's art reception party.

He scanned the first-floor scene. Music from the outdoor venue in the Velvet Muse pounded a bass beat into the gallery. A long buffet of food was set up inside the main door of the Dahlia, and Georgi was serving wine. For a moment, he heard Marilyn laughing and watched her having fun in her colorful dress with hot-pink lips that outlined her smile. She was so pretty.

It was still early in the evening. He went out the back door to the garden for fresh air and sat at a table by boxwood shrubs that lined flower beds. Suddenly, movement from above caught his attention. Aaron was balancing on the fence at the back of the property.

"You just freaked me out," Troy said from below.

Aaron laughed while teetering on a thin board.

"You're always looking for a place to rise above the crowds," Troy teased.

"I love heights! You should come up here." He beckoned to Troy. "It's exhilarating!"

"I'm exhilarated on the ground. Besides, you're so skinny you have less to balance. But I wouldn't mind the solitude up there."

"Come on!" Aaron continued to wave him up high.

"No way! I'd only be good for meatloaf or dog food when they find me splat down on the patio blocks in the morning."

Aaron snickered. "*Sweeney Todd! Cloud Atlas! Eating Raoul*! It means you'll still be useful after you're gone, and maybe they'll make a movie about you."

"What it means is," Troy countered, "you know movies where people become food and are eaten!"

"Well, isn't that what zombies do? Unless you are a zombie. And if you are, which one are you?" Aaron asked. He loved challenging Troy because they enjoyed bantering about any subject. They both had opinions and were willing to share them.

"I like them all, but probably the voodoo zombies most. Hmm…it might be fun to write the screenplay so that I can control the zombies."

Aaron laughed. "That's why your artwork is so good. Your mind goes to the next level."

Troy opened his eyes with a feeling of sadness from the memories of his friends. Suddenly, he jolted upright. His head throbbed again, "Ow!" He held it while he considered his realization. *Karl and Isadore were the last ones to see Aaron. Oh no! I heard he was high on psychedelic mushrooms when he fell! We had mushroom soup for dinner! She poisoned us both!*

"That woman is a witch," he muttered.

CHAPTER 70

The Search for Troy

While Troy remained imprisoned in Isadore's elegant holding cell, beachcombers noticed beach gear left in the same spot for two days on Thursday morning, so they brought the bag to the nearby Thames Yacht Club. Troy's identification was in the bag, which informed the staff that he was not a yacht club member. They called the police department.

Shortly after, the police identified Troy's car nearby and discovered he was a resident artist at the Dahlia studios. The fire department was called in for search and rescue. Chief Samson surmised that if he had gone swimming, it was best to use the fireboat to quickly search the waters along the Thames River and New London Harbor. Yet after a full hour and a half, they had no luck finding him.

Sam made a call. "Roxanne, Troy's belongings, with his identification, were found this morning on the beach by the yacht club. And his car is here too. As far as we can tell, they've been there since Tuesday, and it appears he went swimming. I thought you should know we have been searching for him with the rescue boat since eight-thirty. Do you have a way to find out where he is?"

"Oh, gee, since Tuesday!"

Sam treaded into Roxanne's forte. "Listen, I don't want to think the worst, but can you call anyone who knows him? I'd like to believe his belongings were left behind because he forgot to put them in the car and that he got a ride with someone."

"Of course. I will call Georgi first."

"Also, Morrison has been notified since Troy is a Dahlia artist. Call him if you find anything out. I've got to go, Roxanne, they're calling me."

"Okay, I will. Bye." Roxanne immediately rang Georgi. "Have you heard about Troy?"

Georgi was polishing glasses at his bar in the Vinho Verde for a wine dinner event he was hosting that evening. "I know a few people are looking for him, but I wasn't worried. Why?"

"My gosh, Georgi! I just heard they found his car and belongings on the beach. It seems he went swimming, and no one has seen him since!"

"Uhh! No! Not Troy!" Georgi cried.

"Can you call some of his friends and ask around? I'll meet you at the Vinho Verde in an hour." Roxanne held her stomach in a panic.

"Yes, of course, right away. See you in an hour." Georgi's hand went to his forehead and thought, *who should I call first*? He answered himself loudly, "It doesn't matter, call everyone!" His voice echoed in the spacious brick and granite room.

When Roxanne arrived, he was on the back deck with another call. She walked toward him and listened as he spoke to the person.

"You had an appointment with Troy Tuesday night, and he didn't show? Oh no, and he hasn't called you back? Are you kidding? Let me look while you're on the phone." Georgi checked Troy's social media pages. "Whoa, I see what you mean. He's made no posts. His friends began looking for him on Wednesday evening. He had missed appointments, was a no-show for dinner and wasn't returning their texts, but they've become frenetic today.

"Wait! You said the police contacted you? This morning? Okay, yeah, I'll call you. Bye." He pressed on his temple, feeling a headache coming on.

"Georgi!" Roxanne stepped across the deck.

"Oh, Roxanne. I'm so worried." He opened his arms wide to hug her, and she gladly accepted. "Can you believe this? Our world is upside-down."

"I know. Sam is searching for Troy. Ugh, I hope he is not in the water, Georgi." Her voice cracked. "This is too much for me. How can we reason this out?" She leaned on the railing.

"Come sit down." He took her arm and coaxed her to a chair. "Now let's think about this. When do you last recall Troy mentioning he was going swimming?" He watched her expression.

Squinting her eyes, she considered how long she had known Troy—at least twenty years. "I don't think he's ever mentioned going swimming. He would never go alone if he did because he knows the undertow can be rough." Her mouth gaped open. "But what does that mean?"

"It must mean he was with someone. What else?" Georgi shrugged. "Listen, I know he avoids the sun. Think about it—he's so pasty white. He told me he slathers on SPF 50 suntan lotion before he goes for a walk because he'll turn red as a lobster." Georgi reached out and held Roxanne's arm gently.

Creasing her brow, she locked eyes with him. Suddenly, Georgi gasped, "Oh my god. He's an artist at the Dahlia like the others! Is this a coincidence or an omen? Should we worry? What are we to do, Roxanne?" He fanned his face.

"The tell-tale sign is, why did he leave his car?" she asked. "I don't know what makes sense anymore. The detective's last good lead was Mario Corinthian, who seems to have a hand in all these events. Is it possible he's done something to Troy?"

"Don't forget what happened to Cora!" Georgi reminded. His brain was now humming. "Cora ended up drugged and in her underwear. Who knows, could that happen to Troy too?"

Roxanne's face was priceless. Her cheeks sucked in, and her eyes went wide, moving around, as she wondered if that was something she should even imagine. "Oh, Georgi, that would be weird if they drugged him too and left him to fend for himself. If he is in the water, I hope he can swim."

"If I know Troy, he'll float on his back until he hits land. But what if he's in deep water? This is terrible. I tend to imagine the worst!"

Roxanne put her chin in her hands and leaned on the table. In a defeated monotone, she added, "Search, and rescue must be all over this. We need to wait for their results." She folded her arms, slumped over, and put her head on the table.

"Hey!" Georgi's idea threw his hands in the air and startled Roxanne. She sat straight up. "Ophelia told me Detective Morrison had Troy view a video of Marilyn on Monday. It is the last image they have of her. Troy told her it was spooky seeing Marilyn silhouetted in the fog as she crossed Bank Street. Do you think he would let us see it?"

"I wonder why Dan didn't tell you about it?"

"Well, to be fair, he's not the type to let me cry on his shoulder." Georgi's expression was sweet. "I have an idea. We should, or you should Roxanne, call him and say it would be a good idea for me, Georgi, to see the video, and you'd like to come with me. But, but, but here's the real reason we are going there." Roxanne was all ears. "We will attempt to find out what the detective knows about Troy. Anything we learn will make us feel better, won't it?"

Roxanne rose out of her chair and gave him a peck on the cheek. "I knew you had something cooking under your coiffed hair, so sleek and perfect." Her blonde bob lifted in a breeze, and Georgi laughed.

"I could hose you down with my hairspray if you'd like."

"I'll call the detective," she answered, ignoring his last suggestion.

"Hi, Detective Dan, this is Roxanne. I know you are busy. Sam asked that I call around to see where Troy is, and no one seems to know. What do you have?"

Morrison sighed. "I just got back from meeting with your husband. They've called the Coast Guard to assist in the water search for Troy. The police are all over this too. We aren't taking any chances since he fits the profile, being the third Dahlia artist in a suspicious incident."

"Okay. I'm glad they've sent out the Coast Guard. But I'm calling for another reason too. Is there a chance Georgi and I can see the foggy video we heard you have of Marilyn the night she passed away? Georgi would feel better if he could see her. Do you mind?"

Morrison hesitated. "Sure, come on down. I can give you five minutes, but you must manage Georgi, and I don't need to tell you why."

Georgi's fawning and fussing were imprinted on Morrison's brain from his past experiences. He was in no mood for hysterics.

"Of course, Dan. Thank you. We are on our way."

Reggie Transitions

Over the last few weeks, Morrison kept checking in with Ms. Zelda from the hospitality center and Reggie Crumberton, the Special Force veteran.

Morrison had noticed how meticulous he was about details and observation skills in the fire on Belham Street and seeing Marilyn in the fog on the night of her death.

Ms. Zelda reported that Reggie was doing well and ready to work. His quick reintegration into society was successful due to the assisted therapy treatment he received with MDMA. It successfully shifted PTSD.

The detective's gut told him Reggie's multiple tours had given him the instinct and know-how he needed for investigating and hunting down bad guys. After seeing how well he was doing and discussing the opportunity, he offered him a part-time consultant job, and Reggie agreed.

Morrison placed him immediately with Peabody to assist with his cases and finding Troy.

CHAPTER 71

That's Not Her
Thursday

Isadore was listening to the local NPR news on the radio at noon when a special report was announced.

> The City of Steeples, New London, is involved in a search and rescue for Troy Zaner, a missing Dahlia artist. Mr. Zaner's belongings were on a beach near the Thames Yacht Club. His car was nearby. Authorities have speculated he may have been caught in the undertow currents of Long Island Sound. If anyone has information on his whereabouts, please contact nine-one-one.

Instantly she was at ease. No one would consider Troy was with them. She believed that her hard work in creating a sterling impression as an outstanding philanthropist put them above question.

***

Roxanne and Georgi found Detective Peabody in the lobby of police headquarters. After greeting each other, she bantered purposefully, "Detective, did you know Troy and a few high school students painted the colorful mural in your lobby?" She was warming him up.

A look of surprise was on his face. "I didn't realize that." He led them to the conference room and asked them to sit.

"Has anything new occurred?" she probed. "You know Troy is our friend, and we are so worried to learn that he left things on the beach and that his car was found. Did you find his cell phone?"

Peabody was befuddled by her question. *She's the fire chief's wife and friends with my boss. Can I tell her?* He opens his mouth to speak. Then stops himself. Then saw the intent look on Roxanne's face. His anxiousness swung like a pendulum the other way. Peabody blurted, "His car was unlocked, and his phone was left in the glove box. If he's not in the water, he will have his phone. It looks as though he went swimming alone. We don't have anything to go on. I'm sorry, Mrs. Chief."

"Thank you, Detective." She patted Georgi's arm. "We're ready when you are to see the video of Marilyn."

"I'm going to thank you now for putting up with my sadness, Detective," Georgi warned.

Peabody left his chair and picked up a box of tissues on a side table. He handed it to Georgi. "Just in case you need them," he said with a weak smile. "Detective Morrison asked me to start without him and run the video for you as often as you like. We have lightened and sharpened the images as best we could because of the pea soup fog that night. Here it is."

Roxanne and Georgi faced the big screen on the wall, and the video began. New London looked eerie, devoid of color in the gray, misty, grainy image. A luminous orb formed over the Velvet Muse, but it was mostly a dark video until a car passed. Suddenly, the silhouetted form of someone in a raincoat with bare legs and high heels came from the sidewalk's edge. She wore a large, brimmed hat and carried a rectangular portfolio. Once she crossed the street, the person's image quickly vanished into the thick mist.

"Whoa, that was brief," Roxanne exclaimed.

"Can we see it again?" Georgi asked. Intently, he leaned forward with his elbows on the conference table. Peabody ran it. After seeing it, Georgi motioned with a roll of his hand. "Again, please."

Roxanne watched him. He was not presenting tears or extreme dramatics, which surprised her. *He may still spontaneously fall apart.* She braced for a total collapse, but he looked at the detective with a blank stare. "Can you play it in slow motion?" he asked without reacting.

"Of course, Georgi." They all watched the figure in slow motion. It was pixelated and hard to discern any detail in the gray-on-gray forms.

Finally, Georgi's arms flew up. "That's not her!"

Peabody jolted in his seat, and Roxanne's head snapped toward him.

"That's not her, Roxanne. That's not her, Jack." He glared at them and flung an arm toward the screen. "THAT'S NOT HER!" Georgi's gaze ping-ponged between them. "What do we do? Who is that if it's not her? Is that the murderer, the killer?" Georgi was nearly shrieking.

Peabody stood. "Stay right here. I'll be back in a minute."

However, he did not return. Morrison came into the room instead. Georgi stood and pointed at the screen. "Detective, that's not Marilyn. She doesn't walk like that." Then he pointed at the detective with indignation. "And those are the hat and raincoat I pulled from the trash bin, aren't they? The ones you took from me. You did not disclose whose they were. Why? I could have told you this wasn't her a long time ago. But no. You didn't share the video with me."

Georgi was in a haughty mood. “No, because you are afraid of Georgi’s tantrums and meltdowns, aren’t you?” He paused to take a breath. “Grrr, Detective Morrison, you have me right mad. I could have told you that’s not her a long, long time ago.”

Morrison put his finger to his lips to shush and calm him. “This is what investigations are all about,” he said. “We don’t disclose information to the public because there are too many variables and personal interpretations of what could and could not be. We have our methods on how we verify the facts. Troy knew her the longest, so I showed him the video.

“He didn’t tell me it wasn’t her, and this scene works within the estimated time of death. As you know, Marilyn could have returned through the back entrance within a half hour, where there were no cameras. The perpetrator was either with her or waiting for her. If you believe this is not Marilyn, tell me why you say that.”

“Detective, there is a huge difference between believing and knowing.” Georgi explained, “I know that is not her walk because that’s not how she moves. The smoothness of her strut is like a model on a catwalk. And besides, the hat and coat were in my trash bin. Doesn’t that mean something to you? Someone was wearing these as a disguise because that is not Marilyn!”

“We took the hat and coat to identify if her DNA was on them, and it was. It verifies they belong to Marilyn. There was no other DNA found. I can tell you that this is an ongoing investigation.”

Georgi’s face went lax.

Morrison suspected Marilyn would not dispose of her clothing, but he had no other leads. His tolerance was limited as he was on the hunt for Troy. He gestured toward the door to indicate their time was up. “Thank you for coming in, Georgi, and confirming it isn’t her.”

Roxanne spoke up. “Detective, thanks for seeing us on such short notice.” She tugged on Georgi’s sleeve. “Before we go, is there anything new with Troy? We are very concerned. Georgi has called everyone he knows. Do you think Mario Corinthian has struck again?”

With an understanding sigh, Morrison put his hands in his pockets, relaxed his shoulders, and took a casual stance. “I have nothing to go on yet, Roxanne. And Georgi, thank you for calling around. It appears he went swimming and did not come back. We need more evidence that tells me otherwise. I’m sorry.”

“Okay,” she said dismally. The duo put their arms around each other’s shoulders and glumly left the room.

Once back in Roxanne's truck, Georgi was ready to complain. "It's tough for me to keep my mouth shut, Roxanne. I hope you noticed my restraint. I wanted to make a bigger fuss than I did. I'm glad you were there with me."

She patted his shoulder. "Somehow, it will all work out in the end. At least that's what the Brits say when they don't know what else to say." She tilted her head and gave him a heartwarming, empathetic smile.

Georgi considered everything. "I'm beginning to think we know just as much as they do, and we need to get to work."

"We need to stay out of this evolving situation with Troy and Marilyn," said Roxanne, "or at least keep a low profile," she cautioned. "We can't upset the detective, but here's an idea: do you want to ride with me? I have some questions for Karl on the labyrinth garden I'm designing, and we can drop in on him at the museum. I'll call the detective and tell him what we're doing so the FBI and Dan stay on our side."

"Good idea, I'm up for a drive. On the way, I'll text my friends again about Troy."

Roxanne phoned the detective first, then Karl, to say she had a question about the garden design and asked if she could stop by for a quick visit. He agreed.

Inside the museum, Karl was dusting in the grand gallery. Georgi approached first. "Hello, Mr. Karl Rubens. It's good to see you. How are you?"

Karl perked up with Georgi's formality, and he nodded to Roxanne. "Just fine, Mr. Georgi Algarve. You remind me of how much has happened since we first met. I feel like I'm back on my feet after weeks of instability, and you have been so helpful."

"I have?" Georgi grinned.

"Why, yes. At my grand reopening, you brought in Roxanne and Marco to help with the decor, and you handled the wine and champagne selection superbly. Roxanne, Marco, and you did a marvelous job."

Roxanne was surprised by his profuse acknowledgment.

"Georgi, the event at the Garde went swimmingly well, and you have truly helped me keep my reputation intact. I must say I am most grateful to you."

Thoroughly enjoying the praise, Georgi did a little tap dance, then flared his palms in jazz hand fashion. "That's how your compliment makes me feel, Karl."

Karl hummed his approval and gave a genuine smile.

Since Karl was so amicable, Georgi took the opportunity to ask a question. "If I could be serious for a moment, Roxanne and I are befuddled because our dear friend Troy has been missing for a couple of days, and we were wondering if this person, Mario Corinthian, the supposed art agent, could be at the bottom of all these events. He was linked to Marilyn, Cora, and the BFA painting. Maybe Aaron too. What is your perspective as an art aficionado?"

Karl's amicable demeanor suddenly clouded. "Well, I...I...don't know. I wouldn't know how to think like a criminal, Georgi. They are so unpredictable, yet if these events are all connected, then maybe Troy has fallen victim too. I'm sorry to say that. How long has he been missing?"

"Since Tuesday night, as far as we know."

Roxanne jumped in. "Georgi is just guessing about the art correlation. It's been reported Troy's car was left at the beach, and he went swimming." Noticing Karl was uncomfortable, Roxanne suggested, "Georgi, how about I take a minute to review a few questions about the garden with Karl? Then we'll make more calls about Troy, okay?"

"Sure, I'll look around at the art."

Georgi took his time perusing the works on the far end of the grand gallery. After ten minutes, Karl momentarily left Roxanne to find something in his office, and on returning with a book, Georgi noticed his stride.

"Ohh!" Georgi squealed. "Uh, Uh, I don't know what I was thinking! Roxanne, we will have to leave in five minutes." He pointed at his wristwatch. "I forgot I have an event tonight!"

Karl carried the book back to his office, and Georgi raced to Roxanne and whispered, "I'm going to ask Karl about this painting. Watch him as he crosses the gallery."

Karl returned, and Georgi called out, "Karl, quick question before we leave. Is this a local artist? This painting is just lovely."

Georgi and Roxanne watched as Karl strode across the room toward the painting. Georgi again noted the bend in the elbow, the steel rod posture, and no sway at all. It was the walk of the mysterious figure in the fog! Georgi practically leaped out of his skin while Karl told him about the local artist.

Roxanne quickly gathered her design notes. "Okay, Georgi, we must be going. Let's get you back to New London for your event."

They ran to Roxanne's truck. She mouthed the words, 'Oh my God.' Georgi bit his fingers so he wouldn't wail. She put her truck in gear and restrained herself from gunning the engine. She held back so as not to raise Karl's suspicions.

"Did you see that?" Georgi exclaimed. "He walked like the person in the video, right?"

"He did! But how can we be sure? The detective won't accept us guessing." Roxanne gripped her steering wheel tight.

"I think it was him. Oh my god! It can't be, can it?" Georgi shuddered. "The energy moving through me is too much. This is freaking me out! How are we going to prove it? Is he Mario Corinthian, Roxanne?"

She shot a glance. "Hmm, I doubt it. Gee, Georgi, I think it was him. But we can't prove it. There must be a way.

"I don't want to believe it! Did he kill Marilyn?"

"Until we prove Karl wore the hat and coat, we've got nothing. You heard there was no other DNA found. Let's think and hope the universe gives us something to work with."

"It has to, Roxanne! We're the good guys."

"It will. It just takes time for the next clue or opportunity to appear." She reached out and patted his hand. He gripped hers. "I feel like we're on the edge of a cliff, and we don't know what's going to happen next."

"Hold on. We'll make it through together."

***

The art community organized a search party to look for Troy. Fifty people were combing the shoreline by three o'clock, including two friends with small boats. The Coast Guard kept up the hunt until dark. By then, over one hundred people were involved in the search for Troy.

CHAPTER 72

Posh Dungeon
Thursday

Isadore returned home from shopping, lunch, and cocktails with friends and began a new concoction for Troy to eat. *By now, he'll be hungry.* Once ready, she placed the meal in the warming oven.

At 5:30 p.m., Karl drove his Jaguar into the garage. He left a bag of fruit and protein bars in the car.

"Hello, Mother?" He found her in the living room. "Shall we have dinner at Captain Daniel Packer's tonight?"

"Yes, dear, that would be lovely. Call ahead, would you, and ask for our favorite table. I'll change my clothes. And Karl, take the food I made down to our guest."

He phoned the restaurant as his mother went into her bedroom, then he dashed to the garage. He put the shopping bag over his shoulder, returned to the kitchen, and lifted the food tray. After kicking the carpet back in the hall, he pushed the button with his elbow to reveal the underground staircase. Down he went into the hideaway.

Troy was at the gallery's far end in a standing yoga pose. Karl set the food tray down and watched him from a cushioned bench. He ignored Karl by remaining in the warrior stance. Taking a deep breath, Troy exhaled and stretched into a relaxed standing pose.

In a conciliatory fashion, Karl began, "Troy, my mother has put us both in a trap, and I want to converse about our dilemma. I was caught unaware, just as you, about her plan. Furthermore, the news outlets have announced your disappearance. They report that you may have drowned because your belongings were found on a beach. Since no one will be looking for you here, I have a proposition."

Troy remained quiet to assess his options, yet he was doubtful he had any.

"When I saw the laptop images of your artwork, I was surprised I hadn't seen or heard of them before. They are excellent, and I think there is a way out of this predicament for you, but I need to see them in person. Is that possible?"

Troy nodded.

"If I buy your work to resell, could you forget this has happened? I will set you free and deal with my mother. For all the public will know," Karl waved his arm toward the sea, "the tide will bring you back from whence you came, floating in on a wave." Karl's lack of dealing with people had left him at a disadvantage. He didn't understand how another person felt. He was attempting to buy Troy's trust and keep his mother's deadly secret. Troy's art was his bargaining tool. But could Troy be tempted?

Troy gave a hint of a smile.

Karl added, "I'll get you out of here and drop you at the water's edge somewhere. You can have amnesia and not remember anything. Could this work for you?" *This might put him at ease. If Mother kills him, that will be on my conscience. If I can pay him off, even if his art is rubbish, I can pawn his work on some fool gallery owner. Who can resist me, Karl Rubens, curator/conservator extraordinaire? If I say his work is good, they'll accept it. And if his art is good, I can make a hefty profit. I will deal with my mother's wrath.*

Troy calculated the possibility that his friends could be suspicious of Karl wanting to buy his art, and hopefully, they would alert the detectives. Troy came out of his standing pose to answer, "Yes, my friend runs the Kitchen Gallery in the DuWater Building on State Street. It's part of her yoga and art studio. And my friend Jason handles all my sales when I'm not around. You can call him for an appointment, and he will arrange a viewing."

"Good. I will do so and see them in the morning." Karl was pleased Troy was cooperating. "I brought you a gift." He revealed the bag under his arm. "Here's some fruit and protein bars from the health food store. But it would be best to hide these in the bathroom closet with the towels. I don't want Mother to know I'm giving you food. I'm so mad at her. She should never have done this to you, Troy."

Troy grabbed the food, unwrapped a protein bar, and ate. Karl left and closed the door. As he ascended the stairs, he thought of Aaron's death. It made him cringe that his mother could instigate such things. And worse, she compromised their lovely world again by imprisoning Troy. He had felt hopeless in her web of deceit, but this idea of gaining some control could help them both.

"Mother," he called. She answered as he entered the kitchen. "I found out how I can view Troy's art tomorrow. His friend Jason will show me his work. If they're good, I may buy some. You know the price will only go up now that people think he might be dead."

"Excellent, darling. Why don't you schmooze Troy and find out how many pieces he has? If you like them enough, you should buy his whole collection."

"Yes, I'll see what he says after I get changed for dinner."

Karl had yet to think the facts through. By Thursday morning, most of the poisonous mushroom was out of Troy's system, and he could think more clearly. He had analyzed his quiet companions on the gallery walls. His schooling in art made him well-versed in the masters. He had aced art history and traveled to many fine museums.

The gallery paintings in the clandestine confine were beautifully lit and labeled with attribution and history as if displayed in a museum. Several paintings by Rubens, Caravaggio, Botticelli, and Raphael were recognizable. The captive artist studied the intricacies of the brush strokes, the aged and cracked paint, the composition, style, and tone. He felt they could not be replicas, forgeries, or counterfeits, and Karl and Isadore had either purchased them with their super wealth or inherited these fine works.

Yet the curiosity of them being in a basement confounded him. Finally, he came upon *The Concert* from 1664 by Johannes Vermeer. *This was stolen!* He remembered the tale of the art heist at the Isabella Stewart Gardner Mansion. With this epiphany, he ogled the long-missing, priceless work.

Troy recalled hearing it was Isabella's first significant art purchase. She had only paid $5000, but it was worth millions today. He gazed at the two-foot square oil painting of three bourgeoisie musicians.

Refreshed by the protein bar Troy inspected the gallery's famous art. His wonderment grew as he recognized other stolen works. In front of him were five small Edgar Degas; two were sketch studies for an artistic program. Two others were *Three Mounted Jockeys* and *Leaving the Paddock* because Degas enjoyed horse racing. The last was called *Procession on a Road Near Florence,* an Italian landscape.

Troy then connected with *Chez Tortoni* 1875. An image of a man wearing a top hat, who glances at the painter Edouard Manet staring at him. Troy conspired with him, "We must find a way out of this prison, buddy."

The four remaining paintings astonished Troy as they were Rembrandts and a Flinck. A Rembrandt self-portrait was under two inches square, and *Lady and Gentleman in Black,* 1633, was a serene interior portrait of a husband and wife. The only seascape was the famous painting *Christ in the Storm on the Sea of Galilee*, 1633. Troy was mesmerized by the twelve men with Christ being tossed at sea.

When he peered closer, Troy chuckled at his recognition of a man in a green tunic looking back at him, holding onto his cap and a taut rope. It was Rembrandt himself. He enjoyed playing with the viewers of his paintings by planting himself in them. Troy felt that although hundreds of years had passed, Rembrandt was saying, “Hello! I hope you enjoy my work!”

Last in the line of known stolen art was the *Landscape with Obelisk*, 1638, by one of Rembrandt’s followers, Govaert Flinck. Troy had visited the Isabella Stewart Gardner Mansion and recalled the prestigious spot for the painting with natural light on desk by a window.

He sighed and imagined how amazing it might have been to call any of these artists a friend. He felt privileged to behold the masterworks privately. Only then did he understand what Georgi’s great-grandmother meant by being grateful. Even when things were worse than you could imagine, there was a small ray of light somewhere—but one had to look for it. These paintings were it for him.

His moment of peace broke as a thick feeling of dread hit the pit of his stomach. *I know their darkest secrets. These are stolen paintings. They will never release me. Their ploy is to purchase my art and make money after they kill me.* Suddenly, Troy heard the clicking mechanism to the door. Karl entered and sat in one of the club chairs. Troy sat across from him.

“What do you feed your spirit, Karl? It seems to be pure greed. Look at all these stolen paintings you have.”

Karl was surprised by Troy’s bravado to challenge him while he was trying to be kind and empathetic. Defensive energy brought him to his feet. “Me? I never stole anything. I had nothing to do with these paintings being in this room. You don’t...don’t...don’t understand,” he sputtered, clearly upset. “My mother saved these priceless works of art from being stolen by gangsters who would never appreciate them the way we do.”

Karl paced the room. “I have been put in another awkward position, without my consent, to be the protector and preserver of history for these majestic works from Isabella’s heritage. I’ll have you know that the word on the street back in the eighties and nineties was that fine art paintings were a ‘get out of jail free’ card. Thieves were encouraged to commit daring art heists worldwide.” Karl poured out his defense.

“It was happening to museums, palaces, and mansions everywhere, and I knew thieves were destined to rob the Gardner Mansion if they didn’t invest heavily in security. Without my knowledge, my mother took matters into her own hands and hired a man who organized street thieves to dress up in police uniforms. If nothing else, she proved it was possible and simple to steal priceless works of art."

Karl's face burned red, desperate to be understood. "Don't you see, Troy? Once these works were stolen, the new security system saved the entire mansion's collection.

"Did I answer your question? This isn't greed. This is a passion for fine art. My love is for the art, the artists, the inspiration, and the process of bringing forth a work of art. Yes, we have them here, but they are under my protection. I am one of the finest conservators in the world. There is no better a caretaker."

Troy responded with force, "You must believe you are above the law." "You're a thief, and my friend Aaron is dead. You two were the last to see him alive. Are you able to justify death, Karl?" Troy choked up. "What is wrong with you?"

Karl lunged forward. "I didn't kill anyone! That was my twisted Motherrr." He growled and left the room, slamming the door shut and locking it tight. Karl leaned against the door in the dimly lit hall, exhausted by the encounter.

Troy reclined on his back with legs splayed, and arms stretched out to the sides. He felt miserable knowing Isadore was trying to kill him, and he didn't believe Karl would ever let him go.

Friday Morning

Karl peeked through the peephole. He could see Troy at the far end of the gallery.

Troy heard the vault door open; he was rested and ready to joust. This cat-and-mouse game was infuriating him. "Welcome to my posh dungeon, oh wizard and thief of art," he said sarcastically.

Karl grimaced. "Sure, keep insulting me, and my mother will have her way sooner than you think!"

"You mean death by mushrooms. That didn't work so well. Did it? Why are you even talking to me? Is this some cruel routine where the villain discusses his plan with the victim? Or are you just scared and don't know what to do? I'll tell you. Let me go. You don't have anything to gain with me. Why am I even here?"

"You know too much, Troy."

"Karl, my artwork is worth more than my life to me. I would rather you save my art for posterity."

"Why?" Karl was curious to hear the artist's answer.

"My artwork will live on, as will I as a luminous being. Your mother can't really kill me because my energy lives beyond this body, just like everyone. In fact, you can tell her that when I'm gone, I will enjoy haunting you both until I am satisfied that you are terrified. That is how karma works."

Karl jolted, and his shoulders raised with the thought. He wondered if this could be true.

Troy enjoyed teasing Karl's senses. "It astounds me how you both are so stunningly stupid. You are convinced there are no repercussions for your actions. That couldn't be further from the truth, Karl. You will be like zombies, trudging in an alternate reality, lost and in pain, either mentally, emotionally, or physically because that is the ultimate consequence of any bad behavior. A debt you will repay with your pain, equal to or worse than what you imparted on another.

"Those are the hard and fast rules, Karl, and there is no escape from them. That is karma. It is like looking in a mirror; whatever you've done to someone, you do to yourself. So, it guarantees *you*…." he pointed, "will end up in misery."

Karl's mouth hung open. He had never heard the concept of karma explained this way.

"Selfishness is a form of limited thinking and a lack of knowledge. It will only lengthen your discomfort and suffering. It could be in this lifetime or your next lifetime. And since you and your mother live in a world of selfishness, I don't envy you at all."

Karl's mind took a different tack. "With thoughts like this, you must have extraordinary artwork." He attempted to divert, refocus, and gain the upper hand.

"Jason will show you," Troy grumbled and waved him off.

Before leaving the room, Karl made Troy stand at the gallery's far end, sixty feet away. But when Karl opened the door, Troy rushed at him. Karl scurried and slammed the door. With his heart pounding, he locked it.

Troy's voice carried through the thick barrier. "You think you're scared now, Karl. It will be much worse when my spirit haunts you and your mother for real!"

CHAPTER 73

Isadore's Research

Isadore was committed to her poisoning mission. Her toxic craft was designed to go through one entrance, the oral cavity. This would be her fourth try. Karl had left the food inside the private gallery, but to her dismay, Troy refused to eat. She was frustrated and disappointed he wasn't dead yet.

She tied on her apron, determined to disguise her mushrooms in a dessert recipe to entice Troy. The villainess removed her rings and a diamond watch. The glimmering timepiece held the memory of Milo, the man who gave it to her. She chopped and mixed her ingredients and wistfully recalled how her *love of art* brought her and Milo together.

***

It was in 1975 when news broke of a Rembrandt painting stolen from the Boston Fine Arts Museum. It was of a lovely, round-faced girl with pearl earrings.

Karl was an intern at the BFA at the time and reported to her that a man had joined a museum tour group and swiftly put the Rembrandt under his arm. By his side was his accomplice, a man with a machine gun under wraps. The security guards were alerted to the theft and descended on the men near the museum exit. To keep the guards away, the gunman shot at their feet.

All halted except for one courageous guard who grabbed the painting and held on tightly, and so did the thief. They struggled out the door, but a second gunman came from the getaway vehicle. He was about to shoot the guard when the man holding the painting ordered him not to. Instead, the second gunman hit the guard over the head with the gun, causing him to let go of the painting, and all the perpetrators escaped with the Rembrandt.

This experience made Karl wonder about the security at his beloved Isabella Stewart Gardner Mansion. Later, in 1981, the mansion had its first theft: a Whistler, Matisse, and Sargent were stolen. Isadore could still hear Karl's constant howls. "How could this have happened?" Eventually, the criminal was caught, and the paintings were returned. All seemed well and done.

But this event emboldened Karl, now employed by the BFA Museum. On his own, he decided to do some exploring. He discovered the security stayed the same.

By 1987, Karl had earned his position as a professional fine art conservator at the BFA, and his expertise allowed him to work on collections from around the world. He was very content, but one thing niggled at him. He was still not satisfied with the safety of Isabella's famous art collection, almost to the point of obsession.

Isadore recalled growing tired of hearing him complain and decided to put him at ease with information. Initially, she decided to investigate the facts herself. She had spent time traveling the world with Karl's father to purchase art, and on one of their trips, an international art dealer whispered to her, "If you truly desire a rare, unavailable fine work of art, you can have it for the right price." This secret counsel she had received many years ago brought her attention to the underworld of art collectors.

Her quest to satisfy Karl's and her concern regarding the art security at the Isabella became her first opportunity to tap this resource. Through these channels of personal relationships among art dealers, she came upon a man who knew a man named Milo.

In 1987, she was told, "Milo is known to have international business connections in the art world. He acquires rare fine art but be fair warned. He has spent time in jail for stealing art, which makes him qualified to know how vulnerable the Gardner Mansion is to future theft. He's a cocky son-of-a-gun who will deal with anyone when it comes to art."

Isadore was enticed. She was used to dealing with powerful men. Determined, she decided to seek the information that the mansion was safe and put Karl's mind at ease, or she would convince the decision-makers to add additional security based on her well-informed facts.

Although her intentions seemed honorable, Isadore's tendencies descended from there.

The 1990 Boston Art Theft

On March 18, 1990, one day after the St. Patty's Day celebrations, news media outlets announced that a shocking robbery had occurred at the Gardner Museum in the middle of the night.

Karl's response to the theft was indignation and devastation. Karl wanted to march in and yell at someone in charge. He did not. Yet, he complained to his mother. She kept her secret about Milo as long as possible. Until one day, she needed Karl's help.

In September 1990, Isadore was at home in their Boston Brownstone when Karl came home from work at the BFA Museum. "Karl, I have a present for you, but you will have to do some conservation on the art. I know it will make you happy in the end." He was annoyed with her request. "Not another project, Mother. I'm not your free service. I can't come home from work to work for you!"

"Oh, stop. Come here and see my new acquisitions. I need your expertise. Besides repairs, they will need traditional frames."

He followed her into the basement, and Karl saw several tables covered in sheets. Never had she made such a display. "Mother, what are you up to?"

She posed like Isabella Stewart Gardner in the painting by Anders Zorn with arms lifted and hands pressed against the door frame. Karl recognized the reference immediately.

Wagging his finger at her, he said, "Don't be so dramatic, Mother. You are not Isabella."

"I have a new collection that Isabella would adore!" She smiled mischievously. She gave him a peek by lifting the sheet quickly. She knew he would recognize it. "Are you interested?"

He took one step forward. "You know better than to buy a replica of Vermeer!" He motioned with his hand across the tables. "Who advised you? Are the rest of these fakes?"

"You advised me, my dear."

Karl searched his mother's face. "Are you playing a game with me? Because I am not amused, Mother." With a quick swipe, he lifted one of the sheets away. His face contorted into a scowl, which transformed into wide-eyed horror. Swiftly, he turned toward her, inching forward. "Who sold you these counterfeits, and how much did you pay?" he asked in a hoarse whisper.

"Look more carefully, my son." She handed him a magnifying glass.

"Mother, just because you know I love Isabella's Vermeer doesn't mean you should have paid for a forgery. Why didn't you consult me? You know better! Father would say, 'For Pete's sake at the pearly gates.'"

With the magnifier in hand, Karl's tall form bent over the painting and leaned in for a close-up view. He suddenly jolted straight upright as if he had been electrically shocked. He gasped with childlike wonderment, then softly said, "Mother, you found them. You found Isabella's treasures."

He gently pulled the coverings from the other tables and revealed more objects. "Ohh, Flinck's *Landscape with Obelisk* and the *Three Mounted Jockeys* by Degas! They were Father's favorites. Wow! Did you get Manet's

Chez Tortoni? There it is! Look, *The Concert* by Vermeer! Where are the Rembrandts?" Without waiting for her to answer, he began to laugh with exuberance. "This is wonderful. We will receive the million-dollar reward!"

Karl's arms drew wide in celebration. He leaped toward Isadore, embraced her, and lifted her off the floor. Placing her down, he waltzed her around the tables while singing a tune in three-quarter time. "We're going to be rich, dat-dat, dat-dat." Stepping back, he said, "We're going to be famous! You knew my despair, and you found them, Mother!" He hugged her, giddy from the discovery. "Where did you find them? One of your European connections?"

Isadore had not seen him display such cheerful affection since he had been a child. He became a serious young man after his father's death, and now she was dismayed to break the spell. *Maybe I can wait and tell him later,* she thought, but she knew better. Preparing herself for the outcome, she spoke delicately. "Karl, we don't have many options. In fact, we only have one."

Karl, still bubbling with excitement, looked at her with sparkling eyes. "What do you mean, Mother?"

"My son, this must remain our secret. No one can know. You see, I did this for you." A quizzical expression crossed his brow as she continued, "You were so upset with the security at Isabella's mansion, and you would not stop complaining, especially after the robbery in 1981 when the Whistler, Matisse, and Sargent paintings were stolen. Even though they were reclaimed, you grumbled relentlessly every year after. And then, one day, I discovered a solution to relieve you of your concerns."

Karl stilled. He became a statue of disbelief.

"The one person who cared more than anyone in the world about Isabella's treasures was you. I arranged for a few key pieces to be taken so they would be *forced* to secure the whole property." Isadore moved around the tables of precious cargo.

Karl's form slowly descended until he landed on a footstool. With his knees against his chest, he hugged them and closed his eyes.

"You were the catalyst, darling. I did this for you. It took a great deal of effort to implement this plan. I thought you would be grateful. A new security system has been installed, and now you have a priceless Vermeer!"

He said nothing. To Isadore, his silence was more distressing than any words.

Huddled upon himself, in a monotone of defeat, Karl finally spoke. "Mother, very carefully, you will explain everything to me. Every detail. And once you do, I will decide when I will enter the valley of death via an elixir, for I am doomed."

Isadore realized she unexpectedly may have made a big mistake. Dotingly, she sat near him.

For the first time in his life, Karl heard his mother beg. She begged him to understand.

Unfolding himself, he shook his head. His face appeared sickly. Without looking at her, he held up his hand. "Mother, just tell me your story."

Isadore held her hands against her chest and hoped to assuage Karl. "You know the man named Milo who stole the BFA's Rembrandt in 1975?"

Karl's head remained in his lap as he listened.

"Eventually, the newspapers reported he was caught and, in return for a lighter sentence, he gave up the Rembrandt. You remember it was hidden underneath a woman's bed, and she didn't know what she had. I would know if a Rembrandt were under my bed! Just the vibrations from it would have me levitating."

Karl grunted and waved a hand for her to continue.

"Instead of an eight-year sentence for stealing the painting, he was given four years for returning it. This theft created the myth among thieves that it was a free 'get out of jail' card. They learned that stolen art could be used to negotiate their release from prison, and stealing art became a rampant pastime worldwide during the 1980s. Museums were lax, and thieves were courageous. You said it was the worst day in the art world and constantly lamented it."

"Mother, I know what I said. You're just trying to justify your criminal actions by using me."

She ignored him and continued, "In 1988, I decided to ask around about how tight the security was at the Gardner Mansion. I was told I should meet an art collector who could help me. He performed as a musician in a little beach town. Curious, I drove to where he played, and I watched to see how he handled himself. Finally, I decided to approach him. He was Milo, the thief who stole the BFA's Rembrandt."

Karl shook his downturned head. "Ugh! You stalked an art thief so you could ask him about Isabella's mansion! Mother, you've lost touch with reality."

"Well, I was quite surprised at his intelligence and how he knew all the best museums and masterworks from the fourteenth century onward. He was even a fashionable man who wore Italian-tailored shirts and a fine Swiss watch.

I enjoyed my conversations with him; he was interesting and confident, much like your father."

Karl covered his ears.

Isadore paused. "Listen," she said gently, "I'm trying to explain myself. By 1989, you were annoyed that the security had not improved at the mansion. Remember? I, too, was concerned that her collection was not adequately protected.

"At first, I figured if he could learn the voids in the security system, he could help me understand how to convince the powers that it was too easy to break in. Isn't a thief the right person to ask?"

"You're incorrigible," Karl groused.

"I finally realized we couldn't sway the mansion to invest in a new security system. After much thought, I decided that a bold move was in order. I made Milo an offer to save the art by taking it. Only by losing a few pieces would they feel the pinch to protect the whole mansion with a high-quality security system."

Karl found the energy to lift his head. "Mother, I could go to jail. Everyone will believe I was the inside man because I know Isabella's mansion well. But worse, my own mother is the inside man. I don't know what I'm going to do," he moaned. "I'm ruined. You've ruined me." He folded in upon himself into a heap of distraught humanity.

"No, no, my dear. I have another plan."

"No!" He crossed his arms in front of his face to ward off whatever possessed his mother. "No more!"

Isadore's masterpiece of illusion was still in process. "Not to worry. I promise you won't be going to jail. No one will ever know our secret. Think about it. Isabella's mansion is now as secure as the Tower of London with its Crown Jewels. Do you see? Nothing else will be stolen from our beloved mansion.

"Karl, even though you didn't know until now, you have thanked me repeatedly. Your wish was granted. All Isabella's treasures were secured once these glorious paintings went missing."

CHAPTER 74

The Whole Story on Milo

Isadore knew she would never tell Karl the whole story about her and Milo. A mother cannot share such details with her son.

When she discovered Milo, they were both in their mid-forties. As she grew comfortable with him, she revealed whom she knew in the world of art and her husband's family, the Rubens.

Their many conversations about art delighted her. He was a wealthy and knowledgeable art collector and revealed that when he could not buy art because it was in a museum, he was courageous enough to steal the art.

"Who is your favorite artist at the Isabella, Milo?" Isadore found him disturbingly alluring.

He swigged his whiskey and gave his intriguing companion a genuine smile. His deep voice resonated, "Well, if you must know, it's only Rembrandts for me." She watched his eyes rove to the buttons on her blouse and imagined being agreeable if he plucked them.

Their engaging discussions on art and flirtatious eye contact had Isadore ready to consort. Coyly, she offered up her risky venture. "Milo, dear, I have a job for you, one you will adore because I'm going to offer you a Rembrandt. But there is an exchange—you must get me something in return. Are you willing?"

He cupped his chin in his hand and leaned toward her. "Quite willing, Isadore," he charmingly purred and gazed deeply into her eyes. "You have my full attention."

She moved in close and spoke into his ear. "Since the Gardner Mansion's art will be stolen by someone eventually, I will pay you handsomely to help them realize that they should add security for its protection. I expect this theft to be a very professional job with no one harmed. When you have what I want, we can exchange it through the art dealer in New York. But…," she halted and put her hand on his, "I need to know, how can I possibly trust you?"

He drew in the scent of her perfume and murmured, "How can I trust you, my dear?"

They stared into each other's eyes.

Isadore held her breath, studying him carefully. Finally, she exhaled. "There must be something we can do to prove it to each other, for longevity's sake. Is that possible?"

"I do believe it is, Isadore."

She was entranced by his deep voice saying her name.

"I have something you might like — items from an acquisition not long ago. You may have heard about it in the news. The Captain Bangs Hallet House in Massachusetts had some items go missing. You may choose whatever you like from my collection, and you can trust me to acquire the paintings of your choice from the Gardner. All I want are the Rembrandts."

"Then we shall kill three birds with one stone. One, you will have your Rembrandts. Two, I will have the art I love. And three, it will convince the powers that be to protect Isabella's collection."

They clinked their glasses to seal their nefarious deal.

Milo drove Isadore to his warehouse of art. She willingly made choices from his collection of scrimshaw plus a thirteenth-century Chinese vase.

He took her hand and kissed it. "We were never here, my dear. Agreed?"

"Agreed," breathed Isadore.

Milo was a character with many irons in the fire of life. In 1989, he told Isadore that every gangster knew the Gardner was destined to be hit. It was a race to see who would be first. He had to find the right crew to fit all the details together for the hit on the Gardner Mansion. Therefore, it could take months to a year.

But Isadore surprised Milo with some well-needed assistance. She provided a building map showing all the back doors, secured rooms, and secret hallways. Of course, she knew all this from Karl, but she never revealed that to Milo. She casually pumped Karl for all the guards' names and their demeanors.

Over time, she built into her discussions with Karl what was stored in the basement, where the video cameras were, and where the security recording room with the VHS tapes was located. She handed all these vital facts to Milo. Then she provided a list of the art she wanted with the locations in the building. Milo was staggered by the coveted details.

She smiled at him beguilingly. "I have procured information from a direct source. If you confine the guards first, no one will come, even if an alarm goes off in the building. The alarms…are harmless!"

"They have only one to the outside world, behind the guard's desk. If you remove the guards from that location, you are home-free and will have all the time you need." Smitten with him and the plan, she whispered, "And Milo, I will sweeten the deal. I'll cover your expenses and pay you three hundred thousand dollars upfront. Ultimately, seven hundred thousand will be yours when you place the art into my hands. This will help guarantee a successful job."

Milo was dazzled. "My dear, where have you been all my life?" He kissed her cheek and whispered, "This will be a clean steal."

"If we are to make a deal, Milo, I'd like to seal it with a true kiss."

He grabbed her passionately, enticed by the excitement of their devious partnership. An alliance based on Isadore's twisted mantra: Steal the art to protect the collection from thefts.

She was thrilled that their rendezvous had become passionate. Before he left, he whispered, "We shall have a personal identifier only between us. In France, four kisses are given on the cheek when you meet someone close to you. It also means, 'It is on until the break of dawn.' For us, it represents our eternal secret." She remembered him breathing the words softly into her ear, "*Isadore, I will sign all my messages to you with these words, Four Kisses XXXX.*"

When she heard the news about the breach of the Gardner Mansion, Isadore knew Milo had achieved their goal.

As agreed, Milo chose his booty: the stolen *Chinese beaker, Napoleon's Eagle finial*, and three Rembrandts: *Portrait of the Artist as a Young Man*, *Christ in the Storm on the Sea of Galilee*, and *A Lady and Gentleman in Black.* Isadore had Vermeer's *The Concert*, Flinck's *Landscape with Obelisk*, Manet's *Chez Tortoni*, and five works by Degas.

After Isadore's payment and the art transfer, Milo and Isadore agreed it was safer never to see each other again.

Karl had yet to learn the true purpose of her underground vault. It was built to house Isabella's stolen art collection and completed before 1990.

Milo sent Isadore a gift to her island home,
Twenty years after the theft.

Isadore, my dear partner in….

I cannot care for and display these treasures in the manner they deserve. Please take care of them as I care for you. Although it's been twenty years, I think of you often. Thank you for taking me on your grand adventure. Please think of me when you look at our collection of Isabella's paintings. Fondly, I wish you all the best with double the love and four kisses for good luck!

Yours truly, Four Kisses XXXX

Isadore opened the crated packages and was astounded to see Milo's stolen collection, including the Rembrandts from the Gardner Mansion.

When Karl visited her from Boston in 2010, he arrived to find the staircase exposed to the underground gallery. He stepped into the gallery. She was dusting. Suddenly, his pace quickened as he spied the Rembrandts. Isadore relished the moment. Twenty years had passed since he had seen these fine works on the mansion walls of the Isabella.

"Mother, where did you get these? Tell me they are counterfeits."

"My dear, don't be obnoxious. I only deal with the best."

"But how did they come into your possession? Were they recovered?"

"No, my dear, they were delivered."

"Delivered? What do you mean delivered?" Karl was rightly suspicious.

"Well, you could say I have friends in low places." Isadore smiled, and Karl's hands went to his hips as he stared at her with indignation. "I'm your mother. Don't give me that look. You should be grateful."

He slumped into a club chair. "Oh, Mother, how am I to reason this?" Karl held his stomach, and his face contorted with thoughts of going to jail again. "I am trying to comprehend another dilemma you have suddenly thrust me into. I have encountered a black hole, and her name is Isadore. I am a prisoner of your gravitational pull, and I see no way out!" Wringing his hands, he rocked back and forth in his seat. "I can't change it, I can't stop it, I can't make it go away!"

"Come on, Karl. Relax, sit back, and enjoy the magnificence before your eyes." Isadore drew her arms wide. She spread her flowy outfit, which made her look winged.

Karl raised his head. He disliked this habit. "Mother, you look like a winged fury enticing the winds to destroy my peace. How? I ask you, how am I to resolve this?"

"My darling dear, it's quite easy. You only have to do one thing." Her breast heaved, and she exhaled her air of arrogance. "Accept it!" Tapping one monogrammed velvet slipper, she instructed, "Now enjoy the scenery."

Karl flopped back in the chair. "I am in simultaneous adoration and dismay."

"We have them for the rest of our lives. You bellyached for years about the Rembrandts, and here they are. This is my life's achievement. All your wishes have come true because these are safeguarded with us." She whirled her dress in the spacious gallery. She settled into an angelic pose with her hands against her bosom.

"Mother, I wonder about you. Do you ever surprise yourself?" She laughed, knowing full well he was mesmerized by the paintings.

"When I luxuriate among these hidden treasures, I feel the fire of my glow of contentment keeping me warm," she sang.

Karl crossed his arms in disapproval. "Mother, your inner glow is from a fire-breathing dragon inside you that enjoys sitting on a priceless hoard in an underground lair."

Facts: Isabella Stewart Gardner Museum

In 1990 the stolen art from the Gardner Museum was worth $200 million. On the street, it was worth $20 million. After the theft, the security system was updated to state-of-the-art standards. The museum offered a $1 million reward for the art to be returned. In 1997, they increased it to $5 million. The art is still MISSING, and the reward is $10 million today.

CHAPTER 75

Jason's Art Deal
Friday – six weeks since Marilyn's fatality

While Isadore was crafting a dessert with toxic mushroom powder to feed Troy, Karl arranged to see Troy's art.

Jason had been hyping Troy's disappearance on various social media sites, and now the collector and museum director Karl Rubens was interested. The artist decided to play the game and dress a little classier than usual. He threw a jacket over his T-shirt and wore black jeans and fresh high-top sneakers.

Karl parked his swanky Jaguar in front of the DuWater Building at 10 a.m. Jason was waiting at the door for the prospective client and watched as he rose from the car. Seeing the crisp suit, bowtie, and gold cuff links gave him high hopes for wads of money. "Mr. Rubens, I'm Jason. It's good of you to come by. You're the first to see Troy's collection. God rest his soul."

Caught off guard by the death reference, Karl deflected by saying, "How did you know it was me?"

"My man, you're the only polished dude arriving in a fancy Jaguar this morning. The Thames Club members next door don't usually arrive until lunch. Besides, I was at your grand museum reopening and the fantastic auction you just had at the Garde." He purposely poured on the charm because Karl looked like his winning ticket. *If I act this out, I'm going all the way. Troy and I will have a good laugh over this sale.*

Jason held the door open to the building, then led Karl upstairs. "Many artists have their studios in this building. Right this way, Mr. Rubens." Jason had the key to enter the Kitchen Gallery. Since he cared for Matt, Troy's cat, Jason had let him into the gallery. Matt happily approached Jason, but on seeing Karl, he halted, hissed, and growled.

"Matt, what's wrong with you? That's not how to treat a guest!" Jason turned to Karl. "I'll put him in the other room."

The yoga studio's owner, Kimberly, also a fantastic artist, had colorful paintings on her gallery walls along with Troy's. Karl was impressed by both, but he focused on his goal, Troy's monoprints. The first was a flowering dogwood branch with glistening copper highlights. He noticed Troy's application was intricate, meticulous, and layered with color and texture. Karl moved about and tilted his head. He stepped forward and stopped to analyze the work. *How have I not seen his work? His technique is unusual.*

"Do you have others?" Karl asked without letting Jason know what he thought of Troy's work.

Jason knew this game: view and negotiate without emotion. "Right this way. This series highlights how important bees are to our planet and livelihood." Karl could see Troy had used a pointillism technique, dots of paint, to create an image. In one, a large bee hovered over a giant sunflower; a young woman was in the background.

Next was a series Troy had created in Ethiopia and Bulgaria. Most of these works depicted landscapes or nature close-up. Karl again gazed at the fine detail and layering of color and tone. Some of his works leaned toward impressionism.

Karl's attention was then drawn to a rack with hanging, unframed canvases. "What are these?"

Jason wheeled the rack forward and flipped through the hinged display. "These are all block prints. They are individual flowers or seedpods in a large format, variations on themes of poppies, milkweed pods, dandelion seeds, and cannabis flower buds. Troy carved the design into a wax block, creating these unique prints. After printing, he adds more detail, color, and texture to enhance and customize each one. It is a laborious process and requires patience. Would you like to see more? There must be a hundred in total. He has a storage unit of his artwork."

"No, I've seen enough," said Karl.

Jason's heart sank, but at least he had tried. "Well, others are coming to see the work today from Boston. I'll let you think about what you've seen, Mr. Rubens. I know the collection will be separated; however, I'm trying to sell the themes as a unit. Thank you for coming by."

Karl had bought, dealt, and bartered art his whole life for his mother, her friends, and gallery owners from Europe to Australia, and never had someone brushed him off so quickly in hopes of another sale. "Do you have high hopes with this dealer from Boston?" he asked.

"Why yes, I do, because they only deal in contemporary art and are familiar with Troy's work. I know you prefer classical fine art. I imagined—"

"You know me not, sir," Karl interrupted. "I am keenly interested and deal with galleries far and wide who will show his collection. How much?"

"For which pieces? Do you have a theme you prefer?" Jason was pleased his tactic was gaining results. If this dude was going to throw down the dough, he was prepared to negotiate.

Karl took his pose for high-volume sales that portrayed relaxed and willing to make a deal. His left arm crossed his waist to support his right elbow. His right thumb was neatly tucked under his chin. He considered his offer. "I want them all. The entire collection."

Unprepared, Jason was stunned and had to gather his wits quickly. "This is your field of expertise, Mr. Rubens. Make me an offer I can't refuse. I am not going to give Troy's legacy away."

"One hundred fifty thousand dollars for everything," Karl proposed, testing him.

"No way. I can get double that or more by selling one piece at a time."

Karl pursed his lips as he considered his next move. "But that's going to take time. So why don't you make it easy on yourself and agree to three hundred thousand dollars? Take it or leave it."

Jason was no novice to men seeking treasure. He learned from his father, who worked on classic cars, that if a guy loves something, he'll spend the money, especially if it is unique. "That's a fair offer, and if Troy is still alive, he would tell me to take it. But Mr. Rubens, he's been missing for several days, and his belongings were found on the beach. He hasn't been in contact with friends and missed several appointments. Considering what happened to Marilyn, I'm protecting Troy's family's interest. You and I understand he isn't likely alive." Jason paused, knowing Troy was in Vermont on a well-earned hiatus.

On the other hand, Karl knew Troy was avoiding Isadore's food in their subterranean gallery.

Both knew he was alive, and both were pretending he was dead.

But only Karl knew Troy's life teetered on edge. Either way, this art investment was worth it because there were over a hundred pieces, and they would only go up, up, up in price.

Jason thought, *Troy, you were right, buddy. Everybody wants your art when you're dead. If only more people appreciated the artists who are alive.* "Mr. Rubens, artists are the engines of the Renaissance, the mediums for muses. We interpret the realms beyond eyesight and turn them into masterpieces of matter. What are they worth? They are priceless today. So, I will tell my Boston client that Troy's work is going up in price because I have a serious offer. I will wait and find out if he plans to counter your offer. I'll call you once I have an answer." Jason loved the risk of negotiation as long as he kept Karl in play and didn't offend him.

Karl turned away to process what to do. He usually had the upper hand. *Why am I bothering? The work is excellent, and I know it will fetch more. All I must do is hold it for a year, and I will help build the buzz. I'll be credited with discovering a contemporary artist whose life was cut short.* He glanced toward the flowering dogwood again. "Normally, I would agree to wait for your counteroffer. But why don't you tell me what it will take to buy the collection now." Karl's tone was firm.

Thrilled he had caught his big fish, Jason said, "If you want to make the deal now, I'll take five hundred thousand dollars. You pay all the transaction fees, shipping, and taxes, and you'll receive over one hundred and twenty-five of his original works. You know you will get four times that price in one to five years."

Karl considered the offer. It seemed like an eternity, but it was only thirty seconds. "I believe you're right, Jason. I'll take the deal."

Ready to jump with joy, Jason bit his tongue to keep from smiling.

Karl said, "Write up our agreement and email me an invoice. I'll wire you a fifty-percent deposit today and send a packing service tomorrow morning. I will arrive with the signed paperwork, then wire you the balance. Are you satisfied with this arrangement?"

"Yes, sir, very satisfied." Jason grinned, imagining his fifteen percent fee of seventy-five thousand dollars and how pleased Troy would be for this sale.

Karl nodded. "Send me the routing number for the bank account, and I will wire the funds. Here's my card. Good day, sir."

Jason looked out the window and watched Karl drive away; he started hooting and hollering. He opened the door for the cat, who pranced out, but when Jason yowled over their good fortune, Matt the cat ran. "Hey, Matt, tonight it's tuna juice and shrimp for you. We're living large!"

As Karl drove down State Street, he calculated the numbers for his art transaction. Selling one hundred twenty-five paintings at four thousand each equaled his five-hundred-thousand-dollar investment. But he estimated he could easily sell many for forty thousand dollars each, which would bring him a profit of five million dollars for an excellent artist.

Spontaneously, he decided to peruse downtown's art scene. He had seen the signs for the Marquee Gallery, 1up Gallery, Thames River Gallery, Studio 33, Expressiones Cultural Center, Sparks Makerspace, Hygienic Art Gallery,

Helios Art Association, and of course, the Dahlia Art Gallery. These were just a few options for artists to display their work in the City of Steeples.

Karl let out a long sigh. *Maybe I've been myopic and biased. Here in New London, hiding behind rustic walls in studio apartments, artists manifest their burning desires, sleeping in crowded conditions among their work. That's what many old masters did. Why has it taken me so long to notice that even today, this is where all great art begins?*

The thought made Karl consider that buyers, art dealers, and gallery representatives should be looking in small places like private studios and local galleries to seek out hidden gems and gain a direct connection to the art and the artists. He knew of art investors who had become patrons for artists to promote their careers. He recalled a taxi company mogul in New York who had made a fortune selling art he purchased directly from the artists. Buying from the artist was an investment that helped the artist financially and cut out the middleman.

Karl considered his purchase. *Mother always loved the art of the deal. She will be pleased with me. The problem? Troy is now worth more dead than alive.*

CHAPTER 76

A Villainess
Friday

Isadore was so pleased with Karl's purchase of Troy's art that she decided they should celebrate. "Darling, why don't we call Father Hagerty at the monastery and ask if we can host a dinner tomorrow evening? He told me yesterday that they had an open schedule this weekend due to a cancellation. We can invite twenty or so people. It will be a win-win-win. The monastery will make money from the dinner, and you could even invite Georgi to do an impromptu wine pairing for the meal. Father Hagerty would love it."

Karl contemplated the idea. Her desires seemed to come out of nowhere, like a whirling waterspout suddenly emerging in the ocean. "Mother, why do you do this? Can't we be peaceful? Let's lounge around and luxuriate in our successes. Besides, we have Troy downstairs. Is this the time to be celebrating with a group of people?"

"Why not let people see us out and about, like when we were at dinner yesterday? We are in public, acting normally. I'll set it up. It's a wise choice. Give Georgi a call and tell him to invite a few friends too. Okay?"

"Yes, Mother." Karl shook his head in defeat. She would always get her way no matter what he did or how hard he tried. He gave up fighting.

Friday afternoon

The active search and rescue were still underway for Troy in New London with no results. With little information to verify that he did go into the water, the Coast Guard would soon call off the search.

At the Vinho Verde, Georgi was preparing for an evening wine dinner when he received a call from Karl.

"Georgi Algarve, this is Karl Rubens. I have a last-minute request."

"Yes, Karl, how can I assist?"

"Would it be possible for you to work a private dinner on Edgar's Island at the Franciscan monastery tomorrow night? Mother arranged with Father Hagerty for the monks to prepare a delicious meal for twenty."

Georgi knew he should accept, but he purposely hesitated. "I, well, I'm not sure, Karl. Let me see if I have a server to fill in for me tomorrow. We have a six o'clock wine dinner for fifteen. Um, yes, it looks like I have a competent person who will be here. What can I do for you, and what time would you like me to be there?"

"We will start dinner near five o'clock. You can come as early as three to set up. I will send you the food menu so you can select the proper wines for the five-course meal. How does that sound?"

"Just fine, Karl. Is there anything else I should know?"

"Oh, yes. I nearly forgot. You're welcome to invite four guests of your own. Do you have anyone in mind who could attend?"

"That's very nice. Yes, I do. Roxanne and her husband, and I'm sure I can find another couple too. Thank you for thinking of me."

"Of course. See you tomorrow, Georgi, and thank you for accepting last minute."

Georgi quickly called Roxanne and informed her of the opportunity that had presented itself. Would they be able to expose Karl? After realizing Karl's walk was the same as the video, they decided to sit on the information rather than run to Detective Morrison.

Roxanne said she and Sam would go to the event and that she would put her thinking cap on. "Ooh, what if we were able to get Dan to go? We need him to be there. Let me work on that." They hung up.

Georgi opened his laptop to look for the menu Karl was sending but was interrupted when his doorbell rang. It was Marguerite. He hugged her and welcomed her in. They sat outside on the back deck with a cool drink of mint iced tea. She told him she was recovering well and asked if he had pictures from last Sunday's Celebrate the Arts event. She had left early and knew he might have a few she would enjoy seeing.

"Yes, I have plenty because I take pics for my Vinho Verde social media pages. Let's see…." Georgi swiped through a few on his phone. "Did you meet the people who donated the painting for the big auction? This is Karl and his mother."

"I saw him around," she acknowledged, "but I didn't see her except…wait. That's the nice lady who took me to tea when I went to Mystic. That's her. I don't recall her name. What is it?"

Georgi was shocked. "Isadore? Are you sure this is the lady, Marguerite?"

"Yes, absolutely," she nodded. "I'd like to thank her."

Georgi's brain was spinning. His pulse elevated, and the pitch of his voice increased. "Marguerite, do you mind me asking how you ended up in the water?"

"The doctors told me a blood test showed I had a psychedelic mushroom substance in my body. I told them I had never tried them. They asked me how I think it entered into my body." She shrugged. "I don't know. I…I…oh no, Georgi. They thought I ingested it within an hour of going into the water." She held her stomach. "Detective Morrison said he wanted to meet the lady. Is it possible she drugged me? The detective told me Aaron had the same mushrooms in his system too!"

On the inside, Georgi was screaming, *Yikes! It's Isadore!* But he bit his tongue and kept quiet.

Alarmed by her thoughts, she covered her mouth. "Georgi, she poisoned us, didn't she?" Marguerite began crying.

Georgi wrapped his arms around her. Tears rolled down his face too. He needed to get his distraught friend some help. He drove Marguerite to her parent's house and told her he would get advice about what they should do next.

Roxanne was about to be his first call when Ophelia called him. She revealed that Karl had bought some of Troy's art through Jason. Georgi's sleuthing antennae raised even higher, so he had to call Roxanne immediately.

Through a quick dialogue exchange, a plan was made to visit Jason before reporting these suspicious behaviors of Isadore and Karl to Detective Morrison.

They sat huddled at Washington Street Coffeehouse, each with a drink. Georgi whispered, "Jason, we wanted to meet because I heard you sold some of Troy's art to Karl Rubens. Is that true?"

"Yes, we represent each other if the other is away. He does it for me all the time." Jason took a sip of his coffee.

"But he's missing, maybe a swimming accident," Roxanne said, "and we are afraid he's fallen victim to whatever is going on with the artists. Didn't you find it suspicious that Karl was hot to purchase some of his work so soon?"

Jason turned from side to side to check the room to see who could hear them. "Troy would want me to make a sale, even if he was not around anymore. The money would go to his mother. And hey, I don't know why Karl suddenly showed up, but he didn't buy some of Troy's work…he bought all his work."

Georgi and Roxanne grabbed each other's arms. "Whhaatt?"

"Isn't that unusual?" asked Roxanne.

Jason leaned in. "The guy thinks Troy could be dead. That message brings the art wolves out of their den to see how they can profit from what is left behind. He probably thinks he can make a pretty penny. Marilyn's work is worth triple or higher than what she was selling it for, which is the nature of the business when it comes to the death of an artist. I know it sounds cruel, but that is how it rolls. It's sick, isn't it? But I don't think anything happened to Troy, and when he finds out what Karl paid for his paintings, he'll be ecstatic."

"Well, yes, but don't you think Karl's jumping ahead by thinking Troy's already dead?" asked Roxanne. "It makes me suspicious of him."

"Well, he won't have much profit if Troy is alive. I'm happy with the sale and don't care how it affects Karl." Of course, Jason knew he did it for Troy and his own pocket.

Georgi spoke up, "Listen, you two, Marguerite just identified Isadore as the person who took her to tea on the day she nearly drowned." Georgi air quoted as he finished with, "From being drugged." He was a bit too loud with this statement. Roxanne squeezed his arm to calm him.

And now Jason was surprised. "Oh no! Do you think she is the one? Would Karl be in on it? That means they drugged Aaron too. They were the last to see him at the museum."

"Oh no!" whispered Georgi.

"Did they kill Marilyn too? This is horrible." Jason hung his head, hoping none of this was true.

Roxanne sat up straight and tapped on the table. "This is what we're going to do. We are not saying anything to anyone until we talk to Detective Morrison. Can you agree to that, Jason?"

He nodded. "Of course. I won't say a word." He thought of Troy in Vermont. *Should I ask a neighbor to check in on him and tell him what is happening?*

After Roxanne and Georgi left Jason, they sat in her truck to discuss their next step. "Why haven't they found Troy? I'm concerned. Do you think Karl and Isadore are villains?"

"Wouldn't this be a good time to call Detective Morrison," Georgi wondered.

"Not quite yet," Roxanne said. Shocked, Georgi's head jerked. Her eyes twinkled at him.

"Usually, I would say yes, especially since Dan admonished us with the third degree. But I think he will understand when I tell him why I waited. Besides, he has known Sam and me for fifteen years. I have some clout with him, and don't forget we were his saviors on his last case, so he can't get too angry.

"Here's the deal. I planned to lay out my labyrinth design at the Rubens' house sometime. I can do it tomorrow. The dinner event they planned is practically next door. Let's figure out how to set a trap. Then I'll explain it to our Detective Morrison."

"That sounds great, but let's check back with each other because I have to return to work."

Roxanne busied herself at home while waiting for Sam to arrive so she could share her sleuthing plans. She picked up a book, *Dangerous Women in History*. The tagline read: 'A villainess can only be taken in small doses. Unfortunately, she doesn't come that way.'

Roxanne considered, "Hmm." *Isadore could be in their second edition.*

CHAPTER 77

Lectio Divina – Divine Reading
Friday - afternoon

Troy found the scent of Isadore's home-cooked meals inviting, though he would have none. *That's how a witch tempts you with her deadly brew. It's good Karl brought me a secret stash of food.* The spine-chilling thought of Isadore made him recall a music video by Eric Church called *Creepin'*.

His thoughts were interrupted when he heard the locking mechanism click on the door. Karl returned with a skip in his step and a cherry pie.

"I see you brought me a sweet temptation. Is that another Isadore recipe?"

"Oh no. She's given up on you eating. I bought this for you to celebrate. I saw your work. You have an ingenious technique. Your details and investment of time in the pursuit of excellence are obvious. Troy, you are very, very good. Frankly, I'm impressed."

"Frankly, I'm depressed," Troy replied suspiciously.

Karl's arms drew wide, "I decided to buy all your work. Jason made sure the price was top dollar. My connections in the New York and LA markets will negotiate against each other to own your collection." Troy's mouth hung open with relief that his art sold.

"I thought this would make you feel better. I have granted your wish. But my hands are tied with my mother. You will become famous, posthumously, of course. Your art will live on after your death." Troy's head jerked forward.

"You see, we are going to make you and Marilyn famous. My mother has already bought a collection of Marilyn's art from private investors. And she has locked in your fate with the unscrupulous characters she's hired. I'm sorry, Troy, but she's made her decision. I have no say in the matter."

Troy swallowed hard as a shiver went through him, realizing Karl's cavalier attitude meant he saw Troy's life as a meaningless bump in the road. This mother and son's love of art, and the deal, fed their greedy hunger.

Karl became more insensitive and asked, "Troy, you want your art to be famous, so I want to enhance it by including an exposé about your creative process and inspirations.

Troy considered Karl and Isadore's state of mind. He had been a worrier his whole life for no good reason compared to this. Now his life was on the line, and he knew worrying about it wouldn't help him one bit. He had nothing to lose, so he expounded his words for Karl. "Artists are the interpreters of the divine within them. Everyone has an artist's spirit, even you, Karl, but it all depends on what you feed the spirit."

Karl shifted in his seat.

Troy looked into his eyes to see if he was nearly evil or purely evil. "Lectio Divina. Do you know this term, Karl?"

"Divine reading?"

"Yes, it is what the monks practice. They read spiritual works very slowly, allowing the divine to enter between each word. Pauses are intentional so that the holy spirit can speak to them. I have tried to accomplish this in my artwork."

Karl circled his hand. "Go on."

"As I paint, I enter a contemplative state and allow a creative spirit to assist me. Some might call it universal energy, others might say the muses are whispering to them, but you enter a creative place within yourself. It is how I enhance my work with my spiritual nature.

"There is space between forms. This is the void, and it is just as important as the form itself. It is the same as the contrast between light and dark in my paintings.

"Some allow divine inspiration to enter them by using a personal mantra or tone that resonates within them. Likewise, your painting can resonate with the viewer. Most will not recognize it. They either like or dislike my work.

"But I found that many viewers are superficial and, therefore, can't feel the resonance I have instilled in my work. Or they may feel it but are financially challenged and can't afford it. The dilemma is getting my work appropriately publicized so that the true art appreciators, those with the income, will see and buy it. But you already know that.

"So that is why, my cunning captor, I sell online vintage typewriters that I refurbish and customize. It's a different means for my creative output. In the end, I create less art, like most starving artists, but I have some income when my artwork doesn't sell."

Karl considered the use of the word spirit. "Troy, do you truly believe in revenge? If you believe in the spirit world, do you believe you can come after me as a ghost?"

Good. He's worried. Troy thought.

Continuing his query, Karl asked, "I mean, if I make you famous, surely that must correct my karma with you, and you won't need to haunt me?"

Troy smiled to himself. *How amusing that Karl is negotiating with his afterlife.* "Look, karma exists, and you will incur your retribution. It doesn't matter if you believe in it. It will occur. If my image haunts you and your mother as your retribution, then so be it. It's all in what you deserve. Your mother is a bewitching woman who seduces death. She is evil."

Karl was speechless. He was in awe of Troy's point of view but was experiencing disdain for Troy's crass candor toward his mother—such mixed emotions.

"Is karma like sin?"

Troy smiled. "No, nothing like sin because karma is more exact. Karma means you are never forgiven for wrongdoings. You will and must pay for your actions." Troy paused for emphasis. "If you understood the spiritual worlds, Karl, you would be trembling in your skin for all you've done."

Feeling the sting of his words, Karl attempted to retain composure by looking at his manicured nails. "Where did you learn about these things?"

"Physicists have determined that at least eleven parallel realities exist beyond our own. If you investigated teachings about the soul and the afterlife, you would understand what the ancient masters knew. You have proven to me that you know nothing about reality. Expand your mind, Karl. You are so selfish that you don't realize you are setting yourself up to be a lost, wandering spirit for a long time.

"You've heard people say: Do everything to the best of your ability, cause no harm, and treat others as you wish to be treated. So far, you have failed the test big time. You may wonder who is keeping the score. There is a balance in the universe. Everything must come into balance." Troy was in a fight for his life with logical, poetic, and emotional words. Words were all he had—to try—and sway Karl's conscience to let him live.

"Between you and me is energy, and you are messing with my energy. Worst of all, you are planning to extinguish mine. Your mother has taught you to be evil." He raised his hands and his voice. "Wake up, Karl!"

Karl pulled on his vest in a huff, straightening it over his starched shirt. His gold cuff links caught a bit of the light from the ceiling. He toughened his Teflon exterior. "No matter what you say, I cannot let you go. Mother has already determined your fate. And I, well, I have had quite enough of you."

"What about me? Don't you think I've had enough? No! Because you're mean and insensitive. You've forgotten what fear and discomfort feel like, haven't you? Everything is provided for you on a silver plate, isn't it? Yet, when someone threatens your joy, your love, you become aware because you only think of yourself, your petty little peewee self. You are fifty shades of selfish, Karl! The self who lives in a bubble world with all his toys. You have no compassion. You don't even know what compassion is."

Karl glared at Troy. Never in his life had anyone spoken to him that way. He stomped out of the elegant gallery.

Troy understood Karl would not empathize, so he yelled, "Karl, I'm sure no one has once told you the truth about yourself. You're spoiled rotten, KARL! You're rotting like a zombie's flesh. You're DOOMED, KARL!" Troy's voice rang dully in the posh room with the six-inch padded, triple-lock vault door.

Karl stood on the other side with his fists and teeth clenched. He heard Troy's words through the air vents. Suddenly, Isadore appeared out of the shadows in the darkened hallway where she had been listening. Reaching out her hand, she led him up the staircase. She pushed the button, and the polished hardwood floor slid across and clicked into place, disguising the staircase flawlessly. With a swift kick, her foot caught the corner of the oriental rug, which flipped into position.

"Do you see my point now, dear?" she asked.

"Yes, Mother. It's time. I'm ready now."

"Good!" She brought her fingertips together. "I'll alert my contacts and see when they can fit Troy into their schedule."

Troy sat in the stillness of the gallery, his own words to Karl rang in his head as he thought, *I faked my death to increase the price of my art, and now I'm facing my own creation. My art will be worth more, and I'll be dead. My karma has come to greet me. It manifested almost instantly, but I've been tricked. My fake death will be a real death.*

Troy's only company was his memory and imagination. He had met his enemy, Isadore and Karl. A song queued in his head, "Enemy" by Imagine Dragons. Tapping out the beat, he sang the lyrics to keep himself company.

CHAPTER 78

The Sleuth-inator
Friday - afternoon

Fire Chief Samson pulled his truck into the driveway and ambled up the back stairs. He entered the house to find Roxanne reading. "Hi, doll. How are things?" He peeled off his official uniform.

"I'll know better when I hear about Troy. Any news from the Coast Guard?" Roxanne was concerned but hopeful.

"Sorry, no results. It's a damn shame. The city has been out with search and rescue volunteers in boats and people walking the shoreline. No one saw Troy enter the water. Family and friends have not heard from him either. I spoke to Morrison, and he's frustrated that Troy may be another case to investigate. The mayor wants results, of course, so Dan says he'll bring in a profiler on Monday. He needs hard evidence. It's a royal mystery, isn't it?"

"I think I may have a clue, yet I'm not sure if it applies to Troy."

Sam was surprised.

She patted the sofa. "Here, sit down. This is what's happened since yesterday. Georgi and I saw Morrison's video of a person, supposedly Marilyn, in the fog on the night she died. After visiting Karl, we became suspicious of him when he walked across the room. Get this! His stride was like the one in the video dressed up like Marilyn with the hat and coat. Those are the items Georgi found in his trash bin."

"That sounds bizarre! And you can't prove it. Can you?"

"No, so here's the second part of my story." Roxanne gripped Sam's arm. "Just a short while ago, Georgi was with Marguerite. She identified *Isadore* in photos from the Garde Arts event as the woman she had tea with before she went into the Mystic River! That's suspicious too!"

"And how does this become a lead?" Sam squinted his eyes, wondering if his wife was dreaming up solutions. He tried to imagine the formal, stiff Karl Rubens wearing heels, a hat, and a short raincoat.

"Here's the thing. Who else was at the museum when Aaron was there that night? It was Karl and Isadore at closing near the time Aaron fell off the roof. You learned from Dan that Aaron and Marguerite had that psychedelic mushroom in their body. But family and friends said neither of them was known or claimed to have ever taken the stuff. Isadore had access to Aaron and

Marguerite within the timeframe of the incidents. I can't think of a motive other than the theft of the painting.

"Here's another weird thing. Karl just purchased *all* of Troy's art on display and in storage. Jason sold it to him because he and Troy agreed to sell each other's art. Doesn't that make Karl suspicious? Last, I must say, it did look like Karl's walk in that video. I think we have several leads. Don't you?"

"Ahh, those are all things to ponder. Let's give Dan a call and let him decide."

"Okay, but I have a plan."

Sam gave his wife an 'Oh, no you don't,' look.

"Don't say no, don't say no," she said hurriedly, waving her hands. "Honestly, I have a good idea."

Sam placed his fist against his forehead. "I feel a headache coming on, and I just realized it's you. I egged you on when I said this is a royal mystery. That did it, didn't it?"

"No. I had the idea before you got home. I already discussed it with Georgi, who thinks it's a grand plan. Besides, we've already set it up. We can't go back now because the plan is in play."

"What are you talking about?" Sam's voice held a note of warning.

"I'll tell you what," Roxanne challenged. "Call Dan and tell him to come by because I have information, maybe a lead. We'll let him decide."

"Okay, I can agree, but if he says no, then the answer is no. Will you agree to that?"

Roxanne wobbled in her seat. "Uh, ah, the idea is great. I don't think he'll say no. Come on, call him."

Sam rang him. "Hey, Dan, Roxanne has some good information on your case, and she's got a plan. I can't say if the idea is good because she wants to wait until you are here. I have my dithers if you catch my drift." Sam listened. "Yeah, shillyshally. That's the proper word for it." He paused. "Okay, see you soon." He turned back to his wife. "He's coming right over. He said he'll be here in triple time."

Roxanne jumped up quickly while smirking at her good luck. She ran to the kitchen. "I'm warming some leftovers, so I can feed him well while he's here. He'll slow down and maybe listen."

"I think you'll butter him up, fill him up, then offer dessert and sweeten him up. All for the sake of him buying into your perfect plan." Sam winked at her.

"You just wait. Georgi and I have a good idea. You'll see." Roxanne rustled the meal together quickly. By the time Dan arrived, she was ready to serve.

Sam greeted him at the door. "Hey, Dan. Come in, have a seat, have some food, and hold on. I think we are about to take a ride on the Roxanne and Georgi train."

The handsome, dark-haired, blue-eyed detective needed a lead; if Roxanne had one, he was a willing listener. He gave her a charming smile and took a seat. "Roxanne, you have my ear, my attention, and my stomach. I'm all yours. What have you dug up?"

She recounted the same stories she had told Sam about how Karl walked, Marguerite's identification of Isadore, and Karl's purchase of Troy's art. Morrison's eyes were aglow with interest. Seeing this, she knew it was time to offer up her plan.

"Okay, here's what's next, Dan. Karl has hired me to do a labyrinth garden on their property. The design is done, and I will lay it out by measuring and marking it up on the property tomorrow afternoon. Across the causeway is Edgar's Island, with a Franciscan monastery. Here's the thing, Karl and his mother are hosting a dinner there tomorrow. He has serendipitously invited Georgi to bring wine to pair with dinner.

"He also told Georgi to bring guests. Sam, you, and I can go. You see, Dan, this monastery has a retreat center and regularly hosts meals for large groups. They arranged the impromptu dinner for five o'clock. I'll be arriving directly from laying out the garden at the Rubens' property.

"Georgi was told there will be about twenty guests. We plan to improvise and confront them somehow. With you there, we hope to shock them with all the detailed information we, I mean you have. I think this is the best way to see how they react, to test them, and see their guilt, don't you? It will be full exposure in front of everyone." She outstretched her arms, "What do you say? Are you in?"

Sam chewed a piece of meat and raised one bushy white eyebrow questioningly at Dan.

Dan stopped eating and stared at Roxanne for a few moments. Then he gave a sly smile. "You know, Sam, you have a prize sleuth-inator on your hands. Roxanne, you and Georgi think so far out of the box that you're in an alternate realm of problem-solving. I'm concerned with all this thought and planning that you may pop like a bottle of fizzy water if I say no."

Roxanne pointed her fork at her friend in a mock threat.

Sam laughed. "Ha-ha, you have her number, Dan, and you're welcome to call it any time you need, The Sleuth-inator," he emphasized.

Roxanne's head bobbed between her two jovial companions as she couldn't tell if they agreed with her plan or not. She announced with determination, to obtain the upper hand, "Dessert is on hold, gentlemen until I have a fair hearing and a verdict on Georgi's and my idea."

Dan replied, "Roxanne, you are an exotic and welcome breath of fresh air on a stale night. We have no trace of Troy and no progress on these cases. We know Mario Corinthian is possibly part of an art theft ring, but we don't understand why he is after the artists. Also, Marilyn's art agent is under suspicion, but we have no hard evidence.

"Karl and Isadore have been questionable to me all along, but Detective Hanniford, the FBI, and I are stuck. For me to attend dinner, and see if it turns up anything, is a pleasure and a no-brainer. Just remember, this is not the way we do police business. I'll be there as a guest to see what shakes out."

Sam's eyebrows were now dancing on his forehead. "Well, I'll be." He chomped on his last bite of food and said, "I think you just won dessert, Dan. Good job."

They all chuckled as she went for the chocolate cream pie.

CHAPTER 79

The Labyrinth Garden
Saturday

Roxanne called Dan Morrison Saturday morning to confirm everything was still on schedule with all the plans for dinner at the monastery. "Why don't you bring that nice Angela Storm with you? It will look best if you bring a guest."

"Are you playing matchmaker with me, Roxanne?"

"No, no way. This is sleuthing business only." There was an awkward silence on the line, so she said, "Uh, well, I've got to go now. I'll see you later." She quickly hung up with a smile on her face. *He could use a little female friendship in his life.*

Roxanne packed her truck. It was fully loaded with a measuring wheel, measuring tape, wooden and rebar stakes, a mallet, marking flags, marking paint, a five-gallon bucket, shovels, pruners, loppers, and other standard tools garden designers used.

She planned with Karl to be outside his house at 2:00 p.m. and meet with him around 3:00 after she finished the layout of the labyrinth garden design. They had one of the few two-acre lots on the island. There was an expansive rectangular lawn between a small dirt access road and the house. Roxanne parked her truck in the shade on the access road and unloaded her tools.

The design area ran 200 feet toward the house and was at least 100 feet across. She started measuring and flagging the layout. Karl arrived. Roxanne was keenly aware of keeping her professional demeanor and his focus on the design details. She showed him the paper schematic of the labyrinth garden.

He paced the area she had marked with the flags. "It's much larger than I imagined." He looked from side to side. "But it's perfect. I'm looking forward to walking it for relaxation. I enjoy striding a path. My mother will too. And yes, we can see the water from here and have the shade of the trees on this end."

"If you'd like, Roxanne suggested, "we can put a tall viewing chair in this corner between the house and the shrub border, like a tennis umpire chair. Then you can sit and look down at the labyrinth design too. Would your mother like to see the design at this stage, Karl?" Roxanne was keeping Karl comfortable and unsuspecting of her suspicions of him and Isadore.

He swatted the air and said, "Mother thinks this is a folly. She doesn't believe she will have time to walk the labyrinth with all her socializing and travel. But one day, she will, and then it will have been her idea, not mine. Besides, Mother has already gone to the monastery to have tea with Father Hagerty in the garden. She visits him often, and they sit overlooking the water. I'm on my way there now to join them."

"Georgi invited my husband and me as his guests for tonight's dinner. I'll see you there. And by next week, I will have finished the layout, and we can walk through the labyrinth for your approval."

"That will be wonderful." With his hands clasped behind his back, Karl nodded to her and strutted toward the house. He soon left in his Jaguar. Roxanne clicked her tongue as she watched him drive off. *It will be a shame if he's guilty.*

After an hour, Roxanne finished plotting the critical points of the design with her marking flags. She pulled a few rebar stakes from the truck to pound them in the ground as permanent markers. Driving one in, it hit a rock, so she tried another. Again and again at ten inches deep, the rebar stopped. After six tries, it finally dawned on her. *This isn't normal.* She pulled a shovel out of her truck, dug out a section of soil, and placed it into her bucket. At the bottom of the hole was concrete. *That's weird. He didn't tell me this was here. How am I going to put plants in the ground?*

She needed to figure out where the concrete began and ended. At the far edge of the lawn were some twelve-foot rhododendron shrubs. "Well, these are doing all right," she said aloud. "It must end before them." She circled behind the shrubs and noticed they obscured the view to something else. The land descended. She strode past overgrown weeds and saplings to discover stairs under the overgrowth. She turned around and realized the narrow, dirt-access road led to it. Curious, she bushwhacked through using her hand pruners to cut back the weeds, then waded through years of piled-up leaves on the stairs. After carefully making her way down, she was surprised to find vines entangled in an iron gate. "Hmm, this must be an old entrance to whatever is under the ground."

The rusted but decorative wrought-iron gate had a black oblong handle. She tried to turn it, but the rust had frozen it shut. Peering inside, she could see an alcove made of granite. *I could use this place to leave tools and gardening equipment while installing the labyrinth. I'm sure they won't mind.* Without a second thought, she decided to try to open the gate.

Returning to her truck, she grabbed her loppers and Rust-B-Gone to spray and loosen the handle. While there, she called Sam. "Hi, honey. I'm laying out the labyrinth garden at Karl's. I spoke with him, and we went over the design. He seemed his normal self. He's at the monastery with his mother now. And just so you know, the weirdest thing happened when I was trying to put markers into the ground." Roxanne explained the details of being unable to dig and said, "I found some old stairs leading down to a possible access door. I plan to check it out, so I might be a little late for dinner. I'm just letting you know in case I disappear," she said with a chuckle.

"Don't go investigating on your own. Especially when you suspect them."

"I must, Sam," she insisted. "I can feel it in my gut. My instinct says go, go, go."

"I'm coming over. Wait for me," he ordered, not expecting her to listen.

"I'm really okay."

"Roxanne!" he grunted.

"Don't worry, love. I'll be fine. I'll see you soon."

A dial tone was left in his ear. "Grrr!" Sam hung up the phone and directly called the detective to explain the details of what she was doing. "Dan, she's gone off script and is attempting to enter an underground feature. She says the Rubens are already at the monastery."

"I'll send Peabody over there to make sure she gets to the dinner on time. Then we can all go as planned to the event, and nothing will appear unusual. It will be fine, Sam. I'll see you there."

"That makes sense. Thanks, Dan."

He called Peabody into his office and explained. "Jack, how has Reggie been working out?"

"Excellent, Boss. We get along, and he's been helpful in research and on the streets."

"Call him and pick him up. I want you two to stand by and help us if we need backup at this dinner on Edgar's Island. Head over to the Rubens' house now. Roxanne is outdoors working in their yard, marking out a garden. Just see that she gets to the dinner on time." Peabody complied.

Meanwhile, Roxanne called Georgi to let him know she was still working on the garden and might be a little late, but not to worry.

Georgi had another idea. "Everything is set up for dinner here at the monastery. I'll come by to see you. It's more than an hour before we start." He drove the three minutes, parked near her truck, and then yelled her name. "Roxanne! Roxanne, where are you!"

"I'm over here." She waved her loppers in the air.

Georgi found her rummaging through knee-deep leaves. In shock, he stood with his hands on his hips at the top of the steps she had uncovered. "Roxanne Samson, are you bleeping mad? What are you doing? This looks like an archaeology dig, not gardening."

She bent down and picked up the de-rusting spray to give the hinges and handle another dose. "Let me finish this little cleanup. Then you can come down here and see what I found."

Georgi wrinkled his nose in a quandary. He was simultaneously disgusted and enormously curious at the same time. "There is more than a little bit that needs cleaning, dear lady of the garden. It looks as though you are trying to discover the portal to *Narnia*."

She made good headway by pruning back the overgrowth and then swiped clean the path down the stairs with her rake.

Keeping his hands tucked in close to his body, he complained, "I don't understand why Karl let this become so overgrown. He is such a fuss bucket."

"I think it is an unused, forgotten doorway," she answered. "I'm sure he won't mind me cleaning things up so I can leave my tools tucked away here while I work on his project. Come and see."

He stepped down to a granite slab in front of the iron gate.

"Isn't this interesting? I'm sure they would like this to open." Roxanne's curiosity to know where the underground entrance led was insatiable. Georgi watched as she tried twisting the handle, but it wouldn't budge. "Hand me that tool." He did so, but try as she might, she couldn't lever the latch. He got on the other end to help, but it was too difficult. She resprayed the rust dissolver.

Detective Jack Peabody and Reggie drove to the Rubens' estate in an unmarked car. They pulled in beside Roxanne's truck and Georgi's vehicle. Peabody put the car in park and shut off the engine. "I didn't know Georgi was here too. We'll wait here until they come back."

"Where did she say she was?" asked Reggie.

"Something about an underground feature she was trying to enter."

Reggie opened the door. "Let's go check on her."

"What?" Peabody blurted.

"I know what I'm doing. Let's go." Reggie jumped out, and immediately, so did Jack. They disappeared into the greenery.

Reggie could hear sounds coming from behind the shrubbery. He parted the branches, and Jack looked over his shoulder. They saw stairs that led down into a shadow. Rounding the shrubs, they spied Roxanne and Georgi. They struggled with a handle and latch, huffing and grunting.

"Roxanne, it's Jack Peabody and Reggie Crumberton. Detective Morrison sent us. "Can we help you?" They maneuvered around a few piles of brush and descended the steps.

"Hi, guys!" She welcomed them covered in leaf debris, including her hair. "This is turning into a party," she chimed. Georgi smiled broadly and stood near the iron door in a small, cleared area.

Reggie observed that Georgi's fine clothes were not meant for gardening. Peabody asked, "What's going on?"

"I'm trying to get this gate open to see if it tells me why there is a concrete slab under the lawn. It's very unusual because everywhere you see that I flagged is where I hit concrete ten inches down. I've been hired to create a garden, and the concrete underground won't do."

Jack scratched his head and asked, "Reggie, are you familiar with this?"

"I've encountered underground bunkers in my military profession. It could be for several reasons. I'm curious. Hand me that small sledgehammer. I'll try to open the gate for you." Reggie whacked at the handle, and the latch released. Then he and Roxanne tried to muscle the old iron door open. Jack jumped in to help while Georgi watched. They gave a mighty pull, and a loud, grinding metal squeak came from the hinges.

The four of them slowly entered a small room about eight-by-ten feet. The walls, floors, and ceiling were lined in gray granite.

Roxanne took out her cell phone and turned on the flashlight. At first, Georgi was amazed but suddenly thrust himself against Roxanne's back with a squeal. "Ohh! How can you stand this? There are cobwebs everywhere, Roxanne! And what's that?" he pointed. A plaque came into view under her light. It read:

Rest In Peace - In Loving Memory of
Saul Rubens, Beloved Husband of Isadore Rubens and
Father of Karl Rubens

A separate plaque below it read:

Four Kisses for my Love
XXXX

"This is a mausoleum," Roxanne said softly.

"You mean a crypt for dead bodies? This is creepy!" Georgi cringed. "Oh no, this is not for me." Clenching his arms tight against his chest, he said, "Jack and Reggie, this is your department. Roxanne, my constitution is not designed for this experience with spiders in a dark crypt and dead bodies. I'm going back to the monastery. I'll see you there." He looked at his watch. "We start in less than an hour, Roxanne."

"Yes, of course. I'll pick up and leave soon."

Georgi tiptoed up the stairs, trying not to touch anything, and ran to the safety of his car with his arms flailing in case there were any spiders on him.

In the mausoleum, Roxanne wondered, "This can't just be a crypt. Concrete is ten inches under the whole blooming lawn where I've been marking up a design, but this room is only eight by ten. Doesn't that seem weird?"

Jack wondered, "Could it be a bomb shelter?"

Reggie considered the options. "It does make sense for this location. Concrete bunkers or bomb shelters were built around World War II and were popular in the fifties. Can I see your flashlight, Roxanne?" Shining it on the wall, he analyzed the construction of the granite room. He began pounding to hear if there were any irregularities behind it. Following a grid pattern, he moved up and down.

Suddenly, they heard a thud. "What was that?" said Jack. Reggie didn't move so he could listen intently. He knocked again to make sure it was not an echo. Someone knocked back. Roxanne yelped and jumped. A muffled plea called out, "Help! Help get me out of here!"

"Whoa!" yelled Roxanne and Jack simultaneously. She called out, "We'll try to find a way in."

The voice spoke back. "Roxanne, is that you?"

Shocked, she shouted, "Who are you? And what are you doing in there?"

"It's Troy, Roxanne. Pleeaasse, get me out of here!"

"Troy? Why are you in there?" she asked.

"It's Karl and Isadore. They are bonkers! They locked me up."

"Troy, this is Jack Peabody. Hold on! We'll get you out, buddy.

"Oh wow! You're here too, Jack!"

Reggie pounded on the wall, listening for hollow sounds. "Troy, this is Reggie. We met weeks ago at your apartment. We're looking for a trip switch."

"Thank you, Reggie. I'm glad you're all here."

Frantically, Reggie, Jack, and Roxanne searched for some way to open the crypt. Simultaneously, their hands pressed on the top plaque for Saul Rubens. Nothing happened. They pushed on the next plaque, *Four Kisses XXXX*. Instantly, a small square in the granite popped open on a hinge. Inside it was a clean door handle. Reggie turned it smoothly. "We found something, Troy." A large door swung open along a fine line in the granite. It revealed studs supporting a sheetrock wall on the other side.

Troy yelled, "I can hear where you are."

Reggie said, "Stand back. I'm going to punch this wall open."

"Wait, wait!" Troy insisted. "I have to remove a painting."

Roxanne, Jack, and Reggie looked at each other dumbfounded.

Quickly, Troy removed the Vermeer painting of *The Concert* from his side of the wall. "Okay!" he yelled.

Reggie lifted his leg, kicked the wall with his heel, and cracked it. He grabbed one of Roxanne's gardening tools and dug into the sheetrock, creating a hole, then he kicked again, this time right through to the other side. Troy wrestled with the damaged sheetrock until the opening was large enough between two studs. Roxanne grabbed Troy's arm and pulled. Jack and Reggie pitched in, and Troy squeezed through and landed on the ground, panting from the effort. They got him to his feet.

"Oh my God, you're alive." Roxanne hugged him.

Distressed, Troy pleaded, "Let's get out of here before they come back. They're criminals. They have stolen priceless art, and it's all in there."

"But are you okay?" Roxanne asked.

"I'm okay. They did try to poison me, but I didn't eat Isadore's food after that. Karl brought me protein bars and fruit, so I ate and had access to water from the bathroom. I feared for my life. Karl told me Isadore's lackeys would do away with me soon. They're frigging nuts."

Jack began calculating what they should do next. "Reggie, let's bring him to the event and expose the Rubens. Morrison will be there, and Troy is our physical proof that they are villains."

"Good idea," said Roxanne. "Let's go."

Troy backed away with his hands raised. "Whoa! No, I can't do that. I don't know what event you're talking about. I don't want to see them ever again."

Reggie understood his reluctance. "I have an idea I think you and Jack might like, Troy. The event is at the monastery across the way. I know the place and Father Hagerty. I went to these retreats many years ago. Troy and I will go in the back door and wait in the kitchen until the timing is right. And we'll get some real food in you, Troy. Trust me. You'll be fine with Jack and me."

Troy wanted to hide away in his apartment and hang out with his cat, Matt. But eating sounded pretty good. He looked at Roxanne for confidence.

She encouraged him, "You'll be fine, Troy. Sam is there, and he won't let anyone touch you. The detectives will put the Rubens in jail. Right, Jack?"

"Absolutely, and Roxanne, why don't you attend the event now? Are you ready, Troy?"

He nodded yes, reluctantly. Roxanne hugged him again, then raced to her truck. She jumped in and drove toward Edgar's Island. In the parking lot, she did her best to clean up with some wipes, comb her hair, apply a little makeup, and quickly change her clothes and shoes. Her hands were shaking, nervous about what would happen next. She looked in the mirror and heaved a sigh. *I'm so glad Sam and Dan are here.*

CHAPTER 80

Revenge is Sweet
Saturday

Jack drove Reggie and Troy to the monastery. "You guys pulled me out of that hole in the ground just in time." Troy watched as the view of the water passed by. "It's nice to see daylight," he murmured. "I've been locked in there since Tuesday."

"Troy, everyone, and I mean everyone, has been looking for you," Jack said, trying to make him feel better.

Jack followed the narrow road and drove to the back door for their clandestine work. "I'll cover the front entrance Reggie, while you bring Troy into the kitchen."

Reggie knocked and asked for Father Hagerty. He greeted Reggie like an old friend. On many occasions, Reggie had stayed there between his tours of duty to Afghanistan. He quickly explained that they were working with Detective Morrison, who was in the dining room with Georgi. He signaled Troy to come forth and introduced him. Then he asked the priest to go about everything as usual but requested to know when dessert was to be served.

The monks wore traditional hooded brown robes. The robes represented their lack of need for material things. They dedicated themselves to their spiritual tradition of living a simple life of teaching, performing acts of charity, and social service. The meals they prepared raised funds to hold retreats and maintain the buildings and grounds.

While dinner was served, Troy and Reggie ate in the kitchen. Troy quickly tackled the baked fish and vegetables while humming his delight with the flavors. He thought this was the best meal he had ever had. He even began to wonder if he should become a monk. *A simple life seems reasonable to me right now.*

Reggie stepped away for a moment, and when he returned, he asked Troy to stand up. "Try this on." Reggie held up a brown robe.

"Why?" Troy wondered if Reggie had read his mind about wanting a simple life.

"We'll be in disguise. Believe me. You'll enjoy being undercover."

Troy and Reggie put on the robes, and with the hoods up, they were in perfect camouflage.

"Follow me." Reggie handed him two desserts. "We're going to walk in, and you'll place these desserts in front of Isadore and Karl."

Troy stepped back. "No, I'm not," he whispered with dread.

Reggie explained, "They won't see you because you will be behind them. And besides, you're in a hooded monk's robe. They won't even look at you. I checked out the room. Only Roxanne, Chief Sam, and Detective Morrison will know you because they're on the other side of the table. They'll see you standing behind Karl and Isadore."

Unsure, Troy hesitated.

"Look, buddy," Reggie encouraged, "this is your chance to redeem your confidence. It's like revenge but better. Enjoy it!"

"They even tried to poison me with cherry pie. Revenge sounds so sweet right now." Troy smiled and considered it a rebalancing of karma. "Reggie?" he asked.

"Yes, my man?"

"I look forward to redeeming my confidence."

"There you go, dude. You've got the picture now. Revenge is a sweet dessert. Let's go." Reggie entered with Troy following his lead.

Georgi was pouring champagne for the final course. Several of the monks delivered the dessert for the twenty guests. Troy and Reggie joined them. Troy placed a dessert in front of Isadore and Karl each, and he and Reggie stood behind them.

Chief Sam was surprised to see Troy. He didn't think he had joined the monks. Roxanne hadn't had time to tell him about Troy's escape from his underground prison. She squeezed Sam's hand and gave him a look. Sam understood his wife's secret code, and he stifled his reaction.

Detective Morrison and Dr. Storm did not notice Troy. Neither had Georgi, who stood at the head of the long oval table. He was busy describing the champagne and cake combo. After his explanation, Roxanne tried to get his attention by using her eyes and head to motion to the side where Troy stood, but Georgi thought she was making faces about the champagne.

Suddenly, he saw a familiar face among the robed men. "Troy!" he squealed. "What are you doing here? Did you join the monks? I would have never thought!"

Roxanne jumped out of her seat. Using a spoon to clink her glass, she said, "I have a toast for the monks who are giving Troy sanctuary after being imprisoned by Isadore and her son, Karl, in their underground gallery of stolen artwork. Detective Morrison," she pointed at the Rubens, "you need to arrest them. They are unforgivable."

Karl and his mother tried to rise, but Reggie's large hands held their shoulders to keep them seated.

Isadore exclaimed, "Oh! I never!"

"Shut up, Mother!" Karl ordered under his breath.

Troy announced, "Detective, I was abducted by these two, but more than that, one of the most famous art heist in the world has just been solved. Karl had worked in Boston, only blocks away from the Isabella Stewart Gardner Mansion, and in 1990, they stole several priceless works of art.

"Mother and son have fooled everyone. These two high-class socialites are nothing more than common thieves who have pulled off mind-blowing art thefts and poisonings. I've been a prisoner with the art in their posh, climate-controlled gallery under their home."

Many people in the room gasped and stared at Troy, confused by this monk's fantastic tale.

"And worse," he exclaimed, "they had no plans to release me. I would be dead, just like Marilyn and Aaron."

The room was silent as each person tried to discern if they had heard him correctly.

"Excuse me," a distinguished man said. "Did you say you've seen the stolen art from the Isabella Stewart Gardner Mansion?"

"Yes, sir, I've seen it all. Karl admitted that his mother was the mastermind behind arranging the theft. And she planned to eliminate me to keep their secrets."

With great disappointment, Father Hagerty rose from his seat. "You've been my friend, Isadore, and a great donor to our mission. Greed has overcome your soul. I can do nothing for you but pray that you will be remorseful. I am sorry to see you in this situation. It is disturbing in so many ways. And Karl, I couldn't imagine such darkness in you. You disregard humanity and the blessings of life."

Georgi was furious. Pointing at Karl, he yelled, "You and your mother are the most disgraceful human beings I have ever met. I helped you, trusted you, and you hurt my friends. How could you? We have lost our loved ones! Your ravenous appetite to possess finery has only deprived and demoralized others, causing some to meet their demise. And you were going to kill Troy? How dare you!" Raging emotions overcame him, and Georgi took his water glass and threw the liquid into Karl's face.

Karl had a forlorn expression, and without a word, took his napkin and dabbed his face and clothing. Then he stared at his wet dessert. The conservator of fine art and curator of a museum had no choice but to absorb the disgrace. He and Isadore had been unmasked.

Father Hagerty ended the outburst. "Detective Morrison, will you please remove these imposters of good so we may continue our evening in peace?"

Isadore discreetly reached into her purse and pulled out two pills. Karl looked at her curiously when she slipped one of the pills into his hand. She leaned over, pretending to kiss his cheek. "Cyanide, instant death," she whispered.

Karl was horrified and snarled, "Motherrr…you have manipulated me my whole life. Enough is enough."

Isadore's expression ruffled, but she composed herself with a gentle pat on her son's hand. She said, "Father Hagerty, I will confess right here. Karl is innocent! I was at the Dahlia party, and Marilyn annoyed me. I pushed her away, causing her to fall on her statue's spear. Aaron died because he was a snooper; he was in the way. I planned to have the Mary Cassatt painting taken that night, so I gave him tea laced with psilocybin mushrooms. While high, I persuaded him to do his balancing act on the upper rooftop patio. It was because of me that he fell. I purposely startled him.

"Marguerite visited the museum in sadness. I saw her and invited her to tea. Then I put the same mushroom drug in her cup. I told her to walk by the water to calm herself. I didn't know she would walk into the Mystic River. And to fully clear the air, I was the one who arranged for Cora's meeting with my colleague, Mario Corinthian. His alias was created for the ruse. The purpose was to throw Marilyn's case in a different direction, so anyone but us would be under suspicion."

She flicked her hand toward Troy. "Troy thought he could expose me from the detective's grainy video. Karl knew nothing. He didn't know about the Gardner heist until he discovered the paintings in my possession.

"Yes, Troy eventually would have been gone, too, because my hired hands were ready to pick him up tomorrow. His paintings would have been worth a fortune after his demise. My point for returning the Cassatt painting was to make my son famous. I wanted the Mystic River Fine Art Museum to be the most important art destination in the region. The Dahlia Art Gallery debased my fine art standards, and Marilyn brought attention to the Dahlia. Life is too short for insignificant people to interfere with my son's potential. But alas, my plan didn't work out because of Troy."

"Motherrr!" Karl yelled. His entire demeanor presented thorough humiliation.

A hoarse growl from Isadore's throat was expelled. "Be quiet, son! Don't say another word."

One woman at the far end of the table, who had a few too many glasses of wine, slurred loudly, "Is this a dinner theater? I'm confused." Her date patted her hand and whispered for her to keep listening.

"Alright, that's enough," Morrison decided. "Detective Hanniford is standing by. We'll be escorting the Rubens to New London first." He stood to assist Peabody, who was waiting by the door to remove Karl and Isadore.

Isadore spoke to Father Hagerty, her old friend. "May I be forgiven, Father?"

"I am no longer your conduit to God, Isadore," Father Hagerty grimly replied. "You are on your own. Forgiveness is only for those who are truly sorry, and I believe the devil is your only ally now."

Isadore snapped, "Father, get used to it. There's a woman like me in every town, but no one has been better at the game of life than me. I've fooled everyone long enough. At my age, I am very proud of my accomplishments. I've had a rich, fulfilling life. I don't need your blessing. I have my own conduit!"

Peabody spoke to Morrison in his ear, "Boss, we'll take the Rubens to the station. Enjoy the rest of your dinner."

Morrison glanced over at Angela Storm and nodded. She gave him a wink, knowing that in their business, he was back on duty.

CHAPTER 81

The Millionaire

Jack and Reggie approached their unmarked car just as Detective Hanniford and the Mystic police arrived at the monastery. The two forces finalized where to charge the felons, New London, or Mystic. Since Marilyn's death happened in New London, Jack, and Reggie took the mother-son duo to police headquarters for booking. The Mystic police would have their hands full, assisting the FBI in handling the stolen art from the Gardner Mansion.

Isadore and Karl were placed uncuffed in the rear seat of the unmarked car. Jack steered away from Edgar's Island and drove across the causeway to Mason's Island.

Isadore turned to Karl and held his hand. "I did it because I love you."

"You didn't do it out of love, Mother. You did it out of want. You wanted fine art and to claim my success as your fame and power. You're selfish. Your wants are not love—they are greed, and you taught me that."

Isadore put her hands together in prayer.

"It's too late, Mother! You have broken every sacred rule," Karl admonished her. "You imagine yourself as virtuous as Mother Mary, trying to protect me as if I'm baby Jesus when you know nothing of generosity, compassion, or religious values. You use them to trick yourself into justifying anything you desire."

He took a deep breath. "Mother! You have only tricked yourself into Hell! Good luck! You and the Devil will get along just fine. In fact, like a Greek tragedy, you are doomed to wander forever without rest in the underworld with Hades." Karl looked away. He was finished with fooling himself and done with her.

Jack and Reggie listened silently as they turned onto Route One, and when they passed the Sea Swirl, a strange guttural sound emerged from the back seat. Through the rearview mirror, Jack could see Karl looking at his mother in shock. Reggie turned around to identify the noise.

"Mother! What have you done now?"

Isadore was choking, and foam began flowing out of her mouth.

"Karl!" Jack yelled. "What is going on?" He pulled into a nearby parking lot while Reggie called for an ambulance.

"She took a cyanide pill," Karl said without emotion. "The black widow has taken her poison. She'll be dead soon enough, and you can do nothing."

Reggie jumped out of the car and pulled Karl out from the backseat. He tried to attend to Isadore by cleaning out her mouth. Alas, it was too late. She successfully established her outcome again.

Jack was beside himself, pacing up and down the parking lot. Reggie stood next to Karl, whose arms were crossed with scorn for his mother. An ambulance arrived, and the paramedics recognized there was nothing more to do but take her away. The three men stood and watched as the emergency vehicle made its way onto Route One, sirens off.

A towel was in the car's trunk, and Reggie threw it across the back seat. Karl returned to the vehicle. He placed his head into his hands, contemplating taking the cyanide pill his mother had slipped him. Witnessing the horror of her death convinced him he couldn't do it. He thought about what she had said at dinner to Detective Morrison, that killing Marilyn was an accident. She had taken the blame. If they believed her, he would be off the hook. If so, this would be the one lasting memory of her for which he could be grateful.

***

"Do you need a hug?" Roxanne asked Troy. He nodded gingerly; his eyes were downcast. Roxanne walked around the table, and Georgi followed. They both gave him a big bear hug. They told him how wonderful he was and how happy they were that he survived because he still had much to offer the world. Georgi exclaimed without thought, "You've lost weight, Troy."

Troy laughed and whispered, "I'll share my secret with you…fear of being poisoned."

"Well, you look smashing in a brown robe. You could make a habit of it. Pun intended." They snickered, mostly in relief at the ending tensions.

Georgi used a spoon to chime his glass. "I'd like to make a toast!" Everyone settled down as he cleared his throat. "To Troy, a dear friend and artist, who was almost dead, which would have made his artwork more valuable. But…," Georgi held up a finger to pause his audience, "…he does not need to worry anymore because Troy, whether he knows it or not, is a multi-millionaire! How many of you know a millionaire? Well, you do now! Because Troy will receive the reward for solving the case and finding the art from the Isabella Stewart Gardner Mansion! Let's hear it for Troy! Hip, hip, hooray!"

The guests joined in. "Hip, hip, hooray! Hip, hip, hooray!"

"Whaaat?" As he looked across the room, Troy was stunned and wondered if the dining audience was tipsy from drinking too much fine wine. Maybe they were delirious because he was confused. "Georgi, what are you talking about?"

"You win, Troy! You win the reward. Didn't you know? Whoever finds the art and the thieves wins the reward money! That's you." Georgi hung onto Troy's shoulders and excitedly jumped up and down. "And guess what? Karl paid five hundred thousand dollars for all your art! Whoop-whoop!"

"Wait a minute. Stop that! Are you serious?"

"Yes, you! You silly, brown-robed gnome. You're it! The big IT!"

Troy was overcome. He had been very sad, even depressed, and now he was not only glad but, but…it was a deep feeling he had never felt so intensely before. *What is it?* He wondered. *It's strange, but it's moving through me like a warm, delicious hot chocolate.* He pushed back his monk's hood scratching his head as he realized what it was. It was pure relief.

For the first time in his life, he felt fully relieved. Relief from not knowing if he could pay rent or eat. Relief from knowing he could fix his car and buy a gift for a woman he liked. It was a fantastic feeling. He had never imagined this feeling, not really. He had imagined trying to imagine it, but it never stuck. "Is this really for real?" he asked.

The room answered, "Yes!"

With a sweet, childlike inflection, Troy said, "Wow!" Then he giggled. "I'm feeling happy."

His giggling made Roxanne and Georgi giggle, then laugh. Their laughter was contagious, and the whole room morphed into merriment.

Sam said, "Roxanne, my dear, I don't know how, but you got yourself in and out of trouble again."

Under the table, Dan Morrison squeezed Angela Storm's hand. He beamed her a rare, charming smile. More than being relieved by the resolution to his case, he was grateful for being there with her. "You were right," he whispered, "there was more to the story, and right in front of us too."

"I never saw this coming," she whispered back.

Troy turned to Georgi. "I have a question for you."

"Yes, I'm listening," Georgi responded with anticipation.

"You're a business manager. Can you help me manage my business? I don't know how to handle millions of dollars. I might do something daft and spend it in a month. Will you help me?"

The request so touched Georgi that he started jumping again. "Of course I will, Troy. We'll be frugal enough to last you a lifetime and make sure you have fun all along the way. How does that sound?"

Nodding his appreciation, Troy smiled. "Just great, Georgi. This makes me feel great."

***

When the FBI arrived, the Mystic Police, Detectives Hanniford and Morrison, followed Roxanne and Troy to the mausoleum, where they had busted him out of the posh prison gallery with Reggie and Jack. Chief Sam, Georgi, and Dr. Storm followed along. Roxanne pointed to where Troy squeezed through the wall. A few agents in protective gear entered and began to process the scene.

Morrison had received the house entry keycode from Peabody through Karl, including directions on how to enter the underground gallery. They found the trap door under the carpet in a broad hallway off the kitchen. Then pressed the automatic button, and the floor slid open to expose the staircase.

A team of officers in protective gear descended the stairs and opened the door to the expansive gallery. At the opposite end, they could see the hole in the wall. Speechless, they gazed slowly upon the room in awe. Expressions of wonder shone in their eyes. They were transfixed by the lost art wonders that had been missing from view for over thirty years.

Since 1990, these precious treasures had been only seen in photographs. Soon these finest works would hang again in their rightful place on Isabella's walls. The unanticipated discovery would be one of the art world's most significant celebrations.

Ironically, Isabella Stewart Gardner would have been grateful that her fine art wonders, cut brutely from their frames, had been restored to mint condition by her most dutiful admirer, Karl, the art conservator.

CHAPTER 82

Moondance

Dr. Angela Storm was driven home by Roxanne and Sam after the remarkable revelations at the monastery dinner party. Detective Morrison was left behind to finish his business in Mystic. Around nine o'clock, she drove down Pequot Avenue to the shoreline to sit on a stonewall by the water and relax from the evening's excitement. A full moon shimmered over the harbor, and the beacon on Ledge Light beamed three flashes across the waves. She counted to ten seconds before the light washed past her again.

Silhouetted images were predominant as the fading view was taken over by the main attractions, the stars, moon, and lighthouse. Angela considered all that had occurred over the past few weeks—then thought of Troy's painting in the silent auction of Marilyn looking out to sea just as she was, into her future.

She was about to step down to the beach when her phone rang. She heard a deep and recognizable voice upon answering.

"Where are you?" he asked. "I have something important to tell you."

When she told him, he said, "I'll be right there."

Soon, a vehicle pulled up and parked. A handsome man emerged and approached.

"I did wonder if I would ever see you again, alone," she admitted.

He smiled and reached for her hands. He said softly, "And I was wondering if you would be interested in an arrangement."

"A business arrangement?" she asked.

"Well, yes, it's a covert business arrangement. That is if you can fit it into your schedule."

"What do you propose?"

"An agreement of secrecy to the highest order. Do you think you can conspire?"

"It all depends," she responded. "What are the terms?"

"No one can know about our dealings for a certain period until we both agree to continue or terminate the arrangement. Can you consent to these terms?" He put her hands between his and gently warmed them. He searched her golden eyes. They glowed in the soft moonlight as he waited for her answer. He asked again, "Is it possible we can pull this off and professionally not be compromised?"

The glimmering light and sea breeze enhanced the mood of their secret rendezvous. A smile crossed her lips after having contemplated all he said. Leaning forward, she whispered, "Yes, I agree to your terms because you have absconded with my heart, Detective Dan Morrison."

"Absconded, is that a professional term, Doctor?" he asked, just as Humphrey Bogart might. From behind his back and on cue, Van Morrison's song "Moondance" filled the air around them from his phone. Dan whispered, "It's a wonderful night for a moon dance, Angela."

And much like Lauren Bacall, she whispered, "Kiss me."

Dan did so most passionately. Their shadows commingled and cast a form reminiscent of *The Kiss,* a rapturous sculpture by Auguste Rodin.

The lighthouse beacon swooped across the sound and flashed upon them as a distant boat horn sounded the clarion call of their new beginning. Gentle waves rippled stones on the shore while Dan Morrison and Angela Storm remained entwined in their blissful moment. ♥

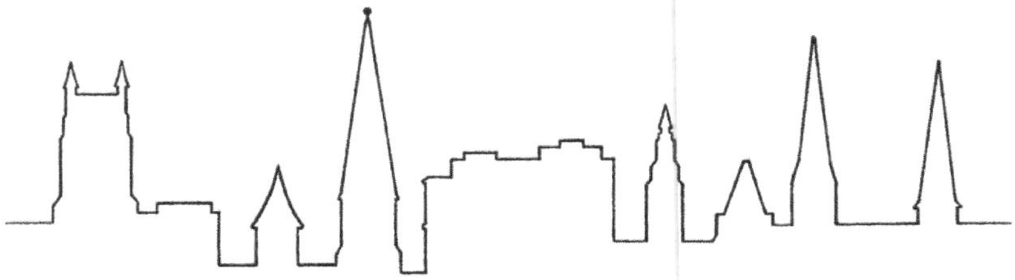

Karl's Finale

Karl cooperated with the police. He found Isadore's methods of contacting Mario Corinthian in her phone. Detective Hanniford's police force set up a sting operation with Detective Morrison and the FBI. Mario and his men were arrested boating in Poggy Bay on their way to the Mason Island home. Their plan with Isadore had been to take Troy into Long Island Sound and dump him. If ever his body were discovered, it would have matched the evidence of his belongings on the beach and the theory that he had gone swimming and drowned.

Isadore's confession allowed Karl to admit only to his knowledge of the art heist. But only after the fact. He professed his infatuation with Isabella, but possessing the art was his mother's obsession. He was extradited to Boston for the art theft trial, where they found him guilty by association and of withholding evidence.

Because Karl was a proficient art expert, the courts decided at the bequest of Interpol, to move him to Europe, where he remained under house arrest. He collaborates on international cases involving forgeries and the recovery of stolen art. Eventually, Lloyds of London would hire him to be their art expert for insurance purposes and art identification. His sentence would amount to twenty years in an elegant London flat.

Troy declined to press charges because he felt Karl would suffer enough. Since Karl and Isadore had entrapped Troy, he realized that being drugged allowed him to feign forgetfulness for questions about the beach or how he ended up in their home. His ploy with Jason to fake his death to sell his art was kept a secret.

Karl saw that Marilyn's two lotus paintings from her apartment and the *Helen Elizabeth* poppy painting from the silent auction were returned to Georgi, who oversaw the distribution of her estate. In its entirety, it went to assist individual local artists in New London. Her parents never did come forward.

***

In a final bird's-eye-view, we visit Troy in his new condominium, happy and content with Matt, the cat. He has been inspired by the book *Dangerous Women in History* that Roxanne found, and the description in the forward of *The Villainess* written by R. Young. He has finished crushing a lapis lazuli stone into a fine blue powder and now mixes it with linseed oil to make an oil paint.

In front of him is a white mural-sized canvas. He dabs a brush into the intense lapis blue color and whirls a massive circle onto the canvas to create a swirling portal. Troy has determined that the center of this portal is where all things dark and negative, like Isadore, will be drawn in and shall disappear away from his reality.

THE VILLAINESS

Whispering in the confines of a female villain's mind is a conspiracy that justifies every plot and warrants every deed. Born scheming, she plans her wicked and manipulative ways, for entwined within her infected heart are the tangled attachments of jealousy and greed. Greed conspires while vanity overtakes her mind, brewing a cocktail of a poisonous kind.

And beware of her ego—it is just as dangerous as greed and its cousin jealousy. When conceited as she, one feels deserving of what others have earned through hard work. The villainess will selfishly justify stealing, assured that what is theirs should be hers, by placing herself above them in some de facto way.

Expertly crafting her desires, obsession is her lover and friend, escorting her on a winding road of malicious means and ends. Yet, when her cup is full and comfort wraps her in a fleece of gold, she finds her satisfaction fleeting when a new desire takes the place of the old. For what has happened, unforeseen to her, are the goblins of greed and jealousy have taken her in their ultimate hold.

The moral my friend, is to be aware of the selfishly needy—only death ends their lustful treaty.

THE END

♥

THE PARADE PLAZA'S SOLDIERS AND SAILORS MONUMENT, NEW LONDON, CT - ERECTED 1896

♥ Admiration ♥

Isabella Stewart Gardner of Boston is inspiring. She was a rousing supporter and collector of world art. Though she may no longer be here physically, she remains remarkably so in essence through her mansion.

Isabella, also known as Belle, or Mrs. Jack, was an ambassador to the arts and feminine freedoms. Her influence has endured for over one hundred years. An art enthusiast, she befriended and supported artists yet went one step further and built a palace-like mansion to display their works. Her towering architectural beauty is known as the Isabella Stewart Gardner Museum, which also houses a magnificent courtyard garden. It is well worth a visit. As of this writing, her stolen art is still waiting to be discovered.

♥ Acknowledgements ♥

Thank you to my New London friends, the Samuls: Ann Samul for inspiring me to write a mystery that includes our joint passion for gardening; and to her husband, Fire Chief Ron Samul (retired), thank you for our chats about NL history, the odd cases, and fires that sparked my imagination.

To the Lyman Allyn Museum in New London: thank you to the curator, Tanya Pohrt, for generously giving me a tour of the museum's collection. Thank you to Peter Anton, the sculptural artist, for permission to place your beautiful dessert art in a scene.

Steve and Jeanne Sigel, Executive Director and Marketing & Development Director of the Garde Arts Center: Thank you for giving us an in-depth tour of the performance hall palace. Ron McKenzie, House Manager, thank you for inspiring a scene. Thank you to filmmaker JoJo LaRiccia, who documented our time at the Garde and produced a short film. YouTube - *Garde Arts Center Video Tour 2020* or go to GardeArts.org.

Slater Memorial Museum in Norwich, CT - Thank you to the staff and docents who gave me a welcoming tour through the magnificent plaster cast collection of ancient sculptures. Your enthusiasm made every trip worthwhile.

Thank you to the Devendittis family of Candace, Bunny, and Chef Rachel for entertaining my whims of creating a fictional representation of your restaurant and for your generous professional input of champagne and food pairings for the story. Dev's on Main is currently a restaurant in Niantic, CT.

Mystic and New London, Connecticut, inspired my story with their long-standing art communities, unique galleries, and marvelous museums worth visiting. New London was designated a Connecticut Cultural District for the Arts in June 2022. This waterside city has a big heart for art. ♥

♥ Acknowledgements ♥

I want to acknowledge these passionate, hard-working artists whom I know or met during my research. You and your creations are exceptional and inspiring: Troy Zaushny, Artist; Elisha Schauer, Tattoo Artist, thanks for the info on Jack Dracula; Casey Moran, Artist/Creator; Lori Neumann, Artist/Sculptor; Katie Fogg, Artist; Kim Abraham, Artist/Author; and Amy Hannum, Artist/Designer your sculpture *The Messenger* inspired mine.

Thank you, Barry and Kim Ford, Woodworker & Potter, and owners of The Red House Cultural Arts Center in Salem, CT. Barry, thank you for your wine knowledge and the process of hosting a silent wine and art auction.

Thank you, Vinnie Scarano, Photographer and Hygienic Art's board president, for inviting me into your studio and discussing decades of the local art and music scene in New London.

Thank you, Frank Bowen-Homets, for inspiring my character for the Parade Plaza scene. I appreciate you and your husband Don's enthusiastic support of my writing and characters.

Paul Maisano, thank you for the golden bridge analogy that your Italian father shared with you. May he rest in peace.

Phil Tuthill, Sexton of Avery Chapel, Groton, CT. Thank you for the impromptu tour of the chapel's dusty glory. May its renovation come true.

Cindy Samul, Illustrator/Author/Artist: Thank you for pouring your thoughtful and professional expertise into my book cover designs. Your attention to detail and color surpassed my expectations!

A big thank you to my supporting friends, fans, and my initial readers: Lana Westgate, Deonn Bunnell, Henry Koster, and E.J. Bloom, MA, retired English professor; thank goodness for your input. It was priceless. Immense gratitude goes to the due diligence and patience of my editor, Heather Doughty.

New England School of Art & Design, thank you for inspiring my love of art and a career of being creative in design and construction.

♥

In Memory of Robert B. Parker, writer of the Spenser detective series and much more. Bob, and his wife Joan, were friends and clients during my career in landscape design. Bob would show me his latest novel or screenplay while working at his computer. I told him he inspired me to one day write a mystery. He said there was too much competition out there…. Well, Bob, I gave it a go anyway! I miss you both, RIP♥ xoxo

♥ Acknowledgements ♥

New London murals mentioned in the story:

"Prince" by Jamie XV
"The Hard Hat Painters" by Troy Zaushny & Michael McNabney
"The Great Sperm Whale" by Wyland
"Hygienic Ladies" mural designed by Terry "Davo" Davis
with Sara Warda and Wendy Kuklinsky
HygienicArt.org has a map of all New London's murals.

♥

Music and bands mentioned in the story:

Ch. 3: The Night Shakers - Blues Band
Ch. 3: Suave-Ski - Hip-Hop Rapper
Ch. 11: "Senorita" by Camila Cabello and Shawn Mendes
Ch. 17: "Dock of the Bay" by Otis Redding
Ch. 18: "City Boy" by Kyven - Steven Scott and Kyle Ewalt
Ch. 64: "Say You Will" by Billy Gilman
Ch. 64: New London Community Orchestra
Ch. 76: "Creepin'" by Eric Church
Ch. 76: "Enemy" by Imagine Dragons
Ch. 82: "Moondance" by Van Morrison

♥

Thank you to the Museum of Fine Arts, Boston for inspiring me at every visit since I was a teenager. The paintings represented fictionally in Chapter 33, can be viewed at the museum except for, Monsieur Returns the Gaze – In the Loge, it is a fabrication.

♥

Suggested Non-Fiction Reading:

Seven Days in the Art World by Sarah Thornton, 2008
Sky Break poems by Lyubomir Levchev, 1997 – Love letters to America
Mrs. Jack by Louise Hall Tharp, 1965 – Biography of Isabella Stewart Gardner
Stolen by the Isabella Stewart Gardner Museum, 2018
Master Thieves by Stephen Kurkjian, 2015

♥

Suggested Documentary Videos:

The Price of Everything – A documentary about the art world on Kanopy, 2018
Garde Arts Center Video Tour 2020 on YouTube by J. LaRiccia & R. Young and on GardeArts.org website called *A Grand Garde Tour*

THE PARADE PLAZA AND THE UNION TRAIN STATION

NEW LONDON HARBOR LIGHT, 1731 RE-BUILT 1801

New London Ledge Light, built 1909

To learn more about the story, my muses, and inspirations visit my website and join my Mystery Fan VIP List.

Details and links are on the following pages.

Note on the Author

Rose Young
Author of: **Roses, Wine & Murder – In the City of Steeples**

Rose loves to find interesting facts to enhance her mindful mysteries. Having lived in New England, she was inspired by an art heist where the facts did not seem to add up. She fashioned this modern-day tale to include her love of art, history, gardens, and unique characters. Rose is a New England School of Art & Design graduate and former designer, who enjoys the research to develop a story.

Join my Mystery Fan VIP List for special pics, videos & more on my website: www.RoseYoungAuthor.com

Facebook: @RoseYoungAuthor
Instagram: #RoseYoungAuthor

See the - GardeArts.org video go to *A Grand Garde Tour* or go to YouTube.com: *Garde Arts Center Video Tour 2020*

Email: BestBooksPublish@gmail.com

Please leave a review on all your favorite book sites or see my website for links. RoseYoungAuthor.com

Thank you! ♥

The first mystery adventure with
Roxanne, Georgi, and Detective Morrison.

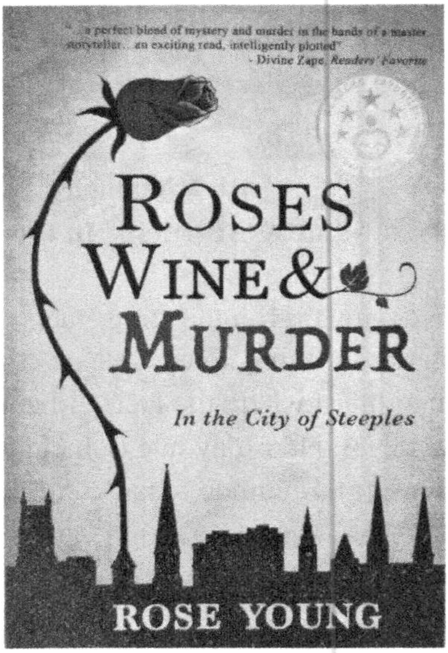

Available as an eBook & audiobook on all sites.
Please go to my website for links.

See the Book Trailer Video
on YouTube: Roses Wine & Murder Mystery

Made in the USA
Monee, IL
17 March 2024

55216221R00216